NICK NEEDHAM

2000 YEARS OF CHRIST'S POWER

VOLUME

THE AGE OF RELIGIOUS CONFLICT

CHRISTIAN
FOCUS

Copyright © Dr N. R. Needham 2016

hardback ISBN 978-1-78191-781-7
epub ISBN 978-1-78191-920-0
mobi ISBN 978-1-78191-921-7

First published in in 2016
reprinted in 2017, 2020, and 2022
by
Christian Focus Publications Ltd,
Geanies House, Fearn, Ross-shire,
IV20 1TW, Scotland, U.K.
www.christianfocus.com
and
Grace Publications Trust
7 Arlington Way
London, EC1R 1XA, England
www.gracepublications.co.uk

Cover design by Paul Lewis

Printed and bound by Bell & Bain, Glasgow

Contents

Introduction

This volume covers roughly the period 1560–1740. Each chapter, however, has a slightly different timeframe, owing to the distinctive nature of the religious tradition involved, with different sets of personalities and events. For example, the English chapters end around 1690, whereas the Roman Catholic chapters go on to about 1750.

A few words about the content:

First, the subtitle *The Age of Religious Conflict* may seem odd. Could that not be the subtitle of any of the preceding volumes in this series? Yes. But as I did the research for the current volume, it struck me forcibly several times that no other period had been so profoundly marked by sheer intensity of conflict: conflict between traditions, conflict within traditions. For instance, when Roman Catholics were not fighting Protestants or Eastern Orthodox, they were fighting each other, and just as fiercely. The epic of the Jansenist controversy must be one of the most explosive and convulsive in Catholic history, and it was fought out within the precincts of the Catholic Church, leaving huge and ugly bloodstains.

Second, some may protest against what seems the exaggerated space devoted to English religious history. I sympathize, and it was not my intention to produce an England-dominated volume. However, three points can be made:

(i) This was surely the great creative epoch of English Christianity. There is just nothing like it before or after in England's spiritual odyssey. To this era we must trace the origins of Puritanism, the documents of the Westminster Assembly, High Church Anglicanism, Broad Church

Anglicanism ("Latitudinarianism"), Congregationalism, Baptists, Quakers, the Arminian-Calvinist divide, the Anglican-Nonconformist divide, and a host of other things that make English Protestantism so distinctive. Where else in the world did Protestantism show itself so bursting with innovative diversity? If we are to tell the story at all, we must give it room to breathe.

(ii) Given the unique impact that English Protestantism has made on world Christianity, through the several centuries of the British Empire, the creation of America as a new Protestant nation, and the King James Bible, we should not scruple to assign appropriate space to seeing how English Protestantism took shape.

(iii) Most readers of this book will in any case welcome the opportunity to immerse themselves in the English story. Who am I to disappoint them, being English myself?

Third, I have omitted several topics from the present volume, because of their more intimate connection with the next one. Chief among these is the scientific revolution and its impact on religious thought. This seems so bound up with the ultimate emergence of the Enlightenment, the distinctive phenomenon of the 18th century, that I decided to treat the two as one. Our next instalment, then, will deal with the rise of modern science and the dawn of the Enlightenment—for good and ill (there were both gains and losses).

Alert readers will also note the absence of the Moravians from the section on Pietism in chapter 1. Again, I postponed coverage of the Moravians to the next volume because of their fairly profound link with the Evangelical Revival in England, especially through John Wesley, who was in some ways an English Moravian.

Finally, I make little apology for not devoting separate sections to nations other than England, Scotland, France, Germany, and (to an extent) Russia. They serve as templates for the wider story. This volume would have more than doubled in length, had I constructed it on a nation-by-nation plan rather than thematically. Those with a special interest in the detailed story of Welsh, Irish, Dutch, Danish, Swedish, Swiss, Spanish, Italian, Polish, Hungarian, Austrian, or Balkan (etc.) Christianity, will be able to find excellent treatments elsewhere. If they appear in this volume, it is by way of particular episodes that had a global impact, e.g. the Arminian controversy in the Dutch Republic.

✦ ✦ ✦ ✦ ✦ ✦ ✦

Samuel Taylor Coleridge, the Unitarian whose agonizing life-journey led him at last to humble Trinitarian faith, was an avid reader, and his comment on histories of the English Civil War (one of the central conflicts of this volume) can be applied more widely to our theatre of events:

> How many books are still written and published about Charles the First and his times! Such is the fresh and enduring interest of that grand crisis of morals, religion, and government! But these books are none of them works of any genius or imagination; not one of these authors seems to be able to throw himself back into that age; if they did, there would be less praise and less blame bestowed on both sides.[1]

---

1. S.T. Coleridge, *Tabletalk* November 9th 1833. Whether the present book has any genius or imagination is for others to say.

List of maps and illustrations

Maps

Illustrations

To the best of our knowledge all these images are in the
public domain (except where acknowledged).

General map of Europe in about 1650

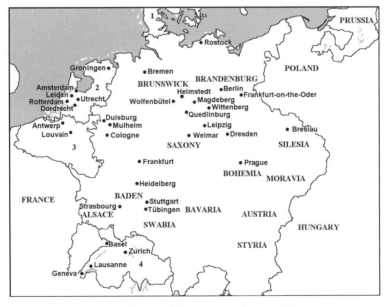

Map of central Europe in about 1650

11

Acknowledgements

Thanks to Phil Arthur, Tim Grass, Alan Howe, Keith Mathison, William VanDoodewaard, Father Richard Conrad of Blackfriars (Oxford), Father Alexis of the St Edward Brotherhood (Brookwood), and Archbishop Chrysostomos of Etna, for valued help and advice along the way. A special word of thanks to my Lutheran friend Paul Williams, whose encyclopaedic knowledge of Lutheranism made chapter 1 possible.

Chapter 1

Germany and the Lutheran Faith

1
A house divided: the post-Luther controversies and the Formula of Concord

1. Lutheranism in the melting pot

Lutheranism was one of the three forms taken by the great 16th century revolt against the Roman papacy (the other two being the Reformed or Calvinist Reformation, and the Radical or Anabaptist Reformation). The Lutheran faith had become the established religion in much of Germany, and in Denmark, Sweden, Norway, Finland, and Iceland.[1]

In the period after Martin Luther's death in 1546, the Lutheran Churches passed through a furnace of severe theological testing. As long as Luther was alive, his titanic personality was powerful enough to drag in its wake Lutherans of every stripe. His right-hand man, **Philip Melanchthon** (1497–1560), who disagreed with his master on several matters, kept silence out of respect for Luther's overwhelming charisma and achievements. When Luther died, however, the Reformer's funeral bells seemed to be tolling not only for his death, but for the end of peace and unity among Lutheran theologians. The fires of controversy were soon blazing fiercely around a number of topics, threatening the entire Lutheran Reformation with self-destruction.

---

1. See *Volume Three: Renaissance and Reformation*, Chapters 2 and 3.

The original heartland of Lutheranism was Germany, and it was here that these disputes raged over a 30 year period. The following century would see Lutheran Germany devastated physically by the horrors of the Thirty Years' War (see section 3); we could say, however, that it had already suffered its Thirty Years' War in a theological sense between 1546 and 1577. Philip Melanchthon became so depressed by the bitter doctrinal conflict that he looked forward to death as a blessed deliverance. A few days before he departed from the world, Melanchthon wrote a brief note on the pros and cons of dying; the advantages, he thought, were simply two—it would free him from sin, and from the fury of theologians!

Eventually, as we shall see, the issues that so troubled Melanchthon and the Lutheran world were resolved comprehensively by the epoch-making *Formula of Concord* in 1577, which (alongside the Augsburg Confession and Luther's Small Catechism) became the chief doctrinal statement for Lutherans throughout Europe. So it remains among conservative Lutherans today. Indeed, far more than Augsburg or the Catechism, the *Formula of Concord* defined who Lutherans were against Calvinism, which had played a role in the controversies.

In the course of these Church-fracturing quarrels, a party emerged within Lutheranism that self-consciously saw itself as defending the heritage of Luther and the original Lutheran Reformation against innovators and corruptors. This conservative party was called the "Gnesio-Lutherans". This term comes from the Greek *gnesios*, "authentic"—hence the authentic or genuine Lutherans. Sometimes the contentions of 1546–77 are perceived as being between the Gnesio-Lutherans and the "Philippists" (disciples of Philip Melanchthon). But this is too simplistic; some of the controversies cannot be described in that way. Gnesio-Lutherans and Philippists were sometimes on the same side against a third party, and on occasion even a Gnesio-Lutheran could go badly off the rails (see the synergistic controversy).

Let us now consider the particular controversies that so tortured the Lutheran Churches over this 30 year period.

2. The antinomian controversy[2]

This controversy had two phases. In the first, the central figure was *Johann Agricola* (1494–1566), who for most of his career was a court preacher in Berlin, capital city of the leading Lutheran state of Brandenberg. Agricola's basic contention was that Law and Gospel are so radically opposed that Christians no longer had any need of the Law to convict them of sin or work repentance in them—the Gospel alone was sufficient to do this. Agricola was opposed by both Luther and Melanchthon, who insisted on the ongoing relevance of the Law to awaken conviction and repentance in the believer. As long as Luther lived, Agricola was kept in check by the sheer personal force of the great Reformer. After Luther's death, Agricola became more outspoken in his views.

The second phase of the antinomian controversy, in the mid 1550s, involved the so-called "third use" of the Law. In Protestant thinking (both Lutheran and Reformed), the Law is traditionally seen as having three uses, often described in Lutheranism as *curb*, *mirror*, and *rule*, which we could summarize thus:

(i) *Curb*: to restrain people from committing sin (partly through the divinely ordained functions of the state, deterring sinners by the threat of physical punishment);

(ii) *Mirror*: to convict the conscience of sin before God by showing the sinner his true condition in the light of God's standards;

(iii) *Rule*: to teach Christians about the holy life they are to live.

Some of Agricola's sympathizers now denied this third use of the law. The foremost figures were Andreas Poach (c.1515–85), pastor of Erfurt and an editor of Luther's *Table Talk*; Anton Otto, pastor of Nordhausen (born 1505, date of death unknown); and Michael Neander (1525–95), rector of a school at Ilfeld, who

---

2. "Antinomian" is from the Greek *anti*, against, and *nomos*, the law—hence "against the law".

had a reputation as one of Germany's most learned men. The distinguished Gnesio-Lutheran *Andreas Musculus* (1514–81), professor at Frankfurt,[3] also became involved (Musculus later retracted some statements about the law's third use which he regarded, in retrospect, as antinomian). These theologians argued that the Law had no teaching or guiding function for the Christian. Indwelt by the Holy Spirit, true believers intuitively knew what was right, and spontaneously did it—they had no need of further guidance. Such views met with the same resistance as Agricola's had. The disciples of both Luther and Melanchthon maintained that the Law was necessary as a moral guide in the Christian life, not least to safeguard believers from false, imaginary views of holiness.

3. *The adiaphorist controversy*

This dispute broke out as a result of the military triumph of Charles V, the Holy Roman Emperor (1519–56), over German Lutherans in the Schmalkaldic War in 1546–7.[4] The Catholic sovereign imposed on most of the defeated Lutherans a religious settlement called the Augsburg Interim in May 1548. On ducal Saxony, however, he imposed a milder settlement—the Leipzig Interim—as a reward for the loyalty of the Saxon Duke Maurice during the war (a loyalty perceived as treachery by other Lutherans, since Maurice had invaded the Lutheran heartland of electoral Saxony on Charles' behalf). The Leipzig Interim maintained the key Lutheran doctrine of justification by faith, but restored medieval Catholic ceremonies of worship, e.g. the way that holy communion was celebrated. Philip Melanchthon, the chief drafter of the Leipzig Interim, defended it on the grounds that the ceremonies were *adiaphora* (Greek for "things indifferent").

However, one place in Germany had managed to defy the imperial victory: the great Lutheran city of Magdeburg. The

---

3. Not to be confused with the better known Reformed theologian Wolfgang Musculus.
4. See *Volume Three: Renaissance and Reformation*, Chapter 6, section 1.

emperor's army put it under prolonged siege, but could not conquer it. In this fortress of Lutheran defiance, the Gnesio-Lutheran theologians **Nicholas von Amsdorf** (1483–1565) and **Matthias Flacius** (1520–75) attacked the Leipzig Interim as a dangerous compromise. Because of the Augsburg Interim, which did not clearly teach justification by faith but did recognize papal supremacy, the Gospel itself (they argued) was under threat. In that situation, even things indifferent could become badges of the enemy, and acceptance of those badges by the faithful Church would confuse the weak and encourage a spirit of surrender. The Catholic ceremonies restored by the Leipzig Interim, therefore, could not be tolerated.

The adiaphorist controversy raged for five years, until Maurice of Saxony in 1552 switched sides, declared war on the emperor, and lifted the siege of Magdeburg. Both of the Interims—Augsburg and Leipzig—now became dead letters; Lutherans had regained their military ascendancy. They also regained their political power through the Peace of Augsburg in 1555. Even so, the issues raised by the adiaphorist controversy had not been resolved, and a running sore of bad feeling was left between Melanchthon and his supporters on the one side, and the Gnesio-Lutherans on the other.

4. The Crypto-Calvinist controversy

"Crypto-Calvinism" was the term used by Gnesio-Lutherans to describe the views of Philip Melanchthon and his followers concerning the Lord's Supper. As we saw back in Volume Three, in the aftermath of the Marburg Colloquy of 1529, Melanchthon moved closer to Reformed pioneer Martin Bucer's understanding of Christ's presence in the eucharist.[5] From the 1540s, Melanchthon's intimate friendship with John Calvin was instrumental in winning Melanchthon over more fully to a Reformed view. This included Reformed Christology, which denied the Lutheran idea of Christ's human body being omnipresent. We could summarize the two views as follows:

---

5. See ibid., Chapter 3, section 7.

(i) Luther's followers taught that in a mysterious manner
that transcended reason, the bread and wine of the
eucharist physically became the body and blood
of Christ, yet without ceasing in any way to be
bread and wine. This latter point distinguished the
Lutheran view from the Roman Catholic doctrine of
transubstantiation, which maintained that the bread
and wine *ceased* to be bread and wine in anything
but appearance; their nature or substance was now
exclusively Christ's body and blood. Lutherans
dissented: the bread and wine, they held, retained their
nature, and coexisted with Christ's body and blood.
For strict Lutherans, the change in the eucharistic
elements was made theologically, if not rationally,
comprehensible by the "communication of attributes"
in the incarnation (in Latin, *communicatio idiomatum*).
This meant that the divine and human natures of Christ
participated each in the attributes of the other. Hence
Christ's human body participated in the omnipresence
("ubiquity") of His divine nature—He was or could be
everywhere in His flesh.

(ii) The Reformed held that Christ's body and blood were
truly given to believers in the eucharist, but to believers
alone—unbelievers would receive only bread and
wine. They rejected, however, any view which might
seem to undermine the localized presence of Christ's
resurrection body in heaven, where He now dwelt as
Man, remaining there physically until the Second
Coming. Hence the only change in the bread and wine
was a change of use: they became *signs* of Christ's
body and blood in heaven, whereby the Holy Spirit
conveyed the Saviour's glorified humanity to the soul
through faith. The Reformed also rejected the Lutheran
understanding of the incarnation; Christ's human
nature had indeed been sanctified, enriched with gifts,
and immeasurably glorified in heaven, but it remained

creaturely and finite. Therefore Christ's humanity did not become omnipresent, omnipotent, omniscient, etc.[6]

It was to this Reformed view of the eucharist, classically expounded by Martin Bucer, Peter Martyr, and John Calvin, that Melanchthon and his supporters now strongly inclined. During Luther's lifetime, however, Melanchthon concealed his shift of opinion for fear of offending Luther. After Luther's death, Melanchthon became far more positive in teaching his Calvinist views. Indeed, almost the entire theological staff at Wittenberg University followed Melanchthon's lead. Wittenberg thus became the stronghold of the Crypto-Calvinist party.

Lutherans often refer to the views of Melanchthon and his sympathizers as "Philippist", by which they chiefly mean Melanchthon's views of the eucharist and of human free will. Confusingly for Reformed readers, however, Philippists are also sometimes presented by Lutherans as essentially Reformed in their entire theology—hence "Crypto-Calvinist". Yet the Philippist understanding of human free will in salvation was radically anti-Reformed. We will examine this further in the section on the synergistic controversy. We should therefore bear in mind that although Philippists were virtually at one with the Reformed in their eucharistic doctrine, we cannot take "Philippist" to indicate closeness to the Reformed on every issue. The Philippists were Crypto-Calvinists only in their views of the Lord's Supper, but certainly not in their exaltation of human free will in salvation; here, they were basically followers of Erasmus ("Crypto-Erasmians", perhaps).

It should also be kept in mind that not all disciples of Melanchthon were Philippists! There were those who learned most of their theology from Melanchthon, accepting his general methods and outlook, but did not follow him in his Crypto-Calvinist views of the eucharist, or his synergist views of grace and free will (see the synergistic controversy). When I use the term

---

6. See *Volume Three: Renaissance and Reformation* for a fuller discussion of how the Lutheran and Reformed views differed.

"Philippist", therefore, I mean those disciples of Melanchthon who embraced their master's Crypto-Calvinism and synergism. As well as the theologians in Wittenberg, others became key supporters of Melanchthon's eucharistic Crypto-Calvinism within German Lutheranism. These included **Caspar Peucer** (1525–1602), Melanchthon's son-in-law, who was personal physician to the lord of electoral Saxony, **Prince Augustus I** (1553–86), and **Georg Cracow** (1525–75), professor of jurisprudence, a valued counsellor of the prince. Peucer and Cracow did everything they could to persuade Augustus to favour the Philippists.

The defining moment in the controversy came with the publication of a theological document known as the *Corpus Philippicum* (or *Corpus Doctrinae*) in 1560. This contained an altered version of the Augsburg Confession and of Melanchthon's *Apology* for the Confession. It also included the latest edition of Melanchthon's *Loci Communes*, the great textbook of Lutheran theology.[7] These all now taught the Crypto-Calvinist view of the eucharist. With Prince Augustus's support, the *Corpus Philippicum* became the official doctrinal standard for electoral Saxony. When Duke John William of ducal or Albertine Saxony lost his throne in 1567 for military adventurism, and was imprisoned for life by Emperor Maximilian II, Augustus became guardian of the duke's two young sons. He imposed the Philippist view in ducal Saxony too. In fact, Augustus now required actual doctrinal subscription to the *Corpus Philippicum* in both Saxonies. One hundred pastors, theologians, and schoolteachers were expelled for refusing to subscribe. The Philippists also now began pressing for a Church union between Lutherans and Reformed. They were in touch with Theodore Beza, Calvin's successor in Geneva, and even had one of his treatises published in Wittenberg.

Resistance to the Crypto-Calvinism of the Philippists came from outside of Saxony. The overwhelming majority of German Lutherans were opposed to this eucharistic departure from

---

7. See ibid., Chapter 2, section 7.

Luther's teaching, and to rapprochement with the Reformed. Often the Gnesio-Lutherans used the same strong-arm tactics as Augustus in Saxony: they resorted to legal force to impose a strict Lutheran view, and expel any who dissented. One fascinating result in Breslau was the expulsion of the Crypto-Calvinist theologian Zacharius Ursinus. He removed to the Reformed Palatinate, embraced the Reformed faith, and (together with Caspar Olevianus) authored the Heidelberg Catechism, which became one of the most widely used confessional standards in the Reformed world.

The dominance of Crypto-Calvinism in the Saxonies came to a sudden and unexpected end in 1574. That year Caspar Peucer, the leading Philippist, wrote a letter to the wife of Christian Schuetze, court preacher in electoral Saxony. He enclosed a Reformed prayer book, asking that it be given to Anna, wife of Prince Augustus. "If first we have Mother Anna on our side," Peucer wrote, "there will be no difficulty in winning his lordship [Augustus] too." The letter somehow fell into hands of another court preacher, Lysthenius, who gave it to Augustus. The prince was outraged by what seemed palpable evidence that the Philippists were manipulating his family. He now changed sides completely, purged the Saxonies of all Philippists (many were locked away in prison, and some died there, including Georg Cracow), and restored the strict Lutherans to favour and office. From now on, Augustus's most trusted advisors were to be the two eminent exponents of Luther's eucharistic theology, **Jacob Andreae** and **Martin Chemnitz** (see below). Henceforth a rigorous adherence to Luther's view of the Lord's Supper was assured.

5. The Majoristic controversy

This took its name from the Lutheran theologian **George Major** (1502–74), who for most of his career was a theology professor at Wittenberg. The dispute he stirred up was over the question whether good works were necessary for salvation. Major affirmed in 1551 that they were. He was attacked by the Gnesio-Lutherans Nicholas von Amsdorf and Matthias Flacius, who feared that Major's position was misleading at best, and would encourage people to think that works merited grace. They preferred to say that good works were necessary, not for salvation, but to glorify God in the lives of the saved. There may have been a degree of verbal confusion in the controversy, since Major (at least sometimes) defined salvation not as initial justification exclusively, but as the entire experience of grace, including sanctification.

Amsdorf added to the confusion when he asserted that good works were positively harmful to one's salvation! For this, he was rebuked by other Gnesio-Lutherans. What Amsdorf meant was that good works, if trusted in as meritorious, were harmful, because they then became an alternative to trust in the Gospel of grace. But Amsdorf's way of putting it only muddied the waters of controversy. In various forms, the quarrel rippled out to other Lutheran territories, such as Frankfurt and Brandenburg.

6. *The Osiandrian controversy*

Andreas Osiander (1496–1552) was the leading Lutheran of Nuremberg from 1522 to 1548. After the Holy Roman Emperor Charles V's victory over Germany's Protestants in the civil war of 1546–7, and the imposition of the Augsburg Interim,[8] Osiander fled to Prussia. Here his friend, Count Albert of Prussia, appointed him chief theology professor in Konigsberg University. In the last two years of his life, Osiander created huge controversy within Lutheranism by his treatise *Concerning Justification* (1550). Here Osiander defined justification, not as a forensic declaration (the imputation of Christ's righteousness to the believer's account), but as the actual indwelling of the divine righteousness of Christ in the believer. In His human nature, Osiander argued, Christ was righteous because of His indwelling deity. When we are united with Christ, His divine nature dwells in us too, and sanctifies us. This indwelling of Christ constitutes our saving righteousness before God.

---

8. See ibid., Chapter 6, section 1.

Osiander's non-forensic doctrine of justification isolated him; both the Gnesio-Lutherans and the Philippists attacked him for what seemed a shocking lapse back into medieval Catholic errors about the nature of justification.[9] His only comfort was Johann Brenz, the celebrated Reformer of Wurttemberg, who thought Osiander was more guilty of misleading language than real error. After Osiander's death, however, Prussia's Count Albert canvassed Lutheran divines for a general view on what Osiander had taught, and found a virtually unanimous rejection of it. Albert swung into line: Prussia would offer no further shelter for Osiandrist ideas.

7. The synergistic controversy

The Lutheran Reformation had originally been stamped by a strongly Augustinian stance on the relationship between divine grace and the human will. Luther himself had given classical expression to this in his *Bondage of the Will* in 1525. Against Erasmus's Semi-Pelagian ranking of the human will alongside God's grace as joint causes in conversion, Luther had insisted that grace was unconditionally sovereign, liberating an enslaved will from sin to make it spiritually free for the first time. Luther's view is known as "monergism" (from the Greek "single energy"—God alone converts), as contrasted with Erasmus's "synergism" ("joint energy"—grace and the human will cooperate in conversion).[10] As long as Luther lived, this monergistic understanding of salvation remained unchallenged within the Lutheran Churches.

Philip Melanchthon had initially been an Augustinian monergist. The earliest editions of his *Loci Communes* taught that the fallen human will was in bondage to sin, and that the causes of its regeneration were wholly divine—the Holy Spirit working through the Word of God. Melanchthon, however, became increasingly ambiguous on the role of the human will in salvation. Later editions of the *Loci* drifted towards a more Erasmian view, positing the human will alongside the Spirit

---

9. See also Calvin *Institutes* 3:11:5-12.

10. See *Volume Three: Renaissance and Reformation*, Chapter 3, section 4.

and the Word as a third factor in conversion. Melanchthon was clearly moving towards a synergist conception of salvation. But no criticism was levelled against him while Luther lived; Luther seems never to have lost his confidence in Melanchthon's theological integrity, which in hindsight is somewhat puzzling (could Luther have been so wholly unaware of his friend's change of mind about monergism and the eucharist?). Luther's death removed the restraints on Melanchthon's journey to synergism. His students at Wittenberg were now going out into schools and parishes, openly teaching that the human will must cooperate by its own energy in its conversion. The storm broke in 1555, when one of Melanchthon's disciples, *Johann Pfeffinger* (1493–1573), professor at Leipzig University in electoral Saxony, published his *Five Questions concerning the Freedom of the Human Will*. The treatise taught synergism in no uncertain terms, quoting Melanchthon as an authority. Pfeffinger was robustly supported by *Victorinus Strigel* (1524–69), professor at Jena University in ducal Saxony.

Melanchthon and his party were attacked by the Gnesio-Lutherans Nicholas von Amsdorf and Matthias Flacius (both lecturers in Jena, like their Philippist colleague Strigel); they upheld Luther's original monergism. By 1559, the controversy had become intense. At the bidding of Amsdorf and Flacius, John Frederick II of ducal Saxony issued a document entitled *The Book of Confutation*, which condemned synergist errors. All pastors in ducal Saxony were to subscribe to this confession. Strigel and others were imprisoned for refusing. But these coercive measures were deemed distasteful, and a colloquy was arranged at Weimar in ducal Saxony in 1560.

The main protagonists at the Weimar colloquy were Strigel and Flacius. It proved a disaster for Flacius; Strigel manoeuvred him into saying that after Adam's fall, sin now belonged to the very substance of human nature. This was Flacius' way of trying to affirm the bondage of the will. But it played into the hands of Strigel and the synergists, because it made sin essential to human nature, rather than an unnatural distortion or perversion of it, as Augustine had maintained. And if sin was essential to human nature, did that not make God the author of sin, since He was the Creator of all essences? Flacius' extremism was disowned by the great majority of the other Gnesio-Lutherans. But Flacius himself would not retract what he had said, and it led to his disgrace. He was expelled from ducal Saxony, and tragically spent the rest of his life as an unwanted wanderer. The colloquy settled nothing, and the synergistic controversy blazed on through the 1560s. John Frederick alternately persecuted the synergists and the Gnesio-Lutherans.

8. *The Formula of Concord*

The controversies that were ravaging Lutheranism almost to desolation finally inspired some theologians (perhaps from sheer desperation) to seek a framework for unity. The movers behind this development were Jacob Andreae (1528–90), professor at Tübingen University in the Lutheran state of Wurttemberg; Martin Chemnitz (1522–86), who spent most of his adult career in the Lutheran state of Brunswick, where he superintended the churches and helped found the University of Helmstedt (see the next section for more on Chemnitz); and **Nicholas Selnecker** (1530–92), based mostly in Leipzig in electoral Saxony, where he was pastor of the Saint Thomas Church. Andreae was a disciple of Johann Brenz, and represented a distinctive "Brenzian" tradition within Lutheranism. Chemnitz and Selnecker were disciples of Melanchthon, but not Philippists (they followed Melanchthon's general outlook, but did not embrace their master's eucharistic Crypto-Calvinism or his synergism).

Andreae was the main wellspring of this theological peace movement. He published in 1573 his *Six Sermons on the Division among Theologians of the Augsburg Confession*. Here he set forth a platform which moderate Gnesio-Lutherans and Melanchthonians could agree on, e.g. he rejected both Flacius' view of original sin, and the Philippist view of synergism. This formed the basis of the Swabian Concord of 1574 (Swabia was the region where Andreae's Wurttemberg was located), a more purely theological document that abandoned the sermon format. It was then revised by Chemnitz and another Melanchthonian,

David Chytraeus (1530–1600), professor of theology at
Rostock (on the Baltic coast). The new document was known
as the Swabian-Saxon Concord.

Meanwhile, Prince Augustus of electoral Saxony, in the
aftermath of purging all Philippists from his domain, involved
another Lutheran prince, Count George Ernest of Henneberg,
in the quest for unity-in-the-truth. In November 1575, George
Ernest, together with Duke Ludwig of Wurttemberg and
margrave Karl of Baden, appointed a number of theologians to
submit proposals for a new doctrinal statement. The theologians
were Wurttemberg's court preacher Lucas Osiander the Elder (not
to be confused with Andreas Osiander), Balthasar Bidembach
of Stuttgart, and a few others from Henneberg and Baden. The
resulting document, after further discussion, was finally published
at Maulbronn (in Wurttemberg) in January 1576.

On the crest of this swelling wave, six of the peace movement
theologians then met at Torgau in ducal Saxony, during May and
June 1576: Jacob Andreae, Martin Chemnitz, David Chytraeus,
Christopher Korner, Andreas Musculus, and Nicholas Selnecker.
After much discussion they produced the Torgau Book. The
Torgau Book became the basis for the final peace platform that
emerged in May 1577, the Formula of Concord. It had 12 articles.[11]

1. Original Sin
2. Free Will
3. The Righteousness of Faith Before God
4. Good Works
5. The Law and the Gospel
6. The Third Use of the Law
7. The Lord's Supper
8. The Person of Christ
9. The Descent of Christ to Hell
10. Church Rites
11. God's Eternal Foreknowledge and Election

---

11. The Five Points of Calvinism are thus matched by the Twelve Points
of Lutheranism!

12. Other Factions and Sects That Never Embraced the Augsburg Confession

The Formula succeeded in blending together in a healthy synthesis the outlook of moderate Gnesio-Lutherans (but not extremists like Flacius), conservative Melanchthonians (but not Philippists), and those who stood in the somewhat distinct tradition of Johann Brenz (like Jacob Andreae). On all the disputed points, a middle ground was staked out that went beyond mere verbal agreement over ambiguous statements; this was much more in the spirit of the ancient Church's Creed of Chalcedon, which had creatively integrated the genuine concerns of Alexandrian and Antiochene theologians.

It would take too long to consider in any detail the positions adopted by the Formula on each of the 12 points. It would be simpler to say what the Formula ruled out. In the main, it excluded the following:

Synergism. Lutherans were now bound to believe in monergism—that God's energy was the sole positive power at work in human conversion. The human will was free in the earthly sphere (free to choose whether to perform this or that earthly action, like keeping or breaking the law of the land), but in the spiritual sphere it was enslaved to sin and needed divine liberation.

Antinomianism. Lutherans would now acknowledge the third use of the law—its capacity to guide believers in the way of practical holiness. Lutherans were also to recognize that good works must (on the one side) be excluded from the sinner's justification before God, but were (on the other side) necessary fruits of true faith, which believers were obligated to do, not to justify themselves, but to render to God the obedience owed to Him.

The Crypto-Calvinist view of the eucharist. Lutherans from now on would be committed to Luther's view of the real presence, stated against Zwingli at the Marburg colloquy. Nothing short of this—not even the "spiritual real

presence" advocated by Peter Martyr and John Calvin—
would be tolerated.

The Reformed view of the relationship between Christ's two natures.
Lutherans were henceforth to confess the "communicatio
idiomatum", the mutual sharing of attributes by the two
natures, so that Christ could be truly omnipresent in His
flesh. This provided the Christological undergirding for
the robust Lutheran view of the real presence.

The 11th article on *God's Eternal Foreknowledge and Election*
was out of keeping with the others, in not being a response
to an existing controversy in Lutheranism. It was instead a
"pre-emptive strike" against what most Lutherans believed was
a dangerous tendency in Calvinism, which could infect the
Lutheran Churches unless the Formula guarded against it. After
all, the Calvinist view of the eucharist had infected many, and
there had been disputes between Lutherans and Reformed over
predestination in Strasbourg and Brunswick.

The danger that the Formula's architects perceived in the
Reformed doctrine of predestination was its view of reprobation.
If election to salvation was balanced by a symmetrical reprobation
to damnation, this might sound logical, Lutherans argued, but
it threatened the genuineness of God's love revealed in Christ.
How could anyone take God's love seriously, or be able to trust
it, if all the time, lurking behind the love, there was an eternal
purpose to damn some? To preserve the reality, the universality,
and the trustworthiness of God's love, the framers of the Formula
maintained that God in Christ was equally intent on saving all.
If some were actually saved, they must credit this entirely to His
grace and not in any sense to themselves. However, if others
were lost, they must not ascribe this to any failure of saving
intent in God, but exclusively to their own resistance to His
grace. If this appeared to violate logic, so much the worse for
logic. We must be content with paradox in this life; in the next,
all will be made clear. Such was the Lutheran view.

The Formula of Concord was officially embraced by around
two thirds of Germany's Lutheran lands, including 23 dukes

and princes and 35 imperial cities. For various local reasons, the remaining third did not subscribe, but often the pastors and theologians of those lands accepted the Formula, even if their prince, duke, count, or city council did not. The rulers of some of these territories later changed their minds and signed the Formula. Frederick II (1559–88), king of Lutheran Denmark, rejected the Formula in a decree of 1580, not wishing to see a German confession of faith obtaining authority in his dominions. However, despite Frederick, the Danish Lutheran clergy generally acknowledged the Formula as a summary of Lutheran teaching. The Swedish Lutheran clergy likewise generally accepted the Formula, but could not persuade their successive monarchs to make it legally binding (it was finally given a limited degree of royal recognition in 1686 by King Charles XI). The Hungarian Lutheran Church endorsed the Formula in 1597.

By and large, then, the Lutheran world received the Formula of Concord, at least at the popular level, even where Lutheran rulers hesitated. This gave Lutherans something the Reformed Churches of Europe never had: an internationally recognized confession of faith.[12]

When the Formula was officially published in 1580, as the Book of Concord, it was bound with all the other authoritative confessional statements of the Lutheran Reformation (the Augsburg Confession, Melanchthon's *Apology for the Augsburg Confession*, Luther's Small and Large Catechisms and his Schmalkald Articles, and Melanchthon's *Treatise on the Primacy of the Pope*) as together constituting the standard of orthodox Lutheranism. Two other documents were also routinely published in each edition of the Book of Concord. There was the Catalogue of Testimonies, a list of passages from the early Church fathers, giving patristic backing to Lutheran theology.

---

12. The canons of Dort did achieve a similar status among the Reformed in the 17th century, but their impact was less enduring. Conservative Lutherans all over the world today still acknowledge the Formula of Concord; but apart from the conservative Dutch Reformed tradition, the same cannot be said about the canons of Dort among Calvinists.

In Saxony, there was additionally the Saxon Visitation Articles of 1592, dealing with a resurgence of the Crypto-Calvinist controversy in Saxony (the topics covered were the eucharist, Christology, and predestination). The Visitation Articles were published with every version of the Book of Concord in Saxony until the early 19th century.

2
Lutheran Orthodoxy

1. *The reign of Aristotle*

The period in Lutheranism after peace had been restored by the Formula of Concord is known as the age of Lutheran Orthodoxy. This is because the Formula provided a fairly detailed standard of orthodox teaching for the Lutheran Churches which they had previously lacked. Lutheran Orthodoxy is also known as Lutheran scholasticism, for reasons that will soon become apparent. Historians usually reckon the Orthodox era to have lasted until around 1730, when Lutheranism entered its Enlightenment phase.[1]

However, there were other distinguishing characteristics of Lutheran Orthodoxy. We can note the following two:

(i) *Systematic theology.* This was the era of the great Lutheran systematic theologians. Philip Melanchthon had, of course, already written the first Lutheran theology textbook in the *Loci Communes* as early as 1521. However, the age of Lutheran Orthodoxy gave a new scientific precision and exhaustive scope to the task of theology. Each theological topic was examined with the utmost

---

1. The Enlightenment was a Europe-wide cultural movement comparable to the Renaissance, although with a different spirit and message—the all-sufficiency of human reason. We can probably say that the Enlightenment began around the end of the 17th century or the start of the 18th, with some "signs of the times" a little earlier, e.g. Descartes' philosophy and the rise of science.

logical rigour and comprehensiveness; all topics were
(often) arranged into an overarching pattern, a "system"
of truth that would explain everything important. (I am
not using the word "system" here in a negative sense to
imply something cold and impersonal; it was the term
employed by the Orthodox theologians themselves. It
derives from a Greek word meaning "an organized whole".)
This emphasis on systematic theology is one reason
why Lutheran Orthodoxy has been called "scholastic",
in imitation of the medieval Catholic scholastics who
delighted in systematic presentations of truth.[2]

(ii) *Aristotelian methodology.* The theologians of Lutheran
Orthodoxy, unlike their predecessors, extensively used
the philosophy of the pre-Christian Greek thinker
Aristotle as a tool for organizing their thoughts. Those
thoughts were not limited to theology; the spokesmen
of Orthodoxy were just as likely to include metaphysics
in their writings (in other words, the rational study of
creation's ultimate principles like existence, time, space,
causation, the structure of the human mind, and so
forth). Both in metaphysics and in theology, Orthodoxy
generally embraced Aristotle's way of analysing and
discussing subjects. Here is another reason for the
"scholastic" label, this time reflecting the tradition of
medieval scholasticism stemming from Thomas Aquinas,
with his high esteem for Aristotle.

This use of Aristotle by Lutherans may seem strange, given
Luther's well-known hostility both to Aristotle himself, and to
Thomas Aquinas, whose Aristotelian theology formed so massive
a segment of the medieval Catholicism Luther rejected. However,
some careful distinctions are needed. What Luther objected to
was not Aristotle *per se*, but the way Luther believed the medieval
Church had allowed Aristotelian philosophy to dictate the content
of Christian theological and moral teaching. As for Thomas

---

2. See *Volume Two: The Middle Ages*, Chapter 7.

Aquinas, it is not clear how far Luther actually knew Aquinas' theology first-hand, or the extent to which his hostility was really targeted at Aquinas' later disciples (one was Cardinal Cajetan, with whom Luther did not exactly have a sparkling relationship[3]). Lutheran Aristotelianism had a number of pioneers in the 16th century, but the principal figure was **Cornelius Martini** (1568–1621) of Helmstedt University in Lutheran Brunswick. With intellectual power and eloquence, Martini disseminated in Helmstedt the more global revival of interest in Aristotle's philosophy that was blossoming in Europe's universities. It provoked bitter controversy with another Helmstedt professor, **Daniel Hoffmann** (1538–1611), a Gnesio-Lutheran who (out of a perceived loyalty to Luther) denounced Aristotle and all his works as a poisoned well of falsehood. In fact Hoffmann said much the same about all philosophy, not just Aristotle. Martini by contrast vindicated Aristotle as a generally sound guide in matters philosophical, although not in theology where divine revelation was the only pure source of knowledge. Aristotelian philosophy and biblical theology could live together as complementary partners, Martini claimed.

Many Lutherans felt torn between Hoffmann and Martini, seeming to sense the voice of Luther in the first and of Melanchthon in the second. It was *Johann Gerhard* (see below) who captured the middle ground, and persuaded Lutheran theologians that there was a right and fruitful way of using Aristotle without becoming uncritically enslaved to him. In essence, Gerhard argued, this consisted in embracing two basic aspects of Aristotle's thought:

> (i) *Aristotle's empiricism*—his belief that experience, not abstract reasoning, was the correct path to knowledge and understanding of all things in the earthly realm. Luther had distinguished between the human sphere, where reason reigned, and the divine sphere, where reason was unreliable and God's revelation reigned. Gerhard convinced

---

3. See *Volume Three: Renaissance and Reformation*, Chapter 2, section 3.

Lutherans that in the human sphere, the "reason" that
should be followed was an Aristotelian reason.

(ii) *Aristotle's way of analysing causes.* Aristotle dissected
causation into a fourfold scheme: material cause, formal
cause, efficient cause, and final cause. To illustrate: let
us imagine a leather football. Its *material* cause is the
matter, the stuff, it is made of: leather. Its *formal* cause is
the form, essence, or idea that makes the football what
it is: a spherical object capable of being kicked about by
human beings. Its *efficient* cause is whoever or whatever
produced it: presumably a football factory, or maybe it
was handmade. Its *final* cause is the purpose for which
it exists: to make a particular game (football or soccer)
possible, thereby giving entertainment to those who play.
Gerhard successfully argued that this Aristotelian scheme
of analysing causes was both legitimate and illuminating,
and could be applied in theology as well as metaphysics.
A theological application might be baptism. Its *material*
cause: water. Its *formal* cause: the act of immersing a
believer or a believer's child in the water.[4] Its *efficient* cause:
Christ who ordained baptism in Matthew 28:19. Its *final*
cause: in order that the Holy Spirit might implant the
seed of faith in a child, or seal the faith of an adult.[5]

Almost as influential as Gerhard in promoting the synthesis
of Luther and Aristotle was Balthasar Meisner (1587–1626)
of Wittenberg. He did not, like Gerhard, write a systematic
theology pervaded by Aristotelianism, but produced a specific
treatise on the right use of philosophy in theology, the *Philosophia
Sobria* ("Sober Philosophy"), published in 1611. Meisner's
arguments, essentially the same as Gerhard's, were a milestone
in the theology-philosophy interface in Lutheran Orthodoxy. All
it needed was the imprimatur of Gerhard's epoch-making *Loci
Theologici* (1610–22) for the Lutheran world to be convinced.

---

4. Baptists, do not panic: this is a Lutheran definition.
5. Again, a Lutheran definition.

Here, then, was the Aristotelianism of the Lutheran Orthodox theologians. They did not take the content of their theology (or not much of it) from Aristotle, or from Aquinas. For example, Lutherans had little to say in their apologetics about the rational proofs for God's existence. What they did was to utilize Aristotle's methods for analysing, categorizing, and discussing their views of metaphysics and theology. It is certainly unjust to characterize Lutheran Orthodoxy as little better than a dry, unbiblical Aristotelian philosophy with a thin Christian varnish, as is sometimes alleged. One can hardly read the actual works of men like Gerhard, Calov, or Quenstedt, and conclude that one is on non-Christian or non-biblical ground.

Let us now consider some representative figures from the ranks of Lutheran Orthodoxy.

2. Martin Chemnitz

"If the second Martin had not come, the first Martin would scarcely have endured." This 17th century epigram sums up how Lutherans in our period (and later) felt about Martin Chemnitz (1522–86). He, the second Martin, by his encyclopaedic learning, brilliant writings, and key role in the *Formula of Concord*, did more than any other man to preserve the legacy of the first Martin (Luther), and ensure it would be transmitted to future generations. Chemnitz stands in the borderlands between the *Formula of Concord*, which he had a pivotal role in creating, and the age of Orthodoxy. We could say that he was the last of the original Lutherans and the first of the Orthodox.

Chemnitz was born at Treuenbritzen in Brandenburg. In his youth he studied theology at Wittenberg under Philip Melanchthon, whom he always regarded as his mentor despite not following him into Crypto-Calvinism or synergism (see previous section). Oddly to the modern student, he did share Melanchthon's fascination with astrology, at least for a time, but this soon dissipated into an all-absorbing passion for theology.[6]

---

6. Many theologians in the medieval and Reformation eras accepted a limited validity for astrology; they thought it could predict some

At Wittenberg Chemnitz sometimes stood in for Melanchthon if the master was unavailable for a lecture; he also gave his own lectures on Lutheran theology, using Melanchthon's famous *Loci Communes* as his textbook. The worsening controversies

that were beginning to tear Lutheranism apart, involving even Melanchthon's views on some issues, convinced Chemnitz that Lutheran unity was an urgently necessary goal to strive after, especially in the face of an increasingly aggressive Roman Catholic revival in the Counter-Reformation.

At the close of 1554, Chemnitz left Wittenberg to become assistant to the distinguished theologian Joachim Morlin (1514–71), superintendent of the Lutheran churches in

Martin Chemnitz (1522–86)
Portrait by an unknown artist

Brunswick-Wolfenbüttel. Morlin stepped down from office in 1567 to become Bishop of Samland in Prussia; Chemnitz took over as superintendent of Brunswick-Wolfenbüttel, a position he held for the remainder of his life. In that capacity, he presided at a gathering of Brunswick's pastors twice a month, where church issues were discussed, particularly cases of discipline. He gave lectures at these meetings from Melanchthon's *Loci Communes*. He also (slowly) won a reputation in Brunswick's churches as a

future events, including the behaviour of people "in the mass" (in large aggregates or populations), but not individual conduct or destiny. This view, found classically in Thomas Aquinas, was based on the belief that real influences emanated from the stars and planets, affecting the human soul. Compare the Geneva Bible translation of Job 38:31, "Canst thou restraine the sweete influences of the Pleiades?" For Aquinas see *Summa Theologiae*, Second Part of the Second Part, Question 95, Article 5.

fine preacher, although his early efforts were unpromising—he improved over time.

Chemnitz was instrumental, too, in setting up the University of Helmstedt in 1575–6, the first Protestant university in that region of northern Germany. It rapidly developed into a large institution; its most famous theological professor would be **Georg Calixtus** (see below). Ironically, the *Formula of Concord*, which Chemnitz had done so much to help create as a bond of Lutheran unity, was not officially adopted in Brunswick; its duke Julius (1568–89) refused to endorse the *Formula*, having been personally offended by criticism from Chemnitz. (Chemnitz had rebuked the duke for having his three sons ordained as Roman Catholic priests in order to get his hands on the Catholic bishopric of Halberstadt. The duke's revenge on Chemnitz was to refuse to ratify the *Formula* in Brunswick.)

We have already considered Chemnitz' part in drafting the *Formula of Concord*. His theology could be described as broadly Melanchthonian, in spirit, method, and content, but keeping Melanchthon's teaching closer to that of Luther, notably on the eucharist and divine sovereignty in regeneration. Chemnitz' powerful influence flowed out to the Lutherans of his own and following times through his weighty treatises, marked by massive learning, sincere but modest piety, a concern to demonstrate the catholic nature of Lutheran faith (that it had continuity with the faith of the early church fathers), and a strong sense that theology existed to serve the Church.

Probably Chemnitz's most accessible work for modern readers is his *Examination of the Council of Trent*, which appeared in four parts between 1565 and 1573. It has been extolled as one of the finest defences of historic Protestantism ever penned. Here Chemnitz exposed the decrees of Trent to a probing critique, especially by comparing Trent's teaching with the beliefs and practices of the patristic era, and pointing out the frequent lack of harmony between the two. His knowledge of the early church fathers was encyclopaedic. Of course, Chemnitz also carefully expounded the Bible to demonstrate Trent's errors; but we should remember that the original Lutheran and Reformed pioneers were not simplistic "Bible alone" people—they were almost as concerned to establish continuity with the early church. This was in order to ward off the otherwise annihilating Catholic accusation that the Protestant faith was a 16th century novelty, unknown to the Christians of the previous 1,500 years. The idea that Christianity had effectively vanished after the death of the apostles, to be miraculously reborn in the 16th century, was an Anabaptist, not a Lutheran or Reformed, view.

Other classic and influential treatises by Chemnitz included his *Repetition of the Wholesome Doctrine of the True Presence* (1561), a defence of Luther's eucharistic views; his *Concerning the Two Natures in Christ* (1570), a defence of Lutheran Christology; his systematic theology textbook, the *Loci Theologici*, published posthumously in 1591 (it was incomplete, based on his Brunswick lectures on Melanchthon's *Loci Communes*); and his *Harmony of the Four Gospel-writers*, completed after his death by Polycarp Leyser (1552–1610) and Johann Gerhard (see below) and published in 1626–7—extraordinarily popular among serious Bible students in the 17th century.

3. Johann Gerhard

Johann Gerhard (1582–1637) was the first of the great Lutheran "scholastics" (see introduction to this section), who persuaded most Lutheran theologians to accept a selective use of Aristotle in philosophy and in theological method. Next after Luther and Chemnitz, he was the third genuinely great theologian of the Lutheran tradition. Popular mythology would probably expect a scholastic thinker who specialized in systematic theology to have been a rather dry and dusty figure; but Gerhard early on absorbed a vibrant spiritual vitality from his pastor in his native Quedlinburg, the famous Johann Arndt, ultimate wellspring of the Pietist movement (see section 4). It was Arndt's influence that inspired the young Gerhard to study theology at Wittenberg and Jena. He immersed himself in the Bible and the early church fathers.

Gerhard then became a lecturer in Marburg University in 1604 while continuing his own studies there. His presence at Marburg coincided with the reign of a new prince of Hesse (where

Marburg was located), Maurice the Learned (1592–1627), who in 1605 converted to the Reformed faith and proceeded to "Calvinize" his lands. Gerhard, a principled Lutheran, left rather than embrace Calvinism. His piety and learning had (despite his youth—he was only 24) attracted the eye of Duke John Casimir of Saxe-Coburg (1596–1633), who made him superintendent of Heldburg in 1606. This gave Gerhard authority over a large swathe of Lutheran churches in John Casimir's lands; he used his authority to reform them in accord with both his pastoral and doctrinal ideals.

In 1616, John Casimir allowed Gerhard to take up an academic post at Jena University, where he taught for the rest of his life—not just systematic theology, but exegetical classes on many New Testament books. The Thirty Years' War (1618–48) was now raging across Germany (see section 3), and on one occasion Gerhard saved the city of Jena from destruction by pleading with the great Catholic general Tilly, commander of the Holy Roman Empire's army. Gerhard visited Tilly as his troops were poised to sack Jena; when Tilly put his fingers in his ears to resist Gerhard's pleas, the Lutheran divine simply drew closer and shouted, "I don't want you to listen to me now; I want you to listen to God!" Tilly was moved, and in consequence, Jena was not destroyed, merely pillaged in a relatively minor way.

Gerhard's masterpiece was his *Loci Theologici*, published in nine volumes between 1610 and 1622. For the rest of the 17th century this would be probably the most influential of all Lutheran systematic theologies (still influential among conservative Lutherans today). For the first time in Lutheran theology, we find in Gerhard a full-blooded use of Aristotelian methodology to analyse and organize the subject matter. It has been said that in comparison with Chemnitz, Gerhard's approach has greater logical clarity, but is less vivid and readable.

However, Gerhard did produce eminently readable treatises, notably his *Sacred Meditations* (1606). This was a work of piety that won international renown, translated at length into most of the world's chief languages (there was an English edition as early as 1627). *The Daily Exercise of Piety* was another popular spiritual treatise (1612). Other important writings included his *Theological Disputes* (1631–3) against Cardinal Bellarmine, most brilliant of the Counter-Reformation theologians,[7] and his *Catholic Confession* (1634–7): together these two works were weighty statements of Lutheran orthodoxy against Roman Catholicism.

4. Jesper Rasmus Brochmand

Jesper Brochmand (1585–1652) is one of the few non-German Lutherans generally regarded as an outstanding theologian from our period. Born at Koge in Zealand, Denmark's largest island, he studied at several Danish and Lutheran universities. Thereafter he spent most of his life in Copenhagen, teaching theology in its university from 1610 to 1639. That year he was appointed Bishop of Zealand; in this capacity, he carried out a number of worship reforms, such as getting rid of Latin choirs.

Much of Brochmand's life was consumed in controversy with Roman Catholicism. His *Controversiae Sacrae* (1626–8) was a three-volume reply to Cardinal Bellarmine; his *Concerning the Roman Pontificate* (1628) was a massive and erudite examination of the history and theological underpinnings of the papacy; and he delivered a series of lectures against the Jesuits, published posthumously in 1653. His reward from the Jesuits was the alarming description "the boldest despiser of the Catholic rulers, a poisonous spider, and a degenerate Absalom." As well as smiting Rome, Brochmand was equally severe against Calvinists, whom he considered to be as deluded and as dangerous as papists. Brochmand also had a tragic controversy with his old friend and tutor Holger Rosenkrantz (1574–1642), a leading Danish noble and member of the king's council, who in 1627 abandoned politics to devote himself to religious writing. A disciple of Erasmus and Johann Arndt, Rosenkrantz taught that justification was initially by faith alone but subsequently by the grace-empowered works that flowed from faith. Brochmand

7. See Chapter 6, section 3.1, for the life and work Bellarmine.

too was influenced by Arndt, but he bitterly condemned Rosenkrantz's teaching as a betrayal of the Reformation.

In the field of systematic theology, Brochmand's masterwork was his *System of Universal Theology* (1633). He brought out an abridged edition in 1649 which became the standard theology textbook in the training of Danish Lutheran clergy for the next hundred years. Brochmand's theology was a blend of the Bible, the *Formula of Concord*, and the methodology of Aristotle. A fourth ingredient was a concern for practical application; the *System* devoted considerable time to solving ethical dilemmas and showing how doctrine made a difference in practice.

Brochmand wrote a number of devotional-type treatises, notably his commentary on James (1640) and a collection of sermons, *Huspostil* (1635), which retained a huge popularity among spiritually-minded Danes for the following two centuries.

5. Georg Calixtus

Georg Calixtus (1586–1656) was an unusual figure among Lutheran theologians in our period, and hardly deserves the name Orthodox; in fact, he was the most articulate voice among Lutherans of a different vision. Still, because of Calixtus' Lutheranism (he thought the Lutheran Church was the purest and best), and his intimate involvement in the world of Lutheran Orthodoxy (albeit as a critic), this is the best place to consider his life. He is of captivating interest, often hailed as one of the trailblazers of ecumenism.

Born at Medelby in Schleswig, a Lutheran duchy bordering on Denmark, Calixtus studied at the University of Helmstedt (founded by Martin Chemnitz). There he found in the writings of Philip Melanchthon the inspiration for his theology—his father had been a pupil and admirer of Melanchthon. From 1609 to 1613 he travelled in Germany, the Spanish Netherlands, France, and England, where he learned as much as he could about Roman Catholicism and the Reformed faith, both generally despised by Lutherans as perversions of Christianity. In the spirit of Melanchthon, however, Calixtus saw Catholics and Calvinists as "separated brethren" rather than mere heretics.

In London Calixtus had a life-changing encounter with Isaac Casaubon (1559–1614), a Genevan Calvinist who had discovered a spiritual home in Anglicanism. Casaubon was one of the most learned theologians and church historians of the 17th century, a formidable critic of the Catholicism of the Council of Trent. He envisaged a Christian unity based on the few doctrines essential to salvation, either taught clearly in Scripture, or confessed by the early church fathers as necessary interpretations of Scripture. Casaubon's influence on Calixtus matched that of Melanchthon. Later on, he would also particularly warm (among the Reformed) to the teaching of Johannes Cocceius (1603–69) and his covenant theology.[8]

Returning to Helmstedt, he became professor of theology in the university from 1614 to his death in 1656. Here he developed his ecumenical outlook in many treatises, such as his *Concerning the True Christian Religion and Church* (1633), and *Judgment Concerning the Theological Controversies Agitated between Lutherans and Reformed* (1650). His basic argument was that Western Europe could resolve its religious strife between Catholic, Lutheran, and Reformed (horrifyingly visible in the Thirty Years' War) by agreeing to work within "the consensus of the first five centuries". This of course embraced the formative period of the Church's creedal theology—the Apostles' Creed, the Nicene Creed, the Creed (or Formula) of Chalcedon, which all three of the warring "branches" of Western Christianity professed.

Calixtus also vigorously advocated colloquies (face-to-face discussions and debates) among Catholics, Lutherans, and Reformed. He was convinced that each of the different traditions simply did not understand what the others were saying, and caricatured their teachings; only free exchange of ideas in a non-confrontational setting could bring real understanding of what it really meant to a Catholic to be Catholic, to a Lutheran to be Lutheran, and to a Calvinist to be Reformed. Calixtus' hand of friendship extended to Eastern Orthodoxy too; he made

---

8. See Chapter 2, section 1.7.

contact with patriarch Cyril Lucaris of Constantinople, himself a Protestant sympathizer.[9]

Calixtus' position was condemned by most Lutheran theologians as "Syncretism" (a relativistic mingling of contradictory faiths), and he spent much of his life defending himself against accusations of heresy. The next theologian we shall consider, Abraham Calov, was a zealous opponent. Calixtus probably did not help matters by developing a distaste for theologizing (we remember the dying Melanchthon's sigh to be delivered from the fury of the theologians), and stressing Christian life as the best basis for the reunion of shattered Christendom. Amazingly, however, Calixtus succeeded in not being dismissed from his post at Helmstedt; he had enough supporters to keep him in place. One thing that helped him was the fact that the *Formula of Concord*, the standard of Lutheran Orthodoxy, did not operate in Brunswick, where Helmstedt was located.

Calixtus took part in the Colloquy of Thorn in Prussia in 1645, where Lutherans, Catholics, and Calvinists discussed their differences while the Thirty Years' War was lurching to its bloody and exhausted close. The colloquy achieved nothing, partly because of the in-fighting among the Protestants—Lutherans and Reformed quarrelled with each other, while Lutherans also managed to quarrel among themselves (Orthodox against Syncretists).

The Syncretist controversy continued after Calixtus' death; his son Friedrich Ulrich Calixtus (1622–1701) energetically advocated his father's ideas. So did others. Although Lutheran Orthodoxy was the reigning pattern of thought in the 17th century, the Syncretist alternative was serious, and meant that Orthodoxy never had its way unchallenged among Lutherans.

6. Abraham Calov

Abraham Calov (1612–86) was Calixtus' most formidable opponent and one of Lutheran Orthodoxy's most militant and learned advocates in the second part of the 17th century. He was

9. For Cyril Lucaris, see Chapter 8, section 1.

born in 1612 at Mohrungen in East Prussia (now in Poland, but part of Brandenburg-Prussia in Calov's day). He studied at Konigsberg University (modern-day Kaliningrad in Russia, but again part of Brandenburg-Prussia in Calov's day), joining its teaching staff as a philosopher in 1632. It seems that Calov was destined to be plunged in theological controversy for the whole of his life; we soon find him attacking the Reformed view of holy communion, and defending the Lutheran view, in response to Brandenburg's court preacher, Johann Bergius (1587–1658). The ruling house of Brandenberg-Prussia, the Hohenzollerns, had embraced the Reformed faith under Prince John Sigismund (1608–19), so that the court both favoured and propagated Calvinism.[10] Many of Brandenburg's nobility, however, remained staunchly Lutheran; impressed by Calov's vindication of their eucharistic beliefs, some of them financed the young theologian to further his studies at Rostock University.

After three years at Rostock, where he published several notable works of philosophy, Calov returned to teach theology at Konigsberg, where he rapidly became a hugely popular lecturer. In 1641 he was also made superintendent of Konigsberg's churches and schools. In 1643, however, he moved to Danzig (modern Gdańsk) to teach in its academy and preach in the Holy Trinity Church. Danzig was an unusual city; theoretically part of Poland, it enjoyed a large measure of autonomy, and its population was multi-ethnic—mostly Poles, Germans, Dutch, and a Jewish community. Not surprisingly, the city had no official confession of faith. Calov found himself among Lutherans who were divided between Orthodoxy and Syncretism, jostling with Calvinists, Roman Catholics, and Jews. Perhaps this helps explain why Calov became such a controversialist; he had to defend Lutheran Orthodoxy against so many alternatives. Still, Calov reserved his chief energies for combating Syncretism, since this was so close to home—a threat from within the bosom of Lutheranism. The Syncretist controversy occupied Calov for the rest of his life.

---

10. For more about this, see section 4 on Pietism.

In 1650, Calov moved again, this time to Wittenberg University; in 1652, he was also appointed superintendent of Saxony's churches. His lectures were so popular, but so anti-Reformed, that the Calvinist court of Brandenburg-Prussia prohibited its citizens from studying at Wittenberg! Calov lived the rest of his life in Wittenberg, teaching the Lutheranism of the *Formula of Concord*, and defending it against its various enemies (e.g. Calvinists, Catholics, Socinians). But even now Calov directed most of his firepower against Syncretism. He and the Wittenbergers led the hard-line Lutheran response to Syncretism, wishing Lutherans to adopt a new anti-Syncretist confession of faith, but they were defeated by the more moderate opponents of Syncretism, led by Johannes Musäus (1613–81) and the theologians of Jena, who thought that such a response would be overkill.

Although Calov came half-way through the development of Lutheran Orthodoxy, he had a big impact on its future course, especially through his understanding of the *ordo salutis* (the order of salvation—the sequence of saving events or experiences in human life). Previous Lutheran theologians had dealt with the subject, but Calov set out his view with such lucidity and learning that it dominated Lutheran thought thereafter. Calov's *ordo salutis* was calling, illumination, regeneration, conversion, justification, repentance, mystical union with Christ, sanctification, and glorification. Calov's scholastic theology is most fully expounded in his *Systema Locorum Theologicorum*, published in 12 parts between 1655 and 1677. This multi-volume systematic theology has been called the brightest zenith of Aristotelian Lutheranism (or its darkest midnight, if one disapproves of Protestant scholasticism).

Calov has an unenviable reputation as the most fiercely intolerant gladiator of Lutheran Orthodoxy, who spent all his time outpouring the vials of wrath on anyone who disagreed with him. His critics called him the Lutheran Grand Inquisitor. Certainly he wrote voluminously against everything and everyone he regarded as deviating from the strictest Lutheranism, and some of his polemics now look patently absurd (especially perhaps his fervent defence of the verbal inspiration of the vowel points in the Hebrew Old Testament).[11]

However, it would be unfair to paint so one-sided a picture of Calov. He was no icy academic theologian, obsessed with correct doctrine and lacking a human soul. Calov was concerned for piety as well as polemics; in his writings, this concern found fullest expression in an edition of the Bible (1682) to which Calov attached a running commentary drawn from the works of Luther. This proved a popular devotional Bible; it made a deep impression on Johann Sebastian Bach (see below), Lutheranism's greatest musical genius. At least equally important was Calov's *Biblia Illustrata*, published in four volumes between 1672 and 1676. This was a complete Bible commentary in which Calov displayed his considerable talents as an exegete. The commentary would keep its hold on Lutheran affections for the next two hundred years.

Finally we should note that Calov, for all his polemical vigour, was an early supporter of Philip Jacob Spener and the spiritual renewal movement that came to be known as Pietism.[12] Calov warmly endorsed Spener's *Pia Desideria* (1675), the manifesto of Pietism: an unimaginable act, had Calov really been all grim head and no gracious heart.

7. Johann Conrad Dannhauer

Johann Conrad Dannhauer (1603–66) was born at Köndrigen in Baden, the son of a Lutheran pastor. He studied theology at Strasbourg, Marburg, Altdorf, and under Johann Gerhard at Jena. In 1628 he was invited to take charge of theological studies at Strasbourg, where he lectured on systematic theology and ethics. In 1633 he became pastor of Strasbourg cathedral, and later the president of the church assembly with wider responsibilities for the Lutheran congregations of Strasbourg. In this latter capacity, Dannhauer established a new scheme of

---

11. Everyone now admits that the vowel points were not part of the original text, but added later.

12. See section 4.

pastoral visitation for the churches under his care, developed the effectiveness of catechizing the young, and strove to improve standards of godliness and learning among the Lutheran pastors. Dannhauer was also the most celebrated preacher of Lutheran Orthodoxy; his 10 volumes of sermons were very influential.

Dannhauer, like most Lutheran Orthodox, turned his hand to polemics against the adversaries of his faith—Roman Catholics, Reformed, and (above all) the Lutheran Syncretists. Unlike Calov, however, Dannhauer produced works of Orthodox apologetics distinguished by their fairness and irenic spirit, remarkably lacking in vitriol. His supreme contribution in this vein was his *Mystery of Syncretism Detected* (1648). The Reformed faith received the same treatment in his *Foolishness of the Calvinist Spirit* (1654), where Dannhauer set out the differences between Lutheran and Reformed theology calmly and clearly, stating his disagreements with Calvinism, and his reasons for disagreeing, without vilifying his opponents.

Dannhauer's masterpiece, however, was his *Way of Christian Wisdom or Positive Theology* (1649), a work of striking originality. It synthesized a rich meditation on biblical imagery with doctrinal teaching about salvation. Dannhauer examined 12 images found in Scripture—e.g. light, pilgrim, path, candlestick, goal, home, stumbling block—and used each image to communicate some aspect of the sinner's ascent to heaven. One commentator has described it as resembling a systematic theology set out in the form of *Pilgrim's Progress*.

There were many other literary works by Dannhauer (he was amazingly prolific), but the final aspect of his life we should consider is his profound impact on Philip Jacob Spener, the "father of Pietism" (see section 4). Spener was born in the Alsace region, where Strasbourg was situated, and in 1663–6 he was based in Strasbourg itself. He therefore came within the sphere of Dannhauer's activities as president of the Strasbourg church assembly. It was Dannhauer who ordained Spener, and Spener may have helped prepare the second edition of the *Way of Christian Wisdom*. Certainly Spener later paid tribute to Dannhauer as his teacher in a poem dedicated to his memory.

Here, then, is one of the many surprising connections between Lutheran Orthodoxy and Pietism.

8. Johannes Andreas Quenstedt

Johannes Quenstedt (1617–88) was the nephew of Johann Gerhard. Born at Quedlinburg, he always hoped to study theology under his uncle at Jena, but Gerhard died before this could happen. Quenstedt studied instead at Helmstedt and Wittenberg. Appointed a lecturer in Wittenberg in 1644 while still completing his studies, he spent the remainder of his life teaching there: he became professor of logic and metaphysics in 1649, gained his theology doctorate in 1650, was appointed theology professor in 1660, and then senior theology professor in 1687. Quenstedt was based at Wittenberg at the same time as the redoubtable Calov. The two giants of Lutheran Orthodoxy, however, had nothing in common at the level of personality; Quenstedt was a quiet, meek, physically weak individual, in contrast to the swashbuckling Calov. They did, however, acquire a family bond, when Calov married Quenstedt's fourth daughter in 1684.

Quenstedt's placid and uneventful life as a lecturer leaves us simply with his literary legacy to consider. This was immense, even though it really consisted of a single work, his *Didactic-Polemic Theology or Theological System*, published just three years before his death in 1685. Together with his uncle Gerhard's *Loci Theologici*, Quenstedt's work ranks as the supreme achievement of Lutheran Orthodoxy in print. In fact, so brilliant was Quenstedt's textbook, such a marvel of clarity and comprehensiveness, that some have said it destroyed the activity of systematic theology among Lutherans, since no one could ever write anything to compete with Quentstedt's work!

The strength of Quenstedt's systematic theology did not lie in any original development of doctrine, but in the masterly way it expounded Lutheran Orthodoxy. Alongside its crystal lucidity and exhaustive scope, it breathed an overwhelmingly calm tone; no opponent of Lutheranism could ever claim that Quenstedt had handled him intemperately. The supporting biblical exegesis occupied fully one third of the volume, and was of a high order: this was a systematic theology that united philosophy and biblical studies.

Quenstedt's work was printed five times within a 30 year period. Lutheran clergy regarded it as the theological textbook of choice.

9. Musical interlude: Lutheran worship

Before ending this section on Lutheran Orthodoxy, we should take note of the musical flowering of Lutheran worship in the same period. It abounded in hymn-writers and composers who left an imperishable mark on Lutheran piety. Among the great Lutheran hymn-writers were **Philipp Nicolai** (1556–1608), **Johann Heermann** (1585–1647), and **Paul Gerhardt** (1607–1676). Gerhardt in particular has become a universal favourite, far beyond the borders of Lutheranism. Often regarded as Germany's most gifted hymn-writer, English versions of Gerhardt (many by John Wesley) include *O sacred head now wounded, Jesus Thy boundless love to me, Commit thou all thy griefs, Extended on a cursèd tree, Holy Ghost, dispel our sadness*, and *All my heart this night rejoices*. Gerhardt, whose theology was shaped by conscientious adherence to the Formula of Concord, proved that Lutheran Orthodoxy could be expressed in heart-warming poetry and song.

It is fascinating to reflect that Gerhardt was a preacher in Brandenburg-Prussia's capital Berlin, at the Church of Saint Nicholas, when Lutheran-Reformed controversy there was at its height. The ruling house of Hohenzollern had converted to the Reformed faith under Prince John Sigismund (1608–19), but the population of Brandenburg-Prussia remained largely Lutheran. The prince in Gerhardt's day was Frederick William I (1640–88), who was becoming impatient with Lutheran polemics against Calvinism, and eventually barred all preachers from attacking each other's beliefs in the pulpit. Since this seemed to many Lutherans incompatible with their allegiance to the Formula of Concord, it resulted in a good number of Lutheran clergy being deprived of their ministries. Yet despite the intensity of the Lutheran-Reformed quarrel, it is on record that many Calvinists attended Gerhardt's church, so impressed and edified were they by his preaching. His admirers included Louisa Henrietta (1627–67), the Dutch Calvinist wife of Prince Frederick William; Louisa was herself an accomplished hymn-writer, and treasured Gerhardt's hymns. But it did not save Gerhardt. His loyalty to the Formula of Concord was unwavering, and he lost his post at the Saint Nicholas Church in 1666. He was back in the pulpit, however, at Lubbën in Saxe-Merseburg in 1668, after two years of poverty.

Among the celebrated Lutheran musical composers of our period were *Michael Praetorius* (c.1571–1621), *Heinrich Schütz* (1585–1672), and *Dieterich Buxtehude* (c.1637–1707). These were not merely musicians who had religious significance for their own day; they are all considered to have permanent importance in the history of European music. We can hardly omit the greatest of them all, *Johann Sebastian Bach* (1685–1750), even though the latter part of his life takes him outside our timeframe. Bach is not only Lutheranism's supreme musical genius, but of course one of the most captivating and influential makers of music of all time. He was a deeply committed Lutheran believer—under *Abraham Calov* we saw Bach's personal study and appreciation of Calov's devotional Bible—and Bach's Lutheran faith inspired much of his music. We have only to think of his *Magnificat, Christmas Oratorio, Saint Matthew Passion, Saint John Passion, Mass in B Minor*, and the many cantatas he wrote for Lutheran worship. Bach always began his compositions with INJ ("In the name of Jesus"), and always ended with SDG ("Soli deo gloria"—to the glory of God alone). Once again, however, the Lutheran-Reformed interface confronts us. Bach spent some time (1717–23) as musical director at the court of Anhalt-Köthen, which was Reformed; hence it required no elaborate church music for its worship. Here Bach concentrated on "secular" music, and produced his six Brandenburg concertos, generally appraised as among the most brilliant compositions from the whole Baroque period (c.1600–1750) of European music.

3
The Thirty Years' War: the holy text of pike and gun[1]

The Thirty Years' War (1618–48) ranks as one of the most devastating conflicts ever to ravage the soil of Europe. Unfortunately for Germany, the Holy Roman Empire provided the theatre of war. Virtually all the major European powers became involved in the clash at one time or another, so that Germany became an international battleground where marauding armies inflicted destruction on each other, on the civilian population, and on the land. Some have called it the "European Civil War".

The war was religious in origin. We could regard it in many ways as part two of the religious civil war between Protestant and Roman Catholic that had flared across Germany from 1547 to 1552. That war had culminated in the Peace of Augsburg, ratified by the German imperial diet in 1555. The Peace generally accomplished its objective; it really did bring peace to most of Germany, most of the time, for the following 60 years. Its fatal defect was that it gave legal recognition to only two forms of Christianity: Roman Catholicism and Lutheranism. The Reformed faith, which at that point had almost no presence in Germany, was not covered by the Peace. Calvinism, however, enjoyed major growth in Germany after the Peace was signed.

---

1. The phrase is from Samuel Butler's *Hudibras*. See a fuller quotation in Chapter 4, section 1.2.

The Palatinate, Nassau, Bremen, Wesel, Julich, Cleves, Berg, Anhalt, Hesse, and Brandenburg (among other German territories) all embraced or extended toleration to the Reformed faith after 1555. Yet technically they were violating imperial law, since the Peace of Augsburg had outlawed any faith but Catholicism and Lutheranism.

The sort of tensions that Calvinism created in Germany can be gauged from the "Cologne War" of 1583–8. Cologne was ruled by a prince-bishop; and in 1583, the reigning prince-bishop, Gebhard Truchsess von Waldburg (born 1547; reigned 1577–88; died 1601), defected from Catholicism to the Reformed faith. This was a disaster for the Catholic Habsburg family that had controlled the Holy Roman Empire since 1438, because Cologne's prince-bishop was one of the seven "electors" among the German princes who chose each new emperor. With Cologne's defection to Calvinism, Protestants now had a four to three majority among the electors. A Protestant emperor was not a prospect the Habsburgs were prepared to tolerate. Invoking the Peace of Augsburg, they declared von Waldburg's position illegal, since the Peace did not recognize Calvinism; Spanish troops (Spain too was governed by the Habsburgs) invaded Cologne, financed by Pope Gregory XIII, and defeated the would-be Reformed elector, replacing him with a Bavarian Catholic. Von Waldburg died in exile in the Calvinist Dutch Republic in 1601.

It was not Calvinism alone, however, that provoked friction in Germany. Lutherans and Catholics, although legally protected by the Peace of Augsburg, did not necessarily live at peace with each other. Violence erupted between them in the free imperial city of Donauworth in Swabia. Lutherans here were in the majority, and their attempt in 1606 to prevent Catholics from holding a religious procession led to a riot. To aid his co-religionists, the Catholic Duke of Bavaria, *Maximilian I* (1597–1651), sent in his troops. They occupied the city and forcibly imposed Catholicism as its official religion. This emboldened the Catholic rulers, and the following year at the German imperial diet they demanded that all lands and properties taken over by Protestants since 1552 be returned to Catholic ownership. The

Protestant delegates, in a minority, stormed out of the diet in outrage, and would not come back until the Thirty Years' War was over. Clearly Germany's system of imperial government was disintegrating under the impact of religious strife.

These events thoroughly alarmed the Calvinists of Germany: if Catholic rulers could act like this toward Lutherans, whose faith was legal, what might they not do to Calvinists, whose faith was not? In response, Calvinists and Lutherans set aside their differences, and banded together as the Protestant Union in 1608, led by the Calvinist prince of the Palatinate, **Frederick IV** (1592–1610). Catholics reacted by forming the Catholic League in 1609, led by Maximilian of Bavaria. Two hostile religious power-blocs now faced each other within Germany. They began searching for allies; the Protestant Union forged bonds with the Dutch Republic, Denmark, and England, while the Catholic League recruited Archduke Leopold of Upper Austria.

The spark that finally ignited Germany's religious civil war came in 1618 in Bohemia. Ironically, Bohemia was not part of Germany, but a Slavic nation with its own monarchy; it had, however, been intimately connected with the Holy Roman Empire since the 11th century, and in 1198 the Emperor Frederick Barbarossa made it an independent kingdom within the Empire. Religiously, the Bohemian population were mainly Hussites; inspired originally by the 15th century Reformer John Huss, they had now enthusiastically put themselves in the Protestant camp.[2] There were also Lutherans and Calvinists in Bohemia, and indeed in 1575 they and the Hussites had signed a joint Protestant confession of faith, the Bohemian Confession, as a way of acting together politically to secure freedom of worship. Their king was none other than the Holy Roman Emperor, the Catholic Habsburg Rudolf II (1576–1612); the Habsburgs had added Bohemia to their Europe-wide dynastic empire in 1526, and since 1555 the Holy Roman Emperors had also worn the Bohemian crown. Despite Rudolf's animosity toward the

---

2. For the Hussites and their origins, see *Volume Two: The Middle Ages*, Chapter 10, section 5.

Reformation, the Bohemian Protestant nobility forced him in 1609 to recognize their liberty in a document known as the "Letter of Majesty".

The next emperor, Matthias (1612–19), who was childless, had his cousin, Archduke Ferdinand of Styria or Lower Austria (born 1578; Holy Roman Emperor as **Ferdinand II** 1619–37), presented to the Bohemian nobility in 1617 as their crown prince and future king. A shiver of dread ran through the country. Ferdinand was an aggressive Counter-Reformation Catholic; having received a brilliant Jesuit training, he had brutally suppressed Protestantism in his land of Styria. Already the 1609 Letter of Majesty was proving ineffective at stopping Emperor Matthias' agents in Bohemia from harassing its Protestants. The fear of what so intolerant a Catholic as Ferdinand might do as their new king drove the Bohemian nobility to outright rebellion. A band of nobles bribed their way into Prague castle, where four of Ferdinand's representatives were meeting, and the nobles threw two of the unfortunate men (well-known inflexible Catholics) out of the third floor window—they landed unharmed in a pile of horse dung. It was May 18th 1618, and it was known as the Defenestration of Prague. (Defenestration is the act of throwing someone out of a window: a bizarre word, but throwing unpopular politicians out of windows was a Bohemian tradition, almost a sport!) From this melodramatic event we can date the outbreak of the Thirty Years' War.

By November 1618, the Bohemian rebels had quelled internal resistance to their revolution and were in full military control of the country. This initial success of the Bohemian revolt led to serious Protestant uprisings against Catholic rulers throughout the entire region: Moravia, Silesia, Upper Austria, Transylvania, even Archduke Ferdinand's Styria. In August 1619, the Bohemians elected a new king—the Calvinist Prince Frederick V of the Palatinate (1610–23), leader of the Protestant Union. The Union would not support him in what they perceived was a dangerous gamble, but he received strong backing and finance from the Dutch Republic. Two days later, Archduke Ferdinand was elected as the new Holy Roman Emperor (Matthias had died in March). Ferdinand was, however, kept busy as emperor for the next year reconquering Styria and Upper Austria with the help of the Catholic League. Having crushed the Protestant rebels there, he was finally able in 1620 to turn his attention to Bohemia. The emperor appealed to the Spanish Habsburg branch of the family for assistance; his young nephew, King *Philip IV of Spain* (1621–65), who ascended the Spanish throne in March 1621, sent an army from the Spanish Netherlands to help vanquish the heretical and mutinous Bohemians and their Calvinist monarch.

The imperial and Spanish armies joined forces, commanded by the fearsome imperial Catholic General, Count *Johann Tserclaes of Tilly* (1559–1632), and wiped out the Bohemian Protestant army at the battle of the White Mountain on November 8th 1621. Frederick V, the Calvinist ex-king, had to flee into exile in the Dutch Republic—even his original German homeland of the Palatinate was now overrun by Spanish Catholic troops. Ferdinand gave the Palatinate to Maximilian of Bavaria. The Protestant Union protested at this Catholic seizure of a Protestant land, but a triumphant Ferdinand, secure amid his menacing army, merely ordered the Union to disband. Fearing that disobedience would plunge them into a ruinous war, the Union meekly disbanded. Two Protestant princes, however— *Christian the Younger* (1616–26), who was the Lutheran duke of Brunswick, together with George Frederick, the margrave of Baden-Durlach—refused to give up the fight. Meanwhile, Bohemia was forcibly Catholicized, its 200 year old Hussite heritage effectively destroyed. A long, dark night of the soul began for the shattered disciples of John Huss. What was left of the Protestant Union's army was now commanded by Christian the Younger of Brunswick; an intense devotee of all things military, he had gained battlefield experience in fighting Spanish Catholics in the Netherlands after Spain had renewed its long war with the Dutch Republic in 1621. Christian's army, however, was decisively defeated by Count Tilly at the battle of Stadtljohn in August 1623.

That might have been the end of the war—a catastrophic defeat for the Protestants, a resounding triumph for the

Catholic emperor—had it not been for the international dimensions of the German conflict. Bordering on Germany lay Lutheran Denmark, whose king, **Christian IV** (1588–1648), also controlled the German duchy of Holstein. Fearing that Ferdinand's victory was creating a new, powerful Catholic Habsburg empire in Germany which would threaten Lutheran Denmark, in 1625 Christian IV led a full-scale Danish invasion of Germany to strike down Ferdinand and restore the fortunes of Protestantism. So began a long series of foreign interventions which kept the flames of war burning across Germany for three decades. What could have been the Five Years' War (1618–23) became the Thirty Years' War (1618–48). By the time the carnage was over, historians estimate that Germany had lost almost a third of its population to battle, disease, starvation, and all the other brutal accompaniments of war. One of the worst atrocities was the destruction of the historic and prosperous Lutheran city of Magdeburg; the army of the Catholic general Tilly stormed the city in May 1631, massacring its inhabitants. Out of an original population of 30,000, only 5,000 survived the onslaught. The city itself was burnt to the ground, and for days afterwards, there was a non-stop carrying of corpses to be dumped in the Elbe river. The whole of Europe was shocked to the core; yet still the war dragged on.

It is beyond the scope of this book to tell the full story of the Thirty Years' War. The most important things for us to observe now are the way its religious and political aspects developed almost out of recognition, and its ultimate outcomes for Europe. We can summarize these as follows.

First, the war fundamentally altered in character as it progressed. It began as a religious conflict between Protestant and Catholic. By the time it ended, it had become a secular power-struggle between the Habsburgs and all their foes (whether those foes were Protestant or Catholic). The single greatest factor that made this change possible was the intervention of France. Led by Cardinal Richelieu (1585–1642), who in effect controlled French affairs as the all-powerful chief minister of

King Louis XIII (1610–43), Catholic France threw its weight behind the Protestant forces in the war.[3]

Cardinal Richelieu feared that a strong Holy Roman Empire, no matter how Catholic it was, would be a serious threat to France on the stage of international diplomacy and war. After all, the Empire was controlled by the Habsburg family, who also occupied the throne of Spain. To prevent France being encircled by Habsburg power, Richelieu decided to help the anti-Habsburg forces in the Thirty Years' War, who happened to be Protestants. He financed the Danish invasion of Germany by Christian IV in 1625. When Christian's intervention ultimately failed to check Habsburg power, Richelieu encouraged Protestant Sweden in 1629 to invade Germany (with much greater success), under the great Lutheran warrior-king **Gustavus Adolphus** (1611–32). Gustavus inflicted a series of devastating defeats on the Habsburg armies, vanquishing their great commander Tilly twice (the second time Tilly died of his injuries). Even after Gustavus' own death in battle in 1632, his brilliant chancellor **Axel Oxenstierna** (1583–1654) kept his forces fighting in Germany; Richelieu massively subsidized the Swedish troops for many years. In 1635, Richelieu finally decided to take direct action, and declared war on Spain, which was the Holy Roman Emperor's greatest ally. French Catholic troops—under the command of a French Protestant general!—were soon fighting Catholic Habsburg forces in Germany.

Richelieu's policy transformed the Thirty Years War into a more purely political struggle, between the Habsburgs and their many enemies (whether Catholic or Protestant) who—for nationalistic reasons—did not wish to see the creation of an over-mighty Habsburg empire that embraced both Germany and Spain. Many Catholics condemned Richelieu for betraying his religion in favour of French nationalism. But there can be no doubting his success. By the time the war ended in 1648, the Habsburg German-Spanish axis was financially bankrupt, and France was ready to assume dominance in Europe.

---

3. See Chapter 6, section 1.1 for more about Richelieu.

Because of these developments in the Thirty Years' War, it was the last great religious war in Europe. The way its nature had been secularized by Richelieu, with Catholic France fighting alongside Protestants against the Catholic Habsburgs, meant that a new, more pragmatic era had dawned in European history. Nations would now be much more ready to fight frankly for their own interests and glory, without a convincing religious motive.

The war finally concluded with the Peace of Westphalia in 1648. Involving several treaties, the signatories were the Holy Roman Empire, Spain, France, Sweden, the Dutch Republic, and the princes and free imperial cities of Germany. The real winner was France: by supporting the Protestants, it had dealt a crippling blow to Habsburg power in Germany and Spain, draining their resources, and causing them to lose territory. France's great rival for national greatness had been effectively neutered. Spain was also finally forced to recognize officially the sovereign independence of the Calvinist Dutch Republic, ending some 80 years of conflict. The Holy Roman Emperor lost all authority over the German princes: if Germany was ever to be unified into a single nation, it could now never be under the Catholic Habsburg emperors (in fact, it would be unified under Protestant Brandenburg-Prussia in the 19th century).

As for religion, the initial cause of the conflagration, the Peace of Westphalia gave legal recognition to the Reformed faith in Germany for the first time. Part of the Palatinate was also restored to Calvinists after its Catholic conquest in 1622. The land of Luther would now be just as much the land of Calvin, especially through the increasingly mighty state of Brandenburg-Prussia, with its Reformed ruling house of Hohenzollern. The old principle that the ruler determined the religion of his subjects was modified in two ways: (i) if more than one faith existed in a territory in 1624, both could continue; (ii) Lutherans and Calvinists agreed that if a Lutheran ruler became Calvinist (or vice versa), this would not affect his subjects—they were free to choose.

4
Pietism: religion of the heart

1. Origins

Pietism was a movement for spiritual renewal within the German Lutheran Churches. It would be no exaggeration to say that it changed the face of Lutheranism—for the better, according to its defenders, and for the worse, according to its critics. There can however be no doubting its colossal impact. Among English-speaking Protestants, Pietism has gained a special interest because of its deep connections with the Evangelical Revival in mid-18th century Britain, particularly its direct and strong influence on John Wesley and early Wesleyan Methodism.

There has been much discussion of the origins of Pietism. In part, it was a reaction against Lutheran Orthodoxy; Pietists felt it had become too dry, lacking in practical piety, and too obsessed with condemning the errors of others. Some have seen in Pietism a symptom of a wider drive across Europe toward a more intense spirituality, also manifest as Puritanism in the Reformed world (see Chapter 3) and as Jansenism in the Catholic world (see Chapter 6). However, historians have also identified some very specific positive sources of Pietism.

One of the most important sources was the Lutheran pastor and writer *Johann Arndt* (1553–1621), who could be called the spiritual grandfather of Pietism. Born at Ballenstedt in Lutheran Anhalt, Arndt originally studied medicine, but ironically illness forced him to abandon a medical career. His mind turned to theology. In 1584 he became pastor of the church at Badeborn in Anhalt. Life became difficult, however, under Anhalt's new

Prince, Christian I (1586–1630), who was Reformed rather than Lutheran. The new Calvinist regime pressurized Arndt to remove religious icons from his church, and drop the traditional Lutheran exorcism in the baptismal rite, but Arndt refused. Eventually Arndt moved from Badeborn to Quedlinburg in 1590, and left the lands of Anhalt altogether for Brunswick-Lüneburg in 1599. He ended up as superintendent from 1611 of the Lutheran churches in Brunswick's Celle region, where the dukes of Brunswick-Lüneburg had a residential castle.

Arndt was a prolific author, but his most epoch-making was *True Christianity*, published between 1605 and 1610 in four books. In this treatise, Arndt emphasized the transforming work of Christ in the soul of the believer. He drew on medieval writings such as the anonymous *Theologica Germanica*, the works of Johann Tauler, and Thomas a Kempis' *Imitation of Christ*, as well as Luther himself, in setting out his theme.[1] It has often been said (rightly) that Arndt wanted to draw attention to Christ's life *in* His people, as a corrective to Lutheran theology's tendency to dwell almost exclusively on Christ's death *for* His people. Indeed many orthodox Lutheran theologians condemned Arndt for allegedly betraying the central truth of justification by faith alone, although it must be said that one of the greatest theologians of the period, Johann Gerhard (see section 2), defended Arndt from these attacks.

At any rate, Arndt's *True Christianity* proved a popular success (20 editions in his lifetime), and had a far-flung influence, well beyond the boundaries of German Lutheranism. For example, it became the favourite spiritual reading of the illustrious Russian Orthodox bishop and saint, Tikhon of Zadonsk (1724–83). Tikhon, in advising a young Russian noble on his religious reading, said of Arndt's *True Christianity*: "Always, morning and night, study the Bible and Arndt; you should only skim other books." Certainly the early Pietists regarded Arndt as their greatest inspiration; they believed they

---

1. For Tauler, the Theologica Germanica, and Thomas a Kempis, see *Volume Two: The Middle Ages*, Chapter 10, section 6.

were trying to implement on a church-wide basis what Arndt had offered to the individual soul.

There were also strong Reformed or Calvinist influences on Pietism. In general, there was some degree of mingling between Lutherans and Calvinists in southwestern Germany, where the immediate "father" of Pietism, **Philip Jacob Spener** lived (see below for his life). For example, we find some instances of Lutheran sponsors at Reformed baptisms, and Reformed people taking part in Lutheran services of holy communion. Spener was particularly impacted by several Reformed figures.

One was *Jean de Labadie* (1610–74). Labadie was a French Jansenist who had embraced the Reformed faith; Spener met him during the former's travels in 1659–61, while Labadie was a pastor in Geneva. Later Labadie became suspect in the eyes of Reformed orthodoxy; he founded a community that practised communist principles (the community's property and children were "owned" jointly by the whole membership), and his theology, critics felt, placed an unbalanced emphasis on the Holy Spirit's role in revealing the Bible's meaning to the individual. Spener, however, met Labadie prior to these developments. He translated into German Labadie's *The Christian Practice of Prayer and Meditation*, publishing it in 1667.

Another Reformed influence on Spener was *John Durie* (1596–1680). Durie was Scottish by birth, but had been ordained as an Anglican clergyman. A very moderate Puritan, Durie was a member of the Westminster Assembly (where his broad views on religious toleration got him into trouble).[2] Committed to ecumenism among Protestants, Durie spent much of his life on the Continent trying to promote Lutheran-Reformed unity, although few Lutherans were interested. Spener, however, said he saw "more evidence of true Christian discipleship in Durie" than he saw in many Lutherans!

Other Puritan influences on Spener came through literature: for instance, Lewis Bayly's *The Practice of Piety*, Daniel Dyke's *The Mystery of Self-deceiving*, and Richard Baxter's *The Necessary*

---

2. See Chapter 3, section 5.6, for the Westminster Assembly.

Teaching of the Denial of Self. These were all Puritan classics that
had been translated into German.[3]

Finally, there was some influence of mysticism on Pietism.
We know that another great Pietist leader, August Hermann
Francke, reprinted the *Spiritual Guide* of the Catholic Quietist
mystic Miguel de Molinos.[4] The strange and possibly
incomprehensible Lutheran mystic, Jacob Boehme (c.1575–
1624), also influenced the more radical Pietists.

2. Philip Jacob Spener

Philip Jacob Spener (1635–1705), Pietism's spiritual father, was
born to devout Lutheran parents at Rappoltsweiler in Alsace
(at that point, Alsace was part of Germany—most of it would
be conquered by France in 1639 during the Thirty Years' War).
After studying at various universities, including Geneva, he had
a three year spell in Strasbourg as a preacher without pastoral
duties (Strasbourg remained part of Germany until annexed
by France in 1681). Then in 1666, Spener became pastor of
the Lutheran church in the city of Frankfurt. Here he became
disillusioned with what he felt was the spiritually dry and dead
orthodoxy of the Lutheranism of his day; in his judgment, it
lacked genuine living faith, especially among the clergy. It was
little more, he felt, than indoctrinating people in strict Lutheran
orthodoxy. Repulsed by this perceived sterility, Spener—together
with a group of sympathetic pastors—argued that the cause of
the deadness lay in the defective training of Lutheran clergy.
He especially blamed the divorce between academic theology
and spiritual life. Clergy, he said, were trained to the fingertips
in book learning, but had little or no experiential knowledge of
Christ and the affairs of the soul.

Spener and his sympathizers began meeting twice a week
in Spener's study from 1670 onwards for spiritual edification.
They became known as "the college of piety". Soon non-clergy

---

3. For Bayly, see Chapter 3, section 4.3; for Baxter, see Chapter 3, section
   6.4.
4. See Chapter 7, section 2.1 for Molinos.

were also allowed to attend, and—very radical for that day and age—even women (although it must be said that the women were not allowed to take part in discussions). The meetings opened and closed with hymn-singing and prayer; they focused on promoting group spirituality through reading and discussing Christian literature. By 1674, the nickname "Pietist" was being applied to the group.

Spener gave classic expression to his ideals in his landmark work *Pia Desideria* (which can be translated "Holy Desires", or "Pious Aspirations"), published in 1675 as a preface to an edition of Johann Arndt's sermons, then reissued in 1676 as a separate treatise. It became the spiritual manifesto of Pietism. It set out concrete proposals for spiritual renewal within the life of the Lutheran Church, summed up under the following six heads:

1. The committed practice of Bible study by all church members, e.g. in small discussion groups.

2. The active involvement of the laity in church life—there must be no "one-man ministry".

3. An emphasis on the living practice of Christian love as more important than a mere head-knowledge of doctrine.

4. An emphasis on what united Christians across denominational divides as against theological quarrels, e.g. between Lutherans and Calvinists.

5. The reform of pastoral training, so that spiritual formation of soul and character were the main focus, not the mere transmission of scholarship.

6. Preaching should be simple and edifying, not mere rehearsals of Lutheran orthodoxy with denunciations of all who disagree. Johann Arndt should be taken as a model of good preaching.

Soon Lutherans all over Germany were reading *Pia Desideria*. An instant best-seller, it went through four editions over the next three decades, and was translated into Latin for the international scholarly market. Some Orthodox Lutherans condemned it as having a disparaging attitude to theology, over-emphasizing the religious role of emotion, and being soft on Calvinists; but as we saw, no less a figure than Abraham Calov, the fire-breathing guardian of Lutheran Orthodoxy, commended the book. By the close of the 17th century, *Pia Desideria* had unloosed a river of Pietist influence that flowed not only in Germany but in Lutheran Scandinavia too (Denmark, Sweden, Norway), and crossed religious barriers to find a friendly reception in Reformed Switzerland and the Dutch Republic.

In 1686 Spener was appointed court preacher at Dresden in electoral Saxony at the invitation of the Saxon prince, John George III (1680–91). Unfortunately John George soon repented of his choice when Spener criticized the moral conduct of the prince's son. There was a tense stand-off between preacher and prince, with Spener refusing to retract his criticism despite intense pressure, and John George hesitating to sack him. The problem was resolved in 1691 when Spener was invited to relocate to Berlin by the margrave of Brandenburg-Prussia, **Frederick III** (he ruled as prince from 1688; in 1701 he transformed his lands into a kingdom, taking the title of king as Frederick I of Prussia, reigning until his death in 1713).

3. Pietism in Prussia: The life and work of August Hermann Francke

The religious situation of Brandenburg-Prussia was highly unusual in Germany. This large, powerful state had a mostly Lutheran population but Reformed rulers, the Hohenzollerns, who had embraced Calvinism under Prince John Sigismund (1608–19). Unable to persuade his Church to follow his example, John Sigismund had to let his people remain Lutheran. But the Calvinist Hohenzollern court in Berlin fostered the growth of the Reformed faith in other ways, e.g. offering financial incentives to Calvinists to immigrate into Brandenburg-Prussia from other parts of Europe, and giving them their own judicial system.[5] Many French Huguenots took up the offer and settled in Prussia to escape persecution in their own country, especially after the Edict of Nantes was revoked in 1685 (see Chapter 7, section 3). There were frictions between the two religious communities; the court sometimes had to order Lutheran and Reformed preachers to stop denouncing each other from the pulpit.[6] Still, this unique Prussian experiment in Lutheran-Calvinist diversity survived all the tensions.

Prussia seems to have suited Spener, who had been so influenced by Reformed spirituality. Although he opposed the Reformed doctrine of predestination, he had a very mild attitude to the Reformed view of the eucharist: both sides agreed that Christ was present, he felt, and disagreed only about the mode. On this basis Spener advocated Lutheran-Reformed cooperation against the "common enemy", Rome. More than anything else, this made Spener abhorrent to many orthodox Lutherans, who accused him of the same laxity over doctrine that had characterized Georg Calixtus and so-called Syncretism. The main opposition to Spener's ideals came from the University of Wittenberg, whose theologians discovered no fewer than 284 heresies in Pietist teaching. In fact Spener personally adhered to the theology of the Lutheran confessions, but he did distinguish in them between what was essential and non-essential. At any rate, he found a spiritual home in Prussia, with its odd combination of largely Lutheran people under a Reformed government. Certainly the Calvinist Prince Frederick III became a zealous supporter both of Spener himself and of his Pietist outlook.

In Berlin, Spener was appointed rector of the Saint Nicholas Church. His greatest achievement, however, was the creation of Halle University in 1694. Funded by Frederick III, Halle

---

5. The idea of minority communities being granted their own judicial system—e.g. Muslims functioning under Sharia law within a larger non-Muslim society—is thus nothing new. Calvinists enjoyed this privilege in Prussia.

6. As we saw in the life of Lutheran hymnwriter Paul Gerhardt.

was deliberately organized as a Pietist university, where Spener's ideals would reign supreme. Spener had the perfect man to teach at Halle and set its spiritual tone: *August Hermann Francke* (1663–1727). A disciple of Spener, Francke was born at Lubeck, the son of a prominent local politician; he studied at several universities, ending up in Leipzig. After various adventures, including a life-changing experience of assurance of salvation in 1687, he went back to Leipzig in 1689 to give exegetical lectures; Hebrew and Greek were Francke's speciality. By now he had identified himself closely with Pietism, and the university authorities took a violent dislike to the spiritual element in Francke's teaching. Under its impact, people were forming Bible study groups; the city fathers of Leipzig frowned on these groups as existing outside the structures of the established Lutheran Church. So Francke was banned from lecturing. Spener found him temporary relief as a deacon in Erfurt in 1690, where his preaching drew a crowd; but eventually the city council expelled him, once again from hostility to his Pietism. Spener now invited Francke to settle in Prussia and teach at the new Halle University, at that point still being planned.

Francke arrived during the Christmas of 1691–2, and to keep him gainfully employed while the university was set up, Spener had him appointed pastor of Saint George Church in Glaucha, near Halle. He remained in this pastorate even after taking up his responsibilities in Halle University when it was finally opened for business in 1694, combining the two roles of pastor and professor very successfully. In the university he taught Greek and Oriental languages (from 1698, he taught theology). Alongside this, he gave practical expositions of Scripture to the entire student body every Thursday morning between ten and eleven. These expositions were crucial in permeating the university with a Pietist spirit: Halle would be equally a centre of academic and spiritual life and training. Apart from the Bible itself, the basic text at the heart of the university curriculum was the homilies of Macarius. The 50 homilies were traditionally attributed to Macarius of Egypt (c.300–91), one of the desert fathers; modern scholarship puts them slightly later, by an unknown author of the

5th century. A treasured part of Eastern Orthodox spirituality, the homilies were universally popular among Pietists, partly because of the homilies' emphasis on the need for an experiential religion rather than mere head-knowledge. ***Gottfried Arnold*** (see below) translated them into German.

Meanwhile Francke's work as a pastor in Glaucha blossomed into a whole range of works. His area was beset with a severe social problem—street children. In 1695, Francke set up an orphanage to care for these children and give them the necessary skills to earn a living. Within a year, Francke had to buy a house for it, so successful had the venture become. A year later he had to purchase a second house. As well as reclaiming the street children, Francke established a school for poor children. The orphanage and school were soon being imitated across Germany by other Pietists; their orphanages were known as Franckesche Stiftungen ("Francke Foundations"), after the pioneer. In his school, Francke did not follow the traditional curriculum based on the ancient Greek and Latin classics; he devised what he believed was a curriculum that enshrined the biblical values of Pietism. Rather than classical Greek and Latin, students learned biblical Greek and Hebrew.

A man of unbelievable energy, Francke also set up a school to train teachers, the Paedegogium. He helped found a "Bible institute" in 1710, the forerunner of the Bible Societies that proliferated in the 19th century. The Bible institute printed and distributed copies of the Bible at cheap prices—some two million, all told, in the 18th century. It also published hymn books, prayer books, and other devotional material. The financial support that enabled the Bible institute to function came from a wealthy Pietist aristocrat, Carl Hildebrand von Canstein (1667–1719).

The Prussian prince, Frederick III—King Frederick I, since his elevation to monarchy in 1701—not only backed Francke's various activities; he and his successors made extensive use of those trained in Halle University. The Prussian army was flooded with Pietist chaplains from Halle, imparting a unique spiritual flavour to Prussian military life. Halle-trained Pietists were appointed to run Prussia's royal school, the Collegium Fredericianum. Prussia's other Protestant University of Konigsberg was restructured in 1726 to conform to the Pietist template of Halle; the order came direct from King Frederick William I (1713–40). When in 1763 the Prussian government introduced compulsory education for all children from the ages of 5 to 13, the new public school system was modelled on Francke's ideals and practices. With this level of state patronage, it is not surprising that some have spoken of Pietism becoming the official state religion of Prussia.

4. Other significant Pietists

Pietism spawned a myriad of fascinating figures. Here we can consider only a few of the more significant. One was certainly **Gottfried Arnold** (1666–1714). Born at Annaberg, in Saxony, he studied at Wittenberg from 1685 to 1689. He then had a spell as a private tutor at Dresden, at the time that Spener was court preacher there; the two men met, becoming friends. Arnold later said he owed his religious conversion to conversations with Spener in Dresden. Thereafter, Arnold's life was very unsettled, as he drifted from one job and place to another, usually having to move on because of his outspoken disagreements with theologians and pastors, generally those of a Lutheran Orthodox persuasion. He retained Spener's affection, however. This was despite Arnold's embrace of a more extreme Pietism that no longer saw any need to work within Lutheranism for its renewal (Spener's governing ideal). Arnold exemplified what historians have called "Radical Pietism" as against Spener's "Church Pietism". The difference was precisely the attitude to the established Lutheran Churches of Germany: while Church Pietists remained within to revitalize the Church of their birth and baptism, Radical Pietists showed a separatist tendency. They would denounce unsatisfactory pastors as unconverted, and refuse to take holy communion from their unworthy hands. Arnold sometimes ended up cut off from any actual church, worshiping by himself. Spener tried to discourage these developments, but only very mildly. He was afraid of quenching the Spirit if he took too hard a line.

It was while Arnold was in the grip of this Radical Pietism that he wrote his masterpiece—his *Impartial History of Church and Heresy*. In this massive work, published in two volumes in 1699 and 1700, Arnold narrated Church history not as the story of an institution, but as the story of God's people who could not be identified with any institution. After the first few centuries, according to Arnold, the institutional Church was increasingly characterized by a power-mad hypocrisy; its ultimate disaster was the conversion of Constantine, which allied the Church with the powers of the world. Thereafter Arnold found God's truth and Spirit mainly in dissenting movements. These, he argued, had the true apostolic succession of spiritual life. To underline his thesis, he published editions of patristic, medieval, and 16th-17th century mystics, who embodied for him the authentic voice of the Spirit. His favourite was the author of the Macarian homilies (see previous section). However, he also travelled far beyond normal Protestant boundaries in editing the works of the Lutheran-turned-Catholic mystic Angelus Silesius (1624–77),[7] and publishing translations of the Catholic Quietists Miguel Molinos and Madame Guyon.[8]

In 1707, Arnold modified his Radical Pietism enough to become pastor the Lutheran parish church of Perleberg in Brandenburg-Prussia, where he ministered for the remainder of his life. He is best remembered today for his hymns, especially among German-speakers; the hymns first appeared in a volume *Sparks of Divine Love* (1697), often reprinted with additions. Many were translated into English by Catherine Winkworth (1827–78).

Arnold's new approach to church history was echoed and promoted by two other Pietists, the jurist and philosopher **Christian Thomasius** (1655–1728) and the theologian **Joachim Justus Breithaupt** (1658–1732). Both men taught

---

7. German name Johann Scheffler. His most well-known hymn in English is *Thee will I love, my Strength, my Tower*, translated into English by John Wesley.

8. See Chapter 7, section 2.

at Halle University after being driven out of their previous homes for their Pietism (Thomasius from Leipzig, Breithaupt from Erfurt). Thomasius and Breithaupt saw the Church in non-denominational terms as the total number of all believers throughout the world. They classed as heretics only those who rejected the utterly basic truths necessary to personal salvation. On that basis, they were willing to regard Calvinists and Roman Catholics as fellow believers. This ecumenical impulse flowed partly from the earlier work of Georg Calixtus (see section 2); it was a key factor enabling the easy spread of Pietism across religious boundaries. English Protestants, for example, were to be deeply impacted by Pietism—which seems only fitting, given the huge input of English Puritanism into early Pietism.

This prompts us to consider one final figure who illustrates the capacity of Pietism to transcend denominations, namely, the Radical Pietist **Gerhard Tersteegen** (1697–1769). Born in the little independent city of Moers in northern Germany, he trained as a merchant in Muhlheim, apprenticed to his brother-in-law. Here, at age 16, he experienced a spiritual awakening which instilled into him a distaste for the grubby pursuit of profit. Convinced that the life of a merchant was no longer for him, Tersteegen became a ribbon-maker. He came to public attention through religious meetings originally organized in Muhlheim by the Reformed Pietist pastor, Theodore Undereick, some decades previously. Tersteegen was encouraged to speak at these meetings in 1725 by an admirer, the Pietist William Hoffman. In 1727 the whole area (the Duchy of Berg) was swept by a spiritual awakening, which gave Tersteegen even more prominence at the Muhlheim meetings. People flocked to Tersteegen to ask his spiritual advice. In consequence, he abandoned his ribbon-making the following year to become a full-time counsellor of souls from his home, the "Pilgrims' Hut" in Otterbeck, near Muhlheim.

Tersteegen represents a Radical Pietism that operated with scant regard for any institutional Church, whether Lutheran or Reformed (although Tersteegen's immediate roots were Reformed). His circle was a purely spiritual gathering, rooted in shared experience; the Pilgrims' Hut became the focus for a sort of unofficial non-monastic religious community of like-minded souls. Meanwhile, Tersteegen translated into German many works of the French Quietists, such as Madame Guyon, and wrote a body of his own intense yet tender religious poetry that has endeared itself to millions. John Wesley translated into English Tersteegen's *Thou hidden love of God* and *Lo, God is here! Let us adore*, which have become well-known hymns. Many of his other poems and hymns were translated into English by Catherine Winkworth and Frances Bevan (1827–1909).

5. Orthodox critiques of Pietism: Valentin Ernst Löscher

There was significant opposition to Pietism from upholders of Lutheran Orthodoxy. Wittenberg University in particular, a Lutheran Orthodox stronghold, was highly critical of many aspects of Pietism.

However, we should not think that the Orthodox opposition was either heartless or mindless. There were solid issues at stake. We can perhaps best gauge the nature of the critique in the life of **Valentin Ernst Löscher** (1673–1749), whose father taught theology at Wittenberg. Born at Sondershausen, Löscher himself studied at Wittenberg University, and then at Jena in central Germany. His studies convinced him that the philosophical ideas of the French Catholic René Descartes were a grave danger to a traditional Christian worldview.[9] Travelling widely in Europe, he especially spent time in the Dutch Republic, whose traditions of intellectual liberty made it the ideal place to learn all the latest fashions of thought; here his negative assessment of Descartes was reinforced by interacting with other critics of the French philosopher. This desire to position Christianity in relation to the thought-currents of the day was to be a lifelong concern of Löscher's. In 1696 Löscher became a lecturer back at Wittenberg. From 1698 to 1701 he was superintendent of the Lutheran churches in Jüterborg, then from 1701 to 1707 in Delitzsch. Two

9. See Chapter 2, section 1.6, for more about Descartes.

years of further lecturing at Wittenberg (1707–9) were followed by another superintendency in Dresden, the cultural capital of German Lutheranism, where he also pastored the Cross Church. He remained in Dresden for the rest of his life.

What, then, of Löscher's relationship to Pietism? He admitted that Pietists had exposed genuine problems and needs in Lutheran Church life. Some of his own reforming activities as a superintendent could easily be perceived as a Pietist programme for reinvigorating church life: he encouraged family devotions, pastoral home visitation, fellowship meals, generous practical care of orphans and the poor. Indeed, Löscher found little to disagree with in the original first-generation Pietism of Philip Jacob Spener, and defended Spener against his critics. It might be said that Löscher had a Pietist side to his own personality. However, he had increasing problems with Spener's disciples, especially the Radical Pietists (see above). This impelled him to a more polemical stance. In particular, he criticized what he believed was a wrong view among many Pietists of the relationship between doctrine and spiritual life, as though the latter could flourish where the former was downgraded. For Löscher, all true piety had to grow out of correct Lutheran doctrine. He defended traditional Lutheran Orthodoxy as the authentic theological expression of Lutheran belief; he strenuously opposed any dilution of its doctrinal content which might blur the differences between Lutheran and Reformed (too many Lutheran Pietists, he argued, were now moving towards a fusion of Lutheranism and Calvinism into a theologically boneless jelly of "mere piety"). He was especially concerned that a right understanding of justification by faith was being lost amid all the zeal for Christian experience and holiness.

To promote his critique, in 1701 Löscher founded Germany's first theological periodical, the *Unschuldige Nachrichten von alten und neuen theologischen Sachen* ("Unbiased News of Theological Matters Old and New"). In a series of articles under the heading *Timotheus Verinus*, Löscher set out his reasons for rejecting the Pietist remedy for the Church's ills. The entire series was then published in two volumes as *The Complete Timotheus Verinus*

(1718–22). Löscher was so eloquent in voicing his concerns that the ranks of Lutheran Orthodoxy came to look on him as their chief spokesman against the massive advances that Pietism, especially in its more Radical forms, was making in their Churches.

On the other hand, for all his robust critique of Pietism, Löscher did not see it as the most urgent threat to Lutheran Orthodoxy. The new philosophical thinking of the period, stemming often from Descartes, was (he believed) a far deadlier enemy. His *Theological Preconceptions* (1709) was an attempt at a comprehensive analysis and criticism of the new thinking, which he argued was essentially human-centred, exalting the human mind as the ultimate measure of all things, and leaving no effective space for a sovereign God or for supernatural divine revelation.

Löscher's conviction that this godless philosophy was the real enemy inspired him to deal fraternally with Pietists as fellow-Christians in spite of their errors. He tried to bring about a rapprochement between the Orthodox Lutherans and Pietists, drawing up a six-point basis of discussion between the two parties. However, as is often the fate of the mediator, he was rebuffed by both sides. The Orthodox wanted to discuss not six, but sixty points; the Pietists were offended that anyone should query their fidelity to Scripture or the Lutheran confessions. Despite this, Löscher arranged a private meeting with August Hermann Francke in May 1719 at Merseburg. Löscher thought the meeting had provided a basis for further friendly conversations. But Francke evidently had other ideas; Löscher was given a sealed letter in which Francke informed the Orthodox theologian that he needed to be born again—only then would Löscher be able to see that the Pietists had the truth! Löscher's attempt at Orthodox-Pietist collaboration bit the dust.

5
Dawn of the Protestant missionary movement

It was August Hermann Francke and the Pietism of Halle that first opened the floodgates of Protestant mission. Francke's mentor, Spener, had gone on record that Protestants ought not to leave the global spread of Christianity in Roman Catholic hands. There had been massive Catholic missionary expansion in the 16th and 17th centuries; there was simply nothing comparable from Protestants. Some Protestant theologians, such as John Calvin, acknowledged in theory that the gospel should be taken to the ends of the earth; the Protestant Churches, however, had not yet experienced any awakening of an effective missionary impulse, except within Europe itself—evangelizing Roman Catholics. But Roman Catholics did not limit themselves to spreading their faith among Protestants; they went out into all the world. Such a global missionary impulse finally awakened in the Protestant consciousness through German Pietism.

However, we should qualify this by acknowledging that there was some Lutheran missionary activity prior to the 18th century. Some of this was within Europe/Russia, for instance the Lutheran missionaries sent by Swedish King Gustavus Vasa (1523–60) to the Sami people (formerly known as the Lapps) in 1559. The Sami inhabited the area of Sápmi (covering parts of Norway, Sweden, Finland, and Russia), and some of this territory had now fallen under Swedish sovereignty. Over a century later, this missionary work found its greatest labourer in **Thomas von Westen** (1682–1727), a Lutheran Pietist nicknamed "apostle to the Sami". Again, some early Lutheran missionary activity took place outside Europe but within the bounds of ancient Christendom, such as the work of the lay theologian and physician **Peter Heyling** (born 1607/8, died some time after 1652) in Ethiopia; working from 1634 as court physician to Ethiopian King Fasilides (1632–67), Heyling translated the New Testament into Amharic.

When Swedish Lutheran colonists arrived in America, their settlement at New Sweden (present day Wilmington, Delaware) was pastored by John Campanius (1601–83), who arrived in 1643. As well as ministering to the Swedes, Campanius took a strong interest in the native Lenape people who lived in the locality. He studied their culture, and invented a written script for their language, translating Luther's Small Catechism. He also preached to the Lenape with (we are told) some positive effect.

These efforts, however, seem like relatively isolated outbursts of missionary zeal, compared to the more focused awakening of missionary consciousness that characterized Francke's Pietism at Halle. Francke himself was possessed with a sense of the necessity of world mission as an integral part of the coming of Christ's kingdom. He did everything in his power to implant this conviction in his students at Halle. There remained, however, the practical problem of how to get missionaries into non-Christian countries and support them while they worked there. Roman Catholic missionaries had the vast overseas empires of Spain and Portugal to ferry them abroad and protect them. What could Protestants do?

The answer came in the shape of a Protestant king—**Frederick IV of Denmark** (1699–1730). Frederick had a German Pietist chaplain, Franz Julius Liitkins (1650–1712), and Liitkins imparted to Frederick the Pietist enthusiasm for mission; the Danish king resolved that he must imitate the zeal of Catholic monarchs in promoting overseas evangelism. There was a Danish colony in Tranquebar, on the coast of south-east India, where the Danes ruled over native Indians whose religion was Hinduism. Frederick decided to send missionaries to work among these

Hindu natives. Where would he find people prepared to surrender their lives to such a calling? He consulted Francke in Halle; Francke immediately recommended two of his students, **Bartholomew Ziegenbalg** (1682–1719) and **Henry Plütschau** (1676–1747). They accepted King Frederick's offer, sailed at the close of 1705, and set foot in Tranquebar on 9th July 1706.

Ziegenbalg and Plütschau were the first Protestant missionaries to India. The Danish Pietist mission they founded at Tranquebar would have a 130 year history (1707–1837), during which 54 missionaries worked in the area. Since Ziegenbalg wrote regularly to his sponsors back in Europe, we know a lot about the early mission, its trials and triumphs. Certainly it enjoyed significant success; when Ziegenbalg died in 1719, he and Plütschau had established a 350–strong Lutheran congregation in Tranquebar. Not all its members were Hindu converts (some were slaves of colonists, some were ex-Catholics), but many were.

Ziegenbalg and Plütschau laid the foundations of an effective mission by the policies they adopted at the outset. These have been summed up as five major points and hailed as guidelines of enduring validity:

1. Christian education must be a priority. All converts must be able to read the Bible; therefore they must be taught how to read. Church and school therefore go hand-in-hand.

2. The Bible must be translated into the native language. Ziegenbalg himself translated the New Testament into Tamil (the first ever Tamil version); it was published in 1714.

3. Preaching must be grounded in an understanding of the native culture and mentality. Ziegenbalg made an intensive study of Hinduism, and made sure his evangelism and teaching took full account of the beliefs of those among whom he laboured.

4. The mission must pursue the goal of authentic personal conversions, not a merely outward exchange of one lifestyle for another.

5. The mission must aim at establishing an indigenous
   Indian church as soon as possible. The first native Indian
   pastor, a man named Aaron, converted from Hinduism,
   was ordained in 1733, which was quick by missionary
   standards.

The Danish Pietist mission actually extended outside of the
Danish territory in Tranquebar. The British had settlements
in that part of India; and the British Society for Promoting
Christian Knowledge (commonly shortened to SPCK), an
Anglican organization founded in 1698, offered to finance
the Danish missionaries if they would extend their work into
British territories, such as Madras and Trichonopoly. The Danes
agreed. The first Danish Pietist missionary to be active in British
territory for the SPCK was a Prussian, **Benjamin Schultz** (1689–
1760), who from 1728 worked in Madras. Now employed by
an Anglican body, the Danish SPCK missionaries used the
Anglican Book of Common Prayer in worship, translating it
into Tamil. Their converts were baptized as Anglicans rather
than Lutherans.

Frederick IV's Pietist enthusiasm for mission also expressed
itself in Greenland. He supported the venture of **Hans Egede**
(1686–1758), a Danish Lutheran pastor, who sailed to
Greenland in 1721 in search of any survivors from the old
Norse colony there which had probably died out in the late
15th century. Instead he found the Inuit people,[1] and worked
as a missionary among them until 1736, winning converts, and
initiating a study of their language that enabled his son **Paul
Egede** (1708–89) to translate the New Testament into Inuit.

Meanwhile, back in Germany, Francke publicized the work
of the Pietist missionaries in a newspaper entitled *Hallesche
Correspondenz* ("Halle Correspondence"), the first ever
missionary journal. It circulated not only throughout Germany
but across Europe, helping to stimulate at last a concerned
Protestant consciousness of the mission field outside the

---

1. Formerly known as Eskimos, a term now regarded as demeaning.

European homeland. It seems that Protestantism owes to Luther the first clarion call to Reformation, and to Lutherans the birth of the modern Protestant missionary movement.

Important people:

Nicholas von Amsdorf (1483–1565)
Johann Pfeffinger (1493–1573)
Johann Agricola (1494–1566)
Andreas Osiander (1496–1552)
Philip Melanchthon (1497–1560)
George Major (1502–74)
Andreas Musculus (1514–81)
Matthias Flacius (1520–75)
Martin Chemnitz (1522–86)
Victorinus Strigel (1524–69)
Caspar Peucer (1525–1602)
Georg Cracow (1525–75)
Jacob Andreae (1528–90)
Nicholas Selnecker (1530–92)
David Chytraeus (1530–1600)
Daniel Hoffmann (1538–1611)
Augustus I of Saxony (1553–86)
Cornelius Martini (1568–1621)
Johann Gerhard (1582–1637)
Jesper Rasmus Brochmand (1585–1652)
Georg Calixtus (1586–1656)
Johann Conrad Dannhauer (1603–1666)
Peter Heyling (born 1607/8, died some time after 1652)
Abraham Calov (1612–86)
Johannes Andreas Quenstedt (1617–88)
Valentin Ernst Löscher (1673–1749)

The Thirty Years' War

Johann Tserclaes of Tilly (1559–1632)
Axel Oxenstierna (1583–1654)
Christian IV of Denmark (1588–1648)
Maximilian I of Bavaria (1597–1651)
Frederick V of the Palatinate (1610–23)

Gustavus Adolphus of Sweden (1611–32)
Christian the Younger (1616–26)
Emperor Ferdinand II (1619–37)
Philip IV of Spain (1621–65)

Hymns and music

Philipp Nicolai (1556–1608)
Michael Praetorius (c.1571–1621
Johann Heermann (1585–1647)
Heinrich Schütz (1585–1672)
Paul Gerhardt (1607–1676)
Dieterich Buxtehude (c.1637–1707)
Johann Sebastian Bach (1685–1750)

Pietism

Johann Arndt (1553–1621)
John Durie (1596–1680)
Jean de Labadie (1610–74)
Philip Jacob Spener (1635–1705)
Christian Thomasius (1655–1728)
Joachim Justus Breithaupt (1658–1732)
August Hermann Francke (1663–1727)
Gottfried Arnold (1666–1714)
Henry Plütschau (1676–1747)
Bartholomew Ziegenbalg (1682–1719)
Thomas von Westen (1682–1727)
Hans Egede (1686–1758)
Frederick III of Prussia (margrave 1688–1701; king 1701–13)
Gerhard Tersteegen (1697–1769)
Benjamin Schultz (1689–1760)
Frederick IV of Denmark (1699–1730)
Paul Egede (1708–89)

Primary source material

Martin Chemnitz: The true doctrine of predestination

In the third place, they [Roman Catholic theologians] erect the
doctrine of predestination, or election, against the assurance of

salvation. To give some plausible colour to this, they say that we must avoid foolhardy presumption concerning the hidden mystery of predestination. True indeed (and it is carefully taught among us), no one should pry into the secret purpose of God, thereby to establish whether we belong to the ranks of the elect. That way leads to a head-first plunge into many errors, ultimately into sheer despair. Where election is the subject, we must not judge by the canons of the human mind and its thoughts, nor by questionable speculations about what God has decreed in His secret purpose concerning each individual's salvation or damnation. We must judge from the Word of God, where God has made His will known to us.

We must not, however, learn this from the Law, which preaches about our works, our merits, and what we deserve; we must go to the Gospel. And the Gospel speaks of election—although not like poets telling fairy-stories about "the books of Fate", where some are predestined to life, others to death, about which we know nothing for certain, since we do not know if we belong to the ranks of those who will be saved, or of those who will be damned. No, the revealed doctrine of predestination in Scripture sets forth God's decrees concerning the causes and way of salvation or damnation, like this:

1. There is God's decree to redeem humankind through the obedience and suffering of Christ the Mediator.

2. There is God's decree to call Jews and Gentiles alike, through the ministry of the Word, to share in the merit of Christ for salvation.

3. There is God's decree that He wills, through the hearing of the Word, to work by His Spirit in human hearts to bring them to repentance and faith in the Gospel.

4. There is God's decree that He wills to justify and save those who, when they feel their sins and God's wrath, flee by faith to the throne of grace, and embrace Christ the Mediator, as He is proclaimed in the Gospel. On the other hand, God has decreed to damn those who

reject the Word, despising the promise, and refusing to embrace it.

This is a précis and outline of the doctrine of predestination, insofar as it stands revealed to us in the Word. It does not teach true believers to doubt whether they belong to the ranks of the elect, but imitating Paul in Romans 8:30, it establishes this sequence of steps: "Those whom He predestined He also called, and those whom He called He also justified." Therefore, those whom God calls and justifies should certainly conclude that they are elected!

If the reader will look at what Scripture says about election, he will plainly see that the doctrine of predestination, as it stands revealed in Scripture, is not given in order to cast doubt and uncertainty on the salvation of believers, but to be a basis of certainty. Eph. 1:4: "He chose us in Christ before the founding of the world." 2 Tim. 2:19: "God's foundation stands firm, bearing this seal: The Lord knows those who are His." John 10:27–28: "My sheep hear My voice… and they will never perish; no one will snatch them out of My hand." Rom. 8:28, 34, 35: "Those who are called according to God's purpose." Therefore, "who is He that condemns? Who shall separate us?" Rom. 11:29: "For the gifts and the calling of God cannot be revoked." 2 Tim. 1:7–9: "God did not give us a spirit of fear… For He has called us because of His own purpose and the grace He gave us in Christ Jesus ages ago, etc."

My intention was not to explain the whole doctrine of predestination at this point, but only to show that divine election, as it is revealed in God's Word, does not beget uncertainty, but rather confirms and establishes the certainty of salvation and the confidence of believers. The Council of Trent is quite wrong when it says, in Chapter 12, that no one can know from God's Word whom God has chosen for Himself, unless He adds a special revelation beyond and apart from the Word. Nor is it true that a true believer cannot establish with certainty from God's Word, without any special revelation, that he belongs to the ranks of the predestined. Trent here clashes with Scripture, as we have just shown. Of course, I am not unaware of the fact that disordered minds conjure up many mystifying and ghastly things about predestination; but I have set out this summary of teaching in what I judge to be a very simple manner.

Martin Chemnitz
Examination of the Council of Trent, Ninth Topic, section 3:23–5

Johann Gerhard: a meditation on how Christ's death profits us

Behold, Lord Jesus, how inadequately I contemplate Thy suffering! It disturbs my heart and greatly saddens my spirit that my own works and merits are not to be found in Thy suffering, although Thy suffering is (even so) my deed and Thy works are my merits. O how inadequately I contemplate Thy suffering because, despite the perfect adequacy of Thy suffering, still I restlessly try to bolster it with my own works! Yet if I could manufacture some righteousness of my own, then Thy righteousness would cease to be of any benefit to me. At any rate, I surely would not have thirsted after Thy righteousness so strongly. If I try to do the works of the Law, then by the Law I shall be condemned. Yet I know that now I am no longer under the Law, but under grace (Rom. 6:14). My life has been intemperate. Holy heavenly Father, I have sinned, and I am not worthy to be called Thy child! And yet Thou wilt not call me Thy servant!

O may the fruit of Thy suffering not be denied me. Thy blood is not infertile; truly it bears fruit, and liberates my soul. My sins have always lived in my fallen nature. Now at last, I plead that they will die with me! Up until now, my fallen nature has always controlled me; O grant that my spiritual nature may gain the victory! May my external self be made subject to perishing and poison, so that my inner self may come forth to glory! Up until now, I have always followed Satan's promptings. O may he at last be bruised beneath my feet! He is always ready to accuse me, but he has no rights over me. The sight of death fills me with fear; yet death will bring an end to my sins and instate me in the life of holiness. Yes, very soon, my God, I will at last be able to please Thee perfectly. The enemy terrifies me by showing me my sins; but in reality, he accuses the One who took My failings upon Him, whom God delivered to death for my sins! How overwhelmingly great is my debt, which I cannot pay at all. But I trust in my Surety's riches and love. He underwrote my debt and sets me free, paying in full for me!

O Lord, I have sinned: how many are my sins, how great beyond calculation. Even so, I will not commit the most awful sin of all, the sin of accusing Thee of lying, when Thou dost testify by Thy words and works and oath that Thou hast made atonement for my sins! Thou art my righteousness: therefore I do not fear my sins! Thou art my wisdom: I do not fear my ignorance! Thou art my life: I do not fear death! Thou art my truth: I do not fear falsehoods! Thou art my resurrection: I do not fear that I may perish! Thou art my joy: I do not fear the pangs of death! Because Thou art my righteousness, I do not fear to stand before the harshest judge.

O may the dew of Thy grace, and the comfort of the resurrection, be outpoured into my parching soul. My spirit shrivels up, but soon it will rejoice in Thee! My feeble flesh droops, but soon it will blossom forth! Necessity is laid upon me; I perish. But Thou hast set me free from all ills, and Thou wilt free me from perishing! Thou hast made me: shall anything destroy what Thy hands have made? Thou hast redeemed me from every foe: how can the final foe, death, triumph over me? Thou hast lavished Thy life, Thy blood, Thy all to save me: how shall death keep its hold on those redeemed at so costly a ransom-price?

Thou art my righteousness, Lord Jesus: my sins will not succeed against Thee. Thou art the resurrection and the life: my death-sentence will not succeed against Thee. Thou art God: Satan will not succeed against Thee. Thou hast given me the gift of Thy Spirit! In this I exult, in this I triumph, in this I most surely believe, not doubting that Thou hast granted me to enter the marriage supper of the Lamb! O my Advocate, Thou art my wedding garment with which my baptism has clothed me. Thou hast covered my nakedness! Forbid that I should ever sew onto this costly and loveliest of garments any patch of my own righteousness; for what is human righteousness but a filthy rag? With what audacity can I sew this foul rag onto the robe of Thy righteousness? I shall stand forth in this robe before Thy face in Thy judgment, on the day Thou dost judge the world in righteousness and equity. I shall stand forth in this robe before Thy face in the kingdom of heaven. This robe is the covering for my embarrassment and my unseemliness, so that none of it may ever again be recorded in eternity. There I shall stand forth in Thine eyes glorious and holy in my flesh; my very body will be imperishable, clothed in the most blessed glory—eternal glory unto the ages of ages!

Johann Gerhard
Sacred Meditations, **Meditation 5**

Johannes Andreas Quenstedt: the difference between Christ's atonement and His merit

The atonement and the merit of Christ are not the same thing. The reasons are:

1. The atonement negatively "pays damages" to God for a grievance against what we have done, recompenses for sin, makes good a debt, and altogether rescues us from penalties that would endure for ever. Christ's merit, however, positively reinstates us into God's acceptance, and secures for sinners an undeserved reward—the free gift of forgiveness of sins, justification, and everlasting life.

2. The atonement is the cause, but Christ's merit is the effect. For merit flows from the fountain of atonement. Christ made atonement for our sins, and for the punishments they had incurred, and *thereby* He merited God's favour for us, sin's forgiveness, and everlasting life.

3. Atonement was given to the triune God and to His justice, not to us, although it was given for our sakes. But when Christ merited, by that merit He secured something for us, not for the Trinity.

4. The acts of Christ's humiliation, such as His obedience to the Law, His suffering and death, etc., are both atoning and meritorious at the same time. But the acts of His exaltation, such as His resurrection, ascending into heaven, and being enthroned at God's right hand, are not atoning acts; they are purely meritorious. In other words, Christ did not atone for our sins by rising from the dead and ascending into heaven; but by doing these things, He thereby merited everlasting life for us and opened the gates of heaven.

5. Finally, the work of atonement originates from debt. Merit, however, is a work that is in no sense owed, but is done freely. It is to merit, then, that reward or recompense belongs.

Even so, not all theologians accept this distinction, but some incorporate Christ's atonement itself into the concept of merit.

Johannes Andreas Quenstedt
Didactic-Polemic Theology or Theological System, **Part 1,
Chapter 2, section 1**

Paul Gerhardt: Christ-centred faith

Jesus, Thy boundless love to me
        No thought can reach, no tongue declare;
Unite my thankful heart with Thee
        And reign without a rival there.
To Thee alone, dear Lord, I live;
        Myself to Thee, dear Lord, I give.

O, grant that nothing in my soul
        May dwell but Thy pure love alone!
Oh, may Thy love possess me whole,
        My joy, my treasure, and my crown!
All coldness from my heart remove;
        My every act, word, thought, be love.

O Love, how cheering is Thy ray!
　　All pain before Thy presence flies;
Care, anguish, sorrow, melt away
　　Where'er Thy healing beams arise.
O Jesus, nothing may I see,
　　Nothing desire or seek, but Thee!

This love unwearied I pursue,
　　And dauntlessly to Thee aspire.
Oh, may Thy love my hope renew,
　　Burn in my soul like heavenly fire!
And day and night be all my care
　　To guard this sacred treasure there.

My Saviour, Thou Thy love to me
　　In shame, in want, in pain, hast showed;
For me, on the accursed tree,
　　Thou pourest forth Thy guiltless blood;
Thy wounds upon my heart impress,
　　Nor aught the mark shall e'er efface!

More hard than marble is my heart,
　　And foul with sins of deepest stain;
But Thou the mighty Saviour art,
　　Nor flowed thy cleansing blood in vain;
Ah soften, melt this rock, and may
　　Thy blood wash all these stains away!

O that I, as a little child,
　　May follow Thee, and never rest,
Till sweetly Thou hast breathed Thy mild
　　And lowly mind into my breast!
Nor ever may we parted be,
　　Till I become as one with Thee.

Still let Thy love point out my way;
> *How wondrous things Thy love hath wrought!*

Still lead me, lest I go astray;
> *Direct my word, inspire my thought;*

And if I fall, soon may I hear
> *Thy voice, and know that love is near.*

In suffering be Thy love my peace,
> *In weakness be Thy love my power;*

And when the storms of life shall cease,
> *Jesus, in that tremendous hour,*

In death as life be Thou my guide,
> *And save me, who for me hast died.* [2]

Johann Arndt: the urgent necessity of sanctification in the life of faith

How can a person who has faith in Christ remain in the sins for which the Lord paid so costly a price as His own most precious blood? When, therefore, O soul, you are tempted to high thoughts of yourself and selfish ambition, think about the scorn and humiliation which Jesus took upon Himself to atone for these sins. When you desire this world, think of the poverty Jesus experienced that He might make atonement for your grasping desires; and surely this will extinguish in you the love of money and material goods. What pain and agony Christ endured because of your sinful desires and pleasures! And are you still pursuing these pleasures whose aftermath will be a deadly sting? Alas! how great must the depravity of our nature be, when we can find sweetness in things for which our Redeemer and Lord underwent sorrow even unto death! Christ died to pay the price for your anger, hatred, and hostility: to atone for your bitterness and malignity, your delight in taking revenge, and your unforgiving spirit. This He accomplished by

---

2. Based on the translation by John Wesley, with very slight alteration.

His utmost meekness and patience, His compassion and long-suffering. And will you become angry for every trivial reason, and consider revenge to be delicious, when your Redeemer drank to the last drops the cup of bitterness and suffering in order to atone for these very things?

In truth, those who take to themselves the name of Christians, and yet do not renounce the pleasures of sin, crucify Christ to themselves anew, and put Him to public disgrace (Heb. 6:6). It is, therefore, utterly impossible that they should share in that merit which they trample underfoot. They defile the blood of the eternal covenant, that is, they do not consider it a purification of their sins. They despise the Spirit of grace; they scorn Him and resist Him; and, by their ungodly lives, they treat as some cheap and despicable thing God's grace offered in Jesus Christ (Heb. 10:29). Thus the blood of the Saviour, which was shed for their salvation, now cries aloud for justice against them; they will have to face the righteous judgment of God, which they attract to themselves by their sin. This thought ought to instil dread into everyone who names the name of Christ. For in truth, how fearful it is to fall into the hands of the living God (Heb. 10:31). For He is a living God, not a dead idol who will allow His grace and mercy to be for ever mocked and scorned…

Even though these truths are certain and self-evident in themselves, many people who say they are Christians have never repented—and yet they have the effrontery to claim a share in the merits of Christ, and in the forgiveness of sins He has procured. They have not stopped indulging their usual anger, worldly desires, pride, ill-will, jealousy, hypocrisy, and injustice to others; in fact, they have fallen into an ever deeper bondage to these things! And yet (alas!) they expect their sin to be forgiven! With false confidence they think the merits of Christ will protect them against the coming judgment of Almighty God. Although this is one of the most crude and blatant errors in the world, they have no hesitation in calling it "faith" by which they expect to be saved! O what a fallacy! These are people who sweet-talk themselves to their own destruction, foolishly imagining they are true Christians merely because they have a head-knowledge of the Gospel, and because they believe that Jesus died for their sins. But sadly, this is not faith. It is mere fancy. You are a wretched and most appallingly self- infatuated counterfeit Christian, if you can let yourself be deceived in this way! The Word of God never taught such a doctrine.

Johann Arndt
True Christianity, **Book 1, Chapter 8**

Philip Jacob Spener: Church Pietism

Thirdly, it might be profitable (I offer this for deeper and more mature consideration) to bring back the kind of church meetings they had of old, in apostolic times. As well as our ordinary preaching services, we could have other gatherings such as Paul sets out in 1 Corinthians 14:26–40. Here, it would not be one person getting up to preach (although this custom would carry on at other times); no, others blessed with gifts of understanding would also speak, giving their godly opinions on the topic proposed, to be evaluated by the rest. All this would be done in a way designed to avoid disorder and conflict.

We could do this acceptably by bringing together a number of pastors, in towns that have more than one pastor in residence. Or a number of church members whose knowledge of God is reasonably good, or who wish to make progress in that knowledge, could meet under a pastor's oversight, read out from the holy Scriptures, and discuss the verses in a brotherly way. They would search for the plain meaning, and whatever the verses contain that serve the purposes of common edification. If anyone at the meeting has some difficulty with a verse, he should be allowed to air his doubts and ask for a better explanation. The more knowledgeable—including the pastors—would be free to give their understanding of the passages in question. All the contributions, assuming they are in keeping with what the Holy Spirit intends in the Scriptures, should be pondered with care by the others (especially the ordained pastors), and the practical application be brought out, so that the gathering might be edified. Everything should be organized with God's glory in view, and also the spiritual progress of group members, bearing in mind their limitations. If anyone becomes impertinent, argumentative, self-promoting, and so forth, the preachers in charge should keep watch against this and diplomatically impose silence on such people.

Considerable benefit might be expected from this kind of meeting. The preachers would get better acquainted with church members, with their weaknesses or their progress in doctrine and godliness; preachers and people would gain a closer confidence in each other, to their mutual advantage. The people would have a wonderful opportunity to get down to some solid study of God's Word, ask questions politely, and get an answer (people do not always feel able to discuss such things with their pastor on their own). The outcome would soon be personal growth, and a greater ability to instruct children and domestic servants in Christian things. Without such meetings, set-piece sermons are not always understood very well, because people have no time to stop and think about each point. Or if they do stop to think, they then lose the thread of what the preacher is saying next. Discussions avoid this pitfall. Or again, reading the Bible in private or out loud to one's family, without anyone present to offer help now and then in understanding this or that verse, does not give us an adequate explanation of all we would wish to understand.

The defects in these two methods—public preaching and private reading—would be remedied by the meetings I have described. No great burden would be laid on the preachers or the people, and it would contribute greatly to fulfilling Paul's exhortation in Colossians 3:16, "Let the word of Christ dwell in you richly, teaching and admonishing one another in all wisdom, singing psalms and hymns and spiritual songs." Indeed, the meetings could sing such songs to praise God and inspire group members.

We can be sure of this: the careful and industrious use of God's Word does not consist merely of listening to sermons! It includes reading, meditating, discussing (Ps. 1:2), and is the chief means of reformation—whether my suggestion above is followed, or some other is adopted. God's Word is ever the seed from which everything good in us must grow. If we can just get people to seek their happiness gladly and seriously in the Book of Life, it will gloriously strengthen their spiritual life, and change them into very different people!

Philip Jacob Spener
Pia Desideria, **Part 3, section 1**

Gerhard Tersteegen: the poetry of Radical Pietism

Still, O soul! the sign and wonder
        Of all ages see:
Christ, thy God, the King of glory,
        On the Cross for thee:
From the Father's bosom come,
Wandering soul, to bring thee home.

Wouldst thou know if Jesus loves thee?
        If He loves thee well?
See Him suffer, broken-hearted,
        All the pains of hell:
Smitten, bearing in thy place
All thy guilt, and thy disgrace.

See Him of His God forsaken,
        Hear His bitter cries
Rise unanswered through the darkness
        Of the silent skies:
See the fountain of the blood
Shed to bring thee back to God.

Mine the sin, O mighty Saviour,
        Laid by God on Thee;
My eternal condemnation
        In Thy Cross I see;
In Thine agony divine
See the curse that else were mine.

See the conquest and the triumph
  Thou for me hast won;
Justice satisfied for ever,
  All God's pleasure done.
Thus, O smitten Rock! from Thee,
Life eternal flows to me.

Unto me, the base, the guilty,
  Flows that living flood;
I, Thine enemy, am ransomed
  By Thy precious blood.
Silent at Thy feet I lie,
Lost in love's immensity.

(from the translation by Frances Bevan)

Chapter 2

The Reformed Faith

Introduction

The Reformed faith, commonly known as Calvinism, had established itself in the cities of Switzerland, and in England, Scotland, the Dutch Republic, and parts of Germany, with a significant Reformed minority in France. In our period it was, theologically and spiritually, a vast, complex, developing entity. The original vision expressed by the first generation of pioneers—Ulrich Zwingli, Heinrich Bullinger, Martin Bucer, Peter Martyr Vermigli, John Calvin, and others—was in many ways only the foundation on which the succeeding generations built the temple of "Reformed Orthodoxy" (see below). But Reformed Orthodoxy was far from monolithic, as we shall discover. It had its internal frictions and controversies, its different voices, its own rich history. To freeze-frame one scene from that history (say, the Westminster Assembly of Britain's Reformed theologians), and treat this as the be-all and end-all of the Reformed story, would be to impoverish our understanding almost immeasurably.

This Chapter will seek to introduce readers to the post-Calvin Reformed world in all its varieties, but with two massive qualifications: Reformed theology in England and Scotland receive separate treatments in Chapters 3–5. The only British[1] theologian given a substantial place in the current Chapter is William Ames, because of his rather special role in the unfolding drama of Continental European Reformed theology.

---

1. For non-British readers: the island of Britain, located off the north-west coast of Europe, includes England, Scotland, and Wales. "British" could therefore mean English, Scottish, or Welsh.

1

Reformed Orthodoxy

1. Scholasticism and Ramism

In the chapter on Lutheranism, section 2, we considered the way that Lutheran theologians, after the Formula of Concord (1577), allied themselves with a revived Aristotelian philosophy. The result, we saw, is generally known as Lutheran Orthodoxy or Lutheran scholasticism. There was a parallel development in Reformed theology. We will therefore spare ourselves from covering the same ground again; the account already given of Lutheran theology, and its relationship with Aristotle, applies in essence to Reformed theology as well. The result was Reformed Orthodoxy or Reformed scholasticism (sometimes called "scholastic Calvinism"). It developed slightly earlier than its Lutheran counterpart, perhaps because Reformed theology never had quite the same animus that early Lutheranism had against Aristotle, or against his great medieval Christian interpreter, Thomas Aquinas. After all, one of the most influential "founding fathers" of the Reformed tradition, Peter Martyr Vermigli, was himself a highly accomplished professional Aristotelian philosopher.[2]

One complicating factor in Reformed Orthodoxy was the presence, not only of a reinvigorated Aristotelianism, but a newly fashioned tool of thought: Ramism. It was named after a French Reformed thinker, **Peter Ramus** (1515–72).

---

2. See *Volume Three: Renaissance and Reformation*, Chapter 4, section 3.

Ramus developed a system of logical analysis that relied on "dichotomy"—breaking concepts down into pairs, and then dividing each pair into another pair, until one finally arrived at basic axioms that could not be further divided. A good many Reformed thinkers embraced Ramism as their method for examining and explaining theological concepts. Others (like Theodore Beza—see below) rejected Ramism in favour of a pristine Aristotelianism. However, it would be too simplistic to set up Ramism and Aristotelianism as stark alternatives; a good many Reformed theologians could and did blend the two. It is also a matter of debate whether Ramism is strictly an alternative to Aristotelian thinking, or whether it is best to see Ramism as itself a form of Aristotelianism—Aristotle redesigned for 16th century Reformed humanism.

Debates about the nature, origins, and consequences of Reformed Orthodoxy or scholastic Calvinism are legion, and will no doubt continue. By locating most of my own discussion under the previous heading of *Lutheran* Orthodoxy, I am gently suggesting that Reformed students should not get too imprisoned in their own Reformed universe, but think about the far wider dimensions of how theological method evolved across the board in the second part of the 16th century.

Let us now meet some of the representative figures of Reformed Orthodoxy—giants who made their mark on the history of Calvinist theology after the pioneers had passed from the scene.

2. Theodore Beza

Theodore Beza (1519–1605) was John Calvin's most distinguished disciple, and indeed Calvin's successor as spiritual leader of Geneva. Born to an aristocratic family at Vézelay in Burgundy, France, he received a first class education from the German humanist Melchior Wolmar (1497–1561), one of the foremost Greek scholars of that time (he had also taught Greek to Calvin, who dedicated his commentary on 2 Corinthians to Wolmar). Wolmar had embraced Reformation views, and these deeply influenced the young Beza. However, he remained outwardly a Roman Catholic for many years, living in Paris as a carefree noble with a private income, and dedicating his energies to classical literature. It was not until recovering from a near-death experience through illness in 1548 that Beza became serious about being a Protestant. He now fled from Paris to the Swiss Reformed city of Lausanne, where he taught Greek for the next nine years at its university. In 1558, the rulers of the powerful Swiss canton of Berne imposed a new religious settlement on Lausanne; although the Bernese were Reformed, Beza objected to the state dictating doctrine and worship to a Reformed Church. So he left in protest, relocating to Calvin's Geneva.

Beza soon became Calvin's closest friend and co-worker; Calvin put him in charge of the Genevan academy in 1559, a position he held for the rest of his life. As well as his general duties running the academy, Beza taught systematic theology there. His devotion to the academy made it one of the most successful Reformed educational bodies of the 16th century, with distinguished lecturers and a huge international student body. From the academy a steady flow of Reformed pastors, evangelists, and church-planters streamed out into the rest of Europe. On Calvin's death in 1564, Geneva naturally looked to Beza for continued leadership, which he provided for the next 40 years.

Beza not only supervised the academy; he was also, after Calvin died, Geneva's chief pastor and chairman of the "company of pastors", which supervised ministerial training and ordination. Much of Beza's energy as a church leader was given to the roller-coaster fortunes of the French Calvinists or Huguenots during France's "wars of religion" (1562–98).[3] He advised the Huguenot nobles; he gave guidance to Huguenot pastors and theologians, especially over matters of church government, where he upheld Presbyterianism (under Peter Ramus' influence, some preferred a more Congregational model, which Beza considered destructive to French Reformed unity). His political philosophy evolved in a more radical direction under the impact of the massacre of Saint

---

3. See *Volume Three: Renaissance and Reformation*, Chapter 6, section 4 for the French wars of religion.

Bartholomew's day in 1572, when some 20,000 Huguenots were slaughtered. The French crown's participation in the massacre (through the young King Charles IX's domineering

mother, Catherine de Medici), inspired Beza to write *Concerning the Power of Magistrates* (1574). Here, Beza argued that if monarchs behaved tyrannically, the lesser political authorities of the realm could lawfully restrain them, by force if necessary. This became the standard Reformed view, acted on not just by Huguenots in France, but also by Dutch Calvinists in revolt against King Philip II of Spain, and by Scottish Covenanters

Theodore Beza (1519–1605)
Portrait by Etienne-Jehandier
Desrochers (1668–1741)

and English Puritans in revolt against King Charles I.

Beza's contribution to Reformed worship was notable. In 1562, he published a complete French metrical psalter. It had been translated in part by Clement Marot (1497–1544)—Beza finished it. He was poetically talented, and the new psalter instantly captured the affections of French-speaking Calvinists across Europe. It formed the basis for English, German, and Dutch Reformed psalters.

Beza was also a notable textual scholar. He published his own critical edition of the Greek New Testament in 1565, intended as a replacement for Erasmus' text which Beza considered inadequate. Beza's version made use of other Greek manuscripts unknown to Erasmus, including one named after Beza, the *codex Bezae*; of French origin, it was given to Beza for safekeeping during the French wars of religion, and he in turn donated it to England's Cambridge University. Beza's edition of the Greek New Testament went through five editions in his lifetime, and had widespread influence on Protestant textual scholarship; it would be a key text used by the translators of the King James Bible.[4]

Beza was the most influential early Reformed theologian to state the doctrine of predestination in its "supralapsarian" form.[5] Most Reformed theologians have been "infralapsarian".[6] The difference lies in the logical order of God's purposes or decrees. According to the majority infralapsarian view, in His predestination of the elect to blessedness, God contemplates them in His foreknowledge as fallen in Adam and in need of salvation. Election is therefore a decree to save from sin. According to the supralapsarian view, by contrast, in God's predestination of the elect to blessedness, He contemplates them simply as persons capable of being created. Election therefore has no link with sin; in His eternal mind, God has chosen the elect "before" He foresees them as sinning and needing salvation. Beza championed this supralaparian view. Perhaps a diagram will make the difference clear (Beza himself produced a famous diagram that was far more detailed):

THE LOGICAL ORDER OF GOD'S DECREES

Infralapsarian order of decrees	Supralapsarian order of decrees
God decrees to create humanity.	God decrees to give eternal blessedness to some (the decree of election).
He decrees to permit the fall of humanity.	He decrees to create the elect and the non-elect.
He decrees to save some sinners out of fallen humanity (the decree of election), and to leave the rest in their sins.	He decrees to permit the fall of the elect and non-elect.
He decrees the mission of Christ to save the elect.	He decrees the mission of Christ to save the elect.

---

4. See Chapter 3, section 4.2.

5. From the Latin *supra* (above or before) and *lapsus* (fall).

6. From the Latin *infra* (beneath or after) and *lapsus* (fall).

Criticism of Beza's "scholasticism" has often focused on his supralapsarian views. Since, however, most Reformed scholastics were infralapsarian, yet no less scholastic, it would seem that a consistent criticism of Reformed scholasticism must reject *all* idea of a logical order in God's decrees, whether supralapsarian, infralapsarian, or any other sequence (see section 3 for the Amyraldian sequence). There was certainly nothing in the scholastic methodology of Reformed Orthodoxy that bound it to Beza's supralapsarianism. The only confession of faith with an international character to be produced by scholastic Calvinism was actually infralapsarian (the canons of Dort—see section 2).

Beza's deepest impact was the way he helped consolidate a distinctive Reformed theological identity post-Calvin. Through his writings, he put clear blue water between the Reformed faith and its competitors in the latter half of the 16th century, engaging with Roman Catholics, Lutherans, Socinians, and even his fellow-Reformed in the shape of Zwinglians (on the Lord's Supper, where Beza rejected the Zwinglian "memorialism" still favoured by a few in favour of the "spiritual real presence" view that Martin Bucer, Peter Martyr, and John Calvin had championed). Beza articulated his theology most fully in his *Confession of the Christian Faith*, originally published in French (1559), then translated into Latin (1560) and other languages (e.g. English in 1563). It was a Europe-wide best-seller.

3. *Amandus Polanus*

Amandus Polanus (1561–1610) was born into an aristocratic family at Opole in Silesia (a region now mostly in Poland, but partly in Germany: in Polanus' time it belonged to the Austrian crown). His spiritual life is a fascinating case-study in the cross-currents of Lutheranism and Calvinism during the doctrinal conflicts that ravaged Lutheranism prior to the Formula of Concord in 1577. Polanus was originally a Lutheran; while studying at Breslau (also in Silesia), we find him adhering to a "Philippist" form of Lutheranism, otherwise nicknamed "Crypto-Calvinism" by strict Lutherans for its embrace of a

Reformed understanding of Christ's presence in the eucharist.[7] Polanus continued his studies in the Lutheran University of Tubingen, but had soon abandoned Lutheranism entirely (he embraced a more Reformed understanding of election). Leaving Tubingen in 1583, he pursued his education at Basel, Geneva, and Heidelberg. In Geneva he fell deeply under the spell of Theodore Beza. After spending two years with the Bohemian Hussites, Polanus returned to the Swiss city of Basel as a private tutor to an aristocratic family. In 1596, he became professor of Old Testament at Basel University.

Here, Polanus' outspokenly Reformed views got him into trouble with Lutheran sympathizers. Basel had gone through several decades of intense religious friction over whether it would remain in the Reformed camp or go over to Lutheranism. Many of its city clergy had favoured Lutheranism, especially Simon Sulzer (1508–85), the *antistes* (chief pastor) of Basel from 1553. Selzer had introduced Lutheran forms of worship (e.g. musical instruments—organ, flute, and kettle-drum), and got all the clergy to subscribe to the Wittenberg Concordat of 1536, a carefully-worded statement on the Lord's Supper which had crafted a Lutheran-Reformed unity on the topic. The only factor that had finally prevented Basel becoming fully Lutheran was (ironically) Lutheranism's 1577 Formula of Concord; the Formula's explicit condemnations of Calvinism proved too strong for most of Basel's clergy and magistrates. When Sulzer died in 1585, the next *antistes* was the robustly Reformed John Jacob Grynaeus (1540–1617), who undid most of Sulzer's work.

Still, there remained Lutheran-inclined people in Basel, and Polanus' lectures antagonized them. He was accused of teaching doctrines in the university he would not dare preach in a pulpit—specifically his understanding of predestination. Polanus defended himself by appealing to Martin Luther himself: had not Luther, in his *Bondage of the Will*, been a full-blooded predestinarian? He also denied teaching anything in the university that he would not preach in a pulpit, although

---

7. See Chapter 1, section 1.

conceding that academic and pulpit methodology was very different. Polanus was successful in vindicating his views, and this seems to have been the last gasp of the Lutheranizers in Basel, which thereafter was solidly Reformed, due in some measure to Polanus' own teaching.

Polanus wrote various treatises, but his masterwork was his *System of Christian Theology* (1609). This was the most comprehensive systematic theology yet written by a Reformed theologian, and exercised great influence. It had a strong anti-Catholic emphasis, championing Reformed teaching against the Roman alternative; Polanus' chief sparring partner was Italian Cardinal Robert Bellarmine, the supreme theologian of the Catholic Counter-Reformation.[8] The extent of Polanus' historic impact on future Reformed thought can be gauged from the great "Neo-Orthodox" movement of the 1920s and 1930s, which revived interest in the theologians of Reformed Orthodoxy. The movement's dominant thinker Karl Barth, in his colossal *Church Dogmatics*, devoted more space to discussing the views of Amandus Polanus than of any other Reformed Orthodox theologian.

Polanus' theological method was a strong synthesis of Aristotelianism and Ramism; he accepted Aristotle's analysis of causation, but also made extensive use of Ramus' dichotomy technique.[9] (This demonstrates that Aristotelianism and Ramism could be combined in Reformed Orthodoxy.) He also, following Ramus' lead, stressed the practical "use" of each doctrine, which gave a new impetus to the moral dimensions of theology. In addition he helped advance the cause of covenant or "federal" theology; his impact as a systematic theologian gave immense credence to the view that the original relationship between God and humanity in Eden had been mediated through a covenant. (See Coccieus below for more on federal theology.)

Polanus was a huge admirer of Theodore Beza, under whom he studied in Geneva, and in some ways he followed his master

---

8. See Chapter 6, section 3.1.

9. For Aristotle's philosophy of fourfold causation, see Chapter 1, section 2, where Aristotle's influence on Lutheran Orthodoxy is examined.

in giving a more logical, structured shape to theology. He insisted that wholesome theology could not merely be biblical exegesis; it equally required a rigorous philosophical method, which was supplied largely by Aristotle. However, in taking this stance Polanus was no slavish follower of Beza. He clearly blended his Aristotelianism with Ramism, which Beza rejected, and he was far less enthusiastic about the supralapsarian view of predestination than Beza, allowing for the possibility of an infralapsarian understanding.

Polanus' lecturing so impressed the rulers of Basel that after his death, they created in the university a new department of systematic theology in memory of Polanus (previously there had only been departments of Old and New Testament).

4. William Ames

William Ames (1576–1633) was born at Ipswich in Suffolk, England. He studied theology at Cambridge, where he became a close friend of his tutor, the celebrated William Perkins, greatest of the Elizabethan Reformed theologians.[10] The English establishment, however, prevented Ames from following an academic career, owing to his strong Puritan objections to aspects of the Anglican Church, e.g. the wearing of clerical vestments. Eventually Ames left England altogether, deciding that its religious climate had become too hostile to his advanced Puritan outlook; he settled in the Dutch Republic in 1610, and the following year became chaplain to the English émigré community in The Hague, location of the Dutch government. He was supported financially by Puritan sympathizer Sir Horatio Vere, who led an English contingent helping the Dutch in their long war with Spain. The English government was still hostile to Ames, however, and forced Sir Horatio to dismiss him in 1618. He therefore had no official position recognized by the English Church or monarchy when they sent delegates to the illustrious Synod of Dort, convened to settle the Arminian controversy— the Synod began meeting in November 1618 (see section 2).

---

10. For Perkins, see Chapter 3, section 2.4.

Despite this, Ames was held in such high esteem by the Dutch Reformed that they paid him to attend the Synod, where he acted as advisor to its chairman, Johannes Bogerman. Ames was not so hard-line against the Arminians as many Reformed Orthodox; while he admitted that the Arminian view of grace was an error, he refused to classify it as a heresy.

In 1622, Ames became professor of theology at the newly created Franeker University on the Dutch Republic's northern coastland. Here he produced the bulk of his literary output: his *Marrow of Theology* (1627), *Bellarmine's Sinews Removed* (1628),[11] *Criticisms of the Synod by Remonstrant Writers* (1629), and *Concerning Conscience, Its Power and Cases* (1632). His lectures secured him a Europe-wide renown; students flocked from all quarters to hear the great Ames. In recognition of his reputation, the university made him its rector in 1626. However, he found the university's Orthodox intellectualism rather stifling; too many, he felt, treated theology as a purely academic discipline, without any obvious impact on lifestyle. It is reported of one of Ames' theological colleagues that he would sometimes drink too much in the evenings, and that his students would then—on the pretext of carrying him home—cart him off to the gates of a different town altogether, so that he could not get back to Franaeker in time for his lecture the next morning.[12] With his insistence on the practical nature of theology, Ames became disheartened.

For whatever reason, Ames tried to leave Franaeker. He made an abortive attempt to emigrate to America, whose Congregational churches in the new Massachusetts colony entreated his pastoral services, and whose climate he hoped would cure his asthma.[13] Then in 1632 he became co-pastor of a Congregationalist church in Rotterdam, where he died a

---

11. Bellarmine was once again cardinal Robert Bellarmine, the most formidable theologian of Counter-Reformation Catholicism. See Chapter 6, section 3.1.

12. Let us hope the story is apocryphal.

13. See Chapter 3, section 4.3.

year later at the age of 57. It is interesting to reflect that of the English theologians who achieved international acceptance as a Reformed scholastic, none was more renowned in the 17th century than Ames—and Ames was a Congregationalist. The Continental scholastics, almost all of whom were all Presbyterian (apart from a few influenced by the more Congregational views of Peter Ramus), do not seem to have held against Ames his minority views on church government.

Ames' masterwork, the *Marrow of Theology*, was hugely influential on subsequent generations of Reformed thinkers. Its attraction lay partly in its method; Ames organized its theological content on a radical, thoroughgoing Ramist model. Ramism was very fashionable at that time, and the *Marrow's* approach must have seemed cutting-edge. Also appealing was Ames' pervasive insistence on the practical nature of theology. Here too he was following Ramus, and his old mentor William Perkins who had defined theology as "the science of living blessedly for ever".

Ames was also influential in his extended exploration of the ethical dimensions of theology, found especially in his *Concerning Conscience*. No Reformed theologian prior to this had so fully analyzed the moral dilemmas of faith. Ames' work was long admired and imitated as a model of its kind.

On the Continent, Ames was known by his Latinized name, Amesius.

5. Johannes Wollebius

Johannes Wollebius (1586–1629) was born in the Swiss canton of Basel, the son of a city councillor. Here he studied philosophy and theology, and was particularly influenced by Amandus Polanus. Wollebius had a solid clerical career in the city of his birth: ordained in 1606, he became pastor of Basel's Saint Elizabeth Church in 1611; in 1618, he was appointed preacher in the city's cathedral church, at the same time taking up the post of Old Testament lecturer in the university. He was also the city's *antistes* or chief pastor, the first native of Basel to hold the post (it was created during the Swiss

Reformation). His 1619 doctorate *On Divine Predestination* took an infralapsarian view. Wollebius died of plague in 1629 at the young age of 42, leaving two sons who were both pastors in Basel.

Wollebius was clearly a man of one city; he was also a man of few treatises. Other than a handful of sermons and his doctoral dissertation, his contribution to Reformed literature was his one-volume *Compendium of Christian Theology*, published in 1626. It was enough, however, to assure his fame; this single work was used throughout the Reformed world for a hundred years and more as a basic textbook of theology. In addition to six Latin editions between 1626 and 1760, the *Compendium* was translated in English in 1650, and into Dutch in 1651. Its popularity in Puritan England is illustrated in the life of John Milton, best known to us as the author of the epic poem *Paradise Lost*, but quite as much a political and theological pamphleteer in his own day, pursuing a highly personalized vision of a Puritan society. When Milton wrote his own systematic theology to undergird his vision, he drew heavily on Wollebius' *Compendium*—it was arguably Milton's chief inspiration, albeit he departed from the Swiss divine's Trinitarian orthodoxy. Often Milton's *Concerning Christian Doctrine* is simply Wollebius, word for word.[14] A generation later and a continent away, we find Wollebius still going strong in Puritan America. In Connecticut's Yale College, founded in 1701 mainly to train Congregationalist pastors, a student remarked (rather sardonically) of Wollebius' *Compendium* in 1714 that it was "considered with equal or greater veneration than the Bible itself".

The *Compendium* earned its place in Reformed theology by its orderly arrangement of topics, its crystal lucidity of expression, its precise treatment of issues, its brevity, and its non-speculative character. Much of its content was taken from Polanus' *System of Christian Theology*, but masterfully condensed. Divided into two parts, the first dealt with the knowledge of God, and the

---

14. For Milton, see Chapter 4 section 1.6.

second with the worship or service of God. For Wollebius the one flowed into the other: all theological knowledge was for the purpose of worship and service. It would be hard to imagine anything more different from the ice-cold, abstract metaphysics that has too often been attributed to the Reformed scholastics. Some historians have detected in the famous catechisms of the Westminster Assembly the direct influence of Wollebius's twofold approach to God's knowledge and service.[15]

6. Gisbert Voetius

Gisbert Voetius (1589–1676) (pronounced *Foot-ius* or *Foosh-ius*) was a Dutch Reformed theologian, arguably the greatest of them in our period. Born at Heusden near Utrecht, as a child he displayed a phenomenal memory, learning by heart vast chunks of Greek and Latin poetry. He developed these linguistic skills at Leyden University, where he also studied theology during the Arminian controversy; he followed the teachings of Arminius' chief critic, Francis Gomarus (see section 2). Voetius was then ordained as pastor of the Dutch Reformed congregation in Vlymen in 1611; in 1617 he accepted a call back to the congregation of his childhood in Heusden. He attended the Synod of Dort as a delegate for six months in 1619.

Voetius' international fame flowed from his time as a lecturer in the University of Utrecht. He was invited to this post in 1634, although the university was not yet built; in the interim, he moved into the city and took charge of one of its churches. The university opened for business in 1636; Voetius delivered the inaugural address. He taught theology and Oriental languages there for the next 30 years till his death in 1676, and was recognized throughout Europe as one of the foremost Reformed Orthodox thinkers of his day. His literary masterpiece and legacy

---

15. Questions 1–38 of the Shorter Catechism relate to the knowledge of God; questions 39–107 relate to the service of God. Yet the two parts of the Catechism are organically connected. This is certainly Wollebian, whether or not he was a direct influence. See Chapter 3, section 5.6 for the Westminster Assembly.

to the Reformed world was his *Select Theological Disputations*, published in five volumes between 1648 and 1669. The 19th century German theologian and Bible commentator, Johannes Ebrard (1818–88), said of these volumes that they contained "an unbelievably clear and precise exposition of Reformed theology, such as one finds nowhere else".

Voetius comes across as a sort of Reformed Abraham Calov:[16] always fighting someone or something, always seeing truth about to be crushed by its host of adversaries, a gladiator for correct doctrine—and yet at the same time, like Calov, a man with a pious heart who wanted true spirituality as well as true doctrine to flourish. Among the enemies he combated were Roman Catholics, Arminians, atheists, mystics (like Jean de Labadie),[17] philosophers (like Descartes—see below), Erastians (those who wanted the Dutch state to control the Church), and fellow Reformed theologians (like Cocceius—see below). Amid the endless controversial writings, however, Voetius penned some devotional gems too, such as *Proof of the Power of Godliness* (1627), *Meditation on the True Practice of Godliness or Good Works* (1628), and *Discipline, or the Exercise of Piety* (1644). The title of Voetius' inaugural address at Utrecht University summed up his ideal: *On Piety Joined with Knowledge*. He was much influenced in this by Thomas a Kempis' *Imitation of Christ* and by English Puritan literature.[18] Voetius' practical Christianity sometimes had political dimensions, e.g. his advocacy of interest-free government loans to the poor. Less politically, he favoured small group meetings for the nurture of practical godliness, and was at the centre of a movement in the Dutch Reformed Church that has usually been compared with English Puritanism—the so-called "Second Dutch Reformation" (or "Further Reformation"). The other great spiritual writer in the Second Dutch Reformation, a generation later, was **Wilhelmus**

---

16. See Chapter 1, section 2.
17. See Chapter 1, section 4.
18. For Thomas a Kempis see *Volume Two: The Middle Ages*, Chapter 10, section 6.

a Brakel (1635–1711), whose *The Christian's Reasonable Service* (1700) proved an enduring masterpiece of piety.

Two controversies in which Voetius was involved have attracted the particular interest of students.

First, he was a vehement opponent of the new and fashionable philosophy of the highly influential French Catholic thinker **René Descartes** (1596–1650). Descartes is often regarded as the first truly modern philosopher, and was undoubtedly a trailblazer in scientific thinking. Voetius, however, fought relentlessly against Descartes. This was partly because the French intellectual's philosophy was a deliberate and provocative alternative to Aristotelianism, and Voetius was an ardent disciple of Aristotle in matters of philosophy. (For the same reason, he opposed Ramism.) Voetius was convinced that Descartes' philosophical method would lead people into atheism, and indeed he actually accused Descartes himself of being a closet atheist. This was because Descartes' worldview was grounded in radical doubt. The French thinker famously set out to doubt the truth and reality of everything that could possibly be doubted; he discovered that the only thing immune to this universal acid of doubt was his own existence. Hence Descartes' statement, one of the most celebrated in the history of philosophy: "I think, therefore I am." In other words, if I doubt everything, there must at the very least be an "I" who does the doubting; therefore I, the doubter, must exist, even if nothing else does.

Descartes, a Roman Catholic, reintroduced God into his universe by a version of the "ontological argument", pioneered by Anselm of Canterbury in the 11th century. Voetius, however—like probably all Aristotelians—failed to find the ontological argument remotely convincing (it had been the medieval Christian Aristotelian, Thomas Aquinas, who in the 13th century had so devastated Anselm's argument that it had ceased to be taken seriously until Descartes revived it 350 years later). It is not hard to see, then, how Descartes' ultra-sceptical approach was, for Voetius, merely the back door to atheism. Equally problematic for Voetius was Descartes' rejection of Aristotelian physics (although here, modern science would follow neither the Dutch nor the French thinker, but the Englishman, Sir Isaac Newton). Descartes further gave an account of natural causation that seemed, to Voetius, to leave no room for God's causal interaction with creation. In 1642, Voetius succeeded in getting the senate of Utrecht University to issue an official condemnation of Descartes' philosophy. Descartes was living in the Dutch Republic at the time, through fear (it would seem) of what the Catholic authorities in his native France would make of his work; the controversy with Voetius dragged unpleasantly on, and was a primary factor in Descartes' departure to Sweden in 1649.

In his own mind, Voetius' all-out war with Descartes was an aspect of a larger war with atheism, which he believed to be gaining ground in Dutch society. His 1639 book *Disputations on Atheism* shows the level of his concern. Together with this, however, we should also take Voetius' general interest in non-Christian worldviews. Although he did not organize any missionary activity, he paved the way for it by extensive writing on what we would call comparative religion, and on how Christianity related to the other (known) faiths of the world.

Voetius' conflict with Descartes fed directly into his second captivating controversy—with a fellow Reformed theologian, Johannes Cocceius—which takes us to our next entry...

7. Johannes Cocceius and covenant theology
Johannes Cocceius (1603–69) (pronounced *Cok-say-uss*) was born at Bremen, in north-western Germany. He studied in Bremen University under the early "covenant" theologians Matthias Martini and Ludwig Crocius (see below). Then in 1626 he went to Franeker University in the Dutch Republic, where he sat under the teaching of William Ames. Cocceius' career as an educator was lifelong; he began by lecturing on biblical languages in Bremen in 1630. In 1636 he moved to Franeker, teaching Hebrew and Oriental languages, adding on theology in 1643. In 1650, he moved to Leyden University as professor of theology, remaining there till his death in 1669. The extent of Cocceius' learning was astonishing; as well as the Bible

in Hebrew and Greek, and Christian theology from a Reformed perspective, he had a thorough knowledge of the Jewish Talmud, and of the Qur'an which he read in the original Arabic. By all accounts, Cocceius was also distinguished by a warm, earnest piety; we know that one reason why he left Germany for the Dutch Republic was (according to his own testimony) his discomfort over poor standards of personal godliness that he found in the German universities.

Cocceius' most famous, influential, and controversial work was his *Doctrine of the Covenant and Testament of God*, first published in 1648, with revised editions in 1653 and 1660. This eloquently presented his "covenant theology" (or "federal theology"). In the process he managed to divide the Dutch Reformed Church into ardent admirers and fierce critics, for reasons explored below.

Understanding God's dealings with humanity in terms of successive covenants was not in itself a novelty coined by Cocceius. It goes back at least as far as Augustine (see *City of God* 16:27—God's covenant with Adam). However, it was given a whole new lease of life by Reformed theologians in the 16th century. There is debate about how early it appeared in the Reformed tradition, and what exactly counts as "covenant theology"—a mere use of the word or concept would not suffice. A key point would probably be whether a particular theologian interpreted God's original relationship with humanity in Adam in covenant terms. In that respect, Cocceius' tutors at Bremen, Matthias Martini and Ludwig Crocius, were certainly among the more influential proponents. A little earlier, *Zacharius Ursinus* (1534–83), chief author of the Heidelberg Catechism, had pioneered the idea of a pre-fall covenant between God and humankind ("the covenant of nature"), and organized his entire *Summary of Theology Expounded through Questions and Answers* (written 1561–2) around the theme of covenant.[19] *Wolfgang Musculus* (1497–1563) and *Andreas Hyperius* (1511–64) were also early developers of covenant thinking. Again, the English

---

19. See *Volume Three: Renaissance and Reformation*, Chapter 6, section 3.

Puritan theologian **Dudley Fenner** (c.1558–87) was significant; he was among the first to describe God's relationship with Adam as a "covenant of works", setting it off against the "covenant of grace" using the Ramist logic of dichotomy (see section 1). Such thinkers began to follow Ursinus in employing "covenant" as an organizing concept for the entire content of their theology. By the mid-17th century, this covenantal way of doing theology had become common currency among the Reformed. It was also called "federal" theology from the Latin for covenant, *foedus.*

The basic idea of federal theology was that human history revolved around two covenants: an original covenant between God and the human race in Adam (variously named: the covenant of nature, the covenant of life, the covenant of innocence, the covenant of works), and the covenant of grace in which Christ played the role of a Second Adam. Through these covenants, God bound Himself to the communities represented by Adam and Christ as heads—all humankind in Adam, the new humanity in Christ. Life and blessedness flowed through the covenant-keeping of the two federal heads; their communities participated in the consequences of their actions. Through union with Adam, humanity fell, because Adam broke the covenant; through union with Christ, the new humanity is redeemed, because Christ kept the covenant.

Cocceius invented none of this. But in his *Doctrine of the Covenant and Testament of God,* he magnified covenant thinking to intense new levels of meaning for the Bible and theology. Federal theology had put the spotlight on the historical outworking of God's purposes, and has often been interpreted as a corrective to forms of Reformed Orthodoxy where the emphasis had been on God's eternal decrees. Cocceius carried this "historicizing" impulse into the covenant of grace itself. It could not be seen as a static entity, he insisted; it was progressive within history, developing from a primitive Old Testament seed into a mature New Testament organism. In modern terms, one can see Cocceius here seeking to express a "biblical theology" against what he felt was an unduly abstract "systematic theology" among other Reformed scholastics. For Cocceius, the overriding reality in the Bible was what 19th century German theologians would call *heilsgeschichte*—salvation history (in other words, the unfolding history of God's saving acts in Israel and the Church).

The controversial aspect of Cocceius' federalism was the way it highlighted differences between the Old and New Testaments. Two such differences in Cocceius' thinking became particular storm-centres of contention:

First, Cocceius saw the Sabbath as a distinctively Old Testament ordinance, rooted not in creation but in God's covenant with Israel at Sinai. It was a sign of the coming Messianic kingdom, he argued, just like other ceremonial ordinances; it foreshadowed the spiritual rest that Christ would procure from the laborious existence of sin. In the New Testament church, he maintained, a day of rest and worship was observed, not from obedience to an obsolete Sabbath command, but simply because Christ's people had always found it edifying to have such a day.

Second, Cocceius made a distinction between the salvation enjoyed by believers under the Old and New Testaments. Before Christ actually atoned for sin by His death, he argued, God "passed over" sin rather than forgave it. So the justification of the Old Testament saints was inferior to that of the New; prior to Christ, justification was by way of "promise", whereas now in Christ it is by way of "fulfilment". Cocceius' exegetical stronghold was Romans 3:25 and Hebrews 10:18. He accused his opponents of flattening out justification into a single unchanging fact, ignoring its historical development between the Testaments—an inbuilt flaw of "systematic theology", he felt, which he was trying to remedy with his exegesis-rich "biblical theology".

The opposition to Cocceius was spearheaded by Gisbet Voetius. It did not help matters that Cocceius and his followers tended to be hospitable to the scientific philosophy of Descartes, which Voetius opposed with such energy. So fierce did the theological warfare become, it threatened to rip apart the Dutch Reformed Church into two mutually exclusive factions, the Cocceians and the Voetians. The Voetians portrayed the Cocceians as merely Arminians in disguise, and did everything possible to discredit and destroy them. But the Cocceians fought back ardently. Where one party gained the ascendancy in a university, the other party was expelled. The Dutch state had to intervene to tell the theologians to calm down and practise a little more Christian forbearance; in fact, to make sure they did, the government coerced the universities into appointing equal numbers of Cocceians and Voetians, so that neither could vote the other out of their places. The dispute between the factions continued for many years after both Cocceius and Voetius had died. It dissipated at last through a combination of sheer exhaustion and the marginalizing of both sides by a new, more liberal Enlightenment theology, which regarded Cocceians and Voetians as equally old-fashioned and irrelevant. Fortunately both parties had their share of men who valued piety as well as doctrine, and the "pious" Cocceians and Voetians coalesced in the 18th century to fight together against the new liberalism.

It should be said that there were important Dutch Reformed theologians who did not fully identify with either side in the Cocceian-Voetian war. The most significant were Samuel des Marets (1599–1673),[20] Balthasar Bekker (1634–98), and **Hermann Witsius** (1636–1708). Witsius was the most influential; his now classic *Economy of the Covenants between God and Man* (1677) was Witsius' deliberate and brilliant attempt to blend into one all that was best in Cocceius and Voetius, whose warfare he deplored. The *Economy* was translated into English in 1803.[21]

8. Francis Turretin

Francis Turretin (1623–87) was born in Geneva to a distinguished Reformed family of Italian origin. He pursued his education in a mind-boggling variety of places—Geneva itself, Leyden, Utrecht, Paris, Saumur, Montauban, and Nismes. His aim

---

20. See section 3 on Amyraldianism for more about des Marets.
21. A modern reprint of this edition had an enthusiastic preface by J.I.Packer.

was to sample as much of the Reformed theological universe as he could by visiting its centres of influence. Among the famous Reformed teachers at whose feet he sat were fellow-Italian Giovanni Diodati (1576–1649), who translated the Bible into Italian; the distinguished German Friedrich Spanheim (1600–49); Gisbert Voetius; and controversial Huguenot thinker Moise Amyraut, and his supporter Jean Daillé (see section 3).

Turretin became pastor of the Italian church in Geneva in 1648 (at the age of 25); although he was by now a naturalised French-Swiss, Turretin still spoke Italian fluently. His preaching, we are told, was full of heartfelt pleading that his hearers should truly embrace Christ for salvation. (It should be clear by now that neither the Lutheran nor Reformed "scholastics" had anything in their makeup that impeded a warm, experiential piety, despite caricatures to the contrary.) In 1653 he was appointed professor of theology in the Genevan academy, stepping into his father's shoes—Turretin Senior had taught theology at the academy from 1618 to 1631. Turretin Junior spent the rest of life and career doing the same, but with far greater distinction.

Turretin's enduring fame rests on *Institutes of Elenctic Theology*, published in three volumes between 1679 and 1685. Within a 50 year period, there were no fewer than six further editions, the last being in 1734. *Elenctic* comes from a Greek word meaning "to refute". The elenctic method in logic was also known as the Socratic method, after Socrates, the most influential Pagan philosopher of Athens. Socrates brought people to a deeper knowledge of truth by asking them to state their beliefs, then subjecting them to relentless questioning; eventually they realized their original belief must have been wrong, once its inconsistencies and absurdities had been exposed by Socrates' inquisition.

This was Turretin's approach. His *Institutes*, rather than construct an all-embracing system, moved through a vast range of specific disputed questions. He covered 20 topics, each divided into distinct questions, sometimes as many as 34. Each question stated a controversy between Reformed Orthodox theology and its critics—Roman Catholics, Lutherans, Amyraldians, Arminians, Socinians, and others. Turretin carefully examined alternatives, refuted them to his own satisfaction, and established the Reformed view. The method is identical to the one used by Thomas Aquinas in his *Summa Theologiae*, and Aquinas indeed was a strong influence on Turretin, including the admiration for Aristotle as a supremely perceptive philosopher. The result is a masterpiece of clarity. To know what the mainstream Reformed view was on any significant issue in the period of Reformed Orthodoxy, and see it stated and defended with a massive and calm rationality, the student cannot do better than read Turretin. It is little wonder his *Institutes* were used as the textbook of choice in many seminaries throughout the Reformed world. In America's famous citadel of Reformed theology, Princeton Seminary in New Jersey, Turretin was the key text far into the 19th century, until finally replaced by Charles Hodge's *Systematic Theology* in 1872.

Turretin's most distinctive contribution to his day was his opposition to Amyraldianism, the system of theology articulated by Moise Amyraut in the French Reformed Church (see section 3 below). After bitter internal controversy, Amyraldianism won the day among French Calvinists; Turretin was determined to exhibit its errors, in case any other Reformed Church felt tempted to follow the French example. Amyraldianism never had a more incisive critic than Turretin. It may have been due to him, more than any other single individual, that popular Calvinism outside France usually had five rather than four points set in its theological concrete.[22]

9. Johann Heinrich Heidegger

Johann Heinrich Heidegger (1633–98) was born in the canton of Zurich at Baretswil, a village just outside the city walls. The son of a Swiss Reformed clergyman, he studied in Zurich under

---

22. The distinctive stance of Amyraldianism was a view of God's saving purpose in Christ as having a hypothetical or potential universality: Christ died to save all sinners on condition that they believe. For more, see section 3.

Johann Heinrich Hottinger (1620–67), one of the foremost linguists of the day. Heidegger later wrote Hottinger's biography. Then he pursued further study at Marburg and Heidelberg. In the latter he became professor of Hebrew in 1656, and then philosophy too. In 1659, Heidegger moved to Steinfurt in north-eastern Germany to teach theology and church history. However, in 1660 the troops of the Catholic prince-bishop of Munster occupied Steinfurt, in what must have been a fearful reminder of the Thirty Years' War, which had ended only a dozen years previously. Heidegger returned to Zurich, where he married an Italian lady, descended from Protestant refugees from Locarno (a Catholic Italian-speaking district of Switzerland) who had settled in Zurich in 1555.

After his marriage Heidegger spent some time in the Dutch Republic, where he got acquainted with Johannes Cocceius (see above). He went back to Zurich again in 1665 to become professor of moral philosophy; he then succeeded his old mentor Hottinger as theology professor in 1667, on the latter's death. Heidegger's growing fame as a theologian brought him invitations from other centres of Reformed academic life, e.g. to take over from Cocceius at Leyden on the German-Dutch divine's death in 1669. Heidegger, however, turned down all invitations and remained in Zurich for the rest of his life.

Heidegger combined a complex theology with a remarkable spiritual breadth of sympathy: he defended his own detailed beliefs, but in a non-controversial spirit. His stricter side was shown in his authorship of the Helvetic Consensus of 1675,[23] designed to safeguard the Swiss Reformed Churches against Amyraldianism (see section 3). After a consultation between Swiss Reformed theologians, Heidegger was chosen as the one to draft the document. As well as rejecting Amyraldianism and several other perceived errors, the Consensus affirmed a full-blooded federal theology, which had by then become the universal Reformed framework for understanding God's dealings with humanity. The Consensus was adopted in all the Reformed

23. *Helvetic* is Latin for "Swiss".

cantons; all prospective preachers had to sign it. It began to be dropped, however, after the Edict of Nantes was revoked in 1685 and the floodtide of French Reformed refugees flowed into Switzerland and elsewhere, many of whom held Amyraldian views (the Swiss Reformed canton of Berne abandoned the Consensus as early as 1686).[24]

Heidegger's broader side was shown in his championship of religious refugees from various regions of Europe where an intolerant Catholicism was making life unbearable for Protestants, e.g. France, Hungary, and Poland. Heidegger may have been opposed theologically to French Amyraldians, but in their hour of darkness he extended the arms of brotherhood to them. He took a special interest in the plight of Hungarian Protestants, both Reformed and Lutheran; the Holy Roman Emperor Leopold I (1658–1705) had annexed most of Hungary, and in the 1670s oppressed Protestants ever more harshly. Heidegger's house in Zurich became a centre for information about persecution in Hungary, and acted as an agency through which contacts with Hungarians were made, monetary aid channelled, and testimonials written as letters of safe-conduct. From Heidegger's abode accommodation for refugees was also organised, and dangerous journeys back to Hungary planned and financed. He sometimes personally sheltered refugees; we know that two Hungarians lodged with Heidegger for 17 months. Not surprisingly, Heidegger has been called both "Professor of Protestantism and Protector of Protestants".

Heidegger also displayed his breadth of spirit in his approach to Lutherans. Despite his disagreements with them, he refused to take up the strongly polemical attitude to Lutheranism that he took towards Roman Catholicism. As we have just seen, he gave practical help to Hungarian Lutheran refugees. In his 1686 treatise, *Direction: A Pathway towards Protestant Ecclesiastical Concord*, he emphasized the common Reformation ground of Lutherans and Calvinists, although without neglecting the differences between them.

---

24. See Chapter 7, section 3 for the revocation of the Edict of Nantes and its consequences.

Heidegger was a prolific theological author, but his masterworks were his *Marrow of Christian Theology* (1696), and his *Body of Christian Theology* (1700). These were regarded as models of clarity, summing up Reformed Orthodoxy in a supremely calm, careful way. The admiration the Reformed world had for Heidegger as a theologian was shown in the funeral oration given by Benedict Pictet for Francis Turretin in 1687, in which Pictet referred to Heidegger as "the esteemed Johann Heinrich Heidegger, the most radiant light not just of Switzerland, but of all Europe."

10. Peter van Mastricht

Peter van Mastricht (1630–1706) was a Dutch-German theologian. Born at Cologne, one of Germany's most important cities (its prince was one of the seven electors of the Holy Roman empire), his family were of ethnic Dutch origin. His name derives from the Dutch city of Maastricht, which between 1579 and 1632 was part of the Spanish Catholic empire in the Netherlands; to escape persecution, the van Mastricht family fled and settled in Cologne. There they became staunch members of the local German Reformed church. Peter van Mastricht returned to his ancestral Holland to study theology at Utrecht under the celebrated Voetius, whose blend of orthodoxy and piety made a lifelong impact on him. He then studied further in the Dutch University of Leyden, and the south German University of Heidelberg; he also spent some time in England (during the English Civil War). In 1652 he was ordained a pastor in the Dutch Reformed Church, serving congregations in Xanten and Gluckstadt. The call of academic life then beckoned, and he returned to Germany to teach Hebrew and practical theology at the university of Frankfurt-on-the-Oder in 1662.[25] He moved to the university at Duisberg in 1669, a city that had recently become part of Brandenburg-Prussia. In 1677 he returned to teach at Utrecht, remaining there for the next 30 years.

---

25. An east German city on the borders with Poland. Not to be confused with the larger and more famous Frankfurt in Hesse.

Van Mastricht's greatest contribution to Reformed
Orthodoxy was his *Theoretical and Practical Theology*, first
published in two volumes in 1682 and 1687; a new enlarged
edition appeared in 1698–99. This comprehensive exposition
of Reformed theology was probably second only to Turretin's
in impact, and in some quarters it even surpassed Turretin to
take pride of place. The illustrious Jonathan Edwards (1703–
58), who would be America's most original and influential
theologian in the 18th century and beyond, famously praised
Van Mastricht's work as simply the best:

> Turretin is [excellent] on polemical divinity, on the five points
> and all other controversial points, and is much larger in these
> than Mastricht, and is better for one that desires only to be
> thoroughly versed in controversies. But take Mastricht for
> divinity in general, doctrine, practice, and controversy, or as
> an universal system of divinity; and it is much better than
> Turretin or any other book in the world, excepting the Bible,
> in my opinion.

Others voiced similar high opinions. The qualities in
van Mastricht's work that provoked such praise were its
comprehensiveness, its orderly structure, its fair-mindedness to
other viewpoints, and the rich vein of piety that ran through its
theologizing.

Van Mastricht wrote other treatises, notably against the
two greatest philosophers of the 17th century—Descartes
(see the previous treatment of Gisbert Voetius), and the
Dutch Jew **Benedict de Spinoza** (1632–77). His basic
problem with both Descartes and Spinoza was the way he
felt they made human philosophy independent of divine
revelation, and effectively gave philosophy the superior place
as source and arbiter of all truth, including truth about God.
Within theology itself, Van Mastricht regarded Cocceius as
an almost equal danger, and wrote strenuously against his
views (see the previous treatment of Cocceius), although he
disapproved of the party-spirit that had polarized many into
Voetians and Cocceians.

2

The Arminian controversy and the Synod of Dort

If Lutheranism experienced its defining controversy in the period 1546–77, resulting in the Formula of Concord, then the equivalent controversy for the Reformed Churches revolved around Arminianism in the period 1603–19, resulting in the canons of Dort.[1] Not that this quenched all controversy within the Reformed world; the next generation would see the far more global and protracted Amyraldian controversy (see section 3). Amyraldianism, however, was an in-house quarrel among the heirs of Dort.

1. Jacobus Arminius

The figure who sparked off the Arminian controversy, giving it its historic name, was *Jacobus Arminius* (1560–1609)—the Latinized form of his Dutch name Jakob Hermanszoon. Born at Oudewater in the Dutch Republic's province of Utrecht, his early life was marked by tragedy. His father died during his infancy; while he was away in Marburg (southern-central Germany) pursuing his education, Spanish troops sacked his native Oudewater, massacring its inhabitants, including Arminius'

---

1. *Arminian* must not be confused with *Armenian*. The first refers to a theological viewpoint. The second refers to a nationality—the nation of Armenia, on the eastern borders of Turkey. There is of course no necessary connection between being an Arminian and being an Armenian!

mother, sister, and two brothers. This was in the early part of
the long and bloody war fought by the Dutch for independence
from Spain's empire in the Netherlands. A young orphaned
Arminius had, however, already found a generous patron in the
wealthy Dutch linguist and mathematician Rudolph Snellius
(1546–1613), who enabled the orphan to study at the Dutch
Republic's Leyden University. Now supported by Amsterdam's
merchant guild, Arminius spent a year studying theology in
Geneva under Theodore Beza. He continued his studies in
Basel University, where his academic success was brilliant.
Arminius finally returned to the Dutch Republic in 1587, and
the following year was ordained a pastor in the Dutch Reformed
Church, serving a congregation in Amsterdam.

Arminius' doubts about the Reformed understanding of divine
predestination and human freedom seem to have begun almost
immediately after his ordination. We should not, however, see him
as a lonely rebel against some overwhelming Dutch Calvinism;
there had in fact always been an alternative outlook within Dutch
Protestantism, taking its inspiration less from Calvin, and more
from a strong tradition of Dutch humanism. This tradition had
been exemplified supremely in Erasmus of Rotterdam, the "prince
of humanists" who had done so much to prepare the way for the
Reformation but not finally embraced it. Erasmus, of course, had
famously defended a more positive view of human free will than
Martin Luther's Augustinian pessimism about the will's bondage
to sin. This Erasmian humanist strain in Dutch Protestantism
was still very much alive in Arminius' day; it was sceptical about
the value of doctrinal theology beyond the basics of the Apostles'
Creed, focusing instead on practical morality and a spirituality
that stressed human freedom and dignity. Long before Arminius
became a figure of contention, the Dutch Republic had already
witnessed frictions between the Reformed Orthodoxy favoured
by most clergy, and the humanism preferred by some. But these
had proved minor controversies compared to the storm Arminius
would provoke.

The seeds of doubt were sown in Arminius' mind by one of
these earlier disputes. It concerned the theological writings of

the great Dutch Catholic humanist *Dirk Coornhert* (1522–90). A many-sided, many-talented thinker and statesman, Coornhert had been a key player in the original anti-Spanish revolt of William the Silent; he drafted William's 1566 manifesto, calling on all patriotic Dutchmen to join him in liberating their land from Spanish tyranny. Among other things, Coornhert dabbled in theology, where he showed himself a second Erasmus in advocating a concept of human free will that gave it virtual autonomy from divine grace. Coornhert expressed his Erasmian views in a critique of Theodore Beza's Calvinism. The ensuing controversy brought Arminius into the arena; he was asked in 1589 to write something in defence of Beza. In studying the issues, however, Arminius found himself repelled by Beza's high supralapsarian views of predestination, and more inclined to sympathize with Coornhert's criticisms. So Arminius wrote nothing, but brooded on the questions Coornhert had raised.

Time would fail us to analyze the complex development of Arminius' theology between the Coornhert controversy and Arminius' eventual appointment as professor of theology at Leyden University in 1603. By then, he had said enough to draw upon himself a widespread suspicion of unsoundness on predestination and related doctrines. The suspicions were well-founded; Arminius had by now abandoned the Reformed view. He seems to have been influenced in the late 1590s by the view of Roman Catholic theologian Luis de Molina on human freedom, divine foreknowledge, and sufficient grace (see Chapter 6, section 4.2). However, the alternative to the customary Reformed view (itself rooted in Augustine) that Arminius constructed has very often been misunderstood or even caricatured by his critics. We can summarize it as follows. Arminius had come to deny that God's predestination of the saved was unconditional. Predestination, he held, was in fact conditional on human faith: God elected to salvation those whom He foreknew would believe. Moreover, their choice to believe was not caused by God's monergistic or efficacious grace; it was rather a choice born of synergistic cooperation between the divine and the human wills.

On the other hand, Arminius did not deny the natural deadness and impotence of the human will in the sphere of salvation, as opponents have often wrongly claimed. His view was more subtle. He accepted that the fall of humankind in Adam had indeed enslaved the will to sin. However, he argued that God's grace had supernaturally restored a measure of liberty to the fallen will, enough to enable it to repent and believe if it so chose. This universal gift of enabling or sufficient grace he termed "prevenient grace" (from the Latin for "going before"). He did not, therefore, base human freedom on the inborn or natural independence of the will, nor on superficial views of human depravity, but on divine grace universally bestowed to remedy the will's otherwise helpless bondage to sin.

2. The beginnings of controversy

By now, Arminius had gained influential supporters both in the Dutch Reformed Church and the government. His most eminent backer in the Church was **Jan Uytenbogaert** (1557–1644), pastor of the Walloon congregation in the Dutch capital, The Hague.[2] Arminius and Uytenbogaert had studied theology together in Geneva and become close friends. The Hague's Walloon congregation, where Uytenbogaert now ministered, was the most politically important church in the land; it was here that the most powerful military figure in the Dutch Republic worshiped— **Prince Maurice of Nassau** (1567–1625), head of the powerful aristocratic house of Orange, and son of the Dutch people's national hero, William the Silent. (He is sometimes called Maurice of Orange.) Maurice, the captain-general of the Dutch army, made Uytenbogaert tutor to his own son. Not only Maurice, but many of the Dutch nobility were members of Uytenbogaert's congregation.

Arminius' most eminent backer in the Dutch government was **Johan van Oldenbarnevelt** (1547–1619), who held the

---

2. Walloon refers to a people-group with a distinct language in the Dutch Republic, the Spanish Netherlands, and northern France. The Walloon language was spoken quite widely among them in the 17th century; it has now largely been replaced by French.

supremely influential political office of "land's advocate of Holland". Holland was by far the largest and wealthiest province of the Dutch Republic, the whole Republic often simply being called "Holland". The land's advocate of Holland was the representative of Holland's nobility, and the virtual prime minister of the Dutch Republic. Oldenbarnevelt had played a central part in holding the various Dutch provinces together politically in their gruelling war with Spain.

It was with such supporters that Arminius secured the theology professorship at Leyden. Even so, he first had to satisfy the university's senior theology lecturer, **Francis Gomarus** (1563–1641), of his soundness at a meeting in The Hague. Gomarus was Reformed Orthodox of the strictest kind, and a man of immense learning; he was to be Arminius' chief opponent. At the meeting, however, Arminius' powerful supporters laid down conditions that favoured Arminius: he would not have to state his own views in general, but only respond to specific questions that Gomarus asked him. Arminius answered these questions without violating Gomarus' keen sense of Reformed correctness, and was duly appointed to teach at Leyden in 1603.

Within a year, Arminius and Gomarus were at war with each other. Gomarus probably felt that Arminius had deceived him at the Hague meeting, which may explain the angry passion with which he now denounced his academic colleague. Leyden University became a theological gladiators' arena; soon Arminius' students were also being accused of taking their master's dubious teachings out into the churches. In a fruitless attempt to restore peace, the Dutch government became involved in the controversy; several times, Arminius and Gomarus had debates in the presence of the civil authorities, and once Arminius read out a statement of his beliefs before the states-general (the Dutch federal council representing its seven provinces). The magistrates tended to favour Arminius, partly because he gave a commanding position to civil authority in governing the Church (see below for more on the "Arminian" view of Church-state relations). A majority of the Dutch Reformed clergy, however, sided with Gomarus.

Long before the controversy reached any resolution, Arminius died of tuberculosis in 1609, at the relatively young age of 49. Most agree that he was a pious man, who sincerely desired to serve God and the Dutch Reformed Church, and was peace-loving despite the many conflicts he became embroiled in. He was certainly a scholarly theologian, a clear thinker, a good preacher, and a talented debater. The one serious question-mark that has been placed over his integrity was his subscription to the Belgic Confession and Heidelberg Catechism, the Dutch Reformed Church's two confessions of faith. Could Arminius honestly have failed to see the gulf between his own views and those taught in the confessions he had sworn to uphold? Perhaps an answer can be found in his lifelong advocacy of a broad tolerance in the Church for all views that did not affect the substance of the Gospel. He may have regarded the confessions as expressing what the majority believed, rather than as objective standards of truth. If so, he could then always plead that he respected majority opinion, as enshrined in the confessions, and would uphold the majority's right to believe as they did, while claiming toleration for his own views. (This explanation does not, however, fit entirely comfortably with his apparent insistence that his views did not in fact contradict the confessions.)

3. Remonstrants and Counter-Remonstrants

Arminius' death removed the central figure around whom controversy had swirled. But it did not end the controversy. By now, there was a vocal party in the Dutch Reformed Church that sailed under the flag of Arminius. Jan Uytenbogaert became their leader. Among the other "Arminians", the most three important were Conrad Vorstius, Simon Episcopius, and Hugo Grotius.

Conrad Vorstius (1569–1622) succeeded Arminius as theology professor at Leyden; Gomarus was so disgusted by his appointment that he resigned, taking up a pastorate at Middelburg in the province of Zeeland, then moving to the Huguenot academy at Saumur in 1615 to teach theology. Vorstius' views were far more radical than those of Arminius, verging on Socinianism; the Dutch government dismissed him in 1612, in order to appease Britain's King James, who in an outburst of orthodoxy demanded the sacking of so unsound a thinker from so prestigious a university as Leyden. Vorstius retired on full salary to the Dutch city of Gouda, where he poured out such a river of fierce polemical writings against Calvinism that even Uytenbogaert despaired of his ill-mannered aggressiveness. All was not lost, however, for the Arminian cause in Leyden; its backers got **Simon Episcopius** (1583–1643) appointed to the post vacated by Gomarus. Episcopius was a courteous man, a talented speaker, especially in debate, and would become the great systematizer of Arminian beliefs. He emphasized the centrality of a scholarly interpretation of Scripture, and the practical, non-speculative character of Christian faith. Erasmus rather than Luther or Calvin was his model.

The last of the three, **Hugo Grotius** (1583–1645), was one of the geniuses of the 17th century, still famous today for his contribution to the philosophy of international law. A protégé of Oldenbarnevelt, he developed into a scholar-politician of impressive dimensions. He held the important offices of advocate fiscal of Holland and Zeeland from 1607, and pensionary (mayor) of Rotterdam in 1613. His intellectual brilliance was displayed most richly in his legal classic, *On the Law of War and Peace* (1625), and his apologetics classic, *On the Truth of the Christian Religion* (1627). The first laid the foundations of international law, based on the concept of natural law: a culture-transcending law that applied to all people and nations, and was universally accessible through human conscience. The second was a landmark work in setting out the truth-claims of Christianity in the context of the plurality of world faiths (in the period we are examining other faiths were increasingly well known, owing to huge overseas expansion by European nations). Translated into Arabic, Persian, and Chinese, *On the Truth of the Christian Religion* was long studied by missionaries as a key text. From 1608, Grotius threw his potent political and intellectual weight behind the Arminian movement. Grotius also pioneered the "moral government" view of the atonement, which had significant popularity as an alternative to the "penal substitution" favoured by Lutheran and Reformed Orthodoxy. According to Grotius, the divine punishment of sin did not spring from any attribute of retributive justice in God, but from His loving concern to maintain good order in the moral universe. Sin upset the harmony and happiness of that universe, and must be deterred. Christ's death did not satisfy God's "personal" justice; it was a public exhibition of God's opposition to sin, demonstrating what all sin deserved, in order that God might pardon the penitent without fostering any illusions about sin's heinousness.

With such significant leadership, the Arminian party was emboldened after Arminius' death to publish a theological manifesto, the Remonstrance (1610). This set out their distinctive beliefs, in opposition to Reformed Orthodoxy, in five points:

1. In the decree of election, God has purposed to save those whom He foreknows will believe and persevere in faith to the end.

2. Christ by His death has purchased salvation equally for all, but this salvation is enjoyed only through faith.

3. Fallen human beings are enslaved to sin, and have no innate power to think, will, or do anything spiritually good, unless they are first regenerated by the Holy Spirit.

4. Divine grace alone enables fallen sinners to think, will, or do anything good; yet this grace is always able to be resisted. The difference between the righteous and the unrighteous is that the former cooperate with grace, but the latter resist it.

5. Believers are given all the help of grace to persevere to the end; but whether a true believer can reject this grace, return to his sin, and be for ever lost, is a question requiring further investigation from Scripture.

The third point may seem strange to modern-day Calvinists, as it basically affirms the "Calvinist" doctrine of total depravity! This warns us not to project current ideas back into a past controversy. The original Arminians believed in total depravity. Their belief was not that the human will had some natural autonomy unaffected by sin, but that God had supernaturally bestowed unmerited grace on humanity's impotent will, sufficient to *enable* each person to believe the Gospel and be saved.

The Remonstrance was drafted by Uytenbogaert, and signed by 41 pastors and two teachers of the Leyden state college for pastoral training. The Arminians now became known as the Remonstrants. They submitted the document to the Dutch Republic's *de facto* prime minister, Oldenbarnevelt, asking him to use his power to secure toleration for their beliefs. Feeling was now running high between the Remonstrants and their opponents. The civil authorities summoned both parties in March 1611 to The Hague; here the Reformed presented their response to the Remonstrance, known fittingly as the Counter-Remonstrance. From then onwards, the two quarrelling parties were known as the Remonstrants and the Counter-Remonstrants.

4. Religion and politics in the Dutch Republic

It would be profoundly wrong to see this as a purely theological conflict. It was just as much political as theological, involving the thorny issue of Church-state relations. The Counter-Remonstrants stood for the principle that the Dutch Reformed Church must be independent of state control; the Remonstrants, however, advocated the subordination of Church to state. Jan Uytenbogaert expressed this view clearly in 1610 in his *Tract on the Function and Authority of a Higher Christian Government in Ecclesiastical Affairs*. He argued that supreme spiritual power belonged to the local civil governments of each Dutch province. It was their right and duty to appoint pastors, monitor preaching, determine forms of worship, and summon and control synods. Hugo Grotius said much the same in his *Resolution for Peace in the Churches* in 1614, emphasizing that the provincial governments had the power to outlaw controversial preaching. For Grotius, the only guarantee of social harmony in

the Republic was a broad-based Church, where all viewpoints
were tolerated (as long as the Trinity was acknowledged), and
the Christian magistrates silenced trouble-making preachers.

It is uncertain whether Uytenbogaert and his colleagues
among the clergy adopted this Grotian view on pure principle,
or whether it was more their way of currying support from the
civil authorities against the Counter-Remonstrant majority in
the Church. Certainly most politicians were ready to back the
Remonstrants, especially with so committed a Remonstrant as
Oldenbarnevelt wielding power as land's advocate of Holland.
With most of the magistrates on the Remonstrant side, and most
of the clergy on the Counter-Remonstrant side, the struggle was
intensely politicized. It also had a dimension of class warfare:
the upper classes tended to be Remonstrant, the lower classes
Counter-Remonstrant.

The controversy was also utterly entangled in disputes over
the Republic's foreign policy. Oldenbarnevelt had negotiated a
12 year truce with Spain in 1609. Prince Maurice of Nassau,
however, had opposed the truce; he believed that war with
Catholic Spain was inevitable and should be prosecuted
vigorously. Maurice was strongly supported by Calvinists in his
pro-war policy. Oldenbarnevelt, however, frustrated all Maurice's
attempts to renew the war. The growing political conflict between
Oldenbarnevelt and Maurice thus became hopelessly embroiled
with the religious quarrel between Arminian Remonstrants
and Calvinist Counter-Remonstrants. The latter, in supporting
Maurice's pro-war policy, were opposing Oldenbarnevelt both
for his peace policy and his championship of the Remonstrants.

By 1617, these internal religious and political conflicts were
beginning to tear the Dutch Republic apart. Literary warfare
between Remonstrant and Counter-Remonstrant theology had
reached fever pitch. Provincial governments prohibited Counter-
Remonstrant clergy from preaching against the Remonstrants,
and suspended or deposed some who disobeyed. Significant
numbers of the laity walked out of churches where the government
had made it impossible for them to hear the preaching they
desired; they now held separate meetings in houses, barns, and

boats. Once again, however, the pro-Remonstrant authorities intervened, and confiscated these alternative meeting places. Oldenbarnvelt and Maurice each feared that the other was planning a coup against him. In July 1617, Maurice openly sided with the Counter-Remonstrants in the religious quarrel, by withdrawing from Uytenbogaert's Remonstrant church in The Hague, where he had worshiped for years, and joining a Counter-Remonstrant congregation. This was not owing to any theological conviction on Maurice's part; he had no real interest in theology, and he confessed, "I know nothing of predestination, whether it is green or whether it is blue." This was a political decision. Maurice was putting himself at the head of the popular Calvinist opposition to Oldenbarnevelt and the Remonstrants in order to topple them from power.

Oldenbarnevelt must have sensed extreme danger in this public coalition between Maurice and the Counter-Remonstrants. To protect himself against the coup he feared Maurice was plotting, and give greater security to the Remonstrants, Oldenbarnevelt issued his famous "Sharp Resolution" in August 1617. It asserted that the provincial governments had supreme power in Church matters, and could recruit troops to defend Remonstrants against attacks from their opponents. Remonstrants were indeed now experiencing outbursts of popular violence against them, especially from the skilled manual workers of the Dutch cities. These people were suffering badly from Oldenbarnevelt's truce with Spain, because it meant that the Spanish Netherlands (bordering on the Republic) was flooding the country with inexpensive cloth. This in turn was causing low incomes and unemployment for Dutch Calvinist cloth-workers. It was easy for them to vent their wrath on Remonstrants who were, after all, Oldenbarnevelt's allies. However, they also rioted against town councils that supported Oldenbarnevelt. On one occasion they sacked the house of Simon Episcopius, the Remonstrant theology professor at Leyden, and chased his wife through the streets, calling her an "Arminian whore".

The Sharp Resolution brought the Dutch situation to boiling point. The provincial governments of Holland and Utrecht raised troops to shore up their power, as the Resolution had authorized them to do. Prince Maurice, however, saw this as a direct challenge to his military authority as captain-general of the Dutch army. There followed a year of intrigue and counter-intrigue. The most important event in this tense period came in November 1617, when Maurice and the Counter-Remonstrants persuaded the states-general, the Dutch Republic's federal council, to summon a general synod of the Dutch Reformed Church to settle the religious quarrel. Such a synod could result only in defeat for the Remonstrants; popular opinion in the Church had always favoured the Calvinism of the Counter-Remonstrants. Holland, however—Oldenbarnevelt's stronghold, and the Republic's biggest and richest province—refused to go along with this decision. So did two other provinces where Oldenbarnevelt's policies held sway. It was clear that Remonstrant political power in Holland would have to be broken before the synod could go ahead.

Prince Maurice finally struck in July 1618. He decided to act with a strong show of legality rather than stage a naked coup; his opportunity lay in the Republic's federal council, the states-general. Although Holland was the Republic's most powerful province, there were seven provinces in total. All seven had only a single vote each in the states-general. Maurice was able to take his stand on a crisis that had developed between the states-general, where five of the provinces now supported the prince, and the provinces of Holland and Utrecht, which supported Oldenbarnevelt. The crisis hinged on whether supreme political authority lay with each province individually, or with the states-general as the country's federal council. Holland had always held to the view that each province was a sovereign state, and could not be ultimately overruled by the states-general. But with Utrecht alone now supporting Holland, the states-general by a 5–2 majority took the view that as the Republic's federal body, it was the supreme authority in the land. It therefore decreed that Holland and Utrecht had acted beyond their lawful powers in raising troops without federal consent. Then it gave Maurice the prize he sought—it authorized him to use the Dutch army to disarm the local troops in Holland and Utrecht.

The local troops were no match for Maurice's veteran army; Utrecht surrendered, and Oldenbarnevelt's power in Holland collapsed. He, Grotius, and several other leading Remonstrant politicians were arrested. Maurice purged Holland's "council of nobles", dismissing all Remonstrants and putting his own men in power. He did the same to Holland's town councils. This was a political revolution which guaranteed that Maurice and his family (the house of Orange) would rule the Republic for the next 30 years. Oldenbarnevelt and Grotius were at length tried for treason by a special political court, and found guilty. Oldenbarnevelt was executed in May 1619: a tragic fate for a 72 year old man who had spent his life serving the Dutch Republic, and done as much as anyone to secure its freedom from Spain. Grotius was imprisoned for life, but his wife managed to get him smuggled out of his cell in 1621, and he fled to France. There he was given refuge by King Louis XIII. It was during his stay in France that Grotius wrote his two masterworks, *On the Law of War and Peace*, and *On the Truth of the Christian Religion*. Never allowed to return to the Dutch Republic, Grotius died in exile in 1645.

5. *The Synod of Dort*

Meanwhile, Maurice and the states-general, having crushed Oldenbarnevelt and the Remonstrants politically, moved to resolve the religious issue too. The general synod of the Dutch Reformed Church they had summoned back in November 1617 now finally met at Dort (or Dordrecht) in the south of Holland. It was composed of 56 ministers and elders, and 5 professors, with 18 political commissioners to report back to the states-general. Reformed theologians from across Europe were also invited to attend. This was to be more than a purely Dutch synod; it was to represent Reformed opinion worldwide. 26 delegates came from various German Reformed territories (e.g. Heidelberg, Hesse, and Bremen), from Switzerland, and from Britain. The British delegates were sent by King James, a devout Calvinist in matters of theology; the six delegates—five Englishmen and one Scot—included the distinguished theologian John Davenant (1572–1641), Bishop of Salisbury

from 1621. All six were either Calvinists (like Davenant) or
had Calvinist leanings. The French Reformed Church also
commissioned four delegates to Dort, but King Louis XIII
would not allow them to attend.

The Synod of Dort proved to be a landmark event in the history
of the Reformed faith. Its membership was overwhelmingly opposed
to Remonstrant theology. When a large Remonstrant delegation
arrived at Dort, only 13 named by the synod were allowed to
appear—and not as delegates, but as plaintiffs on trial for doctrinal
error. They were led by Simon Episcopius, the theologian of Leyden
University; their natural leader, Uytenbogaert, had fled to Antwerp
in the Spanish Netherlands. Episcopius made a speech before the
synod, pleading for a spirit of love and free discussion. Perhaps
understandably, Dutch Calvinists were not very willing to listen,
given the way many of them had been ill-treated by Remonstrant
magistrates under Oldenbarnevelt's government. Episcopius and
his friends were dismissed, while the synod hammered out its
theological rejoinder to Remonstrant theology.

Since the Remonstrance had expressed Arminian theology in
five points, the synod responded by working through these points in
a series of "canons" and presenting a Reformed perspective on each
point. Here is the origin of the so-called "Five Points of Calvinism":
not a summary of Reformed theology, but simply Reformed
theology's response to the five points of the Arminian Remonstrance
on disputed matters concerning salvation. (Reformed theology in
the 16th and 17th centuries was far wider and richer than the
"Five Points", and had other distinctive beliefs in relation to other
controversies, e.g. its doctrine of the Lord's Supper in relation to
Lutheranism.) We can summarize the synod's teaching thus:

1. Predestination is God's eternal purpose to give saving
   faith to some sinners out of the mass of fallen humanity.
   It is unconditional—not based on God's foreknowledge
   of anything in those chosen. (This first article takes the
   infralapsarian view: quite striking, considering that some
   leading Dutch theologians were supralapsarian, e.g.
   Francis Gomarus.)

2. The death of Christ is sufficient to save the whole of humanity, but by God's sovereign will it is effective in actually saving the elect, by enlivening them to a true, justifying, sanctifying, persevering faith.

3. The synod agreed with the third point of the Remonstrance—the spiritual inability of the fallen human will apart from divine grace. However...

4. The synod rejected the Remonstrant view that grace is always resistible. On the contrary, the grace that regenerates is sovereignly efficacious.

5. This grace also ensures that the elect will persevere to the end and enter glory at last. True saving faith can never be entirely lost; and a person can attain an assurance that he or she has this faith, and will therefore persevere.

(The canons of Dort are actually far longer and much more detailed than this. The above is only a very short précis.)

The synod concluded its business on May 9th 1619. Its canons now became authoritative in the Dutch Reformed Church, alongside the Belgic Confession and Heidelberg Catechism (known collectively as the Three Forms of Unity). Some 190 pastors were deposed for refusing to subscribe to the canons—Arminianism was purged out of the ranks of the clergy. (There were around 1,100 pastors altogether in the Dutch Reformed Church at that time.) Of the 190 deposed, 80 were banished, 70 allowed to remain in the Dutch Republic but deprived of their ministries, while 40 eventually conformed to the canons and were restored. Of the other Reformed Churches, only the French adopted Dort's canons as a binding confession of faith (in 1620); nonetheless, the canons were universally regarded by Reformed theologians as summing up orthodox teaching against Arminianism. This made the canons of Dort the nearest Reformed equivalent to Lutheranism's Formula of Concord.

One other thing the synod did: it set in motion a project for a new translation of the Bible into Dutch. Previous Dutch Bibles had not been translated from the original Hebrew or Greek, but from other existing translations (e.g. the Latin Vulgate). The new translation was to be directly from Hebrew and Greek. The project was completed in 1635; the states-general issued it with official sanction in 1637. It was known as the *Statenvertaling* ("States Translation") or *Statenbijbel* ("States Bible"). The new translation—the "authorized version" of the Dutch Reformed Church—was to mould the Dutch language, much as Luther's Bible had moulded German. For the next 300 years it would be the commonly accepted Bible among all Dutch Protestants.

The Dutch Republic's political and religious crisis, which had pushed it to the edge of civil war, had been averted. This enabled a united nation, under the leadership of Prince Maurice and the house of Orange, to face renewed conflict with Spain in 1621: an exhausting struggle not concluded until the Peace of Westphalia in 1648.[3]

With Remonstrant pastors either banished from the Republic or silenced in 1619, congregations that remained loyal to Remonstrant theology were harassed in various ways. Any new pastors they appointed were liable to be imprisoned. The persecution, however, ended on the death of Prince Maurice in 1625; his successor and brother, Frederick Henry (Prince of Orange, and Dutch captain-general, from 1625 to 1647) was more tolerant than Maurice. He allowed the exiled pastors to return. Simon Episcopius came back in 1626 to pastor a Remonstrant church in Amsterdam; he then became head of a Remonstrant theology college, also in Amsterdam, founded in 1630. Uytenbogaert too returned in 1626 and resumed preaching in The Hague. There were some 40 Remonstrant congregations, mostly in south Holland. The movement endured, and was finally given legal recognition in 1795.

---

3. See Chapter 1, section 3, on the Thirty Years' War. Since Spain was part of the Habsburg empire, the Spanish-Dutch war naturally got snarled up in the wider anti-Habsburg war by Europe's Protestants in alliance with France. The treaties that ended the Thirty Years' War thus also ended the Spanish-Dutch war.

3
Amyraldianism: the debate that never died

The Reformed world was to be more convulsed by Amyraldianism than it had ever been by Arminianism. This was because Arminians could fairly easily be identified as holding views incompatible with Reformed theology. It was much harder to make that charge stick against Amyraldians, who claimed to be just as Reformed as their critics—perhaps more Reformed. Some of the most formidable opponents of the Amyraldians admitted that despite their errors, they were Reformed men. Francis Turretin, for instance, the trumpet of Reformed Orthodoxy in Geneva (see section 1.8), consistently recognized Amyraldians as Reformed thinkers, even while disagreeing vehemently with their views. As a quarrel within the Reformed family, therefore, the Amyraldian controversy was more deeply troubling than Arminianism. It involved the question of what it really meant to hold a Reformed theology—especially whether John Calvin himself would have approved of the way his tradition had developed.

1. The life and work of Moise Amyraut

Amyraldianism took its name from the French theologian *Moise Amyraut* (1596–1664); his last name was Latinized as *Amyraldus*. He was born to a Huguenot family at Bourgueil in the west of France. The Huguenots—the French Calvinists—were a tolerated minority in Catholic France, with religious freedoms legally guaranteed in the famous Edict of Nantes (1598), which had effectively ended the long Catholic-Huguenot civil war, so devastating to France in the latter part of the 16th century. In Amyraut's youth, the French government under Cardinal Richelieu destroyed the remaining political and military power of the Huguenots in a war of 1627–8 (see Chapter 6, section 1). The French Reformed community was now unable to defend itself against aggression by a Catholic state, if the latter should ever decide to revoke their religious liberties (see section 5 of Chapter 7).

We know little of Amyraut's family or childhood. We do know that after studying law, Amyraut's reading of Calvin's *Institutes* inspired him to go to the Huguenot theology academy at Saumur, near his birthplace, around 1618. Here he was deeply influenced by the Scottish theologian **John Cameron** (1579–1625), who had himself only just arrived to teach at Saumur. Born in Glasgow, and trained theologically in its university, Cameron spent most of his life in France among the Huguenots. He was co-pastor of a Huguenot church at Bordeaux from 1608, and then moved to Saumur academy in 1618. Since Amyraut's theology so closely mirrored Cameron's, we will not give a separate account of Cameron's theology; in looking at the views of his French disciple, we will see what the Scot believed. Cameron left France in 1621 owing to political difficulties, and taught theology in London for some time, before being appointed principal of Glasgow University by King James I in 1622. However, he returned to France in 1623 to lecture in the Huguenot academy at Montauban. Here he was killed in 1625 by a mob—ironically a Huguenot mob. It seems they objected to Cameron's strong views on the duty of obedience to kings. This was a bitterly controversial belief among the highly politicized Huguenots of that era, with their tendency to constant rebellion against the French crown (a tendency that Cardinal Richelieu was about to crush decisively in the 1627–8 war).

After his studies at Saumur academy, Amyraut became pastor of Saumur's Huguenot congregation in 1626. Soon after, he began lecturing on theology in the academy, part-time at first, but full-time from 1631 (without relinquishing his pastorate). He also helped to supervise publication of the works of his mentor, John Cameron. A memorable encounter with the French court in 1631 throws some light on Amyraut's character. Every year the Huguenots sent one of their number to report to the king any infringements of the 1598 edict of Nantes, which had given them religious liberty. That year Amyraut was selected. However, he refused to kneel in the presence of King Louis XIII; Amyraut saw this as discrimination against Protestants, since Roman Catholic clergy were allowed to remain standing. For 15 days the offended king refused to see Amyraut unless he would kneel; Amyraut persisted in his objection. Finally the king's all-powerful chief minister, Cardinal Richelieu, visited the stubborn Huguenot pastor to persuade him to kneel. But Amyraut displayed such a combination of courtesy and resolve that Richelieu was won over, and Amyraut was allowed to remain standing in the royal presence.

By 1634, Amyraut was becoming well-known among French Protestants as a distinguished theologian. That year, however, he published a treatise which landed like a bomb on the playground of the theologians.[1] It was his *Brief Treatise on Predestination and its Dependent Principles*. From the moment it hit the bookshops, Amyraut's life became one long controversy. A contemporary Huguenot historian, Pierre Bayle (1647–1706), described the subsequent years as "a kind of civil war among the Protestant theologians of France". The war extended beyond France, as we shall see.

2. Amyraut's theology
What ignited the fires was Amyraut's way of countering the view—attributed to Reformed theology by its foes, and possibly held by supralapsarians[2]—that God had created a great portion of humankind (the non-elect) for the sole and express purpose

---

1. To borrow the famous description of the effect produced by the second edition of Karl Barth's commentary on Romans in 1922.
2. See section 1.2.

of damning them. Many French Catholics thought that the Calvinist God was a capricious, unjust, and unloving tyrant, which (Amyraut felt) hindered their conversion to Reformed truth. Meanwhile some Huguenots were drifting away into Roman Catholicism in order to find a more loving God. Amyraut wanted to rescue the Reformed doctrine of predestination from this caricature, as he considered it.

His rescue method was to argue, in effect, that election should be viewed in the light of the cross of Christ, not the cross in the light of election. According to Amyraut, the moving cause behind the coming of Christ was God's love for the whole human race without any limitations. The salvation Christ procured for humanity, however, must be received personally through faith; as Amyraut put it, God had decreed a universal scope to Christ's death, but made its effect conditional on faith. Such faith, unfortunately, was beyond the power of the fallen human will. Election therefore was God's sovereign decision to give faith efficaciously to some sinners, in order that Christ's universal mission might bear at least some fruit among humankind. In this way, Amyraut believed he had woven together God's general love for humanity, the universal applicability of Christ's atoning death, and divine sovereignty in personal salvation, in a tapestry more Biblical, more evangelistically preachable, and more faithful to Calvin, than what was commonly found in the Reformed theology of the day. Amyraut's system became known as "hypothetical universalism", from its synthesis of an unlimited scope to Christ's death (the "universal" aspect) and its effect being conditional on faith (the "hypothetical" aspect).

Amyraut was in reality arguing both with supralapsarians and infralapsarians over the logical order in God's decrees (see section 1, under Theodore Beza). Although Amyraut sometimes preferred not to divide God's decree into any kind of inner sequence, but leave it simply as a single unified purpose, at other times he was prepared to suggest an order of decrees, perhaps as a concession to the human mind's desire for clarity of explanation. We could express Amyraut's view thus:

Amyraldian order of decrees
God decrees to create humanity.
He decrees to permit the fall.
He decrees the mission of Christ to save humanity, its effect conditional on faith.
He decrees to give faith to some (election), so that Christ's mission will bear some fruit.

Another facet of Amyraut's theology that attracted criticism was his distinction between *natural* ability and *moral* ability. He argued that in spite of sin, fallen sinners have a natural ability to believe the Gospel for their salvation—otherwise how could God require them to believe, and hold them blameworthy for not believing? By "natural ability", Amyraut meant all the mental equipment necessary to perform the act of believing. A human was not the same as (say) a tree-stump. A tree-stump has a natural inability to believe: it lacks the mental equipment. A human being is not in that category. Amyraut maintained that human "inability" to believe is spiritual, not natural, in origin: not the lack of the necessary mental equipment, but a voluntary aversion to using it aright. He accepted that efficacious divine grace alone could overcome that aversion. His opponents, however, felt he had diluted the Reformed view of the sinner's inability. Was human nature not corrupted by sin? How then could human inability fail to be an inability of nature—a natural inability? Was Amyraut's distinction not simply a crafty backdoor to Arminianism?[3]

Amyraut's sources for his theology (other than his own meditations on the Bible) were supremely John Calvin himself and John Cameron. There would be bitter disputing about Amyraut's fidelity to the Bible and Calvin; there could be none about his fidelity to Cameron. Amyraldianism might just

---

3. Some may recognize the natural-spiritual inability distinction from the later influential theology of the English Reformed Baptist Andrew Fuller, who popularized it in the Anglo-Saxon world in the 18th century.

as well be called Cameronianism. Another debate, ongoing among scholars, is whether Amyraut's view should be seen as expressing a strand of thought that had always been present in the Reformed tradition, from Heinrich Bullinger onwards. Was he an innovator, or was he giving fresh voice to a genuine aspect of Reformed thinking from its very origins?[4]

Other treatises by Amyraut followed, in which he defended and elaborated his views: *Six Sermons on the Nature of the Gospel* (1636), *Sample of Calvin's Doctrine* (1636), *The Doctrine of John Calvin on the Absolute Decree of Reprobation Defended* (1641), *Four Dissertations* (1645), *A Declaration of the Faith of Moise Amyraut concerning the Errors of the Arminians* (1646), *Disputation on Free Will* (1647).... And even more. In all, Amyraut wrote 90 works. Not all were connected with the controversy over his views on grace. For instance, he penned treatises on the Trinity, the Lord's Supper, Christian ethics, and apologetics. Despite his immersion in theological controversy within the Reformed family, Amyraut was firmly committed to ecumenical unity among all Protestants; he had a special regard for Lutherans, and played a part in the French Reformed Church's decision in 1631 to allow Lutherans to sit at the Lord's Table in Huguenot congregations.

3. Foes and friends

Amyraut's Reformed critics were many and formidable. They especially objected to his formula that Christ died for all on condition that they believe. Such conditionality, they felt, was inconsistent with God's sovereignty. In France, Amyraut's most vehement adversary was **Pierre du Moulin** (1568–1658). A marvel of learning, du Moulin had studied theology at Cambridge University under the famous William Whitaker.[5] Cambridge later awarded him a Doctorate in Divinity. After teaching theology for six years in the Dutch

---

4. Fools and scholars rush in where angels fear to tread; I shall not venture into this particular minefield with my own ill-digested opinions.

5. See Chapter 6, section 3.1.

university of Leyden, du Moulin returned to France in 1599 to pastor the enormous Huguenot congregation in Charenton, near Paris. When Catholic Paris became too dangerous for an outspoken Protestant preacher, he relocated in 1621 to Sedan in the Ardennes, where he pastored another church and taught theology at Sedan's Huguenot academy. He spent most of the remainder of his life there.

From 1634, that life was consumed by literary warfare with Amyraut, whom du Moulin portrayed as a crypto-Arminian. Indeed, the shadow of Arminianism loomed large over the whole Amyraldian controversy. Du Moulin had been instrumental in getting the French Reformed Church to adopt the canons of Dort in 1620. Now he and others feared that Amyraut and his supporters would bring into France the kind of turmoil the Remonstrants had provoked in the Dutch Republic. The accusation of crypto-Arminianism was unfair; although Amyraut shared some Arminian criticisms of supralapsarian Calvinism, he was a different type of man and thinker from Arminius, and Amyraldianism was a different system of thought from Arminianism. But in historical context, one can well understand the anxiety of du Moulin and others. Their suspicions were further kindled by the leniency of the Huguenot churches in the Paris district (where Amyraldian sympathies were strong) toward Dutch Arminian expatriates who wished to join their ranks. It enraged anti-Amyraldians even more when Amyraldians nonchalantly swore their allegiance to the canons of Dort!

Another prominent Huguenot critic was **André Rivet** (1572–1651), otherwise known by his Latinized name Rivetus, who spent much of his career teaching theology in Leyden University. His 1625 work, the *Synopsis of a Purer Theology*, was an exhaustive systematic theology textbook, widely used throughout the Reformed world. Rivet was du Moulin's brother-in-law, and he had been a friend of Amyraut before going into print against him. His criticisms, however, were expressed much more mildly, and with greater clarity and precision, than du Moulin's thunder and lightning. **Samuel des Marets** (1599–1673) (Latinized as Maresius) was another distinguished

French Reformed theologian who entered the arena against Amyraut.[6] From 1643, he pastored a church in the Dutch city of Groningen; his *System of Theology* (1645) was another popular textbook.

The fact that Rivet's and des Marets' opposition to Amyraut emanated from the Dutch Republic shows how the controversy spilled outside France's borders. Rivet and des Marets, however, were still French. Other outstanding Reformed theologians of different nationalities who wrote against Amyraut included the German **Friedrich Spanheim** (1600–49), from the Palatinate, who taught at Geneva and Leyden, the Swiss divines Johann Heidegger of Zurich and Francis Turretin of Geneva (see section 1), and the English Puritan John Owen (1616–83) in his most famous treatise, *The Death of Death in the Death of Christ* (1648), where Owen critiques Amyraut among others for his view on the extent of the atonement.[7] Geneva took particularly strong action, effectively banning all Amyraldians from taking up any pastoral or teaching position in the city.

However, Amyraut had many supporters. In the French Reformed Church, his chief defenders were the two illustrious divines, **Jean Daillé** (1594–1670) and **David Blondel** (1590–1655). Daillé was pastor of the Huguenot congregation at Charenton—ironically, the same church that had previously been pastored by Amyraut's arch-enemy du Moulin. A formidable scholar, Daillé's *Treatise on the Use of the Holy Fathers for Judging Current Religious Differences* (1632) and *Apology for the Reformed Churches* (1633) were internationally renowned masterpieces of controversy against Roman Catholic claims, while many of his sermons were published as valued commentaries, especially on Paul's letters. Blondel was pastor of the Huguenot congregation at Roucy from 1630, then professor of church history at the Athenaeum Illustre in Amsterdam (the forerunner of Amsterdam University) in the Dutch Republic from 1650; he was the Huguenots' church historian *par*

6. See also section 1.7.

7. For Owen, see Chapter 3, section 6.3.

excellence. His most important works (like Daillé's) were anti-Roman Catholic: *On Primacy in the Church* (1641), *Apology for the Opinion of Jerome on Presbyters and Bishops* (1646), and supremely *Pseudo-Isidore* (1628) which exposed the medieval Isidorian Decretals as a forgery.[8] Both Daillé and Blondel were powerful allies of Amyraut and exponents of his theology.

Another supporter was **Louis Cappel** (1585–1658) who taught alongside Amyraut at Saumur. Cappel was above all a Hebrew scholar, and his main work lay not in the Amyraldian debate but in textual scholarship. He stirred up fierce controversy against himself by marshalling his formidable learning to attack the (then widespread) belief that the vowel points in the Hebrew Masoretic text of the Old Testament were divinely inspired. Modern biblical scholarship of all shades is virtually unanimous that Cappel was correct, but in his own day he was perceived as overthrowing the inspiration of Scripture. Perhaps it did not help Amyraut that Cappel, himself suspect for his orthodoxy (albeit unjustly, in retrospect), stood by him.

Amyraut found supporters in other countries too. English Calvinism seemed to produce a fairly rich crop of Amyraldians or sympathizers who constructed similar outlooks: Stephen Marshall (c.1594–1655), Richard Vines (1600–56), Edmund Calamy (1600–66), John Arrowsmith (1602–59), John Howe (1630–1705), Lazarus Seaman (d.1675), and Richard Baxter (1615–91), to name some of the most influential.[9] Some of these had probably embraced a form of universal atonement before Amyraut's controversial treatise exploded on the scene in 1634; the influence has been detected here of Bishop John Davenant of Salisbury, one of the English delegates to the Synod

---

8. The Isidorian Decretals were documents from the 9th century granting allegedly historic powers to the papacy in the government of the Catholic Church, which later popes used as proof of the papacy's supremacy from earliest times. Because of Blondel's exposé, the documents are now universally admitted to be spurious, and are referred to as the Pseudo-Isidorian Decretals.

9. Five of these—Marshall, Vines, Calamy, Arrowsmith, and Seaman—were members of the Westminster Assembly. See Chapter 3, section 5.6.

of Dort (see previous section for the Synod and Davenant's presence). In other words, if we go by chronology, Amyraut was a Davenantian rather than Davenant an Amyraldian. Davenant's "Amyraldianism" was classically expressed in his *Dissertation on the Death of Christ, as to its Extent and Special Benefits*, published posthumously in 1650. The *Dissertation* seems originally to have been given as lectures at Cambridge University, where Davenant was Lady Margaret Professor of Divinity from 1609 to 1621.

Another probable influence on the English was John Preston (1587–1628), a moderate Calvinist, Master of the Puritan Emmanuel College and preacher to the lawyers of Lincoln's Inn. Preston pioneered the evangelistic formula "Christ is dead for you" as consistent with a Reformed view of the relationship between the atonement and divine sovereignty. The formula would be popularized by the celebrated *Marrow of Modern Divinity* (1645), probably by the Presbyterian lay theologian Edward Fisher. The *Marrow* was destined for equal amounts of fame and controversy in 18th century Scotland, where it was republished in 1718, its admirers gaining the nickname "Marrowmen".

English "Amyraldianism" may therefore not have been the exclusive product of Amyraut's influence, but more a case of a native English tradition of moderate Calvinism, articulated by men like Davenant and Preston, creating a ready audience for Amyraut's ideas.

4. The controversy and its outcomes

The French Reformed national synod held at Alençon in 1637 officially investigated the views of Amyraut and another Huguenot pastor, **Paul Testard** (1599–1650) of Blois, who had published a treatise entitled *Peace Proposal, or Synopsis of the Doctrine of Nature and Grace* (1633). Testard, like Amyraut, was a theological disciple of John Cameron. Du Moulin and Rivet sent lengthy submissions to the synod, condemning Amyraut's and Testard's theology. Indeed, the adversaries of Amyraldianism had been very active in preparing for the synod, mobilizing support and quite probably expecting to see Amyraut and Testard overwhelmingly condemned. The synod president was anti-Amyraldian and opened proceedings with a sermon on 2 Corinthians 11:3: "I fear that as the serpent deceived Eve by his subtlety, so your minds may be led away from the simplicity that is in Christ." It seemed obvious that the president was casting Amyraut and Testard in the joint-role of the serpent! The synod took the charges against the two men very seriously, and there was detailed discussion of the disputed views; both Amyraut and Testard explained their beliefs, answered questions, and affirmed their allegiance to the canons of Dort. Ultimately the synod exonerated both men of any doctrinal errors, although it did caution them against using certain phrases (like "conditional decrees") liable to misunderstanding.

It was an astonishing victory for Amyraut and Testard, which historians have struggled to explain. Why did all the anti-Amyraldian opposition, with its widespread support and well-organized preparations, turn into such a spectacular flop at the synod? Three reasons have been suggested. First, much of the theological opposition to Amyraut had come from outside France; deluged with these complaints at the synod, many patriotic delegates may have felt that foreigners were ganging up on a Frenchman—Amyraut was nothing if not typically and classically French in his personality and manner. Second, when actually confronted by the possible consequences of a decision against Amyraut, delegates may have recoiled through a fear that it would produce a schism in the French Reformed Church. In the aftermath of Cardinal Richelieu's annihilation of Huguenot political and military power in 1627–8, French Calvinists probably felt they could ill afford a division in their ranks. Unity prevailed. Third, no one had expected Amyraut and Testard to perform so impressively at the synod. They were eloquent, sincere, convincing. It looked as though their critics had caricatured them: could these really be the bogey-men of heresy they had been made out to be? Putting these three reasons together, perhaps we can begin to understand Amyraut's and Testard's acquittal.

After seven years of peace, the controversy erupted again in 1644, when the German theologian Friedrich Spanheim, now teaching at Leyden in the Dutch Republic, published a disputation against "universal grace". Amyraut believed himself to be the object of Spanheim's criticisms, and published a response. This exchange once again unloosed the storms of contention, with vehement treatises flying back and forth from various authors for the next four years. This was the controversy that ruptured the friendship between Amyraut and Rivet; an anti-Amyraldian treatise by Rivet somehow found its way to England's Westminster Assembly of divines, which Amyraut interpreted as Rivet stabbing him in the back, trying to persuade an English synod to condemn him when a French synod had acquitted him.[10] Spanheim proved a more bitter foe to Amyraut than anyone in France; not content with damning the Frenchman's theology as riddled with absurd errors, he devoted some time to proving that Amyraut wrote the most atrocious Latin.

Amyraut himself was once again put on trial, this time by the synod of Charenton which met from December 1644 to January 1645. Once again he was acquitted. However, another theologian at the Saumur academy, Josué de la Place (1596–1655 or 1665), was condemned—or at least his theology was (he was not named in the condemnation). The synod rejected de la Place's understanding of original sin. De la Place held that Adam's act of sin in Eden was not imputed to all humanity, but that his consequent depravity was inherited by all on the principle that "like begets like". To evade the condemnation, de la Place later expressed a view known as "mediate imputation"—that Adam's sin is imputed only via the medium of the inherited corruption. This can be found in his 1655 treatise *On the Imputation of Adam's First Sin*.[11]

---

10. See Chapter 3, section 5.6.

11. It should be noted that there is an alternative interpretation of the synod of Charenton, which does not think it was condemning any of de la Place's views. According to this interpretation, de la Place's enemies seized on the synod's condemnation of the denial of original guilt and fastened it onto de la Place's theology, illegitimately, as a pretext for denouncing him.

With more and more pastors and divines drawn into the latest fray, it soon began to look like the "civil war among Protestant theologians" described in retrospect by Pierre Bayle. After four years of public acrimony, a top-ranking Huguenot nobleman intervened—Henri-Charles de la Tremoille, Duke of Thouars and Prince of Tarante. He managed to get some of the disputants together on his estate in October 1649, and persuaded them to cease from their public polemics, so damaging to the unity and morale of French Protestantism. Thus by aristocratic authority, peace broke out; the theologians sheathed their swords.

Peace, however, proved short-lived, and the conflict blazed afresh in 1655. This time it was owing to Amyraut's supporters, David Blondel and Jean Daillé. Blondel published a historical account of the controversy—which merely reignited the controversy, as others disputed his interpretation. Jean Daillé published a huge tome, *Apology for the Synods of Alençon and Charenton*, which detailed all the theological arguments; it also had a section containing a myriad of quotations, from the early Church fathers up to contemporary Reformed theologians, all allegedly teaching Amyraut's views or something like them. Once again the literary warfare raged.

By 1659 the latest phase of the controversy had virtually spent itself. That year, when the French Reformed Church met in synod at Loudun, Jean Daillé was elected its moderator. The synod proceeded to affirm the orthodoxy of both Daillé and Amyraut. It was clear that most French Calvinists were now happy to accept Amyraldianism as a valid understanding of the Reformed faith: Amyraut had triumphed in the land of his birth. Outside France, however, controversy continued. Perhaps the most calm and clear critique of Amyraldianism was to come from the hugely influential Francis Turretin of Geneva, in his *Institutes of Elenctic Theology* (1679–85). Even Turretin was prepared to concede the Reformed status of Amyraut and his supporters, albeit the Genevan believed they had sadly strayed from the purest standards of Reformed Orthodoxy.

In the deepest sense, the Amyraldian controversy never went away. Reformed theology would continue to struggle with the issues Amyraut had raised, and still struggles today. Arminianism had been cast out at the Synod of Dort, and would never be seen as a legitimate variety of Reformed theology; but whenever there has been any friction over the extent of the atonement and related beliefs in Reformed circles, as there has often been, the spirit of Amyraut has walked anew.

Important people:

Wolfgang Musculus (1497–1563)
Andreas Hyperius (1511–64)
Peter Ramus (1515–72)
Theodore Beza (1519–1605)
Zacharius Ursinus (1534–83)
Dudley Fenner (c.1558–87)
Amandus Polanus (1561–1610)
William Ames (1576–1633)
Johannes Wollebius (1586–1629)
Gisbert Voetius (1589–1676)
Johannes Cocceius (1603–69)
Francis Turretin (1623–87)
Peter van Mastricht (1630–1706)
Johann Heinrich Heidegger (1633–98)
Wilhelmus a Brakel (1635–1711)
Hermann Witsius (1636–1708)

The Arminian controversy

Dirk Coornhert (1522–90)
Johan van Oldenbarnevelt (1547–1619)
Jan Uytenbogaert (1557–1644)
Jacobus Arminius (1560–1609)
Francis Gomarus (1563–1641)
Maurice of Nassau (1567–1625)
Conrad Vorstius (1569–1622)
Simon Episcopius (1583–1643)
Hugo Grotius (1583–1645)

The Amyraldian controversy

Pierre du Moulin (1568–1658)
André Rivet (1572–1651)
John Cameron (1579–1625)
Louis Cappel (1585–1658)
David Blondel (1590–1655)
Jean Daillé (1594–1670)
Josué de la Place (1596–1655 or 1665)
Moise Amyraut (1596–1664)
Paul Testard (1599–1650)
Samuel des Marets (1599–1673)
Friedrich Spanheim (1600–49)

Others

René Descartes (1596–1650)
Benedict de Spinoza (1632–77)

Primary source material

Theodore Beza: true faith in Christ

We define faith as a sure knowledge which, by God's pure grace and goodness, the Holy Spirit carves ever more deeply into the hearts of God's elect (1 Cor. 2:6-8). By this knowledge, they are assured each one in their hearts of their election, taking and applying to themselves personally the promise of their salvation in Jesus Christ.

Now faith does not just believe that Jesus Christ has died and risen again for sinners; rather, faith actually embraces Jesus Christ (Rom. 8:16, 39; Heb. 10:22, 23; 1 John 4:13; 5:19, etc). Whoever truly believes thereby trusts in Christ alone and is assured of personal salvation, so that there is no more doubting it (Eph. 3:12). That is why Saint Bernard [of Clairvaux] said, in keeping with all Scripture: "If you believe your sins cannot be wiped away except by the One against whom alone you have sinned, this is good. But add this: believe also that He has indeed forgiven your sins. This is the witness that the Holy Spirit bears to our hearts, saying, 'Your sins are forgiven you.'"[12]

Jesus Christ is the object of faith, as He is set forth to us in the Word of God. Since this is so, two consequences should be observed carefully. On the one hand, where the Word of God is not found, but only a human word (whoever may speak it), there is no faith there—only a dream or a mere opinion which will surely deceive us (Rom. 10:2-4; Mark 16:15, 16; Rom. 1:28; Gal. 1:8-9). On the other hand, faith embraces and takes hold of Jesus Christ and all His treasures, since He has been given to us on condition that we believe in Him (John 17:20, 21; Rom. 8:9). One of two things must follow: everything necessary for our salvation is not in Jesus Christ, or if everything is really there, those who have Jesus Christ by faith have everything! But to say that everything necessary for our salvation is not in Jesus Christ is a very foul blasphemy; it would make Him a merely partial Saviour (Matt. 1:21). So we are shut up to the other alternative: having Jesus Christ by faith, we have in Him everything necessary for our salvation (Rom. 5:1). As the apostle says, 'There is no condemnation for those who are in Jesus Christ' (Rom. 8:1)…

We have established that for a person to be assured of salvation, through faith, is neither presumption nor bluster. On the contrary, this is the only way of tearing off all the garments of pride, and to give all the glory to God (Rom. 8:16, 38; Eph. 3:12; Heb. 10:22, 23; 1 John 4:13; 5:19; Rom. 3:27; 4:20; 1 Cor. 4:4; 9:26, 27). This is because it is only faith that teaches us to go outside of ourselves, forcing us to confess most fervently that we have nothing in ourselves except materials for utter damnation.

So then, faith sends us off to Jesus Christ, teaching and assuring us that only through His righteousness will we find salvation before God. Indeed, everything that is in Jesus Christ, all His righteousness and perfection (for in Him was no sin, and He fulfilled the entire righteousness of the Law), is credited to our account—granted to us as though we had done it ourselves,

---

12. For Bernard, see *Volume Two: The Middle Ages*, Chapter 5, section 3, under *The Second Crusade*.

on condition that we embrace Christ by faith. This is why Saint
Bernard said, "The witness of our conscience is our glory: not the
witness given to itself by a deluded mind, such as the boastful
Pharisee gave himself (Luke 18:11, 12); this witness is not true.
But the witness that the Holy Spirit bears to our spirit is true."

Theodore Beza
Confession of the Christian Faith

William Ames: theology is a practical science

1. Theology is the doctrine being alive to God. John 6:68,
   The words of eternal life. Acts 5:20, *The words of this life*.
   Romans 6:11, *Consider yourselves alive to God*.

2. The word "doctrine" is used, not to distinguish it from
   "understanding", "knowledge", "wisdom", "art", or "prudence",
   since these belong to every systematic body of knowledge,
   and they characterize theology above all. Rather the word
   "doctrine" is used to signify that theology is a body of
   knowledge that does not originate in nature and human
   investigation as others do. It originates in divine revelation
   and authorization. Isaiah 51:4, *Doctrine shall proceed from
   Me*. Matthew 21:25, *From heaven. Why then did you not
   believe him?* John 9:29, *We know that God spoke to Moses*.
   Galatians 1:11–12, *The gospel is not according to man. For
   I did not receive it from man, nor was I taught it, but it came
   through a revelation*. John 6:45.

3. Where other arts are concerned, their principles are innate
   to our nature, and can be cultivated through sensory awareness, observation, experience, and logical argument. In these
   ways we perfect the various human arts. But the founda-
   tional principles of theology are not innate to our nature,
   although we can make progress in them by studious labour.
   Matthew 16:17, *Flesh and blood have not revealed this to you*.

4. Every art has its laws, and the art's practitioner conforms
   his work to those laws. The most excellent of all works

is living; therefore no study can be more fitting than to study the art of living.

5. The highest human life is that which comes closest to the living God, the giver of life. Living to God is therefore the nature of theological life.

6. People live to God when they live in harmony with God's will, to God's glory, and by God's enabling energy. 1 Peter 4:2, 6, *That he may live by the will of God, according to God*. Galatians 2:19-20, *That I may live to God. Christ lives in me*. 2 Corinthians 4:10, *That the life of Jesus may be manifest in our bodies*. Philippians 1:20, *Christ will be glorified in my body, whether by life or by death*.

7. This life continues the same in essence from its commencement to eternity. John 3:36 and 5:24, *Whoever believes in the Son has eternal life*. 1 John 3:15, *Eternal life abiding in him*.

8. Although it is possible in this world to live both a happy life and a good life, living a good life is more excellent than living a happy life. The supreme and final goal of our labours should not be happiness (which concerns our own pleasure), but goodness (which looks to God's glory). Therefore, a better definition of theology is the good life by which we live to God, rather than the happy life by which we live to ourselves. The apostle therefore called it by synecdoche,[13] *The doctrine that accords with godliness*, 1 Timothy 6:3.

9. On top of this, this life involves the spiritual work of the whole person, in which he is brought to share in God and to act according to His will. Since this life surely concerns the human will, it follows that theology applies firstly and most fittingly to the will. Proverbs 4:23, *From the heart flow the issues of life*; and 23:26, *Give me your heart*.

---

13. The part standing for the whole.

10. Since this life, pursued by the will, is truly and fittingly our supremely important practice, it is plain to see that theology is not a speculative system of knowledge but a practical one. This is the case, not only in the sense that all systems of knowledge have good practice as their goal, but in a special and distinctive way in theology above all else.

11. There is nothing in theology that fails to refer to the final goal or the means concerned with that goal—all of which relate directly to practice.

12. Theology embodies this practice of life so completely that theology has something to say about all universally true rules concerning living aright, in domestic economy, ethics, politics, or lawmaking.

13. Theology, therefore, is our ultimate and most excellent of all the arts of systematic teaching. It is a guide and blueprint for our highest goal, sent in a special way from God, dealing with divine things, directed toward God, and leading us to God. In addition to the name of "theology", it may therefore rightly be called a living to God, or a labouring towards God.

William Ames
Marrow of Theology, **Book 1, Chapter 1**

Johannes Wollebius: the sin of Adam and Eve.

1. The cause of Adam and Eve's sin was not God, nor any decree of God, nor His withholding any special grace, nor His permission of the fall, nor any motive arising naturally, nor God's providential sovereignty over the fall itself. It was not God, because He had most rigidly forbidden humanity to eat the fruit of that tree. It was not His decree, because the "necessity" involved in the decree is only the necessity of *immutability*, not the necessity of *compulsion*. God's decree never forces anyone to sin.[14] It

---

14. In other words, the decree did not psychologically coerce Adam to sin. What the decree did was to make his sin an unchangeably foreknown

was not God's withholding of some special grace by which humanity might have stayed innocent, for God was under no obligation to give even the grace that He did give to humanity; Adam was given the possibility of willing to remain innocent, but not the actual will inclining him to that possibility. It was not God's permission of the fall, for He was under no obligation to hinder it. It was not any motive arising naturally, for a natural motive in itself is not a sin. It was not God's providential sovereignty over the fall, because bringing good out of evil makes Him the author of good rather than of evil.

2. God both willed, and did not will, the first sin. He did not will it, in its nature as sin. But He willed it by His decree, insofar as it was a means to manifest His glory, mercy, and justice.

3. The external cause of original sin was the incitement and persuasion of that subtle serpent, the devil.

4. Its internal cause was the human will, which by itself was impartially suspended between good and evil, but, when persuaded by Satan, was turned toward evil.

5. When humanity fell from God, the fall went through five stages, one at a time rather than all at once: (i) a careless and meddlesome attitude when Eve spoke with the serpent in her husband's absence; (ii) unbelief, as by degrees she began to agree with Satan's lies, when he called into question God's goodness toward humanity, so that

---

fact. Given that God had decreed to permit Adam to sin, it follows that in relation to the decree, Adam's sin had become an immutable part of the unfolding of world-history (if it had not happened, God's permission and foreknowledge would have been falsified). In relation to Adam's own will, however, his sin was perfectly free—he had the psychological ability to choose otherwise. Philosophers would distinguish between "It is necessarily true that this will happen" and "It is true that this will necessarily happen." Ordinary non-philosophical people might get a headache.

she came to mistrust God; (iii) a desire for the forbidden fruit and for divine glory; (iv) the actual deed; (v) the seducing of Adam and the kindling of unruly desire in him too.

6. If all the parts of this sin are reckoned up, it is correctly called a violation of the entire law of nature.

   Humanity sinned by unbelief, mistrust, unthankfulness, and also idolatry by falling from God and making an idol of self. Humanity also sinned by contempt for God's word, by rebellion, by murder,[15] by lack of self-control, by secretly stealing what was not humanity's without the Owner's permission, by assenting to false statements, and finally by the craving for a more glorious position, indeed, for the glory that belongs only to God. Therefore it is too limited a definition to call this sin merely lack of self-control, or ambition, or pride.

7. Correctly, therefore, in the words of the blessed apostle, we call this sin transgression, offence, and disobedience (Rom. 5:14, 18, 19).

8. In this whole matter, we must look upon Adam not simply as a private individual, but also as a public person, and in this way as the parent, head, and root of the entire human race.

9. Therefore, whatever Adam gained and lost, he gained and lost both for himself and for all his descendants.

   Just as the head contains reason both for itself and for the body, and a nobleman may lose or preserve his privileges for both himself and his descendants, so Adam lost this blessedness for himself and his descendants. Nothing healthy will grow from a poisoned root; likewise, whatever is descended by nature from Adam is born in the guilt of this first sin.

---

15. Eve spiritually murdered her husband.

10. Therefore, this first sin is not only a personal sin, but also a sin of nature, because human nature in its totality has been corrupted by it. That is why the descendants of Adam—that is, all who are naturally sprung from Adam—are held captive in sin.

   Christ is not included in this guilt. He was born *of* Adam, but not *through* Adam: not by natural birth, but by the power of the Holy Spirit.

11. Therefore, as a person corrupted the nature, so now the nature corrupts persons.

12. It is our pious belief that Adam and Eve were taken by God into His grace.[16]

Johannes Wollebius
Compendium of Christian Theology, **Book 1, Chapter 10**

Gisbert Voetius: The necessity of practical theology, in which the English have excelled all others

Is practical theology necessary and useful in schools and churches? And should those training for the ministry be encouraged or required to study it? We reply, yes, against those who have little care for this aspect of theological study, whether they are opposed to godliness, or not much concerned for morality, or glory in their own barren ability, or devote themselves to laziness and ignorance. In heated strife over the ingredients and requirements of theology, they denigrate its practical aspect with ill-sounding words like *scriptural literalism, factiousness, wise folly, Precisianism, Puritanism, Anabaptism, legalistic and anti-gospel theology*, and *superstition*.

Maybe the words *casuistry, morality, patristic, historical, ascetic, scholastic, church polity*, scare them away from studying this challenging branch of theology. Well, we should be relaxed

---

16. Adam and Eve were saved. "Pious belief" means something lower than a dogma. A dogma is a public teaching to be proclaimed in the church to all, so that all may believe it. A pious belief is something the individual is entitled to believe personally, but it is not binding on the church collectively.

about mere words, as long as there is agreement about the underlying reality... Before our own time, this issue was set forth by our most outstanding theologians through the whole of their writings. Look at Luther, Melanchthon, Calvin, Beza, Martyr, Hyperius,[17] Danaeus,[18] Aretius,[19] Francis Junius,[20] Zanchius,[21] Lavater,[22] etc. Later on, these matters were then gathered up to a new standard (as it were) by more contemporary writers, using the words previously mentioned. The word *casuistry* was used by Perkins, Ames, Baldwin,[23] and Alstedt.[24] Consequently, this word is utilized in Reformed schools and churches, together with the phrase *Christian ethics and politics*, which means the same thing...

The word *ascetic*, which means *athletic training*, or *exercise*, or *practice*, or *to exercise in godliness*, is well-known among the lovers of true religion, because of the practical works of Johann Gerhard[25] and Lewis Bayly.[26] Indeed, Bayly has been translated from English into French, Dutch, and German, and possibly into Hungarian (I think the translation was begun, at any rate), and is known in virtually all the Reformed churches...

We demonstrate the necessity and usefulness of practical theology, and the worth of its study, from Scripture. See 1 Timothy 6:3, Titus 1:1, Acts 24:16, and 1 Timothy 4:7, where all theology is called truth and teaching according to godliness and discipline. Therefore we do not deviate from

---

17. For Hyperius, see section 1 under *Johannes Cocceius and covenant theology*.

18. Lambertus Danaeus (c.1535–c.1590).

19. Benedictus Aretius (1522–74).

20. Francis Junius (1545–1602).

21. Jerome Zanchius (1516–90).

22. Ludwig Lavater (1527–86).

23. Frederick Baldwinus or Balduinus (1575–1627): a Lutheran divine.

24. Johann Heinrich Alstedt (1588–1638).

25. See Chapter 1, section 2 for Johann Gerhard.

26. See Chapter 3, section 4.3.

Scripture and the goal of theology, when we hold up the practice of godliness, faith, repentance, conscience, and the application of encouragement, comfort, and exhortation, through all our theology, especially where the topics are themselves practical, and are even called practical. Alternatively, we hold up particular items from the theological topics like a signpost. Either of these approaches can be used. We shall not pursue this argument to a conclusion, but refer students to the oration of Ames that is printed together with his *Cases of Conscience*...

Another argument for practical theology derives from the example of our foremost theologians, mentioned earlier in this essay and in our *Bibliotheca*. The English undertook more labours than other Reformed people in this aspect of theology prior to their Civil War, when popery was extinguished among them and other sects were outlawed. Perkins, the genius of practical English divines to this very day, stands pre-eminent. Some of our own Dutch writers have followed the English example.

Gisbert Voetius
Select Theological Disputations, **Volume**

Johann Heinrich Heidegger: The efficacious merit of Christ

To Christ the Mediator, Arminians credit little or even nothing in the matter of people actually being reconciled and saved. Indeed, they destroy the merit of Christ, because they will not accept that Christ has merited forgiveness of sins, the Holy Spirit, and life everlasting for anyone in particular. They stubbornly affirm that Christ has merely acquired for His Father the right and authority to show compassion to human beings in general, and set down for them whatever conditions He pleases for their being saved. Yet they declare raucously and bluntly that Christ's merit has no direct application to persons, and that all people could be lost without harming His merit at all, should no one fulfil the conditions God sets down. Further, they do not accept any effective power in Christ's merit, because they ascribe calling, faith, and the new obedience, to human choice; that is, the human will is the sole cause why some persons repent and believe, while others do not. The efficacy of salvation, then, depends on the human will, not the grace of Christ; moreover, this efficacy relates to salvation as distinct from faith, since they say that the efficacy follows on from faith, but does not go before it—faith itself is not born in us as a result of Christ's merit or efficacious power.

But Christ is the Saviour by merit, because He has procured our salvation by His blood; and He is also the Saviour by efficacious power, because He imparts the salvation He has procured, and keeps it in being after it is imparted. Justification, forgiveness of sins, and salvation gush from Christ's merit, as the appropriate effect from the appropriate cause. Further, Christ bestows and applies forgiveness of sins, the Holy Spirit, and everlasting life on all those for whom He has merited these gifts.

Johann Heinrich Heidegger
Body of Christian Theology, Book 1, Topic 19.

John Davenant: The universal and particular aspects of redemption

Through the merit of the death of Christ, a new covenant was entered into between God and the human race. By this covenant we understand that which is urged by the Apostle, Gal. 3, *Believe, and you shall live*, and is opposed to the legal command, *Do this and you shall live*. This agreement, which promises salvation to every sinner under the condition of faith, has no foundation or confirmation anywhere else than in the blood of the Mediator; without the effusion of which no mortal man could aspire to eternal life, not even though believing. *But through the death of Christ having been accepted by God as a ransom, now it is lawful for any man indiscriminately to ascend into heaven by believing,* as the Apostle shows in Romans 3:21 to 26; and Christ Himself, Mark 16:15, *Go into all the world, and preach the Gospel to all creatures.* Therefore in this evangelical covenant, confirmed by the death of Christ, which the Apostles published to the whole world, and the ministers of the Gospel preach at the present time, there is no difference of persons made. As well Esau shall be saved, if he should believe in the Messiah, as Jacob shall be condemned if he should not believe.

But it is to be confessed, that there is also another ordination of God, secret and absolute, regarding certain definite persons, and founded likewise on the death of Christ, which obtains the name of the new covenant. But this is understood rather as agreed upon between God the Father and Christ, than between God and us. For it is that which is related by the Prophet Isaiah (53:10), *When You make His soul a sin-offering, He shall see His seed*; and is explained by the Apostle, Hebrews 8:10, *This is the Testament that 1 will make with the house of Israel, after those days, says the Lord, I will put My laws into their mind, and write them in their hearts, and I will be their God, and they shall be My people*, etc. As if he should say, That Christ by His death not only established that conditional covenant which may be published to all men individually in this form, *If you shall believe, whoever you are, you shall be saved through the death of Christ*, but also that secret and absolute covenant concerning the giving of faith to certain persons and infallibly saving them through Christ and for His sake.

But it is to be observed that this latter covenant is known to Christ alone, nor can it be opened to anyone by the ministers of Christ, as to the individual persons whom it embraces. For the Apostles themselves could, and we can preach to every man that conditional and revealed covenant, *If you shall believe, you shall be saved*. But neither could they, nor can we promise infallibly to any one, *You art one of those whom God gave to Christ the Mediator, and to whom, through Christ and for His sake, He will give persevering faith, and will infallibly lead to eternal life*. For this would be the same as if we should declare that we were in the councils of God before the foundations of the world were laid, and could point out with our finger the elect and the non-elect. Without this latter covenant, which is more properly understood to be established between God and men, that first conditional covenant would be in vain to all men through human depravity, and the precious and infinitely meritorious blood of Christ would flow in vain. But since, as it was said, God alone knows them to whom this covenant has regard, it is our business to urge and press that first conditional covenant, which is revealed to us; and this is that which we contend was confirmed by the death of Christ with the whole human race.[27]

John Davenant
A Dissertation on the Death of Christ, **Chapter 4**

Moise Amyraut: Christ, not God's mysterious decrees, the object of faith

I know full well that Calvin has said many things about the impelling *causes* of God's decrees. But I do not find that he has ever said a thing about their *order*. Calvin asserts that the only reason why God has created humanity for the hope of eternal blessedness is God's goodness. Once humanity had fallen into sin and condemnation, Calvin asserts that the only reason why God chose to send His Son into the world to redeem human beings by His death is the wonderful love of God for humankind. Calvin also asserts that the only reason why God has chosen some, and passed by others, in bestowing the grace of faith, is the divine mercy and severity. Further, Calvin does not acknowledge any other reason than purely the perfect freedom of God's will, concerning why God has chosen one person rather than another in the apportioning of this grace. Why He has chosen to save believers and to condemn unbelievers to everlasting punishment, Calvin thinks the reason for the latter must be found in God's justice, whereas the reason for the former must be found in His mercy… But concerning the sequence in which God's eternal wisdom set out all these things—I mean the question of His proposing in thought or will one thing or another first or last—Calvin never offers any account of this, nor does he show the smallest interest in doing so…

We must ever recall to our minds that God is God—that is, He has an infinite mind whose wisdom is wondrously complex and measureless, whose will we cannot fathom completely, and whose majesty we should revere with the utmost wonder and

---

27. For the opposing Reformed Orthodox view of particular redemption, see Francis Turretin's *Institutes of Elenctic Theology* (Phillipsburg, New Jersey: P&R, 1992–7), vol. 2, p. 455ff.

submission. We should accept the things He has revealed to us, take hold of them, and with all our heart convert them into the practice of godliness and sanctification. But the things about which He has chosen that we remain without knowledge (and, O sovereign Lord! how many, how great, are these?), we should not ask questions about them over-curiously. Concerning these things, it does not matter what view our hearts and sentiments embrace, there will always be a huge abyss whose breadth, and length, and depth, and height incalculably transcend our intellects. Abject little human beings that we are, we need not feel humiliated merely because we do not know everything...

In fact nobody at a banquet wonders whether, in the secret counsel of God, it has been decreed whether he will eat or not. If he is wise, he will consult his stomach to see whether he has any appetite; he will look at the meats to know whether they are agreeable to him; he will listen to the praises and the advice of the person who invited him, and find out whether it is sensible to take that advice; and then, when he has thought it over, he will finally decide to have what he judges most appropriate. Thus, in the preaching of the Gospel, whether it is a question of receiving the faith of Christ or rejecting it, nobody bothers to work out what the secret will of God is. Everybody tends to be attracted by hunger and thirst for righteousness, or else put off by the disgust and revulsion caused (so to speak) by bad inner influences which fill and penetrate the soul...

A person, then, must simply fasten his spiritual eyes upon the Lord Jesus; he must focus all the energy of his soul upon Him; he must contemplate every facet of this Object, and reflect how very true He is, how very profitable He is, how very needful He is, how utterly worthy of admiration, and overflowing with contentment, comfort, and joy. In short, he should reflect how divine Christ is, from whatever angle He is seen. This a person must do, so that in Christ he acknowledges and takes hold of the infinite compassion that is made known to us.

Moise Amyraut
Defence of the Doctrine of Calvin on the
Subject of Election and Reprobation (1644)

Herman Witsius: classical covenant theology

In Scripture, we discover two covenants of God with humanity: the covenant of works, otherwise called the covenant of nature, or the legal covenant; and the covenant of grace. The apostle teaches us this distinction in Romans 3:27, where he speaks about the law of works, and the law of faith. By the law of works, he means the doctrine which points out the way in which salvation is obtained by means of works; and by the law of faith, he means the doctrine that directs us to obtain salvation by faith. The form of the covenant of works is, "The man that does these things shall live by them," Romans 10:5. The form of the covenant of grace is, "Whosoever believes in Him shall not be ashamed," Romans 10:11. These covenants of compassion agree in the following particulars:

1. The covenanting parties are the same in both, viz. God and humankind.

2. The same promise of eternal life is present in both, consisting in the immediate enjoyment of God.

3. The condition is the same in both, viz., perfect obedience to the law. It would not have been worthy of God to give humanity an entry into a blessed communion with Him, except by way of a spotless holiness.

4. The same goal is aimed at in both, viz. the glory of the supremely perfect goodness of God.

But in the following particulars the covenants differ:

1. In the covenant of works, the character or relationship between God and humanity is different from what we find in the covenant of grace. In the former, God deals with humanity as the Supreme Lawgiver, and the Supreme Blessedness, rejoicing to make His innocent creature share in His own happiness. In the latter, God deals with us on a basis of infinite mercy, bestowing life on the elect sinner in a way that harmonizes with His wisdom and justice.

2. In the covenant of works there was no mediator. In that of grace, the mediator is Christ Jesus.

3. In the covenant of works, the condition of perfect obedience had to be performed by the human race itself, which had consented to it. In the covenant of grace, the same condition is proposed, as a condition to be performed, or as having already been performed, by a mediator. In this substitution of the persons resides the chief and essential difference between the covenants.

4. In the covenant of works, humanity is considered as working, and the reward is to be given as something owed; therefore, human glorying is not excluded, but humanity may glory, as a faithful servant may do, upon the right discharge of duty, and may claim the reward promised to the work. In the covenant of grace, humanity, ungodly in itself, is considered in the covenant as believing; and eternal life is considered as the merit of the mediator, but as given to humanity out of free grace. This excludes all human boasting, except the glorying of the believing sinner in God, as his or her merciful Saviour.

5. In the covenant of works, something is required of humanity as a condition which, when performed, entitles us to the reward. The covenant of grace, as it bears on us, consists in the absolute promises of God, in which the mediator, the life He will procure, the faith by which we may be made partakers of Him, the benefits purchased by Him, and perseverance in that faith, in a word, the whole of salvation, and all that is necessary to it, are absolutely promised.

6. The special goal of the covenant of works was the manifestation of the holiness, goodness, and justice of God, shining forth in His most perfect law, His most generous promise, and in the recompense of reward to be given to those who seek Him with their whole heart. The special goal of the covenant of grace is "the praise of the

glory of his grace", Ephesians 1:6, and the revelation of His unsearchable and many-splendored wisdom. These divine perfections shine forth radiantly in the gift of a mediator, by whom the sinner is admitted to complete salvation, without any dishonour to the holiness, justice, and truth of God. There is also a demonstration of the all-sufficiency of God, by which not only humanity *per se*, but even sinful humanity (which is more surprising) may be restored to union and communion with God. But all this will be more fully explained in what follows.

Herman Witsius
The Economy of the Covenants between God and Man,
Book 1, Chapter 15

*Map of the British Isles showing the major places
mentioned in Chapters 3–5*

Chapter 3

England: The Puritan Era Part One

1
Puritanism: The problem
of definition

The Puritans have probably been more admired, at least by Reformed believers, than any other body of English Christians. Equally, they have also been more vilified than any other body of English Christians! Yet who were they?

The question finds no easy answer. Some answers that might spring to mind must be rejected. For example, we cannot define Puritanism by its adherence to Reformed theology. The definition would be far too broad. It would make all Calvinists into Puritans. But French, Swiss, German, and Dutch Calvinists were not Puritans. Even if we restrict ourselves to England, there were many English Calvinists who did not identify with the contemporary movement nicknamed "Puritan"—most notably Archbishop Whitgift, the "hammer of the Puritans", whose theology was impeccably Calvinistic, and Richard Hooker, perhaps the Anglican establishment's most creative theologian, whose understanding of salvation was quintessentially Reformed. Finally, there were people who did identify themselves in some sense with the Puritan movement, endorsing much of its agenda, who were not Calvinists in theology: one thinks of those two mighty 17th century Johns—John Goodwin and John Milton— who were Arminians. Milton in particular is routinely described as "the Puritan poet", "the poet of Puritanism", and so forth.

A theological definition focusing on Calvinism, then, will not work. It falsifies history.[1] Others focus on a certain kind of

---

1. If what people admire is Reformed theology, it would be better to say so, and not confuse the issue by introducing the word "Puritan".

spirituality as the heart of Puritanism. Yet it is difficult, again, to pin down what this distinctive spirituality was. If (as often) it is understood as taking the Bible and preaching seriously, insisting on authentic experience of God, and striving after holiness, then the present writer would humbly suggest that these have been hallmarks of most forms of vital Christianity throughout the Christian centuries. By this definition, Basil of Caesarea, Augustine, Simeon the New Theologian, Bernard of Clairvaux, and the Catholic Jansenists were all Puritans. Once again, the word has become so broad as to lose its cash-value.

Could we combine the two definitions, and say that a Puritan was someone who *both* held to Reformed theology, *and* embraced an experiential God-centred spirituality? No: it would still be too wide. There were plenty of genuinely pious Calvinists who did not identify with the label "Puritan". Richard Hooker again comes to mind. There were many others—John Jewel, John Davenant, Daniel Featley, Archbishop Ussher, Samuel Ward, Joseph Hall.[2]

We might be on better ground if we say that Puritanism had a distinctive view of worship. Most students know that conflicts in the English Church from 1559 to 1662 often revolved around worship, and that Puritans believed in the "regulative principle"—that nothing must be done in worship unless authorized by Scripture. Even so, this was a more broadly Reformed ideal, and the history of those times, in England, Scotland, and Continental Europe, shows that the regulative principle itself was capable of widely varying interpretations. The first English Puritans in the 1560s were shocked to find that their European Reformed heroes, like Heinrich Bullinger and Peter Martyr Vermigli, did not share their interpretation of the regulative principle when it came to clerical vestments (see below). It seems, then, that Puritans might have embraced, not simply the Reformed regulative principle, but a particular understanding of how it applied. There were, however, differences among Puritans themselves about its application.

---

2. See below for all these figures.

Did it allow or disallow liturgies, or hymns, or the Lord's Prayer, or the Apostles' Creed, or funeral sermons, or a special sermon on Christmas day? Puritans did not speak with a single voice on these issues.[3]

One interesting theological conviction that many historians think was almost exclusively Puritan was Sabbatarianism—a belief that the Christian Sunday was essentially identical with the Old Testament Sabbath, and should be rigorously kept as a day of rest-for-worship, neither work nor recreation being allowed. This, however, was rather late in developing; the publication in 1595 of the treatise *The Doctrine of the Sabbath* by Nicholas Bownde (d. 1613), Puritan rector of Norton in Suffolk, is commonly held to be decisive for Puritan Sabbatarianism. Even here we must be careful, because some anti-Puritans like Lancelot Andrewes (see section 4.4) were Sabbatarian, and by the second half of the 17th century, Sabbatarianism was the common conviction of virtually all English Protestants, whether "Puritan" in any sense or not. In the earlier part of the 17th century, however, it does seem to have been a likely badge of Puritan sympathies.

Rather than create definitions of our own (possibly framed to include all our heroes and exclude our villains!), perhaps we should try a different tack, and use the word "Puritan" as it was used in the 16th and 17th centuries. Who did the people of *that* time think the Puritans were? Even here we are faced with a problem. At a more educated level, the Anglican establishment used the word "Puritan" to describe those Anglicans who wanted to reform the Church of England still further, e.g. by abolishing certain ceremonies or introducing Presbyterian church government. Other words were also used to label such people—"Precisian" (someone who was too precise) was by far

---

3. Many of these differences (and others) were aired in the debates of the Westminster Assembly, which is covered in section 5. Richard Baxter's *Reformed Liturgy*, which received the assent of the 12 Puritan delegates at the Savoy Conference of 1661 (see Chapter 4, section 1.2), contained the Apostles' Creed.

the most common alternative. On this showing, Puritans were by
definition Anglicans: they were the party within Anglicanism who
sought to reform their Church further than had been achieved
at the Elizabethan settlement of 1559. Thomas Fuller (1608–
61), the professional writer and historian of the 17th century,
a moderate royalist during the English Civil War, gives us the
above definition of Puritan. He adds that within the camp of these
would-be reformers of Anglicanism there were two types: "some
mild and moderate, contented only to enjoy their own conscience;
others fierce and fiery, to the disturbance of church and state".

To set "Puritan" against "Anglican", therefore, as some modern
interpreters do, makes a nonsense of how the people of that
era understood matters. It acquires some kind of sense only
after 1662, when Anglicanism no longer tolerated any clergy
who did not overtly renounce all Puritan aspirations (see
Chapter 4, section 1.2). Even the term "Anglicanism" is dubious;
it was a 19th century invention. There was probably a mindset
to which the term "Anglicanism" could be applied earlier, but
once more that mindset only really emerged in the context of
what happened in 1662. Nevertheless, bowing to general usage,
I shall use the term to describe the national English Church as
established by law, except in the confusion of the Civil War and
Cromwellian period.

But now we have to consider how the word "Puritan" (or
"Precisian") was used at a more popular, grass-roots level.
Here the term was applied simply to anyone who took his
or her Christianity seriously and tried to live a godly life. It
meant nothing more than a "Holy Joe", a "member of the God
squad", a "Bible basher", and other such abusive labels today. The
illustrious Richard Baxter in the 17th century testified that his
own father was insulted as a "Puritan" in this way, although
Baxter Senior had no quarrel with the Church of England, but
simply sought to live an authentic Christian life. In Baxter's
words, anyone was abusively termed "Puritan" if only they "used
to talk of God, and heaven, and scripture, and holiness".

When we arrive at the English Civil War, definitions almost
entirely break down. In the language of the day, the various

religious factions that emerged on the parliamentarian side of the conflict stopped being called Puritans (so Richard Baxter tells us), and began gaining more specific labels—Presbyterians, Independents, Baptists ("Anabaptists" or "Dippers" in contemporary parlance), Quakers, Seekers, Fifth Monarchists. The language of a later time, however, has projected the monolithic label "Puritan" back on many of these factions. It would seem odd to us today, for example, if we did not call John Owen a Puritan, although he was an Independent in the jargon of the day. Just before the Civil War broke out, a writer (either Henry Parker or John Ley) in his *A Discourse Concerning Puritans*, published in 1641, distinguished between "church policy Puritans", "religious Puritans", "state Puritans", and "moral Puritans". Plainly by then the word had ceased to carry any single or obvious meaning.

Our examination thus far seems to have left the name "Puritan" almost as nebulous as ever. Since this volume, however, can hardly avoid using the term completely, some decision must be made. My decision is as follows. When I speak of Puritans *before* the English Civil War, I will be referring to those Anglicans who sought a further reformation of the Church of England. Here I accept the more exact and educated use of the word Puritan within the Anglican establishment of the time, rather than the street-slang that called any spiritually-minded person a Puritan.

What about *during* the Civil War and Cromwellian era? We could perhaps preserve a measure of continuity with earlier and modern usage of the term if we agreed on the following: we could call Puritan those who were willing to work within an established national Church under a parliamentary or Cromwellian regime, embracing its ideal of a more self-consciously advanced Protestantism than had characterized the previous monarchical-Episcopal regime. Such a definition would embrace both Presbyterians and many Independents (even a few Baptists!). It is admittedly a somewhat arbitrary definition, but the historian is struggling here to communicate with the overwhelming assumptions of modern-day believers, who have learned to see a species called "the Puritans" where the people of that day did not necessarily see them.

After the Restoration of the monarchy, and the ejection of Puritans from the national Church in 1662, things are easier. I shall follow contemporary 17th century usage and refer to non-Anglican Protestants as Nonconformists or Dissenters, whatever their brand of theology, spirituality, or church government.

Those who gave up on the established Church, and left her altogether, prior to the post-1660 Restoration regime, I will call Separatists. They could also occasionally be called Puritan in the language of the day; but Separatist was the far more widespread term, and this is the one I will utilize. Of course, they may well have been Puritans before they became Separatists. But we should keep in mind that some Separatists were actually Arminians in their theology. We need to be prepared for the spectacle of an Anglican Calvinist persecuting a Separatist Arminian. That may play havoc with our preconceptions, but history often does.

2

The origins of Puritanism and Separatism

1. The Elizabeth settlement

When Queen *Elizabeth I* (1558–1603) and her first parliament made the Church of England Protestant again in 1559, after the brief but bloody Catholic interlude under Mary Tudor (1553–8), few of the more Protestant-minded Anglican clergy realized that the 1559 religious settlement was to become permanent. Many had spent Mary Tudor's reign in exile, in Reformed communities like Zurich, Basel, and Geneva, where the setting of worship was much freer from medieval ceremony than it was in Elizabethan Anglicanism. These exiles, now that they were back in England and parish ministers in the Anglican Church, expected to see further reforms. In 1563, some of them put up a proposal in convocation (the Anglican clerical governing body) to extend official tolerance to those who had scruples about the wearing of clerical vestments, the sign of the cross in baptism, and kneeling at holy communion, to remove organs from churches, and to reduce the number of holy days in the church calendar. This very moderate proposal was defeated—but only by a single vote. This galvanized those seeking further reform to bypass the Anglican system of church government as hopelessly conservative, and begin campaigning for wider public support.

2. The vestiarian controversy

Meanwhile, there was little uniformity in Anglican worship. The dioceses of London and Norwich in particular had a great

183

variety of practices—some ministers wore vestments, others did not; holy communion was received by some kneeling, by others sitting or standing; and so forth. The bishops of London and Norwich—**Edmund Grindal** (c.1519–83) and John Parkhurst (c.1512–75)—had both been Protestant exiles during Mary Tudor's reign, and were sympathetic to more Continental Reformed ideals of worship. They were therefore reluctant to coerce their clergy into strict compliance with the 1559 settlement. Queen Elizabeth, however, insisted on compliance (she interpreted refusal to conform as defiance of her authority), and ordered her Archbishop of Canterbury, **Matthew Parker** (1504–75), to take action.

Parker held several conferences with the dissident clergy; their demands focused on the issue of clerical vestments (chiefly the "surplice", a white wide-sleeved gown), which they argued were relics of medieval Catholicism, misleading ordinary people into thinking that Protestant ministers were no different from Catholic priests. The anti-vestment party was led by **Thomas Sampson** (1517–89), Dean of Christ Church, Oxford, and **Laurence Humphrey** (1527–90), theology professor at Oxford and dean of the university's Magdalen College. Both Sampson and Humphrey had been in exile during Mary Tudor's reign and absorbed the worship-values of Continental Calvinism. Against their refusal to conform, Parker argued that a minister's garb was essentially a thing indifferent, and that every Church had the authority to institute some practice or other in such matters; to disobey was the sin of anarchy. He could not take very seriously the idea that people would be misled into thinking that men like Sampson and Humphrey were Catholic priests, when their entire teaching said the exact opposite.

When conferences and persuasion failed to win over the dissidents, Parker took sterner practical measures. In 1565 he cancelled all licenses to preach that had been granted before March of that year: from now on, licenses would be given only to those who conformed. The whole body of London's minsters were gathered in Parker's official residence, Lambeth palace, and ordered to conform or be suspended. 61 ministers conformed; 37 refused, and Parker immediately suspended them from duties and cut off their income. Eventually most of the nonconformists did submit. The argument that prevailed with them was whether it was worth losing their congregations over a mere vestment. Most decided it was not.

Sampson and Humphrey tried to save themselves by appealing over Parker's head to Heinrich Bullinger of Zurich. With the recent deaths of Calvin and Peter Martyr Vermigli, Bullinger was now the "grand old man" of Reformed theology. He was also supremely influential on English Protestants; he had sheltered many of them in Zurich during Mary Tudor's reign, forging close pastoral bonds with them. If Bullinger supported Sampson and Humphrey, Archbishop Parker would be in trouble. Unfortunately for Sampson and Humphrey, Bullinger supported Parker! The Swiss Reformer argued that clerical vestments were things indifferent, which for the sake of decency were acceptable garments, and that if the Church authorities had decided that vestments should be worn, then the clergy had no right to disobey. Bullinger also counselled Sampson and Humphrey not to resign over a mere vestment:

> …if the edifying of the church is the chief thing to be regarded in this matter, we shall do the church a greater injury by deserting it than by wearing the vestments.

Sampson and Humphrey were staggered by Bullinger's advice, but persisted in their nonconformity. Consequently Archbishop Parker sacked Sampson from his post as Dean of Christ Church. Humphrey managed to cling on as Dean of Magdelen College, since Parker had no direct authority over that post. Bullinger's attitude, however, may have undermined Humphrey's dissidence; he gradually lost interest in the fight, conformed, and even personally restored the use of vestments in Magdalen College chapel.

3. The birth of Separatism

The vestiarian controversy (as it was called) was the occasion when the term "Puritan" was first used as an abusive label for the Anglican dissidents. It was also around the same time that Puritanism showed its potential for Separatism. In June

1567 in London, the sheriff's officers (the 16th century police) uncovered a group of a hundred holding a meeting in Plumbers' Hall, allegedly for a wedding—but they had in reality gathered to listen to preaching and take part in holy communion. Arrested and questioned by Bishop Grindal of London, the replies made it clear that this was a functional congregation. They had met in secret as Protestants during Mary Tudor's reign. Disillusioned, however, with what they saw as the insufficiently Protestant character of the Elizabethan Anglican Church, most of whose ministers (they said) were mere papists who had conformed to the 1559 settlement, they had decided to resume meeting as a Protestant congregation outside the establishment.

On the whole, however, this group does not seem to have been committed to Separatism; most of them were willing to worship within the Church of England once it was better reformed. A few of them later became Anglican Presbyterians (see below). Their "separation" was a temporary withdrawal, not a principled rejection of the state-established Church. So we should probably think of this congregation as fringe Puritan rather than fully Separatist. Bishop Grindal, a moderate and gentle soul, was rather scandalized by their attitude to his Church, and ultimately treated them severely; some were held in Bridewell prison for at least a year.

However, a mere month before this more famous incident, a genuine Separatist congregation had been unearthed in London, led by a certain Richard Fitz (about whom almost nothing else is known). Here were people who had rejected the entire Anglican Church as hopelessly corrupt, so that true Christians had no option but to depart permanently. Some or all of these Separatists were imprisoned in Bridewell.[4] Even worse was to come for Bishop Grindal. In March 1569, those who had met at Plumbers' Hall, now released from prison, were found to be up their tricks again: the authorities discovered 72 of them meeting as a congregation in the house of a Mr James Tynne, goldsmith, in Saint Martin's-in-the-Fields. Once again, many were imprisoned.

---

4. There must have been more religious dissidents than "real" criminals in Bridewell at this time!

Grindal recorded that some folk seceded from the Plumbers' Hall congregation and joined the authentically Separatist congregation of Richard Fitz. There is some uncertainty about the reason, but it could have been the fact that the Plumbers' Hall congregation used the Geneva liturgy in its worship (in preference to the Anglican Prayer Book), whereas the Separatists used no liturgy at all. This was to be a hallmark of early Separatists—their opposition to any element in worship that was not the immediate, spontaneous utterance of the worshiping soul. That of course meant no liturgies, but it equally meant no hymns and no psalms; all these had been written by persons other than the worshiper, and therefore could not be the worshiper's own heart-utterance. Early Separatists therefore had no liturgies, no psalms, and no hymns. This attitude was to linger long among early Baptists.[5] Puritans, however, were never to take such a view; most were perfectly happy with some sort of liturgy, and all were happy with psalms or hymns.

Thereafter, our knowledge of the radical dissidents of Plumbers' Hall and the Fitz congregation fades away into vague rumour, although we know that Fitz himself died in prison. Our last sight of them may be in 1572, when Richard Cox (c.1500–81), the ardently Protestant Bishop of Ely in Cambridgeshire, referred to dissidents who had broken off completely from the Church of England, meeting in private houses.

Richard Fitz's church, and the seceders from Plumbers' Hall, are the first known Separatist groups in Elizabethan England. We know about them purely because they were discovered. There may very well have been other congregations that managed to stay hidden. Some of them may have been formed in Mary Tudor's reign and *never* gone back into Elizabeth's Protestant Church.

4. Two types of moderate Puritan

In the 1570s, Puritan-minded Anglicans crystallized into three different groups: Puritanism was never a single, uniform outlook.

---

5. See section 4.3 for the first Baptists.

First, there those who still disliked clerical vestments and other aspects of Elizabethan policy, but were convinced that active disobedience would be sinful anarchy. They did not seek any changes in church government, nor did they derive inspiration from Reformed Churches on the Continent. They conformed, told others to conform, and focused all their energies on preaching and teaching which they saw as the real priority. After the 1570s, this group became less and less Puritan in any sense, more and more loyal members of the Elizabethan Church. Their attitude was by far the most widespread one among the sincerely Protestant laity of the Anglican establishment. Prominent leaders in this group included Laurence Humphrey (the original anti-vestment firebrand), John Foxe (the famous chronicler of the martyrs under Mary Tudor), and the bishops John Parkhurst and James Pilkington (1520–76).[6]

Next, there were those who not only disliked vestments and other elements of medieval ritual, but believed that the Anglican Church needed reforming in its organization, if it was most effectively to express and perpetuate a national Protestant faith. Some of them favoured a reformed Episcopacy, with bishops as purely spiritual superintendents of the churches rather than quasi-political figures; others favoured Presbyterianism; in general, they all wished church structures to be made simpler and more accountable. However, they refused to make any changes on their own initiative. If the Church's rulers did not carry out change, these Puritans would not be actively disruptive. Like the first group, they concentrated on preaching and teaching, but hoped by these means to build up such a popular following that eventually parliament would be permeated by their influence. Then lawful reform of the Church would happen naturally and spontaneously. Puritans of this type were supported by significant numbers of leading figures in the social and political sphere—members of the aristocracy and gentry, prosperous merchants, important

---

6. For John Foxe, see *Volume Three: Renaissance and Reformation*, Chapter 7, section 4.

politicians. Among these lay supporters, the most prominent were **Sir Francis Walsingham** (1532–90), head of Elizabeth's security services, and **Robert Dudley, Earl of Leicester** (1532–88), Elizabeth's personal favourite.

This was the brand of Puritanism that had the widest level of backing in Elizabethan England. It was particularly famed for its preachers, such as Richard Greenham, Henry "Silver-tongued" Smith, and William Perkins.

Richard Greenham (c.1535–c.1594) was minister of the small country parish of Dry Drayton in Cambridgeshire, where his preaching excelled in turning theology into pastorally-oriented piety; Thomas Fuller said that "his masterpiece was in comforting wounded consciences". Richard Baxter was to praise Greenham's published sermons as among the premier works of practical divinity in English.

Henry "Silver-tongued" **Smith** (c.1560–c.1591) was reputedly the most popular preacher in Elizabethan London, if indeed not in all England; from his pulpit in Saint Clements Dane he attracted myriads by his spiritual oratory. Antony Wood (1632–95), who wrote the history of Oxford (where Smith studied), remarked that Smith was "esteemed the miracle and wonder of his age for his prodigious memory, and for his fluent, eloquent, and practical way of preaching". His collected sermons, published in 1592, were a best-seller for decades. Particularly popular was the sermon *God's Arrow against Atheists*, which has a curiously modern feel, critiquing not only atheism, but Roman Catholicism and Islam, as the three great foes of biblical Christianity.

William Perkins (1558–1602), a native of Warwickshire, studied at Christ's College, Cambridge University, where he became a fellow (a member of the college's governing council) from 1584 to 1594, when he resigned in order to get married— only single men could be college fellows. In 1585 he was appointed lecturer at Great Saint Andrews Church, opposite Christ's College, a post he held for the rest of his life. Perkins won huge repute as a preacher of plain-spoken, practical Calvinism, and a theologian who used scholastic and Ramist methodology to communicate biblical doctrine.[7] Perkins' definition of theology was famous: "the science of living blessedly for ever". He was also an early exponent of a full-blooded covenant theology.[8]

Among Perkins' many theological writings, *A Reformed Catholic* (1597) was perhaps the most conspicuous; its purpose was to demonstrate that 16th century Protestants were the true Catholics, having more affinity with the patristic heritage than Rome could honestly claim. Even Roman Catholic opponents, taking up the pen to refute so dangerous a book, admitted that it was a monument to scholarship and fairness, and non-Puritan Anglicans referred to it as a masterpiece of anti-Roman polemic. Perkins also blazed a trail of "casuistry" in Puritan theology: the study of "cases of conscience", a well-known feature of medieval Catholic theology, now baptized afresh into a Reformed context. His student William Ames would build impressively on this foundation.[9] Perkins' *Art of Prophesying* (Latin edition 1592; English 1606) became the standard Puritan textbook on preaching.

By the time Perkins died in 1602, he was widely acknowledged as Elizabethan England's most influential Reformed theologian. His works were translated and frequently reprinted for the Continental market, where they made a notable impact on Dutch, Swiss, and German Reformed thinking.

5. Presbyterian dawn: Thomas Cartwright

The third Puritan group were militant Presbyterians who actively and aggressively challenged the Anglican establishment. They believed that Presbyterian church government was the only biblical pattern, so that they could invoke divine authority for its establishment. They also advocated changes in the Anglican confession of faith (the Elizabethan 39 Articles were insufficiently Reformed for them) and forms of worship (they disliked the Book of Common Prayer and wanted a more Continental Reformed liturgy). They were less English, more

---

7. For Ramism, see Chapter 2, section 1.1.

8. See Chapter 2, section 1.7.

9. For Ames, see Chapter 2, section 1.4.

international in outlook; they looked to the model of church life found in the Scottish, French, Dutch, Swiss, and German Reformed Churches. More often than not, they appealed directly to parliament to take control of the Church and introduce these changes in government, doctrine, and liturgy.[10] This Presbyterian group still operated within the Church of England, so we should think of them as Anglican Presbyterians.

Anglican Presbyterianism found its eloquent, scholarly champion in *Thomas Cartwright* (c.1535–1603). A native of Hertfordshire and Cambridge-educated, he was appointed to the prestigious post of Lady Margaret professor of divinity in Cambridge in 1569.[11] Cartwright was already a Puritan; he had actively opposed vestments. He was also a brilliant scholar; Theodore Beza, the post-Calvin leader of Geneva, spoke of Cartwright as the most learned man he knew. A celebrated university preacher, his sermons drew huge crowds. Cartwright now used his new position as Lady Margaret professor to launch a searching critique of Anglican Church government, arguing against both diocesan Episcopacy and any form of clerical hierarchy. Diocesan Episcopacy involved a bishop governing all congregations and ministers in a particular region, a "diocese"— the model Anglicanism had inherited from its medieval Catholic past. For Cartwright, however, there was no office higher than the minister of a local congregation: all ministers were equal. Further, ministers should collectively rule the Church according to the Presbyterian form of government whose outlines Martin Bucer and John Calvin had drawn in the previous generation. Cartwright also criticized various other Anglican practices: the sign of the cross in baptism, fasting at Lent, bowing at the name

---

10. This was not a violation of the classical Reformed belief in the independence of the Church from state control. Reformed theology in the 16th and 17th centuries held that the state could lawfully set up a Reformed Church; only thereafter, the Church having been established by the state, should the state then respect its independence.

11. The oldest professorship in Cambridge university, established in 1502 by lady Margaret Beaufort, the mother of King Henry VII.

of Jesus—all superstitions, according to the Lady Margaret professor, because nowhere commanded in Scripture. More ominously for the Anglican authorities, he maintained that each congregation should choose its own minister: neither landowner nor monarch had any rights here.

Cartwright's critique was given in the course of lectures on the first two chapters of the Acts of the Apostles. The lectures electrified an enthusiastic student body. Moderate Protestants, however, were alarmed; they saw a revolutionary assault on established authority. Several months of frantic controversy finally ended with Cartwright's dismissal by the new university vice-chancellor, *John Whitgift* (c.1530–1604). Whitgift would be Cartwright's arch-enemy throughout the two men's lives. Lincolnshire-born Whitgift had been chaplain to Bishop Cox of Ely, and Cartwright's predecessor as Lady Margaret professor at Cambridge; in the early 1560s he had himself been a Puritan opponent of vestments. Always a strong Calvinist and fierce foe of Rome, Whitgift soon abandoned his Puritanism and became a firm defender of the Anglican establishment. His loyalty would be rewarded; a dozen years later, a grateful Queen Elizabeth would make him Archbishop of Canterbury.

6. The conflict widens: Puritans and parliament

Cartwright's sacking by no means quenched the Presbyterian fire he had ignited. His supporters took the struggle to parliament. Puritan MPs had already tried to enact Church reforms through the House of Commons in 1566 and 1571, led by the intrepid William Strickland (d.1598), MP for Scarborough. Strickland was a former world-explorer with Venetian navigator Sebastian Cabot (whose father John had discovered the coast of North America); his outspoken approach in parliament, which got him into serious trouble with Elizabeth, earned him the name "Strickland the Stinger" from a satirist in 1566. But while Elizabeth was busy trying to shut Strickland up, an anonymous broadside struck the House of Commons in June 1572—a Presbyterian manifesto entitled *Admonition to Parliament*.

The *Admonition* set out the basics of Presbyterian church government, calling on parliament to establish it for England; it also named various other church abuses that parliament should rectify, e.g. replacing the Anglican Prayer Book with a more Continental Reformed liturgy. The treatise was written in clear, energetic English; its authors were **John Field** (1545–88) and Thomas Wilcox (c.1549–1608). Field was a Londoner and an Oxford graduate who preached at Holy Trinity Minories Church in London; here, the preacher was appointed and supported by the congregation (unusually, the church had legal exemption from the Bishop of London's jurisdiction). It was a hotbed of extreme Puritanism. In fact, the very word "Puritan" seems first to have used of the Minories worshipers in 1567. Field had a flair for leadership and was unhampered by the slightest respect for the Anglican establishment. His confederate Wilcox was curate of All Hallows Church, Honey Lane, in London, a gentler sort with a more pastoral turn of mind, but loyal to Field.

Elizabeth was outraged by the *Admonition* and its appeal to parliament. She, not the House of Commons, was supreme governor of the English Church! Field and Wilcox were soon unmasked by the Elizabethan security services as authors of the *Admonition*, and imprisoned for a year for violating the 1559 Act of Uniformity. However, the *Admonition* had stirred up a wasps' nest of controversy, and for several years pro- and anti-Presbyterian treatises swarmed off the printing presses. There was an anonymous *Second Admonition* (1572); a response by John Whitgift (*Answer to the Admonition*, 1572); a counter-response by Thomas Cartwright who had just returned from Geneva (*Reply*, 1573); Whitgift's *Defence* (1574); the *Full and Plain Declaration of Ecclesiastical Discipline* by distinguished Presbyterian preacher **Walter Travers** (c.1548–1635), published in Latin in 1574, but translated into English by Cartwright and published in 1580 at Geneva; Cartwright's *Second Reply* (1575), and *The Rest of the Second Reply* (1577). After a few years' silence, a new spate of tracts from both sides appeared in the 1580s, culminating in the Martin Marprelate tracts of 1588–9 (see below). The whole tone of the literary war was harsh, even bitter, on both sides.

Moderate Puritans were dismayed by the radical aggression of their Presbyterian brethren. One of the Puritan MPs for London, the influential Thomas Norton (1532–84), translator of Calvin's *Institutes* into English, complained that the *Admonition* "was fond [foolishly optimistic], and with unreasonableness and unseasonableness hath hindered much good and done much hurt". Needless to say, parliament did not Presbyterianize the Anglican Church. Few MPs supported the idea, most Puritans were not convinced of the need for anything so drastic, and Elizabeth was implacably hostile. The Presbyterian wing of Puritanism therefore found itself comparatively isolated and weak. Even so, we can glimpse in Elizabeth's early parliaments, and the attempts by Puritan MPs like Strickland and Norton to introduce moderate church reforms, the seeds of a Puritan-parliament coalition of interests.[12] 80 years later, this would be a key ingredient in the outbreak of the English Civil War.

---

12. Very similar to the Jansenist-parlement coalition of interests in Catholic France. See Chapter 6, section 4.

3
Struggles and schisms: the Elizabethan odyssey

1. Education, education

One of the demands common to all varieties of Puritanism was that ministers should be biblically well-educated preachers. Of course, others agreed who could not be called Puritan. But certainly any Anglican who looked for further reformation in the Church of England (our definition of a Puritan) would have given a very high priority to training preachers. Cambridge University fulfilled this aspiration to a significant degree. Some of the individual colleges within the university were marked by Puritan ideals, notably Christ's College, Saint John's College, and Trinity College. Emmanuel College was founded in 1584 specifically to foster Puritan ideals of ministry. Several generations of Puritan clergy and schoolteachers emerged from these institutions.

A method of biblical education utilized in Cambridge was the "conference". Lecturers would meet with students to study the Bible together; each participant had a different speciality assigned to him—Hebrew, Greek, history, logic, rhetoric. The idea was that by pooling their talents and insights, their discussions would lead them to a fuller understanding of the sacred text. The Swiss Reformed canton of Zurich under Zwingli and Bullinger had developed this conference method, and it had caught on in the other Reformed Churches of Continental Europe.

2. The courage and fate of Archbishop Grindal

These conferences spilled out of Cambridge and became popular among the more Protestant-minded clergy and laity in towns and cities; they were known as "prophesyings". This has nothing to do with gifts of prophecy in a charismatic sense. In Elizabethan language, "prophecy" and "prophesying" referred to preaching and teaching. The clergy would discuss a text or a theological subject; the laity would listen. These conferences were not organized in defiance of Episcopal authority; where they took place—in almost all the southern dioceses, by 1577—they had the bishop's approval. Sometimes it was the local bishop who started them on his own initiative. However, it tended to be Puritans who were most active among the clergy and laity who attended.

There was a problem: Queen Elizabeth. She reacted strongly against the prophesyings. To her they smacked too much of democracy and anarchy. No one in Elizabethan England believed in democracy, least of all the imperious sovereign herself.[1] She decided to stamp the prophesyings out; but true to her customary method, she would not do it herself—she would order someone else to do it. The task fell to the luckless Edmund Grindal, who in 1576 had been appointed Archbishop of Canterbury. Grindal was no Puritan. He had experienced some scruples about wearing clerical vestments when Elizabeth made him Bishop of London in 1559, but his mentor, the great Italian Reformer Peter Martyr Vermigli (then teaching in Zurich), advised him not to forfeit such an opportunity over something so trivial as a vestment. Once Grindal was installed as bishop, he enforced the clerical garb of the surplice on his London clergy. However, Grindal was thoroughly Protestant—emphatically Reformed in his theology. He believed in the necessity of an

---

1. The number of those entitled to vote in local and parliamentary elections in Elizabethan England was miniscule. Most people did not have the necessary financial qualifications to vote. Even 200 years later, a survey in 1780 revealed that only 3% of the English population were entitled to vote. So we can forget any idea that anything remotely resembling democracy existed in the England of Elizabeth I.

educated preaching clergy; he saw the value of the prophesyings
as a means to this end. He admitted that Puritans had made
use of the conferences to criticize things they did not like in the
Church, but his answer was to regulate the conferences better,
not to suppress them.

Consequently, when Elizabeth ordered her new archbishop
to suppress the prophesyings, Grindal refused. His letter to
Elizabeth, dated 20th December 1576, was unlike anything for
boldness that Elizabeth had ever heard from any of her subjects:

> ...the speeches which it hath pleased you to deliver unto me,
> when I last attended on your Highness, concerning abridging
> the number of preachers, and the utter suppression of all
> learned exercises and conferences among the ministers of
> the church, allowed by their bishops and ordinaries, have
> exceedingly dismayed and discomforted me...
>
> Public and continual preaching of God's word is the
> ordinary mean and instrument of the salvation of mankind.
> St Paul calleth it the ministry of reconciliation of man unto
> God. By preaching of God's word the glory of God is enlarged,
> faith is nourished, and charity increased. By it the ignorant is
> instructed, the negligent exhorted and incited, the stubborn
> rebuked, the weak conscience comforted, and to all those that
> sin of malicious wickedness the wrath of God is threatened.
> By preaching also due obedience to Christian princes and
> magistrates is planted in hearts of subjects: for obedience
> proceedeth of conscience; conscience is grounded upon the
> word of God; the word of God worketh his effect by preaching.
> So as generally, where preaching wanteth, obedience faileth...
>
> I trust, when your Majesty hath considered and well
> weighed the premises, you will rest satisfied, and judge that
> no such inconveniences can grow of these exercises, as you
> have been informed, but rather the clean contrary. And for
> my own part, because I am very well assured, both by reasons
> and arguments taken out of the holy scriptures, and by
> experience, (the most certain seal of sure knowledge,) that
> the said exercises, for the interpretation and exposition of the
> scriptures, and for exhortation and comfort drawn out of the
> same, are both profitable to increase knowledge among the

ministers, and tendeth to the edifying of the hearers,—I am
forced, with all humility, and yet plainly, to profess, that I
cannot with safe conscience, and without the offence of the
majesty of God, give my assent to the suppressing of the said
exercises: much less can I send out any injunction for the utter
and universal subversion of the same. I say with St Paul, 'I have
no power to destroy, but to only edify;' and with the same
apostle, 'I can do nothing against the truth, but for the truth'...

Bear with me, I beseech you, Madam, if I choose rather
to offend your earthly majesty, than to offend the heavenly
majesty of God.

Elizabeth was incensed. She suspended Grindal from his duties
and placed him under house arrest. He spent the rest of his life
in disgrace, and was only allowed to resume the full functions
of archbishop in 1582, when he was almost blind. He died
the following year. Meanwhile, the queen directly ordered all
the individual bishops to suppress the prophesyings in their
own dioceses. They were suppressed throughout the south of
England, but continued in parts of the north, where the gravest
threat to the Elizabethan Church came not from new-fangled
Puritans but old-fashioned Roman Catholics.

3. Presbyterian subversion: the classis movement
John Field, author of the Presbyterian *Admonition to Parliament*,
had not given up his dream of Presbyterianizing Anglicanism.
In the mid-1570s, he began organizing a secret Presbyterian
structure within the Church: the classis movement. A classis
(plural "classes") was another name for a presbytery. In Field's
movement, it was a meeting of all the ministers from a particular
area (a city, or a country district), who discussed together the
situations and needs of their congregations, providing collective
oversight. No elders were involved, as would be normal in
Presbyterianism, because the Anglican Church lacked an
eldership. It seems that the classis evolved from the conference
or prophesying meetings considered above. But when the
prophesyings were suppressed, the classes continued. Field
acted as a sort of national coordinator for the movement. As his

influence grew, the whole movement took on a more decidedly Presbyterian character, which it originally lacked; certainly the rural classes had started out as little more than secret clerical conferences for moderate Puritans. Field, however, operating from London, succeeded in permeating the movement with his own radically Presbyterian ideals. One classis at Dedham in Essex kept a detailed minute-book of its proceedings, covering 81 meetings between 1582 and 1589: an invaluable source of information for the movement.

By the mid-1580s, Field and his Presbyterian colleagues had managed to move beyond classis or presbytery level. They arranged provincial synods: collective meetings of all of the different classes in particular counties. These provincial synods were well-attended in Northamptonshire, Warwickshire, Norfolk, Suffolk, and Essex. Field's ultimate achievement was to organize several national synods—a sort of Presbyterian general assembly within Anglicanism. One met in London in 1586, another in Cambridge in 1587. This was the zenith of the movement. Walter Travers wrote a Book of Discipline for the classes, provincial synods, and national synod, setting out the rules for church government. Thomas Cartwright, who had been pastoring an English merchants' church in Antwerp, was now back in England again, helping promote the classis movement. The classes even acted as election agents in the general election of 1586, working (sometimes successfully) to get Puritan MPs elected. The national synod held in London that year was timed to coincide with the opening of parliament; a number of radical Puritan MPs went back and forth between parliament and synod.

However, the great parliamentary venture fizzled out pathetically. The Presbyterian MP Sir Anthony Cope (c.1548–1614) presented a bill to replace the Anglican Prayer Book with a Continental Reformed liturgy (a version of the one used in Geneva); attached to the Reformed liturgy was a Presbyterian scheme of church government. Cope's bill also proposed to scrap the entire governmental structure of Anglicanism—all its "laws, customs, statutes, ordinances, and constitutions". Cope was not acting alone; there was a small cadre of Presbyterian MPs backing him.[2] The bill, however, was rejected overwhelmingly by the House of Commons; most Puritan MPs voted against it. Queen Elizabeth, once again outraged by the audacity of her less-than-loyal subjects, had Cope and his collaborators thrown into prison. Their weakness had been pitilessly laid bare: Presbyterianism did not have the blessing of the great bulk of moderate Puritans, could not command support in parliament, and was therefore exposed to the unmitigated force of Elizabeth's hostility.

4. The reign of Archbishop Whitgift

Thereafter, the Anglican Presbyterian movement went into rapid decline, and by the early 1590s it had vanished like smoke. Partly this was owing to the death of John Field in 1588; no one was found to replace his sheer organizing genius. Partly it was because radical Puritanism was brought into utter disrepute both with moderate Puritans, and with the Anglican establishment, by the appearance of the notorious Martin Marprelate tracts in 1588–9. These were seven anonymous satires—no one knew who "Martin Marprelate" was—that poured a merry, scornful ridicule on the unreformed Church of England and its bishops. (Marprelate means something like "Bash-a-Bishop" in modern English.) The queen and Episcopal hierarchy were incandescent with anger; it did not help that the Marprelate tracts were quite popular, and often scandalously funny.

Moderate Puritans, however, deeply disapproved. Richard Greenham, one of their most admired figures, preached against the Marprelate tracts in Saint Mary's College, Cambridge University, on the basis that their effect was "to make sin ridiculous, whereas it ought to be made odious". In fact, almost all those on the Presbyterian wing of Puritanism agreed with Greenham's criticism; but the Marprelate tracts threw a suspicion of tasteless extremism on any Puritan who "rocked the boat" of Anglicanism, as the Presbyterians had certainly done.

---

2. Peter Wentworth, Job Throckmorton, Robert Bainbridge, Edward Lewkenor, and Ranulf Hurleston.

To this day no one is sure who wrote the Marprelate tracts. Some have suggested Presbyterian MP Job Throckmorton, others the Welsh Presbyterian-turned-Separatist John Penry (see below).

Presbyterianism, and indeed Puritanism in general, had acquired a new and powerful foe in 1583. The disgraced Grindal, who died that year, was replaced by Thomas Cartwright's old enemy, John Whitgift. The Presbyterian effrontery in the 1586 parliament, and the Marprelate tracts, which had often lampooned Whitgift, provoked the archbishop into using repressive legal machinery against Puritans on an unprecedented scale. The chief machine was a special church court known as the court of high commission, which had almost unlimited powers to investigate and punish the enemies of the established Church.

Whitgift now employed the court of high commission to discover and shut down the printing presses responsible for the Marprelate tracts; its agents did this successfully, using torture to extract information. They also arrested Thomas Cartwright and some 10 other leading Puritans, who were imprisoned for refusing to take the infamous *ex officio* oath. This was an oath by which a prisoner swore to answer truthfully any and all questions put to him (there was no get-out clause—no right of objecting to questions or claiming confidentiality). Cartwright was kept in prison for some two years altogether, but finally released through the intercession of powerful supporters, including King James VI of Scotland, who saw himself as a marvel of erudition and had a soft spot for scholars. The father of English Presbyterianism soon departed for Guernsey in the Channel Islands, with its new governor, Lord Zouch; Guernsey was under the authority of the English crown but outside its Church—French Reformed influence had made Guernsey Presbyterian. Cartwright was at home here.

Archbishop Whitgift put an efficient Anglican churchman in charge of the court of high commission—**Richard Bancroft** (1544–1610), a Cambridge doctor of divinity and Canon of Westminster Abbey. Bancroft proved a formidably skilful opponent of Puritanism. He managed to discredit the Presbyterian wing of the movement by a dexterous ploy, turning Calvin against them in his 1593 treatise, *A Survey of the Pretended Holy Discipline*:[3]

> And that you may perceive what great difference there is betwixt our men's spirits and Master Calvin's; their outrage, and his modesty: their rashness, ignorance and giddiness, and his sobriety, learning and judgment... But it may peradventure be said that, howsoever Calvin did carry himself in this cause, yet Beza is of another opinion. Indeed he is so: but it turneth more and more daily to his own discredit. He succeeded Master Calvin in place; but neither in his learning nor in all his virtues.

Beza took a far stricter view of Presbyterianism as the divinely ordained and exclusively valid form of church government than Calvin had done. Ironically, Bancroft proved something of a mirror-image of Beza here; he claimed (or seemed to claim) unique divine authority for the Episcopal form of church government. This was an advance on Whitgift, who had defended Episcopacy as merely lawful. Bancroft could therefore be seen as the originator of a "High Church" type of Anglicanism, which has insisted on Episcopacy as an essential mark of the rightly constituted Church. Not even Bancroft, however, was prepared to declare invalid the ministers and sacraments of other Churches that lacked Episcopacy.

5. Separatism's second wind

The 1580s saw the re-emergence of Separatism in Elizabethan England under new, educated leaders. The most significant was **Robert Browne** (1550–1633), a Cambridge graduate who studied under Thomas Cartwright. Browne began as a Puritan, influenced not only by Cartwright but by Richard Greenham, who in 1578 took Browne under his wing, encouraging him to

---

3. The "holy discipline" was a Presbyterian phrase for their form of church government.

finish his divinity studies and accept a parish ministry. However, omitting the tangled complexities of Browne's biography, by 1582 he had rejected both the entire established Church, and also the Puritan ideal of reforming it from within. The only way to have a Scriptural church, he concluded, was to leave Anglicanism and start afresh. Having gathered some like-minded believers, Browne sailed for the Dutch Republic; the Separatist congregation found a home in the city of Middelburg. Browne's church, however, imploded through internal quarrels, e.g. the attitude that should be taken toward believers who conformed to Anglicanism. Browne adopted too exclusive and censorious a stance for most of the congregation, and they eventually sacked him. He left for Scotland.

But before being sacked, Browne had written the first and enduring masterpiece of Separatist theology: *A Treatise of Reformation without Tarrying for any* (1582). Here Browne argued that reforming a corrupt Church like the Anglican involved an ungodly tarrying (waiting)—waiting for bishops or MPs to be won over—whereas Scripture required immediate action. Hence true believers had no choice but to secede and form their own congregations, made up not of everyone living in a locality (as in the parish system), but of genuinely faithful souls. These churches were to be run, more or less, according to what a later generation would call Congregational principles.

After leaving the Dutch Republic, Browne's attempt to propagate Separatism in Scotland failed—he ended up in prison again. After regaining his liberty, this sadly disenchanted Separatist pioneer made his way back into England, where he conformed to the Anglican Church. In 1591 he became minister of the Anglican parish of Achurch-cum-Thorpe in Northamptonshire; he still held this post when he died in 1633. But his name had become attached to the movement he had abandoned—Separatists and Congregationalists were now routinely called Brownists. Further, his *Treatise of Reformation*, and his *A Book which Sheweth the Life and Manner of all True Christians* (1582), which also expounded Congregational church government, had both made a big splash in England;

they continued to influence many, even after Browne himself no longer believed what he had written. The treatises were condemned by special royal proclamation in 1583, and two men—John Copping and Elias Thacker—were hanged in Bury Saint Edmunds for distributing the forbidden literature. The blood of martyrdom was beginning to sanctify the Separatist cause in its followers' eyes.

The other great Separatist leaders at this time were John Greenwood, Henry Barrow, and John Penry. The common date of their deaths in 1593 testifies that all three suffered martyrdom for their Separatist faith in a single savage outburst from the English establishment.

John Greenwood (d.1593) was a Cambridge graduate, originally Puritan, deeply influenced by Thomas Cartwright, but he had now withdrawn entirely from the Church of England and become the foremost Separatist leader in London. Arrested in 1586 when agents of Bishop Aylmer of London broke into a meeting where Greenwood was expounding Scripture, he spent the next seven years in and out of prison.

Henry Barrow (c.1550–93) was another Cambridge graduate, an ex-lawyer who had become consumed by theology after a sudden conversion experience. A friend of Greenwood's, he visited him in prison and was promptly arrested himself. It was during his long imprisonment that Barrow wrote some of the most important treatises of early Separatism, setting forth Congregational ideals of church life, e.g. *A True Description of the Visible Congregation of the Saints* (1589), and *A Brief Discovery of the False Church* (1590), printed by friends in the Dutch Republic. As a result of these influential writings, Brownists were also sometimes called Barrowists.

John Penry (1559–93) was not connected with Greenwood or Barrow prior to being imprisoned with them, but they did develop a sense of brotherhood in captivity. Penry was a Welshman from Llangamarch in Breconshire, who studied at both Cambridge and Oxford; he may have been a Roman Catholic by upbringing, but at Cambridge he embraced Calvinism in an ardent Presbyterian form. At Oxford in 1587

Penry published a plea for more effective evangelism in Wales; he was so critical of the Welsh Anglican establishment, the court of high commission threw him in prison for several days to cool him off. Suspected of authoring the Martin Marprelate tracts of 1588–9 (he certainly helped print them), Penry was arrested again in March 1593. By now his Presbyterianism had passed into outright Separatism.

Greenwood and Barrow were convicted of publishing material "with malicious intent" and hanged on 6th April 1593. Penry was convicted (on dubious testimony) of inciting rebellion, and hanged on May 9th. Separatism had three more martyrs. By killing its leaders, however, the Elizabethan authorities had not stamped out the thing itself. They knew this; the Conventicle Act of 1593 assumed the existence of a significant underground movement of Separatists, decreeing banishment as the first penalty, and death if the banished person dared to return.

Most of Greenwood's congregation emigrated to the Dutch Republic, settling in Amsterdam, where in 1597 *Francis Johnson* (1563–1618) became their pastor. Johnson was an English Presbyterian, a disciple of Thomas Cartwright, who had finally despaired of Anglicanism and embraced Separatism. Unfortunately the Separatist church in Amsterdam was plagued by quarrels and schisms, which at one point involved a solemn examination of a dress worn by Johnson's wife Thomasine, to determine whether it was too flamboyant. Johnson ended up excommunicating as "slanderers" the enemies of the dress, which included his father and his brother. Not surprisingly, further controversies erupted over whether the power of excommunication resided in the eldership or the congregational meeting. Johnson and his followers ultimately withdrew and founded a more Presbyterian-style church in Emden.

6. Questioning Calvinism

The Puritan critique of the condition of the Anglican Church was bound to provoke a theological response sooner or later. In the 1590s, the climate was right for such a response. Roman Catholicism was no longer considered so great a danger, after the failure of Philip II of Spain's attempted Catholic invasion of England in 1588; the mighty Spanish fleet (the "Armada")[4] was smashed by a combination of the English navy and a storm. Philip was the great European champion of intolerant Counter-Reformation Catholicism, and his defeat was a grave blow to Catholic prestige. The Catholic claimant to the English throne, Mary Stuart—"Mary Queen of Scots"—had also finally been executed the previous year, having been Elizabeth's troublesome prisoner for two decades, and the focus of endless Catholic plots to topple Elizabeth and replace her with Mary.[5] With the Catholic threat thus diminished, the Anglican establishment felt no need to soft-pedal its opposition to Puritans, who were strong allies in the struggle against Rome.

One sign of things to come was opposition to the Reformed understanding of salvation that so characterized 16th century Puritans. **Peter Baro** (1534–99), a learned Huguenot, had been Lady Margaret Professor of Divinity at Cambridge since 1574. In the 1580s he began to have second thought about the Reformed view of predestination. He did not, however, aggressively challenge the Reformed Orthodoxy that had the upper hand in the Elizabethan theological world (although a university sermon in 1579 upset some people). But in 1595, Baro's student William Barrett, a fellow of Caius College, did aggressively challenge Reformed Orthodoxy in a sermon preached as part of his Bachelor of Divinity examination. Not only did Barrett openly reject the doctrine of unconditional election and perseverance; he criticized John Calvin, Peter Martyr Vermigli, and Theodore Beza in a way that many thought irreverent. The resulting uproar resulted in the intervention of none other than Archbishop Whitgift. His response, however, was not what modern students might have expected. For all his hostility to Puritanism, Whitgift was

---

4. A Spanish word derived from Latin, meaning a large body of ships.

5. Mary Stuart's claim to the English throne derived from her being the grand-daughter of Margaret Tudor, sister of King Henry VII, first of the Tudor dynasty of English monarchs.

an uncompromising Calvinist in his theology of grace. The archbishop promulgated a doctrinal statement known as the Lambeth Articles which throttled Barrett's anti-Calvinism. The Articles stated:

1. God from eternity has predestined certain people to life; certain people He has reprobated.

2. The moving or efficient cause of predestination to life is not the foresight of faith, or of perseverance, or of good works, or of any thing that is in the person predestined, but only the good will and pleasure of God.

3. There is predetermined a certain number of the predestined, which can neither be augmented nor diminished.

4. Those who are not predestined to salvation shall be necessarily damned for their sins.

5. A true, living, and justifying faith, and the Spirit of God sanctifying, is not extinguished, does not fall away; it does not vanish away in the elect, either finally or totally.

6. A man truly faithful, that is, such a one who is endued with a justifying faith, is certain, with the full assurance of faith, of the remission of his sins and of his everlasting salvation by Christ.

7. Saving grace is not given, is not granted, is not communicated to all people, by which they may be saved if they will.

8. No one can come to Christ unless it shall be given to him, and unless the Father shall draw him; and all are not drawn by the Father, that they may come to the Son.

9. It is not in the will or power of everyone to be saved.

Barrett eventually fled to France where he became a Roman Catholic. His provocative sermon, however, should probably not be seen as an isolated event. There seems to have been a more widespread questioning of Reformed views of salvation

in Cambridge University around this time. Other critics were
Everard Digby (dates unknown), a theologian of Saint John's
College, Cambridge, and Lancelot Andrewes (see below),
later to be Bishop of Winchester, but Master of Cambridge's
Pembroke College from 1589 to 1605. Digby was expelled
(allegedly for unruly behaviour—blowing a trumpet during
daylight hours); Andrewes, however, survived to become
one of the founders of a new "High Church" tradition in
Anglicanism in the reign of King James I. Still, Whitgift had
made it crushingly clear with the Lambeth Articles that there
could be no successful challenge to a Reformed doctrine of
grace as long as he was archbishop. The seeds would blossom
only after his death.

7. Richard Hooker: Elizabethan philosopher-theologian par excellence

The most effective response to Puritanism came not from
the critics of Calvinism, but from a man who largely shared
Calvinist views of salvation. However, he set them within a
larger philosophy of God's ordering of creation, thereby offering
a "sociology of grace" that differed from Puritanism of any
type. The man was **Richard Hooker** (1554–1600). A native of
Exeter, Devon, Hooker studied at Oxford under the patronage
of the illustrious John Jewel (1524–71). Jewel, a Protestant
exile in Mary Tudor's reign, became Bishop of Salisbury in the
Elizabethan Church; his *Defence of the Anglican Church* (1562)
was one of the 16th century's most eloquent and persuasive
statements of English Reformation principles against Roman
Catholicism.

Hooker was ordained in 1579, and became private tutor to
the son of devoutly Protestant Edwin Sandys (1519–88), who
was Bishop of London from 1570 to 1577, then Archbishop of
York until his death in 1588. At the suggestion of Sandys and
Archbishop Whitgift, Queen Elizabeth appointed Hooker in
1584 as Master or rector of London's Temple Church, which
served the legal community. Many of the lawyers would have
preferred the Presbyterian leader Walter Travers (see above),

and decided to hire him as a lecturer; this was a common device among Puritans to give their preachers employment, since lecturers could be appointed by anyone with enough funds, on a purely voluntary basis. The result was a sort of preaching duel between soft-spoken Hooker (the morning preacher) and fire-breathing Travers (the afternoon lecturer); as Thomas Fuller the historian put it, "the pulpit spoke pure Canterbury in the morning and Geneva in the afternoon". Hooker was not built for controversy and sank into depression; he appealed to Archbishop Whitgift to relieve him. Whitgift's response was to silence Travers by a sort of legal injunction served on him while he was in the pulpit. It was probably not what Hooker had in mind, since there was no personal animosity between himself and Travers—they had the highest regard for each other's learning.

Hooker's exposure to Travers' dynamic Presbyterianism inspired him to the true labour of his life, a personal investigation of the deeper issues underlying the debate between Presbyterians and the Elizabethan Church. This bore fruit in his *Of the Laws of Ecclesiastical Polity*, published in five volumes between 1594 and 1597.[6] Hooker's prose is generally recognized as among the noblest in English literature; he holds an exalted place in literary history, whether or not one accepts his beliefs. As for the immediate controversy that provoked the *Laws*, the Presbyterian leaders—Travers and Cartwright—had argued that the New Testament imposed one single detailed form of church government, binding on all Christians in all places at all times, and that failure to follow this pattern was defiance of God. Hooker counter-argued that Scripture revealed no such single detailed pattern. Rather it gave principles that had to be embodied in any form of church government. But the specific form of government varied from one time and place to another, according to need and circumstance. Hooker defended Episcopacy, not because it was imposed by Scripture, but

---

6. Three further books were published much later in 1662, but seem to be (arguably) first drafts that Hooker never finalized.

because the age-long experience of the Church had proven it to be a useful way of enshrining Scriptural principles of oversight, and because it had been appointed by lawful authority for the Anglican Church of which Travers and Cartwright were members.

Stepping back from the immediate dispute, Hooker critiqued the Presbyterian view of Scripture. Travers and Cartwright had set up a stark antithesis between Scripture (which alone carried God's authority) and everything else (which was of merely human authority, and therefore suspect at best and sinful at worst). Hooker argued that this fierce antithesis was over-simplistic and false. God ruled His creation by law. That law was wider than Scripture. Natural law, encoded in the very nature of humanity, was God's law. Therefore reason and conscience had inalienable rights as aspects of God's inbuilt law of nature, and must not be despised in the name of an exclusive Scripturalism.

This facet of Hooker's argument was aimed, in part, at Cartwright's assertion that even the civil laws of the state had to be derived from Scripture—by which Cartwright meant the law of Moses, with a large extension in English law of crimes that should merit the death penalty. In fact, Cartwright argued that the civil authorities now must be *more* severe than Moses: God no longer sent miraculous punishments as He often did in Old Testament times, so that the state must punish more strictly to make up for this apparent divine leniency. "If this be bloody and extreme, I am content to be so counted with the Holy Ghost", Cartwright solemnly pronounced. Hooker rejected this view both of the proper function of Moses' law, and of how civil authority enacted God's will. He appealed again to natural law as God-given. The basic purpose of Scripture was not, as Cartwright seemed to think, to give a detailed blueprint for all of life, without which life was lawless, but to reveal the way of salvation in Christ. When Christians followed the laws of nature, reason, and conscience, in other areas of life, they were still following Christ, because He as Creator was the source of nature, reason, and conscience.

The general and perpetual voice of men is as the sentence of God Himself. For that which all men have at all times learned, Nature herself must needs have taught; and God being the author of Nature, her voice is but His instrument. By her from Him we receive whatsoever in such sort we learn. Infinite duties there are, the goodness whereof is by this rule sufficiently manifested, although we had no other warrant besides to approve them. The Apostle St. Paul having speech concerning the heathen saith of them, "They are a law unto themselves." His meaning is, that by force of the light of Reason, wherewith God illuminateth every one which cometh into the world, men being enabled to know truth from falsehood, and good from evil, do thereby learn in many things what the will of God is; which will Himself not revealing by any extraordinary means unto them, but they by natural discourse attaining the knowledge thereof, seem the makers of those Laws which indeed are His, and they but only the finders of them out.

Of the Laws of Ecclesiastical Polity, then, left behind the original controversy about church government, and became a much larger exploration and vindication of the nature and role of reason in human life. Its philosophy of natural law had roots in Thomas Aquinas, and we would not go far wrong if we envisaged Hooker as a synthesis of Thomist and Calvinist. His treatise certainly remains one of the most majestic expositions of reason and natural law in a theistic setting ever written. It was almost immediately regarded as a literary, political, and theological classic, and moderate Anglican opponents of Puritanism found it both a fortress and arsenal for their beliefs.[7]

Among Hooker's other writings, his *Learned Discourse of Justification* was one of the most eloquently classic presentations

---

7. More extreme "High Church" Anglicans found it more problematic because of Hooker's Reformed stance on matters like the eucharist, and his disbelief in the absolute necessity of Episcopacy. See under *Lancelot Andrewes* in section 4.4 for High Church Anglicanism.

of the Reformation doctrine of justification by faith from the entire 16th century.[8]

---

8. Hooker distinguished between *being* justified by faith, and *believing in* justification by faith. He thought the former was possible in the absence of the latter: a person did not necessarily need an intellectual understanding of the *doctrine* of justification by faith in order to *be* justified by faith. All a person needed was faith. Travers accused him of selling out to Rome, but Hooker has C.H.Spurgeon on his side: see his sermon *Justification by Faith: Illustrated by Abram's Righteousness*, preached on December 6th 1868.

4

The Jacobean Church: of Bibles, Pilgrim Fathers, and High Churchmen

1. *James I and the Hampton Court conference*

When the childless Queen Elizabeth died in March 1603, the English throne passed to the Scottish King James VI, who became *James I* of England (born 1566; King of Scotland, 1567; King of England 1603–25). Elizabeth's chief minister Sir Robert Cecil (1563–1612) was largely responsible for this; technically, under the terms of Henry VIII's will as ratified by the English parliament, the crown should have passed to Edward Seymour or Lady Anne Stanley. But both were nobodies. Cecil used the machinery of the English state to ensure that James, the only realistic candidate, gained the crown. He was, after all, the descendant of Margaret Tudor, sister of Elizabeth's grandfather, King Henry VII.

The personality, formative experiences, and religious policy of James are considered at length in Chapter 5. He was a resolute Episcopalian who had spent most of his reign in Scotland in conflict with Presbyterians; he had managed to outmanoeuvre them, and bring the Scottish national Church largely under royal control. Yet James' beliefs about salvation were undoubtedly Reformed, which perhaps explains why England's Puritans had such high hopes of their new monarch. Their cause had petered out into nothingness in the 1590s, under the heavy hand of Archbishop Whitgift. However, they were biding their time. When Elizabeth

213

died and James was proclaimed king, Puritan clergy in the Church of England organized a petition with astonishing swiftness, signed by a thousand ministers, asking James to reform the Church of his new southern kingdom. The Anglican Church had something like nine thousand clergy, so this petition represented only a small minority of ministers. Nonetheless, there was no other coalition of opinion in the Church so vocal and well-organized. From the fact of the one thousand signatures, the petition is known as the Millenary Petition.

The demands in the petition were nothing new. They were the long-standing Puritan complaints, requesting an end to such things as clerical vestments, the sign of the cross in baptism, bowing at the name of Jesus, the use of wedding rings in the marriage ceremony,[1] and the use of the word *priest* in the Prayer Book. The signatories also objected to pluralism (men holding more than one church appointment, e.g. two parish churches) and ministers who did not preach. Positively, they proposed a conference of scholars to discuss these issues, presided over by King James.

To the alarm of Archbishop Whitgift and the other Anglican bishops, James agreed to the conference. It probably flattered his vanity to think of himself as an erudite monarch dazzling the assembled theologians with the undoubted depth of his learning. The conference was scheduled to take place on November 1st at Hampton Court, a royal palace on the river Thames. An outbreak of plague postponed the conference until January 1604.

Unfortunately we have only one contemporary account of the Hampton Court conference, from a writer violently biased toward the Anglican establishment. However, we can reconstruct what happened. The Anglican establishment was represented by Archbishop Whitgift and eight other bishops, eight deans, and one archdeacon. Their chief spokesman was the

---

1. Puritans regarded wedding rings as Pagan in origin, baptized into Christianity by a corrupt medieval Catholicism, and thus a relic of Paganism and popery alike. They also objected to jewellery as sinfully frivolous.

vehemently anti-Puritan Bishop Bancroft of London. The king's Privy Council selected a group of Puritans to represent the other side; the council chose (probably) four moderate Puritans, led by the scholarly *John Reynolds* (1549–1607), president of Corpus Christ College, Oxford University. Reynolds was the most moderate Puritan imaginable, and certainly no dogmatic Presbyterian—he believed in a reformed Episcopacy. The other three moderates were Laurence Chaderton, Thomas Sparke, and John Knewstubs. Some think a fifth moderate Puritan, Richard Field, was also present. The three-day conference was almost entirely amicable; only Bishop Bancroft kept losing his cool and had to be whipped back into line by the king. James did once see red, when Reynolds used the word "presbyter" (it reminded James of his exhausting struggles with the Presbyterian party in Scotland), but the royal wrath lasted only a moment. By the end of the conference, the king had agreed to a list of moderate requests for Anglican reform.

It seems pointless describing these reforms, since none of them actually happened. The reason was the death of Archbishop Whitgift in February, only a month after the conference—and his replacement at James' command by Bancroft. With Richard Bancroft as Archbishop of Canterbury, there would never be any reforms, moderate or not; he was the most uncompromising opponent of all things Puritan in the entire Episcopal hierarchy. James himself was too lazy over tedious matters of administration to chase up Bancroft to enact what the conference had decided. So nothing happened. Once again, the Puritans were left empty-handed. Worse, Bancroft immediately imposed a new set of canons on all clergy, requiring them to affirm in the most unqualified terms their acceptance of the doctrine, worship, and government of the Anglican Church; some hundred Puritans were deposed or driven into exile for refusing.

2. The King James Bible

James did, however, vigorously pursue one suggestion that emerged unexpectedly from the Hampton Court conference—a suggestion for a new Bible translation. There is debate about

the source of this suggestion. Some think it came from John
Reynolds. However, it was no part of the Millenary Petition.
William Barlow, our only first-hand witness to the conference,
does say that Reynolds *personally* suggested the idea of a new
translation, which may seem conclusive. On the other hand,
Barlow's account is very biased to the Episcopalian side; and
since the Episcopal leader, Bancroft, was opposed to any new
translation (on the grounds that it might be hijacked by Puritans
to smuggle in their pet notions), Barlow may have deliberately
ascribed the suggestion to a Puritan like Reynolds in order to
smear the whole idea of a new Bible.

The official translators' preface to the new version gives a very
different account: it says quite explicitly that King James himself
came up with the idea. This latter opinion is not necessarily
mere flattery; ideas for a new Bible translation had been afloat
in Scotland for several years, prior to James gaining the English
crown. At any rate, whoever originated the suggestion, James
certainly seized on it with ardour. Perhaps he realized that
here was a way to immortalize his name in Christendom, with
Puritan cooperation (many Puritans did indeed favour a new
translation) and without having to change anything in the
government or worship of the Anglican Church.

Up until this point, far and away the most popular English
Bible was the Geneva Bible. Translated by English Protestant
exiles in Geneva during Mary Tudor's reign, the Geneva New
Testament appeared in 1557, the complete Bible in 1560. It was
not favoured by the Anglican establishment on account of its
strongly Puritan, even Presbyterian apparatus of marginal notes.
The preferred translation on the part of the Episcopal hierarchy
was the Bishops' Bible of 1568, enforced by convocation, the
Anglican clerical governing body, in 1571. However, it was the
Geneva Bible that caught the popular imagination. The Geneva
Bible was the Bible of William Shakespeare, England's master
poet, and it was emphatically the Bible of English Puritans of
all types throughout the 16th century. Between 1560 and 1611,
it went through 60 editions. Even after the new translation
sponsored by King James appeared in 1611, the Geneva Bible

remained popular for another half-century; there were 10 more editions. John Milton, England's "second" poet, was still using Geneva (alongside other translations, including the King James Bible) in the middle decades of the 17th century.

James, then, backed the project for a new translation. He personally appointed 47 scholars, who met in various committees in Oxford, Cambridge, and Westminster over a three year period (1607–10). These scholars were not from any single school of thought; James was more concerned, it would seem, about their scholarship than their theology. Some of the translators were establishment Anglicans, strongly opposed to all brands of Puritanism, critical even of Calvinism, such as Lancelot Andrewes, William Barlow, John Overall, and Richard Thomson. Some were Calvinists but not Puritans, such as George Abbott, Samuel Ward, and Daniel Featley. Some were moderate Puritans, such as John Reynolds, Laurence Chaderton, and Thomas Sparke (who had all attended the Hampton Court conference). The King James Bible therefore represented no particular theology, only a broad and general Anglican-style Protestantism.[2]

The completed translation was published in 1611. It included the Apocrypha—the "extra" Old Testament books found in one copy or another of the Greek Old Testament (the Septuagint), but not in the Hebrew canon. All editions of the King James Bible contained the Apocrypha until 1666, when an edition was published without them. Thereafter, King James Bibles varied— some had the Apocrypha, some did not.

Although the King James Bible is often described as a new translation, and James himself thought of it in those terms, it should be pointed out that in fact the overwhelming bulk of its New Testament derives directly from William Tyndale's translation of 1526. Some 80% of the King James New Testament is simply Tyndale. As the King James Bible

---

2. I omit any discussion of the Greek text on which the King James Bible was based. Those interested in these matters can easily enough pursue the topic through an extensive literature.

supplanted the Geneva Bible in popular use (which it did some time in the second half of the 17th century), this meant that Tyndale's literary legacy was given a new and enduring lease of life.[3] No doubt this was not what James intended; but the eventual supremacy of the King James Bible, as the version used throughout the English-speaking Protestant world, and its profound long-term influence on the written and spoken word, meant that James had given Tyndale a place alongside Shakespeare as primary architect of the English language.

3. A Puritan classic, the first Baptists, and the Congregationalists in America

After the false dawn of the Hampton Court conference, Puritanism once again gave up its public attempts to reform the English Church, and concentrated its energies on preaching, pastoral work, and the writing of godly literature. One of its most influential literary expressions appeared around this time, *The Practice of Piety* (3rd edition 1613: the date of the 1st edition may have been 1611) by **Lewis Bayly** (d.1631). There is debate about Bayly's origins. He may have been Welsh, born at Carmarthen; others think he may have been Scottish. Educated at Oxford, he held various posts in the Anglican Church before becoming chaplain to James I's son, Prince Henry, in 1612, then to James himself in 1616. The same year James appointed him Bishop of Bangor (north-western Wales).

Bayly's fame, however, rests squarely on his *Practice of Piety*. The extent to which Bayly was actually a Puritan in any meaningful sense is perhaps debatable; he was accused of allowing Puritan clergy to function in his diocese without fully conforming to the Church's canons, e.g. regarding vestments, the sign of the cross in baptism, etc., although he denied these charges. He may therefore have been a spiritually-minded Anglican Calvinist rather than a Puritan. Bayly's book, however, was certainly embraced

---

3. Theories concerning why the King James Bible finally dislodged the Geneva Bible from popular usage are many and complex. I do not have space to explore them here.

by Puritans of all sorts as a classic of Christian spirituality. Its impact on Puritan piety was enormous. Endlessly reprinted, it was translated into many foreign languages; it had a peculiarly powerful appeal in the Dutch Republic, where it was the best-selling item in all Reformed literature. It was to gain a special place in English spiritual history as the book through which John Bunyan would one day be awakened to the reality of eternal things.[4]

Meanwhile, Separatism was continuing to lead its underground life in Jacobean England. In particular, there was an important Separatist gathering at Gainsborough in Lincolnshire, where we find a number of people who would be of crucial significance for the future of Separatism—*John Smyth* (c.1570–1612), *Thomas Helwys* (c.1575–c.1616), John Robinson, William Bradford, and William Brewster. The meeting became so large that it split into two for safety's sake, one group led by Smyth and Helwys, the other by Robinson, Bradford, and Brewster. Both groups emigrated to the Dutch Republic in search of liberty.

The Smyth-Helwys group arrived in Amsterdam in 1607. Here they made contact with some Mennonites, finding work and lodging with a Mennonite merchant, Jan Munter. The Mennonites were Anabaptists, having originated in the Radical Reformation of the 16th century.[5] Soon John Smyth concluded that the Mennonites were right about believers' baptism, and persuaded Helwys and the other Separatists of their group to follow his lead. Smyth then baptized himself in 1609, after which he baptized Helwys and the others, and they formed the first known English Baptist congregation. (The baptism was by pouring, not immersion.) Smyth, a Cambridge graduate, had therefore travelled from moderate Puritanism, through Congregational Separatism, to this Baptist destination: a not untypical path in the early 17th century. Further, Smyth's engagement with the Mennonites had also prompted him to

---

4. For Bunyan, see Chapter 4, section 1.6.

5. See *Volume 3: Renaissance and Reformation*, Chapter 5, section 1, under *Menno Simons and the Mennonites*.

reject Reformed views of sin and grace in favour of the more Semi-Pelagian views of Mennonites, notably their disbelief in original sin. This is why these first known English Baptists are often called "General Baptists", from their belief in a general or universal atonement made personally effective through human free will. It is striking that they developed these views in a land increasingly torn apart by the Arminian controversy, but Smyth's theology is basically Mennonite, not Arminian (Dutch Arminians did not deny original sin).

Smyth and Helwys soon disagreed over the theology of baptism. Smyth came to think that baptism could rightly be given only by those who had already been baptized (there had to be a historical succession of baptisms). He and some 20 others therefore left the English Baptist congregation and sought to join the Mennonites, although the Mennonites were suspicious, and Smyth died before they decided to accept the English applicants in 1615. Helwys and his group returned to England in 1611 and put down their roots in London's Spitalfield—the first known Baptist church on English soil. Their denial of original sin, however, kept them somewhat apart from other English General Baptists, who were to be mostly Arminian rather than Mennonite in inspiration. Helwys ended up in prison as a punishment for one of the most famous early Baptist tracts, *A Short Declaration of the Mystery of Iniquity* (1612). This was a vitriolic attack on Anglicanism, and a vigorous assertion (one of the first in English) of the principle of absolute liberty of conscience or religious toleration:

> Let them be heretics, Turks [Muslims], Jews, or whatsoever,
> it appertains not to the earthly power to punish them in the
> least measure.

This was anathema to almost all Christians of that time, when religious unity was thought essential to social harmony. Helwys died in prison, and Baptist leadership fell to John Murton (1585–c.1626).

The other body of Separatist exiles in the Dutch Republic, led by **John Robinson** (1575–1625), settled ultimately at

Leyden in 1609. Probably a Cambridge graduate, Robinson had been a Puritan-minded Anglican clergyman in Norwich until his Puritanism crossed the line into Separatism. Unlike the Smyth-Helwys group, Robinson's group of exiles never abandoned infant baptism or Calvinism. Nor were they troubled by internal quarrels, uniquely among the Dutch Republic's various English expatriate congregations—a fact largely due to Robinson's abilities as a peace-loving pastor. In 1620, part of Robinson's church, under the leadership of **William Bradford** (1590–1657) and William Brewster (c.1560–1643), emigrated to North America. They were motivated by economic hardship in the Dutch Republic, fear of the consequences of the Thirty Years' War[6], and anxiety for their children, exposed on all sides to an alien culture with its fair share of temptations. Would it not be better to found their own political community in unspoilt territory? So, with Robinson's blessing, 28 adult members of the congregation and their children booked passage on an English ship, the Mayflower, which sailed from Plymouth in Devon on September 6th 1620. Robinson's "farewell address" to the emigrants has become justly famous. As reported by Edward Winslow (1595–1655), one of the emigrants, it reads:

> We are now ere long to part asunder [said Robinson], and the Lord knoweth whether ever he [Robinson] should live to see our faces again: but whether the Lord had appointed it or not, he charged us before God and His blessed Angels, to follow him no further then he followed Christ. And if God should reveal anything to us by any other instrument of His, to be as ready to receive it, as ever we were to receive any truth by his Ministry: For he was very confident the Lord had more truth and light yet to break forth out of His holy Word. He took occasion also miserably to bewail the state and condition of the reformed churches, who were come to a period [a full stop] in Religion, and would go no further than the instruments of their Reformation: As for example, the *Lutherans* they could not be drawn to go beyond what *Luther* saw, for whatever part

---

6. See Chapter 1, section 3.

of God's will He had further imparted and revealed to Calvin, they will rather die then embrace it. And so also, saith he, you see the Calvinists, they stick where he left them: A misery much to be lamented; For though they were precious shining lights in their times, yet God had not revealed His whole will to them: And were they now living, saith he, they would be as ready and willing to embrace further light, as that they had received. Here also he put us in mind of our Church-Covenant (at least that part of it) whereby we promise and covenant with God and one with another, to receive whatsoever light or truth shall be made known to us from His written Word: but withal exhorted us to take heed what we received for truth, and well to examine and compare, and weigh it with other Scriptures of truth, before we received it; For, saith he, It is not possible the Christian world should come so lately out of such thick Antichristian darkness, and that full perfection of knowledge should break forth at once.

Another thing he commended to us, was, that we should use all means to avoid and shake off the name of *Brownist*, being a mere nickname and brand to make Religion odious, and the professors of it [odious] to the Christian world; and to that end, said he, I should be glad if some godly Minister would go over with you, or come to you, before my coming; For, said he, there will be no difference between the unconformable [nonconformist] Ministers and you, when they come to the practice of the Ordinances out of the Kingdom: And so advised us by all means to endeavour to close with the godly party of the Kingdom of England, and rather to study union then division; *viz.* how near we might possibly, without sin close with them, then in the least measure to affect division or separation from them. And be not loath to take another Pastor or Teacher, saith he, for that flock that hath two shepherds is not endangered, but secured by it.

The Separatist emigrants had intended to create their new community in Virginia; they had been sponsored by English merchants of the Virginia Company, and had legal documents entitling them to live in the colony. (Virginia's Jamestown had existed as an English merchants' colony since 1607.) However, the Mayflower was blown off course and landed instead at Cape Cod in Massachusetts in early November. The emigrants decided to settle here. So the first Separatist community, at once political and religious, was founded in North America. The colonists are nicknamed "the Pilgrim Fathers". They called their colony Plymouth.

It should be noted that the Pilgrim Fathers were not the first English settlers in North America, nor even the first settlers with a serious Christian faith. The Virginia colony of Jamestown, founded 13 years earlier, may have been primarily mercantile, but it took religion very seriously. The Virginia colonists were Anglicans with some Puritan leanings, probably shown in their ultra-strict Sabbath laws. It is true, however, that the second English colony, at Plymouth, was (unlike Jamestown) founded from a specifically religious motive. In the terminology adopted by this book, it was a colony of Separatists rather than Puritans. Plymouth prospered, and William Bradford wrote what would be a famous account of its early trials and triumphs, *Of Plymouth Plantation* (Bradford's journal from 1620 to 1647). Within several decades, there were three more "religious" colonies—Massachusetts, New Haven, and Connecticut, settled by English Puritans who had taken the plunge into Separatism.[7] It has been estimated that something like 20,000 such emigrants arrived on North America's east coast in the "Great Migration" of 1630–40, to escape from an Anglican Church they found increasingly distasteful. Here were the origins of "New England"—the Puritan east coast colonies of America that were to have so formative an influence on the embryonic new nation across the Atlantic.

4. Lancelot Andrewes and High Church Anglicanism

The Jacobean period saw the origin of a "High Church" tradition within Anglicanism. The chief inspiration for this was *Lancelot*

---

7. New Haven was merged with Connecticut in 1664, and Plymouth was amalgamated with Massachusetts in 1691.

Andrewes (1555–1626), one of the most famous preachers and learned theologians of the day. Born at Barking (originally in Essex, now in Greater London), Andrewes studied at Pembroke College, Cambridge, becoming fluent in 15 languages. He did not rise very far under Queen Elizabeth, owing to his sacred conviction that the Church did not exist merely to feed finance to the monarchy (Elizabeth offered him two bishoprics on condition that he divert a good part of the income to her— he turned her down). However, King James, always smitten by erudition, gave Andrewes swift and high promotion. He became Bishop of Chichester in 1605, Bishop of Ely in 1609, and Bishop of Winchester in 1619.

Andrewes seems in his younger days to have moved in Puritan circles; indeed, he never relinquished a Puritan sabbatarianism, to the embarrassment of some of his anti-Puritan disciples. In his maturity, however, he became sceptical about the Calvinist theology that predominated in the Anglicanism of his times, especially its preoccupation with predestination; he thought it pried irreverently into the mystery of God's eternal purposes. Andrewes' theological alternative was to come "down to earth", from God's high decrees to an Episcopal, sacramental Church, where grace was communicated almost physically, chiefly through the eucharist. Bishops were essential, Andrewes taught, to the existence of the Church: they were the successors of the apostles. In this Church-of-the-bishops, the altar rather than the pulpit was the architectural and spiritual focal point. Andrewes held a far more robust view of the centrality of the eucharist in worship, and of the real eucharistic presence of Christ's body and blood, than either Calvinists or even Lutherans. He also expressed a view of the eucharist that used strongly sacrificial language; rejecting any idea of a fresh sacrifice, or Christ being re-sacrificed, he nonetheless taught with emphasis and eloquence that Christ's one perfect sacrifice was made mysteriously present in the eucharist, so that its blessings flowed forth upon the worshiper.

To give sensory emphasis to this theology, Andrewes restored some of the ancient eucharistic ceremonial in his chapel—altar-lights and incense, and the patristic "mixed chalice" (wine mixed with water). He further sought self-consciously to root Christian doctrine in the teachings of the early Church fathers, notably the Eastern fathers, rather than the teachings of the great Reformed divines of the 16th and 17th centuries. He was prepared to acknowledge that there was still much Christian good in Roman Catholicism, despite its admitted corruptions that had made the Reformation a necessity. In all this, we see the themes that went into the making of "High Church" Anglicanism.

None of this meant that Andrewes under-valued preaching. It was for his own preaching that he became famous. After his death, a collection of 96 sermons was published in 1629. The 20th century literary critic T.S.Eliot ranked these among the best English prose the 17th century had to offer. But far more influential were his *Private Prayers*, written mainly in Greek and Latin, and translated in full into English in 1675. They have transcended the boundaries of Andrewes' High Church outlook to become a universal Christian favourite.

Others who helped form the fledgling High Church movement included Richard Montagu (1577–1641), Bishop of Chichester and Ely; Richard Neile (1562–1640), Bishop of Durham and Archbishop of York; Augustine Lindsell (d.1634), Bishop of Hereford; Thomas Jackson (1579–1632), president of Corpus Christi College, Oxford University; and *John Cosin* (1594–1672), prebendary of Durham cathedral, all of whom had felt the influence of Andrewes. The movement would come to occupy the Church's centre stage under James' son, Charles I, and his Archbishop of Canterbury, William Laud.

5
Charles I and the English Civil War[1]

1. The accession of Charles I

When **Charles I** (1625–49) succeeded to the throne on his father James' death in 1625, he brought with him two ingredients for a colossal explosion in English society: a hostility to parliaments and a hostility to Calvinism. On the first point, Charles had inherited from James a belief in the "divine right of kings": the view that monarchs are accountable only to God, not to their subjects as represented in any kind of parliament. James, however, had at least realized the practical value of cooperating with the English parliament. Charles did not, and soon gave up the attempt. From 1629 to 1640, he ruled without summoning any parliament, by methods his opponents found unlawful or destructive of the English constitution. They would refer to this period as "the Eleven Years' Tyranny". Modern historians more impartially call it the period of his personal rule.

Perhaps it would not have mattered so much, had Charles not used those same years energetically to advance the High Church movement within the English national Church. This was more than the usual monarchical assault on Puritanism. It was a much wider assault on the Reformed faith, which had a broad base of

---

1. The English Civil War was one aspect of a larger conflict, engulfing Scotland and Ireland too. The wider conflict is known today as "The War of the Three Kingdoms".

support among Anglican clergy and laity extending far beyond the boundaries of Puritanism. To many, it looked as though Charles was assaulting Protestantism itself: undermining or even undoing the work of the English Reformation. This ignited against him a religious passion which, combined with his inability to work with the English ruling classes represented in parliament, would finally topple him from the throne.

2. High Church Arminianism and Archbishop Laud

Charles' High Church beliefs were sincere, not a tool to achieve political ends. He admired High Church divines like Richard Montagu and John Cosin for their scholarship and devotion to the Church of England. The High Churchman with whom Charles forged the closest and most fateful bond, however, was **William Laud** (1573–1645). Born at Reading in Berkshire, and educated at Saint John's College, Oxford, Laud's career in the Anglican Church overflowed with variety: president of Saint John's College (1611); Dean of Gloucester (1616); Bishop of Saint Davids (1621), of Bath and Wells (1626), and of London (1628); and finally Archbishop of Canterbury in 1633.

Through all of this, Laud was guided by a sense of mission to conform Anglicanism to High Church ideals. Once he had obtained power at the heart of England's political and religious establishment, as Bishop of London and then Archbishop of Canterbury, he used all the legal machinery at his command to compel a reluctant Church to embrace his vision. Some of Laud's policies were offensive only to Puritans, such as enforcing the proper use of the Anglican Prayer Book in worship; no minister was henceforth to leave parts out, or add in parts of his own. Strict conformity or deposition—such was Laud's message to the Anglican clergy. The previous Archbishop of Canterbury, **George Abbot** (born 1562; archbishop 1611–33), had been strongly Reformed, and inclined to give his clergy latitude in how they observed the Prayer Book, as long as they preached soundly. But Abbot's Calvinism meant that he was in disgrace with King Charles, and had little or no influence any longer. Laud, as Bishop of London and the king's confidante, had far more power than Abbot, and was Charles' obvious choice to replace an impotent Abbot at Canterbury when he died in 1633.

Calvinist Abbot's disgrace showed that High Church theology had become permeated by an Arminian stance on salvation. There was no necessary link between the two. High Church views could be held alongside a strict Augustinian understanding of grace, as in the Jansenists (see Chapter 6, section 4). On the other side, there was nothing High Church about the evangelical Arminianism of Jacob Arminius and his Dutch disciples (see Chapter 2, section 2). The combination, however, of High Church and Arminian doctrine proved a uniquely volatile mixture in 17th century England. Dutch Arminianism did undoubtedly have some influence on the English High Churchmen; for example, John Cosin, the erudite High Church prebendary of Durham cathedral, corresponded with the leading Dutch Arminian Hugo Grotius, and is known to have possessed some of Arminius' writings in his library. But Anglican Arminianism was rather different, wedded to the visible Church as the mystical vehicle of grace. In the thinking of Laud and his colleagues, the human will had to cooperate with the grace that flowed through the Episcopal hierarchy and its sacraments.

The High Church party, therefore, with their sacramental Arminianism, did not perceive Puritanism alone as an enemy, but all forms of Calvinism, no matter how conformist it might be in matters of church government and worship. The whole Reformed idea of the bondage of the will and the sovereignty of grace, something far wider than Puritanism, was deemed dangerous by Archbishop Laud and his High Church Arminian confederates. It was under the Laudian regime that all Calvinists began to be labeled "Puritan"—a gross distortion of all previous Elizabethan and Jacobean history. The Calvinist Bishop *John Davenant* (1572–1641) howled in protest:

> why that should now be esteemed Puritan doctrine, which those held who have done our Church the greatest service in beating down Puritanism, or why men should be restrained

from teaching that doctrine hereafter, which hitherto has been generally and publicly maintained, wiser men perhaps may but I cannot understand.

Davenant had good reason to be disgruntled. Laud's policy was only too successful in putting High Church Arminians in power throughout the Anglican establishment, to the detriment of Calvinism. In the words of a popular joke of the time, "Question: what do the Arminians hold? Answer: all the best bishoprics and deaneries in England!"

There were other aspects of Laud's High Church ideals which offended not merely Puritans and Calvinists, but the great majority of Anglicans, who had no zeal for Puritanism, and perhaps no great theological understanding of Calvinism, but who understood themselves and their Church to be Protestant. Anti-Catholicism had entered very deeply into the English soul after several generations of non-stop government propaganda. So when Laud began enforcing changes in the Church that seemed fundamentally at odds with Protestantism, the sense of outrage spread vastly beyond the Puritan constituency. Two of these changes were especially controversial.

First, the communion table was transformed into an altar. This was part of Laud's wider campaign to repair the fabric and restore the beauty of English churches. But this particular architectural act was charged with a contentious theology. Laud ordered all churches to put their communion tables at the east end of the building and rail them off. The east end of a church had symbolic significance in medieval Christianity: the sun rises in the east, so the east end was associated with Christ's second coming. For this reason the medieval altar was traditionally located at a church's east end. At the Reformation, Anglican altars were generally destroyed and replaced with tables in the nave (the central part of the church). Moving the communion table back to its medieval position at the east end seemed ominous in Protestant eyes: was this an attempt to drag the English Church back into the Middle Ages spiritually and doctrinally? Laud further decreed that worshipers must come up to the altar rails to receive holy communion there in a kneeling posture. When he was Dean of Gloucester cathedral, he required all who entered the cathedral to bow to the altar. Such practices were unknown in the reformed Anglican Church; to the popular mind, they meant simply transubstantiation, the mass, Romanism. And if this was the archbishop's outlook, the king must surely agree with it. So the anxiety and hostility aroused by Laud spilled over to envelop Charles as well.

Second, Laud took draconian measures to silence any preaching he did not like (mostly Calvinist). Here he was not only fully supported by Charles, he followed the king's own lead. As early as 1626, Charles had on his own authority, as supreme governor of the English Church, forbidden all preachers to discuss predestination in their sermons. When no less a person than John Davenant, Bishop of Salisbury, James I's chief representative at the Synod of Dort, disobeyed this injunction in 1630, he was summoned before the king's Privy Council and officially rebuked by the High Church Arminian Archbishop of York, Samuel Harsnett (1561–1631). Charles and Laud especially clamped down on "lecturers": that is, clergy unable to find a parish, but appointed as lecturers (preachers under another name) by voluntary subscriptions. Lay patrons of Puritanism had often used this method of finding employment for preachers who could not get a parish church, or who had been deprived by higher authority. In 1629, Charles imposed a new and severely restrictive law on lecturers that tied them closely to the Prayer Book and the disciplinary structures of the Episcopal hierarchy. It made it almost impossible for any lecturer with a Puritan conscience to function.

Archbishop Laud also suppressed an important Puritan organization, the "Feoffees for Impropriations". This group purchased "impropriations" (profits from the sale of church properties, which then became a sort of fund controlled by individual laymen or a corporation) and used them to buy "advowsons" (legal rights to appoint a minister to a particular position in the Anglican Church). The Feoffees of course made sure that Puritan ministers were appointed. The organization was hauled before the courts and dissolved in 1632; all its assets were seized by the crown.

When people saw this crackdown on Reformed preaching at the same time that Laud was turning communion tables into altars, many concluded that it was a conspiracy to undo the Reformation, and make clergy into sacrificing priests rather than teachers of Scripture. Preaching, we should remember, was enormously popular in that era; a good preacher could command the same enthusiasm and crowd-appeal that perhaps only pop stars and media celebrities can today. To silence so many "godly preachers" was to incense and provoke popular opinion, particularly in the cities, in a dangerous way.

High Church Arminians also forged a strong alliance, not just with King Charles personally, but with his view of absolute monarchy unchecked by parliaments or other institutions. One of the most outspoken High Churchmen, Richard Montagu, promised Charles, "defend me with the sword and I will defend you with my pen". This helps explain the political opposition to High Church Arminianism. Those committed to the role of parliament were almost bound to oppose the High Church party for its espousal of the king's absolutism.

The fear that Charles and Laud were Romanizing the English Church found apparent fuel in Charles' marriage in 1625 to a French Catholic princess, **Henrietta Maria** (1609–69), the sister of the French King Louis XIII. The marriage was political in intent: part of an Anglo-French phase in the foreign policy of the English government. However, it meant that Protestant England now had a Catholic queen, and that her Catholic servants and friends (including her father-confessor, the Scottish Catholic priest Robert Phillip) were tolerated in the English court. Henrietta Maria was passionate and flamboyant about her religion, scandalizing Protestant opinion by doing things like praying in public for the English Catholic martyrs—those whom the English government had executed since Elizabeth's reign for alleged treason. Ordinary people began calling

Henrietta Maria "Queen Mary", thereby linking her with Mary Tudor, the arch-persecutor of England's Protestants, who had reigned from 1553 to 1558. No doubt they also remembered the more recent "Gunpowder Plot" of 1605, when English Catholic conspirators (Guy Fawkes was the most famous) had planned to blow up King James, the House of Lords, and the House of Commons, at the opening of parliament on November 5th, and seize control of the country in the name of a restored Catholicism. The plot was of course foiled, but more than any other single event it helped create a national fear of Catholicism as violent and seditious. Most English Catholics were in fact perfectly loyal to England and its monarchy; but in Protestant eyes, bloodshot with fright, they became the dreaded terrorists of the day, always about to repeat the atrocities of Mary Tudor or November 5th.[2]

In retrospect, it is easy to see that King Charles and Archbishop Laud were heading for disaster. Yet monarch and bishop remained strangely blind. Neither man had any understanding of those who differed from them; both were narrow-minded pedants. Laud, however, was the greater offender, and attracted an extraordinary degree of popular hatred. It did not help that he often made himself and his cause seem both pompous and ridiculous. At one service of worship, the choir sang the anthem from Psalm 24:9, "Lift up your heads, ye gates, and lift up yourselves, ye everlasting doores, and the King of glorie shall come in"—at which point the church doors opened, and in bustled Laud. He was a little man, and King Charles' jester caught the public mood when he quipped, "Give great praise to God and little laud to the devil!"

During the eleven years of King Charles' personal rule, many High Church Arminians occupied bishoprics: there was Laud at Canterbury (1633 onwards), Richard Montagu at Chichester (1628) and then Norwich (1638), Richard Neile at York (1631), Francis White at Ely (1631), William Juxon at London (1633),

---

2. *November 5th* had the same resonance back then as *September 11th* does today.

and Matthew Wren at Hereford (1634), Norwich (1635), and then Ely (1638). It may be asked whether there were any Calvinist bishops, and if so, what they were doing. The answer is that there were certainly Calvinists in the Episcopate. In England we find John Davenant of Salisbury,[3] *Joseph Hall* (1574–1656) of Exeter (abidingly famous for his rich devotional writings, especially his *Contemplations*), and Thomas Morton (1564–1659) of Durham. Over in Ireland, at that time wholly governed by Britain, with the Irish national Church part of the Anglican system, there was the esteemed scholar-archbishop *James Ussher* (1581–1656) of Armagh (famous for dating the creation at 4004 BC), and William Bedell (1571–1642) of Kilmore. Perhaps oddly, however, these Calvinist bishops did nothing to oppose the High Church Arminianizing policies of Charles or Laud. Maybe they had been cowed into silence—we remember Davenant's reprimand for daring to preach on predestination. Maybe their reverence for monarchy made it hard for them to resist Charles. Whatever the reason, it would not be from the Calvinist bishops, but from a Calvinist House of Commons, that an effective challenge to Charles and Laud would finally come.

3. Manifestations of spiritual life: Donne, Herbert, and Sibbes

John Donne

John Donne (1573–1631) was one of England's greatest poets and preachers from any age. Born into a Catholic family (his mother was the sister of a Jesuit priest), he attended Hart Hall, Oxford University, followed by further studies, and entered the legal profession in the 1590s. Around this time Donne became deeply concerned about his religious loyalties, torn between the Catholicism of his youth and the Protestantism of his country. His immediate solution was to distance himself from both, and be a simple Christian. By 1598, however, his decision was made:

---

3. See above under *High Church Arminianism and archbishop Laud*, and Chapter 2, section 2.5.

he embraced Protestantism, and would ever after be a faithful member of the Anglican Church. That same year he became private secretary to Sir Thomas Egerton, the Lord Keeper (an important official, who had charge of the crown's great seal, with authority to affix it to public documents). However, Sir Thomas sacked Donne in 1602 for having secretly married his niece the previous year. Donne was actually thrown into prison for a brief spell, along with the minister who performed the marriage ceremony. Years of poverty and reliance on charity followed for Donne and his wife Anne, and their ever-growing family (10 children, eventually).

The turning point for Donne came with two anti-Catholic treatises he published in 1610 and 1611, which brought him to the attention of King James. The monarch exhorted him to enter the Anglican ministry, and after much hesitation and much persistent urging by James, Donne was finally ordained in 1615. In 1621 he was appointed Dean of Saint Paul's cathedral in London, and it was from the cathedral pulpit that he made his mark as a preacher, a popular favourite who also wove his spell over both King James and King Charles.[4]

Donne's literary fame rests on his poetry, his *Devotions* (1624), and his sermons. His poetry can be divided into secular love-poems (largely from his younger days) and religious poems (largely from his years of trouble and poverty). His *Holy Sonnets* and the *Hymn to God the Father* are generally regarded as the most brilliant of the religious poems. Donne is considered perhaps the foremost of a group of poets known as the "Metaphysical Poets". George Herbert (see below) was another. The term was coined by Dr. Samuel Johnson, author of the famous dictionary, in the next century. A characteristic feature of their style is the use of exaggerated and unusual metaphors known as conceits.

Donne's *Devotions* are a series of meditations and prayers on human frailty and mortality, the most famous of which—*Meditation*

---

4. Donne could just as well have been considered under the reign of James I. Since however his Christian fame flowed from his preaching at Saint Paul's, and he spent twice as long there under Charles I as under James, I have placed him in this section.

17—has become almost proverbial ("No man is an island.... Send not to know for whom the bell tolls: it tolls for thee").

Donne's sermons are less well-known today, but they give him a secure place in the literary history of English religion. We have 160 of the sermons, including 34 on selected Psalms, 16 on Matthew, and 16 on John. Donne did not cease to be a poet when he got into the pulpit, and his preaching exploited the English language to the limit of its resources, full of vivid imagery and arresting rhetoric. His chief theme was the overwhelming mercy of God toward sinners; Donne was always overshadowed by a sense of personal sin, and he preached to others what he needed to hear himself. His sermons caught fire whenever he spoke of the love of Christ for the lost; the cross was never far away. They also bristle with quotations from the early Church fathers, especially Augustine: Donne's passion was always blended with learning. Izaak Walton (see below under Richard Sibbes) has left us a graphic portrait of Donne the preacher:

> ...preaching the Word so, as showed his own heart was possessed with those very thoughts and joys that he laboured to distil into others: a preacher in earnest; weeping sometimes *for* his auditory, sometimes *with* them; always preaching to himself, like an angel *from* a cloud, but *in* none; carrying some, as St. Paul was, to heaven in holy raptures, and enticing others by a sacred art and courtship to amend their lives: here picturing a Vice so as to make it ugly to those that practised it; and a Virtue so as to make it be beloved, even by those that loved it not; and all this with a most particular grace and an unexpressible addition of comeliness.

Donne was strongly opposed to Puritanism, but it is difficult to classify him as High Church. In most respects he was more "establishment Anglican" of a Richard Hooker type.

George Herbert

George Herbert (1593–1633) was another master-poet, but more obviously in the High Church mould. Born to the politically important Anglo-Welsh Herbert family in Montgomery, on the border between Wales and England, he was the younger brother of Lord Herbert of Cherbury (1582–1648). Lord Herbert was the founding father of Deism (a view that accepted God as Creator but denied the need for any supernatural revelation or intervention: hugely popular in the 18th century). Unlike his Deist brother, the younger Herbert developed into a devout Christian. Educated at Trinity College, Cambridge, the flowering of his faith came only after his attempt at a courtier's life failed through the death of his various patrons, including King James. Disenchanted with politics by 1625, Herbert's mind turned to spiritual things; he was especially impacted by his friend **Nicholas Ferrar** (1592–1637), founder of a religious commune at Little Gidding, near Huntingdon. This was the first Protestant attempt in England at creating a spiritual community that reflected something of the traditional monastic ethos, but without embracing celibacy—it was family-based. All community members learned a trade; bookbinding was their speciality, and they ran a school for local children. The commune enjoyed the favour of King Charles and Archbishop Laud, but was fiercely denounced by Puritans as "the Arminian nunnery", and deliberately destroyed by parliamentary soldiers during the Civil War.

Deeply influenced by Ferrar, Herbert now studied theology, was ordained, and in 1630 became minister at the parish of Bemerton in Wiltshire, virtually bullied into it by Laud who had to overcome Herbert's sense of unworthiness. By all accounts he was a model pastor, but died after only three years, aged 39. He left a widow, Jane Danvers, and a literary legacy of some of the finest Christian poetry in English. The poems were published after his death by Nicholas Ferrar. They have had a huge influence on subsequent poets of all religious persuasions, depicting the believer's relationship with God in imaginative and intimate yet chaste language. Their distinctive quality has been compared to the parables for a surface simplicity concealing depths of meaning, and a rich use of homely imagery to convey spiritual truth. It is difficult to say whether any of the individual poems have achieved particular fame, but perhaps *Love bade me welcome* would be a front-runner.[5]

---

5. Set to haunting music by John Tavener in 1985.

Richard Sibbes

Richard Sibbes (1577–1635), one of the most influential Puritans
of Charles I's reign before the Civil War, has probably the most
famous epitaph of any theologian or preacher. The epitaph was
written by **Izaak Walton** (1593–1683), who said of Sibbes:

> Of this blest man, let this just praise be given,
> Heaven was in him before he was in heaven.

Walton himself was no Puritan; an establishment Anglican, he
wrote what was in effect a series of "Anglican saints' lives", which
included Richard Hooker, John Donne, and George Herbert.
However, Walton's spiritual tastes were wide-ranging, and he
penned his famous epitaph for Sibbes on reading his treatise
The Returning Backslider (14 sermons on Hosea, published in
1639). Nor was Walton alone in his non-Puritan appreciation
of the Puritan divine. Sibbes' preaching and writings were
treasured by people from all schools of thought, for "the heavenly
Sibbes" radiated the reality of divine things to anyone remotely
receptive. Born at Tostock, Suffolk, he studied at Saint John's
College, one of Cambridge University's Puritan seminaries.
Sibbes experienced a decisive spiritual awakening under the
preaching of the Puritan **Paul Baynes** (c.1573–1617), successor
to William Perkins as preacher at Great Saint Andrews Church.
Sibbes' own pulpit fame (despite a stammer) came when he was
appointed preacher in 1617 to the legal community at Gray's
Inn, London, which he served for the rest of his life. He was
also Master of Saint Catherine's Hall, Cambridge, from 1626.

Although Sibbes was decidedly Puritan in sympathies, and
strongly opposed to Archbishop Laud, he always conformed to
the requirements of the Anglican Church, and had the respect of
Charles I, who appointed him to Holy Trinity Church, Cambridge,
in 1633 (while still retaining his post at Gray's Inn). His collected
writings filled seven volumes, and presented "practical Calvinism"
at its most winsome. Sibbes excelled at raising up the downcast;
his most famous tract in this vein was *The Bruised Reed and
Smoking Flax*, although *The Soul's Conflict with Itself* was perhaps
of equal power. Among those deeply influenced by Sibbes were his

contemporary, the illustrious Congregationalist minister Thomas Hooker, who founded the American colony of Connecticut in 1636, and the great English Puritan divines of the next generation, Thomas Goodwin and Richard Baxter. His influence continued to stream on, and the 19th century testimony of C.H.Spurgeon summed up what multitudes have found in Sibbes:

> Sibbes never wastes the student's time; he scatters pearls and diamonds with both hands. Manton [another Puritan] says of Sibbes, that he had a peculiar gift in unfolding the great mysteries of the Gospel in a sweet and mellifluous manner, and therefore he was by his hearers usually termed the Sweet Dropper, "sweet and heavenly distillations usually dropping from him with such a native elegance as is not easily to be imitated."

4. The first Calvinistic Baptists

The first English Baptists, as we have seen, had abandoned Reformed theology. In the 1630s, however, a momentous step was taken by some London Puritans in renouncing infant baptism but retaining the rest of their Puritan-Calvinist theology and spirituality. The place where this threshold was crossed was a semi-Separatist fellowship in Southwark, gathered by **Henry Jacob** (1536–1624). Jacob had begun as a Puritan-minded Anglican minister who signed the Millenary Petition in 1603. His concerns over an unreformed Anglicanism, however, led him to express moderately critical views in 1605 in his tract *Reasons Taken out of God's Word*, for which he was thrown in prison. On his release he went into exile in the Dutch Republic, pastoring a Separatist church in Leyden. Jacob was the mildest of Separatists; he held that there were true churches (faithful congregations) within Anglicanism, but that the overall system was unscriptural. Hence the label "semi-Separatist" that has been applied to Jacob.

Returning to England in 1616, he helped found the semi-Separatist congregation in Southwark. It often goes under the name of the "JLJ church", after the initials of its first three pastors—Henry Jacob, John Lathrop (or Lothrop/Lothropp), and Henry Jessey. The church was not part of the Anglican establishment, but it allowed its members to attend Anglican services, e.g. to have their children baptized, and continued to recognize some Anglican congregations as true churches. There is some obscurity about the details, but it seems that in 1633 a group of 17, led by Samuel Eaton (d.1639), withdrew from the JLJ church—amicably—in order to form a Baptist congregation. Or at least, it was a congregation of believers baptized on profession of faith: we cannot be absolutely sure whether they rejected all infant baptism, or only Anglican baptism. However, it is certain that six more members of the JLJ church withdrew in 1638 specifically because they had embraced believers' baptism. Contemporary sources say they joined a church led by **John Spilsbury** (c.1593–1668), who was probably now in charge of the 1633 group.[6]

So by 1638 at the latest, there was definitely a Calvinistic Baptist church in London. It was to be the first of many. They are often called "Particular Baptists", because of their Reformed convictions about particular redemption (Christ died not merely to make salvation generally available, but with a "particular" intent to save His elect efficaciously). By 1644, there were seven Calvinistic Baptist congregations in London, and that year they published a confession of faith, in which they distinguished themselves from the Continental Anabaptists (like the Mennonites) and the Arminian Baptists (see section 4.3). It was the Calvinistic Baptists who spearheaded the practice of baptism by immersion; this happened among some Calvinistic Baptists connected with the JLJ church in 1640–41.

5. By the sword divided: the Civil War and its consequences

The circumstances that ended Charles' 11 years of personal rule are described in detail in Chapter 5. The Covenanter movement in Scotland destroyed Charles' authority over his northern

---

6. Either that or he had somehow founded a distinct group: it is difficult to be dogmatic.

kingdom; when the Covenanters invaded England and occupied Newcastle and Durham, Charles was forced to summon an English parliament. Not only did he need money and resources to deal with the northern crisis, which he could only get through parliamentary cooperation, but the Covenanters themselves had also stipulated that they would accept no treaty from Charles unless it was ratified by an English parliament. The first of these parliaments, the Short Parliament, met for a mere three weeks (April-May 1640) before Charles dissolved it again for its rebellious mood. But it was no good; the king could do nothing to solve the crisis without parliamentary help. In November 1640, the Long Parliament met—the longest in English history to that point, since it was not officially dissolved until 20 years later.[7]

Charles once again found parliament in a rebellious state of mind. The vast majority of MPs had no wish to discuss the Scottish crisis. Indeed, some of the foremost MPs had been in correspondence with the Covenanters, treating them as allies against Charles. What the MPs wanted to do was make it impossible for Charles or any king ever to rule again without parliament. So constitutional reform dominated the agenda. A humiliated Charles had to watch parliament strip away his prerogatives one by one: for instance, the Trienniel Act of February 1641 legislated that a parliament had to be summoned every three years, rather than whenever the monarch wished it. At this early stage, there was no division of opinion among MPs into "royalist" and "parliamentarian". The most melodramatic act of the united parliament was to put Charles' chief minister, **Thomas Wentworth**, Earl of Strafford (1593–1641) on trial—with parliament itself serving as the court. Strafford had effectively and ruthlessly enforced the king's will in Ireland; parliamentarians feared he might do the same in

---

7. The Cavalier Parliament of 1661–79 was in reality even longer, since it did not suffer from the military coup that purged the Long Parliament to a "rump" of republican MPs in 1648, and the lengthy interruption that suspended this parliament entirely between 1653 and 1659.

England, perhaps using Irish troops. Charles had promised Strafford absolute loyalty, but when the London mob rioted, crying for Strafford's blood, the king relented, fearing for his family. He signed the parliamentary death warrant for his great minister, who was duly executed on May 12th 1641. The earl's execution was to haunt both sides in the conflict. Charles could never shake off a sense of guilt for having thrown Strafford to the wolves. Parliament, for its part, had "played dirty", by denying Strafford a proper trial and simply voting him to death. (They were terrified he would be acquitted by a lawful trial.)

Archbishop Laud was also arrested, but left languishing in prison for several years. Few shed any tears for him. In 1645, parliament finally disposed of him as it had disposed of Strafford—voted him to the chopping block without a proper trial. It is difficult to see what crime worthy of death the 72 year old archbishop had committed, but the London mob hated him with a passion and would not see him spared. Laud managed to die with dignity, and High Churchmen regarded him as a martyr to Puritan fanaticism.

Once the MPs had cut their king down to size with political reforms, their unity vanished. Religion now came to the fore, and the House of Commons divided more-or-less along the old fault-line of Puritan reformer versus Anglican establishment. By now, Puritanism of one sort or another had managed to win the allegiance of a solid proportion of England's lawyers and country gentleman (those who sat as MPs). Most of the Puritan-minded MPs favoured some sort of Presbyterian or quasi-Presbyterian system of church government, possibly with bishops who would be little more than superintendents of different regions rather than glorified royal servants. It seems plausible that a good number of the staunchly Protestant ruling class had been driven into a more Puritan stance as a reaction against the High Church policies of Charles and Archbishop Laud. They may have felt that the only way to preserve the Protestant character of the English Church was by taking it out of the hands of king and bishops, and putting it under parliamentary control, in alliance with the "godly brotherhood" of Puritan preachers, who had always looked to parliament and exalted it as the best hope of further reformation.

However, many MPs had a sincere attachment to the Anglican Prayer Book, to which Puritans were hostile, and these "Prayer Book" MPs were not prepared to see Archbishop Cranmer's rich and exalted prose replaced by some humdrum Reformed liturgy like Scotland's Book of Common Order. With the harmony of parliament breaking down, Charles began cultivating the support of the Anglican traditionalists. It became increasingly clear to them that their only real guarantee for the worship they prized was an alliance with the king. Hardly any of these MPs wanted to give Charles back the political power they had taken from him; they were, in that sense, still parliamentarians. However, they were ready to stand with the king in a common religious front, defending a more historic Anglicanism against the experiments proposed by Puritan reformers.

Civil war probably became unavoidable in October 1641 because of a massive Catholic insurgency in Ireland. At that point in its history, Ireland was a largely Catholic nation ruled by a British Protestant establishment. King Charles had already been dabbling with ideas of raising a royalist Catholic army to subdue his rebellious English and Scottish kingdoms. This in turn had prompted English parliamentarians and Scottish Covenanters to start talking about invading Ireland, and crushing its Catholics even more thoroughly. Panic swept through the ranks of Irish Catholic landowners, who planned a pre-emptive uprising. Led by Irish Catholic noble Phelim O'Neill (d.1653), the insurgency quickly turned into a popular revolt of apocalyptic dimensions, as the Catholic peasantry vented their long pent-up wrath on their Protestant rulers. Historians argue about the numbers of Protestants killed; a modest estimate accepted by many modern scholars puts the figure at 12,000.

A counter-panic now swept through England. People trembled at the thought of hordes of murdering Catholics crossing the Irish Sea and rampaging through the English counties. Clearly an English army had to be raised to suppress the Irish insurgency. But who should control this army? Traditionally that right belonged to the king; the parliamentarian

MPs, however, were in no mood to trust Charles with an army. He might use it against *them*. So they demanded control of the army: a revolutionary act that had no precedent in the English constitution or English history. This helped deepen the divide in the House of Commons, as royalist MPs began to perceive the parliamentarian opposition as lawless radicals who would stop at nothing to overthrow their country's traditions and erect their own power on its ruins.

To shore up crumbling support for his cause, the parliamentarian leader *John Pym* (1584–1643), devout Puritan MP for Tavistock, Devon, submitted a "Grand Remonstrance" to the House of Commons on November 22nd 1641. The Remonstrance detailed all the alleged failings of Charles' regime since he came to the throne, and set out by contrast the parliamentary reforms achieved in the past year. It proposed two positive measures: to set up an assembly of theologians to help parliament reform the Church, and to make the king's choice of ministers subject to parliamentary control. Pym's strategy was to win support for the revolutionary part of his programme (the second positive proposal) by wrapping it up in an eloquent reminder of Charles' untrustworthiness, and the possibility that all parliament's recent reforms could be undone if so unreliable a king were given personal charge of an army.

The Grand Remonstrance provoked a fiercely heated debate that went on well into the small hours of the following day. Finally, the MPs voted for the Remonstrance by a wafer-thin margin: 159 votes for, 148 against. Royalist MPs made an attempt to protest at the vote's outcome, but a shouting match developed and swords were almost drawn. Even then there was a slim chance that a civil war could be averted; but all was shipwrecked on January 4th 1642, when Charles burst into the House of Commons, with 400 armed men at his back, to arrest the five MPs he regarded as leaders of the parliamentarian faction.[8] This invasion of the Commons by the king was a breath-taking violation of parliament's time-honoured

8. John Pym, John Hampden, Denzil Holles, Sir Arthur Haslerig, and William Strode.

privileges. Now it seemed to be Charles who was trampling on the constitution and acting as a lawless revolutionary. Fortunately for the five MPs, the royal plot had been leaked, and they were already in hiding. Charles left empty-handed. London was now seething with hostility to him, and within a week the king had departed, leaving the capital in the hands of a rejoicing citizen-body that was wildly parliamentarian. Charles would not see London again until he was brought back a prisoner to be tried and executed seven years later.

It is not for us to follow the twists and turns of politics over the next six months which ended with the king "raising his standard" at Nottingham in August—in effect, declaring war on parliament. By then, the royalist MPs had deserted the House of Commons, and set up their own parliament in Oxford. The London parliament, meanwhile, had appointed a "Committee of Safety" to supervise the conflict with Charles, set about raising a parliamentary army, and commissioned Robert Devereux, Earl of Essex (1591–1646), as their troop commander. Parliamentarians began nicknaming royalists "Cavaliers", which meant something like swaggering, licentious bullies (literally it merely means horsemen). However, royalists redefined the word to mean a brave man of honour, loyal to the king for conscientious reasons. The royalist nickname for parliamentarians was "Roundheads". Some have thought this referred to a Puritan male habit of cutting the hair short, but this is not borne out by the evidence of portraits; many Puritans evidently had long hair. It seems more likely that it derived from the London apprentices, who made up a large proportion of the parliamentarian mob that terrorized royalists in the capital. Apprentices typically had close-cropped hair.

The first major battle of the English Civil War was fought at Edgehill in Warwickshire on October 23rd 1642. We will not, however, describe the military progress of the war except when it impacted on, or illustrates, religious events.

6. *The Westminster Assembly and its work*
The assembly of theologians to help parliament reform the Church, proposed in the Grand Remonstrance, began regular

meetings in July 1643. Parliament selected two theologians each from Oxford and Cambridge universities, four from London, two from each English county, one from each Welsh county, and thirteen others. This was the celebrated Westminster Assembly (named from the Jerusalem Chamber of Westminster Abbey, where they met). King Charles sternly forbade anyone to attend, which deterred most Episcopalian Anglicans from taking part. However, the contemporary royalist historian Edward Hyde, Earl of Clarendon, tells us that 20 of the Westminster divines had Episcopalian sentiments. We know that parliament summoned nine Episcopalian divines as delegates, including Archbishop James Ussher who was highly esteemed as a Reformed theologian (he refused to attend). This is significant; it shows that parliament was trying to construct a broad-based Assembly, not one committed in advance to dogmatic Presbyterianism.

The Assembly's chairman was William Twisse (1578–1646), a moderate who wished to see a reformed, downsized Episcopacy, although his doctrinal Calvinism was of the highest kind (a supralapsarian). Twisse's physical frailty meant that his vice-chairman, the distinguished Presbyterian preacher **Cornelius Burges** (or Burgess) (c.1589–1665), often stood in for him. The Assembly gained a new dimension when it was joined by a delegation of Covenanter theologians—Alexander Henderson, Samuel Rutherford, George Gillespie, and Robert Baillie—who arrived in September.

The arrival of the Scottish divines flowed from a new military alliance between parliament and the Covenanters, formalized in the Solemn League and Covenant, which was signed on September 25th 1643. The Civil War had been going badly for the parliamentarians; the last act of their dying leader, John Pym, was to turn the tide of conflict back in their favour by drawing the Covenanters onto the battlefield on parliament's side. Pym succeeded completely; the presence of a Covenanting army on English soil, fighting alongside parliament's forces, proved an irresistible combination that would shatter King Charles and his cause. The Solemn League and Covenant also had a religious aspect, as we will see in Chapter 5; it bound the Scots and English together to embrace uniformity of doctrine and church government, "according to the Word of God and the example of the best Reformed Churches". The Scots trusted that this meant Presbyterianism in church government, but it turned out that the English were not so sure.

The Westminster Assembly was a gathering of glittering theological talent. Richard Baxter, who was not a member, and possessed a theologically independent mind unlikely to grovel before anyone or anything, said of the Assembly:

> The divines there congregated were men of eminent learning, godliness, ministerial abilities, and fidelity; and being not worthy to be one of them myself, I may the more freely speak the truth, even in the face of malice and envy, that, as far as I am able to judge by the information of all history of that kind, and by any other evidences left us, the Christian world, since the days of the apostles, had never a synod of more excellent divines (taking one thing with another) than this and the Synod of Dort.

Not surprisingly, the documents the Assembly produced have enjoyed a widespread and enduring appreciation. These were its confession of faith (the Westminster Confession), its two catechisms (the Larger Catechism and Shorter Catechism), its handbook of worship (the Directory for the Public Worship of God), and to a lesser extent, its Form of Presbyterial Church Government.[9]

The Assembly was not theologically monolithic. It included Presbyterians, Independents, moderate Episcopalians, and Erastians (those who believed that ultimate ecclesiastical authority lay with the state).

The Presbyterians, who formed the majority, were themselves divided into a *ius divinum* (divine right) party, who held that Scripture prescribed a definite and detailed Presbyterian form of church government as binding for all time, and a *ius*

---

9. *Prebyterial* is a 17th century variant of Presbyterian.

humanum (human right) party, who held that Presbyterianism was generally agreeable to Scripture in principle, but that all kinds of details might vary according to need and circumstance. (The Westminster documents reflect the *ius divinum* view.)

The Independents were a distinct minority, some ten or twelve members, but what they lacked in quantity they made up for in theological sharpness, eloquence, and persistence. They exercised an influence far in excess of their numbers.

The moderate Episcopalians were also few in number and exercised little or no influence on the debates, partly through the sporadic nature of their attendance; the king's ban on the Assembly had deeply dampened their enthusiasm. The only Episcopalian member we know for sure attended regularly was Daniel Featley, Provost of London's Chelsea College, founded in 1609 to produce anti-Catholic polemics. He spoke up for Episcopacy at the Assembly, but eventually even Featley withdrew on the direct orders of King Charles.

The Erastians were an even smaller group of two—*Thomas Coleman* (1598–1647), and *John Lightfoot* (1602–75). Like the Independents, they compensated for their fewness by their formidable and vociferous erudition. The Erastian divines were strongly supported by the parliamentary lay delegates (20 from the House of Commons, 10 from the Lords), especially *John Selden* (1584–1654), MP for Oxford, a legal and theological scholar who was quite capable of trouncing the most learned divine in debate. Selden was also unusual in being an Arminian (of the evangelical rather than High Church variety).

There were other differences among Assembly members unrelated to church government. The Scottish delegate Robert Baillie, for instance, lamented the influence that Amyraut and Amyraldianism had on the English divines:

> Unhappily Amyraut's questions are brought in on our Assembly. Many more love their fancies here than I did expect... Amyraut's treatise goes in our Assembly from hand to hand.[10]

---

10. For Amyraut, see Chapter 2, section 3.

The Westminster Confession was the Assembly's greatest achievement. Completed in November 1646, it was a majestic monument to Reformed Orthodoxy (see Chapter 2, section 1), embracing its later characteristic framework of covenant theology. The Confession's chief source was the Irish Articles of 1615, a confession of faith drafted by Archbishop Ussher for Ireland's established Church; the Irish Articles were more fully and explicitly Reformed than the English Church's 39 Articles. The Westminster Confession largely follows the Irish Articles in the order of topics, the chapter headings, and the phraseology.

The Confession was adopted by the Covenanters as the Scottish Kirk's new confession by the general assembly in August 1647; among conservative Presbyterian Churches of Anglo-Scottish origin, the Westminster Confession retains its place today as their doctrinal standard, with slight modifications in some Churches. It failed, however, to function in England as the new confession for the established Church owing to the breakdown of parliament's authority (see below). Even so, the Confession's influence reached far outside its original Presbyterian constituency. In slightly modified form, it was adopted as the Savoy Declaration by the English Independents or Congregationalists at their gathering in the Savoy, London, in 1658. The Independents tightened the Confession's Reformed theology (e.g. by making a much clearer distinction between Christ's active and passive obedience than Westminster). They also added an entirely new appendix on Congregational church government.

The Westminster Confession was also adopted by the English Calvinistic Baptists, modified to teach their distinctive view of baptism and church government (and with some additions from their previous 1644 Confession). The Baptist Confession was first set forth in 1677, but is generally known as the 1689 Baptist Confession since in that year, at a meeting of 107 Calvinistic Baptist churches, their delegates affixed their names to the Confession. Both the Independents and Calvinistic Baptists stated that they embraced the Westminster Confession (albeit in slightly adapted form) to demonstrate their essential unity with their Reformed brethren on all the major issues of theology. Westminster therefore became an exercise in Reformed ecumenism.

The Directory for the Public Worship of God was constructed to give the widest latitude to all shades of Puritan and Covenanter opinion on worship. This was especially the case in the Directory's approach to prayer. It neither imposed nor prohibited liturgical prayer. Many Puritans were happy enough with the idea of a liturgy, but they did not wish to bind all ministers to one exclusive format. Others, notably Independents, were so opposed to all liturgical prayer that they rejected the Lord's Prayer itself as a sub-Christian relic of the Old Testament.[11] So the assembled divines produced guidelines for prayer, which a minister could fulfil either by using a regular liturgy, or by composing his own prayers. It should be noted, however, that no Puritan believed in "extemporary" prayer; the most ardent critics of liturgy insisted that all public prayer must be studiously prepared in advance. What they were contending for was the freedom of each individual minister to prepare his own prayers, instead of all ministers being compelled to use a single prayer-book. The leading Independent, Philip Nye, affirmed in a speech at the Assembly concerning liturgical and extemporary prayer, "I plead for neither, but for studied prayers." The rest of the Directory followed the same pattern: a set of guidelines for how any service of worship should be constructed

---

11. The foremost Independent John Owen rejected the Lord's Prayer thus: "Our Saviour at that time was minister of the Circumcision, and taught the doctrines of the gospel under and with the observation of all the worship of the Judaical Church. He was not yet glorified, and so the Spirit was not yet given... That, then, which the Lord Jesus prescribed unto his disciples, for their present practice in the worship of God, seems to have belonged unto the economy of the Old Testament." Works vol. 15, p. 14 (Edinburgh: Banner of Truth, 1965). This view, however, did not win its way in the Assembly, whose Directory positively commended the Lord's Prayer: "because the prayer which Christ taught his disciples is not only a pattern of prayer, but itself a most comprehensive prayer, we recommend it also to be used in the prayers of the churches."

and conducted, rather than a set of specific forms that had to be followed to the letter.

In addition to the Confession, the other documents of the Assembly—the Larger and Shorter Catechisms, the Directory for the Public Worship of God, and the Form of Presbyterial Church Government—were all adopted by the Scottish Kirk. The Directory replaced John Knox's liturgy. The Shorter Catechism was adopted well beyond the borders of Presbyterianism in modified form, e.g. as Keach's Catechism among the Calvinistic Baptists. Its opening answer became the most famous of any catechism: "Man's chief end is to glorify God and to enjoy Him for ever."[12]

The Assembly also undertook the work of providing a new translation of the psalter for congregational worship. There were already English psalters in use. The most popular was the Sternhold and Hopkins psalter (1562), generally bound with copies of the Anglican Prayer Book and the Geneva Bible. There was also the newer Bay Psalm Book (1640), produced by the American colonists of Puritan/Separatist outlook. The Assembly revised an existing psalter by the Congregationalist *Francis Rous* (1579–1659), MP for Truro in Devonshire; first published in 1638, it was Rous' second edition of 1643 that the Westminster Assembly worked on. The revised Rous was then revised again by the general assembly of the Scottish Kirk, and the result in 1650 was the version commonly called the Scottish metrical psalter.[13] Authorized by the general assembly, it became *the* Scottish psalter, soon hallowed by usage and the object of deep devotional affection that has endured to the present. It was, however, only one among several psalters utilized by the English and Americans. Sternhold and Hopkins, for example, continued in use until the end of the 18th century, while Americans sang from the Bay Psalm Book for a hundred years.

---

12. *Enjoy* here has the older sense of "share in", "experience", "receive the benefit of," as the proof-texts indicate.

13. Given its origins in Rous, maybe it should be called the Devonshire Congregationalist psalter.

6
The English Revolution: the world turned upside down

1. Parliament and its Army fall out

Although the alliance between parliamentarians and Covenanters had smashed King Charles' battalions on the field, at Marston Moor (July 1644) and Naseby (June 1645), it had not led to the desired parliamentary triumph. This was because a third force had emerged to challenge both king and parliament—the parliamentary army.

In the light of previous defeats and problems of strategic coordination, parliament had reorganized its infantry and cavalry into a more centralized, streamlined force in January 1645, known as the New Model Army. Through the "Self-Denying Ordinance", it had also dismissed all members of the House of Commons and the House of Lords from military command; this Army would be run by full-time professional soldiers. Its commander-in-chief was Sir Thomas Fairfax (1612–71), but the dominant figure was his second-in-command, the brilliant cavalry leader *Oliver Cromwell* (1599–1658). (He was in fact an MP in the Commons, but had been exempted from the Self-Denying Ordinance on account of his unique military genius.) Cromwell was a fervent Puritan of the Independent type; a spiritual crisis in his youth had been resolved by a dramatic conversion that he described thus:

> Blessed be His Name for shining on so dark a heart as mine!
> You know what my manner of life hath been. Oh, I lived

Oliver Cromwell (1599–1658)
Portrait by Robert Walker (1599–1658)
Used by permission from The Cromwell Museum, Huntingdon

> in and loved darkness, and hated light; I was a chief, the
> chief of sinners. This is true: I hated godliness, yet God
> had mercy on me.

Cromwell's conversion propelled him into the front rank of
Puritan laymen. Once the Long Parliament was in session, he was
from the start (as MP for Cambridge) a zealous partisan of John
Pym, joining the assault on King Charles' prerogatives and the
Episcopal structures of the Anglican Church. When the Grand
Remonstrance was debated in November 1641, and passed by a
whisker, Cromwell commented, "If the Remonstrance had been
rejected, I would have sold all I had the next morning, and never
seen England more."

Politically passionate as he was, the driving force in
Cromwell's life and personality was his religion. It had a strong
vein of mysticism in it; he felt himself to be in immediate contact
with God, and sought guidance that often came in the shape of
extraordinary providences. Once the Civil War broke out, he not
only discovered a dazzling talent for cavalry warfare, but also an
exhilaration on the battlefield that made his victories, and the
men who won them, seem nothing less than embodiments of
God's will on earth. As he exclaimed amid his triumph at the
battle of Langport in July 1645, "To see this, is it not to see the
face of God?"

Cromwell's radical approach to military training undermined
parliament's control of its own troops. He insisted on recruiting
religiously and politically motivated soldiers, who would fight for
absolute victory without being hampered by the social respect
for aristocracy and monarchy that made others half-hearted in
attacking royalists on the battlefield. In consequence, Cromwell's
men (the backbone of the New Model Army) were largely
Independent and Baptist in religion—Presbyterians were more
socially conservative. Further, the New Model Army was no longer
really fighting for the same goal as its parliamentary masters. The
Presbyterian-dominated parliament wanted a single established
Church, Presbyterian in structure and theology, with no room
for dissent; all who refused to conform would be punished by the

"godly magistrate". The New Model Army soldiers, by contrast, were fighting for liberty of conscience: the freedom for all Protestants to practise their faith without interference or coercion by king, bishops, parliaments, or presbyters. Cromwell himself thoroughly sympathized with his men; he too was fighting for religious freedom. These ideals of liberty and toleration were most forthrightly expressed by the Separatist **Roger Williams** (c.1603–83), who had emigrated to America, but returned briefly to England in 1643 to get legal status for his new colony, Rhode Island. Horrified by the Presbyterian intolerance he discovered in parliament and the Westminster Assembly, Williams produced his classic treatise *The Bloody Tenent of Persecution for Cause of Conscience*, published in London in 1644.[14]

To most MPs, this was a recipe for anarchy, and Williams' book was burned in public. Presbyterians were scandalized by the variety of religious opinions that flourished in the Army: Independents, Baptists, Arminians, Antinomians, Fifth Monarchists, Seekers, Levellers, and (it seemed) everything between A and Z in the theological encyclopedia.[15] As Richard Baxter, then a military chaplain, commented of the Army:

> Independency and Anabaptism were most prevalent; Antinomianism and Arminianism equally distributed.

Independents and Baptists, then, were the most ardent supporters of religious toleration; Presbyterians shunned the very idea. So the opening gulf over freedom of worship roughly matched divisions over church government, which in turn roughly matched the Army-parliament divide. The New Model Army did have some allies in parliament—the so-called Independent MPs (not necessarily Congregationalists, but committed to a more politically and religiously radical agenda). But they were in a minority.

---

14. *Tenent* is 17th century for "tenet".

15. See below for Fifth Monarchists and Seekers. Levellers derived from the Bible what we would call a radically democratic philosophy of society and government.

Once the fighting was over in 1646, parliament tried to disband the New Model Army without giving the considerable amount of back-pay it owed the soldiers. The Army refused to disband, supported by its leaders, Fairfax and Cromwell, who were indignant at the shabby treatment they thought their battle-scarred men were getting. Parliament also debated a fierce Blasphemy Ordinance, which not only prescribed the death penalty for all who denied the Trinity or incarnation, but also life imprisonment for all who held to believers' baptism, Arminianism, antinomianism, soul-sleep, or anti-sabbatarianism, or rejected Presbyterian church government, or denied that the parish churches were true churches of Christ. (The Ordinance was actually enacted as law in May 1648.) Since all these views were widespread in the Army, most of the soldiers would have ended up dead or in prison. With parliament so hostile to religious liberty, it looked as though Cromwell's warriors had fought for nothing.

So a three-cornered power struggle now gripped England, as King Charles, the Presbyterian parliament, and the New Model Army all jockeyed for position. Charles had surrendered to the Scottish Covenanting army; but finding him stubbornly unwilling to sign the Covenants, they had eventually delivered him into the English parliament's custody in 1647 at Holmby House in Northamptonshire. The New Model Army, however, seized Charles to be their "guest". Charles exasperated everybody by playing off Army against parliament, making contradictory promises; he appears to have believed that under duress, a person might promise anything to anyone with no obligations. Ultimately, he betrayed both Army and parliament by entering into a secret agreement with a faction of the Covenanters; they invaded England in July 1648 to restore the king, who had promised to impose Presbyterianism on his southern kingdom for a three-year trial period.[16] The royalists also rose up in a series of insurgencies across England and Wales.

---

16. See Chapter 5, section 3.6, under *Division in the ranks*, for the Scottish situation, and the wrenching split among the Covenanters over the pro-Charles invasion of England.

The New Model Army proved superior to all these challenges. The various royalist risings were all crushed; Cromwell annihilated the Covenanter army in a three-day battle at Preston on 17th-19th August. Then Charles' day of reckoning came. The triumphant Army, burning with anger over the renewed slaughter, decided that the king must pay for all the blood that had been shed. The Presbyterian parliament, however, reopened negotiations with Charles. It was the last straw. The Army marched on London, and on December 6th purged parliament of all Presbyterian MPs. The military coup was known as "Pride's Purge", because Colonel Thomas Pride was in charge of the action. He stood at the top of the staircase leading into the House of Commons with a list of Presbyterian MPs; the radical aristocrat, Lord Grey of Groby (the Earl of Stamford's son), pointed out the MPs as they arrived, and Pride's troops arrested them. By the time Pride had done his work, 45 MPs were under arrest, and a further 96 had been excluded. The much reduced House of Commons now had only around 80 MPs, all Independents and in agreement with the Army's purposes. The remnant parliament earned the derisive nickname "the Rump". They proceeded towards the New Model Army's implacable goal: the execution of the king.

It should be noted that Cromwell played no part in this military coup. He was not in London when the purge began, but on the way there from the siege of Pontefract castle. The coup was not planned by Cromwell, but by the other Army officers and the Independent MPs. Still, Cromwell arrived on the night of the purge, and accepted what had happened. He now threw himself with all the force of his titanic personality behind the need to destroy, not just King Charles, but the Stuart monarchy itself: "I tell you, we will cut of his head with the crown upon it!"

2. The English Republic

The execution of Charles followed with almost indecent haste. It was, of course, quite illegal. There was no court that could try the monarch; the monarch was the very authority the courts represented, from whom they derived their existence and legitimacy. Besides, the court that tried Charles was not really a court at all, merely a group of men nominated by the Army and the Rump. Still, the Army radicals pressed ahead; they were determined that the king must die, partly for religious reasons. One colonel, the Calvinistic Baptist republican Edmund Ludlow (c.1617–92), quoted Numbers 35:33, "blood defiles the land: and the land cannot be cleansed of the blood that is shed therein, except by the blood of him that shed it." In other words, many held Charles guilty of the bloodshed that had "defiled the land", especially in the Second Civil War of 1648. He must die to atone for the defilement.

The decision to try the king in public, however, backfired badly. Charles may have been a disastrous king; he was a stunningly effective martyr. The affections of the London mob were captured by his calm, dignified bearing. Even his usual stammer had miraculously vanished. When he was beheaded on January 30th 1649, there were no cheers from the spectators, only a long, unearthly groan. Charles had virtually destroyed the monarchy by his politically imprudent life; by his heroic death, he sanctified it with the blood of royal martyrdom. The new regime would never recover from the blow the defeated king dealt it by dying so well on January 30th. It did not help the Rump or the Army that a mere 10 days after Charles' execution, a book entitled *Eikon Basilike* ("image of the king") was published, claiming to be Charles' own thoughts on his reign and his approaching martyrdom. The book was a deeply moving portrait of a suffering Christian king, and it was a runaway success, going through 36 editions in its first year. Scholars still debate the extent to which *Eikon Basilike* really was written by Charles. There can be no doubt it was a huge propaganda triumph for royalism.

Having disposed of Charles, the Rump now abolished both the monarchy and the House of Lords, and declared England a republic (for the first and last time in its history). The new English Republic, however, had many enemies. Royalists and Presbyterians alike denounced it at home; this royalist-Presbyterian axis would be responsible, 10 years later, for restoring the monarchy. Royalists denounced the Republic for obvious reasons; Presbyterians denounced it because they perceived the killing of Charles as a violation of the Solemn League and Covenant, which had pledged MPs and Army officers "to preserve and defend the king's majesty's person and authority".

English Royalists and Presbyterians did not, however, present a military threat. The Irish royalists and the Scottish Covenanters did. With awe-inspiring efficiency, the New Model Army dealt with both threats. Cromwell was now commander-in-chief of the Army since Sir Thomas Fairfax had resigned (he opposed Charles' execution). In Ireland, many English and Scottish settlers had united with native Catholics in rejecting the English Republic and proclaiming Charles' son, the Prince of Wales, king (the future Charles II). Cromwell utterly overwhelmed the Irish and beat them into abject submission in a campaign extending from August 1649 to May 1652. English Protestants were now the all-powerful masters of Ireland. Cromwell returned from Ireland in May 1650 to deal with the Scottish menace; his lieutenants completed the Irish conquest. The Scottish Covenanters had also proclaimed the Prince of Wales as their king. Over the next year, however, Cromwell shattered the Covenanters on the battlefield at Dunbar and Worcester, destroying their military and political power for ever. Scotland became an English province, governed by English soldiers and English judges.[17]

In 1653, Cromwell dissolved the Rump, indignant at its plans for perpetuating its power without meaningful elections. The last shreds of constitutional government were gone; the only real power left in the land was Cromwell and the Army. Cromwell ended up ruling Britain as the "Lord Protector" under a written constitution drawn up by the leading Army officers. Once again, we shall not tell the complex political story, but focus rather on religious developments in the 1650s. For in the aftermath of the Rump's Toleration Act of September 1650, which abolished any legal requirement to attend one's parish church, this was a period

---

17. See Chapter 5, section 3.7.

of unparalleled and intoxicating freedom in English history for people to experiment with religion.

3. Religion under Cromwell

We should begin, however, by reflecting that it was a grim time for traditional Anglicans. The parish structures of Anglicanism remained intact, but prior to Pride's Purge and the overthrow of the monarchy, the Long Parliament had set up religious committees that ejected something like 2,000 Anglican clergy (around 20–25% of the total number) from their parishes, either for High Church theology, political royalism, or scandalous morals. Parliament also abolished the Book of Common Prayer, replacing it with the Westminster Directory for Public Worship. Further, it made illegal the celebration of Easter, Christmas, and other traditional festivals in Anglican worship. The Civil War therefore may have brought religious liberty for Puritans and Separatists (and anyone who did not wish to attend his or her parish church), but it brought legal repression for traditional Anglicans and physical hardship for many clergy. Some Anglicans openly defied parliament and continued using the Prayer Book; others conducted secret Prayer Book worship in the houses of those gentry and aristocracy who remained loyal to the old ways.

The plans of the Long Parliament to reform the national Church through the Westminster Assembly came to nothing because of parliament's progressive loss of power to the Army. The intended "Presbyterian Church of England" therefore never materialized on a nationwide basis, although the great capital city of London itself and the county of Lancashire did have a fully functioning Presbyterian system. Despite the failure of a national Presbyterian Church to get established, however, many illustrious Presbyterian pastors and preachers were active in this period: *William Gouge* (1578–1653), *Stephen Marshall* (c.1594–1655), *Richard Vines* (1600–56), *Edmund Calamy* (1600–66), *Obadiah Sedgwick* (c.1600–58), *Thomas Manton* (1620–77), Thomas Watson (c.1620–86), and *Lazarus Seaman* (died 1675)—names that would have to appear in any roll-call of the Puritan heroes of faith.

Meanwhile, outside the boundaries of Anglicanism or Presbyterianism, a variety of other groups flourished. This was the summertime of the Independents, since many Army officers had Independent convictions, and Cromwell was more associated with this than with any other party. Independents could now form churches and worship in public without fear of persecution, and they did so in many parts of the country. When they met at the Savoy assembly in 1658, there were over a hundred congregations. Great Independent pastors and preachers of the period included **Philip Nye** (c.1595–1672), **Hugh Peters** (1598–1660), **William Bridge** (1600–70), **Thomas Goodwin** (1600–80), **Joseph Caryl** (1602–73), **Thomas Brooks** (1608–80), **Peter Sterry** (1613–72), and John Owen who will be given separate treatment (see below). These were all Calvinists; the writings of Bridge, Goodwin, Caryl, Brooks, and Owen continue to edify believers today. The outstanding Arminian Independent pastor was London-based **John Goodwin** (1594–1665), a radical supporter of the Army. Some of these Independent divines played leading roles in Cromwellian politics.

Baptists also prospered. The Arminian Baptists became numerous, and in 1651 thirty of their churches met in the Midlands, probably in Leicester, and adopted a confession of faith. In 1654 they held a nationwide assembly in London, and began functioning much as a "denomination". By the time the monarchy was restored in 1660, there were around 115 Arminian Baptist churches. Important Arminian Baptist pastors and theologians of this period were **Henry Denne** (c.1605–66), William Jeffrey (or Jeffery/Jeffreys) (born c.1616, died after 1660), Thomas Lambe (died 1660s), Edward Barber (died c.1674), and Thomas Grantham (died 1692). The Calvinistic Baptists were less enthusiastic about becoming a denomination, more devoted to the autonomy of the individual congregation; but they too grew in numbers, forming local associations in London, the Midlands, and Wales. These associations met throughout the 1650s and exchanged information with each other. There were about 130 Calvinistic Baptist churches by 1660. Among the prominent Calvinistic Baptist pastors and theologians of the period were *Hanserd Knollys* (c.1598–1691), *Henry Jessey* (1601–63) (the second J in the JLJ church), *John Tombes* (c.1603–76), *Christopher Blackwood* (c.1607–70), William Kiffin (1616–1701), and John Bunyan who will be given separate treatment.[18]

Other groups also sprang up. There were the Fifth Monarchists, who looked for the imminent establishment of Christ's kingdom on earth, perhaps with the Army as His instrument.[19] There were the Ranters, an anarchist movement that espoused pantheism and antinomianism, and were fond of using nudity as a form of social and religious protest. There were the Seekers, not an organized body, but a fairly widespread movement that withdrew from active church involvement to pursue a fuller truth through personal searching; at a local level, however, Seekers commonly met together, often waiting in silence until someone felt inspired to speak. But the most enduring of these alternative groups was the Quakers.

The Quakers probably arose from the Seekers. Their formative figure was *George Fox* (1624–91) of Drayton-in-the-Clay in Leicestershire, where Puritanism reigned. A deeply troubled young man, Fox abandoned his job as a shepherd, and wandered the country, seeking a truth he could never find in Puritanism or in anything else on offer. There was no one who could "speak to his condition", as he put it. His salvation came through a mystical experience in around 1646: "I heard a voice which said, 'There is one, even Christ Jesus, that can speak to thy condition'; and when I heard it my heart did leap for joy." Thereafter Fox became the centre of a new movement, drawn largely at first from among Seekers (the Seeker style of worship carried over into Quakerism). The nickname Quaker originated in an incident in 1650 in Derby, where Fox was on trial for

---

18. For Bunyan, see Chapter 4, section 1.6.

19. They took their name from Daniel's vision (Daniel ch. 2) of the four earthly kingdoms, generally identified as Babylon, Persia, Alexander the Great, and Rome, to be followed by a kingdom that will never pass away—the fifth monarchy.

alleged blasphemy; a judge sneered at his exhortation to "tremble at the word of the Lord", calling Fox and his followers "quakers" (tremblers). Their earliest name, however, was "Children of the Light", then "Friends of the Truth". As a name for his movement, Fox finally settled on "Friends".

Fox's central teaching was that "every man had received from the Lord a measure of light which, if followed, would lead him to the Light of Life" (as Fox expressed it). This exaltation of the "inner light" as the supreme revelation led to many bruising conflicts between Quakers and orthodox Protestants of all sorts, who held that Scripture was supreme. It did not help matters that Quakers were prone to disruptive interruptions of non-Quaker worship. Quaker spirituality grew out of Seeker practice: no sacraments, no Bible exposition, indeed no formal structure other than the silence of the gathered meeting, broken only when a brother or sister felt moved to share some insight. Quaker mysticism was also allied to social radicalism: a message of absolute equality between the classes and the sexes, and a vociferous demand for justice now (which often aroused violent hostility from people of money and property).

Apart from Fox, the earliest outstanding Quaker was *James Nayler* (1618–60), famous for his virtual martyrdom and his dying confession of faith. A charismatic and possibly eccentric figure (even by Quaker standards), Nayler outraged public opinion by re-enacting Jesus' entry into Jerusalem: in October 1656, he rode into Bristol on horseback, while his followers cried "Holy, holy, holy!" and scattered their garments in his path. For this apparent impersonation of Jesus, Nayler was arrested, convicted of blasphemy, and brutally punished: whipped through the streets, his forehead branded, his tongue pierced. The religious toleration even of Cromwellian England had limits. Nayler was physically wrecked by his ordeal. The day before his death in October 1660, however, he penned a confession of faith that has become a treasured classic among Quakers:

> There is a spirit which I feel that delights to do no evil, nor to revenge any wrong, but delights to endure all things, in hope

to enjoy its own in the end. Its hope is to outlive all wrath and contention, and to weary out all exaltation and cruelty, or whatever is of a nature contrary to itself. It sees to the end of all temptations. As it bears no evil in itself, so it conceives none in thoughts to any other. If it be betrayed, it bears it, for its ground and spring is the mercies and forgiveness of God. Its crown is meekness, its life is everlasting love unfeigned; it takes its kingdom with entreaty and not with contention, and keeps it by lowliness of mind. In God alone it can rejoice, though none else regard it, or can own its life. It's conceived in sorrow, and brought forth without any to pity it, nor doth it murmur at grief and oppression. It never rejoiceth but through sufferings; for with the world's joy it is murdered. I found it alone, being forsaken. I have fellowship therein with them who lived in dens and desolate places in the earth, who through death obtained this resurrection and eternal holy life.

By 1660, there were something like thirty or forty thousand Quakers in England, Wales, Scotland, and Ireland. It was clear that the movement was now a permanent part of the religious landscape. A vigorous apostle, George Fox spread his message to Germany, the Dutch Republic, and America; the American colony of Pennsylvania was founded in 1681 by a Quaker, **William Penn** (1644–1718), and gave refuge to Penn's fellow believers from the persecution they often experienced elsewhere from Episcopalian and Puritan alike. Fox's *Journal* (1694) became a landmark document of Quakerism and English mysticism; the theology of Quakerism, to the extent that so subjective a movement had a theology, was given classic form by Scottish Quaker **Robert Barclay** (1648–90) in his *An Apology for the True Christian Divinity* (1676).[20]

---

20. One further point about distinct religious groups: Cromwell is often credited with "readmitting the Jews to England" in 1656 (they had been officially expelled in 1290). In a sense, Cromwell did do this; but it was a private decision to give a greater degree of *de facto* toleration to an existing Anglo-Jewish community—the 1290 "expulsion" had not been completely effective. Cromwell issued no official decree of toleration, and his motives for extending a pragmatic tolerance may partly have been commercial.

The religious scene in the English Republic was not quite the free-for-all the above portrayal may suggest. Cromwell was concerned to provide spiritual nourishment for the English people, and to encourage cooperation between non-royalist Protestants. The result was a scheme established in March 1654, in which Cromwell appointed a commission of "Triers" and (later) "Ejectors" to examine candidates for parish ministry. The Triers were a central body in London, assessing potential pastors, whereas each county had its own body of Ejectors who examined existing pastors. The London committee of 38 Triers was taken mostly from the Independents and Presbyterians. Almost half were Independents, and included famous names like Joseph Caryl, Thomas Goodwin, Philip Nye, John Owen, and Hugh Peters. The slightly fewer Presbyterians included Thomas Manton, Stephen Marshall, and Obadiah Sedgwick. A few Baptists even became involved, notably Henry Jessey and John Tombes. The Triers and Ejectors allowed many Anglican ministers to remain in their parishes as long as they were not politically active royalists, gave evidence of godliness, and promised to refrain from using the Book of Common Prayer. If Presbyterians or Independents were appointed to a parish, they were free to model it along the lines of their own church ideals. Richard Baxter, an opponent of the scheme, nonetheless testified to its benefit:

> The truth is, though some few over-rigid and over-busy Independents among them were too severe against all that were Arminians, and too particular in inquiring after evidences of sanctification in those whom they examined, and somewhat too lax in admitting of unlearned and erroneous men that favoured Antinomianism or Anabaptism; yet, to give them their due, they did abundance of good in the church They saved many a congregation from ignorant, ungodly, drunken teachers,— that sort of men who intend no more in the ministry then to read a sermon on Sunday, and all the rest of the week go with

Jews already lived and worked in London as a prosperous merchant community, and had strong links with a flourishing Jewish business community in Amsterdam which had far-flung financial interests.

the people to the alehouse and harden them in sin; and that sort of ministers who either preached against a holy life, or preached as men who were never acquainted with it. These they usually rejected, and in their stead admitted of any that were able, serious preachers, and lived a godly life, of what tolerable opinion soever they were; so that, though many of them were a little partial for the Independents, Separatists, Fifth-monarchy Men, and Anabaptists, and against the Prelatists [Episcopalians] and Arminians, yet so great was the benefit above the hurt which they brought to the church, that many thousands of souls blessed God for the faithful ministers whom they let in, and grieved when the Prelatists afterwards cast them out again.

4. Other key figures

Richard Baxter

Richard Baxter (1615–91) is probably the most famous Puritan of all. Born at Rowton, Shropshire, he never studied at university; his schoolmaster advised against it, and sent him to study under a friend at Ludlow Castle. Consequently Baxter was largely self-taught. What he lacked in university education, he more than compensated for in the vast extent of his private reading (which included the medieval scholastic theologians) and the subtle genius of his intellect. A spiritual awakening in his teens, partly through reading Richard Sibbes' *The Bruised Reed*, turned Baxter's thoughts at length to the ministry, and he was ordained by the Bishop of Worcester in 1638. From 1641 he was in charge of Kidderminster parish church in Worcestershire. When the Civil War broke out, Baxter's mild Puritanism put him on the parliamentary side, but Worcester was royalist, and Baxter had to flee. He ended up a chaplain in the parliamentary army, where he strove to mitigate the radical religious and political views that were spreading among the soldiers. Ever the moderate, he opposed the Solemn League and Covenant, the execution of the king, and the rise to power of Oliver Cromwell. His verdict on Cromwell was mixed:

> I did in open conference declare Cromwell and his adherents to be guilty of treason and rebellion, aggravated by perfidiousness and hypocrisy. But yet I did not think it my duty to rave against

him in the pulpit, or to do this so unseasonably and imprudently as might irritate him to mischief. And the rather because, as he kept up his approbation of a godly life in general, and of all that was good, except that which the interest of his sinful cause engaged him to be against; so I perceived that it was his design to do good in the main, and to promote the Gospel and the interests of godliness, more than any had done before him; except in those particulars which were against his own interest.

Baxter finally returned to Kidderminster around 1647; his preaching and pastoral visitation over the following decade revolutionized the moral and spiritual state of the parish. His preaching had a matchless power; a 19th century biographer commented that by his sermons Baxter "drew more hearts to the great Broken Heart than any single Englishman of his age".

When the monarchy was restored in 1660 (with Baxter's influential voice assisting), Charles II offered Baxter the bishopric of Hereford, but he declined owing to dissatisfaction with Anglican Episcopacy. He was driven from the Church and from Kidderminster, becoming a leading Nonconformist. Often classed as a Presbyterian, Baxter's views on church government were in fact too eclectic to fit into any system. He suffered grievous persecution for his Nonconformity, especially under the infamous Judge Jeffreys in 1685.[21] He lived to see the overthrow of James II by William of Orange, and rejoiced it in. His autobiography, the *Reliquiae Baxterianae* (1696), is one of the most important (and readable) primary sources for the whole period of the Civil War and Restoration.

Baxter's legacy is huge. He wrote more than any other Puritan, perhaps more than any other English author (a "collected works" would fill 60 volumes); penned in plain, vigorous English, his spiritual writings have been richly prized from that day to this— *Call to the Unconverted, Causes and Danger of Slighting Christ and His Gospel, The Divine Life, The Life of Faith, Now or Never, A Saint or a Brute, A Treatise of Conversion, A Treatise of Self-Denial…* These are the finest flower of Puritan practical divinity.

---

21. For Judge Jeffreys see Chapter 4, section 2.2.

Three of Baxter's works merit particular mention: *The Reformed Pastor* (1656) is the universally acknowledged Puritan classic on the work of the ministry; *The Christian Directory* (1673) is the masterpiece of Puritan casuistry; and *The Saints' Everlasting Rest* (1650), composed after Baxter had almost died of a nosebleed, is an extended meditation on heaven which ranks among the most affecting treatments of the subject ever written.

Baxter's more doctrinally-oriented works have proven more problematic for most mainstream Calvinists because of Baxter's massive independence of thought. As often as he expounded Reformed Orthodoxy, he just as often stepped outside of it, offering his own "Baxterian" interpretation of Law and Gospel, the nature and extent of the atonement, assurance, perseverance, and other themes.[22]

John Owen

John Owen (1616–83) is the most well-known doctrinal theologian among the Puritans. Born at Stadhampton in Oxfordshire, he studied at Queen's College, Oxford, receiving his Master of Arts degree in 1635. He was then ordained as an Anglican deacon and began studying theology, but left the university in 1637, disillusioned with the High Church Arminian theology and worship it was embracing. Once the Civil War broke out, Owen (a parliamentarian) became in 1642 minister of Fordham parish in Essex, moving in 1646 to Coggeshall. By the time he went to Coggeshall, his views on church government had developed from Presbyterianism to Independency. He continued, however, to function within the parish system (now controlled by parliament). His preaching,

---

22. It would take too long to analyze and disentangle what was really distinctive about Baxter's theology, and its thematic motivations. Suffice it to say that it was a highly eclectic system that drew from almost every school of thought, past and contemporary. Critics believed that Baxter's system risked turning the Gospel of free grace into a new kind of law ("Neonomianism"). Baxter of course rejected the accusation, and he has had his defenders as well as his critics. The topic can be pursued through a forest of primary and secondary literature.

and the theological writings that had begun to flow from his pen, brought him increasingly into the public eye; as an Independent, he was appreciated by the leaders of the New Model Army. When Charles I was put to death, the Rump Parliament chose Owen to preach to them the following day. Although he did not specifically mention the king's execution, the sermon was entitled *Righteous Zeal Encouraged by Divine Protection.*

Owen enjoyed high favour throughout the period of the English Republic. He accompanied Cromwell as chaplain on his Irish expedition of 1649 and his invasion of Scotland in 1650. In 1651 Cromwell made Owen Dean of Christ Church Cathedral in Oxford, and in 1652 he became vice-chancellor of the university. He was one of Cromwell's Triers in the ecclesiastical settlement of 1654, and a dominating figure at the Savoy Assembly of 1658, where English Independents adopted a modified *Westminster Confession* as their own doctrinal statement.

When Oliver Cromwell died in 1658, Owen acted as an intermediary between Oliver's son Richard (the new Lord Protector) and the leaders of the New Model Army, who preferred a pure republic under the old Rump Parliament. The republicanism of the Army prevailed and Richard Cromwell was forced to resign. Many blamed Owen as the chief villain in Richard Cromwell's fall; it might be better to say that he played a part. Eventually, however, it was not the English Republic but the Stuart monarchy that was restored in 1660, and Owen was stripped of his civil and ecclesiastical offices. He spent the rest of his life as a nonconforming Independent, ministering from 1666 to a London congregation where many old officers of the New Model Army worshiped.

Owen's theology filled 24 volumes, 16 on doctrinal or practical divinity, the other eight an exhaustive commentary on Hebrews. He was probably the supreme English representative of mature Reformed Orthodoxy; although he wrote no systematic theology, his treatment of different topics was comprehensive and cogent (although his style is generally criticized as cumbersome). Much of Owen's writing is in the key of controversy with others, notably Richard Baxter, Anglicans, Roman Catholics, Arminians, and Socinians, thereby giving an illuminating insight into Puritanism's self-understanding in the post-1640 era. Owen's practical divinity has been as cherished as his doctrine; the two are fused to beautiful effect in his *Of Communion with God the Father, Son and Holy Ghost* (1657). After the monarchy was restored in 1660, amidst persecution Owen offered a nationwide leadership to Independents that was crucial in preserving their faith and morale in a dark time.

Important people:

Elizabethan preachers/theologians

Matthew Parker (1504–75)
Thomas Sampson (1517–89)
Edmund Grindal (c.1519–83)
Laurence Humphrey (1527–90)
John Whitgift (c.1530–1604)
Peter Baro (1534–99)
Richard Greenham (c.1535–c.1594)
Thomas Cartwright (c.1535–1603)
John Field (1545–88)
Walter Travers (c.1548–1635)
John Reynolds (1549–1607)
Henry Barrow (c.1550–93)
Robert Browne (1550–1633)
Richard Hooker (1554–1600)
William Perkins (1558–1602)
John Penry (1559–93)
Henry Smith (c. 1560–c.1591)
John Greenwood (d.1593)
Francis Johnson (1563–1618)

Jacobean preachers/theologians

Henry Jacob (1536–1624)
Richard Bancroft (1544–1610)
Lancelot Andrewes (1555–1626)
George Abbot (1562–1633)
John Smyth (c.1570–1612)

Paul Baynes (c.1573–1617)
Thomas Helwys (c.1575–c.1616)
John Robinson (1575–1625)
Lewis Bayly (d.1631)

Royalty

Elizabeth I (1558–1603)
James I (1603–25)
Henrietta Maria (1609–69)
Charles I (1625–49)

Statesmen and generals

Robert Dudley, Earl of Leicester (1532–88)
Sir Francis Walsingham (1532–90)
John Pym (1584–1643)
Thomas Wentworth (1593–1641)
Oliver Cromwell (1599–1658)

Preachers/theologians: Charles I and the English Revolution

John Davenant (1572–1641)

William Laud (1573–1645)
Joseph Hall (1574–1656)
John Donne (1573–1631)
Richard Sibbes (1577–1635)
James Ussher (1581–1656)
John Selden (1584–1654)
Nicholas Ferrar (1592–1637)
George Herbert (1593–1633)
Izaak Walton (1593–1683)
John Cosin (1594–1672)
Thomas Coleman (1598–1647)
John Lightfoot (1602–75)

Presbyterians

William Gouge (1578–1653)
Cornelius Burges (or Burgess) (c.1589–1665)

Stephen Marshall (c.1594–1655)
Richard Vines (1600–56)
Obadiah Sedgwick (c.1600–58)
Edmund Calamy (1600–66)
Lazarus Seaman (d.1675)
Richard Baxter (1615–91)
Thomas Manton (1620–77)

Independents:

Francis Rous (1579–1659)
William Bradford (1590–1657)
John Goodwin (1594–1665)
Philip Nye (c.1595–1672)
Hugh Peters (or Peter) (1598–1660)
William Bridge (1600–70)
Thomas Goodwin (1600–80)
Joseph Caryl (1602–73)
Thomas Brooks (1608–80)
Peter Sterry (1613–72)
John Owen (1616–83)

Baptists:

John Spilsbury (c.1593–1668)
Hanserd Knollys (c.1598–1691)
Henry Jessey (1601–63)
John Tombes (c.1603–76)
Roger Williams (c.1603–83)
Henry Denne (c.1605–66)
Christopher Blackwood (c.1607–70)

Quakers:

James Nayler (1618–60)
George Fox (1624–91)
William Penn (1644–1718)
Robert Barclay (1648–90)

Primary source material

The English Reformation: we Protestants are the true Catholics

As for our doctrine which we may rightly call Christ's catholic doctrine, it is so far off from new that God, who is above all most ancient, and the Father of our Lord Jesus Christ, hath left the same unto us in the Gospel, in the Prophets' and Apostles' works, being monuments of greatest age. So that no man can now think our doctrine to be new, unless the same think either the Prophets' faith, or the Gospel, or else Christ Himself to be new.

And as for their [Roman Catholic] religion, if it be of so long continuance as they would have men ween [think] it is, why do they not prove it so by the examples of the primitive Church, and by the fathers and councils of old times? Why lieth so ancient a cause thus long in the dust, destitute of an advocate? Fire and sword they have had always ready at hand, but as for the old councils and the fathers, all mum—not a word. They did surely against all reason to begin first with these so bloody and extreme means, if they could have found other more easy and gentle ways. And if they trust so fully to antiquity, and use no dissimulation, why did John Clement, a [Roman Catholic] countryman of ours, but few years past, in the presence of certain honest men and of good credit, tear and cast into the fire certain leaves of Theodoret—the most ancient father and a Greek bishop—wherein he plainly and evidently taught that the nature of bread in the Communion was not changed, abolished, or brought to nothing?...[23]

The old fathers Origen and Chrysostom exhort the people to read the Scriptures, to buy them books, to reason at home betwixt themselves of divine matters—wives with their husbands, and parents with their children. These men [Roman Catholics] condemn the Scriptures as dead elements, and—as much as ever they may—bar the people from them. The ancient fathers,

---

23. In other words, Theodoret did not believe in transubstantiation.

Cyprian, Epiphanius, and Jerome, say, for one who, perchance, hath made a vow to lead a sole [single] life, and afterwards liveth unchastely, and cannot quench the flames of lust, "it is better to marry a wife, and to live honestly in wedlock." And the old father Augustine judgeth the selfsame marriage to be good and perfect, and that it ought not to be broken again. These men [Roman Catholics], if a man have once bound himself by a vow, though afterwards he burn, keep queans [prostitutes], and defile himself with never so sinful and desperate a life, yet they suffer not that person to marry a wife; or if he chance to marry, they allow it not for marriage. And they commonly teach it is much better and more godly to keep a concubine and harlot, than to live in that kind of marriage.

The old father Augustine complained of the multitude of ceremonies, wherewith he even then saw men's minds and consciences overcharged. These men [Roman Catholics], as though God regarded nothing else but their ceremonies, have so out of measure increased them, that there is now almost none other thing left in their churches and places of prayer...

But, say they, "ye have been of our fellowship, but now ye are become forsakers of your profession, and have departed from us." It is true; we have departed from them, and for so doing we both give thanks to Almighty God, and greatly rejoice on our own behalf. But yet for all this, from the primitive Church, from the Apostles, and from Christ we have not departed. True it is, we were brought up with these men [Roman Catholics] in darkness, and in the lack of the knowledge of God, as Moses was taught up in the learning and in the bosom of the Egyptians. "We have been of your company," saith Tertullian, "I confess it, and no marvel at all; for," saith he, "men be made and not born Christians."

John Jewel
The Apology of the Church of England, ch. 5

Reformation now!

They [Anglicans] say, "Behold, we have a Christian Prince, and a mother in Israel." But can they [rulers] be Christians, when they make them [believers] to refuse or withstand the government of Christ in His Church, or will not be subject unto it? If they therefore refuse and withstand, how should they be tarried for? If they be with them, there is no tarrying: and if they be against them, they are no Christians, and therefore also there can be no tarrying. For the worthy may not tarry for the unworthy, but rather forsake them, as it is written, Save yourselves from this froward generation: and cast not pearls before swine, nor holy things unto dogs: and rebuke not a scorner, sayeth the wise man, lest he hate thee: and inquire who is worthy, sayeth Christ. He that will be saved, must not tarry for this man or that: and he that putteth his hand to the plow, and then looketh back, is not fit for the kingdom of God.

Therefore woe unto you, ye blind guides, which cast away all by tarrying for the Magistrates! The Lord will remember this iniquity, and visit this sin upon you. Ye will not have the kingdom of God to go forward by His Spirit, but by an army and strength forsooth: ye will not have it as leaven hid in three pecks of meal, till it leaven all, but at once ye will have all aloft, by civil power and authority: you are offended at the baseness and small beginnings, and because of the troubles in beginning reformation, you will do nothing. Therefore shall Christ be that rock of offence unto you, and ye shall stumble and fall, and shall be broken, and shall be snared, and shall be taken. You will be delivered from the yoke of Antichrist, to the which you do willingly give your necks, by bow, and by sword, and by battle, by horses and by horsemen, that is, by civil power and pomp of Magistrates: by their Proclamations and Parliaments: and the kingdom of God must come with observation, that men may say, Lo the Parliament, or Lo the Bishops' decrees: but the kingdom of God should be within you. The inward obedience to the outward preaching and government of the Church, with newness of life, *that* is the Lord's kingdom. This ye despise. Therefore shall ye desire to see the kingdom of God, and shall not see it, and to enjoy one day of the Son of Man, and ye shall not enjoy it.

Robert Browne
A Treatise of Reformation without Tarrying for any

The difference between justifying and sanctifying righteousness

There is a glorifying righteousness of men in the world to come; and there is a justifying and a sanctifying righteousness here. The righteousness wherewith we shall be clothed in the world to come is both perfect and inherent. That whereby we are justified is perfect, but not inherent. That whereby we are sanctified, inherent, but not perfect. This openeth a way to the plain understanding of that grand question, which hangeth yet in controversy between us and the Church of Rome, about the matter of justifying righteousness...

"Doubtless," saith the Apostle, "I have counted all things but loss, and I do judge them to be dung, that I may win Christ, and be found in Him, not having mine own righteousness, but that which is through the faith of Christ, the righteousness which is of God through faith"... Then, although in ourselves we be altogether sinful and unrighteous, yet even the man who in himself is impious, full of iniquity, full of sin, him being found in Christ through faith, and having his sin in hatred through repentance, him God beholdeth with a gracious eye, putteth away his sin by not imputing it, taketh quite away the punishment due thereunto, by pardoning it, and accepteth him in Jesus Christ as perfectly righteous, as if he had fulfilled all that is commanded him in the law: shall I say more perfectly righteous than if himself had fulfilled the whole law? I must take heed what I say; but the Apostle saith, "God made Him who knew no sin to be sin for us, that we might be made the righteousness of God in Him." Such we are in the sight of God the Father as is the very Son of God Himself. Let it be counted folly, or frenzy, or fury, or whatsoever. It is our wisdom and our comfort; we care for no knowledge in the world but this: that man hath sinned and God hath suffered; that God hath made Himself the sin of men, and that men are made the righteousness of God.

You see therefore that the Church of Rome, in teaching justification by inherent grace, doth pervert the truth of Christ, and that by the hands of his Apostles we have received otherwise than she teacheth.

Now concerning the righteousness of sanctification, we deny it not to be inherent; we grant that, unless we work, we have it not; only we distinguish it as a thing in nature different from the righteousness of justification: we are righteous the one way by the faith of Abraham, the other way, except we do the works of Abraham, we are not righteous. Of the one, St. Paul, "To him that worketh not, but believeth, faith is counted for righteousness." Of the other, St. John, "He is righteous who worketh righteousness." Of the one, St. Paul doth prove by Abraham's example that we have it of faith without works. Of the other, St. James by Abraham's example, that by works we have it, and not only by faith. St. Paul doth plainly sever these two parts of Christian righteousness one from the other; for in the sixth to the Romans he writeth, "Being freed from sin and made servants of God, ye have your fruit in holiness, and the end everlasting life." "Ye are made free from sin and made servants unto God": this is the righteousness of justification; "Ye have your fruit in holiness": this is the righteousness of sanctification. By the one we are interested in the right of inheriting; by the other we are brought to the actual possessing of eternal bliss, and so the end is everlasting life.

Richard Hooker
A Learned Discourse of Justification

Degrees of faith

Lastly, we are to consider the degrees of apprehension,[24] and they are two: there is a *weak apprehension* and there is a *strong apprehension*, as there is a weak and a strong faith. The weak faith and apprehension is, when we endeavour to apprehend. This endeavour is, when we bewail our unbelief, strive against our manifold doubtings, will to believe with an honest heart, desire to be reconciled to God, and constantly use the good means to believe. For God accepts the will to believe for faith itself, and the will to repent for repentance. The reason hereof is plain.

---

24. Apprehension = laying hold of Christ for salvation.

Every supernatural act presupposeth a supernatural power, or gift: and therefore the will to believe and repent, presupposeth the power and gift of faith, and repentance in the heart.

It may be objected, that in the minds of them that believe in this manner, doubtings of God's mercies abound. *Ans.* Though doubtings abound never so, yet are they not of the nature of faith, but are contrary to it. Secondly, we must put difference between true apprehension, and strong apprehension. If we truly apprehend, though not strongly, it sufficeth. The palsie-hand is able to receive a gift, though not so strongly as another. The man in the Gospel said, *Lord, I believe, help mine unbelief. Mark 9:24.* That is, help my faith which by reason of smallness thereof may rather be called unbelief than faith. This is the common faith of true believers. For in this world, we rather live by hungering and thirsting, than by full apprehending of Christ: and our comfort stands rather in this, that we are known of God, than that we know God.

The highest degree of faith is a full persuasion of God's mercy. Thus saith the Holy Ghost, that *Abraham was not weak through unbelief, but strong in faith, Rom. 4:20.* But wherein was this strength? In that *he was fully persuaded, that God, which had promised would also perform it.* This measure of faith is not incident to all believers, but to the Prophets, Apostles, martyrs, and such as have been long exercised in the school of Christ.

And this appears by the order, whereby we attain to this degree of faith. First, there must be a knowledge of Christ: then follows a general persuasion of the possibility of pardon, and mercy, whereby we believe that our sins are pardonable. An example whereof we have in the prodigal child, *Luke 15:18.* After this the Holy Ghost worketh a will and desire to believe, and stirs up the heart to make humble and serious invocation for pardon. After prayer instantly made, follows a settling and quieting of the conscience, according to the promise, *Matt. 7:7, Knock, it shall be opened, seek, ye shall find, ask, ye shall receive.* After all this, follows an experience in manifold observations of the mercies of God, and love in Christ: and after experience, follows a full persuasion. *Abraham* had not this full persuasion, till God had sundry times spoken to him. David, upon much trial of the mercy, and favour of God, grows to resolution, and saith, *Psalm 23:6. Doubtless kindness and mercy shall follow me all the days of my life.*

This distinction of the degrees of faith, must the rather be observed, because the Papists suppose that we teach, that every faith is a full persuasion, and that every one among us hath this persuasion. Which is otherwise. For, certainty we ascribe to all faith, but not fullness of certainty. Neither do we teach, that all men must have a full persuasion, at the first.

William Perkins
Commentary on Galatians 2:15-16

Meditations to stir us up to morning prayer

1. If, when thou art about to pray, Satan shall suggest that thy prayers are too long, and that therefore it were better either to omit prayers, or else to cut them shorter, meditate that prayer is thy spiritual sacrifice, wherewith God is well pleased (Heb. 13:15-16); and therefore it is so displeasing to the devil, and so irksome to the flesh. Bend therefore thy affections (will they, nill they) to so holy an exercise; assuring thyself, that it doth by so much the more please God, by how much the more it is unpleasing to thy flesh.

2. Forget not that the Holy Ghost puts it down as a special note of reprobates, They call not upon the Lord, they call not upon God. (Ps. 14:4, 53:4)… On the other side, that God has promised that whosoever shall call on his name shall be saved. (Rom. 10:13). It is certain that he who makes no conscience of the duty of prayer, has no grace of the Holy Spirit in him, for the spirit of grace and of prayer are one (Zech. 12:10) and therefore grace and prayer go together. But he that can from a penitent heart morning and evening pray to God, it is sure that he has his measure of grace in this world, and he shall have his portion of glory in the life which is to come.

3. Remember, that as loathing of meat, and painfulness of speaking, are two symptoms of a sick body; so irksomeness

of praying when thou talkest with God, and carelessness in hearing, when God, by his word, speaks unto thee, are two sure signs of a sick soul.

4. Call to mind the zealous devotions of the Christians in the primitive church, who spent many whole nights and vigils in watching and praying for the forgiveness of their sins, and that they might be found ready at the coming of Christ; and that David was not content to pray at morning, at evening, and at noon (Ps. 55:16-17), but he would also rise up at midnight to pray unto God (Ps. 119:62). And if Christ did chide his disciples, because they would not watch with him one hour in praying (Matt. 26:40), what chiding dost thou deserve, who thinkest it too long to continue in prayer but one quarter of an hour? If thou hast spent divers hours at a vain ball or play; yea whole days and nights in carding and dicing, to please thy flesh, be ashamed to think that praying for a quarter of an hour is too long an exercise for the service of God.

5. Consider, that if the papists, in their blind superstition, do in an unknown, and therefore unedifying tongue, fit only for the children of mystical Babylon (1 Cor. 14:14, Gen. 11:9, Rev. 17:5), mutter over upon their beads every morning and evening so many scores of ave-maries, paternosters, and idolatrous prayers, how shall they, in their superstitious devotion, rise up in judgment against thee, professing thyself to be a true worshipper of Christ? If that thou thinkest these prayers too long a task, being shorter for quantity than theirs, but far more profitable for quality, tending only to God's glory, and thy good; and so compiled of Scripture phrase, as that thou mayest speak to God, as well in his own holy words, as in thine own native language: be ashamed that papists, in their superstitious worshipping of creatures, should show themselves more devout than thou in the sincere worshipping of the true and only God (John 17:3). And indeed a prayer in private

devotion should be one continued speech, rather than many broken fragments.

6. Lastly, when such thoughts come into thy head, either to keep thee from prayer, or to distract thee in praying, remember that those are the fowls which the evil one sends to devour the good seed, and the carcases of thy spiritual sacrifices; but endeavour with Abraham, to drive them away (Gen. 15:11). Yet notwithstanding, if thou perceivest at times, that thy spirits are dull, and thy mind not apt for prayer and holy devotion, strive not too much for that time, but humbling thyself at the sense of thine infirmity and dulness, knowing that God accepteth the willing mind, though it be oppressed with the heaviness of the flesh (Matt. 26:41; 2 Cor. 8:12), endeavour the next time to recompense this dulness, by redoubling thy zeal, and for the time present, commend thy soul to God in this, or the like short prayer...

Lewis Bayly
The Practice of Piety

A confession of faith

I believe, O Lord, in You, the Father, the Word, the
   Spirit, one God;
that everything was created by Your paternal love and
   power;
that by Your kindness and love to humanity
everything has been gathered into unity in Your Word,
who, for us mortals and for our salvation, became flesh,
was conceived and born, suffered and was crucified,
died, and was buried, and descended,
rose again, ascended, and took His seat on high,
will come again, and will be our judge;
that by Your Holy Spirit's radiant manifestation and
   energy
a people belonging to You has been called out of the
   whole world,
into a community of belief in the truth and holy living,

where we share in the fellowship of saints
and the pardon of sins in this world,
and expect the resurrection of the body
and life for evermore in the world to come.
This most holy faith, which was once entrusted to the
    saints,
I believe, O Lord; O help my unbelief,
enlarge my small faith!
Grant that I may love the Father for His love,
revere the Almighty for His might,
and to Him entrust my soul in doing good, as to a
    faithful Creator.
Grant that I may experience
salvation from Jesus,[25]
anointing from Christ,[26]
adoption from the only-begotten Son;
may I serve the Lord
in faith for His miraculous conception,
in humility for His birth,
in longsuffering for His sufferings, yet with impatience
    toward sin.
For the sake of His cross, may I crucify everything that
    would lead me to sin;
for the sake of His death, may I put to death the flesh;
for the sake of His burial, may I bury evil thoughts in
    the soil of good works;
for the sake of His descent, may I ponder hell;
for the sake of His resurrection, may I ponder the new
    life that He gives;
for the sake of His ascension, may I fix my mind on
    things above;
for the sake of His being seated on high, may I fix my
    mind
on the superior realities found at His right hand;

---

25. Jesus = "God saves".
26. Christ = "the anointed one".

for the sake of His return, may I tremble at His second
    coming;
for the sake of His judgment, may I judge myself before
    I am judged.
Grant that the Spirit may breathe saving grace upon me,
that I may have my calling, my sanctification, and my
    fellowship
in the holy catholic Church,
sharing in her holy things –
prayers, fastings, cries, vigils, weeping, sufferings –
for assurance of the remission of sins,
for the hope of resurrection, and admission to the life
    that knows no end.

Lancelot Andrewes
Private Prayers

It should have been me

Spit in my face, you Jews, and pierce my side,
        Buffet, and scoff, scourge, and crucify me,
        For I have sinned, and sinned, and only He,
Who could do no iniquity, hath died.
But by my death cannot be satisfied
        My sins, which pass the Jews' impiety:
        They killed once an inglorious man, but I
Crucify Him daily, being now glorified.
        O let me then His strange love still admire:
Kings pardon, but He bore our punishment.
        And Jacob came clothed in vile harsh attire
But to supplant, and with gainful intent;
        God clothed Himself in vile man's flesh, that so
        He might be weak enough to suffer woe.

John Donne
Holy Sonnets, sonnet XI

Send not to know for whom the bell tolls

No man is an island, entire of itself; every man is a piece of
the continent, a part of the main. If a clod be washed away
by the sea, Europe is the less, as well as if a promontory were,

as well as if a manor of thy friend's or of thine own were: any man's death diminishes me, because I am involved in mankind, and therefore never send to know for whom the bells tolls; it tolls for thee. Neither can we call this a begging of misery, or a borrowing of misery, as though we were not miserable enough of ourselves, but must fetch in more from the next house, in taking upon us the misery of our neighbours. Truly it were an excusable covetousness if we did, for affliction is a treasure, and scarce any man hath enough of it. No man hath affliction enough that is not matured and ripened by and made fit for God by that affliction. If a man carry treasure in bullion, or in a wedge of gold, and have none coined into current money, his treasure will not defray him as he travels. Tribulation is treasure in the nature of it, but it is not current money in the use of it, except we get nearer and nearer our home, heaven, by it. Another man may be sick too, and sick to death, and this affliction may lie in his bowels, as gold in a mine, and be of no use to him; but this bell, that tells me of his affliction, digs out and applies that gold to me: if by this consideration of another's danger I take mine own into contemplation, and so secure myself, by making my recourse to my God, who is our only security.

O eternal and most gracious God, who hast been pleased to speak to us, not only in the voice of nature, [which] speaks in our hearts, and of Thy word, which speaks to our ears, but in the speech of speechless creatures, in Balaam's ass, in the speech of unbelieving men, in the confession of Pilate, in the speech of the devil himself in the recognition and attestation of Thy Son, I humbly accept Thy voice in the sound of this sad and funeral bell. And first, I bless Thy glorious name, that in this sound and voice I can hear Thy instructions, in another man's to consider mine own condition; and to know, that this bell which tolls for another, before it come to ring out, may take me in too. As death is the wages of sin it is due to me; as death is the end of sickness it belongs to me; and though so disobedient a servant as I may be afraid to die, yet to so merciful a master as Thou I cannot be afraid to come; and therefore into Thy hands,

O my God, I commend my spirit, a surrender which I know Thou wilt accept, whether I live or die; for Thy servant David made it, when he put himself into Thy protection for his life; and Thy blessed Son made it, when He delivered up His soul at His death: declare Thou Thy will upon me, O Lord, for life or death in Thy time; receive my surrender of myself now; into Thy hands, O Lord, I commend my spirit.

John Donne
Devotions upon Emergent Occasions, 17

Divine love's welcome to the sinner

> Love bade me welcome: yet my soul drew back,
> > Guilty of dust and sin.
> But quick-eyed Love, observing me grow slack
> > From my first entrance in,
> Drew nearer to me, sweetly questioning
> > If I lacked anything.
>
> "A guest," I answered, "worthy to be here":
> > Love said, "You shall be he."
> "I, the unkind, the ungrateful? ah my dear,
> > I cannot look on Thee."
> Love took my hand and smiling did reply,
> > "Who made the eyes but I?"
>
> "Truth, Lord, but I have marred them; let my shame
> > Go where it doth deserve."
> "And know you not," says Love, "who bore the blame?"
> > "My dear, then I will serve."
> "You must sit down," says Love, "and taste my meat."
> > So I did sit and eat.

George Herbert
Love (III)

The Christian's true self and best being are in Christ

That which most troubles a good man in all troubles is himself, so far as he is unsubdued; he is more disquieted with himself than with all troubles out of himself; when he hath gotten the better once of himself, whatsoever falls from without is light. Where the spirit is enlarged, it cares not much for outward bondage; where the spirit is lightsome, it cares not much for outward darkness; where the spirit is settled, it cares not much for outward changes; where the spirit is one with itself, it can bear outward breaches; where the spirit is sound, it can bear outward sickness. Nothing can be very ill with us, when all is well within. This is the comfort of a holy man, that though he be troubled with himself, yet by reason of the spirit in him, which is his better self, he works out by degrees whatever is contrary, as spring-water, being clear of itself, works itself clean, though it be troubled by something cast in, as the sea will endure no poisonful thing, but casts it upon the shore. But a carnal man is like a spring corrupted, that cannot work itself clear, because it is wholly tainted; his eye and light is darkness, and therefore no wonder if he seeth nothing. Sin lieth upon his understanding, and hinders the knowledge of itself; it lies close upon the will, and hinders the striving against itself.

True self that is worth the owning, is when a man is taken into a higher condition, and made one with Christ, and esteems neither of himself nor others, as happy for anything according to the flesh. 1. He is under the law and government of the Spirit, and so far as he is himself, works according to that principle. 2. He labours more and more to be transformed into the likeness of Christ, in whom he esteemeth that he hath his best being. 3. He esteems of all things that befall him, to be good or ill, as they farther or hinder his best condition. If all be well for that, he counts himself well, whatsoever else befalls him.

Another man, when he doth anything that is good, acts not his own part; but a godly man, when he doth good, is in his proper element; what another man doth for by-ends and reasons, that he doth from a new nature, which, if there were no law to compel, yet would move him to that which is pleasing to Christ. If he be drawn aside by passion or temptation, that he judgeth not to be himself, but taketh a holy revenge on himself for it, as being redeemed and taken out from himself; he thinks himself no debtor, nor to owe any service to his corrupt self. That which he plots and projects and works for is, that Christ

may rule everywhere, and especially in himself, for he is not his
own but Christ's, and therefore desires to be more and more
emptied of himself, that Christ might be all in all in him.

Richard Sibbes
*The Soul's Conflict with Itself and
Victory over Itself by Faith*, Chapter 9

The spiritual awakening of George Fox

As I cannot declare the misery I was in, it was so great and heavy
upon me, so neither can I set forth the mercies of God unto me
in all my misery. O the everlasting love of God to my soul, when
I was in great distress! When my troubles and torments were
great, then was His love exceeding great. Thou, Lord, makest
a fruitful field a barren wilderness, and a barren wilderness a
fruitful field! Thou bringest down and settest up! Thou killest
and makest alive! all honour and glory be to thee, O Lord of
Glory! The knowledge of Thee in the Spirit is life; but that
knowledge which is fleshly works death…

Now, after I had received that opening from the Lord, that
to be bred at Oxford or Cambridge was not sufficient to fit a
man to be a minister of Christ, I regarded the priests less, and
looked more after the Dissenting people. Among them I saw
there was some tenderness; and many of them came afterwards
to be convinced, for they had some openings.

But as I had forsaken the priests, so I left the separate
preachers also, and those esteemed the most experienced people;
for I saw there was none among them all that could speak to my
condition. When all my hopes in them and in all men were gone,
so that I had nothing outwardly to help me, nor could I tell what
to do, then, oh, then, I heard a voice which said, "There is one,
even Christ Jesus, that can speak to thy condition"; and when I
heard it, my heart did leap for joy.

Then the Lord let me see why there was none upon the earth
that could speak to my condition, namely, that I might give Him
all the glory. For all are concluded under sin, and shut up in
unbelief, as I had been; that Jesus Christ might have the pre-

eminence who enlightens, and gives grace, and faith, and power. Thus when God doth work, who shall hinder it? And this I knew experimentally.

My desire after the Lord grew stronger, and zeal in the pure knowledge of God, and of Christ alone, without the help of any man, book, or writing. For though I read the Scriptures that spoke of Christ and of God, yet I knew Him not, but by revelation, as He who hath the key did open, and as the Father of Life drew me to His Son by His Spirit. Then the Lord gently led me along, and let me see His love, which was endless and eternal, surpassing all the knowledge that men have in the natural state, or can obtain from history or books; and that love let me see myself, as I was without Him.

I was afraid of all company, for I saw them perfectly where they were, through the love of God, which let me see myself. I had not fellowship with any people, priests or professors, or any sort of separated people, but with Christ, who hath the key, and opened the door of Light and Life unto me. I was afraid of all carnal talk and talkers, for I could see nothing but corruptions, and the life lay under the burthen [burden] of corruptions.

When I myself was in the deep, shut up under all, I could not believe that I should ever overcome; my troubles, my sorrows, and my temptations were so great that I thought many times I should have despaired, I was so tempted. But when Christ opened to me how He was tempted by the same devil, and overcame him and bruised his head, and that through Him and His power, light, grace, and Spirit, I should overcome also, I had confidence in Him; so He it was that opened to me when I was shut up and had no hope nor faith. Christ, who had enlightened me, gave me His light to believe in; He gave me hope, which He Himself revealed in me, and He gave me His Spirit and grace, which I found sufficient in the deeps and in weakness.

Thus, in the deepest miseries, and in the greatest sorrows and temptations, that many times beset me, the Lord in His mercy did keep me.

George Fox
Journal, **Chapter 1**

A biblical defence of religious liberty for all

In the multitude of counsellors there is safety: it is therefore humbly desired to be instructed in this point: viz. whether persecution for cause of conscience be not against the doctrine of Jesus Christ the King of kings. The Scriptures and reasons are these.

Because Christ commandeth that the tares and wheat (which some understand are those that walk in the truth, and those that walk in lies) should be let alone in the world, and not plucked up until the harvest, which is the end of the world, Matt. 13:30, 38, etc.

The same commandeth Matt. 15:14, that they that are blind (as some interpret, led on in false religion, and are offended with him for teaching true religion) should be let alone, referring their punishment unto their falling into the ditch.

Again, Luke 9:54, 55. He reproved his disciples who would have had fire come down from heaven and devour those Samaritans who would not receive Him, in these words: Ye know not of what spirit ye are, the Son of Man is not come to destroy men's lives, but to save them.

Paul the Apostle of our Lord teacheth, 2 Tim. 2:24, that the servant of the Lord must not strive, but must be gentle toward all men, suffering the evil men, instructing them with meekness that are contrary minded, proving if God at any time will give them repentance, that they may acknowledge the truth, and come to amendment out of that snare of the devil, etc.

According to these blessed commandments, the holy prophets foretold, that when the Law of Moses (concerning worship) should cease, and Christ's kingdom be established, Isa. 2:4, Micah 4:3, 4, They shall break their swords into mattocks, and their spears into scythes. And Isa. 11:9, Then shall none hurt or destroy in all the mountain of My holiness, etc. And when He came, the same He taught and practised, as before: so did His disciples after Him, for the weapons of His warfare are not carnal (saith the Apostle) 2 Cor. 10:4.

But He chargeth straitly that His disciples should be so far from persecuting those that would not be of their religion, that when they were persecuted they should pray (Matt. 5), when they were cursed they should bless, etc.

And the reason seems to be, because they who now are tares, may hereafter become wheat; they who are now blind, may hereafter see; they that now resist Him, may hereafter receive Him; they that are now in the devil's snare, in adverseness to the truth, may hereafter come to repentance; they that are now blasphemers and persecutors (as Paul was) may in time become faithful as he; they that are now idolaters as the Corinthians once were (1 Cor. 6:9.) may hereafter become true worshippers as they; they that are now no people of God, nor under mercy (as the saints sometimes were, 1 Pet. 2:20.) may hereafter become the people of God, and obtain mercy, as they.

Some come not till the 11th hour, Matt. 20:6, if those that come not till the last hour should be destroyed, because they come not at the first, then should they never come but be prevented.

All which premises are in all humility referred to your godly wise consideration.

Roger Williams
The Bloody Tenent of Persecution for Cause of Conscience

Thou shalt not covet

Remember, man, that thou hast another world to live in; and a far longer life to make provision for; and that thou must be in heaven or hell for ever. This is true, whether thou believe it or not: and thou hast no time but this to make all thy preparation in: and as thou believest, and livest, and labourest now, it must go with thee to all eternity. These are matters worthy of thy care. Canst thou have while [i.e. time] to make such a pudder [fuss] here in the dust, and care and labour for a thing of nought, while thou hast such things as these to care for, and a work of such transcendent consequence to do? Can a man that understands what heaven and hell are, find room for any needless matters, or time for so much unnecessary work?...

Look up to heaven, man, and remember that there is thy home, and there are thy hopes, or else thou art a man undone for ever; and therefore it is for that that thou must care and labour. Believe unfeignedly that thou must dwell for ever in heaven or hell, as thou makest thy preparation here, and consider of this as becometh a man, and then be a worldling and covetous if thou canst: riches will seem dust and chaff to thee, if thou believe and consider thy everlasting state. Write upon the doors of thy shop and chamber, I must be in heaven or hell for ever; or, This is the time on which my endless life dependeth; and methinks every time thou readest it, thou shouldst feel thy covetousness stabbed at the heart. O blinded mortals! that love, like worms, to dwell in earth! Would God but give you an eye of faith, to foresee your end, and where you must dwell to all eternity, what a change would it make upon your earthly minds! Either faith or sense will be your guides. Nothing but reason sanctified by faith can govern sense.

Remember that thou art not a beast, that hath no life to live but this: thou hast a reasonable, immortal soul, that was made by God for higher things, even for God himself, to admire Him, love Him, serve Him, and enjoy Him. If an angel were to dwell awhile in flesh, should he turn an earthworm, and forget his higher life of glory? Thou art like to an incarnate angel; and mayst be equal with the angels, when thou art freed from this sinful flesh, Luke 20:36. O beg of God a heavenly light, and a heavenly mind, and look often into the word of God, which tells thee where thou must be for ever; and worldliness will vanish away in shame.

Richard Baxter
Christian Directory **Part 1, Chapter 4, Direction 2.**

The glory of heaven

Now the poor soul complains, "O that I could love Christ more!" Then thou canst not but love Him. Now, thou knowest little of His amiableness, and therefore lovest little: then, thine eyes will affect thy heart, and the continual viewing of that perfect beauty will keep thee in continual transports of love. Christians, doth it not now stir up your love, to remember all the experiences of His love? Doth not kindness melt you, and the sunshine of Divine goodness warm your frozen hearts? What will it do then, when you shall live in love, and have all in Him, who is all? Surely love is both work and wages. What a high favour, that God will give us leave to love Him! that He will be embraced by those who have embraced lust and sin before Him! But more than this, He returneth love for love; nay, a thousand times more. Christian, thou wilt be then brim-full of love; yet, love as much as thou canst, thou shalt be ten thousand times more beloved. Were the arms of the Son of God open upon the cross, and an open passage made to His heart by the spear; and will not His arms and heart be open to thee in glory? Did not He begin to love before thou lovedst, and will not He continue now? Did He love thee, an enemy? thee, a sinner? thee, who even loathedst thyself? and own thee, when thou didst disclaim thyself? And will He not now immeasurably love thee, a son? thee, a perfect saint? thee, who returnest some love for love? He that in love wept over the old Jerusalem when near its ruin, with what love will He rejoice over the new Jerusalem in her glory!

Christian, believe this, and think on it: thou shalt be eternally embraced in the arms of that love which was from everlasting, and will extend to everlasting; of that love which brought the Son of God's love from heaven to earth, from earth to the cross, from the cross to the grave, from the grave to glory; that love which was weary, hungry, tempted, scorned, scourged, buffeted, spit upon, crucified, pierced; which did fast, pray, teach, heal, weep, sweat, bleed, die; that love will eternally embrace thee. When perfect created love and most perfect uncreated love meet together, it will not be like Joseph and his brethren, who lay upon one another's necks weeping; it will be loving and rejoicing, not loving and sorrowing. Yes, it will make Satan's court ring with the news that Joseph's brethren are come, that the saints are arrived safe at the bosom of Christ, out of the reach of hell for ever. Nor is there any such love as David's and Jonathan's, breathing out its last into sad lamentations for a forced separation. Know this, believer, to thy everlasting comfort, if those arms have once embraced thee, neither sin nor hell can get thee thence for ever. Thou hast not to deal with an inconstant creature, but with Him with whom is no variableness nor shadow of turning. His love to thee will not be as thine was on earth to Him, seldom, and cold, up, and down. He that would not cease nor abate His love, for all thine enmity, unkind neglects, and churlish resistances, can He cease to love thee, when He hath made thee truly lovely?

Richard Baxter
The Saints Everlasting Rest, **Chapter 1**

Chapter 4

England: The Puritan Era Part Two

1

Charles II:
the Restoration regime

1. The return of the king

Oliver Cromwell's death in 1658 plunged Britain into two years of political chaos (see under John Owen in the previous Chapter for some details). Out of the plots and counter-plots of different factions, one dominant power emerged: General *George Monck* (1608–70), a royalist who had switched sides and was Cromwell's military governor of Scotland. Monck now switched sides again, marched his army down into London in February 1660, and restored the Long Parliament, including the Presbyterians who had been excluded by Pride's Purge. The Presbyterians, true to their understanding of the Solemn League and Covenant, had opposed the execution of Charles I, and now favoured the restoration of the monarchy, as Monck himself did. Their only condition was that the exiled *Charles II* (born 1630; reigned 1660–85) would guarantee religious freedom for Presbyterians. After convincing the MPs of his purpose to bring back Charles II, Monck then persuaded the Long Parliament to dissolve itself legally and authorize fresh elections, in order that a new, contemporary House of Commons might give legitimacy to a restored monarchy.

To the horror of Presbyterians, however, Anglican royalists did extremely well in the general election, and the resulting "Convention Parliament" was evenly divided between the two parties. From his exile in the Dutch Republic, Charles played his hand well; on Monck's advice, he issued the "Declaration of Breda"[1] in April 1660, promising religious toleration and an amnesty for all acts committed in the Civil War. Charles was probably sincere in his declaration of intent; he had no stomach for religious persecution, or religious controversy, or indeed religion, and was determined simply to get back on the throne, where he was to become chiefly famous for his extra-marital affairs. The Earl of Rochester allegedly said of Charles:

> We have a pretty witty king,
> Whose word no man relies on;
> He never said a foolish thing,
> And never did a wise one.

If political policy required it, however, Charles could be as intolerant as any religious zealot; note his fairly brutal approach to the Covenanters in Scotland (see Chapter 5, section 4).

On receiving the Declaration of Breda, the Convention Parliament passed the Act of Indemnity and Oblivion, granting the suggested amnesty with a few exceptions (the "regicides"— those responsible for Charles I's execution). Then the MPs invited Charles home; he arrived amid huge popular rejoicing in May. Monck was suitably rewarded by being made Duke of Albemarle. (This re-establishment of the Stuart monarchy is generally known as the Restoration.) Some of the regicides were arrested and executed, including the celebrated Independent preacher Hugh Peters, who had been chaplain to the Republic's council of state; Peters had not signed Charles I's death warrant, but had expressed warm approval of the deed in his preaching, and was widely detested as the embodiment of Puritan fanaticism.

2. The Cavalier Parliament and the Clarendon Code

Parliament was again dissolved in December; new elections produced in May 1661 the "Cavalier Parliament", which was overwhelmingly Anglican-royalist in membership, with hardly a Presbyterian in sight. The head of Charles II's new

---

1. Breda is a city in the south of the Dutch Republic.

administration was ***Edward Hyde, Earl of Clarendon*** (1609–74), a devout Anglican who had led the royalist MPs against John Pym in the House of Commons, after the original unity of the Long Parliament had broken down back in 1641. Clarendon is also important as a historian; his *History of the Rebellion and Civil Wars in England* (first published in three volumes at Oxford, 1702–4) is our most detailed account of the Civil War period from a contemporary royalist.

Under Clarendon's guidance, the Cavalier Parliament proceeded to enact a new religious settlement for the country. The fiercely Episcopalian nature of this settlement, and its oppressive character toward non-Episcopalians, derived from parliament rather than from the king. Charles was prepared to be more tolerant, but the Anglican-royalist MPs were in no mood to be generous to the Presbyterians, Independents, and Baptists who had humiliated them on the battlefield, killed their king, and outlawed their worship. Charles had no choice but to fall in with this vengeful mood; he could rule only through his parliamentary supporters. The whole country indeed seemed to be in an anti-Puritan state of mind, a strange amalgam of Episcopalian religious fervour and sheer licentious rejection of moral restraint. The Puritanism of the Civil War period was now merely a subject for hilarity and ridicule, well captured by satirist Samuel Butler (1612–80) in his poem *Hudibras* (1664). The Puritan "hero" of the poem, a Civil War warrior, was held up to devastating mockery:

> For his Religion, it was fit
> To match his learning and his wit;
> 'Twas Presbyterian true blue;
> For he was of that stubborn crew
> Of errant saints, whom all men grant
> To be the true Church Militant;
> Such as do build their faith upon
> The holy text of pike and gun;
> Decide all controversies by
> Infallible artillery;

And prove their doctrine orthodox
By apostolic blows and knocks;
Call fire and sword and desolation
A godly, thorough reformation,
Which always must be carried on,
And still be doing, never done;
As if religion were intended
For nothing else but to be mended.
A sect, whose chief devotion lies
In odd perverse antipathies;
In falling out with that or this,
And finding somewhat still amiss;
Compound for sins they are inclin'd to
By damning those they have no mind to:
Still so perverse and opposite,
As if they worshipp'd God for spite.

The Cavalier Parliament, reflecting more the religious side of this anti-Puritan frenzy, legally re-established the Church of England as a fully Episcopal Church, worshiping according to a slightly revised Anglican Prayer Book,[2] with the monarch as supreme governor. The Solemn League and Covenant was burned in public by order of parliament—Presbyterianism was now a lost cause. The Act of Uniformity in May 1662 required all parish clergy to renounce the Covenant, submit unconditionally to the doctrine and worship of the restored Anglican Church, promise never to attempt any change to the status quo in church or state, and to receive Episcopal ordination if they lacked it.

The Act came into effect on Saint Bartholomew's Day (24th August). When it did, almost a thousand clergy left the established Church. The figure is often given as two thousand; but this larger number is obtained by adding on a further 700 or so clergy who had already left under the provisions of the

---

2. Richard Baxter thought the revisions made the Prayer Book "more grievous than before".

September 1660 Act for Confirming and Restoring of Ministers (which among other things required an acknowledgment of royal supremacy over the Church), plus some 200 university lecturers (ordained men) also expelled for their Puritanism. In the Anglican Church in Wales, another 120 clergy lost their livings. In all, between 1660 and 1662, the established Church lost roughly one fifth of its ministers.

The 1662 Act of Uniformity did not occur in a vacuum. Prior to the election of the Cavalier Parliament, there had been various attempts, often politically driven, to find some middle way that would allow Presbyterians to remain in the established Church. These efforts reached their high noon in the Savoy Conference of April-July 1661, where 12 Anglican bishops met with 12 Presbyterian divines to discuss the possibility of a national ecclesiastical settlement embracing both Episcopalians and Presbyterians. The Presbyterian delegates included Edward Reynolds, John Conant, and John Wallis (who all conformed to the Anglican Church when the conference failed—see below), and Richard Baxter, Edmund Calamy, and Thomas Manton (who did not conform and were expelled in 1662).

Both sides exhibited a certain inflexibility. The leading Anglican, **Gilbert Sheldon** (1598–1677), the Bishop of London, was a survivor from the days of William Laud, an uncompromising High Church Arminian, deeply averse to Presbyterianism and all other forms of non-Episcopal Protestantism. Sheldon wanted to keep the Presbyterians out of the Church, not to accommodate them. He threw the Presbyterian delegates on the defensive by asking what changes they wished to see in the Church before they would conform. The Presbyterians obligingly walked straight into his trap and produced a list of 99 necessary changes, which of course made *them* look insufferably provocative and pedantic in the eyes of the other bishops (just what Sheldon wanted). The conference fizzled out into futility. The only positive fruit it bore was Richard Baxter's *Reformed Liturgy*, which Baxter offered as an example of how worship might be conducted acceptably to all Reformed consciences. A commendable model of Reformed worship, it nonetheless antagonized the Anglican bishops, since Baxter seemed to be saying that he could whip up a liturgy at a moment's notice that was superior to the venerable Prayer Book.

Reconciliation failed, then, and the Act of Uniformity duly took effect on August 24th 1662. The Church of England thereby lost the majority of its ministers with any kind of Puritan leanings toward reform. It would not be true, however, to say that all spiritually-minded Calvinists left the established Church. A number of such men, including some who in the period 1640–60 had merited the name "Puritan",[3] stayed within the Anglican establishment. Richard Baxter in his autobiography made it clear that there were a good many such men, and that (along with Arminians who were not High Church) they were "laudable preachers and the honour of the conformists".

The most well-known of the Calvinist conformists included *Edward Reynolds* (1599–1676), one of the most highly respected and influential of the Westminster divines, who had already been given the bishopric of Norwich in 1660;[4] the Presbyterian John Conant (1608–94), Rector of Exeter College, Oxford, who married Edward Reynolds' daughter, and after much boggling conformed to Anglicanism in 1670; Robert Crosse (1606–83), another Westminster divine, minister at Chew Magna in Somerset, an expert on the early church fathers and medieval scholastic theologians; John Wallis (1616–1703), a brilliant mathematician (still revered today), one of the Westminster Assembly's scribes, who had several pastorates in London before becoming Savilian Professor of Geometry at Oxford; and most famously *William Gurnall* (1617–79), minister at Lavenham in Suffolk, whose *Christian in Complete Armour* (three volumes, 1655–62) has become one of the most universally esteemed and popular classics of Reformed practical divinity ever published.[5]

---

3. According to this book's definition.

4. This put him in the odd position at the Savoy Conference of being a bishop among the Presbyterian delegation!

5. Gurnall is almost always called a Puritan, but it is debatable; according

Men like this ensured there would still be a Calvinist, evangelical group within the Anglican Church.

The Puritan-minded clergy who left the established Church between 1660 and 1662 were not the only ones to suffer. The Cavalier Parliament enacted a series of repressive measures affecting all non-Anglicans, both ministers and laity—Independents, Baptists, Quakers, and every other brand of nonconforming Protestant in addition to the Presbyterians. Together they made up around 10% of the English population. We can summarize the repressive legal measures against them as follows:

The Corporation Act of 1661 required all who held any kind of public office, from the lowest to the highest, to disown the Solemn League and Covenant, and to take part in holy communion in the Anglican Church within one year of appointment to office. This made it virtually impossible for devout non-Anglican laymen to be MPs, magistrates, university tutors, etc.

The Conventicle Act of 1664 made meetings for unauthorized (non-Anglican) worship illegal, if there were more than five people present who did not belong to the same household. When this Act was reaffirmed and more rigidly enforced in 1670, the Puritan-sympathizing MP and poet Andrew Marvell (1621–78), close friend of John Milton, famously denounced it as "the quintessence of arbitrary malice".

The Five Mile Act of 1665 prohibited non-Anglican ministers from living or even temporarily lodging within five miles of any city, or corporate town, or indeed any town where they had functioned as ministers or theological lecturers. There was a get-out clause: the Act no longer applied if the minister swore that it was never, under any circumstances, lawful to take up arms against the king or his government, and that he would never attempt any change to the status quo in church or state (as specified in the 1662 Act of Uniformity).

---

to this volume's definition, he was simply a spiritually-minded Anglican Calvinist. There is no evidence that Gurnall ever sought any reformation of the Church of England.

Together with the Act of Uniformity, these parliamentary enactments have (since the 19th century) collectively been called the "Clarendon Code", after the Earl of Clarendon. This is probably unfair to Clarendon; he was rather less dogmatic and intolerant than the Cavalier Parliament itself, or than Gilbert Sheldon who became Archbishop of Canterbury in 1663 and pushed hard for the absolute legal suppression of all non-Anglicans. The penalties for violating the Code were severe: crippling fines or imprisonment, including (for a breaking the Code a third time) being shipped out as slave labour to an American or Caribbean plantation for seven years. The overall result was a gruelling persecution of Protestants by a Protestant state that was almost unique in 17th century Europe.[6]

3. Protestant Nonconformists under the Clarendon Code

The next 25 years were to be a long, dark night of the soul for non-Anglican Protestants—Nonconformists or Dissenters, as they were called (Richard Baxter uses both terms in his autobiography). They were now in a worse position than they had ever experienced in English history. All prospect of reforming the Church of England was gone; all prospect of toleration for those outside her precincts was likewise gone. The heady hopes of the Civil War lay in ruins around the heroes of yesterday.

One possible response was violent rebellion. Only a few took this course. In January 1661 there was a Fifth Monarchist uprising in London to replace King Charles with King Jesus, but only some 50 men took part; most were killed by government forces, and the survivors were executed. In March 1663 at Muggleswick Park in Durham, a meeting of Nonconformist conspirators plotted an insurgency, but were betrayed by a Baptist plotter who had second thoughts; many were arrested, many fled. But the conspiracy rumbled on, and the same essential group were still planning an armed revolution when

---

6. Almost unique, because we should remember the parallel persecution of Covenanters by the same government in Scotland.

government agents swooped on them in October, arresting some 90 men. A score of them were executed in January 1664. Still the plotting continued, and it only really fizzled out when the Great Plague hit the country in 1665.[7] These Nonconformist plots and uprisings were the work of a small minority, but they hardened the attitude of a nervous and vengeful government against all Nonconformists; the innocent many suffered for the crimes of the reckless few. The Conventicle Act of 1664 was almost certainly a reaction to these insurrectionary plots.

How did peaceful Nonconformists respond to the Clarendon Code? Some, while retaining their personal convictions, renounced its expression in worship, and attended their parish church. Others sought ingenious ways of complying with the Code without abandoning Nonconformity. Adam Martindale (1623–86), for instance, a Lancashire Presbyterian, preached the same sermon throughout the week to a succession of tiny groups, so that the Conventicle Act was not violated.

Others disobeyed the Code but took precautions to conceal their disobedience. Some congregations met in the thick of night, sometimes in forests or caves. At Olney, in Buckinghamshire, there was an area called Three Counties Point that bordered on Buckinghamshire, Bedfordshire, and Northamptonshire; a Nonconformist group led by John Gibbs (1627–99) worshiped in this area, so that if county officers arrived to arrest them from one county, they could simply slip across the boundary-line into a different county. Others fitted out the house where they met with elaborate escape routes in case government agents turned up: concealed trap-doors into cellars, concealed side-doors into other rooms (e.g. through a cupboard). The government agents could burst into the room where they believed the illegal worship was taking place, only to find it mysteriously deserted. The Independent minister Thomas Jollie (1629–1703) of Wymondhouses, Lancashire, preached in a room from a desk that was really a folded door to a back staircase. If government

---

7. The plague, although it began in London, hit other parts of the country too, hence not "the Great Plague of London".

agents were spotted, Jollie pulled a cord which raised the top half
of the desk, recreating the door. Consequently, agents entering
the room from the front would find a group of people but no
Jollie, who exited by the staircase.

Informers were a constant danger. The Clarendon Code
awarded them a third of the fine imposed on convicted
Nonconformists, so there was a strong financial incentive to
infiltrate and betray illegal worship meetings. In the Calvinistic
Baptist congregation at Broadmead, Bristol, whose pulpit was
filled by a variety of preachers, the speaker gave the sermon from
behind a curtain, so that any visiting informer could hear the
preaching (and hopefully be converted!) but not be able to see
or identify the preacher.

Despite all these dexterous methods of obeying the
Clarendon Code or concealing disobedience, however, many
Nonconformists were arrested, convicted, and punished. Over
200 of the clergy expelled from the national Church in 1660–62
ended up in prison. Between 1682 and 1686, we know that in
London alone, over 3,800 Nonconformists were arrested and
tried for attending illegal worship. It has been estimated that a
total number of between 5,000 and 8,000 Nonconformists may
have died in prison under the Clarendon Code (17th century
prisons were unhygienic places).

How did the three main groupings of Nonconformists—
Presbyterians, Independents, and Baptists—each respond
collectively to the long ordeal?

Many Presbyterians continued to hope that the government
might have a change of heart to the extent, at least, of allowing them
back into a broader Anglican Church. There were conferences on
this between Presbyterian and Anglican divines in 1668, 1674,
and 1680, and one last time in 1689 after the Stuart dynasty had
once again been toppled from the throne. But the conferences
bore no fruit, and Presbyterians remained outside a national
established Church that did not want them. In addition, the
paralyzing restrictions placed on Presbyterian religious activity
by the Clarendon Code meant that Presbyterians could not
function as a genuinely Presbyterian Church. Each congregation

was forced in practice to act as though it were an autonomous Independent church. English Presbyterianism therefore lost its distinctive identity during the years of repression, becoming virtually Independent in practice.

The leading Presbyterian of this period was Richard Baxter.[8] Another who came to prominence was *John Flavel* (1627–91) of Dartmouth in Devonshire; diehard Anglicans of the Restoration era sometimes spoke of an unholy trinity of Richard Baxter, John Owen, and John Flavel as the three great upholders of Nonconformity. Flavel enjoyed unsurpassed success as an evangelistic preacher, and his writings on doctrinal and practical divinity were treasured for their rare marriage of plain speaking and imaginative power. *The Fountain of Life Opened* (1672) was perhaps his most significant work, an extended meditation in 42 sermons on the person and work of Christ. Another Presbyterian who now attained full spiritual stature was *John Howe* (1630–1705); he had had a brief stint as Cromwell's chaplain, but it was in the Restoration period that Howe's theological maturity produced works of enduring value that appealed far beyond the Nonconformist constituency, notably *The Living Temple* (2 vols., 1675–1702) and *The Redeemer's Tears Wept Over Lost Souls* (1684). Intriguingly, Howe had been trained at Cambridge under Henry More and Ralph Cudworth, two of the "Cambridge Platonists" (see below), and some have found Howe's thought a unique bridge between the worlds of Platonism and Puritanism.

The Independents may have profited from the Presbyterians' loss of ethos. Or at least, a significant number of Presbyterian ministers ejected from the national Church between 1660 and 1662 are known to have become Independents. Certainly the Independent-Presbyterian animosities of the Civil War died away; the two great parties were drawn together in a spirit of unity as fellow-sufferers under the Clarendon Code. As Presbyterians lost their church government distinctives, there seemed little to keep the two groups apart. Some Independents drew so close

---

8. Baxter had idiosyncratic views of church government, as he did of virtually everything, but he was most identified with the Presbyterians.

to the Presbyterians that they embraced their desire to return into England's national Church, and joined with Presbyterians in seeking this when the persecution was finally over and a friendly monarch (William of Orange—see below) once again sat on the throne. Perhaps they were harking back to Cromwell's decentralized, live-and-let-live national Church of the 1650s, in which Independents had been given freedom to minister according to their own ideals. But it was not to be, and the sense that some Independents had acquired of being Anglicans-in-exile was doomed to frustration. Many other Independents, however, were glad enough that it should be so; they had held on resolutely to their belief in strict Congregationalism, and saw no way of melding it with the Anglican system.

Until his death in 1683, John Owen was by far the most influential Independent. Thereafter, leading figures in Independency were Thomas Cole, Isaac Chauncey (or Chauncy), and Richard Davis. *Thomas Cole* (1627–97) was minister of Silver Street Independent church in London, which Philip Nye had pastored. He was notable for defending Reformed Orthodoxy against some of Richard Baxter's more debatable ideas on the atonement, imputed righteousness, and the nature of faith and repentance. *Isaac Chauncey* (1632–1712) ministered to the congregation at Mark Lane in London, the capital's most distinguished Independent church; John Owen had been the previous pastor, and the church was full of members who had played a prominent part in the government of Oliver Cromwell, or at least had married into families connected with the old Cromwellian regime. *Richard Davis* (1658–1714) was minister of Rothwell, Northamptonshire; his theology ignited controversy (he was accused of antinomianism), but there could be no denying his passionate commitment to preaching with an evangelistic note. His congregation grew hugely over his 25 year ministry (795 people coming into membership), and he preached regularly to a circle of some 50 Independent churches within an 80 mile radius of Rothwell.

Baptists were also drawn closer to Presbyterians and Independents in the furnace of the Clarendon Code. This probably helps explain why in 1677, during the period of persecution, the Calvinistic Baptists adopted a slightly modified form of the Westminster Confession (Presbyterian) and Savoy Declaration (Independent) as their own doctrinal statement: a self-conscious assertion of pan-Reformed brotherhood. Surprisingly, the Arminian Baptists of Bedfordshire, Buckinghamshire, Hertfordshire, and Oxfordshire, did something similar in 1679 with their Orthodox Creed: Or a Protestant Confession of Faith, where they emphasized what they had in common with all Reformation Protestants, rather than Arminian distinctives. The Orthodox Creed used the framework of Reformed covenant theology, and veered so close to Calvinism (teaching perseverance, for instance) that some have seen it as less an Arminian confession, more an Arminian-Calvinist synthesis. It testified to the desire of at least some Arminian Baptists to join the world of Reformed thought-patterns and language. Their motive was stated in the subtitle of the Creed: "being an essay [attempt] to unite and confirm all true Protestants in the fundamental articles of the Christian religion, against the errors and heresies of Rome". The moving spirit behind the Orthodox Creed was **Thomas Monck** (active 1654–79), who was concerned about the appearance of Christological errors among Arminian Baptists (the old Anabaptist "heavenly flesh" Christology).[9]

The Baptist leadership in this period were mostly the same men we have already considered in Chapter 3 section 6. Still, a few new figures emerged. The most important by far was **Benjamin Keach** (1640–1704), pastor of the Calvinistic Baptist church at Horsleydown in Southwark (south London). A prolific writer, his *Tropologia, or a Key to open Scripture Metaphors* (1682) was long in print as a popular favourite. He is credited with writing the slightly amended Westminster Shorter Catechism for Calvinistic Baptists, "Keach's Catechism", but the attribution

---

9. That is, the view that Christ did not derive His human nature from Mary, but had a separate, specially created "heavenly" flesh. The view was widespread among 16th century Anabaptists.

is doubtful—William Collins (d.1702) seems a more likely candidate. Keach's place in Baptist history, however, is assured by his lively championship of hymn-singing in corporate worship. He published a hymnbook in 1691, and his was probably the first English congregation of any kind to sing hymns, rather than simply psalms and other Bible passages. There were others who argued in favour of hymn-singing—Thomas Manton, Richard Baxter, John Bunyan—but Keach's church took the plunge, setting a precedent that would be largely followed by English Protestants in the 18th century.

One last development provoked by the Clarendon Code should be mentioned. Because the Code excluded Nonconformists from the Anglican-controlled universities (Oxford and Cambridge, the only two at that time), some alternative method had to be found for educating the sons of non-Anglicans. Nonconformists therefore began establishing "academies". These academies were colleges of higher education, usually run by one tutor—often a minister with no church. The tutor would gather 20 or 30 young men in his home, and put them through four years of fairly intensive study. Typical subjects taught in a Dissenting academy were Latin, Greek, Hebrew, maths, history, geography, biology, rhetoric, ethics, philosophy, anatomy, law, and theology. Many of the academies were so effective, Anglicans began complaining that Nonconformists were receiving a superior education than Oxford or Cambridge could provide! The most famous academy was based in Stoke Newington, London, and run by the Independent minister Thomas Rowe (1657–1705).

4. The Church of England: currents of thought

The Church of England in this period had by no means ceased to be a repository of religious life. By this, I mean that it was not just staffed by a bunch of time-servers who had no real beliefs, but were only interested in their salaries. Anglicanism was full of serious faith. Let us consider the strands of thought that were present in the Restoration Church.

The High Church Arminians were certainly there, represented by men like Gilbert Sheldon of Canterbury; John

Cosin, Bishop of Durham; *John Pearson* (1612–86), Bishop of Chester; *Herbert Thorndike* (1598–1672), Canon of Westminster Abbey; and *George Bull* (1634–1710), who held various posts before becoming Bishop of Saint David's in his old age. Calvinists and Nonconformists thought that such men had an insufficiently Protestant faith, but it would be futile to deny that they were devout and sincere in their spirituality. When they were not combating Nonconformity, High Church Arminians were usually combating Roman Catholicism or Socinianism with learned and hard-hitting treatises that all Protestants could admire, e.g. Cosin's *History of Popish Transubstantiation* (1676), or Bull's *Defence of the Nicene Faith* (1685). Pearson's *Exposition of the Creed* (1659) enjoyed a long popularity among Trinitarian believers of all denominations.

Then there were the conforming Calvinists, like Edward Reynolds and William Gurnall. Since we looked at them in the previous section, we will not repeat ourselves here. One point worth making, however, is that conformity to the Church of England was not necessarily painful to Calvinists, and that some not only conformed gladly, they even combined their conformity with high views of the Anglican Church and its Episcopal government. In the case of George Morley (1597–1684), Bishop of Winchester from 1662, one can only use the term "High Church Calvinist". The conforming Calvinists, however, did not exercise much influence over the Church as a whole. Their very Calvinism was now suspect, since it allied them theologically with the disgraced Puritans.

A more novel group that emerged in the Civil War period, but exercised real influence in the national Church only after 1660, was the Cambridge Platonists. Their leading figures were *Benjamin Whichcote* (1609–83), *Henry More* (1614–87), *Nathaniel Culverwell* (d.c.1651), *John Smith* (1618–52), and *Ralph Cudworth* (1617–88). These men studied and/or taught at Cambridge University. All but More were trained in the Puritan seminary of Emmanuel College; More trained in the Puritan-dominated Christ's College. Yet they all moved away from the Puritanism of their youth. Partly this was a reaction against what they perceived to be its intolerance and party-spirit, a charge they levelled equally against the High Churchmen. Never were theologians more devoted to toleration and liberty of conscience than the Cambridge Platonists. Partly it was also a reaction against what they believed was a corrosive irrationality at the heart of much Puritan faith (and non-Puritan Calvinism too), whereby it never really laid any solid foundations for why a person should be a Christian or even a theist. They saw, or thought they saw, far too much lawless subjectivity in Puritan religion—"enthusiasm", in the jargon of the time (emotional fanaticism). They came especially to object to the Calvinist understanding of God's sovereignty, believing it to be destructive of human responsibility and morality, a recipe for a ripe antinomianism.

The positive agenda of the Cambridge Platonists was to cultivate a vision of reason as the essence of religion. By "reason", they did not mean either common sense or the law of non-contradiction; they meant an interior light, a capacity for world-transcending vision, which saw and grasped the basic truths of morality and theism in an immediate way. No religion could be right if it did not validate this vision, enhance it, and foster a morally wholesome character and life. In matters of Christian doctrine, the theologians of this group looked more to the Greek fathers of the early church than to Augustine or the Reformers. They also found lofty inspiration in the Platonist and Neoplatonist philosophers of antiquity (hence the group's nickname, Cambridge "Platonists"); their Christianity was permeated by a sense of the worth and relevance of ancient philosophy for the vital issues of their own day. They took a keen interest in the pioneering work in science that characterized the second half of their century, and sought to correct what they regarded as some of the young scientific enterprise's unhelpful philosophical underpinnings, tending to materialism—notably in the writings of the French Catholic René Descartes, and the English atheist Thomas Hobbes (1588–1679).

Many found the writings and preaching of the Cambridge Platonists captivating; with its synthesis of faith, reason, conscience, and philosophy, it seemed to breathe a freer, nobler spirit than what was often found elsewhere. It was tragic that their heartfelt commitment to religious toleration was not heeded in 1662 by the Church to which they gave their allegiance. The most celebrated treatise to emerge from Cambridge Platonism was probably Nathaniel Culverwell's *An Elegant and Learned Discourse of the Light of Nature* (1652). The most comprehensive philosophical statement by a Cambridge Platonist was Ralph Cudworth's *The True Intellectual System of the Universe* (1678). The most accessible work, however, was Benjamin Whichcote's *Moral and Religious Aphorisms*, collected from his other writings and published in 1703.

The Cambridge Platonists helped to give birth to another new school of thought in the next generation of Restoration Anglicanism, the Latitudinarians (or "Latitude-Men", as they were also called in the jargon of the day). The leading Latitudinarians were **Simon Patrick** (1626–1707), **Edward Stillingfleet** (1635–1699), **Joseph Glanville** (1636–80), Thomas Tenison (1636–1715), **John Tillotson** (1639–94), and **Gilbert Burnet** (1643–1715). Trained or inspired by the Cambridge Platonists, they all rose to top positions in the Anglican hierarchy.[10]

Their "Latitudinarian" nickname stemmed from their insistence that a person needed to believe very little in order to be a Christian: one could tolerate a wide latitude of beliefs, as long as the bare fundamentals were accepted. The Latitudinarians themselves were orthodox enough in their personal beliefs, some even inclining to a mild Calvinism; but their promotion of a minimal approach to fundamental doctrines (sometimes as minimal as "Jesus is the Messiah") was allied to a focus on the

---

10. Patrick was Bishop of Chichester (1689) and Ely (1691); Stillingfleet was Dean of Saint Paul's Cathedral (1678) and Bishop of Worcester (1689); Glanville was Rector of Bath Abbey (1666) and a Fellow of the Royal Society; Tenison was minister of London's eminent Saint-Martin's-in-the-Fields (1680), Bishop of Lincoln (1691), and Archbishop of Canterbury (1694); Tillotson was Dean of Canterbury (1672) and Archbishop of Canterbury (1691); Burnet was Bishop of Salisbury (1689).

moral life as the true heart of Christianity. This view was reflected in their preaching, which often lacked theological depth and risked turning morality into moralism. In the Latitudinarians, the spiritual richness and profundity of their mentors, the Cambridge Platonists, and their almost mystical concept of reason, had rather evaporated; it was replaced by something more like a middle-of-the-road reasonableness. In a famous phrase, Simon Patrick extolled the Church of England as keeping to a "virtuous mediocrity between the meretricious gaudiness of the Church of Rome and the squalid sluttery of fanatick conventicles". "Virtuous mediocrity" summed up what critics felt about Latitudinarians. More positively, their pragmatic view of reason made them strong supporters of the new scientific thought.

The doctrinal tolerance of the Latitudinarians extended to Nonconformity, in the sense that they wished the Anglican Church to be inclusive enough to embrace Nonconformists. At the same time, however, they feared what they perceived as the tendency of Nonconformity to fanaticism ("fanatick conventicles"), and did not exactly protest at the legal restrictions placed on Nonconformists by the Clarendon Code. Latitudinarians were equally opposed to High Church narrowness, and they succeeded in dislodging the High Churchmen from centre stage in Anglicanism. The victory of Latitudinarians over High Churchmen was cemented by the Glorious Revolution of 1688–9, when too many High Church Anglicans refused to give allegiance to William of Orange, whereas Latitudinarians welcomed him with open arms. They were the founders of what became known as "Broad Church" Anglicanism.[11]

5. The Exclusion Crisis

The fate of Nonconformists became deeply entangled with a constitutional crisis between Charles II and parliament that drove

---

11. As distinct from "High Church", which we have encountered at length, and "Low Church", the nickname that became attached to Anglican evangelicalism.

the country to the brink of another civil war. This was owing to Charles' clandestine alliance with the French King Louis XIV, whose Catholic France was now the dominant power in Europe.[12] The two monarchs pledged their allegiance to each other in the secret Treaty of Dover in June 1670. Louis agreed to pay Charles £160,000 a year; Charles in turn would support Louis' foreign policy (by joining him in a war against the Dutch Republic), and would convert to Roman Catholicism as soon as it was politically expedient. In fact Charles was not to convert till his deathbed.[13] But he almost immediately began using royal authority to improve the condition of English Catholics. They were as legally oppressed as Protestant Nonconformists, and had been since Elizabeth I's reign. To disguise his pro-Catholic motives, however, Charles promoted freedom for all non-Anglicans, Catholic and Nonconformist alike. He did this by using his alleged power as king to suspend the discriminatory laws passed against non-Anglicans by parliament. This plunged Charles into prolonged conflict with his MPs over his supposed right to suspend laws properly enacted by parliament.[14]

Charles' suspension of the discriminatory laws came in March 1672, in his "Declaration of Indulgence". Nonconformists were allowed to worship in public, on applying for a license (many did so, despite doubts about the legality of Charles' methods); Roman Catholics were allowed to worship in private. The Indulgence lasted a year. Charles was forced to cancel it in March 1673, however, because of parliament's outrage at what they saw as his gross violation of their constitutional authority by his "suspending power". MPs also suspected the king's motives, fearing that he was leaning towards Rome (as he was). Despite his secret "pension" from Louis XIV, Charles was still desperate for cash (he was in debt, and the Dutch war cost ten times

---

12. See almost the whole of Chapter 6 for the reign of Louis XIV.

13. His motives for agreeing to convert remain rather mysterious. It did not affect his mistress-ridden lifestyle.

14. The "suspending power" was the king's alleged right to suspend the operation of a law *in toto*. He also claimed a "dispensing power", his alleged right to exempt a particular individual from a law's functioning.

more than the pension), and needed parliament's cooperation to raise money legally. So against his wishes, he had to agree to parliament's demand for even stronger anti-Catholic measures. The result was the Test Act of 1673, which required all who held any position of public responsibility to swear an oath denying transubstantiation, and to take part in holy communion in the Anglican way within three months of appointment to office. (This was stricter than the Clarendon Code, which required participation in Anglican communion within one year.)

This anti-Catholic Act was in fact merely the prelude to an outburst of anti-Catholic mania that convulsed the nation, fuelled by the public conversion to Catholicism of Charles' brother James, Duke of York, in 1676. The hysteria reached a pitch of almost insane intensity with the "revelation" of the Popish Plot in 1678. This was an alleged Jesuit conspiracy to assassinate Charles, replace him on the throne with Catholic James, and then massacre untold thousands of Protestants. No such plot existed, save in the twisted mind of Titus Oates (1649–1705), who exposed the imaginary plot for reasons best known to himself. For three years, England was gripped by a paranoia probably unique in its history; scores of innocent Catholics were executed virtually on the say-so of Oates, who was now installed in Whitehall and receiving a handsome salary for his endless perjuries. The paranoia finally burned itself out in 1681. Senior judges reasserted the reign of common sense, and Oates' fall from public favour was spectacular—deserted by everyone, he was arrested, convicted of perjury, and sentenced to life imprisonment. One of his more enduring legacies was a 1678 Act that explicitly prohibited any Catholic from sitting in the House of Commons or the House of Lords. It would not be repealed until 1829.

It was in this atmosphere that the Exclusion Crisis pushed England once again towards civil war. Charles had no legitimate sons (many illegitimate ones, but they did not count). This meant that should he die, his Catholic brother James would inherit the throne. The very idea of a Catholic monarch struck dread into many an English heart: people remembered the persecution of Protestants by the last Catholic monarch, Mary Tudor. A majority of MPs were therefore determined to exclude James from the throne by passing a special parliamentary act to that effect. We shall not follow the political story in detail. Charles dissolved parliaments, summoned new ones, and dissolved them again between 1679 and 1681, trying to fend off an Exclusion Bill; he was adamant that James must be king, partly to give credence to Charles' own secret decision to become Catholic, albeit he was postponing the conversion as long as possible.

The parliamentary leader who masterminded the campaign for excluding James was *Anthony Ashley Cooper, Earl of Shaftesbury* (1621–83), a self-conscious champion of Protestantism and parliament against popery and royal tyranny. A wealthy Dorset landowner with strong business interests, Shaftesbury exploited the hysteria of the Popish Plot for all it was worth in his attempt to keep James from the crown. Shaftesbury had a majority in the various parliaments that sat in 1679–81; his pro-Exclusion party was nicknamed the "Whigs". The name probably derived from the Scottish "whiggamore", a cattle thief; it had been applied insultingly to the faction of Covenanters headed by the Marquis of Argyll, whose "Whiggamore Raid" on Edinburgh in 1648 had ejected the faction allied to Charles I and put Argyll in power.[15] Shaftesbury's Whigs were not only opposed to Roman Catholicism and unchecked kingly authority, they also championed the rights of Nonconformists to freedom of worship. In the anti-Catholic fever that shook England because of the Popish Plot, some Nonconformists were able to elude the Clarendon Code and get themselves elected to the House of Commons as Whig MPs. So was forged the intimate alliance of Whigs and Nonconformists that would play so long and influential a part in English politics.[16]

Opponents of the Exclusion Bill that the Whigs were pushing through parliament were nicknamed the "Tories". The word Tory derived from an Irish word for an outlaw; originally

---

15. See Chapter 5, section 3.6.
16. The Whigs were later re-branded the Liberals, who in turn were the ancestors of today's Liberal Democrats.

it described Irish insurgents against the British. But opponents of James, Duke of York, and his claim to the English crown, applied it to his supporters, perhaps because Catholic James was seen as a natural ally of the Catholic Irish against the Protestant English. Tories were more devoted to the monarchy than Whigs were, and would not let parliament interfere with the line of succession to England's throne.

No matter what Charles II did—suspending parliament, dissolving parliament, new elections—he could not break the grip that Shaftesbury and the Whigs had on the House of Commons. The Exclusion Bill looked as though it would keep getting passed by the MPs. But Charles refused to accept it. As king and parliament confronted each other in an increasingly explosive atmosphere, people muttered that it was "1642 all over again". Charles finally dissolved parliament for the third time, calling a new one in Oxford rather than London. His purpose was to overawe the MPs with a show of force, and for that he had to get them away from the dangerous London mob that supported Exclusion.

In Oxford, Charles summoned the new MPs (still overwhelmingly Whig) into his presence, where—backed by royal troops—he once more rejected the Exclusion Bill, and dissolved parliament again. With no London mob to back them, the Whig MPs were powerless. They dispersed. Charles would never again hold a general election for the rest of his reign. Shaftesbury was arrested and charged with treason. He was acquitted by a Whig jury, but fled the country, dying three years later as an exile in the Dutch Republic.

Charles had made it clear by stationing those royal troops in Oxford that he was ready for violent conflict rather than exclude James from the throne. Were the Whigs ready? Faced with the question, the great majority preferred to bide their time. A small minority of extremists plotted to assassinate Charles (the Rye House Plot of 1683), but the plot was leaked, and several leading Whigs were arrested and executed on flimsy evidence, including Lord William Russell (1639–83), who died with Christian dignity and was hailed by Whigs as a martyr. An anti-

Whig reign of terror was unleashed by Charles in his last two years of life, which destroyed the Whigs' legal basis of power by stripping towns and cities of their right to elect magistrates without the king's consent. Although the Triennial Act required a new parliament for 1684, Charles ignored the Act. He was now ruling as an absolute monarch. Nonconformists were persecuted more bitterly than ever, tainted in Charles' eyes by their alliance with the Whigs.

As he lay dying from a stroke, Charles was received into the Roman Catholic Church in February 1685. On his death, his Catholic brother James succeeded to the throne.

6. Other key figures

Jeremy Taylor

The life of *Jeremy Taylor* (1613–67) straddled the reigns of Charles I and Charles II. However, since his work really "came into its own" during the Restoration, it seems fitting to deal with him here. Born and educated at Cambridge, Taylor impressed Archbishop Laud in the 1630s, and became a chaplain to King Charles I. He then served for several years as chaplain to royalist troops in the Civil War, but was taken prisoner by parliamentary forces at the siege of Cardigan Castle in February 1645. Details are obscure, but that same year Taylor retired from the war, becoming chaplain to Richard Vaughan, the royalist Earl of Carbery, at Golden Grove in Carmarthenshire (south-west Wales). Just before the Restoration, he spent two years in Ireland at Lisburn under the patronage of the royalist viscount of Conway, where he was a "lecturer" (a preacher whose salary came from voluntary subscriptions—royalists were now using the method Puritans had used to find work for their unemployed ministers).

It was during this period of obscurity that Taylor wrote many of the theological and spiritual works for which he would be renowned. *The Liberty of Prophesying* (1647) was a noble appeal for religious toleration. Taylor argued that persecution for religious opinions was utterly inappropriate; human minds were incurably fallible, and endlessly liable to interpret Scripture in conflicting ways. The state should punish people only for criminal behaviour, not for belief; indeed, the best way to judge beliefs was to see what ethical fruit they bore in the lives of those who believed them. The treatise offended King Charles I (not noted for his commitment to freedom of worship), but Taylor had proved with conviction and clarity that one could be a High Church royalist and devoted to liberty.

More influential and celebrated were Taylor's *Holy Living* (1650) and *Holy Dying* (1651), destined to be hailed as classics of non-Puritan Anglican spirituality. *Holy Living* achieved an oddly modern tone in the unsqueamish honesty with which it dealt with lust and chastity. Its companion volume, *Holy Dying*, saw Taylor's prose mature into the dazzling elegance and pregnancy of meaning for which, as an author, he became so famous. It is doubtful whether any other writer in English has scaled such heights of moving eloquence in meditating on death and what lies beyond death. *The Golden Grove* (1655) was, as its subtitle said, "a manual of daily prayers", containing (among other things) an exposition of the Lord's Prayer and a collection of hymns for "younger and pious persons". There were also two volumes of sermons, a comprehensive tome on casuistry, a controversial account of original sin (*Unum Necessarium*, 1655) that seemed vague even to some of Taylor's friends, and a treatise against the Roman Catholic doctrine of transubstantiation, robustly defending a more Reformed-Anglican view of Christ's presence in the eucharist.

At the Restoration, Taylor was immediately honoured by the new regime for his royalism; Charles II made him Bishop of Down and Connor in the Irish Anglican Church, and vice-chancellor of Dublin University, in 1660. The following year, Charles also gave him the bishopric of Dromore. Taylor's Episcopal reign was not a happy one; he met with strong opposition from both Irish Catholics and Scottish Presbyterians who had settled in Ireland. Somehow the "liberty of prophesying" did not seem to find much room to flourish. The Presbyterian ministers treated Taylor with contempt, refusing in any way to recognize his position as bishop;

Taylor rapidly lost patience, referring to them as "Scotch spiders", and declaring that he would rather "be a poor curate in a village church than a bishop over such intolerable persons". He ended up deposing many Presbyterians from the ministry of the Irish established Church for refusing to accept his authority. The only result was a popular body of Irish Nonconformist Presbyterians, who had the loyalty of the Protestant middle classes. Miserable and harassed, Taylor asked the king to bring him back to England, but Charles turned a deaf ear.

Still, Taylor had done his true work in his writings. He ranks as one of the masters of the English language—a "spiritual Shakespeare", as he has often been called. Occasionally his richness of style has (for some) obscured his meaning, but few have disputed the enchanting quality of his image-laden poetic prose, flowing forth in the service of practical Christian truth.

John Milton

John Milton (1608–74) is usually remembered as a poet—England's "number two" after Shakespeare. Before he published *Paradise Lost* in 1667, however, his own generation knew him as a devastatingly eloquent political and ecclesiastical propagandist, and a dedicated servant of the English Republic. Milton's father was a prosperous London scrivener (someone who drew up legal and financial documents on behalf of clients) who gave his eldest son financial independence. Milton Senior was a Puritan convert from Roman Catholicism, and transmitted his faith to Milton Junior. The future poet had a private tutor, the Puritan theologian Thomas Young (1587–1655), later one of the Westminster divines. After studying at the Puritan Christ's College, Cambridge, Milton launched out into a long period of private study, which included a tour of the Continent where he visited famous intellectuals like Galileo. He wrote several great poems during this early period—*Ode upon the Morning of Christ's Nativity*, *Comus*, and *Lycidas*—but they did not establish his reputation.

Everything changed with the collapse of Charles I's government and the Civil War. Milton emerged as a triumphant pamphleteer, pouring out a stream of treatises, first in defence of parliament and Presbyterianism, but then switching his allegiance to the New Model Army and Independency. Milton was horrified and outraged at the religious intolerance of parliament's Presbyterian majority, and scornful of the Scottish Covenanters. His most famous treatise from this period is *Areopagitica* (1644), an animated plea against censorship. When the Army purged parliament and executed the king, the new English Republic found its most brilliant defender in Milton, whose two 1640 treatises *The Tenure of Kings and Magistrates* and *Eikonoklastes* ("Image-breaker", written in response to *Eikon Basilike*) vindicated with a scathing splendour the actions of the Army and the Rump Parliament. Milton argued as George Buchanan and Samuel Rutherford had, that rulers are accountable to the ruled, that tyrants may be lawfully resisted and deposed, and that Charles had been a tyrant.

The English Republic also faced the wrath of almost all Europe, both Catholic and Protestant. At the close of 1649 the erudite French Calvinist, Claude Salmasius, mounted a fierce attack on the Republic, in his *Defensio regia pro Carolo I* ("Royal Defence on behalf of Charles I"). Milton's response in 1651—*Defensio pro Populo Anglicano* ("Defence on behalf of the English People")—demolished Salmasius. The educated European world was amazed to see so learned a defender of the new Republic, and impressed by his arguments and eloquence.

Milton was now appointed "secretary of foreign tongues" to the Republic's council of state, which meant that he translated all diplomatic letters and documents. He remained in this post under Cromwell, whom Milton admired intensely; he expressed his admiration in his 1652 sonnet *Cromwell, our chief of men*. When Cromwell became Lord Protector, Milton wrote:

> …nothing in the world is more pleasing to God, more agreeable to reason, more politically just, or more generally useful, than that the supreme power should be vested in the best and the wisest of men. Such, O Cromwell, all acknowledge you to be.

Milton fought hard to prevent the restoration of the monarchy; once Charles II was back on the throne, it was only the intercession of powerful friends that saved Milton from being hanged. Even so, he had to pay a crippling fine, and his writings were publicly burned. To add to his misery, he was now blind (he had lost his sight, after a period of deterioration, in 1654).

However, in his blindness Milton produced the stunning epic poem *Paradise Lost*, dictated to his daughters[17] and published in 1667. With overwhelming grandeur and dynamic characterization, Milton all but sings the story of humanity's creation and fall, and the hope of redemption, expressing many of the themes of Puritan theology and spirituality. The poem was almost immediately adapted for the stage by John Dryden in 1671 (although the royalist Dryden made Satan bear a remarkable resemblance to a certain Oliver Cromwell). By the end of the 17th century, *Paradise Lost* was being published with explanatory notes, a "first" in English literature. By the early 18th century, it had been accepted as a classic, celebrated as such in a series of essays by foremost critic Joseph Addison in *The Spectator* magazine in 1712;[18] Addison evaluated Milton's achievement as the equal (if not the superior) of Homer's *Iliad* and Virgil's *Aeneid*.

Milton followed up his success with *Paradise Regained* (the story of Christ's threefold temptation in the wilderness) and *Samson Agonistes* (Samson's final hours), both published in 1671: not quite as great as his original epic, but poetry of a high order. Despite the secularization of Anglo-Saxon culture, the deeply religious Milton has never gone away from the literary universe, and books and articles about his work are still legion.

Milton's theology, however, was extremely atypical for one so shaped by Puritan ideals. Some time in the 1640s, Milton abandoned Calvinism for Arminianism. That put him outside the Puritan mainstream, but he was not unique in being a "Puritan Arminian". Far more surprising, a little after this, Milton gave up believing in the eternal pre-existence of Christ. The Son, he thought, was generated from the Father in time,

---

17. Milton's various marriages are an epic in themselves into which I do not propose to enter.

18. Not to be confused with today's *Spectator* magazine.

so that only the Father was eternal. In other words, Milton embraced a Christology that radically subordinated the Son to the Father.[19] He also held that God created the universe, not out of nothing, but out of His own essence, a view verging on pantheism. These views are found most clearly expressed in his *De Doctrina Christiana* ("Concerning Christian Doctrine"), a systematic theology he wrote based on Wollebius (see Chapter 2, section 1) but never published in Milton's lifetime. His unorthodox Christology, however, is not found in the great post-1660 poems, which have been read and wondered at by orthodox Christian believers for nearly 350 years.

John Bunyan

John Bunyan (1628–88) is often labelled a Puritan, but he was never a Puritan as this book defines the term; he was a

From William Cathcart, *The Baptist Encyclopaedia* (Philadelphia, Everts 1881)

John Bunyan (1628–88)

John Bunyan in prison with his blind daughter

Separatist. It remains true, however, that Puritan literature was central in nourishing Bunyan's faith, especially Lewis Bayly's *Practice of Piety*.[20] The details of Bunyan's early life are obscure and matters of debate. We know he was born at Elstow in Bedfordshire of poor parents, that he was a tinker and/or brazier by trade,[21] and that he fought in the Civil War (it is not certain on which side). His marriage to a godly woman (we do not know her name) in 1649 brought him new spiritual impulses; his wife gave him Bayly's book to read, and another Puritan classic, Arthur Dent's

---

19. Many would say Milton became an Arian.

20. For Bayly, see Chapter 3 section 4.3.

21. *Tinker*: a travelling mender of metal utensils used in the household. *Brazier*: one who makes items of brass.

Plain Man's Pathway to Heaven (1601). By 1653, Bunyan had experienced assurance of salvation, after a frightful struggle described in his autobiography; he was (probably) baptized, by John Gifford, pastor of an Independent church in Bedford, which Bunyan joined. The church seems to have tolerated both infant baptism and believers' baptism; its theology was generally Calvinist, and Bunyan himself was a Calvinistic Baptist.[22]

In 1655 Bunyan began preaching; few could equal him in captivating his listeners. The restoration of the monarchy and the Anglican Church in 1660, however, brought persecution, and Bunyan was imprisoned for unlicensed preaching. He spent most of the period 1660–72 in Bedford prison. Conditions, however, were sufficiently tolerable for Bunyan to write, and it was from the prison that he produced his first masterpiece, *Grace Abounding to the Chief of Sinners* (1666). This was a vivid, graphic account of his pilgrimage to Christ, and a classic in the genre of spiritual autobiography. If he had written nothing else, he might be remembered for this.

But in 1678 he published *Pilgrim's Progress*, and English literature would never be the same again. Bunyan's allegory of the soul's journey through the wilderness of this world to heaven was a phenomenal best-seller; between 1678 and 1688 (the year Bunyan died), more than 11 authorized editions of the book appeared in Britain. It was also published in America, and translated into Welsh, French, and Dutch. It owed its popularity in part to the simplicity, immediacy, and descriptive power of its prose, in part to the succession of colourful characters that populate its pages, and the way Bunyan captures the style of ordinary speech in what he makes them say. Beyond that, of course, the very figure of the individual struggling to fulfil his destiny in an uncomprehending world has a universal human appeal. The story is also imbued with orthodox Protestant

---

22. Almost certainly. Some argue that he was a Calvinistic paedobaptist Independent. Some in the "Strict Baptist" tradition argue that his pamphlet *Water Baptism no bar to communion* really makes Bunyan an Independent with Baptist preferences.

theology, seeping out sometimes in direct statement, sometimes in symbol and parable.

Bunyan wrote other godly fiction: a second part of *Pilgrim's Progress* (1684)—parts one and two were always published separately until 1728; *The Life and Death of Mr Badman* (1680); and *The Holy War* (1682). Most of his writings, however, were works of doctrinal and practical divinity in a more typical mould.

When Bunyan died, he had already achieved literary immortality. What John Owen said of Bunyan's preaching has found its echo in the response of millions to Bunyan's writing: "Could I possess that tinker's abilities for preaching, I would gladly relinquish all my learning."

2

James II and the Glorious Revolution

1. A new Catholic king

When *James II* (born 1633; reigned 1685–88) succeeded to the throne in February 1685, all seemed fair. The Whigs who had tried to exclude him from the monarchy had been smashed by Charles II; meanwhile James' allies, the Tories, had made "passive obedience" a first article in their creed—it was never right to resist a lawfully crowned king. The only possible problem was that Tories were ardently Anglican, whereas James was Roman Catholic. Thus far, however, he had played his cards well, never criticizing the Church of England, but praising it for its loyalty to him. He was crowned according to a traditional Anglican ceremony, and he publicly promised to respect and maintain the Anglican Church, disavowing any intent to re-Catholicize England. If that relationship between monarch and Church ever broke down, James would be in trouble. Within three years, it was irreparably broken, and Tories joined with Whigs in ejecting James from the throne.

2. The Monmouth Rebellion and its aftermath

James reassured the country that he was no tyrant by holding a general election. The resulting parliament, which met in May 1685, was Tory-dominated, owing to the way Charles II had stripped towns and cities of their right to elect anyone as MP without royal consent. The Tory MPs were as loyal as James could have wished. They voted him for life the total income Charles had enjoyed.

But there was always going to be some opposition to James; the more fiercely Protestant sections of the population did not believe his moderate pose, and would be only too glad to see James fall. Only a month after parliament met, a violent popular rebellion broke out in the south-western counties (Devon, Dorset, Somerset). It was led by *James Scott, Duke of Monmouth* (1649–85), an illegitimate son of Charles II. Monmouth, a Protestant, had been the Whigs' favoured candidate for the throne in the Exclusion Crisis of 1679–81, and had then been implicated in the extreme Whigs' Rye House Plot in 1683. He was now living in exile in the Dutch Republic.

Monmouth gambled that the strongly Protestant, indeed Nonconformist, people of the south-western counties would back his claim to the throne, and rise up against James, if he (Monmouth) only showed his face and waved the flag of Protestant revolt against a popish king. Many lower class Nonconformists did indeed rally to Monmouth when he landed at Lyme Regis in Dorset on June 11th, but none of the Protestant gentry or nobility would support his hare-brained scheme. Monmouth's ragtag army was butchered by James' professional forces at Sedgemoor in Somerset, on July 6th. Monmouth himself fled but was captured and executed only a week later.

The aftermath of the Monmouth Rebellion was harrowing for Nonconformists. James put judge **George Jeffreys** (1654–89) in charge of the trials of those taken prisoner during and after the uprising. Jeffreys' conduct was fierce in the extreme; some 320 people were executed by hanging, and a further 800 or 900 shipped out as slave labour to the Caribbean plantations. The bodies of the executed were put on display at various spots as a gruesome object lesson in the fate of rebels. Two trials in particular achieved infamy. An elderly lady, Alice Lyle, a member of the royalist gentry, was tried for simply giving compassionate shelter to a Nonconformist minister and his companion who had fled from Sedgemoor; she was sentenced to death by burning, although in the event James mercifully allowed her to be beheaded. Another lady, the devout

Baptist Elizabeth Gaunt, was tried for attempting to help another refugee flee the country; she was not fortunate enough to belong to the gentry, and was actually burnt alive—the last woman to be punished by this method in England. Although most people did not support the Monmouth Rebellion, they were shocked and horrified by the government's brutality in its aftermath. The trials became known as the "Bloody Assizes",[1] and Jeffreys acquired the nickname "the Hanging Judge".

If James' response to the Monmouth Rebellion was not a public relations success, even worse came in October. That month, Louis XIV, Catholic king of France, revoked the Edict of Nantes, which for 100 years had guaranteed the religious liberty of his Protestant subjects, the Huguenots. Huguenot refugees began flooding into England, telling spine-chilling stories of Catholic intolerance in France. James could not prevent his people giving a generous welcome to the Huguenot refugees, but it damaged him badly. The Protestant English began fearing that Catholic James would sooner or later treat them as Louis XIV had treated French Protestants.[2]

When parliament reassembled in November, James unnerved the MPs by demanding huge sums to increase the size of the royal army (he had become paranoid about further rebellions). He also informed them that the Catholic military officers he had appointed, contrary to the Test Act of 1673, would stay in command, because he could not trust any others to be faithful to him. Pro-James though the Tory MPs were, they were alarmed. Was this James creating a Catholic army to impose his religion on England? They would not vote him the large sum he required. So he suspended parliament. In reality he had dissolved it, for this particular parliament would never assemble again.

3. Re-Catholicizing the nation
In 1686, James began taking measures to promote Catholicism. He did this by using the monarch's alleged "dispensing power"

---

1. "Assizes" refers to judges presiding at cases in the English counties.
2. See Chapter 7, section 3, for the persecution of the Huguenots.

to exempt individuals from the discriminatory religious laws against them. James now employed this power to exempt Catholics from the Test Act, and put them in top positions in the army, the universities, and the royal government. James deliberately arranged for an important legal case to come to trial that year. It involved a Catholic army officer, Edward Hales, who argued that the king's dispensing power gave Hales the right to his military commission without taking the anti-Catholic oaths required by the Test Act. Prior to the trial, James had dismissed from office almost all the judges who, on being asked, said they did not believe in the legality of the dispensing power. As a result, the verdict given on June 21st was a great victory for James: 11 of the 12 judges declared in favour of Hales, accepting the validity of his argument about the dispensing power of the monarch.

England's judiciary had checkmated England's parliament, and given James the green light to pursue his policy of staffing the nation's leading institutions with Catholics. 13 Catholics were sworn in as members of the king's Privy Council; Anglican Tories who objected were dismissed. In fact, James now seemed to go out of his way to flaunt his Catholicism in the face of his people. He built royal Catholic chapels at Whitehall and Windsor; he set up a new Catholic printing press in Oxford; the royal printers in London and York became Catholics, and began printing Catholic books; Catholics were put in charge of the armed forces and the civil service; Anglican clergy were forbidden to preach against Catholicism. James also tightened the screws on the universities. He appointed a Catholic as head of University College, Cambridge, with a Jesuit chaplain who celebrated the mass in public. Another Catholic was made head of the Oxford cathedral college of Christ Church. In February 1687, James ordered the vice-chancellor of Cambridge University to confer a degree on a Benedictine monk, Alban Francis. However, Francis declined to take the customary academic oaths (they were Protestant in language). James insisted that Francis must receive the degree without the oaths; the university vice-chancellor, John Peachell (1630–90), refused. Peachell was sacked, after being bullied in public hearings by the infamous Judge Jeffreys.

The public outcry against James' actions was great. Anti-Catholic pamphlets and treatises gushed from Protestant printing presses. So James tried to divide the Protestant opposition by cloaking his pro-Catholic policy in a general good-will to all non-Anglicans; in April 1687, he issued a Declaration of Indulgence, suspending all discriminatory laws against Protestant Nonconformists as well as Roman Catholics. Perhaps the Nonconformists could be won over, and a Catholic-Nonconformist alliance against Anglican intolerance might shore up James' throne? Although Nonconformists took advantage of the Indulgence to worship freely, most of them remained deeply suspicious of James' motives. Two of the foremost Presbyterians, Richard Baxter and John Howe, went so far as to denounce the Indulgence as unconstitutional.

James pressed ahead. One of the most controversial of his acts, following hot on the heels of the Indulgence, was to dismiss from Magdalen College, Oxford, its entire governing body (the "fellows", of whom there were 25) for refusing to have a royally chosen Catholic as head of College. (They had already elected an Anglican.) James forcibly replaced all the fellows with Catholics. A venerable college of Oxford University, the home of Anglican learning and nursery of Anglican piety, had been transformed into a virtual seminary for training Catholic priests. Anglicans were transfixed with horror.

James also outraged the Tory landowners. They no longer trusted him; so he could no longer rely on Tory magistrates to do his bidding. The king therefore carried out a purge, replacing the magistrates drawn from traditional Tory families with compliant non-entities of his own choosing, some of whom were Catholic or Nonconformist. The purge sent howls of anguish through the entire Tory establishment. It led to absurd scenes, for example in Newcastle, where James appointed a Catholic mayor and a Nonconformist council: the council loathed the papist mayor, and kept voting against his every attempt to present an official declaration of loyalty to James.

The alliance between James and Tory Anglicanism was clearly at an end. Since the Whigs were still implacably opposed to him, it left the king with almost no friends in the entire English political class. In August, the leading Tory-Anglican politician, **George Savile, Marquis of Halifax** (1633–95), wrote a best-selling response to the royal Indulgence of February. This was Halifax's *Letter to a Dissenter*, in which he famously told Nonconformists concerning James' advances to them, "You are therefore to be hugged now, only that you may the better be squeezed at another time." 20,000 copies of Halifax's letter were printed, and there were no fewer than six editions. It has been called the most successful leaflet (it was only six pages) of the 17th century. Most Nonconformists found Halifax's argument all too plausible, and refused any alliance with James.

James' position was further undermined by another best-selling pamphlet, published in November by Gaspar Fagel (1634–88), the "grand pensionary" (chief magistrate) of Holland, most powerful of the Dutch Republic's provinces. Fagel was acting on behalf of William of Orange (1650–1702), the Calvinist Republic's "stadtholder" or highest federal official. William's stake in the English scene was his marriage to James' Protestant daughter Mary (1662–94), which meant that if James died without a son, Mary would inherit the English throne. In the November letter, Fagel publicized the fact that William and Mary both disapproved of James' proposed abolition of the 1673 Test Act which prevented Catholics from holding office. It was hinted that they also disapproved of his Declaration of Indulgence. The pamphlet's message spread like wildfire; by 1688, some 55,000 copies had been sold. English Protestants began looking overseas to William of Orange as their great hope of deliverance.

4. The fall of the house of James

In April 1688, James reissued his Declaration of Indulgence. This time he ordered the clergy of the established Church to read it out from their pulpits. Here was a crisis of conscience: ever since the Restoration, Anglican clergy had extolled the virtue of passive obedience to the reigning monarch. Yet now their monarch was commanding them to act as his agents in promulgating a decree they believed to be aimed at the destruction of their Church. They had little doubt that it was a mere cover for the further promotion of Roman Catholicism. Many of them also doubted its legality: could the king ride roughshod over parliament in this manner, by suspending its laws? Was parliament not part of the constitution, as well as the monarchy? Had it not been the Cavalier Parliament that had restored the Anglican Church in 1662? James was sure the spineless clergy would obey and read out the Indulgence. He had a rude awakening.

Seven of the bishops—Archbishop **William Sancroft** (1617–93) of Canterbury, John Lake (1624–89) of Chichester, William Lloyd (1627–1717) of Norwich, Thomas White (1628–98) of Peterborough, Francis Turner (1637–1700) of Ely, *Thomas Ken* (1637–1711) of Bath and Wells, and Jonathan Trelawney (1650–1721) of Bristol—handed in a petition to James, asking to be excused from reading the Indulgence. Several other leading Anglican clergy who did not have bishoprics also signed the petition. **Henry Compton** (1632–1713), the militantly Protestant bishop of London, would have signed, but James had already suspended Compton from his Episcopal functions for his outspoken opposition to royal Romanizing (Compton had refused to discipline one of his clergy in 1686 for an anti-Catholic sermon). Enraged, James had the seven bishops arrested and tried for seditious libel. Meanwhile, those Anglican clergy who did read the Indulgence from the pulpit found that their congregations walked out in protest.

Although the Indulgence gave freedom to Protestant Nonconformists as well as Catholics, even the great majority of Nonconformists opposed the king's declaration: they believed it was unconstitutional, and that its real aim was the re-establishment of Catholicism. The Calvinistic Baptist leader **William Kiffin** (1616–1701) advised churches that shared his faith to make a pragmatic use of their new-found liberty, but to offer no thanks to James, since his motives were bad and the

Indulgence was unlawful. Presbyterian leader Richard Baxter employed the freedom the king had given him by preaching a sermon praising the seven imprisoned bishops for their heroic Christian defiance of a papist tyrant! (Perhaps for the first and last time in English history, Anglican bishops were popular heroes.) The Indulgence therefore brought no great rallying of Nonconformity to James. Paradoxically it had the opposite effect: most Nonconformists rallied to the Anglicans who were suffering for their rejection of the Indulgence. Anglicans responded, and spoke of toleration for Nonconformists being lawfully enacted by a free Protestant parliament. It seemed that the differences between Anglican and Nonconformist had melted away in united Protestant opposition to a greater enemy—Rome, personified in James.

The trial of the seven bishops was held on June 29th. On June 30th, the jury returned a verdict of "Not Guilty". England went wild with celebration. James was stunned and deeply mortified. On the night of the verdict, seven leaders of the opposition to James (including Bishop Compton of London) signed a letter addressed to William of Orange, pleading with him to land in England with his Dutch army and save the liberties of an endangered Protestant people. The letter had even more urgency than it would otherwise have had, owing to the birth of a son to James on June 10th. This meant that James now had his own male heir to the throne. (He already had a grown-up daughter, of course—Mary, wife of William of Orange—but a daughter hardly counted in those days.) The horrifying prospect of a Catholic dynasty drove almost every English Protestant into a state of dread that was prepared to act in a revolutionary manner to preserve a Protestant England. If it took a Dutch Calvinist army to deliver the land, so be it.

William of Orange's motive had in reality nothing to do with English liberty, or not specifically. He had only one objective in life: to destroy the ambitions of Louis XIV to control Europe in the interests of Catholic France. William feared an alliance between Louis and James. James had thus far held back, anxious that such an alliance would alienate his people. But William was taking no chances. He managed to secure the support of the Dutch ruling classes, and of his German allies, especially Prince Frederick III of Brandenburg-Prussia. They could have opposed any expedition of the Dutch army to England on the grounds that it left them defenceless against France, but William convinced them that their long-term safety required a Protestant England. He may even have secured the blessing, or the acquiescence, of Pope Innocent XI. Innocent was as opposed to Louis XIV as William was, because of the French king's assumption of power over the Catholic Church in France in the drawn-out Gallican crisis (see Chapter 7, section 1); indeed the pope had only just excommunicated Louis.[3] Then William waited for a favourable wind. When it finally came on November 1st, William's fleet set sail for England: 600 ships carrying 15,000 troops.

Meanwhile a strong tide of anti-James feeling had been flowing in England. The rank and file of his army were turning against him; so James brought over a contingent of Irish Catholic soldiers. This merely made things worse. Anti-James riots broke out. A satirical anti-James, anti-Catholic ballad, *Lillibullero*, penned by the leading Whig politician Thomas Wharton (1648–1715), caught on with astonishing speed; Wharton boasted later that the ballad "had sung James out of three kingdoms" (England, Scotland, and Ireland). William's troops landed at Torbay in Devon on November 5th. There they waited. There was no general uprising; the people of the south-western counties had been too traumatized by their experience during Monmouth's rebellion to take any further insurrectionary action. But William did not need to do anything. He published a manifesto, disclaiming any intention of conquest, assuring everyone that he had come purely at the invitation of England's civil and spiritual leaders, denouncing James' unconstitutional acts, and calling for a free parliament to resolve the nation's grievances.

---

3. The idea that William of Orange was allied to the pope is of course a rather mind-boggling one, considering the nature of politics in Northern Ireland today.

James ordered his unreliable army to Salisbury. But already some of the foremost English nobles had declared for William. The top Tory statesman, **Thomas Osborne, Earl of Danby** (1632–12), one of the seven who had signed the letter of invitation to William, had mobilized the northern counties against James, and captured York; the top Whig statesman, **William Cavendish, Duke of Devonshire** (1640–1707), who had also signed the invitation, had mobilized the midlands. On November 24th, James' most loyal servant and most capable general, the Tory Lord **John Churchill** (1650–1722), defected from the Salisbury army to William, together with 400 officers and men. James lost his nerve and resolved on flight. He was consumed with fear that he might meet the same fate as his father, Charles I—executed by his own people. The fugitive king was captured by a Protestant mob at Faversham and carried back a prisoner to Whitehall; but William's Dutch troops liberated the fallen monarch, and allowed him to escape to France. William judged it best to have James out of the way.

5. The 1689 Revolution settlement

Once James had left England, the members of the House of Lords, together with those who had been elected MPs in the House of Commons under Charles II, acting as the representatives of the country, entrusted William with its administration. He arranged for a general election to send delegates to a "convention"—a special parliament to settle England's political and religious affairs. The Convention Parliament met on January 22nd 1689. After intense debate, parliament finally declared that since James had abandoned his country, the English throne was now vacant. On this, Whigs and Tories were agreed, after much boggling by the Tories. They were not agreed on a solution to the vacancy. Whigs wanted to give William the crown; Tories preferred to make him a "regent" ruling theoretically in the name of James II's newborn son, so that the strictest principle of hereditary monarchy from father to son would be preserved. The problem with the Tory solution was that William would not accept it. If he was to govern England, he wanted a free hand; he must be king.

The Tories caved in. On 11th April, Bishop Compton of London crowned **William** and **Mary** as joint monarchs of England (William's claim to the throne was through Mary, as daughter of James II—not quite as good as a son, but sufficient). They were crowned on condition that they accepted a Bill of Rights; among other things, the Bill prohibited Roman Catholics from occupying the throne, declared illegal the monarch's power to suspend the operation of laws passed by parliament, and made parliamentary freedom of speech absolute—no MP could be prosecuted for anything said in parliament. William and Mary's acceptance of the Bill of Rights extinguished any idea of absolute monarchical authority in England. They ruled under a constitution.

These events collectively are known in English history as the Glorious Revolution—glorious because bloodless.

The religious settlement of 1689 brought an end at last to the persecution of Nonconformists. As a "reward" for their refusal to ally themselves with James, they were now given legal freedom to worship in the Toleration Act of May 1689. (The Conventicle Act of 1664 and the Five Mile Act of 1665 were both repealed.) There were conditions. The Act did not apply to anti-Trinitarians, only to Presbyterians, Independents, Baptists, and Quakers (who all confessed the Trinity). Unitarians would have to wait until 1813 before parliament granted them legal toleration.

To obtain the benefits of the Act, those of Presbyterian, Independent, and Baptist persuasion had to subscribe to the 39 Articles of the Anglican Church, except the parts dealing with church government and (for Baptists) the article on baptism. Richard Baxter published a treatise, *Mr Baxter's Sense of the Articles*, to enable Nonconformists who still had scruples about some of the 39 Articles to sign them with a good conscience. Quakers were exempt from any allegiance to the 39 Articles; they merely had to declare their faith in the Trinity and the inspiration of the Bible. Nonconformists also had to swear allegiance to the reigning monarch, and subscribe to a statement rejecting transubstantiation. On complying with these terms, Nonconformists became as fully legally protected as Anglicans in their worship. The new freedom was immediately exploited by Nonconformists, and hundreds of new chapels were built and new congregations founded. Nonconformists were required to register their places of worship with the civil authorities, and were not allowed to bar anyone from their meetings, but disturbing Nonconformist worship was now a criminal offence.

However, there was no lifting of the civil restrictions on Nonconformists. They could still not hold public office (therefore not sit as MPs),[4] nor send their sons to Oxford or Cambridge. This exclusion from the political and educational life of the national establishment, however, was not quite as galling as it may sound. Some Nonconformists could and did sit as MPs by "occasionally" taking holy communion in the Anglican Church, thus getting around the Corporation Act of 1662 and the Test Act of 1673. Even where they did not have a Nonconformist MP, Nonconformists could rely implicitly on the Whigs to safeguard their interests in parliament— the Whigs became the political voice of Nonconformity, while the Tories were the political voice of Anglicanism. As for Oxford and Cambridge, Nonconformists could get an equal or superior education at a good Dissenting academy (see this Chapter section 1), to the vexation of envious Anglicans.

One restriction that remained on Nonconformists that was genuinely galling: they still had a legal obligation to pay tithes to the Anglican Church. Tithes had a long and complicated future ahead of them in England, Wales, Scotland, and Ireland.

James II made one attempt to recover his throne. Now that he was in exile in France, his alliance with Louis XIV became a reality; Louis gave him 6,000 French troops, and James landed with them in Ireland in March 1689. The Catholic Irish rallied to his support and threw off the British yoke. However, most Irish Protestants proved to be "Williamites" not "Jacobites".[5] The Williamite military operations in Ireland were led for a year by

4. It would not be until 1828 that Nonconformists could sit as MPs without any religious tests.

5. See Chapter 5, section 5.2. "Jacobite" derives from the Latin for James, *Jacobus*.

the distinguished German Calvinist general, **Frederick Schomberg** (c.1615–90), who had gained French citizenship and lived in France, working for Louis XIV, until Louis expelled the Huguenots in 1685. Schomberg was now general-in-chief of William's ally, the Calvinist Prince Frederick III of Brandenburg-Prussia. Schomberg's progress in quelling the Irish Jacobites was slow, so in June 1690, William himself joined the fray, taking personal command of his forces in Ireland. When William defeated James' army at the battle of the River Boyne in Leinster on July 1st, James' courage failed (although it was not a catastrophic defeat—and on William's side, Schomberg was killed). The ousted monarch fled back to France. His flight demoralized the Irish Jacobites badly. Within a year, Williamite forces had reconquered Ireland; British Protestant rule was once again assured, and the Catholic majority were again second-class citizens in their own land.

6. The Nonjurors

One problem the Glorious Revolution unexpectedly bequeathed to the Anglican Church was a schism. The Anglican clergy had sworn an oath of allegiance to James II. Parliament now required them to swear an oath of allegiance to the new monarchs, William and Mary. Six bishops and 400 parish ministers refused. They believed their oath to James as king was binding; indeed, they held that hereditary monarchy was a sacred institution, and that no act of parliament could exchange one king for another. James II was lawful monarch still, and after his death, his heirs would succeed to the throne. These clergy resigned from the Church of England, which had largely sworn allegiance to William and Mary, and created their own alternative Church, which they maintained was the true Anglican Church. They are referred to as the Nonjurors, and their tradition is known as the Nonjuring movement (the word is derived from Latin: "the non-swearers", i.e., those who would not swear allegiance to William and Mary). The six Nonjuring bishops were replaced by Latitudinarians in the Anglican hierarchy, which helped cement Latitudinarian supremacy as the reigning "party" on into the 18th century.

The Nonjurors included five of the seven bishops whom James II had put on trial for refusing to read out his Declaration of Indulgence. That meant Anglicanism lost its Archbishop of Canterbury, William Sancroft, to the Nonjurors. Sancroft set an uncompromising example to the other Nonjurors by refusing even to worship in the parish church in Suffolk where he had retired; the official Anglican Church, by abandoning James, was now little short of apostate, in Sancroft's view. He was, however, a mild and benevolent man, revered even by his enemies. Equally revered was Thomas Ken, Nonjuring Bishop of Bath and Wells, universally famous for the poetic doxology:

> *Praise God, from whom all blessings flow;*
> *Praise Him, all creatures here below;*
> *Praise Him above, ye heavenly host;*
> *Praise Father, Son and Holy Ghost.*

Ken's declaration in his last will and testament summed up the religious position of the Nonjurors against Anglicans, Nonconformists, and Roman Catholics:

I die in the Holy Catholic and Apostolic Faith, professed by the whole Church before the disunion of East and West: more particularly, I die in the Communion of the Church of England, as it stands distinguished from all Papal and Puritan innovations, and as it adheres to the doctrine of the Cross.

By "the Church of England" here, Ken meant the Church of England as envisaged by Nonjurors, rather than the actual Church of England from which he had seceded. By "the doctrine of the Cross", he meant the High Church Tory doctrine of passive obedience, i.e. that all rebellion against one's sovereign was always wrong.

One Nonjuring bishop, William Lloyd of Norwich, made sure the Nonjuring movement would not rapidly die out by consecrating two more bishops, an act that spawned a series of consecrations which extended the movement's life to the end of the 18th century. There were soon interesting developments within the Nonjuring tradition, notably the restoration by some

Nonjurors of several ancient practices to holy communion—
the mixed chalice (wine and water), the "epiclesis" prayer for the
descent of the Spirit, the offering of the bread and wine to the
Father as a sacrifice of thanksgiving, and prayer for the faithful
departed. There were also fascinating negotiations between the
Nonjurors and the Eastern Orthodox between 1716 and 1725
for some kind of union, but these came to nothing because of
disagreements over a few stubborn issues like the veneration of
saints and the nature of Christ's presence in the eucharist.

By the early decades of the 19th century, the Nonjuring
clergy and congregations had dwindled away into extinction.
Still, the fact that the movement endured for a hundred years,
and boasted some of the holiest and most learned divines in
England, says something for its spirit. By far the most famous
Nonjuror was to be **William Law** (1686–1761); his *Serious
Call to a Devout and Holy Life* (1728) would impact deeply on
many of the leaders of the Evangelical Revival, such as George
Whitefield and the Wesley brothers, and still ranks as one of the
greatest spiritual classics in the English language.

Important people:

Preachers/theologians

Herbert Thorndike (1598–1672)
Gilbert Sheldon (1598–1677)
Edward Reynolds (1599–1676)
Benjamin Whichcote (1609–83)
John Pearson (1612–86)
Jeremy Taylor (1613–67)
Henry More (1614–87)
William Gurnall (1617–79)
Ralph Cudworth (1617–88)
William Sancroft (1617–93)
John Smith (1618–52)
Nathaniel Culverwell (d.c.1651)
Simon Patrick (1626–1707)
Henry Compton (1632–1713)

George Bull (1634–1710)
Edward Stillingfleet (1635–1699)
Joseph Glanville (1636–80)
Thomas Ken (1637–1711)
John Tillotson (1639–94)
Gilbert Burnet (1643–1715)
William Law (1686–1761)

Presbyterians:
John Flavel (1627–91)
John Howe (1630–1705)

Independents:
Thomas Cole (1627–97)
Isaac Chauncey (1632–1712)
Richard Davis (1658–1714)

Baptists:
John Milton (1608–74. Milton teaches believers' baptism in De
    Doctrina Christiana)
William Kiffin (1616–1701)
John Bunyan (1628–88)
Benjamin Keach (1640–1704)
Thomas Monck (active 1654–79)

Royalty

Charles II (born 1630; reigned 1660–85)
James Scott, Duke of Monmouth (1649–85)
James II (1685–88)
Mary II (1689–94)
William III (1689–1702)

Statesmen and generals

George Monck (1608–70)
Edward Hyde, Earl of Clarendon (1609–74)
Anthony Ashley Cooper, Earl of Shaftesbury (1621–83)
Judge George Jeffreys (1654–89)
George Savile, Marquis of Halifax (1633–95)
Thomas Osborne, Earl of Danby (1632–1712)
William Cavendish, Duke of Devonshire (1640–1707)

John Churchill (1650–1722)
Friedrich Schomberg (c.1615–90)

Primary source material

Cambridge Platonism: the excellency and nobleness of true religion

The nearer any being comes to God, who is that infinite fulness that fills all in all, the more vast and large and unbounded it is; as the further it slides from Him, the more it is straitened and confined; as Plato hath long since concluded concerning the condition of sensual men, that they live like a shell-fish, and can never move up and down but in their own prison, which they ever carry about with them. Were I to define sin, I would call it the sinking of a man's soul from God into a sensual selfishness. All the freedom that wicked men have, is but (like that of banished men) to wander up and down in the wilderness of this world from one den and cave to another...

A good man finds not his religion without him, but as a living principle within him; and all his faculties are still endeavouring to unite themselves more and more in the nearest intimacy with it, as with their proper perfection. There is that amiableness [loveliness] in religion, that strong sympathy between the soul and it, that it needs carry no testimonials or commendations along with it. If it could be supposed that God should plant a religion in the soul that had no affinity or alliance with it, it would grow there but as a strange slip.[6] But God, when He gives His laws to men, does not by virtue of His absolute dominion dictate anything at random, and in such an arbitratious [arbitrary] way as some imagine; but He measures all by His own eternal goodness. Had God Himself been anything else than the first and greatest good of man, then to have loved Him with the full strength of all our faculties should not have been the first and greatest commandment, as our Saviour tells us it is.

---

6. Slip = a cutting taken from a plant, in order to graft or plant it elsewhere.

Some are apt to look upon God as some peevish and self-willed thing, because themselves are such: and seeing that their own absolute and naked wills are for the most part the rules of all their actions and the impositions which they lay upon others, they think that Heaven's monarchy is such an arbitrary thing too, as being governed by nothing else but by an almighty absolute will. But the soul that is acquainted most intimately with the divine will, would more certainly resolve us, that God's unchangeable goodness (which makes the divinity a uniform thing and to settle together upon its own centre, as I may speak with reverence) is also the unchangeable rule of His will; neither can He any more swerve from it, than He can swerve from Himself. Nor does He charge any duty upon man without consulting first of all with His goodness: which being the original and adequate object of a good man's will and affections, it must needs be that all the issues and effluxes of it be entertained with an answerable complacency and cheerfulness.

This is the hinge upon which all true religion turns, the proper centre about which it moves; which taking a fast and sure hold of an innate and correspondent principle in the soul of man, raiseth it up above the confines of mortality, and in the day of its mighty power makes it become a free-will offering unto God.

John Smith
The Excellency and Nobleness of True Religion, **Chapter 3**

The grace of humility is exercised by these following rules

Whatsoever evil thou sayest of thyself, be content that others should think to be true: and if thou callest thyself fool, be not angry if another say so of thee. For if thou thinkest so truly, all men in the world desire other men to be of their opinion; and he is a hypocrite that accuses himself before others, with an intent not to be believed. But he that calls himself intemperate, foolish, lustful, and is angry when his neighbours call him so, is both a false and a proud person.

Love to be concealed, and little esteemed: be content to want [lack] praise, never being troubled when thou art slighted or undervalued; for thou canst not undervalue thyself, and if thou thinkest so meanly as there is reason, no contempt will seem unreasonable, and therefore it will be very tolerable…

When thou hast said or done anything for which thou receivest praise or estimation, take it indifferently, and return it to God, reflecting upon Him as the giver of the gift, or the blesser of the action, or the aid of the design; and give God thanks for making thee an instrument of His glory, for the benefit of others.

Secure a good name to thyself by living virtuously and humbly; but let this good name be nursed abroad, and never be brought home to look upon it: let others use it for their own advantage; let them speak of it if they please; but do not thou at all use it, but as an instrument to do God glory, and thy neighbour more advantage. Let thy face, like Moses's, shine to others, but make no looking-glasses for thyself…

Some fantastic [fantasy-indulging] spirits will walk alone, and dream waking of greatness, of palaces, of excellent orations, full theatres, loud applauses, sudden advancement, great fortunes, and so will spend an hour with imaginative pleasure; all their employment being nothing but fumes of pride, and secret indefinite desires and significations of what their heart wishes. In this, although there is nothing of its own nature directly vicious, yet is either an ill mother or an ill daughter, an ill sign or an ill effect; and therefore at no hand consisting with the safety and interests of humility.

Suffer others to be praised in thy presence, and entertain their good and glory with delight; but at no hand disparage them, or lessen the report, or make an objection; and think not the advancement of thy brother is a lessening of thy worth. But this act is also to extend further. Be content that he should be employed, and thou laid by as unprofitable; his sentence approved, thine rejected; he be preferred, and thou fixed in a low employment.

Never compare thyself with others, unless it be to advance them and to depress thyself. To which purpose, we must be sure,

in some sense or other, to think ourselves the worst in every
company where we come: one is more learned than I am, another
is more prudent, a third more charitable, or less proud...

Be not always ready to excuse every oversight, or indiscretion,
or ill action, but if thou beest guilty of it confess it plainly; for
virtue scorns a lie for its cover, but to hide a sin with it is like
a crust of leprosy drawn upon an ulcer. If thou beest not guilty
(unless it be scandalous,) be not over-earnest to remove it, but
rather use it as an argument to chastise all greatness of fancy
and opinion in thyself; and accustom thyself to bear reproof
patiently and contentedly, and the harsh words of thy enemies,
as knowing that the anger of an enemy is a better monitor,
and represents our faults, or admonishes us of our duty, with
more heartiness than the kindness does or precious balms of
a friend.

Give God thanks for every weakness, deformity, and
imperfection, and accept it as a favour and grace of God, and an
instrument to resist pride, and nurse humility, ever remembering,
that when God, by giving thee a crooked back, hath also made
thy spirit stoop or less vain, thou art more ready to enter the
narrow gate of heaven, than by being straight, and standing
upright, and thinking highly. Thus the apostles rejoiced in their
infirmities, not moral, but natural and accidental, in their being
beaten and whipped like slaves, in their nakedness, and poverty.

Jeremy Taylor
The Rule and Exercises of Holy Living

Religion is more than talk

Faithful: Well, if you will, we will fall to it now; and since you
left it with me to state the question, let it be this: How doth
the saving grace of God discover itself when it is in the heart
of man?

Talkative: I perceive, then, that our talk must be about the
power of things. Well, it is a very good question, and I shall be
willing to answer you. And take my answer in brief, thus: First,
where the grace of God is in the heart, it causeth there a great
outcry against sin. Secondly –

Faithful: Nay, hold; let us consider of one at once. I think you should rather say, it shows itself by inclining the soul to abhor its sin.

Talkative: Why, what difference is there between crying out against, and abhorring of sin?

Faithful: Oh! a great deal. A man may cry out against sin, of policy; but he cannot abhor it but by virtue of a godly antipathy against it. I have heard many cry out against sin in the pulpit, who yet can abide it well enough in the heart, house, and conversation. Gen. 39:15. Joseph's mistress cried out with a loud voice, as if she had been very holy; but she would willingly, notwithstanding that, have committed uncleanness with him. Some cry out against sin, even as the mother cries out against her child in her lap, when she calleth it slut and naughty girl, and then falls to hugging and kissing it…

Then Talkative at first began to blush; but, recovering himself, thus he replied: You come now to experience, to conscience, and to God; and to appeal to Him for justification of what is spoken. This kind of discourse I did not expect; nor am I disposed to give an answer to such questions, because I count not myself bound thereto, unless you take upon you to be a catechiser; and though you should so do, yet I may refuse to make you my judge. But I pray, will you tell me why you ask me such questions?

Faithful: Because I saw you forward to talk, and because I knew not that you had aught else but notion. Besides, to tell you all the truth, I have heard of you that you are a man whose religion lies in talk, and that your conversation [i.e. conduct] gives this your mouth-profession the lie. They say you are a spot among Christians, and that religion fareth the worse for your ungodly conversation [conduct]; that some have already stumbled at your wicked ways, and that more are in danger of being destroyed thereby: your religion, and an ale-house, and covetousness, and uncleanness, and swearing, and lying, and vain company-keeping, etc., will stand together. The proverb is true of you which is said of a harlot, to wit, "That she is a shame to all women:" so are you a shame to all professors.

Talkative: Since you are so ready to take up reports, and to judge so rashly as you do, I cannot but conclude you are some peevish or melancholy man, not fit to be discoursed with; and so adieu.

Then up came Christian, and said to his brother, I told you how it would happen; your words and his lusts could not agree. He had rather leave your company than reform his life. But he is gone, as I said: let him go; the loss is no man's but his own. He has saved us the trouble of going from him; for he continuing (as I suppose he will do) as he is, would have been but a blot in our company: besides, the apostle says, "From such withdraw thyself."

Faithful: But I am glad we had this little discourse with him; it may happen that he will think of it again: however, I have dealt plainly with him, and so am clear of his blood if he perisheth.

Christian: You did well to talk so plainly to him as you did. There is but little of this faithful dealing with men now-a-days, and that makes religion to stink so in the nostrils of many as it doth; for they are these talkative fools, whose religion is only in word, and who are debauched and vain in their conversation [conduct], that (being so much admitted into the fellowship of the godly) do puzzle the world, blemish Christianity, and grieve the sincere. I wish that all men would deal with such as you have done; then should they either be made more conformable to religion, or the company of saints would be too hot for them.

John Bunyan
Pilgrim's Progress

How to serve God: Milton on his blindness

> When I consider how my light is spent,
> Ere half my days, in this dark world and wide,
> And that one talent which is death to hide
> Lodged with me useless, though my soul more bent
> To serve therewith my Maker, and present
> My true account, lest He returning chide,
> "Doth God exact day-labour, light denied?"

I fondly ask. But Patience, to prevent
That murmur, soon replies: "God doth not need
Either man's work or His own gifts: who best
Bear His mild yoke, they serve Him best. His state
Is kingly; thousands at His bidding speed
And post o'er land and ocean without rest:
They also serve who only stand and wait."

> **John Milton**
> *Sonnet XIX*

Pride and punishment: Satan's speech on first seeing the sun

Oh thou that with surpassing glory crowned
Look'st from thy sole dominion like the God
Of this new world; at whose sight all the stars
Hide their diminished heads; to thee I call,
But with no friendly voice, and add thy name,
O Sun, to tell thee how I hate thy beams,
That bring to my remembrance from what state
I fell, how glorious once above thy sphere;
Till pride and worse ambition threw me down
Warring in Heaven against Heaven's matchless King.
Ah, wherefore? He deserved no such return
From me, whom He created what I was
In that bright eminence, and with His good
Upbraided none; nor was His service hard…
O had His powerful destiny ordained
Me some inferior angel, I had stood
Then happy; no unbounded hope had raised
Ambition. Yet why not? Some other Power
As great might have aspired, and me, though mean,
Drawn to his part; but other Powers as great
Fell not, but stand unshaken, from within
Or from without, to all temptations armed.
Hadst thou the same free will and power to stand?
Thou hadst. Whom hast thou then or what to accuse,
But Heaven's free love dealt equally to all?

Be then His love accursed, since love or hate,
To me alike, it deals eternal woe.
Nay, cursed be thou, since against His thy will
Chose freely what it now so justly rues.
Me miserable! which way shall I fly
Infinite wrath, and infinite despair?
Which way I fly is Hell; myself am Hell;
And, in the lowest deep, a lower deep
Still threatening to devour me opens wide,
To which the Hell I suffer seems a Heaven.

John Milton
Paradise Lost, Book 4, lines 32–45, 58–78

The loneliness of truth

Servant of God, well done; well hast thou fought
The better fight, who single hast maintained
Against revolted multitudes the cause
Of truth, in word mightier than they in arms;
And for the testimony of truth hast borne
Universal reproach, far worse to bear
Than violence; for this was all thy care,
To stand approved in sight of God, though worlds
Judged thee perverse.

John Milton
Paradise Lost, Book 6, lines 29–37

The beauty of repentance

Henceforth I learn that to obey is best,
And love with fear the only God, to walk
As in His presence, ever to observe
His providence, and on Him sole depend,
Merciful over all His works, with good
Still overcoming evil, and by small
Accomplishing great things, by things deemed weak
Subverting worldly strong, and worldly wise
By simply meek: that suffering for truth's sake
Is fortitude to highest victory,

And, to the faithful, death the gate of life;
Taught this by His example, whom I now
Acknowledge my Redeemer ever blest.

John Milton
Paradise Lost, **Book 12, lines 561–73**

Christ lovely in His offices

He is altogether lovely in His offices: let us consider for a moment the suitability, fullness, and comforting nature of them.

First, The suitability of the offices of Christ to the miseries of men. We cannot but adore the infinite wisdom of His receiving them. We are, by nature, blind and ignorant, at best but groping in the dim light of nature after God, Acts 17:27. Jesus Christ is a light to lighten the Gentiles, Isa. 49:6. When this great prophet came into the world, then did the day-spring from on high visit us, Luke 1:78. By nature we are alienated from, and at enmity against God; Christ comes into the world to be an atoning sacrifice, making peace by the blood of His cross, Col. 1:20. All the world, by nature, is in bondage and captivity to Satan, a miserable slavery. Christ comes with kingly power, to rescue sinners, as a prey from the mouth of the terrible one.

Secondly, Let the fullness of His offices be also considered, which make Him able "to save to the uttermost, all that come to God by Him," Heb. 7:25. The three offices, comprising in them all that our souls do need, become an universal relief to all our distresses; and therefore,

Thirdly, Unspeakably comforting must the offices of Christ be to the souls of sinners. If light be pleasant to our eyes, how pleasant is that light of life springing from the Sun of righteousness? Mal. 4:2. If a pardon be sweet to a condemned criminal, how sweet must the sprinkling of the blood of Jesus be to the trembling conscience of a law-condemned sinner? If a rescue from a cruel tyrant is sweet to a poor captive, how sweet must it be to the ears of enslaved sinners, to hear the voice of liberty and deliverance proclaimed by Jesus Christ? Out of the several offices of Christ, as out of so many fountains, all the promises of the New Covenant flow, as so many soul-refreshing streams of peace and joy. All the promises of illumination, counsel and direction flow out of Christ's prophetic office. All the promises of reconciliation, peace, pardon, and acceptation flow out of His priestly office, with the sweet streams of joy and spiritual comforts which accompany it. All the promises of converting, increasing, defending, directing, and supplying grace, flow out of the kingly office of Christ; indeed, all promises may be reduced to these three offices, so that Jesus Christ must be altogether lovely in His offices.

John Flavel
Sermon 12, in *The Method of Grace*

True faith known by its effects

For a religion that opens such a scene of glory, that discovers things so infinitely above all the world, that so triumphs over death, that assures us of such mansions of bliss, where we shall so soon be as the Angels of God in Heaven; what wonder is it, if such a religion, such truths and expectations, should, in some holy souls, destroy all earthly desires, and make the ardent love of heavenly things, be the one continual passion of their hearts?

If the religion of Christians is founded upon the infinite humiliation, the cruel mockings and scourgings, the prodigious sufferings, the poor, persecuted life, and painful death, of a crucified Son of God; what wonder is it, if many humble adorers of this profound mystery, many affectionate lovers of a crucified Lord, should renounce their share of worldly pleasures, and give themselves up to a continual course of mortification and self-denial, that thus suffering with Christ here, they may reign with Him hereafter?

If truth itself has assured us that there is but one thing needful, what wonder is it that there should be some amongst Christians so full of faith, as to believe this in the highest sense of the words, and to desire such a separation from the world, that their care and attention to the one thing needful may not be interrupted?

If our blessed Lord hath said, "If thou wilt be perfect, go and sell that thou hast, and give to the poor, and thou shalt have treasure in hea···· and come and follow me"; what wonder is it, that there should be amongst Christians some such zealous followers of Christ, so intent upon heavenly treasure, so desirous of perfection, that they should renounce the enjoyment of their estates, choose a voluntary poverty, and relieve all the poor that they are able?

William Law
Serious Call to a Devout and Holy Life, ch. 9

Chapter 5

Scotland: The Crown Rights of the Redeemer

Introduction

The period covered by this Chapter is often considered the heroic age of the Scottish Church—or "Kirk", as we shall call it (it is merely the Scottish word for church). That heroism blazed forth in a long, bloody struggle for Presbyterianism within the national Kirk, against the Stuart monarchy and its determination to reduce the Kirk to a subservient department of state, run by royally appointed bishops.

A student is entitled to wonder how differently things might have turned out, had the Stuart kings themselves been devout Presbyterians. Would the Kirk have developed so stern an insistence on its spiritual autonomy from the state, if the state itself had taken the lead in fostering Presbyterian government in the Kirk? Perhaps a royalist Presbyterianism might have evolved, with Reformed churchmen happy to accept kingly government over the Kirk of Scotland. Of course, it is one of the might-have-beens of history; in reality, the Stuart monarchs loathed Presbyterianism, and vigorously promoted an Episcopalian form of church government as the instrument of monarchical control. For the Scottish Reformed Kirk, then, Presbyterianism went hand-in-hand with independence from royal authority: Calvinists had to secure the latter to enjoy the former.

The story begins where it ended back in Volume Three of the series, with the death of Scotland's first great Reformer, John Knox.

1

Of presbyters and kings: from Andrew Melville to the union of crowns

1. *The death of Knox*

John Knox had done his work. The titanic figure had yielded up his soul in 1572, leaving a reformed Scotland under the government of *James Douglas, Earl of Morton* (c.1525–81). He ruled as regent in the name of a young King *James VI* (born 1566, reigned 1567–1625), who was only six years old. Morton's church policy flowed from the so-called "Concordat of Leith", a religious settlement hammered out between Morton and the Kirk's general assembly in August 1572. Knox's participation in this meeting had been his last act of public significance.

The purpose of the meeting was to settle the question of the Scottish bishoprics that had survived the Reformation. Morton wanted to model the Scottish Kirk on the English Church, with the crown having supreme power, and appointing bishops as royal servants. Knox, however, had weighty objections. A compromise agreement provided that as Episcopal vacancies arose, qualified candidates at least 30 years old should be nominated by the crown, and then examined by a committee of ministers who had the right to accept or reject the nominee. When elected, the bishop was to swear allegiance to the general assembly in spiritual matters, and to the crown in civil matters. Knox acquiesced in this compromise settlement; he probably felt that it was the only practical way to secure finance for providing the spiritual oversight of certain areas of Scotland, previously visited by temporary commissioners of the general assembly. (Other areas had full-time "superintendents".)

Morton enforced the Concordat of Leith vigorously. Within four years, he had filled all vacant bishoprics with his own nominees. They were not, however, very popular; the contempt in which they were held is shown by their nickname—"tulchan" bishops. A tulchan was a dummy calf used to persuade a cow to give milk more freely. This was applied to Morton's bishops because their incomes were used to provide pensions for Morton's friends!

2. Andrew Melville and the Second Book of Discipline

Opposition to Morton's self-interested policies soon found a mighty champion in *Andrew Melville* (1545–1622), sometimes called Scotland's second Reformer (after Knox). If anyone other than Knox shaped the Reformed faith in Scotland, it was undoubtedly Melville. He was less rugged, more scholarly, than his predecessor, but no less intrepid, and probably no less influential. Born at Baldovie in Angus, Melville studied at a variety of Europe's academic centres—Saint Andrews, Paris, Poitiers, and Geneva. By the time he returned to Scotland in 1574, still a young man, he was one of the foremost scholars of the age: a brilliant linguist, fluent in Latin, Greek, Hebrew, Chaldee, and Syriac; a Ramist philosopher who used Ramist methods to liberate the teachings of Aristotle from what he considered medieval misinterpretations (Melville's mastery of Aristotle in the original Greek was unequalled);[1] and an erudite Reformed theologian, trained by the illustrious Theodore Beza.[2] His personality had both infectious fire and large-minded generosity. Certainly no one could accuse him of lacking the courage of his Reformed convictions, as we shall see.

---

1. See Chapter 2, section 1.1, for Ramism and its place in Reformed thinking in our period.

2. See Chapter 2, section 1.2, for Beza's life and work.

On returning to his native land, Melville was (at the surprisingly youthful age of 29) appointed principal of Glasgow University, which he radically reorganized. He especially demoted the medieval version of Aristotle in favour of Ramist thinking. His educational reforms extended far beyond Glasgow; he helped restructure teaching at Aberdeen University in 1575, and in 1580 he moved to Saint Andrews University, carrying out similar changes there. Saint Mary's at Saint Andrews became a divinity college, with Melville as principal. His ideals also shaped Edinburgh University when it was created in 1583. So gifted a figure could hardly remain obscure in the Kirk; he was elected moderator of its general assembly four times (in 1578, 1582, 1587, and 1594).

Melville was soon involved in a bold new movement to promote a more fully Presbyterian model of church government for Scotland. The Concordat of Leith was becoming obnoxious to some of the best minds in the Kirk, especially the way that regent Morton was taking advantage of it with his tulchan bishops. In the general assembly of 1575, the Edinburgh minister **John Durie** (c.1537–1600), a strong Calvinist and opponent of Episcopacy, sparked a debate on whether bishops were warranted by Scripture. By "bishops" he meant "diocesan bishops"—those who ruled a diocese, having a whole region of congregations and pastors under their authority. (This was the traditional Roman Catholic and Eastern Orthodox pattern, inherited and perpetuated by the Anglican Church, and now half-present in the Scottish Kirk.) Melville responded to Durie's overture with a forceful speech arguing for the full-blooded Presbyterian scheme of church government, as it had been conceived by Martin Bucer and John Calvin in the previous generation, and fleshed out in Calvin's Geneva. In the New Testament, Melville maintained, the "bishop" was equivalent to a simple congregational pastor or minister, and all ministers were equal in rank and dignity.

Melville's speech was well received: Presbyterian sentiment clearly had a following among Scottish ministers and elders. Consequently the assembly appointed a committee of six, including Melville, to investigate the question. The committee finally reported that "the name of bishop is common to all that have a particular flock over which they have charge to preach the word, minister the sacraments, and execute the ecclesiastical discipline with consent of the elders". The committee accepted that the Kirk might appoint some ministers as superintendents, with a wider oversight above local congregational level; but this, contended the committee, was a special commission which required the consent of the ministers over whom the superintendent was appointed, and the consent of his own congregation that their minister should take on this extra duty.

The general assembly of 1576 debated and approved this report, encouraged at this point by regent Morton, who perhaps did not quite grasp how serious Melville and his colleagues were in their ideals and commitment. The assembly appointed another committee to submit draft proposals on the proper constitution of the Kirk. Morton's initial flexibility, however, turned into angry hostility when the assembly opposed the regent's chosen candidate (Patrick Adamson) for the vacant archbishopric of Saint Andrews. When Morton went ahead and appointed Adamson over the assembly's head, the assembly charged Adamson with unlawfully intruding himself into the archbishopric. Morton was incandescent with rage. As a result of this rupture between the regent and the general assembly, the latter's proposals on the constitution of the Kirk, drafted chiefly by Melville, were stillborn; Morton was now in no mood to be conciliatory to a Kirk that had snubbed him by rejecting "his" man for the archbishopric. The proposals, however, did win the allegiance of a large party in the Kirk, and are of colossal historical significance as the manifesto of Scottish Presbyterianism—or at least Melvillean Presbyterianism, as it is often known. The manifesto took the shape of the Second Book of Discipline.[3]

---

3. The First Book of Discipline was the blueprint for Kirk and society drawn up by John Knox in 1560. See *Volume Three: Renaissance and Reformation*, Chapter 7, section 8.

The Second Book of Discipline made a clear distinction between Church and state. Each had its own God-given sphere of authority: they were distinct but should cooperate. (In modern terms this is the doctrine of "sphere sovereignty".) The godly magistrate had the power to reform a corrupt Church; but once the Church was Reformed, the magistrate must then support it in its functions, and submit to its discipline if he sinned. Within the Church, the Second Book of Discipline distinguished four offices: pastor, minister, or bishop; doctor or teacher; presbyter or elder; and deacon.

Pastors preached the word, administered the sacraments, and oversaw the spiritual life of the congregation.

Doctors were chiefly theology tutors in the universities, although the title could include catechizers and locally appointed lecturers.

Elders cooperated with the pastor in church discipline; they were to be elected for life (a change from the Reformation settlement of 1560, where elders were elected annually). Pastors and elders together formed the assemblies of the Kirk, which were of four kinds—congregational (the kirk session), provincial (presbyteries and synods), national (general assembly), and ecumenical (a theoretical global assembly for Presbyterians of all nations).

Deacons made sure the Kirk's income was collected, and distributed it to the pastors, the schools, and the poor.

The Second Book of Discipline ended with a list of abuses to be corrected: bishops must be pastors of particular congregations, and should not be distracted by holding political office (hence they should have no seat in parliament); the general assembly should be free to meet and determine all Kirk affairs without any interference by the state; the system of patronage—ministers being chosen by local landowners—should be abolished so that congregations could elect their own pastors.

3. King versus Kirk: the wheel of fortune

Regent Morton refused to enact the Second Book of Discipline in any way, shape, or form. But his days were numbered; he had made too many enemies. Ironically these included not just the Reformed Kirk, with Melville as its spokesman, but also two powerful Roman Catholic nobles, the Earl of Argyll and the Earl of Atholl. With no one left to support him, an isolated Morton was compelled by his foes to resign in 1578. However, Scotland was almost plunged into civil war by Morton's successful bid to regain power by sheer brute force (he kidnapped the young King James, who was to have more than his fair share of kidnappings); but after two more precarious years of regency, Morton's adversaries toppled him for good. The disgraced earl was executed in 1581—ironically, by a guillotine he had himself brought to Scotland because he had been so impressed by its efficiency. The regency now passed into the eager hands of the youthful monarch's new favourite, Esmé Stewart, soon elevated to be Duke of Lennox.

The year of Morton's execution witnessed a far more important event for Scotland's Kirk—a new confession of faith, not supplanting but supplementing the Scots Confession of 1560. This new confession was known as the King's Confession (or sometimes the Negative Confession). It was a specifically anti-Roman Catholic confession of faith, the product of an anti-Catholic panic that had seized the country: from king to peasant, everyone seemed suddenly to be seeing murderous papist conspirators hiding under every bed. The panic grew from Scottish fears of the increasing militancy in Europe of the Catholic Counter-Reformation, especially the aggressive anti-Protestant policies of King Philip II of Spain; Philip was at that time waging a savage war against Dutch Protestants, and within seven years would launch an invasion of England. In Scotland itself, these anti-Catholic anxieties were focused on the figure of regent Lennox, an ex-Catholic whose conversion to Protestantism many thought was insincere.

The King's Confession was an attempt to flush out Scottish Catholics and solidify the nation's Protestant faith. It was written by *John Craig* (c.1512–1600), one of the royal chaplains and an old friend of John Knox (he had served as Knox's co-pastor in Edinburgh's Saint Giles Kirk). As well as the King's Confession,

Craig wrote a famous catechism (also in 1581), which would be widely used in our period.

The King's Confession came in four parts:

1. It reaffirmed the theology of the Scots Confession.

2. It denounced in detail various distinctive Roman Catholic doctrines and practices.

3. It imposed an oath disowning any inclination towards Roman Catholicism.

4. It imposed a declaration of fidelity to king, country, and the Protestant religion.

The King's Confession became a colourful symbolic flag for future Scottish Presbyterians to rally around. It came to be seen as a national oath, perpetually binding on the Scottish people; when the Covenanting movement arose in the mid-17th century (see section 3), this was to be one of their most powerful and persuasive arguments—they were simply practising a godly loyalty to the King's Confession.

The King's Confession, however, failed spectacularly in its most immediate aim, because the dubious Lennox signed it. So some nobles decided on more direct action. In 1582, the Earls of Gowrie, Mar, and Glencairn—Protestant zealots and extreme opponents of Lennox—lured King James to Ruthven castle (it belonged to Gowrie), took him prisoner, and for 10 months ruled the country in his name. They forced James to banish Lennox, who sailed away to France, where he died a few months later. James' lamentation was passionate, outpoured in a poem *A Tragedy of the Phoenix*. Most Reformed ministers approved of the "Ruthven Raid", as it was called, and the general assembly hailed the three earls as Protestant heroes. Queen Elizabeth of England also gave them her backing. The God-fearing government of the three earls did not last, however; in 1583, James managed to escape from their clutches, re-establishing his authority through his old ally James Stewart, Earl of Arran (d.1595), who saw this as his opportunity to make himself master of Scotland. Gowrie was arrested and executed for treason.

James' new administration, headed by a dictatorial Arran, did not look kindly on a Kirk that had extolled the king's kidnappers as spiritual heroes. In February 1584, Andrew Melville was summoned before the Privy Council,[4] charged with preaching treason; he refused to accept the council's authority over his pulpit utterances, and was given a prison sentence in the notorious Blackness Castle, on the Firth of Forth. Rather than enjoy the king's hospitality in Blackness, Melville fled to Berwick-upon-Tweed, just over the border with England.

In May, at Arran's bidding, a subservient parliament passed a series of anti-Kirk acts, which Presbyterians deplored as the "Black Acts". These statutes decreed the king's supreme authority in all matters both spiritual and civil. His subjects were forbidden to gather in assemblies (including those authorized by the Kirk) without the king's command. Preachers were forbidden to say anything in sermons detrimental to the king or his policies. Finally, the bishops—dependent on royal patronage—were given greater legal authority to examine and discipline ministers. All parish ministers were required to subscribe to the Black Acts on pain of deposition. Most subscribed; some subscribed with the reservation "as far as the Word of God allows"; Andrew Melville and a minority of steadfast Presbyterians refused to subscribe at all, and went into exile in England. There they joined a group of refugee Protestant nobles who had supported the Ruthven raid; they were being treated cordially by Queen Elizabeth.

In 1585, these nobles marched back victoriously into Scotland with an army. The wheel of fortune had turned again. The anti-Presbyterian Arran was deposed (he fled), and a new Presbyterian government was formed under **Sir John Maitland of Thirlstane** (1543–95), a good friend of the Kirk for political reasons. The synod of Fife excommunicated Archbishop Adamson of Saint Andrews for his part in passing the godless Black Acts. Preachers became bold again, and administered a verbal lashing to the unfortunate King James in their sermons.

---

4. The Privy Council was the king's council, made up of men of his choosing; it had almost unlimited powers, and its decrees carried the force of law.

4. No bishop, no king!

In the aftermath of this latest Presbyterian triumph, James and the Kirk—perhaps surprisingly—made various attempts at compromise; maybe both sides were weary of the wheel of fortune. Bishops, however, proved a sticking point. James was now 19 years old, a prodigy of scholarly learning, and more than capable of forming independent and sophisticated policies of his own. He wanted bishops of the old Catholic and new Anglican type: powerful figures in the Kirk, but owing their power to royal favour—instruments, effectively, of the royal will. Elizabeth of England had them: why shouldn't James? The general assembly, scenting an attempt to subordinate Kirk to monarchy, was not willing to accept anything more than someone already in the parish ministry being made a special commissioner of the assembly. James backed down. In July 1587 he got parliament to pass the Act of Annexation, whereby the landed properties of bishoprics were taken over by the crown. This enriched the king, but it weakened the prospects of Episcopacy in Scotland.

There seemed to be a more emotional kind of rapprochement between James and the Kirk after his marriage to Anne of Denmark in 1589. The king even lavished approval on Andrew Melville, publishing a poem of Melville's celebrating Anne's coronation in 1590. At the general assembly of that year, James referred to the Scottish Kirk as "the sincerest [purest] Kirk in the world", and even made disparaging remarks about the Church of England. In 1592 a parliamentary act—the "Golden Act"—was passed at the bidding of Sir John Maitland. The Act confirmed the Presbyterian character of the Kirk, incorporating statements from the Second Book of Discipline. The general assembly was accorded the right to meet annually, in the presence of the king or his commissioner who were to appoint the time and place of the next meeting. If neither king nor commissioner were present, the assembly had the right to fix the next time and place. The powers of bishops were transferred to presbyteries.

With the Golden Act, the future now seemed set for harmony between James and the Kirk. But this fair prospect proved deceptive. Popular suspicions began to be inflamed against the

HMP

Andrew Melville (1545–1622)
Andrew Melville upbraids a bishop at the court of James VI
Unknown Victorian artist

king by his conciliatory attitude to Roman Catholics. For example, the Catholic Earls of Huntly, Errol, and Angus had entered into treasonable correspondence with King Philip of Spain, the European champion of intolerant Catholicism; James merely banished them, and soon allowed them to return. This scandalous leniency led to public criticism of James in the general assembly of March 1596. This was the famous or infamous occasion when Andrew Melville plucked James by the sleeve, called him "God's silly vassal" (God's feeble servant), and informed him pointedly:

> Sir, as diverse times before, so now again I must tell you, there are two kings and two kingdoms in Scotland; there is Christ Jesus and His kingdom the Kirk, whose subject King James the Sixth is, and of whose kingdom he is not a king, nor a head, nor a lord, but a member; and they whom Christ has called and commanded to watch over His Kirk, and govern His spiritual kingdom, have sufficient power of Him and authority so to do, both together and severally, the which no Christian king nor prince should control and discharge, but fortify and assist, otherwise they are not faithful subjects nor members of Christ.

Probably no Scottish king had ever been given such a lecture by any of his subjects. Following Melville's intrepid lead, preachers once again used their pulpits to denounce James for his lack of loyalty to the Reformed faith.

This was the last straw for James. He now conceived an absolute, lifelong hostility towards Presbyterianism. It "as well agreeth with a monarchy as God and the devil", he declared bitterly. Royal government in the state demanded bishops in the Kirk: "No bishop, no king!" James also began ever more fervently advocating and practising the theory of "the divine right of kings"—the view that monarchs are accountable only to God, not to their subjects, and certainly not to any Church. James published his divine right theory to the world in 1598 in his *The True Law of Free Monarchies; or, The Reciprocal and Mutual Duty Betwixt a Free King and His Natural Subjects*, a learned and eloquent statement of monarchical absolutism.

In his indignation against Melville, and Melville's apparent belief in a clergyman's right to lecture his sovereign, a newly militant James decided to make a sacrificial victim of one of the Presbyterian leader's foremost disciples, David Black (c.1550–1603), minister of Saint Andrews. Black was cited before the Privy Council for preaching sedition. As Melville had done in 1584, Black refused to recognize the council's authority over ministers' pulpit utterances; he was backed by many other ministers who signed a petition in his favour. The trial went on for months. Eventually Black was found guilty and sentenced to "internal exile" in the area beyond North Esk river (in Angus and Aberdeenshire). Popular support for Black spilled over into a riot in Edinburgh, inflamed by rumours of a Catholic plot. Faced with mob violence, James moved swiftly; seizing the moral and legal high ground, he threatened to strip Edinburgh of its status as Scottish capital unless it made a complete submission to his will, and demanded the arrest of its obnoxious Melvillean ministers. The ministers fled in panic, leaving the field in James' hands. Flushed with triumph, he took severe punitive measures against the overawed city; from now on, none of its clergy or magistrates could be appointed without royal consent.

This dramatic event marked the effective end of Andrew Melville's ascendancy in the Kirk. James now deliberately isolated Melville, deposing him from his office as Rector of Saint Andrews University, and forcibly preventing him from attending any ecclesiastical gatherings (other than Sunday worship). It was an unlawful use of royal power, but it was successful. The king also began to implement a single-minded programme of consolidating his personal authority over the Kirk; his weapon was a crafty use of the right granted him in the Golden Act to fix the time and place for each new general assembly. James chose venues like Perth, Dundee, and Montrose, where he could secure the attendance of ministers from the north of Scotland. They were more open to royal manipulation; James could persuade them to feel ill-will towards southern clergy, who had until then dominated the general assembly when it had met in Edinburgh. In pursuit of this policy, James launched a campaign of systematic flattery toward the northern ministers. It paid rich dividends in the general assembly at Dundee in 1597: the assembly agreed to set up a commission of 14, with a broad range of powers, to confer with James on all ecclesiastical matters.

Before the close of 1597, the commission recommended that the Kirk be represented in parliament—a gross violation of the Melvillean ideal of sphere sovereignty (see above). The proposal played into James' hands, because it meant he would be able to control which churchmen were represented in parliament, who could then claim to be the Kirk's parliamentary voice when in reality they were the king's voice. Through these churchmen in parliament, James could guide legislation affecting the Kirk. And of course, why not designate these churchmen as bishops? Here was James' perfect opportunity to smother Presbyterianism and smuggle in Episcopacy by the back door. Accordingly parliament passed an act that those ministers whom the king appointed to the rank of bishop (or equivalent) should have a seat in parliament. This was fiercely debated in the general assembly in Dundee in 1598, but the motion passed by a small majority. James barred Andrew Melville from taking part in the assembly, even though he was a properly elected delegate.

Although Melville had now been shunted to the sidelines, effectively isolated by James, one of Melville's most intimate disciples who had not been quite so marginalized was doing what he could to promote his master's ideals. This was **Robert Bruce** (1554–1631). If Melville was Knox's successor, Bruce was Melville's: the spiritual lineage passed directly from one to another of these giants of Scottish Presbyterianism.

Bruce was a native of Kinnaird, near Stirling, son of a Catholic mother and a Reformed father. After studying law, he decided to devote his life and talents to the Kirk, feeling an irresistible inward call of God to preach; he became minister of Saint Giles in Edinburgh in 1587. Bruce rapidly came to be held in outstandingly high regard by the Kirk for his piercingly eloquent sermons and his saintly character. At first he even enjoyed the favour of King James, who was intimidated by the majesty and authority of Bruce's preaching and the sanctity of his person.

However, as relations progressively broke down between James and the Kirk in the 1590s, so the king increasingly withheld his smile from Bruce.

The final rupture between monarch and preacher came in 1600. In a white heat of Reformed zeal, the young Earl of Gowrie (son of the Gowrie who had been executed for the Ruthven Raid) tried to emulate his father by kidnapping James, or even killing him—the accounts are confused. The outcome, however, was that Gowrie and his brother were slain. Many suspected a conspiracy by King James to murder the brothers. James ordered the five ministers of Edinburgh—which included Bruce—to read from their pulpits the royal version of what had happened; they refused, on the grounds that their business in the pulpit was solely to proclaim the Word of God. The king was incensed, and banished Bruce and the other four ministers. The four eventually relented and read out James' account from the pulpit. Bruce however remained obstinate, and fled from the king's wrath to France. He was allowed to return in 1601 but kept under house arrest. It was time, James decided, to isolate Bruce as he had isolated Melville. The next stage was to send Bruce far away from the southern centres of Scottish power, yet keep him in Scotland where he would still be within the king's reach; so James dispatched Bruce to "internal exile" in the extreme northern town of Inverness from 1605 to 1613. However, he was allowed to preach, and his ministry was by all accounts marked by great spiritual power. Scotland had not heard the last of Robert Bruce.[5]

5. Other key figures

George Buchanan

George Buchanan (1506–82) was Scotland's foremost humanist, generally hailed as the most vividly eloquent writer of Latin in 16th century Europe. His life was mostly lived in the timeframe covered by Volume Three of this series, but his

---

5. See below for his further life.

supremely enduring achievement fell in our period—which no doubt highlights the artificiality of human divisions of time. However, there can be no history without them, and it is here that we must explore Buchanan's significance.

Born near Killearn, Stirlingshire, Buchanan studied at Saint Andrews and Paris universities. Back in Scotland he was imprisoned for his Protestant sympathies by Cardinal Beaton, who then ruled the land; but Buchanan managed to escape to France. He ended up teaching in Portugal at the University of Coimbra—but was again charged with heresy, and imprisoned in a Lisbon monastery. Finally acquitted for lack of evidence in 1552, he returned to several teaching posts in France, finally finding employment as tutor to a young Mary Queen of Scots. Buchanan returned to Scotland with her 1561. He and Mary remained good friends until the murder of Darnley; then Buchanan turned violently against his one-time pupil, becoming more hostile to her even than John Knox was.[6] Now an openly declared Protestant, he was accorded the unusual honour for a layman of being elected moderator of the general assembly in 1567. He was also appointed tutor to the young King James VI, for whose royal person he showed little tenderness. The story is told that one day, screams of agony were heard coming from the room where Buchanan was teaching the young monarch. A concerned member of the royal court burst in and saw the youthful king laid out over Buchanan's lap, receiving a thorough dose of corporal punishment. "What are you doing to his majesty?" the courtier asked in horror. Buchanan replied, "I am skelping his majesty's backside," and carried on.[7]

Buchanan wrote a brilliant and fact-packed history of Scotland (published 1582), but his most influential work was his masterpiece of political philosophy, *De Jure Regni apud Scotos* ("On the Right of Kingship among the Scots"), published in 1579. It proved a prophetic work: the 17th century would see

---

6. For these people and events, see *Volume Three: Renaissance and Reformation*, Chapter 7, sections 6-9.

7. Skelping is Scots for smacking.

the fulfilment of virtually all Buchanan's political ideas, in the struggle of Scottish Covenanters and English Puritans against the Stuart monarchy, and its eventual overthrow. Buchanan taught that kings were elected by the people, and subject both to God's law and to human law. The Scots, he maintained, had always claimed and exercised the right to call wicked kings to account, rather than merely passively suffer under their misrule. Buchanan also justified tyrannicide—a tyrant was a public enemy, he argued, and could be lawfully slain by any citizen whose conscience would permit him to do the deed.

Not surprisingly, the *De Jure Regni apud Scotos* made Buchanan abhorrent to King James;[8] in 1584, during the virtual dictatorship of the pro-James, anti-Presbyterian Earl of Arran, the book was condemned by special act of the Scottish parliament. Nonetheless, in the 17th century Buchanan's political philosophy was taken up, and successfully popularized, by the eminent Covenanting theologian Samuel Rutherford, the sublime English poet John Milton, and the epoch-making English philosopher John Locke. When the Stuart monarchy was restored after the turmoil of 1637–60, Buchanan's book was once again condemned by act of parliament in 1664. It was granted the singular honour of being publicly burnt by Oxford University in 1683.

Robert Rollock

Robert Rollock (1555–99), a native of Powis near Stirling and graduate of Saint Andrews, was the first principal of Edinburgh University, founded in 1583 according to Andrew Melville's academic ideals. He also preached every Sunday morning in Edinburgh's East Kirk. Rollock's fame, however, rests not on his educational activities, but on his theological writings—five volumes of sermons and nine biblical commentaries. These were highly prized in the age of Reformed Orthodoxy, continuously in print in Britain and on the Continent between 1590 and

---

8. Or it was one of the things that made Buchanan abhorrent to James. The skelping of his majesty's backside was doubtless another.

1634. Rollock had a particular significance in being one of the first Scottish exponents of a full-blooded covenant or federal theology.[9] He taught that in paradise, God had entered into a "covenant of works" with Adam, as representative-head of all humankind, promising eternal life on condition of obedience. After Adam transgressed, God appointed Christ as the Second Adam to succeed where the First Adam failed; Christ obeyed perfectly, thus securing eternal life for His people, the elect, who entered into the covenant of grace by faith alone. This faith was a condition of the covenant from the human side, but a gift of effectual grace from the divine side.

Federal theology was to be systematized and made normative for Scottish Presbyterianism the following century in the Westminster Confession.[10]

---

9. See Chapter 2, section 1.7.
10. See Chapter 3, section 5.6.

2

South wind blowing: the Anglicizing of the Kirk

1. James gains the English crown

The situation and prospects of the Scottish Kirk changed very dramatically in 1603 when Queen Elizabeth of England died, and James succeeded to the English throne.[1] So came the union of the Scottish and English crowns, with fateful consequences for both countries.[2] James left Scotland and took up residence in his new southern kingdom. In fact, he only ever visited Scotland once thereafter! In England, James found a Church far more to his liking: an Episcopalian body whose bishops were appointed by the crown, and who were therefore dependent on the crown for their position—and tended to be very subservient. The adulation that the English Church hierarchy paid to the monarch was a vivid and welcome contrast for James to the constant criticism to which he had been subjected by the likes of Andrew Melville and the Scottish Presbyterian clergy. He now became absolutely determined to remodel the Kirk on the Anglican pattern.

---

1. For a more detailed account from the English point of view, see Chapter 3, section 4.1.

2. The event is customarily called the union of crowns, but the Scottish and English crowns remained technically distinct. It was merely that the same person now wore both.

Little can James have realized that he was sowing the seeds of a revolution that would see Scotland fight its king on the field of battle, and the entire Stuart dynasty toppled from the throne.

2. The bishops restored

James' determination to Anglicize the Kirk was part of a wider shift in his attitude. The fact that he was now living in England, the larger, stronger, and richer of his two kingdoms, led to an Anglicizing of James' entire outlook. It was not merely that English bishops were more deferential that Scottish presbyters; the English aristocracy was also more deferential than its Scottish counterpart. Traditionally, the Scottish nobility had a less rigid, more relaxed ethos in relationships between people of differing social rank. The English court was more strict and formal, more prone to a cult of monarchy. James enjoyed the English ways, and it helped persuade him of the superiority of all things English over all things Scottish.

Slowly but effectively, James carried out his campaign to remodel the Kirk. First he undermined the status of the general assembly. He cancelled its meeting for 1604, and then again for 1605. When a band of 19 ministers loyal to Melville's ideals met of their own accord in Aberdeen in July 1605, the Privy Council charged them with treason and they were banished. In 1606, James had Melville himself and six of his disciples brought to London, and forced them to sit through a series of lectures by Anglican divines on the superior merits of Episcopacy as a model of church government. Melville was not impressed; he was so outspokenly rude about the ceremonial form of worship observed in the English royal chapel that James lost all patience and threw him out of the country. Melville spent his final years in northern France, as a theological teacher in the French Huguenot college at Sedan, dying there in 1622.

Next, James fully restored Episcopacy to the Kirk. It already had several bishops, but only in the shape of parliamentary commissioners, in accordance with the decision of the 1598 general assembly at Dundee (see section 1). James now had three men fully consecrated to the Episcopal office by the traditional method, the laying on of hands by existing bishops. Anglican bishops performed the consecration in 1610; then the three Scottish bishops (of Glasgow, Brechin, and Galloway) consecrated several more. All the bishops were chosen personally by James, and he give them back their secular lands and income which had been seized by the crown in 1587. An interesting point was raised by Lancelot Andrewes, Anglican Bishop of Ely. He argued that without Episcopal ordination, a minister could not validly hold a ministerial position. This would have meant that all Scottish ministers would have to be reordained by bishops! However, Andrewes was opposed by Archbishop Bancroft of Canterbury. Bancroft took the more moderate view that in the absence of bishops, ordination of presbyters by other presbyters was valid—"otherwise it might be doubted if there were any lawful ordination in most of the Reformed Churches". Bancroft's position triumphed over Andrewes', which was just as well for James; had Andrewes prevailed, an attempt to force all Scottish ministers to be Episcopally reordained would have provoked widespread and serious opposition in the Kirk.[3]

James' campaign was remarkably successful; there was very little in the way of resolute opposition to his reintroduction of full Episcopacy. Perhaps this was because he left intact the traditional Presbyterian structures of internal church government—local kirk session, presbytery, synod, and general assembly. However, though they were allowed to remain, they were made completely captive to the greater power of the king and his bishops. Some have seen the Kirk in this period as a compromise between Presbyterianism and Episcopalianism, combining elements of each. Others have argued that it is of the essence of Presbyterianism that the Church must be independent of state control, and that all its ministers enjoy equal status; in that case, the Scottish Kirk had now lost the essentials of Presbyterianism, and become effectively royal and Episcopalian.

---

3. For more about Bancroft and Andrewes, see Chapter 3, sections 3.4 and 4.4.

If we ask why the opposition to James was so ineffectual, it was partly because potential opponents lacked strong leadership, with Andrew Melville in exile in France, and Melville's greatest disciple, Robert Bruce, in "internal exile" in Inverness. It was also partly because James initially confined himself to remodelling the Kirk's authority structures, which did not really impinge on the life and worship of ordinary Scottish churchgoers at grass-roots level.

3. The brink of conflict

However, having enjoyed such success in reforming the government of the Kirk, James next turned his attention to bringing Scottish worship more into line with Anglican worship. In 1617, James visited Scotland with his chaplain, William Laud, the foremost figure in the High Church movement within Anglicanism.[4] James wanted five controversial articles included in a new Scottish book of canon law. These required the following practices to be introduced into the Kirk:

1. Receiving holy communion in a kneeling posture.

2. Private celebrations of communion (e.g. in a nobleman's house).

3. Baptism administered privately whenever circumstances demanded.

4. Confirmation by a bishop of those preparing to receive communion for the first time.

5. The observance of the main holy days in the Christian year, e.g. Christmas and Easter (these had been discontinued in Scotland, rather unusually—other Reformed Churches generally retained them in some form).

These proposals provoked immediate resistance. A group of 55 ministers met in Edinburgh and declared their opposition to

---

4. See Chapter 3, section 5.

the king's scheme; the Kirk, they affirmed, was independent of royal control, its own master in all matters of doctrine, worship, and government. Opponents of the Five Articles argued against them on the following grounds:

1. Forms of worship not commanded in Scripture should not be imposed.

2. Kneeling at communion tended to idolatry—it was too much like the Roman Catholic adoration of the eucharistic bread as Christ's very body.

3. Baptism and communion must not be separated from the preaching of the Word in the gathered congregation.

4. Episcopal confirmation wrongly implied that baptism was defective without laying on of hands by a bishop.

5. Religious festivals like Christmas and Easter diminished respect for the Lord's Day, the only divinely appointed "festival".

James treated this display of clerical defiance with contempt, and demanded that the general assembly accept his Five Articles; when it hesitated, he cut off the income of rebellious ministers. The following year, 1618, the Scottish bishops brought the king's Five Articles before the general assembly in Perth (hence their common name, "the Five Articles of Perth"). The assembly was presided over by John Spottiswoode, the new Archbishop of Saint Andrews. Many of the ministers were present at the king's special request—James' yes-men. The assembly voted to endorse the Five Articles by a majority of 86 to 42.

Despite this, there was serious popular opposition to the Articles. This grew more intense after James issued, later that year, his notorious Book of Sports, which promoted dancing and games on Sunday. Ministers who openly defied the Articles were punished. James' most famous victim was **David Dickson** (c.1583–1663) of Irvine in Ayrshire, later celebrated in Covenanting times as an outstanding theologian and Bible commentator (an exposition of the Psalms and of all the apostle Paul's letters would long remain in print); Dickson was deposed from his church and sentenced to internal exile in Aberdeenshire in 1622-3. However, when it became evident that opposition to the Five Articles of Perth was widespread, James drew back from enforcing them with any vigour, and abandoned plans for further remodelling of Scottish worship. He had the sense to know when enough was enough.

But in a real sense, the damage was already done. The Five Articles had rekindled a Presbyterian flame, albeit not in such a way as to engulf the entire Kirk and country in a conflagration. Many Scots who had reluctantly gone along with James' ecclesiastical policies now became convinced that the diehard Presbyterian minority had been right all along: the king's policies were dragging the Kirk down a path which could end only in the ultimate destruction of its traditionally Reformed faith and worship.

Particularly ominous was the fact that a sizeable number of Scottish nobles joined with ministers in opposing the Five Articles. These nobles would, in the 1630s, step forth as leading Covenanters. It has been argued that James perceived this potentially deadly coalition between Presbyterian ministers and disaffected members of the aristocracy, and backed away, for fear of provoking the coalition into militant life. This would be precisely the fate of James' less politically astute son, Charles I.

The events surrounding the Five Articles revealed very painfully how King James was increasingly losing meaningful contact with the state of public opinion in his northern kingdom. The way that opposition to the Articles had come not just from ministers, but from members of the Scottish aristocracy and gentry, was probably a symptom of a growing alienation between Scotland and its absentee monarch. It was becoming all too possible for the Scottish ruling classes to feel that their land had been degraded to the condition of a mere province, governed in the interests of England, with Scottish concerns not being understood—or if they were understood, being ignored. James' own political skills managed to prevent this situation from developing into a national crisis; for example, throughout his reign the Scottish Privy Council continued to meet in Edinburgh, and James engaged in genuine policy discussion with the council through exchange of letters. Still, this was not the same as person-to-person interaction, and some historians have argued that James merely delayed the inevitable Scottish reaction against an Anglicizing Stuart monarchy. His son was about to reap the bitter consequences.

4. The spiritual succession: Bruce and Henderson

Meanwhile those consequences were being prepared, in part, by Robert Bruce. We last saw him in internal exile in Inverness, creating a deep impression by his preaching. In 1613, James relented somewhat, and allowed Bruce to return to his native Kinnaird, near Stirling, although he was still basically under house arrest. However, he was allowed to preach for other ministers during communion services; and when it was known that Bruce was to preach, people would come flocking from far and wide to sit under his articulate, powerful, and moving ministry.

On one such occasion (either 1615 or 1616), one of his hearers was a young man named **Alexander Henderson** (1583–1646), and Henderson experienced a profound religious conversion through Bruce's preaching. The story is remarkable. Henderson was no Presbyterian; he was an Episcopalian in his beliefs about church government, and had recently been appointed by Archbishop Gladstanes of Saint Andrews to the parish of Leuchars in Fife. His appointment, however, was against the wishes of the congregation, who nailed the kirk doors closed in protest on the day of Henderson's ordination: rather than enter by the door, he had to climb in through the windows. Learning that the famous prisoner of conscience, Robert Bruce, was to preach in Forgan, Henderson went along, more out of curiosity than anything else. Bruce's sermon was on John 10:1—"He that entereth not in by the door into the sheepfold, but climbeth up another way, he is a thief and a robber."

Henderson was thunder-struck. Was this God Himself speaking through Bruce? Henderson fell under deep conviction of sin for the way he had forced himself on the people of Leuchars. From that moment, his life changed; he now became a disciple of Bruce, an earnest preacher, a godly and beloved pastor, a committed Presbyterian—and he would go on to become the architect of the Covenanting movement which would overthrow the Stuart monarchy. As the spiritual torch had passed from the hands of Knox to Melville, and from Melville to Bruce, so it passed from Bruce to Henderson.

Bruce's location varied with the fluctuating intensity of royal disfavour. In 1622–4, he was back in internal exile in Inverness again. Then from 1624 until his death in 1631, he was back at Kinnaird. His spiritual legacy in the Kirk, through his preaching, was deep and enduring. His literary legacy was also not to be despised. A volume of 17 of his sermons in the Scottish dialect has survived. His masterpiece, however, was a separate series of sermons on the Lord's Supper, delivered at Saint Giles Kirk, Edinburgh, in 1589. The sermons, bristling with quotations from the early Church fathers (especially Augustine), expounded the classic Reformed doctrine with a warm evangelical spirituality, charting a middle way between the emptiness of a bare memorialism and the superstition of Catholic transubstantiation. If Bruce is still known today, it is for these rich sermons on the Supper.

3

The Covenanters: days of power

1. A new king: Charles I

Charles I (1625–49) came to throne in 1625. He had a higher moral character than his somewhat dissolute father, but Charles' religious convictions were even more hostile to Melvillean Presbyterianism. James had opposed it on political grounds, but shared its Calvinistic theology. Charles opposed Presbyterianism on religious grounds; his theology was strongly anti-Calvinistic. Charles was a High Church Arminian; he believed that salvation was a joint work shared between the divine and human will, and that God's grace normally flowed through the Episcopal Church and its sacraments. The theology favoured by Charles—"Caroline" divinity (from *Carolus*, Latin for Charles)—was represented most effectively in Scotland by a group of theologians linked with Aberdeen University: William Forbes (1585–1634) and Robert Barron (1596–1639) were the outstanding figures. The Caroline divines not only opposed those in the Church who dissented from royal theology; they also forged a strong political alliance with the Stuart monarchy. Charles protected and promoted Scottish Caroline divinity and its spokesmen, while they taught the highest doctrine of the divine right of kings against all claims that kings were subject to law or to parliament.

2. Charles loses Scotland: a nation in revolt

Almost immediately on being crowned, Charles succeeded in badly alienating the Scottish nobility by the Act of Revocation in 1625. By this Act, he took back into the crown's power all royal and church lands which had been granted to the nobility since 1542. This produced lengthy, complicated, and bitter legal and parliamentary wrangling between Charles and the nobility, which finally ended in compromise. But the blow dealt to Charles' popularity among the nobles was fatal. They no longer trusted their monarch.

In 1633 Charles visited Scotland for the first time. It was a public relations disaster. He was accompanied by his chief advisor on religious affairs, William Laud, Bishop of London (later that year elevated to be Archbishop of Canterbury). Laud decorated the royal chapel in Holyrood with an altar and candles. At Saint Giles Kirk, Edinburgh's chief church, clergy in ecclesiastical vestments conducted the service from the Anglican Prayer Book. This was a shock to the system for Scottish Protestants: it all seemed far too Roman Catholic. Were not these vestments, candles, and altars the relics of the papal Antichrist?

Charles further ruined his cause during his visit by holding a parliament. The king was seen to be noting down the names of all who spoke in opposition to his proposals. The dissenters submitted a supplication to Charles, written in very humble language, complaining about his ecclesiastical policies, but he refused to read it, and ordered it suppressed. One of the supplicants, **John Elphinstone, Lord Balmerino** (d.1649), was arrested and tried for treason, when a copy of the supplication with additional comments of his own was discovered. After a long drawn-out trial, Balmerino was convicted of publishing a seditious document (the supplication) and condemned to death. Public opinion was outraged. Perhaps prudently, Charles pardoned Balmerino, but again it was too late: the trial had inflamed Scottish national feeling against the king. Balmerino was to be a leading Covenanter (see below).

Charles was determined to carry on the remodelling of the Kirk into the image of the Church of England. He asked the Scottish bishops to submit proposals for reforming the Kirk's law and worship to Archbishop Laud, who then revised them.

The result in 1636 was Canons and Constitutions Ecclesiastical. It did not begin very auspiciously for Presbyterians: chapter one asserted the royal supremacy over the Kirk, and threatened to excommunicate anyone who denied it. In fact, throughout the Canons, it was simply taken for granted that the king had the absolute right to structure the Kirk according to his own arbitrary will. Among the new laws in the Canons, distasteful to Scottish Reformed opinion, was the banning of any prayer in worship except from the authorized liturgy, the requirement to kneel to receive communion, the re-establishment of the confessional, and the forbidding of all meetings in presbyteries and kirk sessions. The Canons also required that worship be conducted according to a novel liturgy, the Book of Common Prayer (not the Anglican one: a new Scottish one), which had not yet even appeared—it would not be published until 1637.

The Scottish Book of Common Prayer was, like the Canons, drawn up by the Scottish bishops, and probably revised by Archbishop Laud. Charles fixed on July 23rd as the day for its introduction throughout Scotland. All ministers in all city churches were instructed to announce this on the preceding Sunday, the 16th. The way the Edinburgh ministers responded to this royal instruction was ominous: one refused to have it read at all, another read it in a deliberately careless and contemptuous manner, another pointedly refused to read it himself, but handed it down to a Scripture reader to read out.

When July 23rd came, it marked the beginning of the end for Charles' monarchy. The Prayer Book met with a violently hostile reception. Famously, in Saint Giles Kirk, a riot broke out when the Dean of Edinburgh, James Hanna (or Hannay), tried to conduct the service. This was the occasion when Jenny Geddes, who sold herbs for a living, is supposed to have thrown a stool at Hanna, yelling, "Villain! Do you say mass at my lug [ear]?" In reality, Jenny Geddes (or this particular Jenny Geddes) may not have existed; she may just be a piece of Scottish folklore. The riot itself, however, is well attested. Even the presence of Archbishop Spottiswoode and David Lindsay, Bishop of Edinburgh, could not restrain the hostilities. There is debate as to whether the outburst was spontaneous or organized, but it was certainly uproarious. Similar antagonism greeted the new liturgy in many other parts of the kingdom. Walter Whitford, Bishop of Brechin, managed to conduct the Prayer Book service in peace only because he read it over a pair of loaded pistols!

Why this hostile reception? It was not really because of any principled rejection of liturgy—that was not yet a feature of Scottish Presbyterianism. People were quite happy to hear the written prayers of John Knox read out in worship from Knox's Book of Common Order. (See section 5.3 for the growth of anti-liturgy sentiment.) There were probably two reasons for the hostility:

(i) The new Prayer Book was perceived as being the work of Archbishop Laud of Canterbury. And Laud, in turn, was perceived as a crypto-Catholic. Scottish Protestants were not about to let a popish English bishop dictate to them concerning how they must worship God.

(ii) The Prayer Book was imposed on the Scottish people merely by the will of the king. There was no consultation, no discussion in the Church, no authorization by a general assembly. The king's arbitrary action was regarded as an outrageous violation of the constitutional freedom of Scotland's Kirk and people.

Charles' response to Scotland's anger was simply to order the Privy Council to enforce the Prayer Book. But the resistance was now becoming organized. Meetings were held throughout the Scottish Lowlands; petitions were signed, largely by the nobility, gentry, and ministers. The leaders of the opposition among the nobility were Sir Thomas Hope (Scotland's Lord Advocate or chief legal officer), Lord Balmerino, Lord Rothes, the Earl of Loudoun, and the Marquis of Montrose. Among the clergy, the opposition leaders were Alexander Henderson of Leuchars, Scotland's foremost proponent of Presbyterianism in the tradition of Andrew Melville and Robert Bruce; David Dickson, who had been deposed from the ministry by James VI for opposing the Five Articles of Perth; and Samuel Rutherford, minister of Anwoth, who was in internal exile in Aberdeen. (See below for more on these men.)

This alliance between Scotland's nobility and clergy proved invincible. The Privy Council, besieged in Edinburgh by a hostile mob, was forced to negotiate, and invited the city to appoint commissioners. Four nobles, four lairds, four burgesses, and four ministers were elected; this committee, given a powerful de facto authority by the Privy Council, became known as the Tables. Its most influential members were Lord Loudoun, Alexander Henderson, David Dickson, and the radical Presbyterian lawyer **Archibald Johnston of Wariston** (1611–63). Johnston, son of a leading Edinburgh merchant, was a graphic blend of legal expert and religious zealot; he was to alienate almost everyone by the end of his life, through an abrasive and humourless lack of courtesy. There could be no doubting, however, the consuming sincerity of his faith in Christ and in the cause of Presbyterianism.

3. The National Covenant

Meanwhile, King Charles (still in London) responded by simply declaring again that the Prayer Book must be enforced at all costs. The anti-Charles resistance, now spearheaded by the Tables, decided to show their strength by binding themselves together in a covenant. This was an old Scottish custom; it had also been given a powerful religious and Protestant sanction at the time of the Scottish Reformation, when the Lords of the Congregation had bound themselves together by a covenant and helped secure the victory of Protestantism.[1] Alexander Henderson and radical Presbyterian lawyer Archibald Johnston drew up a National Covenant. The Covenanting movement had begun.

The National Covenant was divided into three sections:

    (i) Section one was the ultra-Protestant King's Confession of 1580. This served as a rallying cry to

---

1. See *Volume Three: Renaissance and Reformation*, Chapter 7, section 7.

an anti-Catholic, solidly Reformed understanding
of the Scottish Kirk. It was also an appeal over the
head of King Charles to the sacredness of established
constitutional law and precedent; after all, the King's
Confession had been signed by King James VI, and (at
the order of the Privy Council and general assembly)
by the entire Scottish establishment—nobles, gentry,
ministers, university lecturers, etc. The Covenanters
were therefore claiming to be defending the Scottish
constitution against the arbitrary will of Charles.

(ii) Section two was a comprehensive list of acts of
parliament from 1560, against Roman Catholicism
and in favour of the Reformed Kirk.

(iii) Section three set out the obligations the Covenanters
were taking upon themselves when they signed the
document: to oppose Charles' religious innovations, to
uphold the true Reformed religion, and to defend the
person and authority of the king. (Obviously they had
a strictly limited interpretation of what royal authority
involved—Charles had no authority to ride roughshod
over the worship and practice of the Church.)

It should be noted that the Covenanters were not fighting for
religious liberty. They were fighting for their own vision of a
Presbyterian Scotland, in which there would be no place for
religious dissent. When the English Independents later began
flying the flag of "liberty of conscience" for all godly Protestants,
whatever their views on disputed issues of theology or church
government, the Covenanters were both horrified and incensed.
Their leading theologian Samuel Rutherford condemned the
whole idea at length in his ominous treatise *A Free Disputation
Against Pretended Liberty of Conscience* (1649).[2]

The National Covenant was read out in Edinburgh's
Greyfriars Kirk on February 28th 1638, to an assembly of

---

2. See Chapter 3, section 6, for religious toleration in the English Civil War.

nobles and gentry, who then signed. Alexander Henderson described the scene:

> This was the day of the Lord's power, wherein we saw His people most willingly offer themselves in multitudes like the dewdrops of the morning, the day of the Redeemer's strength, on which the princes of the people assembled to swear their allegiance to the King of kings.

The next day, ministers and common people also signed, amid scenes of emotional fervour. Copies were then distributed throughout Scotland, and were signed with great zeal everywhere—except in the Scottish Highlands, where Protestantism had still not taken root at a popular level in many regions. In the Highlands, people's primary loyalty was to their clan chief rather than to any particular set of religious convictions. The only Highland chieftain who was a devout Protestant was **Archibald Campbell** (1607–61), Lord Lorne, acting head of the Campbell clan. Lorne was the son of the disgraced Earl of Argyll (he had become a Roman Catholic—the Campbells had been Protestants since the days of John Knox); Lorne succeeded to the earldom after his father's death later on in 1638. He was the most powerful man in Scotland, with 20,000 men of clan Campbell under his personal command. King Charles hoped Lorne would support the royal cause, but after some hesitation, he committed himself completely to the Covenanters. This brought his formidable, well-disciplined Campbell clan onto the Covenanting side. Lorne was also an artful politician, and used his cunning to promote the cause of the Covenant and (his critics said) his own power.

However, despite the factor of clan loyalty in the Highlands, in many places the signing of the Covenant was accompanied by what can only be described as religious revival. **John Livingstone** (1603–72), minister of Stranraer, recorded the scene thus:

> I may truly say that in all my lifetime, excepting at the Kirk of Shotts [where a famous local revival had occurred under Livingstone's preaching some years earlier], I never saw such motions from the Spirit of God. I have seen more than a

thousand persons all at once lifting up their hands and the tears falling down from their eyes.

Faced with an entire kingdom in revolt, Charles finally gave in and announced the meeting of a general assembly in Glasgow in November 1638. It was attended by 140 ministers and 98 ruling elders. The elders were mostly members of the gentry and nobility. The assembly was so overwhelmingly pro-Covenanting that the Scottish bishops protested it was not a genuinely free assembly—it was in the pocket of the Covenanters. Charles' representative in Scotland, the Lord High Commissioner, the Marquis of Hamilton, dissolved the assembly. But the general assembly refused to recognize his authority to do so, and carried on its proceedings. Led by its moderator, Alexander Henderson, the assembly abolished Episcopacy, deposed the bishops (and excommunicated some of them), and got rid of the Book of Canons, the new Prayer Book, and the hated Five Articles of Perth.

Meanwhile, the exalted religious atmosphere that had now gripped large parts of Scotland was nowhere more evident, if in a strange way, than in Edinburgh. Here, Margaret Mitchelson, the daughter of a minister, began falling into trance-like states, during which she prophesied. The content of her prophetic utterances was always in favour of the Covenanters. The National Covenant, she declared, had been made in heaven. She referred to Christ as "Covenanting Jesus". Many were profoundly moved and impressed by her prophecies; Archibald Johnston was so impressed that he took Margaret into his household. Here she delivered her prophecies, which sometimes lasted for hours, to admiring audiences, among whom Lord Rothes and Lord Lorne were to be found.

King Charles decided that armed force was now his only option to defeat the Covenanters. So began the so-called "Bishops' Wars". Charles raised an English army of 20,000 in summer 1639, and marched it to the border with Scotland. But his path was blocked by a Scottish army of equal numbers, far superior in discipline and generalship, led by *Alexander Leslie*

(1582–1661), who had gained great military experience and risen to high rank in the Swedish army in the Thirty Years' War. The Scottish Covenanting army marched under a banner on which was printed in gold letters, *For Christ's Crown And Covenant*. Faced with this awe-inspiring opposition, Charles gave in again, and signed the Pacification of Berwick. In this treaty, Charles still refused to recognize the acts of the Glasgow general assembly, but accepted that all disputed questions should be settled by another assembly or by parliament. A few weeks later a new general assembly met, and simply re-enacted all the acts of the Glasgow assembly! The Scottish parliament, when it met, proved to be Charles' worst nightmare: it was even more zealously Covenanting than the general assembly, and had to be suspended by the Lord High Commissioner, Hamilton. He kept prolonging the suspension until finally, after the tenth suspension, parliament lost patience and decided to meet on its own authority. It legally abolished Episcopacy.

Confronted with this open and complete defiance of his will by both Church and state, Charles responded by raising another army. He got no help from the English parliament, summoned and dismissed with dizzying swiftness between April and May 1640; parliament was so opposed to what it considered Charles' tyranny in England, it treated his troubles in Scotland as the perfect lever to curb his power. So the king dissolved the unaccommodating parliament within three weeks of its meeting; he had to fight on alone against the Covenanters. But his army was a disorderly rabble that had no chance against the well-disciplined, religiously motivated Covenanting troops; many English soldiers deserted rather than meet Leslie's army in battle. In August 1640 the Covenanters crossed the border, routed the English at Newburn, and occupied Newcastle and Durham. The Covenanters declared they would accept no further treaty from Charles which was not ratified by an English parliament. So Charles was compelled once again to summon England's representative legislature—the most famous parliament in English history, the Long Parliament, which did so much to destroy for ever Charles' ideal of absolute monarchy.

4. The Solemn League and Covenant

When the English Civil War between king and parliament broke out in summer 1642,[3] the Covenanters at first did not take sides. They watched anxiously while consolidating their own power at every level in Scotland. But the Covenanters' religious sympathies were with the Puritan-dominated parliament. In 1643, hard pressed by royalist victories on the battlefield, the English parliament appealed to the Scots to join the struggle against the king. This proposed military alliance was made irresistible to the Covenanters by an offer to help undertake a reformation of the Church in England and Ireland by means of an assembly of theologians, already meeting in Westminster, to which Scottish delegates were invited. The Covenanter ministers who were deputed to take part were Alexander Henderson, Samuel Rutherford, George Gillespie, and Robert Baillie (see below). Among the lay deputies who attended was Archibald Johnston of Wariston. The Westminster Assembly was to give Scotland a new confession of faith, the Westminster Confession; a new popular catechism, the Shorter Catechism; and a new manual of worship, the Directory for Public Worship.[4]

All this flowed from the Solemn League and Covenant, the name of the treaty signed on September 25th 1643, between the English parliamentarians and the Scottish Covenanters, in a new and powerful anti-Charles alliance. The Solemn League and Covenant pledged its supporters to

> the reformation of religion in the kingdoms of England and Ireland, in doctrine, worship, discipline and government, according to the Word of God and the example of the best Reformed Churches; and shall endeavour to bring the Churches of God in the three kingdoms [England, Scotland, and Ireland] to the nearest conjunction and uniformity in religion, confession of faith, form of church government, directory for worship, and catechising.

---

3. See Chapter 3, section 5.5.
4. See Chapter 3, section 5.6.

To the Covenanters, the clause "according to the Word of God and the example of the best Reformed Churches" could only mean Presbyterianism. But some of the foremost English parliamentarians, notably Oliver Cromwell, did not see the Solemn League and Covenant this way at all.[5] They were Independents (Congregationalists), and they believed that the clause "according to the Word of God" left space to argue for Independency as the best system of church government. Here lay the seeds of the future breakdown of relations between the Covenanters and the English parliament, and the conquest of Covenanting Scotland by an English Independent army under Cromwell.

As 1644 began, a Covenanting army crossed into England under Alexander Leslie. Together with Oliver Cromwell's Puritan warriors of faith, Leslie's Covenanters decisively crushed the royalist army at the battle of Marston Moor in July 1644.

5. Montrose: The nemesis of the Covenanters

But while King Charles' forces were being destroyed in England, they made an unexpected and spectacular recovery in Scotland. *James Graham, Marquis of Montrose* (1612–50), originally one of the foremost Covenanters among the Scottish nobility, had become disillusioned with what he saw as the self-serving ambition of other Covenanter leaders. Another factor in his disenchantment was probably the intense rivalry between himself and Archibald Campbell, Marquis of Argyll, who had become the supreme political leader of the Covenanting cause. (Campbell had been Earl of Argyll until King Charles had awarded him the more exalted title of marquis in 1641, in the vain hope of winning him over to the royalist side.) The two great aristocrats simply did not get on with each other; there seemed to be a deadly personal chemistry that made them natural enemies. Montrose felt, or claimed, that Argyll had hijacked the Covenant to advance his own personal power.

---

5. See Chapter 3, section 6.1.

When the Solemn League and Covenant was signed between the Covenanters and the English parliament in 1643, Montrose regarded it as a treasonable military alliance whose deliberate aim was to destroy King Charles. This was not why Montrose had signed the National Covenant in 1638. Driven as he always claimed by his conscience, he now switched his allegiance decisively from the Covenanters to the king, although he was an unswerving Calvinist in his theology, and always maintained he was faithful to the National Covenant itself.

Montrose is certainly one of the most colourful and popular figures in Scottish history. This is probably because his life— once he had entered Charles' service—was one long, breathless adventure, in which he always, or almost always, triumphed against huge odds by sheer personal courage, charisma, and skill. His exploits have gained an added charm for those who see his enemies (the Covenanters) as a gang of grim and sanctimonious persecutors. His ultimate and tragic defeat and death lend him something of a martyr's halo, too.

In August 1644 Montrose raised an army of Highlanders to restore Charles' fortunes in Scotland. In this hazardous enterprise, he was powerfully aided by **Alistair Macdonald** (1610–47)—or MacColla, as he was known—a native of the Outer Hebridean island of Colonsay, who brought a contingent of Scots-Irish Macdonalds from Ulster to fight for the king alongside Montrose. MacColla was a Roman Catholic, and there was bad blood between him and the Marquis of Argyll's Protestant Campbell clan; the Campbells had already invaded the Outer Hebrides in 1638 and taken MacColla's father prisoner, forcing the son to flee to Ireland. MacColla has been called the last and greatest of the Celtic generals: he was the one who perfected the fearsome "Highland charge". In this manoeuvre, Highland troops would descend at break-neck speed on an enemy force, which had only one chance to fire at them with their slow-loading muskets, before being swept away by the onrushing Highland host.

Under Montrose's skilful leadership, MacColla proved an invaluable military ally. In a series of devastating campaigns,

Montrose now defeated Covenanting armies time and again, at various points capturing Aberdeen, Dundee, and Glasgow. To the appalled Covenanters it must have seemed that the sovereign God they served had mysteriously raised up (or had allowed Satan to raise up) in Montrose an adversary who threatened the destruction of everything they held dear. Yet despite his amazing successes on the battlefield, Montrose was never able to capitalize on this politically. The Scottish Lowlands not only remained staunchly Covenanting in loyalty, they were also shocked and alienated by the barbarity of Montrose's army of Highlanders and Irishmen—particularly by what had happened in Aberdeen, where Montrose's forces had raped and massacred defenceless civilians.

Even more galling to the Marquis of Argyll was Montrose's victory over a Campbell army at Inverlochy in February 1645, where Montrose's and MacColla's Highlanders gave no quarter and slaughtered something like 1,500 Campbells. MacColla also settled scores with the hated Campbells by going on a rampage and killing as many Campbell men as he could. Montrose, who was personally a very chivalrous and civilized man, always innocently claimed he could not control his Highland troops when bloody events like this took place; but this claim has been treated with a degree of scepticism by many historians.

Montrose ran rings around the Covenanters for a whole year, humiliating them both militarily and spiritually. But it was not to last. The Covenanters finally had their vengeance on their arch-enemy at the battle of Philiphaugh in September 1645. King Charles had just been completely defeated in England the previous month at the battle of Naseby by Oliver Cromwell's "New Model Army", a fighting force of radical soldiers, Independent rather than Presbyterian in outlook. This victory over the English royalists at Naseby freed thousands of Covenanting troops to return to Scotland to deal with Montrose. On 13th September he was caught and crushed by a much larger army at Philiphaugh, near Selkirk. The triumphant Covenanters were in no mood to show mercy to this unholy anti-Covenanting crew; most of the Highlanders and Irish were killed without pity on the battlefield, including their wounded, and their women and children—just one of the atrocities committed by both sides in the war. The few survivors were arrested, tried, and executed. It was a total military disaster for Montrose and the king's cause in Scotland. Montrose himself escaped, but Scotland was now once again firmly in the hands of Charles I's Covenanter opponents.

6. Division in the ranks

In 1647, however, a worse disaster than Montrose struck the Covenanters: division in the ranks. They became fatally split by a political treaty called the Engagement. This was made between Charles and one faction of the Covenanters, who were alarmed at the way the English political landscape was increasingly dominated by Oliver Cromwell and his Independent army. Independency was as repellent as Episcopacy to the Presbyterian Covenanters, and they saw Cromwell's rise to power as a grave danger to all they had fought for. Given the choice between English Independency, with its horrifying belief in complete religious toleration, and King Charles who at least shared the Covenanting ideal of a single Church enforced on all citizens by the state, this faction of Covenanters opted for Charles. Hence the Engagement. Charles proved so desperate for any ally against Cromwell's army, that he was ready to swallow his Episcopalianism and agree to give England a Presbyterian Church.

But the Engagement did not commit Charles to a permanent establishment of Presbyterianism in England, only to a three year trial period. So the more full-blooded Covenanters refused to have anything to do with the iniquitous treaty. The anti-Engagement zealots were led by the Marquis of Argyll and Archibald Johnston, the lawyer who had drafted the National Covenant. The Engagement also opened up a destructive breach between the estates (the committee representing parliament when it was not in session) and the general assembly: most members of the estates approved of the Engagement, but the assembly condemned it. The anti-Engagement party were totally vindicated when Cromwell annihilated the Engagement's army at the battle of Preston in August 1648. Covenanter hardliners seized their opportunity, marched on Edinburgh in the so-called "Whiggamore Raid",[6] overthrew the discredited pro-Engagement government, and made the Marquis of Argyll master of the land.

At first Argyll and Cromwell, the two religious and political giants of their respective countries, cooperated; the Scottish parliament passed the Act of Classes, which prevented anyone who had fought for the king from holding office. But everything was transformed overnight through the execution of King Charles on January 30th 1649, by a purged English parliament controlled by Cromwell's army. A shudder of shock and horror convulsed all of Scotland. The Covenanters regarded the beheading of Charles as an unholy violation of the Solemn League and Covenant; had it not committed its supporters "to preserve and defend the king's majesty's person and authority"? So when Cromwell's victorious army seized power, executed Charles, and abolished the monarchy, the Covenanters responded by denouncing the godless new English Republic.[7] As for Cromwell, he was from that moment "the Judas of the Covenant" in the eyes of Scottish Covenanters. They rallied fervently around Charles' son, proclaiming him their king as **Charles II** (Charles was at that point in virtual exile in The Hague, capital of the Dutch Republic). The Covenanters, suddenly royalists, had drawn their swords against the English Republic. The Civil Wars had become a war between two nations.

However, to get the practical support of the Covenanters against the might of the English Republic, Charles II had to become a Covenanter himself. In proclaiming him king, the Scots had stipulated that he could not actually exercise the powers of a king unless he first "should give satisfaction for religion and peace". That meant signing the Covenants; and Charles was initially unwilling to do this. He had a profound

6. A whiggamore was a cattle thief.

7. For a more detailed account of these events, see Chapter 3, section 6.

distaste for all things Presbyterian, and unlike his late devout
father, could not even comprehend religious motivation—the
new king had an essentially secular mind.

So instead of submitting to the wearisome Covenants,
Charles commissioned the Marquis of Montrose to resume his
adventures: to invade northern Scotland with foreign mercenaries
and an army of recruits from the Orkney Islands, and try to
deliver Scotland to his king without Covenanter support. It was,
however, a forlorn hope. Montrose did not have enough men,
and all his military brilliance and personal charisma were in vain.
He was defeated by a Covenanter army at Carbisdale (north of
Inverness), paraded all the way as a prisoner to Edinburgh, and
publicly executed as a notorious villain by the grisly method of
being hanged for three hours and then quartered (sliced up).
The humiliating treatment backfired; it merely turned the mob's
affections toward the dashing, dignified marquis. They sobbed
rather than cursed, as he died with an unearthly serenity.

7. The English conquest of Scotland

Montrose's death left Charles with no alternative: he signed
the National Covenant, and the Solemn League and Covenant,
sailed from the Dutch Republic, and landed in Scotland in
summer 1650. Not all the Covenanters were happy with this;
John Livingstone, for example, felt that Charles had subscribed
the Covenants insincerely, and that the Covenanters were making
themselves partners in the young king's hypocrisy. Still, the deed
was done. Oliver Cromwell, in a pre-emptive strike, promptly
invaded Scotland with his republican army. The Scots who
confronted him at Dunbar lacked thousands of Scotland's best
and most professional soldiers, excluded from military service
by the Act of Classes because of their theological impurity—
they had fought for Charles I (either under Montrose, or with
the pro-Engagement Scots defeated at Preston). This was an
army of none but the purest Covenanters, relying not on guns
or strategies, but on God.

It was one of the most heart-breaking scenes in the wars
that had engulfed Britain. Two intensely religious armies faced

each other: the most committed of the Covenanters against Cromwell's God-fearing Independents. Each side prayed and sang psalms to the same Lord. But only one side could win. On September 3rd 1650, Cromwell smashed the Covenanters at the battle of Dunbar, in one of his most stunning victories (he attacked uphill after a daring night manoeuvre, against a force twice as strong as his own). Nearly a thousand Covenanters lay dead. Some 5,000 were taken prisoner, of whom 3,500 died of ill-treatment. The 1,500 survivors were shipped out as slave labour to English plantations in America or the Caribbean

Yet the humiliated Covenanting government of Argyll refused to learn its lesson. Argyll personally crowned Charles II king at Scone on January 1st 1651. Argyll's day of power, however, had faded; the Scottish parliament defied the marquis by repealing the Act of Classes, in order to combine all Scotland's fighting men into a single great army, whatever their degree of theological purity. This provoked a savagely bitter and enduring schism between the Resolutioners, who were willing to cooperate with those who had fought for Charles I, and the Protesters, who were not willing. The Resolutioners got their name from two public resolutions passed in December 1650 and March 1651, which declared it lawful to reinstate all but a small minority of those whom the Act of Classes had excluded from the Scottish army. The Protesters were the ultra-orthodox Presbyterian zealots; they regarded the Resolutions as acts of religious apostasy against the Covenants, an unholy alliance between Covenanters and those who had fought for Covenant-hating Charles I. This schism between Resolutioners and Protesters utterly wrecked the unity of the Covenanters throughout the rest of their time in government. A celebrated treatise by Covenanting divine James Durham (1622–58), *The Dying Man's Testament to the Church of Scotland; Or, A Treatise Concerning Scandal* (1658), written as the title suggests while Durham was dying, was intended to heal the breach between Protesters and Resolutioners. A glowing testimony to Durham's belief in the vital significance of church unity, it did nothing to accomplish its aim.

The new Covenanting army of Resolutioners invaded England—but it was a trap set by Cromwell. Exactly one year after the battle of Dunbar, the English general caught and shattered the Scots at the battle of Worcester on September 3rd 1651. Charles II himself was one of the few who escaped the catastrophe. It proved to be the final defeat of the Covenanters on the field of battle. Their armies destroyed, Scotland was now at Oliver Cromwell's mercy, and became a conquered land, ruled by Cromwell and his English soldiers. The Scottish parliament was dissolved, the Scottish Privy Council was replaced by a committee of eight English officials, and the Court of Session (Scotland's supreme legal body) was replaced by seven English judges. New English fortresses were built at Leith, Perth, and Ayr to keep the conquered Scots in subjection.

In 1653, Cromwell forbade the general assembly from meeting; it had in any case degenerated into a sterile ecclesiastical battleground, in which Resolutioners and Protesters fought each other tooth and nail over ministerial appointments and points of technical procedure. *James Kirkton* (1628–99), the ultra-Covenanting minister and historian of that period, acknowledged that Cromwell's dissolution of the strife-ridden assembly was no bad thing! Indeed Kirkton says of the whole Cromwellian era in Scotland, "I verily believe there were more souls converted to Christ in that short period of time than in any season since the Reformation." This has been attributed to the enforced silence on political and party matters, which left the clergy no option but to preach exclusively on spiritual matters.

In 1654, for the first time in history, a combined Anglo-Scottish parliament met in Westminster, with 30 Scottish MPs taking their seats alongside their English counterparts. Cromwell had incorporated Scotland into the English system far more effectively than King James VI or Charles I had ever managed. Still, unlike the Stuart monarchs, Cromwell allowed the Covenanters the freedom to preach and practise their Presbyterian worship; to the annoyance of the Covenanters, he also allowed all other Protestants to preach and practise their brand of worship too. For the first time, Scotland had complete religious freedom for Protestantism in all its forms. Baptist churches, for example, first made their appearance in Scotland at this time, founded by English soldiers stationed in Scotland.

8. Other key figures

Alexander Henderson

Alexander Henderson (1583–1646), unofficial leader of the Covenanters, we have already met in section 2.4; he was the young minister forced on an unwilling church in Leuchars who had been converted under the preaching of Robert Bruce. A native of Creich in Fife, he studied at Saint Andrews University from 1603, and then taught philosophy and rhetoric there until 1613. After his conversion under Bruce, Henderson became a zealous Presbyterian. In the general assembly of 1618 which enacted the notorious Five Articles of Perth, he was one of the opposition leaders, for which he was reprimanded before the court of high commission. Over the next 20 years, Henderson became the focal point of Presbyterian resistance to the Episcopalian policies of James VI and then Charles I.

When Charles I's religious policies provoked Scotland to rebellion in 1637, Henderson stepped forth as the universally acknowledged chieftain of the Presbyterian party. Samuel Rutherford wrote to him, "As for your cause, my reverend and dearest brother, ye are the talk of the north and south"— everyone was looking to see what Henderson would do. When Charles ordered all ministers to buy copies of the new Prayer Book for use in their churches, Henderson agreed to buy a copy, but refused to use it. Threatened with prison, he lodged a petition with the Privy Council to suspend the king's order, on the grounds that the book had not been approved by a general assembly nor by parliament. The council upheld his appeal.

This act of defiance by Henderson was instrumental in consolidating the opposition to the Prayer Book, and in propelling Henderson to the foremost place of leadership in that opposition. He became the chief architect of the National Covenant (1638) and the Solemn League and Covenant (1643).

The revolutionary 1638 Glasgow assembly unanimously elected him moderator. The same year he moved from Leuchars to be minister of Saint Giles Kirk in Edinburgh. He was also made Rector of Edinburgh University. When the Westminster Assembly was convened in 1643, he headed the Scottish delegation, and was regarded on all hands as their undisputed head. Despite constant ill-health, Henderson provided wise and statesmanlike leadership to the entire Covenanting movement throughout its first decade, without which it is hard to see how it could have achieved so much. Certainly after his death it seemed to lack that quality of leadership, as the movement succumbed to internal disintegration and conquest by Cromwell. Henderson's thoughtful moderation and warm piety commended him even to Charles I—Henderson was perhaps the only Covenanter that Charles genuinely liked and trusted.

Henderson's legacy of spiritual writings is unfortunately almost non-existent (there is a collection of papers on public affairs), so that he is undeservedly forgotten by most evangelicals today. This is in vivid contrast to our next figure, who is globally famous.

Samuel Rutherford

Samuel Rutherford (1600–61) was probably the greatest theologian of the Covenanters, although some would award the title to George Gillespie (see below). Beyond question, however, Rutherford was their greatest devotional writer, and indeed one of the greatest from any era in the English language. His nickname "the saint of the Covenant" is well-merited. Born at Nisbet near Roxburgh, Rutherford studied at Edinburgh University from 1617 to 1626. He then became minister of Anwoth in Galloway in 1627; many anecdotes clustered around his decade of ministry there, illustrating his spiritual-mindedness and his profound influence over the parish. Famously he was described as "always praying, always preaching, always visiting the sick, always catechising, always writing and studying." But he got into trouble for his publication in 1636 of an anti-Arminian theological work, which outraged the new Bishop of Galloway, Thomas Sydserff, an ardent Arminian.

The bishop prosecuted Rutherford, resulting in his being barred from preaching, and a sentence of "internal exile" in Aberdeen.

When liberty for Presbyterians dawned anew and the National Covenant was signed, Rutherford returned briefly to Anwoth. His Covenanter brethren, however, would not allow him to hide his brilliant light under a bushel in an obscure parish, and the general assembly appointed him professor of divinity at Saint Mary's College, Saint Andrews, in 1639, although Rutherford insisted on the freedom to preach to ordinary folk every Sunday

In 1643, Rutherford was one of the Scots commissioners to the Westminster Assembly, where his learned contributions were manifold. Afterwards he went back to Saint Andrews, becoming rector of the college in 1651. In the bitter Protester-Resolutioner schism, Rutherford was an outspoken Protester—which rather isolated him in Saint Mary's, leading to much tension and unhappiness. With the restoration of the Stuart monarchy in 1660, Rutherford was a marked man; he was summoned by name to appear before parliament on a charge of treason (as well as being sacked from his job and put under house arrest). However, he was already in the grip of his final illness, and in his own words, he went to appear before a higher tribunal than a mere earthly parliament.

Rutherford's most famous non-devotional writing was his political treatise *Lex Rex* ("The Law and the King") published in 1644. Rutherford here promoted the philosophy of George Buchanan (see section 1). With massive erudition, bristling with quotations from ancient philosophers and the Bible, the treatise argued that kings did not have unlimited sovereignty; they could rule only under God's law, and in accordance with the constitution of their country. The citizen body was at liberty to resist a tyrant, by force if necessary. Needless to say, *Lex Rex* was massively popular among both Covenanters and English parliamentarians during the Civil Wars: here was one of Britain's most learned theologians giving overwhelming sanction to the armed struggle against Stuart tyranny. Also needless to say, *Lex Rex* was abominated as a piece of devilish incitement to treason once the monarchy had been restored in 1660. The book was publicly burnt by order of the triumphant royalist regime. It enjoyed an unexpected revival of popularity in the late 20th century, when Reformed philosopher Francis Schaeffer made it the basis of his own political philosophy in *A Christian Manifesto* (1981).

Rutherford's theology and politics paled into near non-existence beside the impact of his devotional writing. This came after his death in a collection of his *Letters* published in 1664. These had mostly been written during his internal exile in Aberdeen back in the 1630s. They had not been intended for publication; the letters were collected and printed in the Dutch Republic by Rutherford's former student, Robert McWard, under the original title *Joshua Redivivus* ("Joshua Reborn", "Joshua Alive Again"): the idea was that Rutherford had been a spiritual Joshua, spying out the heavenly promised land and reporting on its glories to God's pilgrim people. Once the *Letters* had seen the light of day, they for ever secured Rutherford's reputation as possessing and communicating a rapturous Christ-centred spirituality. The volume was easily his most popular work, and it has been more or less continuously in print to the present day.

There are about 365 letters (there is some variation depending on the edition); they are addressed mainly to Anwoth folk, especially godly ladies. Their style is pastoral, modelled on the letters of Paul, and their overriding theme is "the loveliness of Christ". One of the most celebrated anecdotes about Rutherford brings out the centrality of this idea in his spirituality:

> An English merchant said of him [Rutherford], even in days when controversy had sorely vexed him and distracted his spirit, "I came to Irvine, and heard a well-favoured, proper old man [David Dickson], with a long beard, and that man showed me all my heart. Then I went to St. Andrews, where I heard a sweet, majestic-looking man [Robert Blair], and he showed me the majesty of God. After him I heard a little, fair man [Rutherford], and he showed me the loveliness of Christ."

Rutherford commended Christ with the passion of a lover, utilizing the lush and picturesque language of the Song of Songs. Many readers have found the piety of the *Letters* reminiscent of Bernard of Clairvaux. Critics have objected to some of Rutherford's expressions as crude and tasteless, e.g. his exhortation to spiritual drunkenness:

> let us come near, and fill ourselves with Christ, and let His friends drink, and be drunken... Drink, and spare not; drink love, and be drunken with Christ!

Such language, however, is not peculiar to Rutherford. It is found in other great spiritual writers, such as Augustine. The "God-intoxicated" soul is a recurring theme in devotional literature through the ages.

Rutherford's Christ-centred ecstasies were not some form of false mystical escape from earthly trials. He continually spoke of the cross, not as something Christ alone endured, but as the necessary experience of all Christ's people. Nothing was clearer in Rutherford's *Letters* than the centrality of crucifixion for the believer here below. It was not easy to be a Christian, Rutherford warned: "No man hath a velvet cross." The way to heaven was only and ever through being conformed to the suffering of Christ. To forsake Christ because of suffering betrayed a fundamental misunderstanding of the very nature of a true relationship with Him:

> ye contracted with Christ, I hope, when first ye began to follow Him, that ye would bear His Cross. Fulfil your part of the contract with patience, and break not to Jesus Christ.

Rutherford's *Letters* also attained renown for their homely, proverbial language and images; he was especially fond of sea imagery, and metaphors drawn from the weather and seasons. In one of his most celebrated sayings, "Grace groweth best in winter." More surprisingly, he tells us that Christ, as the representative of sinners, went through the fiery baking oven of God's wrath, and came out as fresh hot bread for the King's table!

Rutherford's *Letters* became an immediate favourite with all evangelically-minded people; the great English Puritan, Richard Baxter, spoke for many when he said of Rutherford's *Letters*, "Hold off the Bible, such a book the world never saw." Two centuries later, Charles Haddon Spurgeon would say:

When we are dead and gone, let the world know that Spurgeon held Rutherford's Letters to be the nearest thing to inspiration which can be found in all the writings of mere men.

Perhaps the best summary of the piety and language of the *Letters* is the 19th century poem *Immanuel's Land* by Anne Ross Cousin (1824–1906), based on the *Letters* and on Rutherford's deathbed sayings.

George Gillespie

George Gillespie (1613–48) was arguably the greatest theologian of the Covenanters, if we do not grant the distinction to Rutherford. A radical Presbyterian well before the National Covenant was drafted, he trained for the ministry of the Kirk, but refused to accept Episcopal ordination. He responded to the Scottish Prayer Book with the anonymously published *A Dispute Against the English-Popish Ceremonies Obtruded Upon the Church of Scotland* (1637). The treatise was banned by the Privy Council, but it made Gillespie's name as the brilliant young author. After the Covenant had been unfurled as a flag of Presbyterian revival, Gillespie signed it, and was ordained (non-Episcopally) to the parish of Wemyss. He was appointed a Scottish commissioner to the Westminster Assembly, where he became one of its most valued members; the theological quality of his contributions in debate was unsurpassed.

Gillespie died young of tuberculosis in 1648, but left behind a large literary output. His most famous work was *Aaron's Rod Blossoming* (1646), which discusses with erudition, incisive logic, and careful exegesis the nature and relationships of civil and ecclesiastical power. It remains a tour de force to the present day, expounding the classical ideal of a Reformed Church in a Reformed state.

Robert Baillie

Robert Baillie (1602–1662), son of a Glasgow merchant, and distinguished graduate of Glasgow University, was minister at Kilwinning in Ayrshire when the Scottish revolt against King

Charles erupted. He began as a moderate Episcopalian, but opposed the imposition of Laud's Prayer Book, played a part in drafting the National Covenant, and was a member of the revolutionary 1638 Glasgow Assembly, although he retained something of his moderation, arguing against the decision to make Episcopacy illegal. In 1642, he was appointed professor of divinity in Glasgow, and then from 1643 to 1646 he was one of the Scots commissioners at Westminster Assembly. After Charles I's execution, Baillie became an ardent supporter of Charles II. In the schism between Resolutioners and Protesters, Baillie was a leading Resolutioner; he regarded the Protesters as traitors for not rallying to the support of king and country against the godless English Republic of Oliver Cromwell.

Baillie helped negotiate the restoration of Charles II to power in 1660; the king offered him a Scottish bishopric, but Baillie declined. He opposed the re-establishment of Episcopacy in the Scottish Kirk, prophesying that it would lead to the dire persecution of many conscientious Presbyterians—a prophecy fulfilled in blood. It was reported that Baillie died of a broken heart. His gossipy letters and journal are one of our most valuable sources of information about the earlier half of the Covenanting era. He was also one of the most learned scholars of the day, knowing some 13 languages, including Ethiopic and Chaldee.

James Guthrie

James Guthrie (1612–61), nicknamed "the short man who could not bow" by Oliver Cromwell, was a dominating figure in the Covenanting general assemblies.[8] Born at Guthrie in Forfarshire, and educated at Saint Andrews, he became one of its regents; his philosophy lectures earned him much distinction. He was at first an ardent Episcopalian, but Samuel Rutherford won him over to the Presbyterian cause after Scotland's spiritual revolution of 1637. Guthrie signed the Covenant in

---

8. Not to be confused with William Guthrie (1620–65), author of *The Christian's Great Interest*, a popular Covenanting work of practical divinity.

1638, apparently prophesying, "I know I shall die for what I have done today, but I cannot die in a better cause." In 1642 he became minister of Lauder in Berwickshire, and thereafter found recognition as one of the most active and well-known of the Covenanting clergy. In 1649 he moved to the parish church of Stirling. He wrote a judicious *Treatise of Ruling Elders and Deacons* in 1652.

During the controversy between Resolutioners and Protesters, Guthrie was a leading Protester. He published a tract in 1653, *Causes of the Lord's Wrath Against Scotland*, in which he asserted the supreme duty of upholding true religion (by which he meant the Covenants), and denounced the exercise of unchecked, unconstitutional power in the state as the chief source of Scotland's maladies. After the Restoration of the monarchy in 1660, this tract was publicly burned alongside Rutherford's *Lex Rex*.

That same year of 1660, Guthrie and nine other Protesters met in Edinburgh and published a "humble petition" to the restored Charles II, declaring their loyalty to him and reminding him of his obligations to the Covenants. However, Guthrie was arrested and tried for treason. Presiding at his trial was the Earl of Middleton, whom Guthrie had mortally offended in 1650 by excommunicating him for plotting to turn Charles against the Scottish parliament. Despite his vigorous defence at the trial, where his knowledge of Scots law and his eloquent final speech electrified the proceedings, Guthrie was condemned, and hanged on 1st June 1661. He made a huge impression by his dignity in dying. "I take God to record, I would not exchange this scaffold with the palace or mitre of the greatest prelate in Britain", were among his final words. Some said they had experienced more of God's presence in Guthrie's death than they had in most celebrations of holy communion. Almost immediately, miraculous stories became attached to Guthrie's remains: it was said that a few weeks after his execution, fresh blood gushed out of his head (which was on public display on one of the city gates), falling on the coach of his arch-enemy, Middleton, and that the blood made stains which could by no means be washed away.

4
The Covenanters: days of blood

1. Episcopacy triumphant

The Restoration of the Stuart monarchy under Charles II (1660–85) in 1660 was, in Scotland, the work of the Resolutioner party of the Covenanters.[1] The leading figures among the Protesters were summoned by parliament to face charges of treason. Among the intended victims were Samuel Rutherford, the Marquis of Argyll, Archibald Johnston, and James Guthrie. Rutherford escaped by dying of natural causes, but Argyll, Johnston, and Guthrie were all executed. Poor Johnston was by now a wreck in body and mind, but the new royal regime showed him no mercy. The vanquished men of yesterday died with the courage of their convictions, and were hailed as Christ's martyrs by their fellow-Protesters.

The Resolutioners were, however, deceived in their expectation that Charles II would confirm the Presbyterian constitution of the Kirk. The new government, determined to show the extent of its loyalty to the king, systematically undid everything the Covenanters had worked for since 1637. All members of the Scottish parliament had to swear a new oath of allegiance in which they acknowledged Charles as "supreme governor of this kingdom over all persons and in all causes"—the monarch was master of the Kirk. An act was passed annulling everything that the Covenanting parliaments had done, which destroyed

---

1. See Chapter 4, section 1.1-2, for a more detailed account of the Restoration in England.

412 2000 Years of Christ's Power

the legal basis on which Presbyterianism existed in Scotland. Synods in southern Scotland objected, especially the synod of Galloway, which was completely dominated by the Protesters.

But Charles ignored these rumblings of discontent and pressed ahead with the re-establishment of Episcopacy. He was persuaded by his leading English advisor, Edward Hyde, Earl of Clarendon, that if he permitted Presbyterianism in Scotland, it would undermine the stability of Episcopalian Anglicanism in England. So in September 1661, a royal proclamation was issued for the re-constituting of the Kirk on an Episcopal basis. Only one bishop survived from the pre-Covenanting era, so fresh ones were appointed to the vacant positions. Most of them were Resolutioner Presbyterians who had made their peace with the new regime. The new Archbishop of Saint Andrews, the chief bishop of all Scotland, was James Sharp (1618–79), the leading Resolutioner. Oliver Cromwell had summed the man up: "Sharp of that ilk"—in other words, Sharp by name, sharp (cunning and selfish) by practice.

The summoning of a new parliament in 1661 saw, within days, a decree that the National Covenant should be publicly burned, and an act declaring the Solemn League and Covenant illegal. Some Covenanters denounced this act as defiance of God, since no mere parliament could nullify an oath. Those who took this line were banished, many settling in Rotterdam in the Dutch Republic. Here they set up a strict Covenanting presbytery, which kept up a constant war of words against the government of Charles II. The most important of these exiles was the learned and high-minded *John Brown of Wamphray* (c.1610–79), ejected from the ministry for refusing to submit to Episcopal reordination (see below). From his Dutch exile, Brown wrote outstanding doctrinal works on justification by faith and the Sabbath, and also withering condemnations of Charles II's government for its religious policy.

In May 1662, the entire Presbyterian structure of the Kirk was legally abolished, and it was made unlawful for anyone to preach without an Episcopal licence. However, hardly any changes were made to worship; certainly the 1637 Prayer Book was not re-introduced. Although the Westminster Directory was prohibited, and shorter sermons were encouraged by the bishops, there was virtually no outward difference between Covenanter worship and the new Episcopal worship. The crucial difference was in the realm of ecclesiastical government; the new Kirk was totally state-controlled, with the king as supreme governor, and the bishops as the agents of his will. Presbyteries became purely clerical bodies, with a moderator appointed by the bishop. Theoretically there was a national synod; but it could meet only by the king's will, and in fact it never met.

Parliament also declared that all charges to which ministers had been inducted since 1649 were vacant, and that all such ministers must apply to the bishop and the local patron for authorization. The year 1649 was picked on, because a Covenanting parliament in that year had abolished patronage (the choice of ministers by local landowners) and granted the right of choosing ministers to kirk sessions. Since the new regime had restored patronage, it would not recognize ministers appointed under the kirk session scheme since 1649. In the north and east, ministers generally applied to the bishop and patron, and were authorized. But in Lanarkshire, Ayrshire, Dumfries, and Galloway, resistance was almost universal. These more principled Presbyterians regarded parliament's demand as a denial of the legitimacy of their ordination, and they were not prepared to compromise.

The Privy Council decreed that all such ministers must depart from their churches by November 1st 1662. Most did so, and the churches were deserted and closed. In February 1663, 270 of the recalcitrant ministers were officially deposed. Since there were roughly 1,000 Kirk ministers, this meant that over a quarter were ejected. We may compare this with what had happened in England in 1660–62, when some 2,000 ministers (roughly one fifth of all Anglican clergy) had been ejected from the Anglican Church for refusing to conform to the new Episcopal regime. The places of the ejected Scottish ministers were taken by licentiates, whom the people referred to scornfully as "curates".[2] The deposed ministers were forbidden to reside

---

2. Curate = assistant to an Episcopal minister.

within 20 miles of their former churches. To ensure that the people attended the parish churches under the new ministers, parliament passed an act known as the "Bishops' Drag-Net", which inflicted crippling fines for non-attendance.

2. The Pentland Rising

There was widespread popular defiance of the Bishops' Drag-net in Galloway and Ayrshire; people boycotted their parish churches and held meetings of their own. These came to be called "conventicles". Parliament defined a conventicle as any meeting for worship outside the established Kirk at which more than five people were present. These were deemed illegal. They flourished, however, in Galloway and Ayrshire, as large numbers of Covenanters met in the open air to worship outside the state system. The government responded by sending troops under the command of Sir James Turner (1615–86) to enforce obedience. Turner, a minister's son, had been a faithful royalist throughout the Covenanter wars, and was a very capable strategist and military historian. The harsh behaviour of Turner and his troops, however, provoked resentment and rebellion. On November 13th 1666 in Kirkcudbrightshire, some of Turner's soldiers beat up an old man who could not pay a fine for non-attendance at his parish church. Four Covenanters intervened, a fight developed, and a soldier was shot and wounded; by the time it was over, others had joined the Covenanters, overpowering and disarming the soldiers. Flushed with victory, they then marched on Dumfries, surprised Turner himself in his bed, and took him prisoner in his dressing gown.

Led by Colonel James Wallace (d.1678), an experienced Presbyterian soldier, the insurgents (now numbering roughly 1,000) marched on Lanark, where they pledged themselves afresh to the Covenants, denied that they were political rebels, protested against oppressive treatment, petitioned for the abolition of Episcopacy and the restoration of Presbyterianism, and affirmed their faithfulness to the crown. Their numbers now swollen to 3,000, they marched on toward Edinburgh to present their grievances. Fierce rainstorms, however, demoralized them, leading to desertions; when they found the city of Edinburgh closed against them, and no support in the city, they decided to march home, now numbering only some 900. They were, however, met, attacked, and crushed by superior government forces on November 28th at Rullion Green, on the Pentland hills, just outside Edinburgh. The insurgent leader Wallace managed to escape, and died in exile in the Dutch Republic; but some 50 were killed in the battle. Around 120 survivors were then publicly executed for treason in various places, to instil terror into any other Covenanters contemplating disobedience. The executions may well have been counter-productive; many people were taken aback by the government's ruthlessness in putting so many obscure, ordinary people to death, and some of the victims made a deep spiritual impression by their dying speeches. The most notable of these was the young preacher Hugh Mackail (1640–66), who famously declared on the scaffold:

> Farewell father and mother, friends and relations—farewell the world and all delights—farewell meat and drink—farewell sun, moon, and stars—welcome God and Father—welcome sweet Jesus Christ, the Mediator of the new covenant—welcome blessed spirit of grace, and God of all consolation—welcome glory—welcome eternal life, and welcome death.

So began the government killings of Covenanters in response to perceived Covenanter disloyalty. The total number of Covenanters killed by the government between 1660 and 1690 has traditionally been put as high as 18,000. Most modern historians think the number was probably considerably smaller but still substantial. As well as the deaths, we should also take into account the emigration of Covenanters to Ireland. It was estimated that about 30,000 fled and resettled in Ulster between 1660 and 1690; the government even expressed its concern that many Scottish landlords would have no tenants left!

3. The life and work of Robert Leighton

Robert Leighton (1611–84) was Charles II's Bishop of Dunblane. He had, however, not only been a Covenanter—he virtually remained one in doctrine and piety. There is some question about his birthplace; he may have been born in London (some think

Edinburgh). He was, however, of Scottish Presbyterian parentage. After studying at Edinburgh University, he spent a decade broadening his mind on the Continent; for example, he befriended some Jansenists in the famous Catholic seminary at Douay in the Spanish Netherlands, and discovered in them a depth of sincere Christian faith and spiritual life he had not thought possible in Roman Catholics. It seems they reminded him of the Christians of the earliest centuries. There was always to be a Jansenist leaven in Leighton's own piety; in particular, he admired monasticism and the celibate life—he himself never married.[3]

However, Leighton's attachment to key Protestant distinctives remained unshaken, and on returning to Scotland he was appointed minister of Newbattle, near Edinburgh, in 1641. Here he preached the sermons which became the basis for his famous commentary on 1 Peter. According to his friend Gilbert Burnet (a Scot who became Anglican Bishop of Salisbury: see Chapter 4, section 1.4), Leighton's preaching was almost literally out-of-this-world:

> His preaching had a sublimity both of thought and expression. The grace and gravity of his pronunciation was such that few heard him without sensible [deeply felt] emotion .... His style was rather too fine; but there was a majesty and beauty in it that left so deep an impression that I cannot forget the sermons I heard him preach thirty years ago.

In 1653, Leighton became Principal of Edinburgh University, where his Latin lectures attracted crowds who could not even understand Latin—Leighton's mere manner, it was said, radiated heavenly realities.

Leighton fell into an increasing disenchantment with the Covenanting movement. He perceived a tendency to quarrelsomeness and divisiveness, and a focus on political and ecclesiastical issues instead of eternal truths. Other Covenanting ministers rebuked him for not "preaching to the times" (i.e. preaching on current affairs, a favourite Covenanter practice).

---

3. For the Jansenists, see Chapter 6, section 4.

Leighton famously replied, "If all of my brethren preach to the times, may not one poor brother be suffered to preach on eternity?"

In 1660, with the restoration of the monarchy, Leighton accepted the bishopric of Dunblane, where his Episcopal rule was distinguished by its tolerance and moderation toward Presbyterian dissenters. In 1667, after the Pentland Rising, he made proposals for reform which he hoped would restore some measure of unity to a divided Kirk. He suggested that the government of the Kirk should again be vested in presbyteries and synods, with the bishops acting as moderators. Ordinations should be carried out by the presbytery, the bishop presiding simply as chief presbyter. Synods of the two dioceses of Glasgow and Saint Andrews should meet every three years, with authority to censure bishops.

Leighton's fellow bishops rejected his proposals, and they fell into complete oblivion when an assassination attempt was made on the life of Archbishop Sharp by an extreme Covenanter. The would-be assassin was James Mitchell; he escaped, and became the first of the Covenanters to defend in print the right and duty of private individuals to kill "idolaters" (by which Mitchell meant enemies of the Covenant), especially bishops. This view, although a minority view among Covenanters, was exploited by the government to portray all Covenanters as murderous fanatics and terrorists.

The government tried a different tactic in 1669; a royal indulgence was issued which allowed the ejected ministers of 1663 to return to their parishes, or be settled in new ones, as long as they had obeyed the law in the meantime. Some 40 of the 270 ejected clergy returned to the Church on these terms. Most of them were settled within the diocese of Glasgow. Its archbishop, Alexander Burnet (not to be confused with Gilbert Burnet), protested at what he saw as government interference, and was summarily deposed. Charles II replaced Burnet with Leighton, who from 1670–4 supervised Glasgow and its churches. At the same time, the Scottish parliament passed a new act asserting in the most forceful and unqualified language the king's absolute supremacy over the Kirk. Leighton worked tirelessly at trying to reconcile Presbyterian ministers and people to the established Kirk, both theologically and in practice, but his best efforts made little headway. His "ecumenism" paradoxically made him an object of suspicion and distaste to staunch Presbyterians, because his godly life and soul-stirring preaching made Episcopalianism seem more attractive! He was also thwarted in his idealism by the hostility of the other bishops, and the persecuting policies of the government.

Where Leighton's methods failed, the king's met with better success: in 1672 a second royal indulgence was issued, and another 50 of the ejected ministers returned to the Kirk. This, however, was a merely pragmatic solution without theological or spiritual substance, and it formed no part of Leighton's idealistic ecumenism. In 1674, weary of it all, he resigned and was allowed to retire to Broadhurst in the south of England. He refused all inducements to resume active church life, and died of pleurisy in 1684. Future generations of evangelicals have treasured Leighton's commentary on 1 Peter, his sermons, and his theological lectures, as pristine models of evangelical spirituality.

4. The battle of Bothwell Bridge

The king's indulgences introduced serious divisions into the ranks of the Covenanters. Three positions were taken with respect to the indulgences:

1. It was lawful for a minister to return to the Kirk through an indulgence.

2. It was not lawful, but Covenanters could still cooperate with indulged ministers and attend their ministry.

3. It was not lawful even to cooperate with an indulged minister or attend his ministry.

This third view hardened into a refusal to cooperate, not only with indulged ministers, but with anyone who had cooperated with them. The vast bulk of Covenanters held position 2 or

3, rejecting the indulgences but dividing over the attitude that should be taken towards the indulged. Position 2 was championed by prominent open-air preachers *John Welsh* (c.1624–81) and *John Blackadder* (1615–86), who bent their efforts towards maintaining Covenanter unity, relegating to a secondary issue the question of indulged ministers. Position 3 was championed by John Brown of Wamphray and the exiles in the Dutch Republic.

In 1674, government policy veered again. The laws against unauthorized religious gatherings were made more severe; the death penalty was decreed against unauthorized preaching; everything just short of death was threatened to anyone who gave shelter to a Presbyterian preacher. Diehard Presbyterians responded by more open and more frequent defiance of the law. In 1678, the government brought a Highland army of 6,000 into the Covenanting heartland of western Scotland, and "quartered" it on the people (gave the troops the right to commandeer property and take whatever they wished from civilians). This time the response of the most militant Covenanters was more violent; on May 29th 1679, they ambushed and assassinated Archbishop Sharp while he was riding in a carriage on Magus Moor, near Saint Andrews. Sharp, the apostate Covenanter, had always pursued the most repressive policies against his one-time religious confederates, and consequently aroused the most intense fury against himself. He paid with his life on Magus Moor, repeatedly stabbed and shot in the presence of his terrified, sobbing daughter. Strangely, the leader of the Covenanter band, David Hackston (d.1680), had a change of heart during the ambush and pled unsuccessfully with the others to spare Sharp's life. (Hackston was nonetheless executed in 1680 as an accessory to the murder.)

Most Covenanters disowned Sharp's assassination as the work of the fanatical few, but in its wake a serious Covenanter rebellion broke out in the west. A band of 80 Covenanters on horseback rode into Rutherglen, near Glasgow, and read out a testimony against Episcopacy and the forsaking of the Covenants. *James Graham of Claverhouse* (1648–89), the viscount of Dundee (the "Bonnie Dundee" of Jacobite lore: "Bloody Clavers" to his opponents), a ruthless professional soldier, was put at the head of a body of government troops, and sent to stamp out the rebellion. He attacked an illegal religious gathering of Covenanters at Drumclog in Lanarkshire, but many of the Covenanters were armed, fought back, and surprisingly routed the government forces—Claverhouse narrowly escaped with his life.

The victorious Covenanters now gathered at Bothwell Bridge, where many flocked to their standard. Numbers hovered between 5,000 and 8,000. However, with numbers came dissension. The division of opinion over the indulged ministers came to the fore: some were implacably opposed to all who had not subscribed in the strictest terms to the Covenants; others wanted a more broadminded restoration of Presbyterianism, with lenience for indulged ministers and those who cooperated with them. Some were committed to direct military action against a tyrannical government; others argued that it was the place of God's people to suffer, rather than to fight for their own deliverance.

In consequence of these divisions, many Covenanters deserted the camp, leaving an army of some 4,000. On June 22nd, they were crushed by a government force of 10,000 led by Charles II's illegitimate son, the Duke of Monmouth: some 500 Covenanters were killed and 1,200 captured.[4] After most of them solemnly promised not to take up arms against the government again, they were released; but 257 of the most dangerous, who refused to give any undertaking not to rebel again, were condemned to slavery in the Barbados Islands. The prison ship carrying them there was wrecked off the Orkneys with the loss of all hands.

Charles now put his Roman Catholic brother James, Duke of York, in charge of Scottish affairs. James' Catholicism was sending waves of alarm across the whole of Britain. In the English parliament, the Whig party, led by the Earl of Shaftesbury, were pushing the country to the brink of civil war in their attempts to exclude James from succeeding to the throne

---

4. For more about Monmouth, see Chapter 4, section 2.2.

after Charles' death (Charles had no legitimate children).[5] Strangely for Scotland, which had once been a Covenanted nation, its parliament was far more docile and submissive. In 1681 it recognized the unconditional right of James to the Scottish throne regardless of religion. At the same time, to show that its acceptance of James did not mean the abandonment of Protestantism, it passed a Test Act applicable to all office-holders in Kirk and state. The Act required them to maintain the Protestant religion as set forth in the Scots Confession of 1560, to acknowledge the king's supremacy over the Kirk, and to disown the Covenants. A number of clergymen were deposed for refusing to subscribe. The leading Scottish noble, the Earl of Argyll (son of the Covenanting marquis who had been executed at the Restoration), was condemned for treason because he would subscribe to the Test Act only with reservations. Argyll saved his life by fleeing to the Dutch Republic.

5. The Cameronians

Charles II's problems in Scotland had been complicated by an event that had occurred on June 22nd 1680. On that day, the first anniversary of Bothwell Bridge, in the town of Sanquhar in Dumfries-shire, a band of 20 Covenanters gathered and read out a declaration—the "Sanquhar Declaration"—renouncing all allegiance to Charles II as a Covenant-breaking tyrant.

> We being under the standard of our Lord Jesus Christ, Captain of Salvation, do declare a war with such a tyrant and usurper, and all the men of his practices, as enemies to our Lord Jesus Christ, and His cause and covenants; and against all such as have strengthened him, sided with, or anywise acknowledged him in his tyranny, civil or ecclesiastic.

The declaration also disowned "that professed papist" James as heir to the throne.

The Sanquhar Covenanters belonged to the hard-line wing of the movement, and were led by a young, idealistic, charismatic,

---

5. See Chapter 4, section 1.5.

and militant preacher, **Richard Cameron** (c.1648–80). Those who accepted his leadership were nicknamed Cameronians. They believed in absolute loyalty to the Covenants, the unlawfulness of any Scottish Kirk or government which did not adhere to the Covenants, the complete independence of the Kirk from state control, total noncooperation with indulged ministers or with those who did cooperate with them, and the lawfulness of killing would-be persecutors in self-defence.

Charles regarded the Sanquhar Declaration as an open declaration of civil war, and sent troops into the west to root out and annihilate the Cameronians. James Graham of Claverhouse was one of the troop commanders; his savage conduct earned him an undying notoriety in Scottish folk memory. Richard Cameron was killed in a skirmish at Ayrsmoss in 1680. His last words before the battle, addressed to his brother Michael, breathe the fiery, battling, almost jihad-like spirit of the Cameronians:

> Michael, come, let us fight it out to the last; for this is the day that I have longed for, and the death I have prayed for, to die fighting against our Lord's avowed enemies; and this is the day that we will get the crown.

Cameron's successor **Donald Cargill** (c.1627–81) was executed in 1681; his successor **James Renwick** (1662–88) was executed in 1688. Although the Cameronians were seen as extremists by other Presbyterians, they were nonetheless admired for their heroic loyalty to the Covenants, their courage and integrity under savage persecution, and the purity and sincerity of their Protestant faith. The government rendered itself hateful by making martyrs of such people.

Along with these Cameronian martyrs, considerable numbers of ordinary people were killed by the government troops, often without trial, merely for their passive sympathy with Cameronian principles. The most famous were the Wigtown Martyrs, **Margaret Lauchlison** (an elderly widow) and **Margaret Wilson** (aged 18). In May 1685, the two women were tied to stakes in the sand on the Solway Firth where the incoming tide would drown them. The older Margaret was positioned further out so that she would be drowned first, while government officials tried to persuade the younger Margaret to renounce her Covenanting principles, while she watched her comrade gasping for air as the waters rose above her head. But the younger Margaret rejected all persuasion and said of the older Margaret, "What do I see but Christ wrestling there?" Both were drowned.

This period of persecution from 1680–88 is the epoch usually designated as the "Killing Times" in Scottish Church history, because of its concentrated anti-Covenanter severity.

5

James VII: Presbyterians victorious

1. James VII: Rome on the throne

When *James VII* of Scotland (James II of England) came to the throne in February 1685, he was determined to bring both his kingdoms back into the Roman Catholic fold.[1] At first his northern kingdom was loyal. The only sign of things to come was an attempted rebellion by the Earl of Argyll, who returned from his Dutch exile to raise a Protestant standard against the popish monarch. But Argyll was forced to disband his army because of fierce internal disputes. The militant Covenanters would have nothing to do with Argyll's rising, perceiving it to be politically and personally motivated, rather than a genuine crusade for the Covenants. Argyll was captured and executed. Despite their non-involvement in Argyll's rebellion, the Covenanters suffered for it in a fresh wave of persecution.

James converted the royal chapel at Holyrood into a centre for Roman Catholic worship. Jesuits were based there, together with a Catholic printing press. James also began systematically dismissing Protestants from all positions of authority, even from town councils, replacing them with Catholics. He used royal power to exempt his Catholic nominees from the Protestant "Test Act" of 1681. Some of the more fiery Kirk ministers preached against popery; James silenced them. He even dismissed the Bishop of Dunblane and the Archbishop

---

1. See Chapter 4, section 2.3.

of Glasgow for opposition to his Catholicizing policies. In 1687, he issued a royal Indulgence in which all the penal laws against Roman Catholics were lifted, although Presbyterians were merely given permission to worship in private houses. A second Indulgence the same year suspended all laws against all nonconformists, whether Catholic or Presbyterian, but worship in the open air—the standard Covenanter practice—was still prohibited.

2. The Glorious Revolution and the 1690 settlement

Charles II's Episcopalian policies had been opposed by staunch Presbyterians. James VII's Romanizing policies were opposed by the entire kingdom—in England as well as Scotland. The English lost patience first, and invited William of Orange, chief magistrate of the Calvinist Dutch Republic (and husband of James' Protestant daughter Mary) to come to England at the head of an army to save the nation from Romanism.[2] James, remembering what had happened to his father Charles I, panicked and fled the country in December 1688, leaving the way clear for a peaceful assumption of power by William of Orange. The event is known in British history as the Glorious Revolution. When news of James' fall from power reached Scotland, there was a popular Protestant uprising in Edinburgh; Catholic chapels were destroyed by a rampaging Protestant mob. In the Covenanting heartland of the west, the Episcopalian clergy were forcibly driven out of their churches and manses ("rabbled" out) by their own insurgent parishioners.

Agents of the Scottish Protestant establishment met William in London, where an agreement was made that William would administer Scotland's affairs until a national assembly settled matters on a more permanent basis. In March 1689, William summoned the Scottish convention of estates (a historic institution representing the traditional social orders: a quasi-parliament) as the promised national assembly. Supporters of James were present, but they were outnumbered by aggressive

---

2. See Chapter 4, section 2.4.

supporters of William, and soon deserted the convention. Following England's example, the convention declared the Scottish throne vacant, and then offered it jointly to William and Mary. Supporters of James were henceforth known as "Jacobites" (from the Latin for James, *Jacobus*). James Graham of Claverhouse, the infamous persecutor of Presbyterians, raised a Highland force for the Jacobite cause, and smashed William's troops at Killiecrankie in July. But Claverhouse himself was killed in the battle, and without his charismatic leadership the Highlanders eventually lost heart and melted away, especially after encountering invincible resistance from a body of Cameronian troops at Dunkeld.

In June 1689 William recalled the convention as his first Scottish parliament. His ecclesiastical policy was guided by his Scottish Presbyterian chaplain, **William Carstares** (1649–1715), who had suffered imprisonment and torture under Charles II, before fleeing to the Dutch Republic and entering William's service. Parliament issued a proclamation calling on all ministers to pray for William and Mary as Scotland's rightful sovereigns; 182 ministers were dismissed for refusing to comply. Episcopacy was then abolished. William was still reluctant to commit himself to legally establishing Presbyterianism as the national Scottish Kirk, but it soon became clear that he had no alternative—the Episcopalians were showing themselves to be strongly Jacobite in their loyalties. So in 1690, the Kirk was constituted in law as a fully Presbyterian body. The royal supremacy over the Kirk was abolished. The Westminster Confession was recognized as the national Confession of Faith. The Presbyterian ministers ejected in 1663 were restored; the Episcopalian ministers who had been removed in 1689, either by popular pressure or for refusing to pray for William and Mary, were officially declared deprived of their livings. Patronage was abolished, except in the case of town councils.

In October 1690, the general assembly met—the first since 1663. The Presbyterians were poised to take full advantage of the Glorious Revolution to press their cause, and there was real danger of anti-Episcopalian persecution. King William recommended moderation to the assembly. It was tacitly accepted that the days of the Covenants were over; the three surviving Cameronian ministers were received back into the Kirk as an uncovenanted body. Episcopalian clergy were allowed to remain in their parishes on condition that they subscribed to the Westminster Confession, prayed for William and Mary as Scotland's lawful sovereigns, and obeyed the Kirk's Presbyterian courts (presbytery, synod, assembly).

The restoration of Presbyterianism brought some changes in Scottish public worship. During 1660–90, the use of the Lord's Prayer and the Apostles' Creed had come to be associated, in many Presbyterian minds, with the detested Episcopal regime which persecuted Presbyterians. Prior to this, these practices had been Presbyterian norms. But these "liturgical" elements were now dropped by most Presbyterians in the post-1690 Kirk, although a few retained them. It was from 1690 onwards that Scottish Presbyterianism became anti-liturgical, which certainly the original Scottish Reformers had not been.

Another practice that became widespread among all Presbyterians in this period was the "communion season". This had been pioneered by the Protesters. The minister in the local church where the Lord's Supper was to be celebrated would be helped by his colleagues from neighbouring churches, and from Saturday to Monday sermons would be preached in the open air each day. People would come from all the churches of that area to take part, and throughout Sunday they would sit in relays at the Lord's Table. The communion season became a settled feature in Scottish Presbyterian life, a kind of sacramental festival, and to some extent compensated for the infrequency of the Lord's Supper.

So was created the abiding Presbyterian form of the Church of Scotland which has endured to the present day (so far). However, the 1690 settlement was not based on the Covenants, which persuaded many Cameronians to remain outside the settlement, although their three ministers did go in. The Cameronians thus became a small lay movement, Presbyterian but estranged from the national Kirk, lacking both ministers and sacraments. They continued the pre-1690 practice of meeting as praying societies, until in 1706 they gained the loyalty of John McMillan (1669–1753), who had been the minister in the established Kirk at Balmaghie, in Galloway. Eventually McMillan was joined by Thomas Nairn (1680–1764), a minister from the First Secession Church (a breakaway Presbyterian Church, dating from 1733). McMillan and Nairn, together with some ruling elders, constituted themselves as a Presbytery in 1743, under the title of "the Reformed Presbytery". This body, as the Reformed Presbyterian Church, still exists today (there are only a few Scottish congregations, but very many more in Ireland, North America, and Canada).

3. The fate of the Episcopalians

What happened to the Episcopalians? Some 200 Episcopalian clergy had been evicted by the mob in 1688 in the south-west, the Covenanting heartland. Another 200 had been expelled by the new government for being Jacobites (refusing to take the oath of allegiance to William and Mary). The general assembly set up two commissions for the regions north and south of the river Tay, in order to inquire into the state of the parish ministry and to eject "scandalous" clergy. The northern commission interpreted its remit stringently to mean that all Episcopalians were automatically scandalous, and to be ejected. The result was that in the period 1690–1710, the parishes of the Episcopalian north-east were not allowed to have the clergy they wanted, and they themselves refused to accept Presbyterian clergy. This meant that they were often without a parish ministry of any kind. Disillusioned, Episcopalians began to withdraw from the parish system and meet on their own. This was an ironic reversal of what had happened in the period 1660–88, when it had been Presbyterians who withdrew and met as private conventicles. Now the boot was on the other foot: the Episcopalians were the dissidents who worshipped in conventicles!

This was regarded as unacceptable by the new Presbyterian establishment. Matters came to an ugly head in 1711 when an Episcopalian clergyman, James Greenshields (active 1700s), was convicted and imprisoned by the Court of Session for conducting Episcopalian worship in Edinburgh. Greenshields appealed to the House of Lords, which upheld his right to conduct Episcopalian worship in Scotland. The Westminster parliament then passed a new Toleration Act in 1712 to enshrine the House of Lords' ruling. However, there was a sting in the tail: the Act required Scottish Episcopalian clergy to renounce the exiled Stuarts, and swear allegiance to Queen Anne and her designated successor, the German Protestant Princess Sophia of Hanover. Greenshields was prepared to do this, but many of the Episcopalian clergy were not, owing to their Jacobite sympathies. The Toleration Act therefore brought only a very limited relief to Episcopalians.

Having lost the government machinery of the national Church, Episcopalians did not survive or thrive so well as the Presbyterians had done in 1660–88. A significant number of Episcopalians drifted into full-blooded Jacobitism, and thus became liable to the death penalty for treason; this had the psychological effect of enhancing their sense of alienation from the Scottish political and religious establishment. Episcopalians increasingly became a virtual sect. However, they did survive, and by the latter half of the 18th century they constituted an enduring minority Church in the life of Scotland, reconciled to their marginal status. In reaction to the prevalent Presbyterianism, Episcopalians became rather more "High Church" in their theology, indeed much higher and closer to Roman Catholicism than were the Episcopalians (Anglicans) of England.

4. Other key figures

Henry Scougal

Henry Scougal (1650–78) was a native of Leuchars, and son of Bishop Patrick Scougal (1607–82) of Aberdeen. He studied at Aberdeen University; he was ordained in 1672, and appointed to the parish of Auchterless. In 1674 he became professor of divinity in Aberdeen, but died four years later (aged only 28).

He is remembered for his devotional classic, *The Life of God in the Soul of Man* (1677). This book has taken an honoured place alongside such select works as Bernard of Clairvaux's *On Loving God*, Thomas a Kempis' *The Imitation of Christ*, and John Bunyan's *Pilgrim's Progress*, as a landmark of Christian spirituality. The true nature of religion was its theme. Scougal argued that this consisted not primarily in intellectual belief or in moral practice, but in a spiritual union between the soul and God, in which God's very life was transfused into a person. The root of this supernatural life was faith; its fruits were love for God, charity to our neighbour, purity of life, and humility. The chief means of promoting the divine life in the soul were "fervent and hearty prayer", and frequent participation in the Lord's Supper. *The Life of God in the Soul of Man* has had an enduring impact on the piety of the English-speaking world, and often been reprinted. The great 18th century English evangelist, George Whitefield, testified that it was through Scougal's book that he was saved from a reliance on external religious works to seek the new birth in Christ.

Alexander Peden

Alexander Peden (1626–86), or "Peden the Prophet" as he was nicknamed, was born in Ayrshire, educated at Glasgow University, and trained for the ministry. However, just as he was about to receive his license to preach, a young unmarried mother accused him of fathering her child out of wedlock. The charge was eventually proved groundless, but Peden was so shaken by the episode that he apparently vowed never to take a wife. In 1660 he became minister of New Luce in Galloway, but his ministry was ended prematurely by the great ejection of 1663 of all those ministers who would not submit to Episcopal reordination.

So began Peden's career of preaching at secret Covenanter meetings in southern Scotland, a career marked by many hair's-breadth escapes from the persecuting hand of Charles II's government. Peden joined the Pentland Rising of 1666, but left just before their defeat at the battle of Rullion Green, having (it

seems) foreknowledge of the defeat. His mere presence among
the Pentland Covenanters was enough to have him declared
a rebel by the government. He was finally seized in 1673 and
imprisoned on the Bass Rock in the Firth of Forth, where
many Covenanters were held captive. In 1677 the government
ordered Peden to be shipped out as a slave to the American
plantations, together with other Presbyterian prisoners. But
Peden prophesied to his fellow captives that they would never
suffer this fate; and when they arrived in London, the captain of
the ship that was to transport them discovered that they were
prisoners of conscience, and refused to take them. Thus they
regained their freedom.

Peden spent the next nine years in Ireland and Ayrshire,
preaching again to secret gatherings. Remarkable, even
miraculous, deliverances from capture are recorded. On one
occasion, a squad of royal troopers were approaching Peden
and several companions. A slight elevation of ground came in
between the troopers and the fleeing Covenanters. Peden called
a halt, and prayed:

> Lord, it is Thy enemy's day, hour, and power; they may not
> be idle, but hast Thou no other work for them but to send
> them after us? Send them after them to whom Thou wilt give
> strength to flee, for our strength is gone. Twine them about
> the hill, Lord, and cast the lap of Thy cloak over Old Sandy
> and these poor things, and save us this one time, and we will
> keep it in remembrance, and tell it to the commendation of
> Thy goodness, pity, and compassion, what Thou didst for us
> at such a time.

A mist descended on the hill, and Peden and his friends were
safe.

Peden's last days were lived in a cave on the banks of the
river Ayr. A few hours before his death, he had a presentiment
of the approaching end, and so left the cave and went to his
brother's house where he died. Peden's reputation as a preacher
and saint of the Covenant was perhaps surpassed only by
Samuel Rutherford. After his death, Patrick Walker collected

all known examples of Peden's prophecies and published them in 1724. They are one of the greatest literary monuments to the supernatural and miraculous aura that surrounded Covenanting piety at its most exalted.

Important people:

George Buchanan (1506–82)
John Craig (c.1512–1600)
John Durie (c.1537–1600)
Andrew Melville (1545–1622)
Robert Bruce (1554–1631)
Robert Rollock (1555–99)
Alexander Henderson (1583–1646)
David Dickson (c.1583–1663)
Robert Baillie (1599–1662)
Samuel Rutherford (1600–61)
John Livingstone (1603–72)
John Brown of Wamphray (c.1610–79)
Robert Leighton (1611–84)
James Guthrie (1612–61)
George Gillespie (1613–48)
John Blackadder (1615–86)
John Welsh (c.1624–81)
Alexander Peden (1626–86)
Donald Cargill (c.1627–81)
James Kirkton (1628–99)
Richard Cameron (c.1648–80)
William Carstares (1649–1715)
Henry Scougal (1650–78)
James Renwick (1662–88)
Margaret Lauchlison (d.1685)
Margaret Wilson (d.1685)

Political and military

James Douglas, Earl of Morton (c.1525–81)
Sir John Maitland of Thirlstane (1543–95)

King James VI (1567–1625)
John Elphinstone, Lord Balmerino (d.1649)
Alexander Leslie (1582–1661)
Archibald Campbell, Lord Lorne, Marquis of Argyll (1607–61)
Alistair Macdonald "MacColla" (1610–47)
Archibald Johnston of Wariston (1611–63)
James Graham, Marquis of Montrose (1612–50)
King Charles I (1625–49)
King Charles II (1649–85)
James Graham of Claverhouse (1648–89)
King James VII (1685–89)

Primary source material

The Second Book of Discipline: the pastoral office

Pastors, bishops, or ministers, are they who are appointed to particular congregations, which they rule by the word of God, and over the which they watch: in respect whereof, sometimes they are called pastors, because they feed their congregation; sometimes *episcopi* or bishops, because they watch over their flock; sometimes ministers, by reason of their service and office; and sometimes also presbyters or seniors, for the gravity in manners which they ought to have in taking care of the spiritual government, which ought to be most dear unto them.

They that are called unto the ministry, or that offer themselves thereunto, ought not to be elected without [unless] one certain flock be assigned to them.

No one ought to ingyre [force] himself, or usurp this office, without lawful calling.

They who are once called by God, and duly elected by man, after that they have once accepted the charge of the ministry, may not leave their functions. The deserters should be admonished; and, in case of obstinacy, finally excommunicated.

No pastor may leave his flock without license of the provincial or national assembly; which, if he does, after admonition not obeyed, let the censures of the kirk strike upon him.

Unto the pastor appertains teaching of the word of God, in season and out of season, publicly and privately, always travailing to edify and discharge his conscience, as God's word prescribes to him.

Unto the pastor only appertains the administration of the sacraments, in like manner as the administration of the word; for both are appointed by God as means to teach us, the one by the ear, and the other by the eyes and other senses, that by both knowledge may be transferred to the mind.

It appertains, by the same reason, to the pastor to pray for the people, and namely for the flock committed to his charge; and to bless them in the name of the Lord, who will not suffer the blessings of His faithful servants to be frustrated.

He ought also to watch over the manners of his flock, that the better he may apply the doctrine to them, in reprehending the dissolute persons, and exhorting the godly to continue in the fear of the Lord.

It appertains to the minister, after lawful proceeding by the eldership, to pronounce the sentence of binding or loosing upon any person, according to the power of the keys granted unto the kirk.

It belongs to him likewise, after lawful proceeding in the matter by the eldership, to solemnize marriage betwixt them that are to be joined therein; and to pronounce the blessing of the Lord upon them that enter in that holy bond in the fear of God.

And generally, all public denunciations [announcements] that are to be made in the kirk before the congregation, concerning the ecclesiastical affairs, belong to the office of a minister; for he is a messenger and herald betwixt God and the people in all these affairs.

Second Book of Discipline, **Chapter 4**

Christ's work, finished yet ongoing

Now, I go to the next voice. When He hath drunk, He says, "It is finished," that is, "That wearisome work is now put to an end; now the ransom is paid; now the work of redemption is ended." Brethren, that ye may understand this; the Lord when He was in the garden [of Gethsemane] had two works; the first was, to buy heaven, to conquer life to us; the second, to put us in possession of it. The first work, He began it in the first moment of His conception, and continues still from that time to that moment He gave up the spirit to the Father. Now, that work being ended, He proclaims on the cross, cries out in the audience of them all, *Consummatum est*, "It is finished. Now that wearisome work is ended; the dear work is ended; heaven, and life, and righteousness, are conquered to the world for ever." This is the sum of the Gospel: "The work of our redemption is ended." This is all our preaching; heaven, life, and glory, are conquered again to the lost world. Thou needest not to give one penny out of thy purse for heaven. Cursed are they, from the high heaven to the low hell, that open their mouth to say, thou must pay some of that ransom out of thy purse. Woe to the Papists who will stand up and say, thou must pay some part of that ransom; woe to that foul mouth that dare be so bold to open it and say, "Pay thou a part of that ransom with thy money," seeing that Jesus Christ hath proclaimed that all is finished and bought by His blood; woe, vengeance, and everlasting damnation, shall light on the Pope, and all the Papists that dare open their mouths to speak such presumptuous words.

Yet there is another work remaining, which is to put us in possession of heaven, and He began this at His resurrection, and He holds it on yet, and shall continue it unto His coming again; and at that day of His coming, ye shall hear Him crying, "All is ended," not on His cross, but in glory; and all the angels and all the saints shall cry, "All is ended, glory to Him who hath ended all!" and no more shall be. Look down to His heart, and to the sense, from whence this voice arose, when He says this, ye shall find that Jesus felt the wrath of His Father assuaged. Before, He was in agony, now He feels the agony to cease; where before He found no joy, now joy returns; on the sense of all these things falls out this voice, "All is ended." When I look to this, I think I see the image of a godly saint dying; for the godly are like to Him in death and life. Before the last moment they are in a battle, and suddenly they will say, "I have gotten the victory in Jesus"; and then last they will yield up the spirit.

Robert Rollock
21st Lecture on the Passion of Christ

The real reception of the whole Christ in the Lord's Supper

The reason why I call them [the bread and wine] signs is this: I call them not signs for the reason that men commonly call them signs, because they signify only; as the bread signifies the body of Christ, and the wine signifies the blood of Christ: I call them not signs because they represent only; but I call them signs, because they have the body and blood of Christ conjoined with them. Yea so truly is the body of Christ conjoined with that Bread, and the blood of Christ conjoined with that Wine, that as soon as thou receivest that Bread in thy mouth (if thou be a faithful man or woman) so soon receivest thou the body of Christ in thy soul, and that by faith: and as soon as thou receivest that Wine in thy mouth, so soon receivest thou the blood of Christ in thy soul, and that by faith: In respect of this exhibition chiefly, that they are instruments to deliver and exhibit the things that they signify, and not in respect only of their representation, are they called signs. For if they did nothing but represent or signify a thing absent, then any picture or dead image should be a sacrament; for there is no picture, as the picture of the King, but at the sight of the picture, the King will come in your mind, and it will signify unto you that that is the King's picture. So if the sign of the sacrament did no more, all pictures should be sacraments: but in respect that the sacrament exhibits and delivers the thing that it signifies, to the soul and heart, so soon as the sign is delivered to the mouth, for this cause, especially, it is called a sign. There is no picture of the King that will deliver the King unto you; there is no other image that will exhibit the thing whereof it is the image; therefore there is no image can be a sacrament.

Thus, in respect the Lord has appointed the sacraments, as hands to deliver and exhibit the thing signified, for this delivery and exhibition chiefly they are called signs. As the word of the Gospel is a mighty and potent instrument to our everlasting salvation: so the Sacrament is a potent instrument appointed by God to deliver to us Christ Jesus, for our everlasting salvation. For this spiritual meat is dressed and served up to us in spiritual dishes: that is, in the ministry of the word, and in the ministry of the sacraments. And though this ministry be external, yet the Lord is said to deliver spiritual and heavenly things by these external things. Why? Because He has appointed them as instruments whereby He will deliver his own Son to us. For this is certain, that none has power to deliver Christ Jesus to us, except God and His Holy Spirit: and therefore, to speak properly, there is none can deliver Christ but God by His own Spirit. He is delivered by the ministry of the Holy Spirit; it is the Holy Spirit that seals Him up in our hearts, and confirms us more and more in Him: as the Apostle gives Him this style, 2 Cor. 1:22…

Now I come to the thing signified, and I call the thing signified by the signs in the sacrament, that which that old writer, Irenaeus, calls the heavenly and spiritual thing: to wit, whole Christ with His whole gifts, benefits and graces, applied and given to my soul. Thus I call not the thing signified by the signs of Bread and Wine, the benefits of Christ, the graces of Christ, or, the virtue that flows out of Christ only: but I call the thing signified, together with the benefits and virtues flowing from Him, the very substance of Christ Himself, from which this virtue doth flow. The substance with the virtues, gifts and graces that flow from the substance, are the thing signified here. As for the virtue and graces that flow from Christ, it is not possible that thou canst be partaker of the virtue that flows from His substance, except thou be first partaker of the substance itself. For how is it possible that I can be partaker of the juice that flows out of any substance, except I be partaker of the substance itself first? Is it possible that my stomach can be refreshed with that meat, the substance whereof never came into my mouth? Is it possible my thirst can be slaked with that drink, which never passed down my throat? Is it possible that

I can suck any virtue out of anything except I get the substance first? So it is impossible that I can get the juice and virtue that flow out of Christ except I get the substance, that is Himself first. So I call not the thing signified, the grace and virtue that flow from Christ only; nor Christ Himself and His substance, without his virtue and graces; but jointly the substance with the graces, whole Christ, God and man, without separation of His natures, without distinction of His substance from His graces.

Robert Bruce
Sermons on the Sacrament, **Sermon 1**

Samuel Rutherford: selections from his letters

My dear brother, let God make of you what He will, He will end all with consolation, and will make glory out of your sufferings; and would you wish better work? This water was in your way to heaven, and written in your Lord's book; ye behoved to cross it, and, therefore, kiss His wise and unerring providence. Let not the censures of men, who see but the outside of things, and scarce well that, abate your courage and rejoicing in the Lord. Let not the Lord's dealings seem harsh, rough, or unfatherly, because it is unpleasant. Howbeit your faith seeth but the black side of Providence, yet it hath a better side, and God shall let you see it. Learn to believe Christ better than His strokes, Himself and His promises better than His glooms. Dashes and disappointments are not canonical Scripture...Hence I infer that losses, disappointments, ill tongues, loss of friends, houses or country, are God's workmen, set on work to work out good to you, out of everything that befalleth you. When the Lord's blessed will bloweth cross your desires, it is best in humility to strike sail to Him and to be willing to be laid any way the Lord pleaseth: it is a point of denial to yourself, to be as if ye had not a will, but had made free disposition of it to God, and had sold it over to Him; and to make use of His will for your own is both true holiness, and your ease and peace. Ye know not what the Lord is working out of this, but ye shall know it hereafter.

For there be many Christians most like unto young sailors, who think the shore and the whole land doth move, when the

ship and they themselves are moved; just so, not a few do imagine
that God moveth and saileth and changeth places, because their
giddy souls are under sail, and subject to alteration, to ebbing
and flowing. But "the foundation of the Lord abideth sure." God
knoweth that ye are His own. Wrestle, fight, go forward, watch,
fear, believe, pray; and then ye shall have the infallible symptoms
of one of the elect of Christ within you.

For your afflictions are not eternal; time will end them, and
so shall you at length see the Lord's salvation. His love sleepeth
not, but is still working for you. His salvation will not tarry or
linger; and suffering for Him is the noblest cross that is out of
Heaven... and this is the fruit, the flower and bloom growing
out of your cross, that ye be a dead man to time, to clay, to gold,
to country, to friends, wife, children, and all pieces of created
nothings; for in them there is not a seat nor bottom for soul's
love. Oh, what room is for your love (if it were as broad as the
sea) up in heaven, and in God!

We may indeed think, Cannot God bring us to heaven with
ease and prosperity? Who doubteth but He can? But His infinite
wisdom thinketh and decreeth the contrary; and we cannot see a
reason of it, yet He hath a most just reason. We never with our
eyes saw our own soul; yet we have a soul. We see many rivers,
but we know not their first spring and original fountain; yet
they have a beginning. Madam, when ye are come to the other
side of the water, and have set down your foot on the shore of
glorious eternity, and look back again to the waters and to your
wearisome journey, and shall see, in that clear glass of endless
glory, nearer to the bottom of God's wisdom, ye shall then be
forced to say, "If God had done otherwise with me than He hath
done, I had never come to the enjoying of this crown of glory."

It is your part now to believe, and suffer, and hope, and wait
on; for I protest, in the presence of that all-discerning eye, who
knoweth what I write and what I think, that I would not want
[lack] the sweet experience of the consolations of God for all the
bitterness of affliction. Nay, whether God come to His children
with a rod or a crown, if He come Himself with it, it is well.
Welcome, welcome, Jesus, what way soever Thou come, if we

can get a sight of Thee! And sure I am, it is better to be sick, providing Christ come to the bedside and draw by the curtains, and say, "Courage, I am Thy salvation", than to enjoy health, being lusty and strong, and never to be visited of God.

Keep God's covenant in your trials; hold you by His blessed word, and sin not; flee anger, wrath, grudging, envying, fretting; forgive a hundred pence to your fellow-servant, because your Lord hath forgiven you ten thousand talents: for, I assure you by the Lord, your adversaries shall get no advantage against you, except you sin, and offend your Lord, in your sufferings.

Christ is worth more blood and lives than either ye or I have to give Him. When we shall come home, and enter to the possession of our Brother's fair kingdom, and when our heads shall find the weight of the eternal crown of glory, and when we shall look back to pains and sufferings, then shall we see life and sorrow to be less than one step or stride from a prison to glory; and that our little inch of time-suffering is not worthy of our first night's welcome-home to heaven. Oh, what then shall be the weight of every one of Christ's kisses! Oh, how weighty, and of what worth shall every one of Christ's love-smiles be!

Our Father in heaven

He is indeed our Father (Acts 17:28), as the author of our being, beyond all the visible creatures. He breathed upon man the breath of life. But the privilege of this our natural relation, the sin of our nature hath made fruitless and comfortless to us, till we be restored by grace, and made partakers of a new sonship. We are indeed the workmanship of God, but, being defaced by sin, and considered in that estate, our true name is, children of wrath. But the sonship that emboldens us to draw near unto God as our Father, is derived from His only-begotten Son. He became the Son of Man, to make us anew the sons of God. Being thus restored, we may indeed look back upon our creation, and draw out of it, to use in prayer with God, that we are His creatures, the workmanship of His hands, and He in that sense our Father. But, by reason of our rebellion, this argument is not strong enough alone, but must be supported with this other, as the main ground of our comfort, that wherein the strength of our confidence lies, that He is our Father in His Son Christ; that by faith we are invested into a new sonship, and by virtue of that may call Him Father, and move Him by that name to help and answer us. John 1:12, "To as many as received Him, He gave power to become the sons of God." Our adoption holds in Jesus Christ as the Head of this fraternity…

But this adoption is accompanied (that we think it not a naked, external name) with a real change, and so great a change that it bears the name of that which is the real ground of sonship; it is called regeneration. And these are inseparable. There be no sons of God by adoption, but such as are withal His sons by regeneration and new birth. There is a new life breathed into them from God… He gives them a supernatural life by this Spirit sent into their hearts: and the Spirit, by that regeneration which He works, ascertains [assures] them of that adoption which is in Christ Jesus; and in the persuasion of both, they call upon God as their Father.

So then, you who would have this confidence in approaching to God, to call Him Father, lay hold on Jesus Christ, as the fountain of sonship. Offer not to come unto God but through Him, and rest not satisfied with yourselves, nor your prayers, till you find some evidence that you are in Him. And know, that there is no evidence of your portion in the Son, but by the Spirit, therefore called the Spirit of the Son, by which we call God Father. Gal. 4:6. See whether the Spirit of God dwells and rules in your hearts… If you then call on the name of God, and particularly by this name, our Father, depart from iniquity. Be ashamed to pretend to be His sons, and yet be so unlike Him, wallowing in sin: it cannot be, that the sons of so holy a God can be altogether unholy, and delight to be so: no, though they cannot be perfectly free from impurity, yet, they who are indeed His children, do certainly hate impurity, because He hates it.

Do you draw near unto God in His Son Christ? Do you give yourselves up to be led by His Spirit? Then you may account and call Him your Father. And if you may use this word, there is abundance of sweetness in it: it is a spring of comfort that cannot run dry. And it hath influence into all the petitions; as likewise the other word, which art in heaven; Thou who art so great and so good. Whose name and whose kingdom should we desire to be advanced so much as our own Father's, our heavenly Father? And whose will to be obeyed on earth as it is in heaven? Of whom should we seek our daily bread, but of our Father? And especially, so rich a Father, possessor of heaven and earth! And forgiveness we may ask of our gracious Father, and conduct, and protection. In the hardest condition that can befall you, ye may come to your Father: all the world cannot bar your access. And there is no child may go to his father with any suit, with more confidence than you may to your Father; and if there be mercy and power enough in God, thou canst not miss of help.

Archbishop Robert Leighton
Exposition of the Lord's Prayer

The true nature of religion

I cannot speak of religion, but I must lament, that among so many pretenders to it, so few understand what it means: some placing it in the understanding, in orthodox notions and opinions; and all the account they can give of their religion is, that they are of this and the other persuasion, and have joined themselves to one of those many sects whereinto Christendom is most unhappily divided.

Others place it in the outward man, in a constant course of external duties, and a model of performances. If they live peaceably with their neighbours, keep a temperate diet, observe the returns of worship, frequenting the church, or their closet, and sometimes extend their hands to the relief of the poor, they think they have sufficiently acquitted themselves.

Others again put all religion in the affections, in rapturous hearts, and ecstatic devotion; and all they aim at is, to pray with passion, and think of heaven with pleasure, and to be affected with those kind and melting expressions wherewith they court their Saviour, till they persuade themselves they are mightily in love with Him, and from thence assume a great confidence of their salvation, which they esteem the chief of Christian graces. Thus are these things which have any resemblance of piety, and at the best are but means of obtaining it, or particular exercises of it, frequently mistaken for the whole of religion: nay, sometimes wickedness and vice pretend to that name. I speak not now of those gross impieties wherewith the Heathens were wont to worship their gods. There are but too many Christians who would consecrate their vices, and follow their corrupt affections, whose ragged humour and sullen pride must pass for Christian severity; whose fierce wrath, and bitter rage against their enemies, must be called holy zeal; whose petulancy towards their superiors, or rebellion against their governors, must have the name of Christian courage and resolution.

But certainly religion is quite another thing, and they who are acquainted with it will entertain far different thoughts, and disdain all those shadows and false imitations of it. They know by experience that true religion is a union of the soul with God, a real participation of the divine nature, the very image of God drawn upon the soul, or, in the apostle's phrase, it is Christ formed within us. Briefly, I know not how the nature of religion can be more fully expressed, than by calling it a Divine Life: and under these terms I shall discourse of it, showing first, how it is called a life; and then, how it is termed divine...

By this time I hope it doth appear, that religion is with a great deal of reason termed a life, or vital principle, and that it is very necessary to distinguish betwixt it and that obedience which is constrained, and depends upon external causes. I come next to give an account why I designed it by the name of Divine Life: and so it may be called, not only in regard of its fountain and original, having God for its author, and being wrought in the souls of men by the power of His Holy Spirit; but also in regard of its nature, religion being a resemblance of the divine perfections, the image of the Almighty shining in the soul of man: nay, it is a real participation of His nature, it is a beam of the eternal light, a drop of that infinite ocean of goodness; and they who are endowed with it may be said to have God dwelling in their souls, and Christ formed within them.

Henry Scougal
The Life of God in the Soul of Man, **Part 1**

Chapter 6

The Roman Catholic Church Part One

1
Introduction: the glory of France

In the period covered by this volume, the character and destiny of the Roman Catholic Church found expression, to a remarkable degree, in one nation—France. It would not be going too far to describe the 17th and 18th centuries as "the age of France", at least as far as Roman Catholicism is concerned. This is not to say, of course, that Italian, Spanish, or German Catholicism made no worthy contributions. However, it was undoubtedly French theologians, French spiritual writers, and French crises and conflicts, that formed the heart of Roman Catholicism in this period. Even those leading Catholic figures who were not French, like Cornelius Jansen (Dutch) and Miguel de Molinos (Spanish), discovered their most receptive soil in France, where their ideas became national and controversial movements. This has huge advantages for the student. In taking France as a template for our study of Catholicism, we gain focus and clarity, without sacrificing anything essential in the wider story.

1. The reign of Richelieu
France began the 17th century still recovering from the wreckage of its "wars of religion", which had pitted French Protestants (Huguenots) and Catholics against each other for forty years, spilling blood on an epic scale. The wars had concluded when the Valois dynasty of kings, which had ruled France for 250 years, perished with the assassination in 1589 of Henry III, by the hand of a fellow Catholic who thought his royal master had

447

drawn too close to the Huguenot heretics. Ironically, the laws of succession meant that the Huguenot leader, Henry of Navarre, now became France's lawful monarch as **Henry IV** (1589–1610). The new king converted to Roman Catholicism in 1593 in order to cement the loyalty of his Catholic subjects. Whatever people may have thought, then and now, about the ethics of Henry's conversion, it was a spectacular political success. The civil wars were over. Huguenot and Catholic could live at peace again as fellow-French under the tolerant Henry IV, and the task of rebuilding a shattered country could begin.

It is not our task to tell the political story in these pages, except when it blends with the religious story. But we do need to know a few facts. Henry IV set France on the path to a dramatic recovery of fortunes. When he died in 1610 (assassinated by another fanatical Catholic), his son **Louis XIII** (1610–43) was only eight years old. For a time, power lay in the hands of Louis' mother, Marie de Medici (1575–1642). However, the following decade saw the rise to power of one of the 17th century's most famous, powerful, and enigmatic figures, Armand Jean du Plessis de Richelieu—**Cardinal Richelieu** (1585–1642), as history knows him. The son of a prominent aristocratic family of Poitou, a bishop at the age of 21, by the 1620s Richelieu was all-powerful as Louis' chief minister. It seems pointless to speculate on the sincerity of his Catholic faith. Some have considered him a complete cynic, interested only in political power. Others have defended his integrity. Rather than debate his character, it is more important for us to consider his impact on the France of his day. In many ways it was Richelieu who lifted his country to greatness as a nation-state, centralizing political power in the royal court (or in Richelieu's hands as chief minister), unifying the country culturally and spiritually around the monarchy, and making sure that France emerged as the real winner of the Thirty Years' War that engulfed most of Europe between 1618 and 1648.

Richelieu's domestic policy, as well as helping establish an "absolute" monarchy (the king exercising an active and virtually unchecked supremacy in church and state), was also instrumental in revitalizing the fortunes of French Catholicism.

On the one hand, Richelieu warmly supported the French Catholic Church as embodying the true faith; France was to be a Catholic kingdom to the core in its beliefs, values, and symbols (he inspired Louis XIII to dedicate France to the Virgin Mary in 1638). In particular, Richelieu gave strong support to the very successful methods of Vincent de Paul for training an effective parish clergy (see section 3.4). On the other hand, he dealt a staggering blow to the political status of French Protestantism. Henry IV had, in the Edict of Nantes in 1598, granted a generous measure of religious freedom and civil privileges to the Huguenots. Richelieu took away the civil privileges. When he was officially appointed chief minister in 1624, the Huguenots were virtually running an independent state of their own, including their own army, in their heartland of southern France. They were also capable of defiantly rebellious behaviour, e.g. seizing for themselves the islands of Ré and Oléron near La Rochelle, one of the most important Huguenot fortress-cities.

Richelieu would not tolerate this Protestant state-within-a-state or its acts of rebellion, and by 1627 there was open war between his government and the Huguenots. The conflict was centred on La Rochelle; Richelieu personally led a military force to besiege the city. The English invaded and occupied the island of Ré to aid the Huguenots (and stir up trouble for the French Catholic government), but suffered a serious defeat when they also tried to occupy the island of Saint Martin. Deprived of English help, the citizens of La Rochelle were finally starved into submission by Richelieu's army by November 1628. The siege had been devastating; only 5,000 of the city's original 25,000 inhabitants were left alive. In the aftermath, Richelieu had all Huguenot fortresses destroyed, dismantled the Huguenot southern army, and stripped Huguenots of all the political rights they had enjoyed under the Edict of Nantes (e.g. there would be no more government grants to help educate Huguenots for the pastorate). Richelieu had annihilated the pretensions of French Protestantism to be anything other than a minority faith, existing solely by the reluctant permission of a Catholic state.

Paradoxically, however, Richelieu's foreign policy favoured Protestantism outside of France. As we saw back in Chapter 1, when it looked as though the Holy Roman Empire, under the Catholic Habsburg Emperor Ferdinand II, was about to defeat the Protestant forces in the Thirty Years' War, so creating a powerful Catholic Empire, Richelieu threw France's weight behind the Protestant cause. Catholic French armies fought alongside Protestants against the Catholic Habsburg armies of Spain and the Holy Roman Empire. Even when Richelieu was not sending French armies into Germany, he was financing Protestant armies, whether from Germany, Denmark, or Sweden, to keep the Habsburgs in check. His policy ensured the exhaustion and bankruptcy of the Catholic Habsburg empire, and the future dominance of France on the European military and political stage.[1]

2. The majesty of a king

The dominance of France aimed at by Richelieu was achieved by *Louis XIV* (1643–1715), who came to the French throne the year after Richelieu's death. He was only four at the time, and affairs were governed by Richelieu's successor as chief minister, *Cardinal Jules Mazarin* (1602–61). However, once Louis had begun to rule in his own name in 1661, he soon drove France to heights of political, cultural, and military glory. If we imagine Europe as a single country, and the nations as cities, we could say that France became Europe's capital city under Louis XIV. Its political unity, military strength, language, literature, and art all contributed to its splendour. The glory of France so captivated people's minds that French now became the preferred language of the educated classes across Europe. Louis' palace at Versailles became the eighth wonder of the world for its beauty and opulence.

Louis was a remarkable man. He inspired awe in everyone; his majesty was not borrowed from royal robes, but emanated from his personality. He both believed and acted on the most exalted view of his authority. The "divine right of kings" was to Louis an absolute truth, embodied in his own person: he was the

---

1. See Chapter 1, section 3 for a fuller account.

representative of God on earth, anointed with supernatural power over all persons and institutions within his realm. French kings were, as a matter of fact, anointed to office with "holy oil" in a coronation ceremony that almost made the king look like a priest as well. The oil, it was believed, had been sent down from heaven to Saint Remigius, who had baptized Clovis, first Christian king of the Franks in the late 5th century. With all the dynamism of his imperious character, Louis acted the part—an absolute monarch whose will was law. Into his strong hands fell the whole machinery of the centralized French state built up by Richelieu.

There has been much debate about Louis' piety. Certainly he conformed to the outward religious practices required of a devout Catholic, and there is every reason to think he did so with serious intent. No one could survive in Louis' court unless they too conformed. The day always began and ended with worship. The king observed all the festival days of the Church; during Lent, he fasted rigorously, and expected everyone around him to do the same. Beyond these formal structures of piety, however, there seemed little to indicate any personal spiritual-mindedness in the great monarch. It was as though he related to God, not so much as an individual soul, but as a king to the only King whose majesty transcended his own. Archbishop Fénelon, one of the most outstanding of France's devotional writers in our period (see Chapter 7 section 2 on Quietism), once wrote a letter intended for Louis and published in Fénelon's works:

> You do not love God. You merely fear Him, with a slave's fear. Your religion is made up exclusively of superstitions and trivial, superficial customs. You are like the Jews of old, whom God charged with honouring Him only with their lips, and not their hearts. You are meticulous about petty things, yet stubborn in other things which are horribly wrong.

The "horribly wrong" things no doubt, in Fénelon's mind, included the king's mistresses. Louis had a number of these during his reign. However, in 1683 or 1684 he finally married Madame de Maintenon, the devout former governess of his illegitimate children by his third mistress, Madame de

Montespan. The marriage was marked by mutual fidelity; the era of royal mistresses was over. Madame de Maintenon herself loved Louis with a love permeated by a higher light:

> Lord God, I desire through the whole of my life to adore whatever Your providence decrees for me. I submit without reservation. Grant that I may be of service to the king in the salvation of his soul. May I be saved together with him!

Yet even when, prior to his marriage, Louis had been dallying with mistresses, he would sit and listen to bold preachers rebuking him to his face for his immorality. We marvel at the courage of these preachers, such as Bishop Bossuet (see section 3.5, below); we can hardly help marveling, too, at Louis, who took these rebukes without a murmur, and never punished those who uttered them. As one historian commented, no modern dictator would allow anyone to address him in this way. In part it testifies to the paradoxes in Louis' personality.

The relationship between monarchy and Church under Louis was deep and pervasive. It was Louis who appointed bishops, abbots, and abbesses, although technically the right of "investing" his appointees belonged still to the pope. Nor did this lead to the French higher clergy becoming a servile body of royal yes-men. Some were of that type, but a surprising number were not. The French Catholic Church under Louis had its fair share of men possessing moral and spiritual integrity, as we shall see. A body known as the Council of Conscience existed to advise the king in all Church affairs, including the choice of bishops; Louis was president of the Council, and took its meetings and deliberations very seriously. There can be no doubt that the Church's profile and dignity in French society were enhanced by this intimate alliance with the great king. However, one cannot help thinking that Louis knew how strongly he benefited from the bond between Church and crown. It lit up his already dazzling monarchy with the radiance of religion. As his official title proclaimed, he was "the Most Christian King". The sanctions of religion bestowed a majestic credibility on the popular French motto, "One faith, one law, one king" (in French, *une foi, un loi, un roi*).

2
Roman Catholic piety

France in our period was overwhelmingly Roman Catholic in religious sentiment. Indeed it is very challenging for a modern Christian, living in a secular country, to imagine the extent to which the whole fabric of 17th century French life was saturated in its religion. Even the casual glance of the eye revealed the presence everywhere of the Catholic Church and its piety. Places of worship abounded in cities large and small. Paris, of course, was the vibrantly religious heart of the nation, but even in a little community like Gray, in Burgundy, whose inhabitants numbered 4,000, there were 14 churches and 22 chapels. Nor was Gray an unusually religious place. Almost every village in France, no matter how tiny, had a Catholic priest. The outward tokens of faith were ubiquitous—crucifixes and statues of the saints wherever one looked, and at night, lamps burning beneath omnipresent shrines to the Virgin Mary. Every intersection of four roads in the countryside was marked with a cross.

Ordinary daily life was ordered by the Church's calendar. Days of work and holidays ("holy days") were religious in nature, and all significant dates were marked by public religious processions. Some people even complained that there were too many holidays—it interfered with their work! The parish church was the centre of community life, like a large family gathering. The local priest would have been the head of the community, knowing everything about everyone; the practice of confession to one's priest was obviously an important channel of this knowledge. He advised his parishioners about life issues in general, whether religious or worldly. On the other hand, parish life was not necessarily dominated by the priest. Many churches had an active parish council made up of laymen, who met to make important decisions about many local matters; in some parishes they had the power of choosing the priest's assistant, the curate.

The practice of Catholic piety was widespread. The vast majority of French Catholics were present at mass every Sunday, although they did not necessarily "take communion". As the 17th century wore on, however, a more frequent participation in holy communion became the norm; one of the century's most successful spiritual guides, Francis de Sales, taught that Catholics serious about their faith would take communion two or three times each month. Sermons, too, were popular and prized among Catholics. It would be a Protestant prejudice to think that only Protestants valued preaching. An almost unbelievable fascination for sermons gripped the Catholic heart of France in our period, and lasted far into the 18th century. One English Protestant visitor, a Mrs Cradock, spoke of Catholic churches packed with congregations who delighted in hour-long sermons. It is on record that in 1755, at Aubais in southern France, the population rioted when the preacher for Lent gave a mere three sermons a week!

Some of the most eloquent preachers in Christian history were French Catholics of this period: Bossuet, Fénelon, Claude Massillon (1663–1742), Louis Bourdaloue (1632–1704), Esprit Flechier (1632–1710), Jules Mascaron (1634–1703)— these were men who delivered spell-binding expositions of basic Christian truths (the existence of God, creation, providence, the incarnation, the resurrection, final judgment) and basic Christian duties (faith, charity, heavenly-mindedness, reverence for God, submission to His providence, respect for the family) that would have been admired in any branch of Christianity.

Edifying literature was also widely read. The most popular work among Catholics was Thomas a Kempis' *Imitation of Christ*, regularly reprinted. Perhaps the next most popular was Francis de Sales' *Introduction to the Devout Life*. We shall encounter other well-read spiritual books and treatises as we consider various individuals and their contributions to Catholic life and faith. The Bible itself was commonly read in French translations—it would once again be a Protestant prejudice to think that Protestants alone loved the Bible. French Catholics had a number of translations to choose from. There was the version by the 16th Century humanist reformer Lefevre d'Étaples, others by Michel de Marolles, Amelotte, and Godeau, and the Jansenist translation by Le Maistre de Sacy. In many pious Catholic households, the father would read the Bible to his family at the close of day, sometimes making comments on the text, followed by family prayers. Pious families also ensured that their children learned a Catholic catechism by heart.

Another increasingly popular practice among French Catholics was "going on retreat". Retreats were held in special "retreat centres", where for seven to ten days people would practise silence (retreats were not to be excuses for worldly chatter and gossip!), read spiritual literature, pray, and listen to talks by a "spiritual director" (an accredited spokesperson of the Church). The retreat would be crowned by holy communion. Retreats became so much in vogue for the pious that soon every city had one or more retreat centres; many towns and even villages had them too. A Catholic would return to ordinary life from a retreat feeling refreshed and invigorated in his or her faith.

Another way in which Catholic piety soaked the fabric of French life was the complete ascendancy of the Church in the spheres of education and relief of poverty. In a secular culture, we think of the state as universal provider of these benefits; in 17th Century France, it was the Catholic Church. In many dioceses, the local bishop made sure that every parish had a school for the young. Secondary schools were not as widespread, but by the 18th century France had some 900 of these, staffed by Catholic clergy as tutors. The universities, too, were run by the Church. Public libraries were popular, and these too were frequently religious in origin, established by the local bishop or a religious order such as the Jesuits. In our day, the Church is likely to be criticised for being anti-intellectual; in Catholic

France in our period, it was accused of being too intellectual! Some people complained that the Church was obsessed with educating people, whereas what society really needed was more uneducated peasants to work in the fields.

The relief of poverty, too, was the province of the Church, not the state. France had no state welfare system. But it did have a vast Church welfare system. The various Catholic religious orders expended time, personnel, and money on a staggering scale to build and maintain orphanages, hospitals, and other centres of care. They also provided assistance and work for the unemployed, land for housing, insurance, food during times of famine, and a whole host of other social services now offered by the state. The idea of Christian care for the deprived entered so deeply into the Catholic consciousness that it was considered a normal part of life for young Catholic ladies from richer families to devote themselves to helping the poor.

3
Key figures

In this section we look at significant figures in the Catholic history of our period—theologians, spiritual writers, preachers—of whom I have not given an extended account in the narrative of different movements and controversies.

1. Robert Bellarmine

Robert Bellarmine (1542–1621) was in many ways the greatest theologian of the Catholic Counter-Reformation: an intellectual giant by any benchmark. Born at Montepulciano, Italy, into an aristocratic family, his mother (sister of Pope Marcellus II who reigned a mere three weeks in 1555) wanted him to become a Jesuit, despite his father's more secular ambitions for his son. The mother was triumphant; Bellarmine entered the Jesuit order in 1560. He was then sent to study theology at the universities of Padua in 1567 and Louvain in 1569. At Louvain he was ordained to the priesthood; he also became one of the university's lecturers, its first Jesuit—he taught on the *Summa Theologiae* of Thomas Aquinas. His preaching attracted huge audiences.

In 1576 Bellarmine returned to Italy, partly in hope of finding better health in its sunnier climate. Pope Gregory XIII (1572–85), recognizing his brilliance, appointed him lecturer in polemical theology in a new papal college in Rome (now the Pontifical Gregorian University). Bellarmine devoted himself to reading and refuting Protestant writings. His particular "sparring partner" was the great Anglican theologian William Whitaker (c.1547–95) of Cambridge University, whose portrait

Robert Bellarmine (1542–1621)
16th century portrait from the "Italian school"

hung in Bellarmine's study. When asked why he had a picture of a heretic in his study, Bellarmine said, "He may be a heretic, but he is a brilliant heretic." Bellarmine's studies in Protestant thought bore fruit in his *Disputations on Controversies about the Christian Faith*, published between 1581 and 1593. Here was the definitive Roman Catholic response to all Protestant arguments. Catholic Europe glowed with admiration; Protestant Europe immediately made the *Disputations* the standard against which any true Protestant theologian must test his mettle.

Meanwhile Bellarmine rose ever higher in his Church's hierarchy: He became rector of his college in 1592, a cardinal in 1598, and Archbishop of Capua in 1602. He took his spiritual responsibilities as archbishop very seriously, devoting himself to the care of his diocese. His later life was famous or infamous for the part he played in the controversy surrounding the pioneer scientist Galileo and his championship of a sun-centred theory of the solar system (heliocentrism). Acting as representative of Pope Paul V (1605–21), Bellarmine ordered Galileo in 1616 to stop teaching heliocentrism. However, Bellarmine's personal views on the issue were more flexible; he believed in the need for further research before heliocentrism could be definitely rejected or confirmed.

Bellarmine spent his last years in retirement in the Roman College, where he wrote a number of devotional treatises for ordinary Catholics, notably *The Art of Dying Well* (1619).

Although Bellarmine became the supreme theological enemy in the eyes of Protestant theologians, they also gave him a certain respect. This was not only owing to his intellectual stature. They observed with approval Bellarmine's rejection of the pope's direct authority in the political sphere, an opinion that had earned him the wrath of Pope Sixtus V (1585–90). Bellarmine was, however, a strong defender of the pope's supreme authority in spiritual matters. Protestants also admired Bellarmine's concessions on the doctrine of grace; in his treatise on justification, he concluded the whole matter by saying, "because of the uncertainty of our own righteousness and the danger of vainglory, it is safest to place one's entire confidence in the mercy and kindness of God alone." In keeping with this, in Bellarmine's last will and testament he begged God "not as the valuer of merit, but as a giver of pardon, to admit me among His saints and elect".[1]

2. Pierre de Bérulle

Pierre de Bérulle (1575–1629) was one of the giants of Roman Catholic spirituality in our period; his personal or literary influence had a deep impact on many other leading figures, e.g. Vincent de Paul, Saint-Cyran, Pascal, and Bossuet. Indeed, every person given his own pen-portrait below was, in one way or another, a disciple of Bérulle. He stands at the fountainhead of that rich harvest of Catholic spirituality which so marked France in the 17th century.

Born into an aristocratic family in Cérilly, north-west France, Bérulle was educated by the Jesuits, studied theology at the Sorbonne, and was ordained priest in 1599. He was introduced to the writings of the great Catholic mystics by his female cousin, herself a distinguished mystic, Barbe Jeanne Acarie (1566–1618), later known as "Mary of the Incarnation". With Bérulle's help, she transplanted Teresa of Avila's Reformed Carmelite order from Spain into the soil of France in 1604.

Bérulle's deepest attachment, however, was not to the Carmelites, but to Philip Neri's Oratorian movement.[2] The Oratorians were one of the important new religious orders that flourished in Italy as part of the Catholic Counter-Reformation in the 16th century. Bérulle established an Oratory in Paris in 1611, and acted as its superior-general. The Oratory became a wellspring of reforming influences that eventually reached out into almost all sectors of the French Catholic clergy. However, Bérulle's activities extended far beyond the Oratory; he was

---

1. Perhaps unsurprisingly, a later Protestant—C.H.Spurgeon—thought highly of Bellarmine's devotional writings, saying of his commentary on the psalms, "Popish, but marvellously good for a Cardinal. He is frequently as evangelical as a Reformer."

2. See *Volume Three: Renaissance and Reformation*, Chapter 8, section 5.

involved in the highest levels of French politics. In particular he was instrumental in supervising the marriage between Henrietta, sister of Louis XIII, and King Charles I of England, in 1625, as a result of which Roman Catholicism enjoyed a brief renaissance in the English court. He alienated Richelieu, however, by opposing his foreign policy (aiding the German Protestants against the Roman Catholic Habsburgs in the Thirty Years' War). Pope Urban VIII recognized Bérulle's spiritual and political services to his Church by making him a cardinal in 1627.

Bérulle's literary legacy was large and impressive. His most enduring work was his *Discourse on the Greatness and Glories of Jesus* (1623), which helped foster a new and potent stream of French Catholic spirituality. Its twin focal points were the awesome majesty of God, before whom we are as nothing, and our access to Him in Jesus Christ alone, God-in-the-flesh. By becoming man, God the Son had bridged the otherwise infinite gulf between deity and humanity, redeeming and sanctifying human nature in Himself as God-Man; the supreme duty and privilege of the Christian was to know God in Christ (Bérulle emphasized the historical Jesus of the Gospels), and be conformed to Him in every aspect of the believer's life. This involved the destruction of all self-will, so that God's interests became the Christian's sole concern. Flowing out of Bérulle's profound attachment to the Redeemer's human life and personality as the medium of revelation and salvation, he conceived a special interest in, and devotion to, the child Jesus.

The glory of the incarnation, then, dominated Bérulle's mind and heart, and positively glowed in his writings. It was therefore very apt when Pope Urban VIII described him as "the apostle of the incarnate Word". The title well expresses Bérulle's Christ-centred spirituality, which was to have such a far-reaching influence on French Catholicism in his own lifetime and in the decades following his death in 1629.

3. Francis de Sales

In *Francis de Sales* (1567–1622), we meet perhaps the most influential Roman Catholic spiritual writer of our period,

whose impact has been felt far beyond the bounds of his own
Church—that is, if we discount the writings of Fénelon and
Madame Guyon, who came under censure for their Quietism,
and may therefore be said not to represent their Church's fully
authentic voice. Francis, by contrast, was entirely orthodox in
his Roman Catholicism, and was canonized (declared a saint)
in 1665, and recognized as a "Doctor (teacher) of the Universal
Church" by Pope Pius IX in 1877.

Francis was born to a high-ranking Catholic family at Sales in
what was then the independent duchy of Savoy, nestling between
Italy, Switzerland, and France (the inhabitants were French-
speaking). He studied at the Jesuit college of Clermont in Paris
in the 1580s, followed by a legal training at Padua University.
The young Francis seems to have undergone a spiritual crisis
while at Paris, his peace temporarily shattered by anxieties over
the doctrine of predestination. He feared he might be one of
the reprobate. A decisive experience of self-abandoning trust in
God's love freed him from this torment.

In 1593 he was ordained to the priesthood—nominally to a
position in Geneva, although the city was of course in reality the
citadel of Reformed Protestantism. Francis worked as a Catholic
evangelist in Chablais, a province of Savoy, bordering on Geneva.
Although part of Catholic Savoy in Francis' day, Chablais had
once belonged to the Swiss Reformed canton of Berne. The Duke
of Savoy had gained it back from Berne, only on condition that
its people be left in peace to practise their Reformed faith. When
Berne broke this treaty by a fresh invasion (which failed), the
duke now set about re-Catholicizing the province.

Francis was appointed to spearhead this enterprise as a street
preacher. He proved outstandingly effective, and won many back
to Roman Catholicism, braving considerable physical danger
from Calvinist zealots who threatened him with violence (it is
said that Francis twice miraculously escaped being murdered!).
Among his evangelistic strategies was holding public debates
with Reformed ministers. To judge by his phenomenal success
in winning converts, Francis must have given most of his
opponents in these debates a serious drubbing. Another strategy

was distributing religious tracts. If Calvinists were unwilling to talk with him, he would slip the tracts under their doors. We should not, however, idealize Francis' evangelism in Chablais. It was backed by military force: the troops of the duke of Savoy were not necessarily too gentle in their treatment of the Reformed population, which may help explain why some over-zealous Calvinists tried to murder Francis!

The most famous encounter between Francis and a Reformed minister took place in 1597, when he paid several visits to Theodore Beza, Calvin's successor in Geneva.[3] By all accounts these were friendly meetings, where the two men—a youthful Francis and an aged Beza—discussed theology in a civilized manner in Beza's home. Francis at first seems to have had high hopes of converting Beza, but the Reformed patriarch was his match in debate, and Francis left disappointed.

In 1599 Francis became assistant Bishop of Geneva (since the Reformation, the Catholic bishops of Geneva had resided in Annecy, France). His bishop sent him to Paris on business in 1602; here he fell under the spiritually fertilizing influence of Bérulle. In 1603 he was appointed Bishop of Geneva. As bishop, he earned a reputation for captivating preaching, skilful personal direction of souls, and championship of the poor. Together with Jane Frances de Chantal, whose spiritual director he was, he founded in 1610 the Visitandine order of nuns (the Order of the Visitation of Holy Mary), a "contemplative" order (devoted to prayer rather than to good works in the wider community).[4]

Francis' widest and most lasting impact came through his spiritual writings, especially the classic *Introduction to the Devout Life*. This was originally a series of letters of spiritual advice, written to Madame Louise de Charmoisy, but rewritten in a more general format and addressed to the imaginary Philothea ("lover of God"). The collection was first published in 1609, and

---

3. See Chapter 2, section 1.

4. Francis originally intended the Visitandines to be socially active in works of service, but the archbishop of Lyons did not approve. Francis submitted and remodelled the order along contemplative lines.

was a runaway bestseller. Francis revised it several times; the *Introduction* known today is the final 1619 edition.

The *Introduction* was a novelty in being directly applicable to Christians living in the world: a handbook of lay piety (although there was nothing to prevent its use by a monk or nun). Its more famous predecessor, Thomas a Kempis' *Imitation of Christ*, had been written specifically for those living in religious communities. Francis' work transplanted the piety of the monastery and nunnery into the soil of the world.[5] Louise de Charmoisy, the original recipient of the work, was the wife of one of the Duke of Savoy's ambassadors, concerned about living out her faith in her secular life. Francis' advice struck a loud chord with many lay Christians throughout Europe who shared those aspirations. The *Introduction* was translated into all the major European languages, in editions both authorized and unauthorized. Many Protestant translations were produced, which omitted and adapted some of Francis' advice to make it more acceptable to Protestant readers. The work has endured to the present day as one of the most loved classics of spirituality in Christian history.

Another classic by Francis, not so well-known, was his *Treatise on the Love of God* (1616).

The example of Francis' life is treasured today in a special way, and his writings promoted, by a religious order named after him, the Salesians. The order, however, was not founded until 1859.

4. Vincent de Paul

If we judge people by their embodiment of a lovable humanity, as well as their influence on others, **Vincent de Paul** (c.1581–1660)[6] was probably the greatest Roman Catholic saint of the 17th century.

---

5. That may be the distinction between Francis' treatise and Erasmus' handbook of lay piety, *Dagger of the Christian Soldier* (published 1503). Erasmus hated monasticism; the piety he instils in the *Dagger* is more "secular" than the piety of Francis' *Introduction to the Devout Life*, which still breathes the air of the cloister.

6. Other sources date his birth in 1576 or 1580.

Vincent de Paul was born in south-west France, in the tiny village of Pouy, near Dax. Of peasant stock, he was at first a shepherd, but wanting to escape his tedious surroundings, embarked on a career in the Church when he was 15. After studying at Toulouse University, he was ordained priest in 1600. Remaining in Toulouse as a tutor, by his own account he was captured by Muslim pirates in 1605 during a sea journey from Marseilles. For two years he was a slave in Tunisia, before escaping back to France in 1607 with his master, a French Christian apostate to Islam whom Vincent re-converted. (Some historians dispute this story, arguing that Vincent made the whole thing up to conceal less respectable adventures at this time.)

The spiritual turning point in Vincent's life came in 1608. That year in Paris he met and fell profoundly under the spell of Bérulle, who became Vincent's role-model for the rest of his life. It was Bérulle who in 1611 sent Vincent to his first parish, as priest of Clichy in Paris's northern district. A year later Bérulle removed him to serve as tutor to the Gondis, a wealthy Italian banking family that had settled in France. Here began Vincent's practical commitment to evangelism; at the urging of the pious Mademoiselle Françoise de Gondi, he conducted effective preaching missions among the peasants on the lands owned by the Gondis in north-eastern France.

After five years of this, however, at Vincent's own request, Bérulle sent him back into parish ministry, at Chatillon-les-Dombes. It seems that Vincent felt uneasy at the comfort of his circumstances in the Gondi household; he must share the hardships of the ordinary parish priesthood. Although he served at Chatillon only five months, it had a profound impact on Vincent in two respects. First, he learned to think charitably of Protestants, several of whom made him feel welcome in his geographically and morally rugged parish—and in turn were so impressed by Vincent's life and teaching that they became Roman Catholics. Hereafter Vincent would always think of Protestants as "separated brethren" to be reconciled with Rome by kindness, rather than monsters to be despised and persecuted. Second, it was in Chatillon that Vincent founded his first "Congregation of

Ladies of Charity".[7] This was a lay society devoted to the relief of the destitute, governed by a detailed code drawn up by Vincent (similar to a monastic rule, although the ladies were not nuns). The idea would soon blossom and bear abundant fruit in the remainder of Vincent's life.

In 1617, Vincent returned to the Gondis, at the insistent plea of Mademoiselle Françoise, who wanted him to resume his preaching missions. Bérulle added his voice, now convinced that Vincent's place was not in the settled parish ministry, but on a wider stage. So he returned to his itinerant evangelism on the Gondi estates, also founding Congregations of Charity in many places. It was a year later, in 1618, that he met Francis de Sales; the two men became spiritually close, and the foundation laid in Vincent's soul by Bérulle was now crowned by the influence of Francis. When dying in 1622, Francis entrusted to Vincent the spiritual care of the Visitandine order of nuns he had founded in 1610.

Vincent's commitment to the poor had by this time possessed him as a mission from heaven. In Paris, where the Congregations of Charity were first established in 1629, he pioneered a momentous new development; to aid the Ladies of Charity, Vincent helped create a movement that became the Sisters of Charity (he preferred to call them Daughters of Charity, but "Sisters" was the name that stuck). What set them apart from the Ladies of Charity was that the Sisters were all recruited young, and lived together in community—in the house, initially, of Mademoiselle Louise de Marillac (1591–1660), who with Vincent was cofounder of the movement. The widow of Antoine Le Gras, a middle-class lawyer, she was known by his name, Mademoiselle Le Gras. Antoine had died in 1625, and Louise had been a close disciple of Vincent from 1626. The nucleus of the Sisters of Charity was formed under her immediate direction in 1633.

Nurtured by the preaching of Vincent, the Sisters grew in number, and became the greatest single agency of social

7. The Congregations are also known as Conferences or Confraternities.

welfare in France, at work in hospitals, orphanages, prisons, schools for the poor, charity-houses for beggars, asylums for the insane, homes for the old, and in providing general relief for the destitute. The relief work was not just for the poor, but included (for example) the victims of war. North-eastern France was ravaged in the Thirty Years' War by an Austrian invasion in 1636, leaving desolation and anarchy in its wake that lasted for years. Paris and its provinces were devastated by civil war in 1648–53, when the French nobility in alliance with parlement rebelled against the young King Louis XIV and his chief minister, Cardinal Mazarin. Wherever social need cried out, the Sisters of Charity rushed in to help.

In 1642, the Sisters began to take the traditional vows of a religious order (poverty, chastity, and obedience), yet without "enclosure"—their daily work was outside the community, in the world. This was a novelty that caused difficulties, since nuns were supposed to live strictly within the walls of a convent. Vincent, however, who drew up the movement's religious rule, managed to persuade the Archbishop of Paris to give his approval in 1646. Louis XIV granted royal authorization in 1657. Finally, soon after the death of Vincent and Mademoiselle Le Gras, Pope Clement IX gave the whole movement papal endorsement in 1668. As a religious order, the Sisters of Charity were nicknamed "the Grey Sisters" from the colour of their garments.

Although Mademoiselle Le Gras must be commemorated as the practical organizer of the Sisters of Charity, their spiritual inspiration always remained Vincent de Paul, whose preaching, example, and influence in high places, carried the movement forward. "Visit the poor instead of praying", he advised the Sisters. "In this way, you are leaving God in order to serve God." By the time of Vincent's death in 1660, there were 40 communities in France; by the time of the French Revolution in 1789, there were 426. The movement spread into other Roman Catholic countries—Italy, Spain, Portugal, Austria, Poland, and the Catholic cantons of Switzerland. It is still active today, a living monument to Vincent's humanitarian commitment. This is how he is remembered in his native France: not so much as the Catholic saint, as the friend of the poor and the orphan. Yet it has been remarked that it was not charity that made Vincent a saint, but his saintliness that made him truly charitable. Vincent's works were the fruits of his faith.

Vincent's other great contribution to French Catholic spirituality lay in the training of the priesthood. Seminaries were at a low ebb in France in the early decades of the 17th century. The 40 years of civil war ("the French wars of religion") in the previous century had devastated Catholic seminaries. In 1625, there were only ten throughout the country. Emergency measures were necessary; the Bishop of Beauvais asked Vincent in 1628 to prepare some candidates by means of a short ten-day "retreat". Vincent's methods of instruction were a huge success (a combination of his own inspirational personality and a ruthless focus on giving what he considered the bare essentials a priest needed to know). Further retreats followed, and as they gained in popularity, they became longer and longer: from ten days, to two or three months, and finally to two or three years. The retreats were soon being transformed into actual seminaries, staffed initially by those whom Vincent had personally trained.

Even before the Bishop of Beauvais launched him on this path, Vincent had already, in 1625, founded a community of "secular" priests (not bound by monastic vows) at the priory of Saint-Lazare in Paris. He had intended them to extend his practice of preaching missions throughout France, but the Lazarists (their popular nickname: technically the Congregation of the Mission) were soon hugely active in training men for the priesthood through Vincent's retreats and seminaries. Vincent also held special conferences for clergy at Saint-Lazare to provide ongoing spiritual input into their lives and ministries; he organized retreats there for pious laymen as well. These conferences and retreats attracted hundreds every year. Not quite single-handedly, but as the fountainhead of inspiration, Vincent raised up a whole new generation of dedicated, successful parish priests for Catholic France, and spread a lively Catholic piety to myriads of ordinary Catholics.

He also made an impact through the Council of Conscience, the body that advised the court on Church affairs, including the choice of bishops and abbots. Vincent was secretary of the Council for nine years, during which he exerted himself to improve the spiritual quality of the Church's men and ministries. On one occasion, his refusal to bestow a bishopric on a young aristocratic drunkard led to a stormy interview with the lad's mother, which ended with her throwing a wooden stool at Vincent's head, causing the blood to gush. But the drunkard was not given the bishopric. Unfortunately for Vincent's reforming endeavours, the Council of Conscience eventually ceased to meet, owing to the hostility of Cardinal Mazarin, who then controlled the French court and regarded Vincent as an interfering busybody. Mazarin preferred to hand out bishoprics as political bribes.

Time would fail to tell of Vincent's other activities. By his death in 1660, aged around 80, he had won a deep and enduring place in Catholic affections. Even Voltaire, arch-critic of Christianity in the following century, exempted Vincent from his bitterness—"my favourite saint is Vincent de Paul." He especially endeared himself to his native land of France, where the memory of "Monsieur Vincent" lingers on today, with something of the flavour of a French Francis of Assisi.

5. Jacques-Bénigne Bossuet

Jacque-Bénigne Bossuet (1627–1704) enjoys an exalted reputation, not only as the most brilliant pulpit orator of 17th century France, but as one of the greatest orators of all the Christian centuries—perhaps *the* greatest, in terms of his sheer mastery of majestic language in the service of spiritual truth. The Sanders Theatre in Harvard has busts of the eight supreme orators of all time, and Bossuet is among them, alongside such Pagan titans as Demosthenes and Cicero, and Christian giants like Chrysostom and Augustine.

Born at Dijon, the son of a judge, Bossuet was educated in his youth by the Jesuits (although, ironically, they would later regard him as an enemy because of his leniency towards Jansenism).

Jacques-Bénigne Bossuet (1627–1704)

A 1723 engraving by Pierre Imbert Drever
(1697–1739)

He then went to Paris to train for the priesthood. Here, at the age of 21, Bossuet underwent the great religious crisis of his life, from which he emerged as a serious, committed Christian man. He then became a disciple of Vincent de Paul, under whose direction he flourished spiritually. The other great influence on him was the writings of de Paul's own mentor, Cardinal Bérulle. After Bossuet's ordination as priest in 1652, he spent some years attached to the cathedral of Metz, where his intellectual powers matured in controversies with Protestants and Jews. It was at Metz that Bossuet conceived his lifelong dream of winning Protestants back into the Roman Catholic Church. Most unusually for his day, Bossuet did not regard Protestants as loathsome adversaries to be crushed, but separated brothers to be reconciled—a generosity he absorbed, perhaps, from his master Vincent de Paul, who held the same rare view.

In 1657, de Paul persuaded Bossuet to settle in Paris, where his ability in the pulpit would receive wider exposure and be put to better use. He was soon the celebrity preacher of the age—audiences hung entranced on his every word—and often preached to the court in the royal chapel. Louis XIV was sufficiently impressed to make Bossuet the personal tutor of his son from 1670–81. Then in 1681 Bossuet was appointed Bishop of Meaux, a position he held for the rest of his life, from which comes his nickname, "the Eagle of Meaux".

Bossuet was now on the centre stage of French Catholic life, and took part in all the great religious and political events of the day: the Gallican crisis (see Chapter 7, section 1), the Jansenist controversy (see section 4, below), the Quietist controversy (see Chapter 7, section 2), and the running sore of Protestantism within Catholic France. On the last point, Bossuet approved of the revocation of the Edict of Nantes; he wished to see a religiously united France—"one king, one Christ, one Church", as he put it. But he did not support the more brutal methods employed by royal troops to force Huguenots to convert to Rome (see Chapter 7, section 3). Peaceful reunion between Roman Catholics and Protestants remained Bossuet's deepest aspiration, and to that end he engaged in a 17 year long friendly correspondence (1683–1700) with the great German Lutheran thinker and pioneer ecumenist, Gottfried Wilhelm Leibniz (1646–1716).

In this brief cameo of Bossuet, we may perhaps focus a special gaze on two aspects of his life and work: Bossuet the preacher, and Bossuet the writer.

As a preacher, Bossuet was without any serious rival in his combination of superb gifts. His physical presence was noble, his voice a well-tuned trumpet; his sermons blended depth of doctrinal knowledge, luminous clarity of thought, piercing scrutiny of the human heart and its motives, an unsurpassed musical command of French prose which never became contrived or hollow, and a fiery ardour of soul that was never melodramatic or out of control. In a Catholic France which was, at that time, passionately addicted to sermons, Bossuet was in endless demand to fill pulpits. Even the despotic Louis XIV acknowledged the power of his preaching; although the king might feel no affection for the Eagle of Meaux, he was compelled to reverence him. Bossuet particularly excelled in delivering set-piece sermons on great occasions; his masterworks are considered to be his funeral orations on Henrietta of France (1669), Henrietta of England (1670), and the Prince of Condé (1687). Other great examples of his pulpit splendour include his sermons on *Death, Ambition, Providence, The Dignity of the Poor*, and *Submission to the Law of God*.

Bossuet's literary legacy is perhaps best seen in the following two treatises:

Discourse on Universal History (1679). Generally acknowledged as Bossuet's greatest work, this was his equivalent to Augustine's *City of God*: a Christian philosophy of history. Bossuet argued that the proper concept of God was not simply as Creator of the universe, but also providential ruler of history. All history was shaped by divine sovereignty, and found its culmination in the incarnation of God's Son, which brought the Church into being as the new humanity. However, God normally governed history through secondary agencies. In the political sphere His agent was the state, especially in the shape of the king (Bossuet believed passionately that monarchy was the true and divinely sanctioned form of government). In the spiritual sphere, His agent was the Catholic Church. Rebellion against either of these bodies was tantamount to rebellion against God Himself. Bossuet's belief that God usually worked through secondary causes impelled him to try to discern patterns in history. Rather than a random series of unconnected scenes, history was a process of development, working according to God-given laws; the perceptive historian could see how the elements of each era gave birth to its successor.

History of the Variations of the Protestant Churches (1688). This was Bossuet's masterpiece of anti-Protestant argument. He traced the evolution of Protestantism from its origins, and sought to show that it had no principle of unity—that without the guidance provided by Roman Catholic tradition and teaching, Protestantism was doomed to helpless instability and endless change. The book was especially challenging to Protestants because Bossuet, rather than highlight the differences between Protestantism and Roman Catholicism, made every possible religious concession to his opponents, in order that their real errors (as he saw them) might stand out all the more starkly. In fact, rather remarkably, he reduced the ultimate difference between Roman Catholics and Protestants to a single point— the doctrine of transubstantiation. Protestants recognized in Bossuet one of their fairest and most moderate, yet most intellectually formidable, Roman Catholic critics.

4
Jansenism: the war about grace

1. Michael Baius and the seeds of Jansenism

Jansenism was the gravest and longest internal crisis experienced by the Roman Catholic Church in our period, provoking political and religious turmoil, persecution, and even schism, on a scale unknown since the Protestant Reformation a hundred years previously. France was once again the land where the drama was largely played out; yet to understand this, and indeed the whole context from which Jansenism was born, we have to step back for a while into the sixteenth century and ponder the life and work of a theologian born in Flanders (then a region in the south-west of the Netherlands, now divided between France, Belgium, and Holland). This was *Michael Baius* (1513–89), whom we could consider the spiritual "grandfather" of Jansenism.

Baius spent his entire academic life teaching at Louvain University in the Spanish Netherlands. Louvain was one of northern Europe's foremost centres of learning, and a citadel of Roman Catholic orthodoxy. Alongside this, it was also steeped in the humanism of Erasmus, determined to study the pure, original texts of Scripture and of the early Church fathers. Baius' own humanist ideals were focused on retrieving the theology of Augustine from what he believed was the diluted and distorted Augustinianism of the medieval schoolmen. Unfortunately for him, Baius' interpretation of Augustine seemed virtually identical with what Luther and Calvin had said about original sin, predestination, free will, and grace, and this would-be

475

champion of Augustine found himself under attack from the anti-Protestant militants of his Church from 1560 onwards.

The controversy became so intense that in 1567, Rome intervened, and in the bull *Ex Omnibus Afflictionibus*, Pope Pius V condemned 79 propositions extracted from Baius' writings. The bull, however, neglected to name Baius as the author of the obnoxious propositions, which enabled Baius to shrug it off by simply claiming that the bull did not refer to him. Twelve years later, in 1579, Pope Gregory XIII remedied the oversight of his predecessor and condemned Baius in the bull *Provisionis Nostrae*. This time Baius could not wriggle free; he recanted. But it was, in a sense, too late. The damage was done; Baius' revived Augustinianism was now in circulation, especially in his own university. And his later writings still seem permeated with the essence of his "recanted" views.

The most ardent foes of Augustinian theology within Roman Catholicism were the Jesuits. The fact that such a famous Catholic university as Louvain was playing host to Baius' ideas prompted the Jesuits to try to capture it for their own doctrinal outlook, which gave a much bigger role to human free will. Among the Jesuit zealots who arrived in Louvain to test their mettle against "Baianism" was Leonardus Lessius (1554–1623). The duel between Lessius and Baius went in the latter's favour; in 1587, he persuaded the university authorities to condemn most of Lessius' teaching as Semi-Pelagian or worse.

2. Molinism and the De Auxiliis controversy

At this point, the quarrels in Louvain became linked with a parallel controversy that had broken out in Spain. (Since Louvain was in the Spanish Netherlands, the two disputes were politically within the same domain, the lands of King Philip of Spain.) The Spanish Jesuit **Luis de Molina** (1535–1600)[1] had systematized the anti-Augustinian perspective of Jesuit theology, and given it to the public in his landmark treatise

---

1. Molina must not be confused with Molinos. For Molinos, see Chapter 7, section 2.1.

The Harmony between Free Will and the Gifts of Grace, Divine Foreknowledge, Providence, Predestination, and Reprobation, with regard to Certain Articles of Saint Thomas' Prima Pars, published in 1588. Since the form of Augustinianism that prevailed in Spain was that of Thomas Aquinas and the Dominican order, Molina chose to subvert the Augustinian view by radically reinterpreting the teachings of Aquinas ("Thomism", as it was called, from Aquinas's first name Thomas).

Molina's argument can be summarized as follows. God gives everyone sufficient grace to be saved, but it hinges on our free will to make use of this grace. So far, this sounds like simply a form of Semi-Pelagianism. But Molina then introduced the sophisticated concept of God's "middle knowledge" (in Latin, *scientia media*). By this, Molina meant God's knowledge of what any person's free will would do in any situation—not just situations that actually occurred, but hypothetical or imaginary situations too. Traditionally theologians had ascribed to God two kinds of knowledge of His creation: (i) knowledge of all that He might possibly decree, and (ii) knowledge of what He had actually decreed. Molina introduced this third category "in the middle" of the other two: God's knowledge of "what would happen if "—middle knowledge (*scientia media*). Molina argued that God knew what every created will would do if it were placed in any possible set of circumstances. This knowledge was not based on what it was within God's power to decree, nor on what He had actually decreed, but was a mysterious and inexplicable knowledge of what any created will would freely choose to do, were it placed in this or that situation.

Perhaps we can illustrate what Molina meant with a parable. Suppose that a man—let us call him John—hears the Gospel preached. God knows (by His middle knowledge) that if He gives John only *fifty* units of sufficient grace, John will not freely respond with repentance and faith. But God also knows that if He gives John a *hundred* units of sufficient grace, John will respond more positively, so that he freely chooses to repent and believe.

In other words, Molina saw sufficient grace as imparting an impetus or momentum to free will to move in the right direction. Since the will was free, it could always resist. Even so, by virtue of

His middle knowledge, God knew the amount of sufficient grace to which anyone's will would respond positively in any situation. Therefore, in order to bring about anyone's salvation without violating their freedom, all God had to do was give a person the amount of sufficient grace to which He knew the person would freely respond in a specific situation, and then place him or her in that situation. Predestination was therefore God choosing, in the case of some people, to give them the amount of sufficient grace to which He foreknew they would respond freely by their own wills. To the rest, God still gave grace sufficient in itself to save them, even though they did not make a right use of it. In this way, Molina believed he had reconciled the universality of God's grace (everyone had sufficient grace to be saved), the reality of divine election (some were given a quantity of sufficient grace to which God foreknew they would actually respond), and the freedom of the human will (what made grace effective was always a person's free response).

Molina's new synthesis of grace and free will proved explosive. The Spanish Dominicans, who were faithful Thomists, were outraged by this reconstruction of Aquinas's theology into what they saw as a Semi-Pelagian enthronement of the human will as the decisive factor in salvation. They tried to prevent the publication of Molina's book, then to have it condemned by universities and the Inquisition. Eventually the conflict became so serious that in 1597, Pope Clement VIII set up a special commission, the *De Auxiliis Divinae Gratiae* ("concerning the helps of divine grace"), to arbitrate between the contending parties. Dominicans maintained that *scientia media* was utterly foreign to Aquinas, and that Molinism was driven by a Pelagian exaltation of the human will. Jesuits maintained that Thomism (as expounded by the Dominicans), and the teachings of Baius in Louvain, were indistinguishable from Calvinism. The whole acrimonious debate took its name from this commission, and is known as the *De Auxiliis* controversy.

The commission sat through three papal reigns—Popes Clement VIII, Leo XI, and Paul V. Clement and Leo teetered on brink of condemning Molinism. But the Jesuits were finally saved from condemnation by the fact that they were the undoubtedly successful spearhead of the whole Roman Catholic Counter-Reformation, and were noted for their special devotion to the papacy. In 1607, after ten years of fruitless argument, Pope Paul V dissolved the commission and imposed silence on both sides. However, both ignored this "silence" and carried on disputing. In 1610, Baius' great Jesuit antagonist Leonardus Lessius published a vast tome on the doctrine of grace, setting out Molinist views; but he was once again condemned by the University of Louvain, which stayed loyal to the Augustinianism of Baius (who had died 20 years previously). The decree of silence was reimposed in a new form by Pope Urban VIII in 1625.

3. Jansen, Saint-Cyran, and the grand project

This, then, was the background at Louvain University when a young Dutchman, **Cornelius Jansen** (1585–1638), arrived there. Born at Accol, from a poor family, Jansen became a brilliant theological student at Louvain, where he was exposed to the Augustinian tradition of Baius. It is not entirely clear exactly when Jansen personally embraced Baius' legacy and made it his lifelong passion. What is clear, however, is that very little fruit would have emerged from this, had it not been for Jansen's friendship with another remarkable figure, the Frenchman Jean-Amboise Duvergier de Hauranne, best known to history by his title of the *Abbé de Saint-Cyran* (1581–1643). A native of Paris, born into a rich Basque family, Saint-Cyran was educated by the Jesuits, studying at the universities of Paris and Louvain. After ordination to the priesthood, he was given the plush parish of Ixtassou in 1607, and later the wealthy abbey of Saint-Cyran, whose name passed to the man himself.

Jansen and Saint-Cyran may have met as students at Louvain; they certainly became well acquainted in Paris in 1609. At any rate, the wealthy French priest and the poor Dutch scholar grew to be intimate lifelong friends. They spent the period 1611–14 closeted together on land owned by the Saint-Cyran family, studying Scripture and the early Church fathers. After this Jansen returned to Louvain, where he entered the priesthood and lectured in theology. He and Saint-Cyran kept up a lively correspondence.

In September 1616, Jansen penned a letter to Saint-Cyran which gives us our first glimpse of the grand project that was beginning to dominate his life. Jansen had now come to believe that the only subject that really mattered to him as a Christian and a theologian was divine grace, and that the only teacher worth studying on this exalted theme (outside the Bible) was Augustine. "I love him uniquely", Jansen wrote. "It seems to me that nothing among the ancients and moderns comes near him by a hundred leagues. The more I read him, the finer I find him."

So began a long series of letters between Jansen and Saint-Cyran on the Augustinian doctrine of grace. Considering that Pope Paul V had imposed silence on this topic as a result of the *De Auxiliis* controversy, the two men adopted an elaborate code to prevent condemnation if their letters were discovered. Interestingly, Jansen kept a close eye on the proceedings of the Synod of Dort from 1618–19, declaring that the Dutch Calvinists were thoroughly sound Catholics on the matter of predestination! (By "Catholic" he meant "in harmony with the true doctrine taught by Augustine".) From 1621, Jansen's project took concrete shape: he would read and re-read Augustine's writings against the Pelagians and Semi-Pelagians on the doctrine of grace, distil the essence, and write a commentary. He referred to the commentary by the codeword "Pilmot"; its actual name was *Augustinus*. Jansen's hope was that the book would rescue the Roman Catholic Church from the debased theologies of free will so beloved by the Jesuits, and restore the truth as taught by Augustine and his successors (such as Baius).

There is little more to tell of Jansen's life. He began writing *Augustinus* in 1627; in 1635 he became Bishop of Ypres; in 1638 he died, having just finished his great treatise, which he entrusted to his chaplain Lamaeus. It was published in 1640 in Louvain. When the Jesuits learned the nature of the work that was rolling from the presses of the printer, a certain Zegers, they made every effort to stop him; but Zegers, incensed by their interference, made his men work night and day to get the *Augustinus* into print before Jesuit efforts to suppress it could bear fruit. Little could its author have foreseen the convulsive movement his book would launch, bearing his name—Jansenism.

4. The Arnauld family and Port-Royal

Some historians have argued that Jansenism should really be called Cyranism, because Saint-Cyran was the man who transformed Jansen's teachings into a spiritual movement with the potential for wide appeal. Where Jansen had been above all a scholar and thinker, Saint-Cyran was a leader of men and women, exceptionally gifted at seeing into the human heart and inspiring others to lives of devotion. He also possessed an almost messianic sense of mission, believing that he had been chosen by God to make Jansen's ideals into a vital reality in the French Church of his day. Sometimes this attitude provoked negative reactions; one critic described Saint-Cyran as "an insulting and violent person, lacking any respect for those who in any way disagree with him". More often, Saint-Cyran's single-minded enthusiasm kindled an answering fire in the souls of others, especially those who had submitted to his spiritual guidance.

Saint-Cyran was propelled into greater prominence by his relationship with the great Cardinal de Bérulle (see section 3.2, above) from 1620 onwards. They became enduring friends. Bérulle admired Saint-Cyran's patristic learning; Saint-Cyran admired Bérulle's blend of spirituality and practical energy, and found his own piety quickened to new heights under Bérulle's influence. Ominously for the future of Jansenism, Saint-Cyran's friendship with Bérulle thrust him into conflict with the Jesuits, who begrudged the growth of Bérulle's Oratorian movement. Saint-Cyran sprang to his friend's defence; in 1632, for example, he wrote a series of pamphlets under the pseudonym "Petrus Aurelius", attacking the Jesuits comprehensively. Collected into a book, the *Petrus Aurelius* won the enthusiastic approval of all critics of the Jesuits in France; in 1642, the French Assembly of the Clergy ordered it to be printed afresh and presented to every bishop and cathedral in the kingdom.

Despite being the titular head of the abbey that bore his name, Saint-Cyran settled in Paris and established a growing influence there. Refusing all offers of bishoprics, he became the personal spiritual director of a large company of men and women prominent in the secular world. His direction of their consciences was rooted in his Augustinian theology; in particular, he taught them a demanding doctrine of *contrition*. This was a technical term, meaning that in repentance, the fear of hell ("attrition") was an insufficient motive; true repentance must involve a genuine love for God ("contrition"). This again was aimed against the Jesuits, who taught the sufficiency of attrition.

The spark that finally ignited Jansenism—other, of course, than Jansen's *Augustinus*—was the association of Saint-Cyran with the Cistercian convent of Port-Royal. Port-Royal had been founded in 1204, in the depths of a slender valley some sixteen miles from Paris. By the sixteenth century it had become very worldly, and would probably have remained unknown but for a truly extraordinary abbess, **Mother Angélique** (1591–1661), real name Jacqueline Arnauld. Placed in the convent at the mere age of seven, she became its nominal abbess in 1602 aged 10. Things took a suddenly serious turn, however, when in 1608 the sermon of a visiting preacher deeply moved the thoughtless young abbess. She reformed her own life, gathered an inner circle of like-minded nuns, and exercised her authority to impose a rigorous observance of the original Benedictine rule on Port-Royal. In 1609, she enforced "strict enclosure" on the convent—banished outsiders from the precincts and locked the doors against the world, including her family.

Mother Angélique's illustrious family, the Arnaulds, were of Huguenot stock. Her grandfather had reconverted to Rome after the infamous St Bartholomew massacre in 1572 during the French wars of religion. It was a family of lawyers; Angélique's father Antoine was legendary for lawsuits against the Jesuits on behalf of Paris University. Antoine at first violently opposed the enclosure of Port-Royal by his newly serious-minded daughter, but afterwards relented and became her warmest supporter.

Under Angélique's leadership, Port-Royal became a magnetic centre of French Catholic piety; many of the nation's distinguished preachers and counsellors were active there, including Cardinal de Bérulle and Francis de Sales (see section 3, above). Angélique now had spiritual star status. She was especially devoted to Francis de Sales; after his death in 1622 she sought a new mentor in vain, till at last she met Saint-Cyran. He and Angélique had an instant and profound rapport, and she yielded herself entirely to his guidance. The first spiritual director of the Port-Royal nuns had been Sébastien Zamet (1587–1655), Bishop of Langres and disciple of Bérulle. Fatefully in 1633, Zamet handed the task over to his friend Saint-Cyran, who was soon the intensely admired father-confessor of all the nuns. So was formed the axis that would make Port-Royal the pulsing heart of Jansenism for two generations.

A sign of Port-Royal's mushrooming celebrity was its relocation to the outskirts of Paris (the unhealthy conditions in the valley had led to too many premature deaths). Nestling now on the borders of France's capital, the convent scaled new heights of fame. It broke away from the Cistercian order and took an independent identity as the "Institute of the Holy Sacrament". The nuns adopted a new garb—a white scapular distinguished by a red cross. Soon they were the spiritual heroines of all Paris. It became the highest ambition of young girls to join Port-Royal. Unknown to most, however, Saint-Cyran was quietly nurturing an Augustinian spirituality in these eminent nuns, paving the way in their minds and hearts for the great book his friend Jansen was writing, which would be God's instrument in restoring the true doctrine of grace to His true Church.

5. Jansenist spirituality

What was the pattern of spirituality that was growing up under the fostering hand of Saint-Cyran, soon to be identified (by its foes) as "Jansenism"? At the risk of over-simplification, we can perhaps pick out the following as prominent elements:

> (i) Jansenists were serious-minded people. Their whole religion was marked by an earnestness and intensity that could be rather disturbing to

other French Catholics who wore their faith more lightly. This seriousness found a focus in Saint-Cyran's doctrine of contrition (see above), which broadened out into an insistence that love for God was the only truly ethical motive. Even natural affection was suspect: one should not be too concerned about the death of a loved one. For Jansenists, the Creator was an all-absorbing object of devotion. Any attachment to created things or persons was regarded as sinful, unless they were loved for God's sake.

(ii) Related to this was a profound feeling of tension and discord between the Christian and the world. Jansenists distanced themselves as far as possible from the culture of their society, especially its amusements; fiction and the theatre were particular targets of criticism. The Augustinian sense of the fallenness of life led to an extreme pessimism about this world, and an other-worldly preoccupation with the next. Jansenists tended to think that the only worthwhile use of life on earth was to prepare oneself for life in heaven. The light of eternity was their sole illumination amid the darkness of a fallen existence.

(iii) The Bible became uniquely central in Jansenist spirituality. In its sacred pages, God spoke the truth of salvation to His elect. Jansenists stressed that every devout Christian, not just priests or theologians, should read the Bible. This spilled over into an enthusiasm for translating the Bible into French (or other languages, in other countries affected by Jansenism). A negative counterpart to this biblical emphasis was a general Jansenist distaste for mysticism, on the grounds that it was too subjective, drawing people away from the objective word of the Bible into a maze of dubious experiences.

(iv) Jansenists had a reforming mindset. They saw themselves as having a divine mission to call their Church back to the true doctrine of grace, taught in the Bible and classically formulated by Augustine. For philosophy and scholastic theology they had little or no time. They took up this stance in a quite uncompromising manner: the Church had been infected by Pelagian and Semi-Pelagian error, and it was the calling of Jansenists to engage in a life-and-death struggle for the Church's soul. Had it not been for this reforming militancy, the popes would probably have been content to leave Jansenism alone as a viable school of thought within the wide embrace of Rome. It was the determination of Jansenists to capture the Church for their own view exclusively that projected them into fateful conflict with the Jesuits and collision with the papacy.

From this crude outline, we can understand why some have compared the Jansenists with the Puritans. In some ways, we could indeed say that Jansenism was a sort of French Catholic Puritanism.[2]

However, we could also ask why, given all the troubles they were to bring upon themselves from the papacy, Jansenists did not just leave the Roman Catholic Church and become Protestants.[3] The answer is that they combined their Augustinian theology of grace with equally strong convictions about the Bishop of Rome as the divinely ordained visible head of the Church, transubstantiation as the true doctrine of the eucharist, the cult of the Virgin Mary and the saints, the apostolic succession of the priesthood, and the superior worth of celibacy and the monastic life. Since most Jansenists were unwilling to part with these cherished convictions, becoming Protestant was not a live option. Their only choice was the attempt to conquer their own Church and make it a citadel for their Augustinian theology.

---

2. See Chapter 3, section 1 for Puritanism and problems of definition.

3. Some of them did, such as Jean de Labadie. See Chapter 1, section 4.1.

Thus the stage was set for a prolonged and painful struggle, by turns heroic, hilarious, and heart-rending, which was to leave enduring scars on the body of the Roman Catholic Church.

6. *The Augustinus and the Great Arnauld: Jansenism becomes a movement*

In 1638, Saint-Cyran was arrested by Cardinal Richelieu, all-powerful chief minister of King Louis XIII during the latter part of his reign. Complicated political factors were driving Richelieu to annul the marriage of the king's brother, Gaston d'Orléans; Richelieu needed the support of the theologians, and sought that of the influential Saint-Cyran, offering him a bishopric. But Saint-Cyran refused, declaring the annulment to be a moral scandal. Richelieu was incensed and decided to make an example of the uncooperative cleric. Consequently Saint-Cyran was kept in prison for the next five years, a living martyr in the eyes of his many spiritual devotees. His detention, however, was not overly restrictive, and he was allowed to receive visitors and write to correspondents. He also penned his classic *Christian and Spiritual Letters*, to be published in 1645.

It was during Saint-Cyran's imprisonment that Jansen's life-work, *Augustinus*, finally appeared in print, in 1640 at Louvain (Jansen having died in 1638). Here was the theological masterpiece on which Saint-Cyran was pinning his hopes, under God, for the revival of the true doctrine of grace in the Roman Catholic Church. And things went well, at first; *Augustinus* proved hugely popular in France—it was reprinted in Paris in 1641. In the Dutch Republic, too, the Reformed sang the praises of *Augustinus*. It seemed to vindicate everything they had established at the Synod of Dort.[4] Although the book purported to be a historical commentary on Augustine's arguments against Pelagianism and Semi-Pelagianism, there could be little disguising Jansen's underlying intent to win over his readers to

---

4. See Chapter 2, section 2, on the Arminian controversy.

Augustine's point of view. Jansen made it fairly clear that he understood Augustine to be teaching as divine truth a doctrinal scheme we could summarize thus:

1. Eternal life can be attained only through God's grace.

2. Before the fall, even Adam needed *sufficient* grace in order to obey.

3. After the fall, sinners need *efficacious* grace, which sovereignly inclines the will.

4. Outside of grace, all efforts of will are sinful, and hence no effort of the unregenerate sinner can secure grace.

5. Only those predestined to life receive grace, the rest being justly passed by in their sin.

Further, Jansen named and condemned the opponents of this true Augustinianism, especially Jesuit theologians. Jesuits accordingly tried to suppress the book, but this merely aroused all their many enemies to rush to its defence. Saint-Cyran of course encouraged the nuns of Port-Royal and his other disciples to take a positive stance towards Jansen's teaching; after all, he had been instilling an Augustinian spirituality into them for years.

Saint-Cyran was finally released from prison in February 1643 shortly after Richelieu's death (December 1642), by his successor Cardinal Mazarin. (Louis XIII died soon after Richelieu, in May 1643; his son Louis XIV was only five years old, and political power lay with Mazarin.) On Saint-Cyran's release, he was thronged with acclamations by the nuns of Port-Royal and his many other supporters. The Jansenist martyr died, however, a few months later. His body was treated as a holy relic; people treasured napkins dipped in his blood. Among those who venerated Saint-Cyran was the illustrious Vincent de Paul, who had often visited and comforted him during his imprisonnment, and was now the first to sprinkle his body with holy water. (Vincent, however, was no Jansenist, and would oppose the movement. His regard for Saint-Cyran was purely personal. See section 3.4 above for more about Vincent.)

With the death of Saint-Cyran, leadership of the budding Jansenist movement passed to **Antoine Arnauld** (1612–94), youngest son of the Arnauld clan, nicknamed "the Great Arnauld" for his intellectual genius. Antoine Arnauld was an ardent disciple of Saint-Cyran, converted under his influence, and virtually anointed by him as his successor. A gawky young man physically, Arnauld nonetheless had the most brilliantly glowing eyes that seemed to penetrate to the heart of any onlooker, and his literary skill as an advocate for any cause in which he believed was formidable. His output was astonishing; the first edition of his collected works filled 45 volumes. Having been ordained to the priesthood in 1641, Arnauld wrote in 1643 (under Saint-Cyran's supervision, just before his death) his first major treatise, destined to become a Jansenist classic—*On Frequent Communion*.

Arnauld's treatise was provoked by the case of a Jesuit confessor allowing a fashionable lady of the French court to attend a mixed dance[5] immediately after taking part in holy communion. Many were outraged, and Arnauld both articulated their indignation and gave it a theological framework. He argued that over-familiarity with the eucharist degraded the sacrament itself and the person partaking; true penitents must approach the altar thoughtfully, not rush to it and from it. Arnauld also maintained, as Saint-Cyran had, the necessity of contrition (repentance flowing from love for God) to a fruitful participation in the sacrament; mere attrition (repentance flowing from fear of hell) was not enough. He further criticized hasty absolutions and superficial penances.

On Frequent Communion was written in French rather than Latin, to reach a wider audience. It struck a chord with many devout French Catholics, and numerous bishops and theologians endorsed it. Jesuits, however, condemned it fiercely; Arnauld

---

5. Mixed, that is, women dancing with men: generally regarded as irredeemably lust-inducing by Catholic and Protestant moralists alike.

was denounced from their pulpits as "a scorpion, a serpent, and a lunatic". This misfired—it just made people more eager to read the book. When Arnauld's Jesuit enemies proposed to send him to Rome to face papal interrogation, he was saved by the protests of his fellow theologians at the Sorbonne, and also the protests of Paris's parlement. Gallican sentiment did not like seeing French theologians dispatched to Rome for discipline. This background of Gallicanism would be a crucial factor in allowing Jansenism to survive and flourish in France.

7. The Five Propositions

Unfortunately for Arnauld, the Jesuits had been straining every nerve in Rome to crush everything he held dear ever since the publication of *Augustinus*. As early as 1641, they had pressurized Pope Urban VIII into signing a bull, *In Eminenti*, which condemned *Augustinus* for reviving Michael Baius' views; it also renewed the *De Auxiliis* prohibition on all discussion of these matters. Urban, a conciliatory man, managed to delay publication for two years, but in 1643 the bull was at length promulgated. Arnauld's response, however, the following year was to publish an *Apology for Jansen*. The treatise was anonymous, but everyone knew Arnauld was the author. Like *On Frequent Communion*, it was written in popular French, not scholarly Latin, and the result was a more widespread diffusion of Jansenist ideas.

Anti-Jansenist forces in France were galvanized into frantic life. A famous preacher of the day, Father Véron, denounced the Jansenist publicly as "Calvinists". The Jesuits now began speaking in alarmist tones of a "Jansenist party" which threatened to seize control of the French Church. (The Jansenists never called themselves Jansenists; they called themselves "disciples of Saint Augustine". The name "Jansenist" was invented by the Jesuits.) The Jesuit accusation was not really true; Jansenism was not an organized party. A witty cardinal once said, "A Jansenist is a Catholic who does not like Jesuits", which despite its sarcasm captures a genuine aspect of the situation. To the extent that Jansenism really existed as a distinctive entity, it was a network of relationships whose focus was the eminent and numerous Arnauld family, and whose visible symbol was Port-Royal, welded together by a vision of the Christian life as a supernatural product of grace which set the converted in opposition to the standards of a corrupt world. Those who had caught this vision could, however, sometimes seem like a self-conscious sect, especially in the way they often referred to themselves, not only as "disciples of Saint Augustine", but also as "Friends of the Truth".

Still, there can be no doubt that Jansenism, in the sense of a spiritual outlook rooted in the life and ministry of Saint-Cyran, underwent spectacular growth in the 1640s. Port-Royal in particular was reaching new heights of influence, especially in Paris. There was now a body of eminent male solitaries living on the grounds, giving basic education to considerable numbers of children in their celebrated and highly successful "Little Schools". And Port-Royal had powerful patrons at court.

Jansenists responded to Jesuit accusations of heresy by demanding that the Sorbonne vindicate them. The matter was taken up by Nicolas Cornet (1572–1663), doctor of the Faculty of Theology and devotee of the Jesuits. He read the *Augustinus* and extracted a number of propositions which he thought summed up Jansenism. On 1st July 1649 he submitted these propositions to the Sorbonne. There were originally seven propositions, but it was five that were ultimately condemned and which are remembered today. They are:

1. It is impossible for the righteous, with the forces at their disposal, to obey some of God's commands, despite their will and effort, because they lack the grace that would make such obedience possible.

2. In the state of fallen nature, interior grace is never resisted.

3. In the state of fallen nature, in order to acquire merit or lose it, it is sufficient that human beings have freedom from compulsion, but not freedom from necessity.

4. The Semi-Pelagians acknowledged the need for prevenient grace for all particular acts, including the beginning of faith, but erred in holding that this grace might be either resisted or obeyed by the human will.

5. It is a Semi-Pelagian error to say that Christ died or shed His blood for all people in general.

At this stage, Arnauld and his fellow Jansenists became uneasy, and persuaded the parlement to prohibit the Sorbonne from examining the propositions. Clearly Arnauld feared a negative outcome, which could shipwreck the grand plan of the Jansenists—how could *Augustinus* be an instrument of renewal in the Church if its theology was condemned? The Sorbonne angrily referred the propositions to the Assembly of the Clergy, the ecclesiastical equivalent of parlement. Anti-Jansenists drafted a petition for all bishops to sign, asking the pope to judge the propositions. Ominously, the great Vincent de Paul swung his influential weight behind this; he was anxious about the practical effects of Jansenism in driving folk away from holy communion (which had, in fact, been one consequence of Arnauld's *On Frequent Communion*—its emphasis on the necessity of serious spiritual preparation had led to a very visible drop in the numbers attending mass). Eighty-five bishops signed the petition; eleven Jansenist bishops drew up a counter-petition. **Pope Innocent X** (1644–55), however, accepted the majority petition, and in 1651 appointed a commission to assess the propositions.

The commission sat for two years, and was plagued by pressure groups and political manoeuvring. But at length, on 31st May 1653, Pope Innocent condemned the Five Propositions (as they were now known) in the bull *Cum Occasione*. All five were "heretical", and some were "blasphemous, ungodly, and an insult to divine mercy".

8. Law and fact

Cum Occasione seemed like a catastrophe for the Jansenists. But their foes had reckoned without the resourceful subtlety of

Arnauld. He wrong-footed them completely, and gave Jansenism much-needed breathing room, by employing a distinction that was to become famous or infamous: the distinction between law and fact. The pope, he admitted, had authority to pronounce on points of law in the Church (e.g. doctrine); but the pope had no special authority about matters of ordinary fact. He could, for example, declare that this or that doctrine was erroneous, but there was no God-given guarantee he would quote accurately from another man's treatise. In other words, papal authority covered theological doctrines, not the facts of history. Based on this law-fact distinction, Arnauld conceded that the Five Propositions were erroneous, but denied that they were to be found in the pages of *Augustinus*.

With all the delicacy of a skilful surgeon's scalpel, Arnauld dissected the Five Propositions, and argued that Jansen's teaching in *Augustinus* was different from each of them, and therefore not affected by the condemnation of *Cum Occasione*. We may briefly examine how he dealt with the Second Proposition to see how he constructed his defence. The Second Proposition, condemned as error, was: "In the state of fallen nature, interior grace is never resisted." This was indeed an error, Arnauld conceded. After all, faith, hope, and love were interior graces, but they could be resisted in the sense that every Christian sometimes acted against faith, hope, and love. Jansen's *Augustinus*, however, nowhere taught that a Christian *never* resisted faith, hope, and love, for it was integral to the teaching of *Augustinus* that even the best Christian fell short of perfection. Therefore the pope was right to condemn the Second Proposition as an error (here was the matter of law), but wrong to say that this Proposition could be found in the pages of *Augustinus* (here was the matter of fact). Arnauld dealt in the same fashion with the other four Propositions. In every case he found a plausible non-Augustinian meaning in the Propositions, agreed that this was an error, and denied that it was taught in *Augustinus*. Jansen's treatise, therefore, had not been condemned.

There has been much discussion about Arnauld's honesty in putting forward the law-fact distinction. Did he really believe it? Or was it just a cunning tactical device to save himself and his friends from being convicted as heretics? Perhaps there were elements of both. On the one hand, Arnauld did not invent the law-fact distinction (it had been around for some time), and it could be defended within a Roman Catholic framework as both plausible and useful in understanding the nature and extent of papal authority. It is also true that the Five Propositions will nowhere be found in *Augustinus* in the precise phraseology used by Innocent X in the *Cum Occasione* bull, and that the Propositions are worded loosely enough to bear a non-Augustinian meaning. On the other hand, Arnauld occasionally came close to admitting that his real motive in suggesting the distinction was basically pragmatic: to create living space for Jansenism in the Church. At any rate, the Jansenists embraced the law-fact distinction from now onward as their typical response to *Cum Occasione*.

Anti-Jansenists seized on *Cum Occasione* and did their best to enforce it. Before giving absolution, some priests would now demand that penitents give assurance that they accepted the bull. One priest, Father Picoté, refused absolution in 1655 to an important Jansenist noble, the duc de Liancourt, because he denied that the Five Propositions could be found in the pages of *Augustinus*. In de Liancourt's defence, Arnauld published two long and flaming letters, in which he denounced Picoté and audaciously reiterated the Jansenist doctrine of grace. This act of boldness or impudence, however, provoked the government into putting overwhelming pressure on the Sorbonne to condemn Arnauld, reject the law-fact distinction, and demand that Arnauld submit on pain of having his doctorate of theology removed. Arnauld would not submit, and so the Sorbonne had no choice but to vote on his expulsion.

On the eve of the vote, the first of a series of Jansenist pamphlets appeared. They were in the form of anonymous letters, defending Jansenist theology and attacking the Jesuits in a biting theological satire unequalled in Christian literary history. The letters took France, especially Paris, by storm, and had people weeping tears of laughter at this merciless lampooning of the Jesuits. Overnight, it seemed, everyone sympathized with the Jansenists, and hated their Jesuit foes as malignant persecutors and enemies of Christian morality. Who could have written these masterpieces of polemic and wit—the *Provincial Letters*, as they are called? For two years no one knew, as the letters continued to pour from the press, eighteen in all (the first was dated January 23rd 1656, the last March 24th 1657). Then in 1659 the secret was out: they had been written by a young Jansenist scientist named **Blaise Pascal** (1623–62).

9. Blaise Pascal and the Pensées

Pascal was one of the greatest intellects of the 17th Century. The history of science knows him for his seminal contributions to geometry and mathematics (especially probability theory); he was also the first to demonstrate experimentally the truth of Torricelli's theory of atmospheric pressure, and the inventor of an early calculating machine. In his own lifetime Pascal achieved international recognition as a scientist. Our interest in him, however, is as a spiritual thinker.

Pascal's family had been won over to Jansenism in 1646. Pascal himself fell under the spell of Arnauld, but his sister Jacqueline was more deeply influenced, becoming a nun at Port-Royal in 1652. Pascal was rather in awe of Jacqueline's spirituality, and felt himself to be very worldly by contrast. However, a near escape from death precipitated Pascal's "second conversion" in 1654. He was riding in a carriage drawn by four horses when it swerved off the road and plunged down a steep river bank. Pascal himself was left dangling on the wall. His nerves shattered, he lost the ability to sleep, and would lay awake at nights reading his Bible, fearing nightmares about the accident. On the night of November 23rd 1654, Pascal was overpowered by a sense of the presence of God. This experience (the "night of fire") lasted for two hours, and he recorded it in a document (the "Memorial") which thereafter he always carried about with him.[6]

---

6. Some dispute that the carriage accident occasioned his conversion.

Pascal's experience brought him into a new harmony with the Jansenist circles of Port-Royal and the Arnauld family. When the Sorbonne threatened to expel the Great Arnauld, Pascal was galvanized into writing in his defence—hence the series of *Provincial Letters* that so effectively portrayed Jansenists as victims of Jesuit spite. The earlier letters defended the Jansenist understanding of grace; the later letters mounted a far-reaching and devastating critique of the Jesuits as a malevolent force for evil that threatened to eat away the moral heart of Church and society. The Jesuits as an organisation never really recovered from the damage Pascal inflicted on them in the eyes of French public opinion; in that sense, the *Provincial Letters* paved the way for the ultimate suppression of the Jesuit order in France in 1764.

In particular, Pascal mocked and attacked the then popular system of Jesuit ethical thinking, "Laxism". This system tried to solve difficult moral cases through a calculus of probabilities about what were right and wrong actions, measured by the number of recognized authorities (theologians, moralists) who recommended one or other option. Some Jesuits were employing the system to permit actions regarded by many as outrageous, by the expedient of finding perhaps just one authority who spoke in favour of the action (although everyone else was against it), and on that slender basis granting the action a "probable" status among permissible choices. One example Pascal gave was killing someone for slapping your face, or even killing him to stop him delivering the slap. Some few authorities had justified this (Jesuit authorities, as Pascal pointed out), and therefore it was permissible, said Laxist Jesuits, despite the vast weight of Christian moral opinion against it. Pascal's ruthless exposure of Laxism led to its downfall; in 1665 and 1666, Pope Alexander VII condemned the system, and in 1679 Pope Innocent XI condemned sixty-five propositions extracted from Laxist writings.

Pascal's other great literary contribution was his *Pensées* (thoughts). He intended this to be an apologetic treatise commending Christianity, especially against the budding forces of atheism and materialism that were beginning to make themselves felt in connection with the new scientific and philosophical thought of the 17th century. Pascal died before he could finish the treatise, but the fragments of his writing were gathered together by his friends and published posthumously in 1670. The *Pensées* has, since then, occupied the front rank in works of Christian apologetics.

We can sketch the main themes of the *Pensées* thus. Human nature is corrupt (Pascal's Augustinianism was much in evidence here); humanity finds itself suspended between potential greatness because of our capacity for understanding the universe, and actual weakness and futility, notably in our bondage to passions and inability to experience true happiness. Pascal emphasized the insufficiency of reason to grasp spiritual and eternal truth. He proposed a threefold view of knowledge:

(i)   the *senses*, which put us in touch with material realities;

(ii) *reason*, which he defined as logical reflection on the knowledge supplied by the senses;

(iii) the *heart*, which Pascal took to be different from and deeper than reason—a power of grasping by intuition those first principles that form the basis of all true knowledge. Not reason but the heart was the seat of aesthetic experience (the perception of beauty) and spiritual life (the perception of God). Thought 110 in the *Pensées* helps us to understand Pascal's meaning:

It is not through reason alone that we know the truth, but through the heart also. It is through the heart that we know first principles. Reason, which has no part to play here, tries in vain to disprove these principles. Sceptics are always trying to do this, but their efforts are wasted. We *know* we are not dreaming; we may be unable to prove this rationally, but our inability proves only how weak reason is. It does not prove (as sceptics claim) that all our knowledge is uncertain. The knowledge of first principles—space, time, motion, number—is as assured as anything derived from reason. In fact, reason has to depend on these first principles, and base all its arguments on them—and these principles come from the heart and from intuition. The heart knows intuitively that there are three dimensions of space and an infinite series of numbers; reason then demonstrates that there exist no two square numbers of which one is twice the other. Principles are *sensed*; propositions are *proved*. Both have certainty, although by different means. It is futile and ridiculous for reason to demand that the heart offer proof of first principles before reason will consent to accept them—just as ridiculous as if the heart were to demand an intuitive sense of all the propositions proved by reason, before the heart would consent to accept them.

Given these views, Pascal was sceptical about the role of reason in knowing God, especially philosophical arguments for God's existence. These arguments are so complicated, he complained, that they can only convince us while we are actually thinking them through; but an hour later, we start wondering whether we made a mistake! Part of Pascal's apologetic, therefore, was to put reason in its place, and to elevate the heart as the true organ of spiritual knowledge. "It is the heart, not the reason, that perceives God. This is faith: to perceive God by the heart, not by the reason" (thought 424). Not that Pascal rejected reason entirely, but he gave it a different area to work in—namely, the historical evidence of Christianity, especially the prophecies of the Old Testament and the miracles of Christ, where God had manifested Himself in the world of the senses.

Ultimately Pascal's apologetic was aimed at leading the seeker to find God, not simply as Creator, but as Saviour, a knowledge accessible only in Jesus Christ. "Knowing God without knowing our own poverty produces pride. Knowing our poverty without knowing God produces despair. Knowing Jesus Christ strikes the true balance, because in Him we know both God and our own poverty" (thought 192). Perhaps Pascal's whole method is best summed up in thought 12:

> People despise Christianity. They hate it, fearing that it may be true. The remedy is first, to demonstrate that Christianity is not contrary to reason, but is entitled to reverence and

respect. Next, make it attractive: make good people *wish*
that it were true. And then show them it *is* true! Entitled
to reverence, because it has a real understanding of human
nature. Attractive, because it promises real blessing.

From 1659 Pascal, who had never enjoyed good health, was
increasingly sick from an unknown cause. His long, drawn-out
death was made worse by incompetent medical procedures.
Before he died in 1662, aged 39, he made an unconditional
submission to Rome, which has often been interpreted as
Pascal's final repudiation of Jansenism. Its true intent may have
been to suspend his judgment on controversies that now seemed
remote and redundant as he faced death and eternity, coupled
with a yearning to die in full communion with the Church he
had always believed was Christ's true body. His literary legacy,
however, was certainly to work strongly and consistently in
Jansenism's favour.

10. The Formulary of Alexander VII

From this excursion into Pascal's thought, let us now return to
the wider story of Jansenism. Despite the sensation created by
the *Provincial Letters*, authority in Church and state continued
to frown on the Jansenists. Soon after the first of the Letters,
the Sorbonne voted to expel Arnauld and strip him of his
doctorate (at the close of January 1656). Arnauld's supporters
at the Sorbonne walked out in protest at the vote; Arnauld
himself went into hiding for the next thirteen years. In the
wake of Arnauld's condemnation, the government moved
to disperse the male solitaries of Port-Royal and close down
the Little Schools. They would have taken further repressive
action, but were temporarily discouraged by the popular success
of Pascal's *Letters*, and by the celebrity of an alleged miracle at
Port-Royal—the healing of a ten year old girl (Pascal's niece)
by a thorn from Christ's crown.

In October 1656, Pope Alexander VII issued the bull *Ad
Sacram*, ratifying an anti-Jansenist "Formulary" which had
been submitted to him by the French Assembly of the Clergy.

The Formulary stated: "With heart and mouth I condemn the doctrine in the Five Propositions of Cornelius Jansen contained in his book *Augustinus*." The wording skilfully disposed of Arnauld's law-fact distinction. It created a crisis of conscience for Jansenists: should they subscribe to the Formulary? Some counselled submission, others that one could subscribe to the Formulary with mental reservations, others that one should openly defy it. Among the defiers were Pascal, his sister Jacqueline, and Mother Angélique. Pascal commented, "there is no difference between condemning Jansen's teaching on the Five Propositions and condemning effectual grace, Saint Augustine, and Saint Paul." Within five months, Pascal had to bring an end to his *Provincial Letters*—it had now become too dangerous to carry on such public opposition to the political and religious establishment. In September 1657, the Inquisition placed the *Provincial Letters* on the Index of Forbidden Books.

The next few years saw only half-hearted attempts by Cardinal Mazarin's government to impose the Formulary on clergy and monastics. Gallican sentiment disliked having to compel French citizens to submit to a papal decree, and the popular impact of Pascal's *Letters* and the miracle of healing at Port-Royal both acted as a deterrent to persecution of Jansenists. After the death of Cardinal Mazarin in March 1661, however, the young French King Louis XIV (aged twenty-two) took the reins of power into his own hands; and Louis was a decided opponent of Jansenism. Almost immediately, in April 1661 he forcibly removed from Port-Royal all its "novices" (nuns in training) and all its boarders (many of whom were not intending a monastic life, but lodged at Port-Royal to benefit from its spirituality). Mother Angélique is said to have died of a broken heart in August; Jacqueline Pascal, also grief-stricken, died shortly thereafter. The new head of the convent was **Mother Angélique de Saint-Jean** (1624–84), the niece of Mother Angélique Arnauld. The new Angélique became the mainspring of hard-line Jansenist defiance, emboldening the other nuns to refuse to sign the Formulary unless they could express their reservation on the question of fact (whether the Five Propositions were really in *Augustinus*).

A quarrel between Louis XIV and Pope Alexander VII gave the Jansenists a respite for the next few years. In 1664, however, king and pope were reconciled, and a new determined effort was made to impose the Formulary on all French clergy and monastics. The Archbishop of Paris, Hardouin de Péréfixe, exasperated by the Jansenist tenacity of the Port-Royal nuns ("as pure as angels and as proud as demons", he called them), resorted to force. Armed officers arrested twelve of the nuns, including Mother Angélique, and dispersed them to other convents. The dispersed maintained their Jansenism in their new convents and wrote accounts of their sufferings. A new pliable Mother Superior, Mother Eugénie, was appointed to Port-Royal from the religious order of Francis de Sales, the Visitandines, along with other nuns from the same order to assist her. But they were unable to secure submission from the remaining Jansenist nuns. At length these impenitent Augustinians were taken back to the old rural site of Port-Royal, cut off from all contact with the outside world, and barred from holy communion. Port-Royal itself, the visible soul of Jansenist piety, seemed to have been extinguished.

Another problem Louis XIV had to deal with was the small minority of Jansenist bishops. In the spring of 1664, he ordered parlement to register a decree that all parish priests must sign the Formulary or else be deprived of their livings. Four bishops—Pavillon of Alet, Caulet of Pamiers, de Buzenval of Beauvais, and Henri Arnauld of Angers—protested, arguing that the king, as a secular ruler, had no right to legislate for the Church. But Louis appealed to Pope Alexander VII, who issued the bull *Regiminis Apostolici*, making it obligatory for the first time to sign the Formulary on direct papal authority. The Jansenist community was shaken to the core: should they submit or defy? The four Jansenist bishops told their flocks to submit to the Formulary in regard to law (the heretical nature of the Five Propositions), but maintain a "respectful silence" in regard to fact (whether the Five Propositions were truly in *Augustinus*). This quibbling manoeuvre prompted pope and king to set up a special commission to pass judgment on the refractory bishops. Matters had clearly reached boiling point in the French Church; but everything was suddenly defused by the death of Pope Alexander VII in 1667.

11. The Clementine Peace

The new pope, Clement IX (1667–9), was a conciliatory man, and the Gallicans now rallied to the Jansenists (they did not like direct papal intervention in French affairs). Hence, after secret negotiations, Clement announced in 1669 a sort of amnesty for Jansenists—the "Clementine peace", as it became known. Clement died at the end of 1669, but his "peace" endured for the next ten years. The contentious Formulary was now understood to mean, not that the Five Propositions were necessarily found in the pages of *Augustinus*, but that they were to be regarded as heretical in whatever book they in fact appeared. On these terms, even Arnauld and the Port-Royal nuns finally submitted. Arnauld came out of his 13 year concealment; the Sorbonne restored his doctorate, and he was received at court by Loius XIV and hailed by the crowds as a hero. "Jansenism is dead!" was suddenly the prevailing view—in other words, no longer a live issue. The French Catholic Church could now bury the squalid quarrel, and get on with its real business: preaching and teaching, fostering the holy life, winning over the Protestants.

Jansenism, however, was far from dead. It was merely no longer a convulsive agent in the body of French Catholicism. The Clementine peace of 1669–79 proved a golden decade for the Jansenists, initiating their period of greatest growth. Port-Royal opened for business again and became hugely fashionable, both with upper and lower classes of society. Pilgrims flocked there, girls were educated there, the dying wanted to be buried there.

At the same time, another brilliant new Jansenist leader emerged onto the centre stage, **Pierre Nicole** (1625–95). He was the brother of a Port-Royal nun and a Sorbonne divinity graduate. Nicole initially made his mark collaborating with Pascal on the *Provincial Letters* (including a Latin translation for the international market), but then went independent, producing a steady stream of writings on behalf of Jansenism (or "the Truth", as he called it) for the rest of his life. His writing style had a captivating beauty, and he mitigated the severity of Jansenist morality by a strong dose of common sense. Nicole finally had a reputation equal to that of the Great Arnauld. Indeed the two great Jansenist leaders worked together on a lengthy and significant work against Calvinism, *The Perpetuity of the Catholic Faith regarding the Eucharist* (1669–74). Despite his prolific Jansenist output, Nicole at the very end of his life underwent a change of mind; in a posthumously published work, *Treatise on Universal Grace* (1715), he signalled the abandonment of his exclusive allegiance to the Augustinian tenets of Jansenism, essentially by trying to construct a universal viewpoint in which the different views of grace (Jansenist, Thomist, Molinist) could all be reconciled.

The Clementine peace saw a great new wave of Jansenist publications. The collected works of Saint-Cyran, Pascal's *Pensées*, Nicole's writings, and a translation of the Bible into beautiful French **by Isaac le Maistre de Sacy** (1613–84, nephew of Arnauld and spiritual director of Port-Royal) all rolled off the press. So did one of the seminal works of scholarly church history, the *Guide to the Church History of the First Six Centuries* by Louis Tillemont (1637–98), a treatise which to this day has not been surpassed for its blend of learning and comprehensiveness. The Jansenist educational system, formed in the Little Schools of Port-Royal, also now spread far and wide throughout France, commended by its intrinsic merits, especially its deliberate cultivation of the French language as a subject in its own right (a novelty at that time). At the heart of Jansenist education lay the influential treatise *Logic, or the Art of Thinking* (1662) by Arnauld and Nicole: an easy-to-read textbook on mental training which achieved huge popularity, and was translated into many other languages.

The Jansenist educational scheme operated in many French schools throughout the 18th Century. The most famous pupil thus educated was **Jean Racine** (1639–99), one of France's greatest playwrights. His strict Jansenist upbringing did not save Racine from a rather disreputable life, but at the end he repented of his worldliness and embraced again the Jansenist piety of his youth. In this last phase, he wrote a favourable history of Port-Royal, while his 1689 play *Esther* (an allegory on the persecution of Jansenists) depicted Mordechai in terms of Arnauld, and Esther's maidens as Port-Royal nuns.

The Clementine peace was the period when Jansenism really began to get a grip on the wider French Catholic mind and heart. It was not so much the theology as the spirituality of the Jansenists that flowed out into the lives of parish priests and people, based on an ardent admiration for the monastics of Port-Royal—"angels on earth". The Jansenist spirit also penetrated other French religious orders, notably the Benedictines and Visitandines. The crucifix favoured by the Jansenists (Christ with His arms stretched taut above His head) now became universally popular.

12. Renewed controversy: Quesnel and the Reflections

The Clementine Peace, however, was not to last longer than a decade. Louis XIV began to become hostile again to Jansenists; he feared they were collaborating with the new Pope **Innocent XI** (1676–89) in the ongoing Gallican controversy. Two Jansenist bishops (Pavillon and Caulet) were outspoken foes of Gallicanism, rejecting the right of the French monarchy to determine church affairs. Innocent himself was nicknamed "the Jansenist pope" for his leniency to the Jansenists. This unholy coalescence of Jansenists and the papacy against Louis' ambitions for a quasi-independent French Church reawakened the king's suspicion and wrath.

The turning point came in 1679, when Port-Royal's greatest advocate in the French court died—the Duchesse de Longueville (1619–79). She had been one of the few people Louis allowed to speak to him candidly. Within weeks of her death, the new Archbishop of Paris, Harlay de Champvallon, took action against Port-Royal. He ordered all young boarders, priests, and candidates for monastic life to leave. Port-Royal was now forbidden to accept novices, and the number of nuns was restricted to a maximum of fifty. Essentially Port-Royal had been sentenced to extinction. A month later Arnauld and Nicole fled to the safety of Belgium. Nicole returned to France in 1680, but Arnauld never—he continued to champion the Jansenist cause in exile until his death in 1694.

The third of Jansenism's great spiritual leaders was now beginning to emerge in succession to Saint-Cyran and the Great Arnauld: the Paris-born Oratorian priest *Pasquier Quesnel* (1634–1719). Quesnel was the spiritual director of the students of Saint-Magloire, the Paris Oratory, where he taught an Augustinian theology and tried to encourage a subversive attitude to the anti-Jansenist Formulary of 1656. Jansenism had many sympathizers at Saint-Magloire; it had even given secret shelter to Arnauld when he was under threat from the authorities.

Quesnel's own increasingly grand reputation, and ultimate position of spiritual leadership among Jansenists, rested on a book he first published in 1668 entitled *Words of the Word Incarnate*. In 1671 he changed the title to *Moral Reflections on the New Testament*, commonly known as *Quesnel's Reflections*. This was an abridgment of the New Testament festooned with edifying comments; it stressed the unrivalled benefit of a careful reading and study of Scripture in the cultivation of a holy life. Many of its religious ideas were akin to Pascal's *Pensées*; contemporaries deemed it an excellent work, and it found its way outside the boundaries of the Roman Catholic Church into the library of many a Protestant preacher. The problem was that Quesnel kept revising the *Reflections* and reissuing it in new editions—and each new edition became more definitely Jansenist in outlook. As the teachings of the *Reflections* were criticized, the book also increasingly propounded the Gallican, conciliarist theories of Richer (see chapter 7, section 1).

None of this was so evident in the *Reflections* at this early stage. But Quesnel's own mind was clearly inclined to Jansenism, as shown in his dislike of the Formulary; and the fact was unexpectedly revealed to the world when someone published his private notes on the New Testament without his approval. They were undoubtedly Jansenist. When the General of the Oratory,

Father Abel de Sainte-Marthe (1621–97), was forced to stand down 1681 because of his scandalous friendship with Arnauld, Quesnel fell from favour too. He was relocated from Paris to Orleans. Three years later, in 1684, his ecclesiastical superiors enforced an anti-Jansenist formula; Quesnel refused to sign and fled to Brussels in Belgium, where he lived with Arnauld. By 1694, the *Reflections* had been denounced both by the Sorbonne and the Inquisition.

In the period 1682–93, there was an eleven year quarrel between Louis and the papacy, triggered by Gallican articles drafted by the lawyers of parlement (see chapter 7, section 1.4). In this rupture, Jansenists supported the pope. A great Jansenist network of secret correspondence spread across France; in Rome, a body of Jansenist partisans established a powerful presence. Louis' wrangle with Rome, however, ended in 1693 with a concordat which struck a balance between Gallicanism and the claims of the papacy over the French Church. Louis rewarded bishops who had been loyal to him during the rupture with new levels of authority over the lower clergy, and he curtailed the capacity of parlement to intervene in the jurisdiction of bishops. Paradoxically, this had the ultimate effect of catapulting parlement itself into the role of Jansenist stronghold against episcopal persecution, on the back of the resentment of the legal magistrates at Louis' curbing of their traditional power over the bishops.

In 1695 there occurred an event of crucial significance for the future of Jansenism: the appointment of the Bishop of Châlons-sur-Marne, ***Louis-Antoine de Noailles*** (1651–1729), as Archbishop of Paris—not a committed Jansenist, but a fervent anti-Jesuit. His ecclesiastical stature increased further in 1700 when Pope Innocent XII made him a cardinal. Son of a duke, Noailles was a man of blameless life, stern and rigorous in personal morals but kind-hearted to others, especially the poor. He had, however, mediocre practical judgment which was often to get him in hot water. He also unfortunately boasted a large red nose which made him look rather ridiculous. Noailles' hostility to the Jesuits, coupled with his staunch Gallicanism, soon entangled him in a strange alliance with the Jansenists in the final phase of the movement in France.

The whole controversy flared up again with a vengeance in 1702. It was rekindled by a Jansenist pamphlet, *A Case of Conscience*, which maintained (in the aftermath of a debate in the Sorbonne) that a priest could absolve a penitent despite the penitent's maintaining a respectful silence on the "fact" of whether the notorious Five Propositions were in the *Augustinus*. The pamphlet reopened all the old wounds over the anti-Jansenist Formulary of 1656, and passions erupted.

13. The destruction of Port-Royal

In 1700, Louis XIV's grandson Philip of Anjou had inherited the Spanish throne as King Philip V, which gave him sovereignty over the Spanish Netherlands (modern Belgium). Louis now convinced Philip to take severe repressive measures against the Belgian Jansenists. In 1703, the "Friends of the Truth" in that previously safe haven were arrested *en masse*, including Quesnel himself (although he managed a dramatic escape within three months to the safety of Amsterdam in the Calvinist Dutch Republic). As a result of the clamp-down, the Spanish authorities got their hands on a multitude of letters and other documents which exposed the huge Jansenist network of correspondence, including Jansenist sympathizers in Rome, and evidence that Jansenist books and pamphlets were published, not at random, but according to a coordinated plan. These documents were sent to Louis; the French king was aghast at what seemed irrefutable proof that Jansenism was a mighty living conspiracy, its tentacles extending both within and beyond France.

Louis wasted no time in arresting Quesnel's foremost French correspondents. Pope **Clement XI** (1700–1721) joined in the anti-Jansenist reaction, publishing the bull *Vineam Domini* in 1705, which declared that it was insufficient to subscribe the anti-Jansenist Formulary of 1656 without positively confessing Jansenism to be a heresy. This was the final annihilation of Arnauld's law-fact distinction. Surprisingly, one of the prime movers behind *Vineam Domini* was Archbishop Fénelon of

Cambrai, often admired by Protestants as a truly spiritual man (see Chapter 7, section 2.3). Having been utterly defeated by Bishop Bossuet of Meaux in the Quietist controversy, this anti-Jansenist outburst was Fénelon's revenge, for Bossuet had always been ambivalent about Jansenism, and in recent times had even supported Quesnel's *Reflections*. Fénelon's diocese of Cambrai was swarming with Jansenists, and he detested their austere piety—"these so-called Augustinians".

In 1706, the nuns of Port-Royal were asked to subscribe to the *Vineam Domini* bull. They reluctantly signed, but added the phrase "without prejudice to the Clementine peace". Their obstinacy on this point was punished by denying them the sacraments, but not even this could break their spirit. The patience of Louis XIV finally snapped with these stubbornly Jansenist nuns. He now asked Pope Clement XI to issue a bull suppressing Port-Royal. Clement hesitated long, but at last consented.

In October 1709, Louis' chief of police, the Marquis d'Argenson, entered Port-Royal with his men, and read out a royal decree, based on Clement's bull. The twenty-two surviving nuns were forcibly dispersed, each of them escorted by troops as if they were deadly threats to public well-being. Then in 1711, Port-Royal itself was destroyed—the convent, the houses, the church, even the cemetery, all pulverized to rubble. The corpses of around three thousand devotees of Port-Royal were disinterred from their graves in the cemetery; some rich families rescued the bodies of relatives and relocated them, but the bodies of the poor were simply thrown into a common pit. In this ignominious fashion ended the life and history of Port-Royal, the visible heart of Jansenist spirituality, once made illustrious by Mother Angélique, Saint-Cyran, the Great Arnauld, and Blaise Pascal.

Port-Royal was gone, but Jansenism as a movement was still alive in France. There were a number of Jansenist convents and bishops, and countless Jansenist sympathizers among the lower clergy. Further, there had by now developed a total convergence between Jansenism and Gallicanism. Gallicans who regarded the 1693 concordat between Louis and Rome as a betrayal of the

French Church now aligned themselves with the Jansenists as the victims of the new Louis-Rome axis. Hence many Gallican politicians and lawyers were enlisted on the Jansenist side.

14. The Unigenitus crisis

A new round of conflict was sparked off by Quesnel. The Inquisition had promulgated a condemnation of the *Reflections* in 1707 after fourteen years of hesitant boggling. The implementation of this condemnation in France was also entrusted to the Inquisition, and on that ground was opposed by Gallican ministers in Louis' cabinet. This inspired Quesnel to issue yet another edition of the *Reflections*, much enlarged, to which he attached a commendatory preface of the celebrated Bossuet, France's greatest preacher, which he had written in private some years previously. (Bossuet had died in 1704.) As we have already noted, Bossuet was ambivalent about Jansenism. He disliked their insubordination and distinction of law and fact, but admired their moral integrity and opposition to Laxism.

The new edition of the *Reflections*, with Bossuet's preface, provoked a fierce reaction against Jansenists in France. An enraged Louis had a "directive" drawn up endorsing the Roman condemnation of the book. Archbishop Fénelon, still crusading against Jansenism, was again highly active in this policy, as were the Jesuits. Any persons who had approved the *Reflections* were described in the royal directive as "abettors of heresy". Based on this, Fénelon then got two bishops under his jurisdiction to publish pastoral letters condemning the *Reflections*. The letters were posted up on the palace walls of Archbishop Noailles of Paris, a well-known foe of the Jesuits and admirer of the *Reflections* who had recommended Quesnel's book to his clergy. Noailles retaliated with a scathing attack on the entire Jesuit order, accusing them of being behind the whole business, and deprived all Jesuit priests in his diocese of the right to preach or hear confession.

King Louis and the anti-Jansenist faction now asked the pope to issue another formal condemnation of the *Reflections*, with the promise that Louis would force all French bishops to submit. In consequence, on 8th September 1713, Clement XI issued one of the most famous bulls in Roman Catholic history, the bull *Unigenitus*. It was a comprehensive condemnation of the *Reflections* in particular and Jansenism in general. The ill-fated Quesnel was described as "a ravening wolf, a false prophet, a teacher of lies, a knave, a hypocrite, and a poisoner of souls". *Unigenitus* condemned one hundred and one theological propositions, a few of them not Jansenist but Gallican. The Catholic faithful were prohibited not only from speaking but even from thinking about the propositions! Embarrassingly, some of the condemned propositions turned out to be direct quotations from the writings of Augustine, prompting some to comment that the Church had now officially condemned its greatest patristic saint as a heretic.

Archbishop Fénelon made himself the champion of *Unigenitus* in France. Taking charge of the Assembly of Clergy, he skilfully manoeuvred it into supporting the new anti-Jansenist campaign. Subsequently one hundred and seventeen French bishops submitted unequivocally to *Unigenitus*. Fifteen, however, only submitted with qualifications, while eight openly refused. An extraordinary theological uproar gripped the nation. In 1714 alone, some two hundred books and pamphlets were published about how French Catholics should respond to *Unigenitus*. Those bishops who objected to the bull received the complete support of the Gallican party, and appealed over the pope's head to a general council of the Church. The Jansenist-leavened parlement saw the bull's condemnation of Gallicanism as intolerable, and bitterly resisted it; they declared that they would not register it legally, until or unless the bishops of France collectively accepted it. Meanwhile, disputes about *Unigenitus* unleashed an anarchy of verbal civil war in the Sorbonne.

But Louis was determined to force *Unigenitus* on Church and nation, and he menacingly overawed parlement by his personal presence into registering the bull (although with a qualifying clause preserving Gallican liberties). The Sorbonne was also cowed into submitting to the implacable king.

Louis' victory was not, however, complete. Archbishop Noailles of Paris stunned him by a devious move, issuing a pastoral letter in which he forbade all priests in his diocese to recognize *Unigenitus*, on pain of suspension, yet also condemned the *Reflections*! To compound matters, defences of Quesnel continued to be printed, and active sympathy for him among the lower clergy was substantial. Henri François d'Aguesseau (1668–1751), Louis' procurator general, added to his king's misery by declaring that *Unigenitus* did not have the force of law in France, because parlement had registered it under duress:

> No papal constitution in matters of doctrine may be invested
> with the king's authority, without a legitimate and sufficient
> acceptance by the Gallican Church; to do otherwise would be
> to recognize the pope as the infallible and sole judge of faith,
> against the fundamental maxims of our liberties.

Louis was now insane with rage, and his wrath spent itself on the hapless Noailles, who was banned from the Assembly of the Clergy, and prohibited from leaving France to argue his case in Rome.

Louis now tried to get parlement to register a decision that parlement itself adhered to *Unigenitus*, and that all bishops in France must sign a declaration submitting to the bull. This time there was stubborn opposition to the king's measures which he could not overcome. The police arrested some two thousand suspected Jansenists, and took in about ten thousand more for questioning. In the summer of 1715, Pope Clement finally surrendered to remorseless pressure from Louis, and agreed to summon a national French council for the purpose of deposing the still recalcitrant Noailles, and enforcing *Unigenitus* once and for all on the French clergy.

15. The Regency: Jansenism breathes again

At the height of the crisis, in September 1715 Louis died. His heir was his great-grandson, **Louis XV** (born 1710, reigned 1715–74), a mere baby, and so a Regency took power under the powerful noble **Philippe d'Orléans** (1674–1723), nephew of the late king. To the joy of the Jansenists, Philippe overturned all the anti-Jansenist measures of the previous reign. All Jansenist prisoners were set free; Father Le Tellier, the old king's Jesuit confessor, was dismissed from court, and bishops throughout France forbade Jesuits to preach in their dioceses. Noailles was restored to high favour. It was a remarkable turnabout.

Why this impressive swell of support for Jansenism under the new Regent? Among the secular clergy (those not belonging to a religious order), it has been suggested that Jansenist sympathy arose because a new generation had entered the priesthood. Proper pastoral seminary training (as mandated by Council of Trent) became effective in France only in the second half of the 17th Century. Between 1642 and 1698, no fewer than one hundred and four seminaries were established. Hence the secular clergy who faced *Unigenitus* were different from their predecessors. Their seminary training had instilled two principles into them: (i) the primary duty of pastoral care—and in that regard, Quesnel's *Reflections* was one of most helpful books around; (ii) the special role of parish priests in the life of church—a conviction that made them identify with the Gallican views condemned in *Unigenitus*. The Jansenism of this new generation of priests was driven less by theology, more by practical pastoral concerns. They saw in Jansenism a devout spirituality and an earnest morality that seemed the crying need of the hour, and the very thing priests should be trying to cultivate among their parishioners.

The regular clergy (those belonging to a religious order) were more theologically motivated in their Jansenism. Those orders that prized humanist scholarship, like the Benedictines, sympathized with the Jansenist appeal to the Bible and Augustine—it seemed part of the "ad fontes" (back to the sources) quest of all humanism. The Dominicans for their part, dedicated to Thomist theology, were increasingly appalled by Jesuit Pelagianism, and so drew closer to Jansenists, especially since they thought they saw in the Jansenists a drawing closer to Aquinas.

Finally there was also by now a widespread antipathy to the Jesuits among the lower clergy. This produced a reactive sympathy for Jansenists as the victims of Jesuit persecution.

Attitudes to *Unigenitus* changed overnight under the new Regency government. The Sorbonne declared it had submitted to *Unigenitus* only under duress. Twenty-five more bishops retracted their apparently full submission, stating that it had been conditional. By the end of 1716, parlement had withdrawn its submission. Dislike of *Unigenitus*, allied with strong Gallican feeling, was pushing significant sections of the French Catholic Church towards openly contemplating some sort of formal break with the papacy. A key work published in 1716 which expressed much of this mood was *Of the Overthrow of the Liberties of the Gallican Church in the Affair of the Constitution "Unigenitus"*, by Nicolas Le Gross (1675–1751). Gross's treatise exalted the ordinary parish priest as essentially equal with the bishop in the government of the Church.

Four Jansenist bishops now appealed against *Unigenitus* to a general council of the whole Church (they were nicknamed the "appellants"). They were supported by a huge majority in Sorbonne and by twelve other bishops, including Archbishop Noailles. Pope Clement XI, fed up with Paris's troublesome prelate, wanted to strip him of his rank of cardinal, but the Regent resisted this move. In 1718, Clement condemned the four appellants in the bull *Pastoralis Officii* and excommunicated them. The bull required all the faithful to submit to *Unigenitus* or be likewise excommunicated. Noailles, however, appealed against the new bull. Ten thousand copies of his appeal were sold. This was the zenith of Jansenism's numerical strength: some ten per cent of all the French clergy, and seventy-five per cent of the parish clergy of Paris, declared themselves on Noailles' side.

But the Regent now drew back from the abyss. Philippe d'Orléans was a worldly-minded aristocrat who had no deep religious convictions and no stomach for the ultimate step of schism, with all the disorder it would inevitably bring. Pope Clement, too, had seen the wisdom of a more conciliatory approach. He therefore empowered Philippe's personal secretary Dubois to effect a compromise. On Dubois' advice, the Regent now browbeat the Jansenist intransigents by having

Jansenist writings burned in public. Then he won over the bothersome Noailles to head up an episcopal committee, whose remit was to draft a vaguely worded acceptance of *Unigenitus* that everyone could subscribe without violating their conscience. Noailles' committee produced the goods in 1720: a statement known as "the Accommodement", graced by Noailles' own signature.

16. The winter of Jansenism

The year of the *Accommodement*, 1720, can be taken as a convenient marker for Jansenism's fourth and final phase. The distinguished French Catholic historian, Daniel-Rops, compared the four phases of Jansenism to the four seasons: the springtime of Saint-Cyran, the high summer of Arnauld, the autumn of Quesnel, and now the winter, which lacked any dominating figure of spiritual stature. Quesnel had died in Amsterdam in December 1719, still refusing to accept *Unigenitus*, and appealing to a future general council of the Church to justify him. With his death came the onset of Jansenism's winter.

The *Accommodement*, despite bringing official peace, left the Jansenist movement still present and capable of causing major problems within French Catholicism. In December 1720, the four Jansenist bishops—the appellants—repeated their appeal over Pope Clement's head to a general council. Many parish priests subscribed the appeal. Clement died the following year, and his successor, Innocent XIII (1721–4), entered into diplomatic discussions with the Jansenists which can only be described as confused, if not anarchic. The next pope, Benedict XIII (1724–30), took a much harder line. He declared *Unigenitus* to be an article of faith for all loyal sons of the Church. This, however, created the backdrop for a new furore: in 1726, Bishop **Jean Soanen** of Sénez (1647–1740) published a pastoral letter withdrawing his submission to the *Accommodement*, condemning *Unigenitus*, extolling the appellant bishops as "sole defenders of the truth", advocating that the faithful read Quesnel, and virtually calling for schism along Gallican lines.

An incensed government ordered Soanen's archbishop, de Tencin of Embrun, to gather a provincial council to try Soanen. But thirty-one bishops declared their support for Soanen, and he managed to drag out the proceedings by endless appeals and legal quibbles. At length, however, in 1727, the council suspended him. Soanen was banished to the monastery of Chaise-Dieu, where he died in 1740, still defiant. For those last thirteen years he was a living Jansenist martyr. Why, we may ask, was Soanen was singled out for such persecution, while other Jansenist bishops were left undisciplined? Basically it was simply because Soanen was not of noble rank; he had no connections among the great families of France to protect his interests—extremely unusual for a French bishop at that time. His martyrdom was as much a social class phenomenon as a theological one.

The Soanen case ignited the Jansenist flames again. Across the country, Jansenists acclaimed the bishop as a martyr for truth. During this fresh upsurge, a new Jansenist newspaper, the *Ecclesiastical News*, was founded, first appearing in February 1728. Printed and distributed secretly, it was read far outside Jansenist circles, and continued publication till 1803. Its achievement in defying the most efficient police force in Christian Europe (the French authorities could never trace its writers or printers) gave the newspaper a high celebrity and a devoted readership. With journalistic invective, it kept up a steady stream of criticism aimed at clerical corruptions, the Jesuits, and anything else that offended Jansenist sensitivities.

Archbishop Noailles would have assumed leadership of this new manifestation of Jansenist feeling, but death cut him off in 1729. Under intense pressure from Cardinal **André Hercule de Fleury** (1653–1743), the new ruler of France during Louis XV's minority (Philippe d'Orléans had died in 1723), Noailles died professing complete submission to Rome and *Unigenitus*, and condemning Quesnel and the *Reflections*. The people of Paris were unimpressed, and sang mocking songs about the fickle archbishop. But Noailles had the last laugh. He had prepared a secret document recanting his submission, and it was published after his death!

The new Archbishop of Paris, de Vintimille, was no Jansenist. France's capital city had now lost the thirty-four years of episcopal protection for Jansenism it had enjoyed under Noailles. De Vintimille's instalment initiated a new fierce crackdown: the Sorbonne was purged of Jansenist sympathizers; suspect Parisian clergy were suspended; suspect seminaries were shut down, or put under new anti-Jansenist leadership. In 1730, Cardinal Fleury issued a declaration that *Unigenitus* was both a binding judgment of the Catholic Church and a law of the French state. From now on, all clergy who did not submit to *Unigenitus* in the plainest terms would be deprived. Appeals to parlement were prohibited. This declaration was registered by parlement, but only under extreme duress, involving the intimidating personal presence in parlement of the young King Louis XV (now twenty years old). Even then some Jansenist magistrates were intrepid enough to try to hold things up. The declaration, however, was registered. This scared most of the clergy into submitting.

But not all. Jansenism was bloodied but unbowed: a substantial minority of parish clergy remained defiant, along with many magistrates inspired by a mixture of Gallicanism and Jansenism. Parlement therefore rallied to the defence of the persecuted Jansenist clergy, despite Fleury's prohibition; and when the government refused to give heed, the entire legal profession went on strike in August 1731.

17. The Convulsionaries and the final transformation of Jansenism

The strangest episode in the entire history of Jansenism now arrived on the scene: the movement entered a pentecostal-charismatic phase. The outburst was focused on the tomb of a young deacon, François de Paris, a divinity graduate of the Saint-Magloire seminary, distinguished by his devoutness and hostility to *Unigenitus* (he had cursed it on his deathbed). The Jansenist deacon had been buried in the Saint-Médard parish of Paris 1727. Extraordinary religious events now began to occur at his tomb: healings, speaking in tongues, prophesyings, dancing in the

Spirit, and convulsions. From the last of these phenomena, those affected were nicknamed the "Convulsionaries". Many flocked to Saint-Médard to watch and take part. The more sober Jansenists found it distasteful, but most gladly hailed it as divine intervention supporting the Jansenist cause. The miracles were popularized in the *Ecclesiastical News*. For a while, it seemed that the eyes of all France were on the charismatic antics of Saint-Médard, and Cardinal Fleury's government was temporarily wrong-footed by this apparent heavenly vindication of Jansenism.

However, Fleury finally took action. First, he ended the damaging legal strike by an ambivalent formula that allowed the lawyers to claim they had won. Second, he shut down the Saint-Médard cemetery by resolute police action in January 1732. Someone put up a satirical placard on the gates of the forcibly closed cemetery:

> God, take note: by royal command,
> Miracles are in this place banned.

The dispersed Convulsionaries carried on a separate life of their own to the end of the century, meeting in private houses to prophesy, speak in tongues, and convulse. Ultimately the majority of Jansenists disowned them, embarrassed by their perceived irrationalities.

In the aftermath of the Saint-Médard affair, Jansenism underwent its final transformation into a largely non-clerical movement. It was no longer led by priests or monastics like Saint-Cyran, Arnauld, Quesnel, or the nuns of Port-Royal, but by the middle class laity, which flexed its muscles through parlement. Jansenism's greatest figure in this last phase was the lawyer **Louis Adrien Le Paige** (1712–1802). He was "bailiff of the Temple", a feudal position which the great noble, the Prince de Conti, had in his power to bestow on whom he wished; the position was exempt from all the normal jurisdictions of French government. Le Paige transformed it into a nerve centre of Jansenist activity. His masterpiece was his treatise *Historical Letters on the Essential Functions of the Parlement* (1753–4), which for the rest of the century supplied a battery of legal

methods to French dissenters (whether Jansenist or not) for
resisting the demands of authority.

When Cardinal Fleury died in 1743, King Louis XV
assumed personal government over the realm. A new mood
of anti-Jansenist belligerence was now gripping many of the
clergy, which Fleury had restrained because he did not wish
to create martyrs (perhaps he was haunted by the spectacle of
Soanen). With Fleury's restraining hand gone, anti-Jansenist
clergy now began demanding that, as a condition of the last
rites, the dying must produce a "letter of confession" signed by a
properly authorized priest. Convinced Jansenist laypeople could
easily find themselves without such a letter—not being able to
find an authorized priest who was himself a Jansenist and would
sign the letter for them.

The new Archbishop of Paris (from 1746) Christophe de
Beaumont, an aggressive opponent of Jansenism, pursued this
policy in his diocese. It resulted in a great scandal in 1749—the
funeral of Charles Coffin, former Rector of Paris University and
notorious Jansenist. Denied the last rites through not having a
letter of confession, he had to be buried in unconsecrated ground.
Four thousand people attended his funeral, demonstrating
solidarity with him. This sparked a new outbreak of Jansenist-
inspired militancy in parlement. It was in the wake of this
controversy over the letters of confession that the anti-Christian
French philosopher, Voltaire, made a famous remark:

> Would it not be fair and reasonable to suggest that the
> whole matter would have been brought to a satisfactory end
> by strangling the last Jesuit with the intestines of the last
> Jansenist?

The magistrates of parlement, at any rate, intervened in the
controversy and prohibited priests from demanding letters
of confession, or even from attacking Jansenism in sermons.
Further, they accused Archbishop Beaumont of promoting
schism through his persecution of Jansenists. Louis XV stepped
in, and overruled parlement by decreeing that no priest could
be legally prosecuted for refusing to administer the sacraments.

Parlement, however, countered the king by issuing a defiant statement. The situation was complicated by Archbishop Beaumont's attempt to purge Jansenists from the governing body of Paris's General Hospital (an association of charitable institutions for the care of the poor and destitute). The governors appealed to parlement, who championed their cause.

Two years of strife ensued between parlement and King Louis, from 1749 to 1751, culminating in another all-out strike by the legal profession. Louis forced the magistrates back to work by direct royal decree, only to see them take up a swathe of complaints by Jansenist laypeople who had been refused the sacraments by anti-Jansenist priests. Once again parlement defied all Louis' attempts to stop them. Early in 1753, a committee of Jansenist magistrates drafted a "Grand Remonstrance" against all the alleged crimes of the French bishops. This was then promulgated in the name of parlement. Louis reacted furiously by banishing all the magistrates of parlement in May 1753, and replaced parlement itself with a new royal chamber.

At length, after fifteen months of confrontation, Louis drew back and reached a compromise with the banished parlement, which he then recalled. To settle the "letters of confession" controversy, Louis promulgated a law of silence: neither side in the dispute was henceforth to raise the matter. When Archbishop Beaumont broke this law by supporting one of his priests who refused the last rites to a Jansenist woman, the king angrily exiled the Archbishop. Louis also persuaded Pope Benedict XIV to issue the bull *Ex Omnibus* in 1756, which prohibited priests from refusing the last rites to any but notorious sinners, or any who openly avowed their rejection of *Unigenitus*. So moderation triumphed.

By the close of this series of controversies, Jansenism had been almost completely transformed from its originally clerical, monastic, doctrinal-spiritual character into something like a lay political faction led by lawyers, whose overriding motive was to curb abuses of power by the French political and ecclesiastical hierarchy, and to promote a more republican ethos. Its history as a spiritually driven movement was largely over. Historians have discerned in this final politicized form of Jansenism one of the forces that would lead France to its earth-shaking revolution of 1789, when religion-sanctioned monarch and aristocracy were overthrown, and secular democracy established in their place.

18. Jansenism outside France

Although France was the heartland of Jansenism, it penetrated into other countries too, notably Belgium and northern Italy. Its greatest success, however, was in the Dutch Republic. Here Roman Catholicism was a minority faith in a land where the Dutch Reformed Church commanded the allegiance of most. However, this worked in Jansenism's favour, as it meant that the Dutch Catholics were under no pressure from a Roman Catholic government to conform to papal decrees, especially *Unigenitus*. Their freedom from political entanglement also gave them an openness to nonconformist ideas that no state-connected church could afford. The great Dutch city of Utrecht in particular became a Jansenist hotbed. Meanwhile Dutch Calvinists themselves encouraged Jansenism, because it seemed to them so close in spirit to their own Reformed theology.

The Dutch Catholics were governed by a "vicar apostolic". This figure was elected as Dutch Catholic archbishop by the priests attached to Utrecht Cathedral (known as the "chapter" of the Cathedral), but he was thereafter accountable to the pope. A number of these vicars apostolic in the 17th Century were sympathetic to Jansenism; the sympathy swelled to positive commitment in the case of Peter Codde (1648–1710), who in 1699 refused to sign the anti-Jansenist Formulary of Pope Alexander VII. In consequence he was suspended from office by Pope Innocent XII, who also dissolved the Cathedral chapter of Utrecht. In fact Codde ignored the suspension and carried on governing the Dutch Catholic community. This was made possible by the fact that the vast majority of Dutch Catholic priests were by now Jansenists. Their support was considerably augmented by Jansenists from Belgium, fleeing from persecution, especially in the aftermath of Unigenitus in 1713. When Codde died, the Dutch Catholics were without an archbishop, and could not elect a new one, since the Cathedral chapter had been dissolved.

But they kept up a supply of new priests, ordained for them by
French bishops sympathetic to Jansenism.

Finally in 1723, the Dutch Catholic clergy in Utrecht, firmly
committed to Jansenism and hostile to *Unigenitus*, had clearly
reached the parting of the ways with the papacy. On their own
initiative, they re-established the Cathedral chapter of Utrecht,
and elected a new archbishop, Cornelius Steenhoven, who was
consecrated in 1724 by an accommodating French bishop. So was
born the Dutch Jansenist Church, no longer in communion with
Rome. It was numerically quite strong in the 18th Century, but
dwindled in the 19th. The Dutch Jansenists found themselves an
object of high regard from many Protestants and reform-minded
Catholics outside their own country, owing to their plain style of
worship, their practice of electing their clergy, and their use of a
Dutch Bible and liturgy (i.e. not in Latin, but in the native language
of their country—remarkable in Roman Catholicism prior to
the Second Vatican Council of 1962–5). They also printed and
distributed a vast number of Jansenist writings, aided by the fact
that Holland was then the centre of the European printing industry.

The Dutch Jansenist Church still maintains a small existence
today as the Dutch "Old Catholics", in communion with the
Anglican Church.

19. The long-term effects of Jansenism

It is difficult to sum up the long-term effects of so complex a
movement as Jansenism. Negatively, its defeat (especially through
the *Unigenitus* bull of 1713) entailed the virtual obliteration of
the Augustinian doctrine of grace within the Roman Catholic
Church. In condemning Jansenism, Rome had unwittingly and
indirectly condemned Augustine. The long-running controversy
also served to poison the Church life of French Catholicism,
helping to make it increasingly vulnerable to the attack of anti-
Christian forces in the 18th century, culminating in the de-
Christianization campaign of the 1789 revolution.

After Jansenism had ceased to be a significant spiritual force
for reformation in the French Catholic Church, it nonetheless
survived in other, less tangible ways. Generally it had succeeded

in permeating large sections of French Catholicism with the leaven of a new seriousness about moral and religious life, even where the distinctive Jansenist theology was not understood or embraced. (In the France of today, the word "Jansenist" has persisted as a description of a person of unusual moral strictness and earnestness, much like the word "Puritan" in English.) A number of religious orders inspired by Port-Royal continued to function after its demolition in 1711, such as the Sisters of Saint Martha. Schools modelled on the Port-Royal "Little Schools", imbued with a Jansenist spirit, also lived on in France until the end of the 19th century.

The 19th century also witnessed the growth of a fascination (largely in France) with the history of Port-Royal, and the lives of its nuns and male solitaries, seen as spiritual heroes. This "cult" of Port-Royal has had a large dose of romanticism in it—admiration for rebels against authority, and sympathy for the persecuted. Even so, it has generated a colossal amount of literature, and helped keep alive the memory of Jansenism as it was in its springtime and summertime.

The greatest source of modern Jansenist influence, however, lies in the writings of Blaise Pascal, now widely accepted as an important philosopher (a designation that would have surprised him, as all he wished to be was a Christian apologist). Pascal's *Provincial Letters* to a limited extent, but much more his *Pensées*, continue to introduce each new generation to the mind of Jansenism's greatest thinker. There may not be much overt Jansenist theology in the *Pensées*, but it is pervaded by the typically Jansenist sense of human frailty and corruption, and of the inadequacy of reason or morality as a basis for finding God. To that extent, it perpetuates the outlook fostered by Jansen and Saint-Cyran.

Important people:

Michael Baius (1513–89)
Luis de Molina (1535–1600)
Robert Bellarmine (1542–1621)
Francis de Sales (1567–1622)
Pierre de Bérulle (1575–1629)

Vincent de Paul (c.1581–1660)
Jacques-Bénigne Bossuet (1627–1704)
Jean Racine (1639–99)

Jansenists

Saint-Cyran (1581–1643)
Cornelius Jansen (1585–1638)
Mother Angélique (1591–1661)
Antoine Arnauld (1612–94)
Isaac le Maistre de Sacy (1613–84)
Blaise Pascal (1623–62)
Mother Angélique de Saint-Jean (1624–84)
Pierre Nicole (1625–95)
Pasquier Quesnel (1634–1719)
Jean Soanen (1647–1740)
Cardinal Noailles (1651–1729)
Louis Adrien Le Paige (1712–1802)

Kings, popes, politicians

Cardinal Richelieu (1585–1642)
King Henry IV (1589–1610)
Cardinal Mazarin (1602–61)
King Louis XIII (1610–43)
King Louis XIV (1643–1715)
Pope Innocent X (1644–55)
Cardinal Fleury (1653–1743)
Philippe d'Orléans (1674–1723)
Pope Innocent XI (1676–89)
Pope Clement XI (1700–1721)
King Louis XV (1715–74)

Primary source material

Robert Bellarmine: the necessity and benefit of prayer

Holy Scripture emphasizes the necessity of prayer so often, nothing is more plainly commanded than this duty. Of course the all-powerful God knows what we need, as our Lord Himself says in Matthew's Gospel; yet He wants us to ask for what we need, and by prayer to grasp hold of it, just as though we used spiritual hands or suchlike. Listen to our Lord in Luke's Gospel: "We ought always to pray, and not to faint"; and again, "Watch therefore, praying at all times" (ch. 18 and 21). Listen to the apostle: "Pray without ceasing," and the book of Ecclesiasticus, "Let nothing hinder you from praying always" (ch. 18).

These commands do not mean that we should do nothing else but pray. Rather they mean that we should never neglect this healthy exercise, and should often engage in it. So our Lord and His apostles have taught us. They did not "always" pray, in the sense of omitting to preach to people, confirming what they said by signs and miracles. Yet it could be said they were always praying, because of the frequency with which they prayed. That is also how we should understand these words: "My eyes are always towards the Lord"; and again, "His praise shall always be in my mouth"; and the words about the apostles, "They were always in the temple, praising and blessing God"...

In short, prayer can secure many gifts for us, as Saint John Chrysostom teaches us so beautifully in his two books on prayer. He compares prayer with our hands. When a human being is born, he is naked, helpless, and in need of everything. But he cannot protest against his Creator, because He has given him hands, and these are incomparable organs, which enable a person to get food, clothes, house, and so on, for himself. Likewise in a spiritual sense, we can do nothing without God's help; but we do have the ability to pray, the supreme spiritual organ, by which we can easily acquire everything for our souls...

There are also many other blessings that flow from prayer. First, prayer brings light into the mind. The eye of the soul cannot be fastened directly on God, who is the light, without being illuminated by Him. "Come to Him and be enlightened", says David.

Second, prayer strengthens our trust and confidence; for the more often we speak to someone, the more confidently we draw close to him.

Third, prayer sets our hearts on fire with charity, and so makes our souls capable of receiving even greater gifts, as Saint Augustine says.

Fourth, prayer deepens humility and wholesome fear. This is because whoever prays confesses that he is a beggar in God's sight, and therefore humbles himself before God, and takes care not to grieve Him, since he needs God's help in every situation.

Fifth, prayer breeds up in our minds a disdain for all the good things of this world. All the objects of this fleeting life must appear cheap and contemptible in the eyes of one who continually meditates on things spiritual and eternal.

Sixth, prayer gives us an unspeakable joy, because in prayer we begin to taste the sweetness of the Lord. How great this sweetness is, we may gather from this fact alone, that I have known some people pass not just nights, but even entire days and nights in prayer, without any difficulty or trouble. In short, prayer is not only useful and delightful, it also bestows nobility and glory upon us. The very angels themselves venerate the soul whom they see is admitted so often and so intimately to converse with the divine Majesty.

Cardinal Robert Bellarmine
The Art of Dying Well, Chapter 7

Francis de Sales: be gentle in your repentance

One of the best acts of gentleness we can carry out is toward ourselves, in never getting upset with ourselves and our own faults. Reason of course does demand that we should be sad and sorry for any sins when we commit them. Even so, we should not give way to a harsh, grim, vindictive passion against them. Many people go seriously wrong here. They are angry with themselves for being angry, vexed with themselves for yielding to vexation, and upset with themselves for getting upset. And so they keep their heart for ever churned in anger. It seems as though the second anger drives out the first, but its actual effect is to open a door for fresh anger the moment the opportunity arises.

Besides, these feelings of anger, vindictiveness, and frustration against ourselves encourage pride; they stem entirely from self-love, which is disturbed and disquieted to see itself so imperfect. We should be displeased by our defects in a peaceful, unruffled, and firm way. A judge punishes wrongdoers much better when reason guides his sentences, and he proceeds in a calm spirit, rather than acting with fury and resentment. If he judges in a rage, he punishes the faults not according to their actual nature, but according to his own nature. Likewise we correct ourselves much more effectively by a serene and temperate repentance, rather than by a violent, hasty, and angry repentance. Repentance in rage does not proceed according to the nature of our faults, but according to our feelings.

For example, a person who aspires to chastity will be upset with an unbalanced bitterness at the smallest offence committed against that particular virtue, and yet will laugh off a terrible slander he or she has committed. On the other hand, a person who hates slander will be tortured over some little grumble against another, and yet make nothing of a flagrant offence committed against chastity. And so on and so forth. Now all this flows entirely from this cause, that such people are guided not by reason but by emotion in assessing their consciences.

Believe me, Philothea, the rebukes of a father given in a gentle and affectionate way have far greater power than fury and fierceness to set a child right. Likewise, when our heart has committed any sin, if we take it to task with gentle and calm rebukes, having compassion for it rather than passion against it, and encouraging it to change its ways, our repentance will last much longer, and penetrate much deeper, than a petulant, reproachful, and furious repentance.

Francis de Sales
Introduction to the Devout Life, **Part 3, Chapter 9**

Bossuet: the death of the Prince of Condé

[Louis de Bourbon, the Prince of Condé (1621–86), was one of France's greatest 17th century generals. His military brilliance in the Thirty Years' War against the Habsburgs initiated France's dominance of Continental Europe; by the time he died, he had earned the nickname "the Great Condé" for his battlefield skills.]

As I begin this oration, in which I propose to celebrate the deathless glory of Louis de Bourbon, the Prince of Condé, I feel myself weighed down both by the lofty nature of my subject and, in all honesty, by the futility of my attempt. Is there any part of the inhabited globe that has not heard of the Prince of Condé's victories, and the amazing events of his life? People speak of them everywhere. The Frenchman who extols them to foreigners tells them nothing they do not already know. No matter how exalted the pitch in which I might sing his praises, I would still sense a conviction in your hearts that I deserved a reprimand for coming so far short of doing him justice…

What was transpiring in that soul at that moment [when he died]? What new light was breaking upon him? What sudden radiance pierced the cloud, and immediately scattered all the darkness of sense, and even the very shadows of faith—shall I dare to say the holy obscurities of faith? In that moment, what became of the titles of earthly dignity that flatter our vanity? On the very brink of glory, in the dawn of such beauteous light, O how quickly the phantoms of the world fade away! O how dim the splendour then seems of the most illustrious victory! How deeply then we despise the glory of this world; how deeply we deplore it that our eyes were ever beguiled by its glitter! Come now, people, come now—or rather, you princes, masters, and judges of the earth, and you priests who open the gates of heaven. Above all else, you princes and princesses nobly sprung from a long line of kings: the luminaries of France, but in shadows today, overcast with clouds of grief—come now, come and see what little is left of a birth so honourable, a majesty so elevated, a glory so ravishing! Look around you on every side. See everything that pomp and devotion can do to honour such a towering hero. See titles and inscriptions, empty tokens of what is no more. See shadows weeping around a coffin: frail images of a sorrow swept away by time, along with everything else. See columns looking as though they would lift to heaven the grandiose evidence of our nothingness. Indeed, nothing is lacking in all these honours: nothing save the very one to whom they are offered! Weep, then, over this insubstantial residue of human life; weep over the cheerless immortality we bestow on heroes.

But come close, all you who so ardently pursue a career of military glory—you brave and warlike spirits! Come especially close. Who was worthier than he to lead you? Did you ever find a leader so honourable? Weep for that great captain, and as you weep, say: "Here is the man who led us through all dangers, whose influence moulded so many other famous captains, inspired by his example to the highest honours of battle. His very shadow might yet win battles! In his silence, his mere name rouses our souls. And yet at the same time, it warns us: if we would find, when we die, some rest from our labours—if we would arrive prepared for our eternal home—then we servants of an earthly king must also serve the King of Heaven."

Yes, serve that King immortal and always merciful. He regards a sigh or a cup of cold water given in His name, much more than the world regards the shedding of your blood. Begin to count the time of your profitable service from the day on which you surrendered yourselves to so loving a Lord.

And you, whom the prince honoured by making you his friends—will you not come too? In whatever degree you enjoyed his trust, come all of you, and surround this sepulchre. Let your tears be mingled with prayers. And as you admire in this great prince a friendship so wonderful, and a fellowship so sweet, do not neglect the memory of a hero whose bravery in battle was matched by his personal goodness. Then he will continue to be your treasured teacher; you will reap dividends from his virtues; and his death, which you mourn, will minister to you both a comfort and an example.

Jacques-Bénigne Bossuet
On the Death of the Great Condé

Pascal's Pensées

172. God orders all things gently, and His way is to infuse Christianity into our minds with reasoned arguments, and into our hearts with grace. Trying to infuse it into our hearts and minds with force and with threats would merely infuse terror, not Christianity.

173. If we submit everything to reason, there will be nothing mysterious or supernatural left in Christianity. But if we violate the principles of reason, our Christianity will be silly and nonsensical.

190. The philosophical proofs for God's existence are so inaccessible to human reasoning, and so complicated, that they make little impression. Even if they helped some people, it would be only for the brief duration of their attending to the proof. An hour later, they would be afraid they had made a mistake!

192. Knowing God without knowing our own poverty produces pride. Knowing our poverty without knowing God produces despair. Knowing Jesus Christ strikes the true balance, because in Him we know both God and our own poverty.

380. Do not be surprised when you see simple people believing without argument. God causes them to love Him and hate themselves. He inclines their hearts to faith. We will never believe with an effective assent and faith unless God inclines our hearts. But the moment He does this, we shall believe. David knew this perfectly well: "Incline my heart to Your testimonies" [Psalm 119:36].

417. Not only do we know God through Jesus Christ alone; we know ourselves through Jesus Christ alone. We know life and death through Jesus Christ alone. Apart from Jesus Christ, we cannot know the meaning of our life, our death, God, or ourselves. Therefore, without Scripture—whose sole theme is Christ—we know nothing and can see nothing in the nature of God, or in nature herself, nothing except shadows and confusion.

423. The heart has its reasons of which reason knows nothing.

424. It is the heart, not the reason, that perceives God. This is faith: to perceive God by the heart, not by the reason.

688. What is the self?... What about a man who delights in a woman on account of her beauty? Does he delight in *her*? No, because smallpox will destroy her beauty without destroying her person, and will bring to an end to his delight in her. What if someone delights in me for my intelligence or memory: do they delight in me, myself? No, because I could lose these attributes without losing my self. Where is this "self", then, since it seems to be neither in the body nor in the soul? And how can we delight in body or soul except on account of their attributes, which can perish and therefore do not define the basic self? Are we to delight in the essence of a person's soul, in the abstract, regardless of the attributes it might have? That is both impossible and wrong. Therefore we never delight in persons, only in attributes.

> **Blaise Pascal**
> *Pensées*

Pascal's Memorial

The year of grace 1654
Monday 23rd November, Saint Clement's Day,
pope and martyr, and others in the martyrology.
The eve of Saint Chrysogone's Day, martyr and others.
From about half past ten in the evening until about half past
  midnight,

FIRE

GOD of Abraham, GOD of Isaac, GOD of Jacob
not that of the philosophers and scholars
Certainty. Certainty. Emotion. Joy. Peace
GOD of Jesus Christ
My God and your God[7]
Your GOD shall be my GOD[8]
Forgotten by the world and by all, apart from GOD

---

7. John 20:17.
8. Ruth 1:16.

He can only be found by the ways taught in the Gospel
Value of the human soul
Righteous Father, the world didn't know You, but I knew
    You[9]
Joy, joy, joy, tears of joy
I went away
They abandoned Me, the fount of living water[10]
My God, will you leave me?
May I not be eternally separated from Him
This is eternal life, that they might know You, the one true
    God, and the One whom You sent, Jesus Christ[11]
Jesus Christ
Jesus Christ
I went away; I fled from Him, denied Him, crucified Him
May I never be separated from Him
He only saves in the ways taught in the Gospel
Total and sweet renunciation
Total submission to Jesus Christ and my director[12]
Eternally in joy in exchange for one day's exertion on earth
I will not forget your words. Amen

Quesnel: select passages from his
Reflections on the New Testament

The ceremonial law, which is no more than a type and shadow
of Christ, destroys itself by revealing Jesus Christ to us, who is
the truth and the substance of the ceremonies. The moral law, by
leaving us to our own inability under sin and the curse, makes us
perceive the necessity of having the law written on the heart, and
of a Saviour to bestow this upon us. To the old self belongs the
law, in its ministry of terrifying us and treating us as slaves; and
together with the old self, that law was crucified and died with

---

9. John 17:25.

10. Jeremiah 2:13.

11. John 17:3.

12. Pascal's "spiritual director", the Jansenist Isaac de Maistre la Sacy, who
    exercised spiritual supervision over Port-Royal.

Christ upon the cross. The new self, and the new law, require a new sacrifice. What need has a person of other sacrifices, if he or she has Jesus Christ? They in whom this Sacrifice lives, themselves live to God alone. However, none can live to Him except by faith; and this life of faith consists in dying with Christ to the things of the present world, and in expecting, as co-heirs with Him, the blessings of the eternal world. Who can work all this in us, but He alone who lives in us? That person has arrived to a high degree of mortification, who can say "Christ lives in me, and I am crucified to the world." Such a person must have renounced not only earthly things, but self too.

See here the perfect pattern of an evangelical preacher:

1. To go and seek out sinners on every side, that he may show them the way to heaven.

2. To preach the gospel of the kingdom, not with a servile spirit, but with a freedom worthy of the King whom he serves, and of the kingdom which he proclaims.

3. To make his reputation and the confidence of the people subservient, not to his own interest, but to the good of souls, and to the establishing of the kingdom of God.

4. To speak nothing but what may lead toward salvation.

5. To join to preaching the exercise of works of mercy, and assistance in the things of this world, as often as he can.

6. To visit all those who apply to him as penitents, however great their sinfulness, and whatever their condition in life.

7. To take care to make people conscious that diseases, and all kinds of worldly evils, are the effect of sin; that whether God is pleased to remove them or not, it is for the good of the soul and to promote our eternal salvation; and that the power which He makes to appear in healing them is a sure sign of the power of His grace to heal our souls.

Everything is contrary to salvation without Jesus Christ. He leaves us sometimes to ourselves, on purpose that we may know ourselves, and the need we have of Him; but He never loses sight of us. This is a picture of the church guided by its pastors. If people would but consider pastors as mariners, always tugging at the oar, always rowing against the wind, and always in danger, they would not envy their condition. Their comfort is, that Christ has His eye continually on the boat, that He sees their pains and difficulties, and will certainly come to their assistance. He frequently lets a great part of the night pass away, without succouring His church in a plain and obvious manner. This is to give us occasion to exercise our trust and confidence toward Him, and to await His proper time.

Let the crown of thorns make those Christians blush who waste so much time, trouble, and money, in beautifying and adorning a sinful head. Let the world do what it will to render the royalty and mysteries of Christ contemptible, it is my glory to serve a King thus debased; my salvation, to adore that which the world despises; and my redemption, to go to God through the merits of Him who had thorns for His crown.

Since Jesus Christ only ever wrote once that we hear of in His whole life; since He did it only in the dust; since it was only to avoid condemning a sinner; and since He would not have what He wrote so much as known; let us learn from this never to write but when it is necessary or useful; to do it with humility and modesty; and to do it from a principle of charity.[13]

Pasquier Quesnel
Moral Reflections on the New Testament

---

13. Useful thoughts when posting anything on the internet.

Chapter 7

The Roman Catholic Church Part Two

1

Gallicanism: who rules the French Church?

1. The foundations of a theory

Gallicanism[1] was an attitude that grew out of the French monarchy's claim to a special relationship with the papacy, which (it was said) gave special privileges to the French Catholic Church. The Church in France, according to Gallicanism, possessed a certain independence from the papacy, with the French king exercising many of the pope's powers. In the 17th century, this view gained impetus from the success of absolutism in government: the concentration of power in the person of the French king lent itself to seeing him as the proper governor of Church as well as state within his kingdom. It is not very surprising, then, that during the reign of Louis XIV, when absolutism reached its pinnacle, Gallicanism also prospered as never before. Indeed, it acquired such a grip on French Catholic sentiment, especially within the royal court, that it pushed the Church in France to the brink of schism with the papacy.

Gallicanism had a long growth. It had been taught in seed-form by the theologians of Paris University's theology faculty, the Sorbonne, soon after its founding in 1257.[2] It first achieved

---

1. From the Latin word for "French", *Gallus*. The old Roman name for France was Gaul.

2. The Sorbonne was initially a university college for students training for the doctor of theology degree. In 1554, it became the meeting place of Paris University's theology faculty.

dramatic visibility in 1438, amid the crisis of the conciliar movement,[3] in the "Pragmatic Sanction of Bourges". By this affirmation, the French clergy asserted the right of the French Church to manage its property independently of the pope, and prohibited popes from nominating men to vacant French bishoprics. A new compromise agreement was struck in 1516, the Concordat of Bologna: the French king could nominate men to be heads of metropolitan and cathedral churches, and abbeys, but the right returned to the pope if two invalid nominations were made. Gallican sentiment was sufficiently entrenched at the time of the Council of Trent for the Council's decrees on church organisational matters to be ignored in Catholic France.[4]

Three of the most significant Gallican theorists flourished in Trent's aftermath: Pierre Pithou, Edmond Richer, and Pierre de Marca. **Pierre Pithou** (1539–96) was a notable lawyer. Raised a Huguenot, he survived the massacre of Saint Bartholomew's Day in 1572 by a hair's breadth; traumatized, he converted to Roman Catholicism the following year. The first to articulate clearly and forcefully an overall theory of Gallicanism, he set this forth in his sensation-making treatise *The Liberties of the Gallican Church* (1594), which was to be the basic manual of Gallicanism for the next 200 years. In essence, Pithou restricted the powers of the pope to purely spiritual matters; in organizational matters, he made the French monarch effective head of the French Church. For instance, Pithou maintained the power of the French crown to prevent French bishops communicating with or travelling to Rome (e.g. to protest against a royal decision), and denied the pope's right in France to assemble Church councils or publish papal decrees without the crown's consent.

Edmond Richer (1559–1631) was a member of the Sorbonne senate. His contribution to Gallicanism was his influential *De*

---

3. For the conciliar movement, which sought to make the papacy accountable to the wider Church, see *Volume Two: The Middle Ages*, Chapter 10, section 3.

4. The Council of Trent formulated the Roman Catholic response to the Reformation in the mid-16th century. See *Volume Three: Renaissance and Reformation*, Chapter 8, section 3.

Ecclesiastica et Politica Potestate Libellus ("Tract on Ecclesiastical and Political Power"), published in 1611. In somewhat democratic vein, Richer taught that Church power belonged primarily to the whole body of believers, which they delegated to the clergy. Christ had not appointed Peter as sole head of the Church, but had committed leadership collectively to all 12 apostles. Church government was thus corporate in nature, not a papal monarchy—hence the right of national Churches (all the faithful in a particular nation) to a measure of autonomy from Rome. These views were in many ways a revival of the conciliarism of the 15th century. Richer also exalted the status of parish priests, whom he made essentially equal to bishops; in this respect, his view has been called "Catholic Presbyterianism". It was all part of his philosophy of decentralizing power, whether in pope or bishop.

Pierre de Marca (1594–1662) was a canon lawyer. A committed Gallican, he wrote a number of dissertations on the subject which impressed Cardinal Richelieu. At Richelieu's bidding, Marca published his dissertations in a single volume in 1641, his De Concordia Sacerdotii et Imperii ("On the Harmony between Priesthood and Kingship"). The strong Gallican tenets of this influential treatise (for instance, that papal laws are not binding until the nation to which they apply gives its consent) so outraged Pope Urban VIII that he had it put on the Index of Forbidden Books in 1642. Even so, the book was republished in an enlarged edition in 1663, a year after de Marca's death. This edition too was placed on the Index. De Marca himself, despite the papal fury heaped on his book, achieved high eminence in the French Church; he eventually submitted to Rome's correction, becoming Archbishop of Toulouse in 1652, and of Paris in 1662. Regardless of his recantation, however, his Gallican theories bloomed.

The climate of opinion in 17th century France, then, allowed Gallicanism to flourish. Pithou, Richer, and de Marca all contributed to a swelling tide of feeling that the Catholic Church of France, under the monarch (especially the awesome Louis XIV), was no mere province of the Roman papacy, but a semi-independent body with its own cherished rights and traditions, which popes disrespected at their peril. Indeed, in 1663, the Sorbonne itself, the most illustrious theological college in Roman Catholic Christendom, issued a firm declaration of Gallican principles: it denied that the papacy had any political power over the French monarchy, that popes were superior to general councils of the Church, or that a pope was infallible unless his pronouncements were ratified by the whole Church.

2. *The crisis: 1673–93*

This thriving Gallican sentiment in France erupted into positive crisis in the period 1673–93. The spark that lit the blaze was the *régale*—the right of the French king to receive the revenues of a vacant bishopric (the *régale temporelle*), and to appoint clergy in certain dioceses (the *régale spirituelle*). This royal right did not as yet apply to large parts of southern France; the legal existence of the *régale* dated back to the Concordat of Bologna in 1516, when much of the south was not directly under the French crown's sovereignty. Since 1608, debate had churned over whether the *régale* should be extended to southern France. King Louis XIV decided to bring the debate to an abrupt end by decreeing unilaterally, in 1673, that the whole of France was now subject to the *régale*. The decree impinged on 59 of France's 130 bishops. Only two bishops protested, Pavillon of Alet and Caulet of Pamiers, both Jansenist sympathizers (see the previous chapter for Jansenism). After Pavillon's death, Caulet battled on alone, strongly backed by Pope *Innocent XI* (1676– 89), who overturned all decisions against Caulet by his royalist archbishop. Caulet died in 1680, but Pope Innocent by now was locked in conflict with Louis over the principles involved.

Relations between Louis and Innocent deteriorated rapidly. Innocent (real name Benedict Odescalchi, born 1611) was a man of high ethical integrity, a scholar who had been a model priest before his elevation to power in the Church. It is said that he often wept while celebrating mass, emotionally overcome by the glory and love of God, and his own unworthiness. The ordinary people of Rome looked on him as a living saint. Quite immune to the French king's threats and bullying, Innocent took issue with him over matters other than the *régale*, especially his military policies. For example, he criticized Louis' alliances with the Muslim Ottoman Empire against Christian countries, and his habit of annexing territories by simply marching his troops in without any legal declaration of war.

Faced with such unbending opposition from high-principled Innocent, Louis' patience finally snapped. He summoned a general assembly of the French clergy, which met from October 1681 to May 1682, in order to unite the French Church behind him in defying the pope over the matter of the *régale*. There was little doubt of the assembly's support for its monarch, but how to formulate that support proved to be a matter of lengthy controversy. The Archbishop of Paris, Harlay de Champvallon (1625–95), was an extreme Gallican who championed Louis' cause with unrestrained fervour; but he was opposed by Jacques-Bénigne Bossuet, Bishop of Meaux, France's greatest preacher, whose Gallicanism was of a much more moderate type (see chapter 6, section 3.5 for more on Bossuet).

3. The Four Articles (1682)

The assembly discussed the *régale*, but this was soon swallowed up in a furore of passionate debate about more basic issues. Arguments for and against papal infallibility raged back and forth; the most radical Gallicans among the clergy even spoke of disowning the papacy altogether. At length Bossuet's moderation prevailed; he was determined to guide the French Church to a mediating position that would uphold the king's authority and the "liberties of the Gallican Church", without severing ties with the papacy. To that end, Bossuet drafted what became known as the Four Articles, which the assembly unanimously approved on 19th March 1682. Although in temperate form, the Articles set forth a definite Gallican position, which we could summarize thus:

1. God has given the papacy and the Church dominion over spiritual matters only, but not political matters. Therefore the pope has no power to depose kings, or

to absolve citizens from their duty to submit to their rightful rulers.

2. The pope's "plenitude of power" in things spiritual does not detract from the sacrosanct decrees of the Council of Constance (1414–18), contained in its fourth and fifth sessions (these laid down the conciliar theory of Church government, in particular that popes were subject to ecumenical councils).[5]

3. The pope's authority must be exercised in accordance with the established laws, liberties, and customs of the French kingdom and Church, which have their own inviolable dignity.

4. Although the pope takes the lead in defining the faith for the universal Church, his judgement is open to correction until approved by the whole Church.

The Four Articles were immediately endorsed by the parlement of Paris, and announced as the law of the land. Unlike the English Westminster parliament, a French parlement was not an elected institution, but more like a corporation of lawyers. Every major French city had a parlement. The Paris parlement was the most important, because to it belonged the right to "register" (ratify) the king's edicts, giving them legal force. It also had the right to complain about proposed new laws without fear of punishment. Often the Paris parlement was at the forefront of opposition to royal policy. In matters pertaining to Gallicanism, however, king and parlement were usually at one.

Determined to place the stamp of his authority on his kingdom, and root out any pro-papal sentiment, Louis ordered that the Four Articles be taught as official doctrine in all French universities and seminaries; all candidates for a theological degree had to subscribe to the Gallican manifesto. Pope Innocent, however, condemned the Articles indignantly—"with

---

5. For the Council of Constance, see *Volume Two: The Middle Ages*, Chapter 10, section 3.

a shudder of disgust"—and for the next seven years, the French court and the papacy were virtually at war with each other. Innocent, unimpressed by the rallying of the French clergy to Louis, refused to recognize any of the bishops Louis appointed to vacant dioceses by means of the disputed *régale*; by the end of the crisis, 35 French dioceses had "king's bishops" out of communion with the pope.

(Incidentally, this state of affairs means that when Louis revoked the Edict of Nantes in 1685, stripping French Protestants of their religious liberty in order to force them back into the Roman Catholic Church, Louis was himself at daggers drawn with the papacy over the Gallican conflict— indeed, within two years, Louis would be excommunicated! This must count as one of the greatest ironies of Church history in the period covered by this volume. See section 3, below for the revocation of the Edict of Nantes.)

Relations between Louis and Innocent hit rock-bottom in 1687. Innocent annulled a diplomatic immunity enjoyed by ambassadors in Rome which had exempted them from police supervision; all governments save the French agreed to this. Louis refused to submit; Innocent excommunicated the French ambassador; Louis promptly put the papal nuncio (Innocent's diplomatic representative in France) under arrest. For Innocent this outrage was the last straw, and on 16th November 1687, he excommunicated Louis. Out of consideration for Louis' commanding stature as the greatest Roman Catholic king in Christendom, however, Innocent did not make the excommunication public; he informed Louis privately that he was now cut off from the sacraments of his Church.

4. Peace restored

The deadlock between Louis and Innocent was broken only by the latter's death in August 1689. The French king was by this time becoming weary of the struggle; the religious side of his nature felt keenly his disharmony with the visible head of his Church. His foreign wars were starting to go badly; a favourable pope would be a comfort, both spiritually and diplomatically.

Besides, Louis needed papal support if he was ever to resolve
the Jansenist controversy that was still disrupting the internal
peace of French Catholicism (see previous chapter). The death
of Innocent XI enabled Louis to claim that the quarrel of the
past decade had been a purely personal one between himself and
the late pope; to Louis' relief, more flexible men now sat on the
papal throne, willing to hear the French king's claims.

After negotiations, the Gallican crisis ended at last in
1693, when Louis and new pope Innocent XII (1691–1700)
agreed terms. Louis withdrew the Four Articles, and made his
"king's bishops" each write to the pope disowning the Articles.
For his part, Innocent accepted the extension of the *régale*
over the whole of southern France, and (on receiving their
letter of apology) recognized the "king's bishops" as properly
ordained. Catholic France was once more in full communion
with Rome.

The immediate crisis was over; but Gallicanism itself was
far from dead. It lived on as a powerful sentiment within the
body of French Catholicism. Most of the parlements of France
declined to recognize the withdrawal of the Four Articles,
and suppressed any writings that questioned their teaching;
the Articles continued to be taught in many universities and
seminaries, albeit without royal sanction; and they remained the
belief of most French Catholics, laity and clergy alike.

2

Quietism: to be or not to be mystical

The third of the internal crises within Roman Catholicism in our period was the movement known as Quietism (from the Latin for "stillness", "absence of activity"). Although not as convulsive in its effects as Gallicanism or Jansenism, it nonetheless catapulted two of France's greatest Catholic thinkers, writers, and preachers—Bossuet and Fénelon—into sensational conflict, resulting in Fénelon's ruin. Quietism was also destined to spread far beyond the boundaries of the Roman Catholic Church through its spiritual impact on the Protestant world.

1. Miguel de Molinos
The originator of Quietism was a Spanish priest, *Miguel de Molinos* (1628–96).[1] Born at Muniesa in Aragon, Molinos studied under the Jesuits, and was ordained to the priesthood in 1652. As a priest in Valencia, he was an admired preacher; his mind glowed with the energy of intense thought, and his services as a spiritual director were much sought after. He moved to Rome in 1663, where he soon became an influential father-confessor, counting cardinals among his spiritual clientele, including the future pope Innocent XI (then Cardinal Odescalchi). Molinos was also very popular with the religiously

---

1. Not to be confused with his compatriot Luis de Molina: see Chapter 6, section 4.2 for Molina.

minded female aristocracy of Rome. In 1675 he published two important treatises, both in Italian—his *Brief Tract on Frequent Communion* and his *Spiritual Guide*. The *Guide* was the real charter of Quietism. Drawing on the great 16th century Spanish mystics, Teresa of Avila and John of the Cross, although pressing beyond them, Molinos elaborated a vision of the Christian life which many found enthralling.[2]

At the heart of Molinos' spirituality lay the rejection of all human effort. For a human being to act towards God, he taught, was in itself sin. Spiritual perfection required total passivity in God's presence, and the annihilation of the human will. This state of annihilation he termed "mystic death". How did one achieve mystic death? By a process of mental prayer, which discarded all meditation and all distinct acts of will; instead, the soul simply rested passively before God. In this perfect state, a person would no longer care even about his own salvation, heaven or hell. All external acts were now redundant; indeed, sin was now impossible. Satan might force the perfect soul to do things that would be sinful in the imperfect, but they could not truly be sins in one whose will had been annihilated. In fact, Molinos said, it was positively harmful to resist temptation, since resistance was an act, and human acts were improper in the spiritual sphere.

At this juncture in his career, Molinos and his Quietist teaching were very fashionable; critics of his writings were censured by the Inquisition. Within a decade, however, the tide of opinion had turned against the Spaniard. This was partly because some confessors alerted their superiors to the fact that a number of Molinos' disciples (especially female ones) were giving an alarming spin to his teachings, using them to justify sexually dubious conduct. Ardent piety and audacious sensuality seemed to be blending. But how could their actions be wrong, these Quietists asked, when their wills had been annihilated in the perfection of mystic death? Some too, in their enthusiasm for mental prayer, were abandoning or even denouncing vocal prayer. In some convents, apparently,

---

2. See *Volume Three: Renaissance and Reformation*, Chapter 8, section 6, for Teresa and John.

Quietism had got such a grip that vocal prayer had actually been suppressed. Unsavoury rumours also began circulating about Molinos' personal relations with his female disciples. And Pope Innocent XI's confessor, father Marrachi, was pressing hard for action against Molinos. It has been suggested that Marrachi, a Jesuit, saw Quietism as an anti-authority sect within the Church, akin to Jansenism; having declared war on one such sect, the Jesuits could hardly tolerate the other.

In consequence, Molinos was arrested by the Inquisition in 1686. Many of his disciples were also arrested, some of whom confessed to immoral conduct. In November 1687, in the bull *Coelestis Pastor*, Innocent XI condemned sixty-eight propositions from the treatises of Molinos. All his writings were placed on the Index of Forbidden Books. The Spanish Quietist submitted unreservedly, but spent the rest of his life in prison. Innocent refused, however, to let his one-time confessor be put to death, as some demanded.

2. Madame Guyon

The story of Quietism did not end with the condemnation of Molinos. In a modified form, the movement gained a new lease of life in France, through one of Christianity's most famous and controversial feminine mystics, *Jeanne Marie Bouvier de la Mothe Guyon* (1648–1717), usually known simply as Madame Guyon. Born at Montargis, she was a strange child and teenager, who even at that early age claimed supernatural visions. In 1664, aged sixteen, she married her cousin Jacques Guyon, an easy-going invalid twenty-two years her senior. The day after the wedding, Madame Guyon decided that marriage was odious to her, and that she should have been a nun! Perhaps unsurprisingly, there followed a lengthy bad experience with her husband and his mother. As though in compensation, the disappointed young wife began having intense spiritual experiences, during one of which Jesus appeared and put an invisible ring of "mystical marriage" on her finger, claiming her for Himself.

After her husband's death in 1676, Madame Guyon (now twenty-eight) used her new liberty to become a sort of freelance instructor in the true Christian life. She was extremely eloquent; few could resist her torrent of edifying words. She had already met her ideal soul-mate while still married: a Barnabite priest and disciple of Molinos, named ***François Lacombe*** (1643–1715).

Father Lacombe was born at Thonon, on the south side of the Lake of Geneva. After entering the Barnabite order, he became the head of its community at Thonon. He appears to have been a highly emotional and impulsive personality, lacking in intellectual clarity. On visits to Rome he became a convert to the doctrines of Molinos. Madame Guyon, now free of marriage ties, remembered the fascinating Barnabite priest, sought him out at Thonon, and placed herself under his spiritual direction. The two seemed to become fused into a single soul; Father Lacombe's influence on Madame Guyon was so profound, he could cure her of headaches simply with a touch. The young widow and the priest were utterly devoted to each other, to the extent that rumours were soon flying around of the impure nature of their relationship. Madame Guyon, under duress, would later confess to exchanging "innocent kisses" with Father Lacombe, but nothing more.

Since Lacombe was a zealous follower of Molinos, the partnership between himself and Madame Guyon became a channel through which Quietism now began flowing into the most respectable religious circles in France. The two spiritual companions engaged in a five year trek over France to disseminate Molinos' teaching. Madame Guyon made a particular hit in Paris, where the feminine upper classes, hungry for a dimension to their lives that would transcend the glitter of the world, went into a state of collective rapture over this magnetic "high priestess" of Quietism. Madame Guyon summed up her teaching in a treatise entitled *A Short and Easy Method of Prayer* (1685), which proved very popular. In essence, the treatise taught a toned-down version of Molinos' Quietism, leaving out his contentious claim that Satan could compel the annihilated will to sin. Even so, Madame Guyon did hold that, by its very detachment from external things, the annihilated will could be led to perform acts which, if committed by imperfect souls, would be sin. (The treatise was placed on the Index of Forbidden Books in 1688.)

Madame Guyon's celebrity status in Paris, however, disturbed its archbishop, Harlay de Champvallon, who was far from impressed by the apostle of Quietism or her soul-mate priest (perhaps because his own life lacked either Quietist or any other kind of spirituality—he was a notoriously worldly bishop). Immediately after Molinos' condemnation in Rome in 1686, Harlay took swift and ruthless measures, and had Father Lacombe arrested. He was to spend the rest of his life in prison, a Quietist saint and martyr; at length, thirty years later, he died insane in an asylum at Charenton.

Madame Guyon was also arrested and confined to a Visitandine convent. However, she was more fortunate than Father Lacombe in having a powerful champion at court— Madame de Maintenon, the devout former governess of Louis XIV's illegitimate children by his third mistress Madame de Montespan. Madame de Maintenon had secretly married the king in 1683 or 1684. Through her influence, Madame Guyon regained her freedom. She was then appointed to teach at a girls' school in Saint-Cyr, which Madame de Maintenon had founded to educate the young female upper class as a moral and spiritual elite. It was at Saint-Cyr that Madame Guyon met her second great spiritual companion—**François de Salignac de la Mothe Fénelon** (1651–1715).

3. Archbishop Fénelon

Fénelon was by all accounts a remarkable man: of commanding presence, stunningly handsome, personally charming, an eloquent preacher, with a brilliant intellect that found expression in notable works of philosophy and theology. He was also spiritually sensitive and wracked with inner anguish over his sins and doubts. "I cannot explain my inner self", he lamented. "It escapes me, and appears to be for ever changing. I have no idea who I am." Of all the Roman Catholic figures in our period, Fénelon is perhaps the most complex and captivating personality.

Born at Périgord, of noble family, Fénelon studied at the Saint-Sulpice seminary in Paris, and was ordained to the priesthood in 1675. In 1678, he became the superior of Nouvelles Catholiques, an institution for teaching Roman Catholic doctrine to converts from Protestantism. He conducted a special mission in the period 1685–6 in the Saintonge region (a surviving stronghold of Huguenots), to evangelize those who had lost their religious liberties through the revocation of the Edict of Nantes (see section 3, below). He was, however, opposed to forced conversions, and secured the withdrawal of royal troops from his mission field. Fénelon preferred to rely on patient, loving instruction, in Bible classes and public preaching, to win Protestants over. "When hearts are to be moved", he wrote, "force is of no avail. Conviction is the only true conversion."

Then Fénelon—fatefully—took up a teaching post at Madame de Maintenon's Saint-Cyr school. Here, in autumn 1688, he made the acquaintance of Madame Guyon, and was deeply impressed both by her piety and her Quietist doctrine. A profoundly emotional but physically chaste relationship swiftly sprang up between the two kindred spirits, Fénelon filling the void left in Madame Guyon's life by the imprisonment of Father Lacombe. Fénelon came to regard Madame Guyon as his "spiritual mother", and she at times even referred to him as her "baby" (although she was only three years his senior). We can gauge something of Fénelon's attitude by these words he wrote to his new mentor: "My confidence in you is complete, because of the brilliance of the light you bring to bear on interior things, and God's designs through you."

However, Fénelon tried to correct some of the more unbalanced dimensions of Madame Guyon's spirituality, which under his influence was refined into something more sane and sensible (it has been called "Semi-Quietism"). Nevertheless, many pious but traditional-minded French Catholics found distasteful elements even in Fénelon's more restrained version of Quietism, especially its somewhat erotic language about the "spiritual nuptials" enjoyed by Jesus and the perfect soul. When a Quietist priest, a disciple of Fénelon, described these spiritual nuptials to one young lady in the confessional, she is said to have exclaimed in shock, "Fancy talking like that, Father, to a girl of my age!"

The period 1689–94 was a sort of spiritual honeymoon period for Fénelon and Madame Guyon. Under the benevolent eye of Madame de Maintenon, they enjoyed an intimate soul-friendship and gathered a circle of admiring disciples. They entertained romantic visions of reforming the whole of France through Louis XIV's young grandson, the Duke of Burgundy, to whom Fénelon was appointed tutor in 1689. Fénelon wrote a famous novel, *Télémaque*, dedicated to the duke and finally published in 1699, in which he set out his ideals of true kingship. Among other things Fénelon insisted that a good king would engage in no wars of aggression, and would be no self-willed autocrat but subject to God's moral law. Fénelon and Madame Guyon hoped that the Duke of Burgundy would grow up to be this king; Madame Guyon prophesied that as the new monarch's spiritual advisor, Fénelon would become the light of France, leading other nations to Christ.[3]

Fénelon and Madame Guyon's honeymoon period, however, ended in 1694, when an extreme form of Quietism began developing at Saint-Cyr. One of the school's young ladies, Mademoiselle de la Maisonfort, an ardent devotee of Madame Guyon, began teaching that prayer and good works were unnecessary in the true and perfect Christian life. Other students at Saint-Cyr were caught up in this blossoming of radical Quietist spirituality. When it came to the notice of Madame de Maintenon, it turned her against Madame Guyon, whom she blamed for the extremism. Madame de Maintenon entrusted a full-scale investigation of the affair to no less a figure than the celebrated Jacques-Bénigne Bossuet, Bishop of Meaux and arguably France's greatest preacher.[4]

Bossuet read Madame Guyon's works carefully, and interviewed her several times. Unfortunately for the feminine

---

3. In fact Louis XIV's successor would not be the duke of Burgundy but Louis' great-grandson, Louis XV.

4. See Chapter 6, section 3.5 for a full account of Bossuet.

apostle of Quietism, the illustrious Bishop of Meaux became convinced that she was mentally disturbed. Madame Guyon, sensing Bossuet's hostility, asked for two more judges to be appointed—these were Bishop Noailles of Châlons-sur-Marne, and Louis Tronson, director of the illustrious Saint-Sulpice Society, devoted to training priests of high moral and spiritual calibre. The investigation was conducted in the Saint-Sulpice summer house at Issy, near Paris, and it lasted eight months. In February 1695, Fénelon was appointed Archbishop of Cambrai; he used his new position of influence to have himself added to the Issy tribunal. Eventually, 34 articles extracted from Madame Guyon's works were condemned later in 1695. Fénelon tried to defend his "spiritual mother", but succeeded only in toning down the condemnation; the high priestess of Quietism was imprisoned, moved from one convent to another, and finally locked away in the Bastille in 1698.

Madame Guyon remained a prisoner in the Bastille until 1703. By then her ordeal had worn her down, and she submitted unreservedly to the Church's condemnation of her teaching. She spent the rest of her life in Blois in the custody of her son, who kept a close watch on his mother to prevent any relapse into Quietist error. The one-time spiritual celebrity behaved herself and did nothing more to antagonize the religious establishment, although she did write religious poetry which was not entirely free from the taint of her old teachings.

When Madame Guyon died in 1717, her influence through her writings passed out of the Roman Catholic Church and into the Protestant world, where her brand of Quietist mysticism attracted many new admirers. The chief propagator of Madame Guyon's spirituality among Protestants was the Huguenot preacher Pierre Poiret (1646–1719). Based in Rijnsburg in Holland, Poiret edited the complete works of Madame Guyon, which appeared in 39 volumes between 1712 and 1722 (the last volumes were edited by Poiret's disciples). Poiret's labours enabled Madame Guyon's Quietism to find its way into German Pietism, especially through Gerhard Tersteegen (a disciple of Poiret—he translated many French Quietist writings into

German).[5] Madame Guyon's literary mentor, Molinos, also found an appreciative response among Pietists; the great Pietist leader August Hermann Francke reprinted Molinos' *Spiritual Guide*.[6]

Madame Guyon's influence flowed into English Evangelicalism too, especially through two great admirers, John Wesley (who published an edited version of Madame Guyon's autobiography), and the Calvinist poet William Cowper (who translated many of Madame Guyon's religious poems into English). Wesley also printed an edited English translation of Molinos' *Spiritual Guide*.

4. Clash of giants: Fénelon and Bossuet

Madame Guyon's condemnation and imprisonment, however, did not end the Quietist controversy in France. It continued in the shape of pungent conflict between Fénelon and Bossuet— the greatest clash of spiritual titans in the Roman Catholic Church in our period. The quarrel began in 1696, when Bossuet wrote his *Pastoral Instruction on the States of Prayer*. This was an exposition of what Bossuet believed to be the true Catholic teaching on prayer, based on the articles of Issy. Bossuet sent a copy to Fénelon, as a member of the Issy tribunal, asking him to approve it. Fénelon, however, refused, detecting in Bossuet's treatise a condemnation of aspects of Madame Guyon's Quietism which Fénelon believed were spiritually sound. Fénelon wrote in 1697 his own *Explication of the Maxims of the Saints concerning the Interior Life*, often considered his masterwork, in which he defended the Quietist doctrine of disinterested love (love for God in which the soul rises above concern about its salvation or damnation), and quoted extensively from reputable Roman Catholic spiritual sources to demonstrate the orthodoxy of the doctrine. Provocatively, Fénelon's treatise was published a month in advance of Bossuet's.

Bossuet was incensed; he launched an all-out attack on Fénelon's *Explication*, which sparked off two years of vitriolic

5. See Chapter 1, section 4.4, for Tersteegen.
6. For Francke, see Chapter 1, section 4.3.

pamphlet warfare between the two bishops. History has
harshly judged the conduct of both men in this prolonged and
acrimonious controversy, as utterly unworthy of their talents
or characters. Bossuet accused Fénelon of destroying the virtue
of true Christian hope, by replacing it with an easy-going
sentimental assurance; Fénelon accused Bossuet of destroying
the virtue of true Christian love by his opposition to the Quietist
doctrine of "disinterested love" for God. Meanwhile, those in
France who cared little for Christianity of any sort laughed
heartily at the sight of their country's two foremost bishops
tearing each other to pieces in print. Bossuet's and Fénelon's
quarrel over hope and love seemed, by its public bitterness, to be
undermining faith. The satirists of Paris turned this unedifying
spectacle into a popular song:

> *Two bishops of France fiercely wrangled*
> *In quest of the Truth so entangled.*
> *"Hope's lost in your scheme!"*
> *"Love's gone, it would seem!"*
> *Alas, it was Faith that got mangled.*

Bossuet managed to get King Louis on his side in the quarrel,
which prompted Fénelon to appeal over the head of the French
monarchy to Pope Innocent XII. This completely alienated
Louis, who banished Fénelon from court in the summer of 1697,
confining him to his diocese of Cambrai. The royal disgrace
lasted for the rest of Fénelon's life.

With Fénelon's appeal to Rome, factions within the Church
and the papal court began to line up and take sides. Supporting
Fénelon were the Jesuits, who suspected Bossuet of Jansenist
sympathies, plus a considerable body of bishops and cardinals
who feared that Fénelon's condemnation would discredit true
mysticism along with false. On Bossuet's side were the formidable
powers of King Louis and the French court, including Madame
de Maintenon and the quasi-Jansenist Archbishop Noailles of
Paris, and in Rome all the enemies of Molinos, the Spanish
father-figure of Quietism, who had only just died in prison for his
errors. In March 1699, under extreme pressure from Louis XIV,

a reluctant pope Innocent finally gave his decision: he condemned 23 propositions from Fénelon's *Explication*. Bossuet had won the battle of the titans. Fénelon submitted unreservedly. The Quietist controversy was over. Fénelon devoted the rest of his life to the spiritual welfare of his Cambrai diocese, only emerging again into public controversy to lend his efforts to defeating Jansenism (see previous section); there were many Jansenists in Cambrai, and Fénelon disliked their austere anti-mystical spirituality.

Fénelon's influence, like Madame Guyon's, was to live on rather in the Protestant than the Roman Catholic world. His *Explication of the Maxims of the Saints concerning the Interior Life* was translated into English as early as 1698; his later classic, *Treatise on the Existence of God*, published in full in 1718, was translated in 1720. Fénelon's life was published in English by A.M.Ramsay in 1723. His main English disciple was John Wesley.

3

Persecution: the fate of
the Huguenots

As we saw in Chapter 6, section 1, Cardinal Richelieu had destroyed the political and military independence of the French Protestants or Huguenots in 1627–8. From that point, they were a religious minority existing in France by the bare permission of the state. They still had the legal rights of toleration guaranteed by the 1598 Edict of Nantes; but if the French crown chose at any time to revoke the Edict, the Huguenots no longer had the strength to resist an onslaught of Catholic intolerance.

Louis XIV was not a monarch to tolerate for long an entire community in his domain who rejected, cursed, and preached against his religion as the superstition of Antichrist. He could barely refrain from annihilating the Jansensists, but they at least were Catholic; Huguenots were simply damnable heretics outside the precincts of the one true Church. The king was egged on in his intolerance by the Catholic clergy, who had never accepted the Edict of Nantes; it was to them a permanent insult to the truth and glory of the Church they served. They wished to see a united Catholic France. "One faith, one law, one king" was their motto.

Inspired by such sentiments, Louis began to pressurize his Protestant subjects with ever increasing harassments and discrimination. From 1681 onward, these became unbearable in the extreme. Huguenot churches were demolished in great numbers, as a punishment for having allegedly proselytized

Catholics and baptized them as Protestants. Huguenot schools
and colleges were shut down. Huguenots were barred from
government service and from most of the trade guilds. Huguenot
pastors were forbidden to live in the same area for more than
three years. In a particularly anguish-inducing measure, Louis
decreed that any Huguenot child was legally entitled, from the
age of seven, to declare himself or herself a Roman Catholic;
on the slightest pretext, government agencies would then
forcibly remove from their families any child who was deemed
to have turned Catholic. Faced with such treatment, thousands
of Huguenots began to leave France in search of religious
freedom elsewhere. Meanwhile, Louis offered financial rewards
to Huguenots who would convert to Catholicism; a special
"treasury of conversions" was set up to pay handsome dividends
to ex-Protestants. The policy worked; many converted.

Finally, on October 17th 1685, Louis officially revoked the
Edict of Nantes. All Protestant pastors were banished from
the kingdom, but their congregations were not allowed to
follow them; Louis wished to destroy the Huguenot religious
leadership, in order to make it easier to force the laity back into
the Catholic Church. His method of choice to shepherd souls
into the Church was the *dragonnade*. This meant handing over
entire Protestant regions to military control; the troops had the
right to do virtually as they pleased with the civilian populace,
and the result was vandalism, outrage, torture, and (for resisters)
death. If any Huguenots were caught trying to flee the country,
the men were made galley slaves in the French navy, the women
were imprisoned, and the children were sent to convents to be
educated as Catholics.

But this did not deter people from making the attempt to
escape the land, and something like 200,000 succeeded in leaving
France, establishing themselves in other countries. Many found
new lives in the Dutch Republic; many were welcomed as refugees
in Britain (ironically under a Roman Catholic king, James II, who
could not withstand the overwhelming Protestantism of British
popular opinion that clamoured to receive the Huguenots); the
Calvinist government of Brandenburg-Prussia made generous

provision for many who settled there, as part of its policy to promote the Reformed faith in its largely Lutheran lands.

It was a catastrophe for France. Some regions, such the Pays de Gex (bordering on Geneva), were almost completely depopulated. In others, such as Normandy, local industry was destroyed, since it had been Huguenot-run; terrible poverty ensued. The armies of France's Protestant enemies were strengthened by the tide of refugees. Nor did Louis' policy bring any internal peace within France itself. It merely renewed the old wars of religion, when the remaining Huguenots of the Cevennes region (southern-central France) rose in rebellion in 1702 against the *dragonnades*. Led by prophets who claimed direct divine inspiration, the Camisards (as they were known) drained French military resources while Louis strove to crush the revolt.[1] As an army in the field, the Camisards were finally defeated after two years of epic conflict in 1704, but the survivors used brutal guerilla tactics for another decade.

A famous "ordinary" victim of the persecution was the young Huguenot lady **Marie Durand** (1715–76). Arrested at the age of 15, Marie was locked away in the Tower of Constance in Aigues-Mortes, a prison for women. She spent the next 38 years there, in wretched conditions, refusing all pressures to renounce her faith, and ministering to the other women prisoners. She was finally released in 1767. Many of her letters survive, revealing her intrepid character and efforts to publicize the sufferings of the women inmates of the prison.

The Camisard rebellion only really ended with the death of King Louis in 1715, and new leadership provided for the Camisards by **Antoine Court** (1696–1760). Court suppressed the "prophets", and reestablished a more traditional Huguenot spirituality and church government and discipline. He was supremely successful, and has often been called the "Restorer of French Protestantism". The Huguenots under Court's guidance became an underground movement, "the Church of the Desert",

---

1. The name Camisard seems to come from the French *camise*, a peasant's smock.

meeting in secret. They survived, and were finally granted full rights of citizenship in 1790 during the French Revolution. On almost all counts, Louis XIV's treatment of the Huguenots was both a disaster for his country and a failure.

4

Roman Catholic Mission: experiments in the East

1. *The Sacred Congregation for the Propagation of the Faith*

The huge missionary growth of Roman Catholicism beyond Europe that had begun during the 16th century continued in our period. The century of the Reformation and Catholic Counter-Reformation had seen Roman Catholic expansion into the Americas, the Philippines, India, Malaysia, Malaku (the Moluccas), and Japan. Catholic missionaries in our period consolidated and extended this work.

The massive extension of Roman Catholic influence outside Europe in the 16th century had largely taken place in the wake of Spanish and Portuguese empire-building. In the early 17th century, the papacy finally decided that Catholic mission should be centrally planned. *Pope Gregory XV* (1621–3) took the momentous step. He was the first Jesuit-trained pope; Jesuits had been at the forefront of Catholic mission in the East, and had become active in South America from 1609. Gregory established in 1622 the Sacred Congregation for the Propagation of the Faith, a body of 13 cardinals and two bishops entrusted with the supervision of Catholic world mission. From its Latin name, the body was usually known simply as "the Propaganda".[1] In one sense, this was the papacy striking a

---

1. This is Latin for "propagation" and has little to do with propaganda in the modern political sense.

blow against the Catholic secular rulers of Europe. The pope, not any mere king or emperor, was responsible for directing missionary activity. Naturally this created friction between the papacy and the Catholic kings, since the latter saw the Propaganda as papal interference in their colonial enterprises. But the papacy would not back down, and Gregory appointed a brilliantly effective first secretary of the Propaganda, *Francesco Ingoli* (1578–1649).

Ingoli is better known for his controversy with the trailblazing scientist Galileo, in which Ingoli disputed the evidence for the Copernican theory of a sun-centred solar system. But it was as secretary to the Propaganda that Ingoli found his true talent; his pioneering work has earned him a reputation as one of the greatest missionary directors in Christian history. Ingoli amassed information about every aspect of the various mission fields as the basis for discussion and decision-making. His guidelines for Catholic mission were to be decisive for the future: Christianity must be uncoupled from the colonial power of Spain and Portugal; the pope must create many more new bishops to act as spiritual guardians of newly evangelized areas and peoples, to be a living link between new churches and the pope, and to protect those churches from secular, colonial control; indigenous priests must be trained as swiftly as possible. The plan for bishops ran into trouble with the Spanish and Portuguese monarchies, which (rightly) claimed that they alone had the legal authority to create new bishoprics in their colonial territories. But Pope Urban VIII (1623–44) sidestepped the problem by creating "vicars apostolic" instead of bishops for the mission field. They were bishops in all but name, representing the pope and accountable only to him. The kings of Spain and Portugal fumed with impotent rage.

In the period 1658–63, the Propaganda set up the Society of Foreign Missions of Paris. The Society's seminary soon became the foremost training centre for Catholic missionaries. This meant that France once again found itself at the heart of Catholic life, especially with the Spanish and Portuguese empires now sinking into decline, and the French empire flourishing.[2]

The most celebrated aspects of Catholic mission in our period are found in the life and work of Robert de Nobili in India, and the Chinese Rites controversy that dragged on from the 1630s to 1715.

2. Robert de Nobili

Robert de Nobili (1577–1656) is one of the most famous Catholic missionaries of the 17th century, and indeed one of the most celebrated missionaries of all the Christian centuries. Born to a wealthy Italian family at Montepulciano, Tuscany, a nephew of the distinguished Cardinal Bellarmine, he joined the Jesuits in 1596, and after his training was sent to India, arriving in 1605. Here he mastered the Tamil language within months; his superiors then stationed him in the city of Madurai, part of the Nayak kingdom in Tamil-speaking southern India. Madurai was effectively the capital city of Tamil culture, and a Portuguese Jesuit mission was already at work here, although without much success. Nobili disagreed deeply with the methods the mission was using; they converted native Tamils not only to Catholic Christianity, but also to Portuguese national customs—converts were taught to act, dress, and live as Portuguese. This provoked fierce contempt from the higher Indian castes (the Brahmins) of Madurai. Was their ancient and rich native culture so shallow, or even wicked, that it had to be disowned by anyone embracing this new religion?[3]

Nobili resolved that the message of Christ had to be disentangled from the trappings of European culture. He would become an Indian to win Indians. His particular desire was to gain converts from the Brahmin caste—to reach Indian society

---

2. By the middle of the 18th century, when this chapter concludes, France's overseas empire included parts of Canada, North America, the Caribbean, South America, West Africa, and India.

3. Brahmins are the highest order in the traditional Indian Hindu caste system: the educated "scholar" caste providing Hinduism with its priests.

through its natural leaders. So he immersed himself in Brahmin culture, learned their "classical" form of Tamil (later learning Telegu and Sanskrit too), studied their scriptures (the Vedas), and virtually turned himself into a Christian Brahmin. He now went about with the shaven head and robe of a *sannyasi* (an Indian holy man), eating a strict vegetarian Brahmin diet, and presenting himself, not as a representative of any European belief or way of life, but as a teacher of universal truth from the God of all peoples. The higher castes were astounded and impressed by his knowledge of their language and scriptures, and respected his holiness—they could understand Christian sanctity when it appeared in Indian garb. He gave lectures on Christian theology, illustrating his points at every turn from classical Indian literature.

By 1609, Nobili had won some 63 converts from the higher castes, including some Brahmins. However, he now came under fierce attack both from native Indians and his Catholic superiors. Indians opposed to his work stated publicly that Nobili was Portuguese, and that in accepting his religion his converts had defiled themselves by embracing a Portuguese way of life. Nobili defended himself by asserting (truthfully) that he was not Portuguese but Italian, from a "high caste" Italian family. The controversy was murky; the word "Portuguese" had different meanings for different people. Indians referred to all Europeans as Portuguese, owing to the predominance of Portugal's overseas empire in India—most Europeans encountered by Indians were in fact Portuguese. Nobili's insistence that he was Italian, not Portuguese, was a possibly over-subtle way of making a valid point, namely, that neither he nor his religion had any necessary connection with the Europeans, whether merchants or priests, currently present in India, or their detested ways.

Nobili also faced serious criticism from his ecclesiastical superior, Archbishop Cristovao of Goa,[4] and from the papacy. His critics in the Church said that he was throwing a Christian veneer over Hindu superstitions, and creating his own little

---

4. Goa was the capital of Portuguese India.

church of converts separate from the Catholic Church. Nobili answered these charges in his important treatise of 1610, *A Reply to the Objections Raised against the Method Used in the New Mission of Mandurai for the Conversion of Gentiles to Christ.* Pope Gregory XV referred the matter to a tribunal, headed by Archbishop Peter Lombard of Armagh;[5] Lombard sifted through the documents of accusation and defence, and finally exonerated Nobili.

This decision of 1623 enabled Nobili to continue his work, which now reached beyond Madurai into Trinchonopoly and Salem, and began gaining converts from lower castes as well as Brahmins (although he kept the two groups of converts separate, with different missionary co-workers for each, as a concession to the host culture). By the time Nobili died, sick and blind, in the city of Myalapore, near Madras, he had acquired a permanent place in Christian missionary history for his radically experimental thinking and practice. He left behind a literary legacy too: a Tamil catechism, and a number of Tamil theological treatises. These brought him the nickname "the father of Tamil prose" (poetry rather than prose had previously been the Tamil vehicle for these religious topics). He also left a body of Tamil hymns.

3. The Chinese Rites controversy

If Nobili's methods proved contentious in India, it was nothing compared to the controversy that erupted over Jesuit missionary practice in China. Francis Xavier had reached the Chinese island of Shangchuan, where he died in 1552.[6] Others followed, and soon there was a Jesuit mission in mainland China, once again (as in India) under Portuguese protection—Portugal had established a trading post at Macao, beside the Canton River, in 1557.[7]

---

5. Not to be confused with the medieval scholastic theologian Peter Lombard. See *Volume Two: The Middle Ages*, Chapter 7, section 3.

6. See *Volume Three: Renaissance and Reformation*, Chapter 8, section 7.

7. Macao was handed over to the Chinese government by Portugal as late as 1999.

The first great Catholic missionary in China was the Italian Jesuit *Matteo Ricci* (1552–1610). Born in the city of Macerata, his studies at the Jesuit college in Rome included mathematics and astronomy, which would serve him well in China. His first missionary posting was in Portuguese India in 1578, but he was then sent to the Portuguese trading centre at Macao in 1582. For the next 20 years he travelled about, immersing himself in the Chinese language and culture. One of the fruits of this immersion was a Portuguese-Chinese dictionary, produced jointly with another Jesuit missionary, Michele Ruggieri (1543–1607), probably between 1583 and 1588. This was the first ever dictionary of Chinese for any European language. Ricci also translated into Latin the "Four Books" of Confucianism, the basis of all Chinese scholarship at that period. This, together with his general work on principles for translating Chinese into European languages, has earned Ricci the title "founder of Western Sinology".[8]

Finally, in 1601, Ricci managed to gain access to Peking or Beijing, the capital city of the Chinese Empire.[9] The Emperor Wanli (1572–1620) of the Ming dynasty invited Ricci to his capital largely on the strength of the Jesuit's astronomical skill; Ricci's ability to predict solar eclipses was highly valued in Chinese culture, since eclipses were considered heavenly signs of coming events on earth. Ricci was the first Westerner to be allowed into Beijing; the Chinese regarded theirs as the only true civilisation in the world, and despised foreigners, so that Ricci found himself in a unique position. He had proved that a foreigner could be as learned as the Chinese, and could treat their culture with respect and sympathy. The emperor's favour enabled Ricci to remain in Beijing until his death in 1610. He established a Catholic congregation in the city, with converts from the highest and most educated classes; they worshiped

8. Sinology: the study of Chinese culture and history by Western scholars.
9. Peking and Beijing derive from different Chinese pronunciations of the city's name, depending on dialect.

in the Cathedral of the Immaculate Conception—the building dates from 1605.

Ricci's study of Confucianism, the prevalent Chinese worldview, led him to some controversial conclusions. One was about translation. How should the concept "God" be expressed in Chinese? The term *T'ien Chu* ("lord of heaven") was available, and Ricci used it in a Chinese catechism. More contentious was his use of two other words, *Shangi-Ti* ("sovereign lord") and *T'ien* ("heaven"). These Confucian terms were generally taken to refer to an impersonal reality (something like "ultimate being"), but Ricci argued that in their original usage they had described a personal God. He also maintained that the term *Sheng* meant "worthy of reverence" rather than "holy" (as it was often understood). It was therefore permissible for Confucianists who embraced Christianity to continue to call Confucius *sheng*.

More problematic were the ceremonies of veneration that Confucianism required Chinese families to pay to their ancestors, e.g. bowing to a tablet on which one's ancestors' names were written. Was this Pagan idolatry? Or did it lack religious dimensions? Was it really like (say) a Western European family gathering on a dead grandparent's birthday to recite poems and sing songs in celebration of his or her memory? Ricci argued that Confucian ancestor-veneration was essentially about honouring the family, not worshiping gods or spirits. So he allowed his converts to carry on venerating their ancestors. He certainly knew that any break with this custom would be seen by Confucianists as a vile dishonouring of the family—and honouring the family lay at the heart of Chinese culture. Ricci's methods were adopted by the Jesuit missionaries. The policy undoubtedly led to remarkable success in making Christianity accessible to Confucianists. Reliable statistics are hard to obtain, but it does seem that by the closing decades of the 17th century there were many thousands of Chinese Christians from a high-class Confucian background.

At first the Jesuit methods received support from the Sacred Congregation for the Propagation of the Faith back in Rome.

In 1659 it issued a famous statement to its missionaries in the Far East:

> Do not see it as your task, and do not pressurize the peoples, to change their manners, their customs, and their ways, unless they are obviously contrary to religion and wholesome morality. What could be more ridiculous than to transplant France, Spain, Italy, or some other European country into China? Do not take all that to them; take only the faith, which does not deride or uproot the manners and customs of any people, assuming of course that they are not actually evil, but rather wishes to see them preserved intact. It is human nature to love and cherish above everything else one's own country and its ways. Consequently there is no greater cause for alienation and hatred than when someone attacks local customs, particularly when these customs have a long and venerable history. This is more especially the case, when an attempt is made to bring in the customs of some other people to replace the customs that have been abolished. Do not make odious contrasts between native and European customs; do everything possible to adapt yourselves to their customs.

The **Chinese Emperor Kangxi** or Kang Hsi (1661–1722) was so impressed by the respectful attitude of the Jesuits to Chinese culture, and their contributions to it (e.g. as linguistic experts and interpreters) that he issued an edict of toleration in 1692:

> The Europeans are very quiet; they stir up no disturbances in the provinces, they injure no one, they commit no crimes, and their teaching shares no part of what is taught by the false sects in the empire, nor does it have any tendency to stir up sedition... We decree therefore that all temples dedicated to the Lord of heaven, wherever they may be found, should be preserved, and that permission is given to all who would worship this God to enter these temples, offer Him incense, and perform the rites practised by the Christians according to their ancient custom. Henceforth let no one offer them any opposition.

There were, however, problems brewing for the Jesuits in China. They were not the only Catholic religious order working there; Dominicans and Franciscans were now at work among the peasant peoples of the Chinese coast. The new missionaries, who had often worked in the Spanish Philippines, brought a completely different approach to evangelism and conversion. They insisted that converts must break with their culture—in effect, adopt the manners and customs of their European preachers. This was their policy in the Philippines, and they saw no reason to pursue a different path in China. When they became fully conscious of the level of Jesuit concession toward Confucian customs, they sent a fierce denunciation to Rome, accusing the Jesuits of selling out the Gospel to Paganism.

Pope Clement XI (1700–21) was convinced by this complaint, and in 1705 sent a papal ambassador to Emperor Kangxi, informing him that Chinese Christians were no longer allowed to observe the disputed Confucian customs. Kangxi was so offended that he banished the ambassador from Beijing. Clement confirmed his decision more authoritatively in 1715 with a papal bull, *Ex illa die*. This time Kangxi's outrage knew no bounds; he banished all Christian missionaries from China. The imperial decree of 1721 said:

> Having read this proclamation, I must conclude that the Westerners are utterly petty-minded. One cannot reason with them; they do not understand the bigger issues as we in China understand them. There is not even one Westerner who has mastered Chinese literature, and their comments are often unbelievable and absurd. If this proclamation is anything to go by, their religion is just the same as the other tiny, intolerant sects of Buddhists or Taoists. Never have I laid eyes on a document that had so much nonsense in it. Henceforth, in order to avoid further trouble, no Westerners should be allowed to preach in China.

It was not only the Jesuit policy in China that was suppressed. The same policy pioneered by Robert de Nobili in India suffered the same fate. Pope Benedict XIV (1740–58) condemned the Jesuit approach in both China and India in the papal bull *Ex quo singulari* in 1742. In practice it dealt a staggering wound to the work of Catholic mission in the Far East. The Catholic cause in China never really recovered.

The Chinese rites controversy transcends its 18th century Catholic limits to touch on two issues that arise again and again in the area of cross-cultural mission. The first is "contextualisation": to what extent can Christian missionaries be "all things to all men" (1 Corinthians 9:22) without compromising the gospel itself? The second is that the misunderstandings that often arise between workers on the field and committees back home. If that is so today, in our age of rapid communication, how much more was it likely back in Nobili and Ricci's era when personal contact was so difficult?

Important people:

Pierre Pithou (1539–96)
Matteo Ricci (1552–1610)
Edmond Richer (1559–1631)
Robert de Nobili (1577–1656)
Francesco Ingoli (1578–1649)
Pierre de Marca (1594–1662)
Antoine Court (1696–1760)
Marie Durand (1715–76)

Quietists

Miguel de Molinos (1628–96)
François Lacombe (1643–1715)
Jeanne Marie Bouvier de la Mothe Guyon (1648–1717)
François de Salignac de la Mothe Fénelon (1651–1715)

Kings, popes, politicians

Pope Gregory XV (1621–3)
Chinese Emperor Kangxi (1661–1722)
Pope Innocent XI (1676–89)
Pope Clement XI (1700–21)

Primary source material

The Quietism of Molinos: inward mortification and complete resignation are necessary to acquire inner peace.

Never disquiet yourself for any accident. Disquiet is the door by which the enemy gets into the soul to rob it of its peace. Resign yourself and deny yourself entirely; for though true self-denial is bitter at the beginning, it is easy in the middle, and becomes very sweet in the end. You will find yourself far from perfection if you do not find God in everything. Understand this: pure, perfect, and essential love consists in the cross, in self-denial and resignation, in perfect humility, in poverty of spirit, and in a low opinion of yourself…

There are many who, however much they have been dedicated to prayer, still have no relish for God, because at the end of their prayers, they are not mortified, nor do they attend upon God once they have stopped praying. In order to obtain a peaceful and continual attending upon God, you have to get a great purity of mind and heart, great peace of soul, and a resignation in all things.

To the pure-hearted and the mortified, the recreation of the senses is a sort of death: they never go to it, unless compelled by necessity and edification of their neighbours.

The depth of our soul, you will know, is the place of our happiness. There the Lord shows us wonders. There we engulf and lose ourselves in the immense ocean of His infinite goodness, in which we keep ourselves fixed and immoveable. There resides the incomparable fruitfulness of our soul, and its supreme and sweet rest. A humble and resigned soul, which has come to this depth, seeks no more than simply to please God; and the Holy Spirit of Love teaches it everything with His sweet and enlivening anointing.

Among the saints, there are some giants, who continually and patiently suffer indispositions of body; God takes great care of them. But what high and sovereign gift belongs to those who, by the power of the Holy Spirit, suffer both internal and external crosses with contentment and resignation. This is the sort of holiness that is rare, and therefore so much more precious in the sight of God. The spiritual ones who walk this way are rare, because there are few in the world who totally deny themselves, in order to follow Christ crucified, with simplicity and poverty of spirit, through the lonely and thorny ways of the cross, without thinking about themselves.

A life of self-denial is above all miracles of the saints; and it does not know whether it is alive or dead, lost or gained, whether it agrees or resists. This is the true resigned life. But although it may be a long time before you come to this state, and you think you have not made a step towards it, do not disquiet yourself at this, for God often bestows upon a soul that blessing in one moment which was denied it for many years before...

Tribulation is a great treasure, with which God honours those who are His in this life. Therefore evil persons are necessary for those who are good; and so are the devils themselves, which, by afflicting us, try to ruin us. But instead of doing us harm, they do us the greatest good imaginable.

There must be tribulation to make a person's life acceptable to God; without tribulation, it is like the body without the soul, the soul without grace, the earth without the sun. With the wind of tribulation God separates, in the floor of the soul, the chaff from the wheat...

Those saints are to be pitied who cannot find it in their hearts to believe that tribulation and suffering are their greatest blessing. Those who are spiritually mature ought always to be desirous of dying and suffering, of being always in a state of death and suffering. How empty is the person who does not suffer! Humans are born to toil and suffer: much more so the friends and elect of God.

Miguel de Molinos
Spiritual Guide, **Book 2, Chapter 7**

Fénelon: a holy life is possible anywhere and everywhere, even in the royal court of France

Our salvation should engage our energies every single day and hour. There is no time better for it than the time God in His mercy gives us right now. Today is ours; but we do not know what tomorrow may bring forth. Nor shall we accomplish salvation by merely wishing for it; we have to seek after it vigorously. Life's uncertainty should make us realize that we have to pursue this purpose with all our powers, and that all other pursuits are empty of value, since they do not bring us closer to God. He is the proper goal of everything we do—the God of our salvation, as David continually calls Him in the Psalms. Why do we think carefully about how to make progress towards the perfecting of our souls? Because we believe it to be necessary to our salvation. Why, then, do we delay carrying out our resolutions, when it is just as necessary to seek salvation now, as it will be ten years from now? Yes, right now, in the royal court, as afterwards in a more retired life!

Wisdom surely dictates that we should always take the safest course in everything to do with our salvation; for this is a thing in which we lose everything or gain everything. The position in life to which God has called us is safe for us, as long as we fulfil all its obligations. If God foresaw that it was impossible for us to be saved in the royal court, He would have forbidden us to live there. This, however, is not so. God has appointed kings and their courts; God gives people that birth and position which puts them in those courts. So we may be sure it is God's will that souls in the royal court should be saved, and find the narrow way to heaven, the way of truth, that way which Jesus Christ has said will make us free: the way, that is, which will guide us out of all the perils which the world rains down on us. The more you meet these perils in your present position, the more you must keep watch over yourself, so that you do not give way beneath them. Keeping watch over self means listening to God; it means always abiding in His presence, always being calm and collected, never plunging into wilful dissipation or distraction amid the things of this world. It means devoting ourselves to solitude, prayer, and reading good books, as far as we can; it means what David calls "pouring out your heart before God", feeling His inner presence, seeking Him heartily, loving Him supremely, shunning everything that is displeasing to Him.

This godliness, Madame, is suitable for every position in life. It will be most useful to anyone living in the royal court. Indeed, I do not know anything more effective for teaching you to be *in* the world without being *of* the world. Adopt this method. Make every effort to remember at all times that you are with God, and

God is with you, so that you may keep on serving Him faithfully. Build into your life the habit of often adoring His holy will, by submitting humbly to whatever His good providence ordains. Ask Him to hold you up, in case you fall. Beg Him to perfect His work in you, so that after infusing the desire for salvation into your heart in your present position in life, you may actually work out your salvation just where you are.

God does not require you to do great things in order to make triumphant progress. Our Lord Himself said, "The Kingdom of God is within you." We can find His kingdom there whenever we choose. Let us just do whatever we know He requires from us. The moment we see His will in anything, let there be no reluctance— only complete fidelity. Such fidelity need not lead us to do great things for His service and for our salvation; but it will surely lead us to do whatever lies close at hand, whatever is relevant to our position in life. If we could be saved only through great deeds, how few could ever hope for salvation! But salvation actually depends on fulfilling God's will. When God requires them from us, the littlest things become great. They are only little in themselves; they become instantly great when we do them for Him, when they lead to Him, and when they help unite with Him eternally. Remember what He said: "Whoever is faithful in what is least is faithful also in much, and he that is unrighteous in the least is unrighteous also in much!" In my view, a soul that honestly longs for God never thinks about whether a thing is little or great. It is enough to know that the One for whom we do it is infinitely great, and that it is His right to see all creation devoted to His glory alone: and this can be the case only when we fulfil His Will.

Archbishop Fénelon
Spiritual Letters to Women, Letter 17

Madame Guyon: the soul that loves God finds Him everywhere

O Thou, by long experience tried,
Near whom no grief can long abide;
My Love! how full of sweet content
I pass my years of banishment!

All scenes alike engaging prove
To souls impressed with sacred love!
Where'er they dwell, they dwell in Thee;
In heaven, in earth, or on the sea.

To me remains nor place nor time;
My country is in every clime;
I can be calm and free from care
On any shore, since God is there.

While place we seek, or place we shun,
The soul finds happiness in none;
But with a God to guide our way,
'Tis equal joy to go or stay.

Could I be cast where Thou art not,
That were indeed a dreadful lot;
But regions none remote I call,
Secure of finding God in all.

My country, Lord, art Thou alone;
Nor other can I claim or own;
The point where all my wishes meet;
My Law, my Love, life's only Sweet!

I hold by nothing here below;
Appoint my journey and I go;
Though pierced by scorn, oppressed by pride,
I feel Thee good—feel nought beside.

No frowns of men can hurtful prove
To souls on fire with heavenly Love;
Though men and devils both condemn,
No gloomy days arise for them.

Ah then! to His embrace repair;
My soul, thou art no stranger there;
There Love divine shall be thy guard,
And peace and safety thy reward.

Madame Guyon
translated by William Cowper (1731–1800)

Chapter 8

Eastern Orthodoxy

Introduction

Eastern Orthodoxy was the shape taken by Christianity in Eastern Europe, Russia, and the Middle East, existing in unbroken continuity from the days of the early church fathers. The Roman papacy had never exercised its supremacy over Eastern Christians, who cherished their own identity, traditions, and independence.

In the period covered by this volume, Orthodoxy was, in some ways, the unwilling and unwitting victim of the Protestant Reformation and the Catholic Counter-Reformation. Both made deep inroads into Orthodox territory and theology. Amid the struggles for ascendancy between Protestantized and Romanized Orthodox people, it can be hard at times to discern where, if anywhere, the authentic face and voice of Orthodoxy can be seen and heard. Perhaps the following narrative will provide at least the framework for readers to ask and answer that key question.

We begin our account with the man who was undoubtedly the most famous and most tragic figure of the entire period, whose life so poignantly sums up the inner conflicts of 17th century Orthodoxy.

1

Cyril Lucaris: the
Calvinist patriarch?

1. Cyril's early days

Cyril Lucaris (pronounced loo-ka-rees) [1] is often called the greatest patriarch of Constantinople in the modern era. If greatness is measured by religious devotion, intellectual gifts, heroic striving against the odds, and the capacity to generate deep-seated controversy long after one is dead, he certainly qualifies.

Cyril was born in Crete, at that time a colony of the Italian republic of Venice. But its inhabitants were largely Greek, and even the Venetian ruling class had "gone native" and embraced Greek culture. (Cyril's baptismal name was Constantine, but we shall call him by the more famous name he took on becoming a monk prior to his ordination as an unmarried priest.) We know virtually nothing of Cyril's parents, although he described them as "prominent both in the state and in the Church". Cyril's father seems to have been a prosperous butcher, with a solid commitment to his son's education. The greatest Cretan centre of Orthodox spiritual life and learning was the monastery of St Catherine in the town of Candia, which ran a school for boys, with high academic standards. Here the young Cyril found a mentor and lifelong friend in the schoolteacher Meletios Blastos.

After Cyril's schooling at St Catherine's, in 1584 his father sent him to a more advanced school for Greek boys in Venice.

---

1. Spelt Loukaris in Greek.

The school was attached to the Greek Orthodox church in Venice, which had a thriving Greek enclave. The inquisition hardly functioned in Venice; the republic was jealous of its political liberties and commercial enterprise, and would not allow the Church to interfere in such matters. Hence Venice has been called the most intellectually free city in Europe at that epoch. Some have traced Cyril's (alleged) adult freedom and

independence of thought to his time in Venice. Certainly he always looked back with immense affection to his four years of study there.

After a year back in Crete, young Cyril returned in 1589 to Italy, this time to the University of Padua, an international centre of academic excellence. Padua was famous for medicine and law; later generations would remember it as the university where the great Galileo taught maths. Here Cyril studied the "humane" subjects, especially philosophy, graduating with honours in 1595. His future was by now set for a church career, owing to the influence of his uncle, **Meletios**

Cyril Lucaris
(1572–1638)

Portrait by an
unknown artist

Pegas (d.1601), Patriarch of the Orthodox Church in the Egyptian city of Alexandria. This meant that Pegas was head of one of the four historic patriarchates of the East, the other three being Constantinople, Antioch, and Jerusalem. Most Egyptian Christians belonged to the Coptic Orthodox Church, which was Monophysite[2] in its theology. Cyril's uncle headed the Chalcedonian or Byzantine Orthodox community in Egypt, a much smaller body than the Coptic Orthodox, and marked by its fidelity to the Creed of Chalcedon (451 AD), which was the touchstone of what we call "Eastern Orthodoxy" throughout the old Byzantine

---

2. The belief that the the divine and human natures of Christ blended into a single divine-human nature. See *Volume One: The Age of the Early Church Fathers*, Chapter 12.

world. Pegas had the warmest affection and admiration for his nephew, thinking of him as his "son in the Lord"; he expected great things of Cyril in the Church. So around 1595, Cyril was ordained priest in Constantinople. His uncle ordained him; Pegas was then administering Constantinople's vacant patriarchal throne, and indeed spent much of his time in Constantinople—his flock in Alexandria was not numerically large.

2. Cyril in Poland-Lithuania

In 1596, Cyril was sent by his uncle to minister to the minority Orthodox population within the Roman Catholic kingdom of Poland-Lithuania. Cyril was accompanied by another priest, **Nicephorus Cantacuzinos** (dates unknown). They walked into an explosive situation that requires some explanation.

The king of Poland at this time was Sigismund III, an ardent Roman Catholic who threw the whole weight of the Polish state behind the Catholic Counter-Reformation and its "shock troops", the Jesuits. This made life very difficult for Poland's Orthodox population. These were Ukrainians. Ukraine (or "Little Russia") was the heartland of old Kievan Russia, including the city of Kiev itself, but it had been absorbed into Poland-Lithuania in the later Middle Ages. This created an anomalous situation: a Catholic kingdom with a large Orthodox minority. The Polish monarchy assumed autocratic powers over the Ukrainian Orthodox Church, appointing its bishops, often for political rather than religious reasons.

In the wake of the Catholic Counter-Reformation, and the harassment inflicted on the Ukrainian Orthodox in Poland by King Sigismund III, a pro-Rome movement emerged among the Ukrainian Orthodox leadership. It was spearheaded by Michael, metropolitan of the Ukrainian Orthodox Church in Poland, and Bishop Ignatius of Vladimir. They conducted secret negotiations with Rome to submit to the pope on the terms laid down by the 15th century Council of Florence.[3] In December

---

3. For the Council of Florence, see *Volume Two: The Middle Ages*, Chapter 9, section 4.

1595, at a council of the Ukrainian Orthodox Church held in Brest-Litovsk, six of the eight Orthodox bishops voted to submit to Rome. This brought about a very bitter schism in Ukrainian Orthodoxy. Many followed the lead of the six bishops (they became known as the "Greek Catholics"), but others were outraged and remained defiantly Orthodox. The Greek Catholics were permitted to retain their Orthodox liturgy, married clergy, the old Julian calendar,[4] and holy communion in both kinds (the wine as well as the bread given to the laity), but they accepted papal supremacy, purgatory, and the *filioque* clause.[5] The Greek Catholics were also known as the Uniates (Greeks united with Rome).

The remnant Orthodox in Poland now underwent a previously unknown degree of persecution. It served, however, to quicken their energies, and led to an unusual outcome: Ukrainian Orthodoxy acquired a new lay character, as the laity more than the clergy rallied to defence of Orthodoxy (most of the higher clergy had become Uniates). These lay religious leaders were organized as *bratsva* (brotherhoods); they produced literature

---

4. The Julian calendar was replaced by the Gregorian calendar, first promulgated by pope Gregory XIII in 1582. It was then adopted by Western European nations—by Britain in 1752. The Gregorian calendar was more accurate in its timing of the spring equinoxes. It meant that in adopting the Gregorian calendar, a country had to skip a number of days—10 in the 16th century (11 by the time Britain adopted it). Many Protestant countries resisted adopting the Gregorian calendar from anti-papal feeling. So did many Eastern Orthodox countries, along with a sense that that it was more important to keep the traditional Christian calendar out of reverence rather than adopt the new one for the sake of technical accuracy.

5. For the controversies surrounding the *filioque* clause, see *Volume Two: The Middle Ages*, Chapter 3, section 4. The Latin word means "and from the Son". It was added by the Western Church into the Nicene Creed's statement on the procession of the Holy Spirit, which originally said simply that He proceeds from the Father. The East stuck to the original version of the Creed, arguing that the Spirit does not proceed *from* the Son within the eternal Trinity, but at most proceeds *through* the Son in the experience of salvation: the Father remains the ultimate source.

to counter Jesuit propaganda, and organized Orthodox schools to check the influence of Jesuit schools.

Among the greatest lay defenders of Orthodoxy in Poland was *Prince Andrei Kurbskii* (1528–83). Kurbskii set up a school to translate the Latin fathers into Russian. He was also a great Byzantinist; that is, he wanted to bring riches of Byzantine Orthodox theology into Ukrainian Orthodox life. Another lay champion of Ukrainian Orthodoxy was *Prince Konstantin Ostrozhskii* (1526–1608), who established a school at Ostrog, where Latin, Greek, and Slavonic were all taught. Ostrozhskii was responsible for the first printed translation of the whole Bible into Church Slavonic. This is still the standard text for most Russian translations. Under Ostrozhskii's influence, schools and printing presses were created to aid the work of the Orthodox brotherhoods of Lviv and Vilnius. These taught in Latin and Polish, and unwittingly began to bring Western intellectual influences into Ukrainian Orthodoxy. It would not be long before the Ukrainian Orthodox were fighting Rome with weapons forged in Roman workshops: the Latin language, Jesuit educational methods, and medieval scholastic theology, with unforeseen results for Orthodox theology and spirituality (see next section).

Cyril and his companion Nicephorus arrived in Poland just after the first council of Brest-Litovsk, where the majority of Orthodox bishops had submitted to Rome. A second council met in October 1596 to ratify the decision of the first, now that the six bishops had been to Rome and been absolved of their erstwhile Orthodoxy by Pope Clement VIII. The second council was a furious affair; the anti-Uniates, led by Prince Ostrozhskii, now outnumbered the Uniates, and the council split into two, each anathematizing the other. Cyril and Nicephorus were present as anti-Uniates.

Cyril spent a good part of the next four years in Poland, trying to build up the Orthodox in their faith, and fight off the belligerent evangelism of the Jesuits. Cyril diagnosed the greatest problem as the ignorance of the Orthodox clergy: they were poorly educated in their own religion, and could offer little depth of teaching or argument to offset the brilliant Jesuit propaganda. Cyril dedicated himself to improving Orthodox schools and establishing an Orthodox printing press, first in Vilnius, then Lviv. It was a dangerous life; Cyril's companion Nicephorus was arrested and killed by the Polish police in 1598, and Cyril himself only escaped the same fate by being smuggled out of Poland and fleeing to Constantinople. (He was able to return later.) It was undoubtedly his experiences in Poland that made Cyril a lifelong and uncompromising enemy of Rome. This in turn was a factor that disposed him to look positively on Rome's other implacable enemy, the Protestant Reformation. Indeed, Orthodox and Protestants had suffered alike in Poland under Roman Catholic persecution, and in the Polish city of Vilnius, Cyril had enjoyed courteous relations with Lutherans.

3. Patriarch of Alexandria

At this point, Cyril's life again intersected that of his uncle Meletios, Patriarch of Alexandria. Meletios was dying; he sent for Cyril, who arrived in Alexandria in September 1601, and two days later, Meletios was dead. On his dying recommendation, the Alexandrian Church instantly elected Cyril as their new leader. Cyril's patriarchal regime seems to have been outstandingly efficient and benign. Among other things, he relocated the residence of the patriarch from Alexandria (a moribund port) to the vibrant capital city of Cairo, put his Church's finances on a sound footing, and continued to pursue the educational vision he had embraced in Poland, reorganizing the Greek schools under his jurisdiction.

It was in Alexandria, as far as we know, that Cyril first undertook a serious study of the Protestant Reformation. This was made possible by a member of the Dutch Reformed Church, Cornelius van Haag, whom Cyril had met when van Haag was a traveller in the Middle East—he was now Dutch ambassador to the Ottoman Empire in Constantinople. Cyril himself was back in Constantinople in 1602, where he renewed acquaintance with van Haag, and asked the Dutchman to supply him with theology texts written by Protestants. This request was passed back to

Holland, and Cyril received his books. Through van Haag, Cyril became acquainted with the Dutch Arminian theologian, Jan Uytenbogaert, supporter of Arminius and his successor as head of the "Remonstrant" (Arminian) party in Holland.[6] Cyril and Uytenbogaert corresponded for many long years. In 1617 Cyril met another Dutch theologian, David le Leu de Wilhelm, who was visiting Middle East, and kept up a lively correspondence with him too. He also corresponded with the Archbishop of Canterbury, George Abbot, whose theology was Reformed. Abbot initiated the contact, inviting Cyril to send some Greek youths to be theologically educated in England, all costs met by its king, James I. Cyril sent Metrophanes Critoboulos, who would succeed Cyril as Patriarch of Alexandria.

Over these Alexandrian years, Cyril assiduously compared Orthodox and Reformed theology. The outcome, especially in Cyril's famous Confession of Faith (1629), has been a subject of vigorous debate ever since. Some historians—Orthodox, Reformed, and those of other persuasions—think that Cyril really abandoned Orthodoxy altogether, and became a Calvinist in Orthodox robes.[7] This, however, does not seem wholly convincing to the present writer; it would convict Cyril of dire hypocrisy or gross imbecility (there is little evidence of either) in thinking that a pure Genevan Calvinist could be an Orthodox patriarch. Others have accused him of an unprincipled theological adaptability ("all things to all men" in the worst sense), continually tailoring his beliefs to whichever person or group he was trying to impress or mollify.[8] But this would merely paint Cyril as a different sort of hypocrite, and it fails to explain his uncompromising hostility to

---

6. See Chapter 2, section 2.

7. Modern Orthodox scholars who support this view include one of Orthodoxy's most influential 20th century theologians, Vladimir Lossky; the distinguished Orthodox historian, Nicolas Zernov; and Orthodoxy's most successful communicator and popularizer in the English-speaking world, Kallistos Ware.

8. Some modern Orthodox scholars essentially take this view, although expressing it more politely; they are listed in Hadjiantoniou's *Protestant Patriarch* (London: Epworth Press, 1961), p. 103.

Roman Catholicism—no adaptability there! Within Orthodoxy, some have argued strongly that Cyril remained impeccably Orthodox in his theology, as testified by his other public writings, and that the 1629 Confession was a mischievous forgery either by Calvinists or Jesuits. This view, however, seems to sit light to the evidence of Cyril's large private correspondence with Protestant friends, where he clearly expresses keen sympathy with various aspects of Protestantism, and also says that he *is* the author of the Confession.[9]

4. Cyril, Orthodoxy, and Calvinism: a possible perspective

The controversy over Cyril's "Calvinism" will probably never die away. Still, at the risk of introducing even more confusion, the present writer will offer an interpretation different to the three mentioned above.

It seems plausible to me that Cyril was at heart Orthodox, but that he saw in Protestantism both a powerful ally against Counter-Reformation Catholicism, and also a practical model for reforming and renewing church life that could be "baptized" into an Orthodox context. This twin perception of Protestantism goes a long way towards explaining Cyril's attitude and conduct as an Orthodox church leader. At a more deeply personal level, it is credible that Cyril increasingly found considerable elements in Orthodoxy and Reformed theology to be compatible, perhaps even complementary. The result was that he incorporated some facets of a Reformed outlook into his expression of Orthodoxy, both in concept and in terminology. Probably one of his purposes in doing so—arguably his chief purpose—was to cement alliances with powerful Reformed countries, especially Britain and the Dutch Republic. Their ambassadors in Constantinople

---

9. The evidence of Cyril's private letters to Protestant friends is presented in various sources: Hadjiantoniou's *Protestant Patriarch*, Sir Steven Runciman's *The Great Church in Captivity* (Cambridge: CUP, 1968), George A. Maloney's *A History of Orthodox Theology since 1453* (Belmont, Massachusetts: Nordland Publishing Company, 1976).

gave Cyril invaluable support against all too effective Roman
Catholic attempts to subvert Orthodoxy in the Ottoman Empire,
as it had been subverted in Poland.

None of this means that Cyril was a Calvinist in Orthodox
robes. It is clear that on some key issues, his beliefs remained
firmly within an Orthodox template. For example, Cyril
remained trenchantly Orthodox in his utter rejection of
Western views of the Trinity; the *filioque* clause was simply
anathema to him, and his Protestant friends could never get
him to budge on this point. His high views of the sacramental
efficacy of baptism and the eucharist were also typically
Orthodox: a robust belief in baptismal grace and in the
real eucharistic presence of Christ's body and blood.[10] He
never deviated from the patristic and Orthodox belief in the
perpetual virginity of Mary.[11] Cyril also retained an Orthodox
faith in the lawfulness of icons, albeit admitting to Protestant
friends that their veneration was open to grave abuse. It would
appear that, in Cyril's pastoral judgment, some Orthodox
folk never got beyond a superstitious veneration of icons to
an appreciation of the heavenly realities depicted—especially
"the true and spiritual worship and adoration which are due to
God alone" (to quote Cyril). But he never actually condemned
icon-veneration; what he explicitly condemned was the *worship*
of icons. The distinction between veneration and worship was
well-known within Orthodox theology. Cyril was probably
saying to his Protestant friends that he feared the distinction
sometimes failed to filter down into popular Orthodox practice.

10. It should be noted that Cyril distinctly rejected transubstantiation.
    Despite Western misunderstandings, however, transubstantiation
    is not a characteristically Orthodox way of understanding the real
    presence; Orthodox language equivalent to transubstantiation in the
    16th-18th centuries stems from Romanizing influences.
11. This, however, was also a common Protestant view in the 17th century.
    See the defence of Mary's perpetual virginity in the systematic theology of
    Francis Turretin, one of the greatest and most influential of the Reformed
    theologians of that era. For Turretin, see Chapter 2, section 1.8.

His understanding of church government also seems to have kept within an Orthodox Episcopal standpoint.[12]

Alongside this Orthodox structure of belief and piety, however, it seems undeniable that Cyril had also developed a sympathetic attitude to various aspects of Reformed theology. For example, he recognized value in the Reformed stress on man's *need* of grace—the humanly incurable state of sin, articulated in the Reformed view of man's total spiritual inability to respond to God apart from grace—"total depravity", in popular Reformed parlance. This assimilation of an Augustinian perspective on sin and grace was the most awkward aspect of Cyril's attempt at stating Orthodoxy in Reformed language, since Orthodoxy traditionally has held to "synergism"—the cooperation of divine grace and human free will.

And yet even at this point, some caution may be needed in evaluating Cyril's position. We must keep in mind that he numbered among his friends and correspondents, not only Reformed Protestants, but Arminians too, especially Jan Uytenbogaert. Arminian theology was a variety of Protestantism whose doctrine of salvation aligned itself with the traditional synergism of Orthodoxy. Uytenbogaert remained a close lifelong friend and supporter of Cyril. This could of course be taken as evidence for the "all things to all men" interpretation of the patriarch. It may be suggested, however, that it could instead be seen as mitigating somewhat the "pure Genevan Calvinist" interpretation. Perhaps Cyril's use of Augustinian language in speaking of the incompetence of the human will and the sovereignty of divine grace did not represent some absolute "fundamentalist" stance. It may have functioned more as a stern reactive protest against the perceived Pelagianism which the Jesuits were at that time busy enthroning within Roman Catholic theology—and hence within Orthodoxy too, under its relentless assault and infiltration

---

12. In ch. 10 of the Confession, Cyril says that "particular visible churches" each have a "chief", who is "the principal member" of that church, who is, albeit improperly, called the "head" of that church. In ch. 12, he uses "mediatorial" language of all the clergy, in the sense of mediators of truth.

by Jesuit-inspired Catholicism.[13] When Pelagianism is the enemy, Augustinian language and models of salvation can appear the most attractive and effective way of trumping it.[14]

Cyril expressed the Protestant formulation of salvation in terms of "justification by faith", although he was equally insistent that true faith will always do good works. His view here was not unOrthodox; it was more a case of stating the faith-works-salvation complex in a theological framework not particularly utilized by Orthodoxy. Cyril also appreciated the Reformed stress on the place of Scripture in theology, as the supreme source and norm of doctrine. It has been thought that Cyril here abandoned the Orthodox coordination of Scripture with Church and tradition, but it seems more likely that he simply resonated with the Magisterial Reformation's "Tradition 1" view of tradition in the life of the Church—critical rather than authoritarian reverence for tradition[15]—and that this illuminated his own interpretation of the Orthodox view. It is certain that Cyril did not regard himself as a freelance Bible interpreter, accountable to none; when France's Roman Catholic ambassador interrogated him in 1631 about the Confession, the patriarch replied:

> I am under no obligation to give an account of my beliefs to the pope. There are the metropolitans and bishops of the

---

13. See Chapter 6, section 4, for Jesuit Pelagianism and the storms of contention it aroused even within the Roman Catholic Church.

14. There is evidence in Cyril's Confession that he was not espousing an Augustinian "fundamentalism". In ch. 14, Cyril uses both "dead" and "wounded" imagery for the fallen will. The analogies are incompatible from a logical standpoint, and "wounded" is the more synergist of the terms. Also, even when speaking of predestination, Cyril insists in ch. 3 that the fate of the lost is not arbitrary but due to justice on God's part, while in ch. 4, he places an unusual stress on God's not being author of sin. These seem like the Orthodox element in his synthesis.

15. As explained in *Volume Three: Renaissance and Reformation*, Chapter 2, section 3. Tradition 1 = critical reverence for tradition (the Reformation Protestant view). Tradition 2 = authoritarian reverence for tradition (the Roman Catholic view, at least prior to the Second Vatican Council). Tradition 0 = no reverence for tradition (often the modern evangelical view).

Greek Church, and to these, assembled in council, I am ready
to justify my position, by reference to the Word of God and
the Fathers of the Church.

Even Cyril's seemingly unOrthodox view that the Church on
earth may err is quite conceivably a way of expressing Orthodoxy
in Reformed language: for it is counterbalanced, in the same
breath, by an affirmation that this Church "is sanctified and
instructed by the Holy Spirit" sent by the Father through the Son
"to teach the truth and expel darkness from the understanding
of the faithful". In other words, the Church is capable of error
considered from its human side, as a company of sinful human
beings, but is preserved from error considered from its divine
side, as the body of Christ and temple of the Holy Spirit.[16]
  Cyril's theology, then, should perhaps be seen neither
as Calvinism masquerading deceitfully in Orthodox dress,
nor as cynical opportunism which varied according to his
audience, nor as pure and simple Orthodoxy which others have
mischievously misrepresented as Reformed. Rather, it may
have been a deeply personal exploration of common ground
between Orthodox and Reformed attitudes and formulas,
quite possibly intended more for Protestant than home
consumption—an honest attempt by Cyril to restate aspects
of Orthodoxy in a form that Protestants could understand and
accept. This is not to deny that Cyril himself may have found
the attempt congenial. Cyril's restatements of Orthodoxy in
Protestant terms may also perhaps have been underpinned
in his own mind by an Eastern "apophatic" perspective on the
inability of human language to express spiritual truth in ways
that could avoid paradox.[17]

---

16. Some Reformed theologians have attributed a Spirit-given indefectibility
    to the Church with respect to the fundamentals of the faith, appealing
    to 1 John 2:26-7.

17. Hence perhaps the use of both "dead" and "wounded" imagery in his
    treatment of the human will, as previously noted. This should not, however,
    be interpreted as doctrinal relativism on Cyril's part, else he would surely
    not have refused so utterly to shift his ground on the *filioque* clause.

In the present writer's opinion, what will strike the Orthodox eye as strange and suspicious in Cyril's Confession of Faith (apart from his Augustinian-leaning formulations of sin and grace) is not so much what it says, as what it leaves unsaid. Cyril puts "up front" an interpretation of Orthodoxy consisting in all the points where it is most obviously compatible with Reformed theology, and downplays everything else. This, coupled with Cyril's fairly numerous uses of a Reformed terminology with which most Orthodox were then unacquainted, probably accounts for the anxious rejection his Confession encountered in his own day from the majority of theologically trained Orthodox (apart from Cyril's little team of devoted supporters). What Cyril's critics could not have anticipated, however, was the huge flourishing in the 18th century of a virtually identical style of Protestant-friendly "Cyrillian" theology in Orthodox Russia (see below).

5. Patriarch of Constantinople

By the time Cyril was called to the patriarchate of Constantinople in November 1621 (1620, according to some), his personal interpretation of Orthodox-Reformed congruity seems to have been complete. He was now in the highest office in the Orthodox Church, which has traditionally accorded primacy of honour to the Patriarchs of Constantinople (hence their title, "ecumenical patriarch"). His patriarchal reign is perhaps second only to that of the medieval giant Photius the Great in its religious interest and dramatic colour.[18]

The driving force behind Cyril's 17 years as patriarch was, in a sense, negative: the conflict with an aggressive Counter-Reformation Roman Catholicism. We must remember that Constantinople was no longer a Christian city; it was now the capital of the Islamic Ottoman Empire, which controlled all four of the historic Eastern patriarchates (Constantinople, Antioch, Jerusalem, and Alexandria). As Patriarch of Constantinople, therefore, Cyril was caught in a complex set of power-

---

18. For Photius, see *Volume Two: The Middle Ages*, Chapter 3, section 4.

relationships. He owed allegiance to the Ottoman Sultan, an Islamic despot; but the Sultan and his ministers were susceptible to the influence of the Western world's stronger states through their ambassadors. And through the French and Austrian ambassadors in Constantinople, the Roman Catholic Church was expending every effort to win over the Greek Orthodox population of the Ottoman Empire, either by conversion, or (more subtly) by persuading Orthodox to embrace a Roman Catholic type of theology within Orthodoxy.

Cyril's experiences in Poland, with Rome successfully splitting off many Ukrainian Orthodox into a Uniate Church, had given him a very negative slant on all things papal. He found this all too relevant as leader of the Greek Orthodox in Constantinople. The agents of Rome—the papacy itself, the Jesuits, the French and Austrian ambassadors—saw Cyril as a menace of the highest order who had to be overthrown at all costs. Pope Urban VIII (1623–44), Cyril's archenemy, described him as "that son of darkness, that athlete of hell, the pseudo-patriarch Cyril".

The Jesuits were already active in Constantinople prior to Cyril's arrival. Protected by the French ambassador, they ran a school offering free education to Greek children. Jesuit schools were the most efficient and successful in Europe, and the Constantinople school was an instrument for converting Greeks to Roman Catholicism. The children were a hook to draw in the parents. One Jesuit commented, "Through these children, we have reconciled many of their parents and even whole families with the Roman Church." The Orthodox women of Constantinople proved especially susceptible to Jesuit methods. An Orthodox contemporary, Chrysosculos the Logothete, lamented:

> The women were easily influenced by the eloquence and the charming manners of these new guides of conscience [the Jesuits], who succeeded in persuading them to come to them for hearing confession of their sins, without intimidating them and without imposing any rigorous penance or severe fasting.

A partisan report, perhaps, but it was grounded in fact.

There was also, among the Orthodox clergy, a party favourable to Rome. It owed its greatest impetus to the College of Saint Athanasius in Rome, founded by Pope Gregory XIII in 1577 for the express purpose of educating young Greeks and imbuing them with Roman sympathies (see Volume Three, Chapter 9, section 3). As a result, there were now Greek Orthodox clergy who had "unionist" sentiments: they supported Orthodox reunion with Rome, along the lines of the Uniate Church in Poland. One of these unionists, in the period 1603–1608, had managed to become Patriarch of Constantinople—Raphael II, a graduate of the Saint Athanasius College, who did all he could to advance crypto-Romanism within Greek Orthodoxy.

The context of Cyril's work, then, was dictated by this contest with a militant Counter-Reformation Catholicism.

Cyril's initiatives as patriarch to defend and build up Orthodoxy within the Ottoman Empire included the following. He gathered a group of Orthodox scholars in Constantinople to spearhead a sort of intellectual rearmament of Orthodox theology. One of these scholars, **Theophilus Corydalleus** (1563–1645), was appointed head of the patriarchal academy; the aim was to reform the academy, in order to offset the influence of the Jesuit school. Corydalleus was a good choice; he was one of Greek Orthodoxy's most celebrated and brilliant thinkers and teachers, who had been principal of a philosophical college in his native Athens. Corydalleus also sympathized warmly with Cyril's attitude towards Orthodox-Reformed rapprochement against Rome. A successful head of the patriarchal academy, Corydalleus raised it to standards of excellence, especially in science, that made it the equal of any Western university.

Convinced that religious ignorance among the Orthodox was a chief cause of Jesuit success, Cyril tried to reinstate preaching as a tool for raising Orthodox consciousness. Contemporary testimony tells us that preaching had fallen into widespread neglect in the Orthodox Middle East—"the custom of preaching had been abolished," according to the French traveller Pitton de Tournefort. We do not know what large-scale success Cyril enjoyed in reviving the art of preaching, but we do know he appointed the eloquent Archbishop of Ephesus, *Meletios Pantogalos* (1596–1646), as a sort of missionary preacher. In his preaching tours, Pantogalos bore with him a commendatory letter of authority from Cyril, in which the patriarch addressed all clergy and laity, comparing Pantogalos to a good physician who must not be limited to one locality. Pantagolos, like Corydalleus, supported the Cyrillian Orthodox-Reformed alliance.

Another aspect of Cyril's attempt to dispel ignorance was the publication of good literature. An Orthodox printing press was set up in Constantinople in June 1627, under the protection of the British ambassador, Sir Thomas Roe. This was the first ever printing press in the Greek world. Its first production was a work by Cyril's uncle, Meletios Pegas of Alexandria—a polemic against the supremacy of the pope. This shows with naked clarity the anti-Roman thrust of Cyril's strategy. The press also turned out two further books on the subject by Nilus of Thessalonica and Gabriel of Philadelphia, and other items aimed against Rome. The Ottoman government intervened, however, incited by Constantinople's Jesuits, and destroyed the press in January 1628; the Jesuits had persuaded the Grand Vizier (prime minister to the Sultan) that a book by Cyril against Judaism had insulted Islam. The judgment was later reversed, but by then it was too late; the precious printing machinery had been wrecked.

This incident, however, brought one great benefit to Cyril: it resulted in the expulsion of the Jesuits from Constantinople. After the destruction of the press, the Grand Vizier had been shaken by the solemn judgment of Ottoman religious experts that Cyril's book had not in fact insulted Islam. An alarmed Vizier now felt he had been manipulated and conned by the Jesuits. This, coupled with the outrage of Sir Thomas Roe, the British ambassador, who had provided a house for the printing press, moved the Vizier to wrath against the Jesuits, and they were driven from Constantinople. From that point, Rome had to rely on members of the Capuchin order in its campaign against Cyril.

Cyril also authorized a translation of the New Testament into modern Greek (rather different to New Testament Greek). The translator was Cyril's friend, the monk Maximos

Callioupollites; Cyril wrote a preface, vindicating the right and duty of all Christians to read the New Testament in a language they could comprehend. The new translation was published in 1638. It contained the original Greek text and the modern version in parallel columns, with some uncontroversial marginal comments. Some years after the death of Cyril, the prominent Greek Orthodox monk-theologian, **Meletios Syrigos** (d.1667), vigorously denounced the translation as a Protestant perversion, but he was silenced and banished to the island of Chios by Patriarch Parthenios II, who sympathized with certain aspects of Cyril's work. The new translation seems to have achieved some popularity; forty years after Cyril's death, an English diplomat in Smyrna reported that Cyril's New Testament was being used for public readings in some Orthodox churches. There are still signs of the work in 1714, when the Greek writer Alexander Halladios urged Orthodox to burn any copies of the book they found. Thereafter, it fades from view. Greek Orthodox opposition to the new translation was rooted largely in reverence for the ancient Greek in which the New Testament was written. Any tampering with this venerable old Greek was seen as a kind of sacrilege.

While we are on the topic of the Greek New Testament, it should be noted that it was Cyril who, in 1627, donated the illustrious Codex Alexandrinus to the British government, in recognition of all the help he had received from the ambassador Sir Thomas Roe. Codex Alexandrinus is one of the most important manuscripts of the Bible in Greek, dating from the 5th century. It contains the Greek Old Testament (the Septuagint), and an almost complete New Testament, lacking only portions of Matthew, John, and 1 Corinthians. It also has the two Epistles of the apostolic father Clement of Rome, from which the earliest English editions were taken.

The last aspect of Cyril's activities to note is the publication of his Confession of Faith in 1629 in Geneva, initially in Latin. It was published in Geneva, not because of the Confession's "Calvinism", but because by then, Cyril's own printing press in Constantinople had been destroyed. At this period in Orthodox history, apart from the brief six months when Cyril's press functioned, all Orthodox literature had to be printed in the West. Geneva was simply one of several good international printing centres. A second edition of the Confession, both Latin and Greek, followed in 1631. Questions of authorship and content have already been considered; we will see its fate after Cyril's death. It is almost impossible to assess its diffusion and influence within the Orthodox world, unless we judge that its planned condemnation in a pan-Orthodox council or synod in Jassy (in Moldavia), and its actual condemnation in a council in Jerusalem, indicate a pervasive awareness of the Confession. In Europe, it was widely translated: for example, into English twice, and into French four times.

6. *Cyril's final downfall and death*

Cyril's patriarchate was stormy. Through the scheming of Jesuits, Capuchins, and the French and Austrian ambassadors, often in conspiracy with Romanizing Orthodox clerics, Cyril was deposed from office and then reinstated no fewer than five times. At last, however, a plot by the Austrian ambassador, Schmid-Schwarzenhorn, and the ardently Romanizing Orthodox Bishop of Aleppo, Cyril Contari (who had been trained by Jesuits), brought about Cyril's deposition for the last time in 1638. Schmid-Schwarzenhorn and Contari persuaded the Ottoman sultan, **Murad IV** (1623–40), that Cyril was plotting with Murad's military enemies, the Cossacks. Murad, a notoriously savage despot, had Cyril arrested, condemned without trial, and— on the evening of June 27th—strangled to death by imperial troops in a remote spot near the port of Saint Stephanos, south of Constantinople. When the news of Cyril's execution became public, the Greek Orthodox population of Constantinople almost rioted in protest against Contari; they congregated outside the Romanizing bishop's house, crying, "Pilate, give us the body!" This indicates the high level of affection in which Cyril was held by his flock, and their contempt for his betrayer.

Cyril's death brought an end to his experiment in enlisting Reformed support for Orthodoxy against Rome. His team of co-workers dispersed. For example, Theophilus Corydalleus, head of the patriarchal academy, was sacked, and retired from Constantinople. But he was soon appointed Bishop of Artos and Naupactos by Patriarch Parthenios I, who had a high personal regard for Cyril, despite not sharing his "ecumenism" towards Protestants. It seems, however, that Corydalleus' Cyrillian views got him into trouble as bishop, and led to his disgrace. He died in abject poverty. The Archbishop of Ephesus, Meletios Pantogalos, Cyril's missionary preacher, ended up in the Dutch Republic at the University of Leyden, where he enjoyed great esteem. In Pantogalos, at least, the Orthodox-Reformed amity lived on.

7. Controversy continues

Cyril's enemies within Greek Orthodoxy were determined to blacken his memory. Contari, who overthrew Cyril and then succeeded him as Patriarch of Constantinople, summoned a council in September 1638, at which both Cyril himself and his Confession were anathematized. The 13 anathemas were signed not only by Contari, but also by the patriarchs of Jerusalem and Alexandria, as well as 24 archbishops and bishops. However, Contari was (as we have seen) motivated by ardent pro-Roman sympathies, and when in December that year he actually submitted to Pope Urban VIII as head of the Church, the Holy Synod—the governing body of Constantinople's church—was outraged. So was sultan Murad, and Contari was deposed and banished.

Controversy over Cyril rumbled on, however. Among Cyril's enemies were Peter Moghila, leader of the Ukrainian Orthodox (see next section), and Meletios Syrigos (he who denounced Cyril's New Testament). Moghila and Syrigos were working closely with **Basil the Wolf** (1634–53), king of the independent Slavic domain of Moldavia, by the western shores of the Black Sea. Basil saw himself as a latter-day Byzantine emperor, the lay head of Orthodoxy; the patriarchate of Constantinople was now deeply in his debt, since he had personally restored its solvency after Cyril's death. Basil, Moghila, and Syrigos pressurized Patriarch Parthenios I into convening a new council in Jassy, Basil's capital city, in 1642.

Made up of both Greek and Slavic representatives, the council's overall purpose was to define Orthodox doctrine in response to the challenges of Counter-Reformation Catholicism and Cyril's perceived crypto-Protestantism. Top of the agenda, in fact, was the condemnation of Cyril's Confession. The Russian delegates, however, scuppered the plan by insisting that the Confession was (a) probably a forgery, (b) if not a forgery, a purely personal statement by Cyril, which thus had no actual authority for Orthodoxy at large and therefore did not need to be condemned. Basil, Moghila, and Syrigos were forced to rest content with a condemnation of a catechism written by one of Cyril's supporters (although ascribed to Cyril); nothing was said about Cyril himself. Ironically, the Council of Jassy has itself been judged by most later Orthodox as leaning too far towards Rome, especially in the confession of faith it adopted, authored by Peter Moghila (see next section).

The story was still not over. Cyril's Confession was condemned 30 years later in 1672, at a synod in Jerusalem, summoned by its patriarch, **Dositheos II** (1669–1707). Here Cyril himself was vindicated: the Council of Jerusalem declared the good patriarch not to be the author of the bad Confession.[19] The furthest the Council of Jerusalem would go in casting aspersions on Cyril was to say in its fifth decree that if he really wrote the Confession, he was a heretic worthy of eternal anathema and excommunication. But the Council left the world in no doubt that the Confession itself was bad. The Council's own statement of faith, written by Dositheos, has (like that of Peter Moghila) been regarded by later generations of Orthodox as rather too laden with Roman ideas and terms, although less so than Moghila's.

8. Epitaph

So ends our treatment of Cyril Lucaris. The extremely varying interpretations his life and work have provoked may mean that he remains ultimately an enigma to many. The verdict of this book is that he was a fundamentally Orthodox theologian,

19. A view shared by many modern Greek Orthodox.

with an ecumenical vision (in the best sense of the much abused word) enabling him to appreciate the Christian virtue of spiritually-minded Protestants, to recognize value in the Protestant Reformation as a model for church renewal, and to exploit whatever theological and practical armaments the Reformation had to offer the East, in the common struggle with an aggressive Counter-Reformation Catholicism. He went as far as he could in restating Orthodoxy in a way his Reformed supporters could understand, even to the point of insufficiently guarded formulations that gave hostages to his foes, particularly among the Romanizing Orthodox.

Whatever view one takes of Cyril's theological stance, however, through all of his personality and labour there shines a single-minded, energetic commitment to build up Orthodox people in the understanding and practice of their faith. Religious ignorance was his enemy, education was his weapon. Much of this endeavour had nothing to do with an Orthodox-Reformed rapprochement. And there was one thing Cyril would never countenance: compromise with Rome. For this, he paid with his life.

2
Peter Moghila and his disciples

A controversial issue in Orthodoxy today is the extent to which Orthodoxy absorbed alien Western elements into its theology in the 17th and 18th centuries. Few would dispute that in trying to restate Orthodoxy for a contemporary constituency, some Orthodox (notably Cyril Lucaris) used Protestant theological methods, terminology, and concepts, to stiffen Orthodoxy's resistance to Rome, nor that other Orthodox thinkers, by a parallel or reactive movement, used Rome's theological methods, terminology, and concepts to stave off Protestant influences. Some contemporary Orthodox have seen in these developments a virtual "fall of Orthodoxy", requiring a thoroughgoing reformation to purge out both Protestant and Roman elements, and restore a pristine Orthodox faith. Others have rejected this interpretation, emphasizing that the Church cannot defect from the faith. They see the Westernizing period as a perhaps unfortunate variation from the norm, but not in any sense having derailed Orthodoxy; hence, no reformation is required, only a prudent and discerning attitude to those 17th and 18th century sources which veered too far towards either Protestantism or Rome.

We have already considered the rapprochement between Orthodoxy and Protestantism exemplified in the life and work of Cyril Lucaris. Now we must consider the opposite tendency, whereby Orthodoxy drew closer to Rome. This tendency, it has been argued, was itself exacerbated by the need to roll back the apparent inroads that Protestant thinking was making into Orthodoxy. Ready-made theological weapons for that purpose were to hand in the Jesuit-led armoury of anti-Protestant apologetics developed in the Catholic Counter-Reformation.

1. Peter Moghila

The most successful Orthodox leader of this type was **Peter Moghila** (1596–1646), metropolitan of Kiev. Born in Moldavia into an aristocratic family, he and his family fled from political upheaval in their homeland, taking refuge in Catholic Poland. Here (as we have seen) a large Orthodox minority lived, in the Ukraine region, then part of the Polish kingdom. Moghila was educated in a Brotherhood school in Lviv (see previous section for the Orthodox Brotherhoods of Ukraine), and in the Sorbonne, the Roman Catholic theological college in Paris— the most illustrious Catholic seminary in the world. This time at the Sorbonne did not necessarily indicate any sympathy on Moghila's part towards Rome; there was an established tradition of Orthodox men going to Western Catholic universities for an education unavailable to them in their own countries. Moghila then served for a time as an officer in the Polish army, but his deepest attraction was to the life of an Orthodox monk. In pursuit of this calling, he entered Kiev's historic Monastery of the Caves in 1625. Tonsured as a monk in 1627, he was later ordained to the priesthood, and then became archimandrite (head) of the monastery.

Here in the Monastery of the Caves, Moghila founded an influential Orthodox school. In 1632 this monastic school united with Kiev's Brotherhood school to become the Kiev College. Moghila's religious and educational ideal, embodied in the College, was the opposite of Cyril Lucaris's—Moghila wanted to "baptize" into Orthodoxy the methods and standards of the Jesuits, who stood at the cutting edge of Roman Catholic education. The College was thus modelled closely on Polish Jesuit academies. Historians have come to differing conclusions about Moghila's motives here. Did his policy spring from a desire for ultimate union with Rome? Or did it grow out of

Moghila's conviction that in Catholic Poland, where Orthodox Ukraine was situated, Orthodoxy's best strategy for survival was to steal its Catholic enemy's armour and weapons? In assessing Moghila's intentions, interpreters have found him as controversial a figure as Cyril Lucaris. Whatever was driving Moghila, it is certainly true that his method paralleled Cyril's: where Cyril had used Protestant resources to give shape and vibrancy to Orthodoxy, Moghila would use Rome's resources. Hence in his Kiev College, great attention was given to learning Latin, the language of Catholic thought, together with the most up-to-date Catholic philosophy, based on Aristotle, and an Orthodox theology expressed in Latin-Catholic terms.[1] Under Moghila's inspiration, the Kiev College achieved a quality of academic excellence unique in 17th century Orthodoxy.

In 1633, the new Polish king, Vladislav IV (1632–48), recognized the legal right of the Ukrainian Orthodox to their own bishops (up till now, the Polish state had thrown its weight behind the Uniates or Greek Catholics, one-time Orthodox who had submitted to Rome, and persecuted the Orthodox who would not submit: see previous section). Moghila thereupon became metropolitan of Kiev, and thus leader of Ukrainian Orthodoxy. He used his new-found authority to stamp the Ukrainian Church with his own vision of reform. In the educational sphere, he introduced Latin as the language of all Orthodox schools in Ukraine, and began using Roman Catholic theological textbooks in the training of his clergy. This Western-style teaching had two effects: it helped to disarm Catholic hostility to the Orthodox, and to equip the latter to understand Catholicism and respond intelligently to its claims.

It was in this context that Moghila's famous Orthodox Confession appeared in 1640. Written in Latin, its structure and spirit were based in large measure on Catholic systematic theologies. The Confession was approved by the joint Russian-Greek Synod that met at Jassy in Moldavia in 1642, whose

---

1. The Polish monarchy initially forbade the College to teach theology or philosophy, but soon relented.

chief purpose was to distance Orthodoxy from Cyril Lucaris's perceived quasi-Protestantism (see previous section). However, the Synod sanctioned Moghila's Confession only after it was translated into Greek and amended by the Greek theologian, Meletios Syrigos (another vocal critic of Cyril—see previous section). In the original draft of the Confession, Moghila had accepted the Roman Catholic view of eucharistic consecration (that the bread and wine are made into Christ's body and blood by the words of institution spoken by the priest) and also a doctrine of purgatory. Syrigos corrected these elements, reinstating the traditional Orthodox view of consecration (it is effected by the "epiclesis" prayer, when the priest prays that the Holy Spirit will consecrate the bread and wine), and rejecting purgatory.

There were some other strictly Orthodox non-Roman elements in the final text of the Confession: for example, the *filioque* clause was absent, Christ not the pope was declared head of the Church, and primacy of honour among churches was given not to Rome but Jerusalem (not to Constantinople, interestingly). Nonetheless, Moghila's Confession, even as revised by Syrigos, remained laced with heavy doses of Roman Catholic thought-patterns. It has been called the most Rome-leaning statement of belief ever sanctioned by an Orthodox council—it was adopted not only by the Synod of Jassy, but the Synod of Jerusalem too, in 1672. As a result of its quasi-Roman flavour, Orthodox theologians since the 19th century, no longer so close to Rome, have accorded the *Confession* only a relative authority; wherever it goes beyond the teachings of the seven ecumenical councils, they have felt no obligation to uphold it.

Moghila's *Euchologion* (a prayer book for use in services) also leaned significantly towards Roman forms; although lacking the sanction of a synod, it had widespread influence. Later Orthodox critics have highlighted its denial that the epiclesis prayer is essential to the eucharist, and its acceptance of purgatory (the same two elements that Syrigos struck out of Moghila's Confession). Further, Moghila added explanations before the text of each ritual; the explanations were couched in the style of Catholic scholastic theology.

2. Moghila's disciples

Peter Moghila fathered a whole school of thought which, for over a hundred years, would pursue his vision of Orthodoxy. The extent to which this school was capable of veering Romeward was shown in its use of the writings of the great medieval Catholic scholastic theologians, Thomas Aquinas and Duns Scotus, as textbooks for training Orthodox clergy. Among Moghila's disciples, the most important were the following.

Simeon Polotski

Simeon Polotski (1629–80) was born at Polotsk in Belarus (after which he is named). He studied at Moghila's Kiev College, and at the Jesuit college in Vilnius. He then became a monk in the Bogoyavlenie monastery in his native Polotsk in 1656, after it had been liberated from Polish Catholic rule by the Ukrainian Cossacks. Here his literary career began, with poetic and other works in Latin, Polish, and Slavonic. When some of these were presented in 1660 to the Russian tsar Alexei I (1645–76), he was deeply impressed. The tsar discerned in Polotski's writings an attractive statement of Russian imperial ideology—especially Moscow as the "third Rome", inheriting the authority of old apostate Rome and conquered Constantinople.

Polotski moved to Moscow in 1664, after Polish power had been restored in Polotsk, and established in that year Moscow's first Latin school. Tsar Alexei also appointed Polotski tutor to his children; he became a powerful court preacher, helping to awaken a new popular taste for sermons, especially among the Russian nobility (two thick volumes of his sermons were published shortly after his death). He wrote a systematic theology, the *Corona Fidei* ("crown of faith"), which—as one would expect from a disciple of Moghila—framed Orthodoxy in a significantly Catholic way. Polotski was also a fierce enemy of the Old Believers (see section 3).

Dimitri Tuptalo

Dimitri Tuptalo (1651–1709) was born at Makariv near Kiev, and studied at Moghila's Kiev College in 1662–5. He then embraced a monastic life in 1668 in the Saint Cyril Monastery of Kiev, and from 1675 he was in charge of several Ukrainian and Belarusian monasteries. *Tsar Peter the Great* (1682–1725) appointed him metropolitan of Tobolsk in 1701, although illness prevented him taking up his duties; the following year he became metropolitan of Rostov. In the internal controversies of Russian Orthodoxy, Tuptalo opposed both the Old Believers and Peter the Great's subordination of church to state.

Tuptalo's major work was a collection of lives of the Russian saints, the *Menaion*, arranged for daily readings within the framework of the Church calendar.[2] It was published in a series of volumes between 1689 and 1705, and became hugely popular among clergy, monks, and laity. Tuptalo was also a celebrated preacher, although it was only in the last century that a collected edition of his sermons was published. In addition to theological treatises (e.g. *The Mirror of the Orthodox Faith*), he also wrote religious plays which were staged (e.g. *A Comedy on the Day of Christ's Birth*); this "baptism of the theatre" was another example of Jesuit influence on Moghila's disciples. (In the Jesuit-Jansenist controversy that dominated 17th century French Catholicism, the Jesuits championed the theatre, while Jansenists were stern critics.) Finally, Tuptalo produced musical versions of the penitential psalms which attained widespread popularity in Ukraine, entering into its folk tradition.

Stefan Yavorsky

Stefan Yavorsky (1658–1722) has been called the greatest of Moghila's disciples. Born at Yavoriv in western Ukraine, he studied at the Kiev College, and at several Polish Jesuit colleges—he temporarily became a Uniate or Greek Catholic

---

2. The term "menaion" has other and wider meanings than this within Orthodoxy; Tuptalo's *Menaion* was specifically a calendar of readings on the lives of Russian saints.

to pursue these studies. After embracing the monastic life, he ended up back at the College in 1690 as a tutor, teaching rhetoric, philosophy, and theology. His philosophical and theological lectures were based on the Catholic scholasticism of Duns Scotus and William of Ockham. Tsar Peter the Great of Russia (see section 4 for Peter's reign) was impressed by his preaching and his Western outlook; he appointed Yavorsky metropolitan of Ryazan in 1700. When Patriarch Adrian of Moscow died, and Peter decided to suppress the patriarchate, he made Yavorsky the "exarch" of Moscow (administering the affairs of the patriarchal throne, but without the rank of patriarch).

Yavorsky brought with him to Moscow many theologians from Kiev, in order to mould Moscow's Orthodoxy along Moghilan lines. Yavorsky himself was profoundly influenced by the Jesuits and their aggressive Counter-Reformation Catholicism. This set him on a collision course with Peter the Great, who had a strong admiration for Lutheranism. When Yavorsky wrote his theological masterpiece, *Rock of Faith of the Orthodox Catholic Eastern Church*, in 1718, its vehement anti-Protestantism was an acute embarrassment to Peter, who had just granted religious freedom to Protestants throughout Russia. The tsar suppressed the treatise; it would be published at last after both Yavorsky's and Peter's deaths.

Yavorsky's militant hostility to Protestantism, as well as his opposition to Peter's plans for stripping the Russian Church of its autonomy from the state, had already cost Yavorsky the tsar's favour long before *Rock of Faith*. In 1712, Peter prohibited him from preaching; in 1718 he was sent into "internal exile" in St Petersburg, where he was exposed to non-stop political harassment. When Peter replaced the Moscow patriarchate with the Holy Synod in 1721 (see section 4), he appointed Yavorsky its first president, though Yavorsky detested the Synod as a tool of state control. He died the following year. It has been said that his troubled life embodied the contradictions of early 18th century Russia, as Yavorsky simultaneously promoted the Westernisation of Russian religion in one area (conforming it to Jesuit Counter-Reformation ideals), while opposing it in another (resisting Western-style state control of the Church, which was just as pronounced in Catholic as in Protestant countries).

3
The Old Believers: schism
in the heart of Russia

Orthodoxy in our period suffered one of its greatest and bitterest schisms—the schism of the Old Believers. Russia was the land where the schism occurred. This was no accident; the whole controversy erupted because of Russian Orthodoxy's real or alleged departure from the more ancient Greek Orthodox Churches in patterns of worship.

1. Patriarch Nikon

The man who was instrumental in sparking the conflagration was **Nikon** (1605–81). Born in 1605, he was the child of peasants in Valmanovo (a village some 60 miles from the great Russian city of Nizhy Novgorod). An adventurous early life saw him running away from home, becoming a priest, seeing all three of his children die,[1] retiring to a hermitage, joining a monastery (of which he became abbot), and finally coming to the attention of **Tsar Alexei I** (1645–76). A year after his coronation, Alexi met Nikon when the latter was in Moscow on monastery business. The new tsar was a sincere and devout practitioner of his religion, and felt a spiritual rapport with Nikon. He transferred him from his monastery in Kozhezersky to the Moscow monastery of Novospassky in 1646; two years later, the tsar made Nikon metropolitan Bishop of Veliky

---

1. Protestant readers should remember that the Orthodox priesthood is normally married.

Novgorod, the celebrated city where Alexander Nevsky, one of Russia's folk heroes and Orthodoxy's saints, had reigned in the 13th century.[2] Its bishop ranked second only to the Patriarch of Moscow in importance in the Russian Church. In 1652, Nikon attained to that supreme position.

There was a reform movement in the Russian Church at that time, fostered by the tsar himself. Its supporters are commonly known as the "Zealots of Piety". Among the clergy they included the tsar's confessor, archpriest at Moscow's Annunciation Cathedral, **Stefan Vonifatiev** (d.1656); Mikhail Rogov, archpriest at Moscow's Archangel Cathedral; Ivan Nasedka, priest at Moscow's Dormition Cathedral; **Ivan Neronov** (1591–1670), archpriest of Moscow's Kazan Cathedral; and archpriest **Avvakum Petrovich** (c.1620–82), a disciple of Neronov who also served at Kazan Cathedral. Other Zealots were high-ranking members of the laity. The reformation they envisaged meant the suppression of Pagan folk customs that still survived, especially in rural Russia, the revival of effective preaching at parish level, the promotion of a strict morality, and the orderly and correct conduct of worship.

It was this last element that was to provoke controversy and schism. When Moscow became a centre for printing, many religious texts were published which had existed only in manuscript until then. Scholars and printers were dismayed to find so many textual variations in the manuscripts. The quest for the correct text became something of an obsession. This obsession particularly affected liturgical texts, because the issue there assumed practical dimensions of vast size: how should a congregation be worshipping? Corporate worship lay at the innermost heart of Orthodoxy. And Orthodox worshipers believed that they were simply practising the age-old form of worship bequeathed to them by their ancestors. They were not interested in innovating; they wanted to know what the correct tradition was. The textual variations in liturgical books therefore had the capacity to awaken deep disturbance, and the search for the correct text here took on a passion absent in other areas.

---

2. See *Volume Two: The Middle Ages*, Chapter 6, section 3

2. *The passion for all things Greek*

A dominant group among the Zealots of Piety had a simple, clean-cut answer to the question of liturgical correctness. They were enamoured of all things Greek; they admired the Greek Orthodox liturgy as the absolute pinnacle of genuine worship. For these Zealots, then, the solution to the liturgical textual problem was obvious: the Greeks had the correct text. Godly reformation demanded that Russian worship be brought into complete conformity with Greek worship. They were encouraged in this attitude by many Greeks, who pointed out to them the peculiarities of Russian worship. One argument was that Greek worship was older and more pristine, closer to the ancient sources, than Russian worship. After all, the Greeks had been worshiping God since the first century, whereas it was not until the 10th century that the Russians were converted. It sounded persuasive to many, and many still find it persuasive. A counter-argument from some scholars is that Greek worship had not been static; it had undergone certain developments over the centuries. It was therefore possible that the Russian tradition was actually based on an older pattern of Greek worship than the Greeks now practised in the 17th century. Perhaps Russian worship was in reality more pristine! This argument, however, has not found huge support beyond the ranks of scholars sympathetic to the Old Believers.

The Greek-loving Zealots, spurred on by Greek Orthodox contacts, were committed to conforming Russian worship to Greek ways. Among the differences they set out to eradicate were the following:

Russian	*Greek*
The sign of the cross made with the index finger straight, the middle finger slightly bent, and the thumb joined to the other two fingers fully bent.	The sign of the cross made with the index and middle fingers extended and joined to the thumb, and the other two fingers fully bent.

Russian	Greek
Two alleluias in the prominent formula: "Alleluia, alleluia, glory to You, O God!"	Three alleluias in the formula: "Alleluia, alleluia, alleluia, glory to You, O God!"
The Nicene Creed: "I believe in the Holy Spirit, the true Lord and Giver of Life."	"I believe in the Holy Spirit, the Lord, the Giver of Life."
Seven loaves used in holy communion and another service known as the *artoklasia* ("breaking of bread").	Five loaves used in holy communion and the *artoklasia*.
Eight-pointed star on church buildings and on the bread of holy communion.	Four-pointed star.
Church procession: circle left to right.	Circle right to left.

There were some other differences (e.g. the number of prostrations and bows in the Lent services), but these were the most significant. If there had been only a single change, it is possible that the controversy might have been less uproarious. But with such an accumulation of changes, it seemed to many that a revolution in worship was being forced on them. If Protestants think it was all a fuss over nothing, perhaps they should imagine how they would feel if a new Bible translation, a new hymnbook, a new style of music, and a new way of celebrating the Lord's Supper, were suddenly forced on their church, all at the same time, without consultation. An equivalent sense of alienation and resentment was felt among many Russian Orthodox when Patriarch Nikon began enforcing the Greek forms of worship in 1653.

However, it is true that Russian Orthodox attached a greater significance to external worship-forms than most Protestants have done. For the pious Russian, the complex of actions that together made up corporate worship was nothing less than an image of heaven. To tamper with that image was to risk damaging or destroying the Church's union and communion with God. Hence the spiritual shock felt by many Russian believers at the visible and audible changes thrust upon their worship. Was this any longer the true image of heaven?

3. Nikon's papal aspirations

Nikon's response to opposition from many clergy, monks, and laity was harsh. He had opponents of the Greek reforms branded as heretics and excommunicated. He also invoked the oppressive machinery of the Russian state: dissenters were imprisoned, exiled, and eventually even put to death. Nikon's opponents included some of the Zealots of Piety, former friends and co-workers who could not share the patriarch's enthusiasm for Greek worship. The most prominent Zealots to oppose Nikon were Ivan Neronov and Avvakum. Neronov was excommunicated and banished to a distant northern monastery; Avvakum was banished to Siberia. Here were the beginnings of the schism of the Old Believers (or Old Ritualists)—those who held onto Russian Orthodoxy's older ways of worship. Old Believers were called *raskolniki* (schismatics) by their opponents. Old Believers called those who accepted the Greek worship-forms "Nikonites".

Nikon's authoritarian response to Old Belief was partly owing to his personality. A very capable man intellectually, and a gifted if long-winded preacher, he could not stomach opposition to what seemed to him his obviously correct and well-thought-out ideas. To Nikon, such foolishness was insufferable. It was not only Old Believers who suffered from his severity; anyone in the Church who failed to live up to his ideals could expect savage treatment. Archdeacon Paul of Aleppo, on a visit to Russia, wrote a detailed diary of events, in which he recorded with horror many of Nikon's deeds.

> He was a real butcher among the clergy [Paul wrote]. His Janissaries[3] are always patrolling the city. When they discover

---

3. Paul is comparing Nikon's ecclesiastical police with the notoriously brutal personal troops (the Janissaries) of the Ottoman sultan.

any priest or monk who has had too much to drink, they drag
him off to prison, strip him, and whip him. Nikon's prisons are
full of them, tormented with heavy chains and wooden logs on
their necks and legs, or on the bakery treadmill, sifting flour
day and night.

That is one of the milder things reported by Archdeacon Paul.
He was also fairly unimpressed by Nikon's sermonizing:

The patriarch was not content with the worship-service; he
also had to crown it with an exhortation and a voluminous
sermon. God give him moderation! His heart had no feeling
for his emperor, nor for the young children, standing there in
the intense cold without adequate clothing. What would we
say to this if he did it in our country?

So Nikon's rough, uncompromising personality explains in part
his severity toward Old Believers. The harshness, however, was
also owing to Nikon's exalted views of the Moscow patriarchate.
He regarded his office almost as a kind of Russian papacy. The
Church, he believed, should be a streamlined organisation with
himself at the top as a virtual autocrat, ruling with ruthless
efficiency. Any kind of dissent was ungodly disobedience. Some
have conjectured that Nikon's motives in enforcing the Greek
worship-forms on Russian Orthodoxy may have included a
desire to make it easier for the Greek Orthodox world to accept
his leadership as a sort of Orthodox super-patriarch. Allied to
this, Nikon also wished to acquire independent political power
for the Church: rather than be a purely spiritual institution,
relying on the state for material support, he wanted the Russian
Church to be a strong political force in its own right. To
symbolize this, Nikon assumed the title *Veliky Gosudar* (Great
Lord), previously given only to the tsar.

    We may wonder how the tsar reacted to this. Alexei I at
first yielded to Nikon's exaltation of his patriarchal authority;
after all, Alexei was a pious man, with a profound reverence
for Nikon. By 1658, however, after five years of Nikon's high-
handed attitude toward religious dissent and civil government
alike, the patriarch and the tsar finally fell out with each other.

Alexei failed to resolve certain conflicts between Nikon and his opponents in a way that satisfied Nikon; in anger, the patriarch shook Moscow's dust off his feet, and retreated into the New Jerusalem monastery he himself had founded in 1656, beside the river Istra outside of Moscow. He left the daily running of the Church to the Bishop of Krutitsy. But Nikon did not resign from office; he was still patriarch, and was still treated as such by his own party in the Russian Church. Mediators made many journeys between Moscow and New Jerusalem, carrying letters from the tsar and the patriarch to each other, but the breakdown in relations proved final. Alexei could not accept the quasi-political power claimed by Nikon for the patriarchate; Nikon could not retract that claim.

4. Nikon's downfall

The personal fate of Nikon, and the fate of the Greek reforms in worship he had initiated, became strangely separated. Tsar Alexei, finally wearying of Nikon's intransigence, summoned a Church council in 1667 to decide what should be done. In order to transcend Russian problems, the council was to represent the wider Orthodox world; the tsar invited the other Orthodox patriarchs to preside, although only those of Antioch and Alexandria turned up. The council decided that Nikon had behaved intolerably, especially towards the tsar; the patriarchs of Antioch and Alexandria had no sympathy for Nikon's aspirations towards a Russian papacy. They deposed him, banishing him to the northern monastery of Ferapontov. Nikon's attempt to elevate the patriarchate to an independent political power had failed. The old idea was restored, with patriarch and tsar each having their own spheres of authority; the patriarch's sphere, it was agreed, was strictly the spiritual affairs of the Church. A new Patriarch of Moscow, Joasaphus II (1667–72), was appointed. So ended Nikon's career, somewhat ingloriously (although a faction in the church continued to regard him as the true patriarch).

However, the same council that deposed Nikon decreed in favour of his Greek worship-reforms. Whichever of the

contested customs was really the most ancient, it was clear
that the Greek Orthodox Churches of that time held to the
practices Nikon had embraced and enforced. The wider Greek
world would no longer tolerate Russian peculiarities; these were
seen, not as offences against the Greek way, but as violations of
the universal Church's worship by one faction of one country's
Church. The tsar and his government swung behind the council's
decree: from now on, Russian believers would have to worship
in the same way as global Orthodoxy, on pain of having the state
against them—not at Nikon's bidding, but in the name of the
Church universal. The tsar might not in theory have spiritual
authority over the Church, but he would use the state's power
to enforce the views of what was believed by the majority to be
genuine Orthodoxy..

The council was a devastating blow to Old Believers. They
had hoped for vindication, or at least toleration, from the council.
Instead they found themselves condemned both by the council
and by the tsar's government. From this point onwards, their
conflict was unavoidably with the Russian state as much as it
was with the reformed Russian Church. The leading spokesmen
of the old ways, present at the council (including Avvakum),
were punished for their defiance—deposed from the priesthood
and banished to an underground prison on the arctic coast (two
also had their tongues cut out for insulting the tsar). It was
here that Avvakum wrote his life story, *The Life of Archpriest
Avvakum by Himself*, the first Russian autobiography; it has
been generally regarded as a masterpiece of Russian religious
literature. It is written, not in literary Russian, but in the down-
to-earth language spoken by ordinary people: in that respect,
a Russian *Pilgrim's Progress*. It also unveils Avvakum's strong,
vivid, occasionally crude personality, in all its fascinating blend
of gritty humanity and ardent piety—a great soul in a narrow
mind, as it has been evocatively said.

From their arctic prison, Avvakum and his fellow captives
smuggled out exhortations to their followers in Moscow and
elsewhere, fanning the flames of opposition to the Greek
reforms. As the government became increasingly appalled at the

extent and depth of the resistance (see below), the treatment the prisoners received became steadily harsher, and Avvakum himself was at length executed in April 1682 (burnt at the stake), Old Belief's most renowned martyr.

5. Persecution: Antichrist has come!
Attitudes were now hardened on both sides beyond the possibility of reconciliation. For the rest of the century, Russia was troubled by popular uprisings of Old Believers against a government they now perceived as utterly corrupt and apostate. These outbreaks were not entirely religious in motive; other more earthly grievances, local in nature, were often mingled with the opposition to the new forms of worship. Sometimes an Old Believer uprising would get attached to a separate rebellion, most notably when Old Believers joined forces with a mutinous army unit in Moscow in 1682; the resulting clash with government forces brought terrible bloodshed as the rebellion was crushed. The most spectacular defiance of the government, however, occurred at the Solovetsky monastery, which rejected the new worship, and heroically endured an eight year siege by government troops between 1668 and 1676. When Solovetsky finally fell, the troops showed no mercy, slaughtering all those left alive after the ordeal. But such butchery was counter-productive for the government; the Solovetsky dead were hailed as martyrs by other Old Believers, inspiring them to resist with even greater resolve.

In December 1684, the government—now in the hands of Princess **Sophia Alekseyevna** (1682–9), acting as regent for her two young brothers, Peter and Ivan—lost whatever little patience it had left for the obstinate dissenters. It decreed the death penalty for all Old Believers (unless they renounced their creed), and stiff punishments for anyone who gave them shelter. Old Believers responded with an overpowering sense that they were living in the end times, and that Russia had been taken over by the Antichrist. Russian Orthodox piety had always had a strong view of God's historical purposes being played out in "Holy Russia"; this now became a white-hot conviction in the

Old Believers that they were taking part in the final conflict between light and darkness, Christ and Satan.

A great number of Old Believers fled as far as they could from all signs of the government's unholy presence, into the remote, unpopulated areas of Russia's vast landscape. There they created their own self-sufficient communities, some of which flourished and survived into the 20th century to face the different horrors of the Russian Revolution. In these isolated regions, Old Belief often became the dominant faith. Others fled Russia altogether. Still others, rather than flee, went on the offensive, attacking and capturing monasteries and villages. When government troops appeared to reclaim the monastery or village, the Old Believers chose collective suicide rather than surrender, burning themselves to death. Between 1672 and 1691, there were some 37 of these mass suicides by burning, resulting in the deaths of over 20,000 Old Believers, according to some estimates.

Meanwhile the Old Believers became divided among themselves into two parties, the *Popovtsy* ("Priestists") and the *Bezpopovtsy* ("Priestless"). The Priestists were closer in spirit to the official Orthodoxy that now persecuted them; they were simply an alternative Orthodoxy, with their own clergy and sacraments. The Priestless were more radical. They held that a universal apostasy, headed by Antichrist, had corrupted the entire Church. Consequently there was no true Church on earth any longer: no clergy, no sacraments (except baptism—the term "sacrament" was applied more widely in Orthodoxy than merely to baptism and eucharist). The only means of communion left between God and believers was therefore prayer. The Priestless divided into many smaller groups with their own distinctives.

The Old Believer schism in Russian Orthodoxy proved enduring. Statistics are almost impossible to obtain or calculate, but one estimate is that Old Believers may have comprised 10% of the Russian population before the Revolution of 1917. The Priestist Old Believers survive today, with anything between one and ten million adherents worldwide (figures vary hugely depending on source).

4

Peter the Great: the East looks West

1. Peter's politics

Peter the Great was one of Russia's most colourful and powerful tsars, influencing his country's character and destiny in profound ways, not least in religion. Although he officially became tsar in 1682, he was only 10 years old, and his elder sister Sophia ruled as regent. Peter also had an older half-brother Ivan, who was recognized as co-tsar. In 1689, however, Peter managed to sideline his sister and her chief minister by a coup. Although his half-brother Ivan continued to be co-tsar until his death in 1696, he played no part in government; Peter now controlled the Russian empire in his own name. A giant of a man (nearly seven feet tall), he radiated both physical energy and mental restlessness. His thirst for personal control of government could have led to paralysis and disaster, had it not been allied to a hugely capable intellect. A self-taught individual with wide learning, a successful military commander, a ruler who knew how to take advice but ultimately followed his own independent judgment, Peter took hold of his country and devoted his extraordinary powers to remaking it in his own image.

Once government was firmly in his hands, Peter set about reforming Russia on a massive scale, largely with the aim of "Westernizing" it—i.e., bringing its social and political life into harmony with the norms of Western European nations. Some of this may seem superficial to a modern student, such as forcing the Russian nobility to dress in Western clothes and forbidding the men to sport the traditional Russian beard (there was a "beard tax" for any who refused). However, in other areas Peter's reforms were aimed at the structures of Russian society. It is not the purpose of this book to investigate them, but they embraced educational, cultural, administrative, financial, military, and religious dimensions which together brought Russia into the family of Western nations in important ways.

2. Peter's Church policy

It is Peter's religious reforms that command our interest. He took a strong interest in the Russian Church and the role it played in society. In harmony with his desire to conform Russia to Western ways, he at first promoted Peter Moghila's conception of Orthodoxy (see section 2): in other words, an Orthodoxy Westernized along Roman Catholic lines. The Russian tsar therefore put disciples of Moghila in positions of power as bishops. Opponents of Moghila were frowned upon. For example, the Likoudes brothers, *Joannikos* (d.1717) and *Sophronios* (d.1730), monks whom Patriarch Dositheos II of Jerusalem had sent to Moscow as theological advisors, were expelled by Peter in 1704 and banished to a remote monastery. Through their printing press, the Likoudes brothers had poured out treatises opposing Moghilan Romanized Orthodoxy, especially its doctrine of the eucharist (where it switched the key moment of consecration from the Eastern epiclesis prayer to the Catholic formula "This is My body").

However, Peter began to see problems in Moghila's form of Orthodoxy. Chiefly, it had a too militant hostility to Protestantism, at a time when Peter's Westernizing policy required a spirit of openness to the Protestant culture of leading Western nations like Prussia, Saxony, Denmark, and Britain. So Peter ultimately abandoned his support for Moghilan Orthodoxy, transferring his patronage instead to the non-Moghilan *Feofan Prokopovich* (1681–1736). Prokopovich, a native of Ukraine, had become a Uniate in order to complete his education in Poland and Rome, but reverted to Orthodoxy on his return to Kiev. Here he became a lecturer, and finally rector, of the theological college founded by Moghila. Prokopovich, however, had turned against Moghila's Romanized Orthodoxy; he thoroughly reshaped the college's outlook into one resembling the vision of Cyril Lucaris—an Orthodoxy that saw Rome as the chief enemy and corrupter of Orthodoxy, and was ready to borrow Protestant weapons to combat the papacy.

Prokopovich was well read in Lutheran theology, and had a real sympathy for some Lutheran ideas. In his mission to purify Orthodoxy of Roman elements, he drew inspiration from the weapons forged against Rome by Lutherans, especially the great Lutheran divines Martin Chemnitz, Johannes Quenstedt, and Johann Gerhard (Prokopovich's favourite).[1] However, Prokopovich was not motivated by purely theological concerns; he was equally driven by the same passion as Peter the Great to Westernize Russian culture, which included subordinating the Russian Church to the government along the church-state model of Western Europe. This was the man whom Peter chose to spearhead his anti-Moghila campaign in Russia. Prokopovich was brought to St Petersburg in 1716, and appointed Bishop of Pskov in 1718, and then Archbishop of Novgorod in 1724.

Prokopovich's Westernized version of Russian Orthodoxy swung it behind a more Protestant attitude to the canon of Scripture, favouring the Hebrew Old Testament, with the apocrypha being downgraded to a secondary status ("deuterocanonical"). He also took a more Protestant slant on the authority of extra-biblical tradition: the fathers and councils were not on a par with Scripture, but gained their value as faithful expositors of Scripture which alone was the infallible Word of God. Prokopovich taught a Protestant-leaning view of salvation too; it was through faith alone, albeit such faith is always accompanied by holiness. The Church was the whole body of believers who accepted the truth revealed in Scripture, as expounded by the fathers and councils. In Prokopovich's Lutheran view of church-state relations, the tsar became the divinely appointed head of the church.

---

1. See Chapter 1, section 2 for cameos of these figures.

It would be going much too far to say that Prokopovich transformed Russian Orthodoxy into a Protestantized body. Many clergy distrusted him; some dared to denounce him. The spiritual and theological character of Orthodoxy was too deeply rooted to change quite so drastically or globally. Prokopovich's influence was limited. Even so, the next two centuries would undeniably see flourishing in the Russian Church a form of Orthodoxy which had, like Prokopovich, drunk deeply of Protestant sources. Not everyone shared it; but among many who did, the result was not so much a loss of historic Orthodoxy, as a realignment of its attitudes along the lines envisaged by Cyril Lucaris in Constantinople in the previous century.

3. The abolition of the patriarchate

Peter was determined that no future Patriarch of Moscow should try to repeat Nikon's attempt to create a political force in the Church that could challenge the state. His solution was to subordinate Church to state on the pattern of Lutheran Germany, where the Church was governed by a state-appointed "consistory", a board of lawyers and theologians. By Peter's time, the conflict with the Old Believers had gravely undermined the power of the Russian Church, making it relatively easy for Peter to accomplish his purpose. It was already the prerogative of the tsar to nominate a man to the patriarchate; when Patriarch Adrian (1690–1700) died, Peter left the office vacant for 20 years. He appointed Stefan Yavorsky (see section 2) to administer patriarchal affairs, but without the rank or authority of a patriarch.

In 1721, Peter officially abolished the patriarchate, replacing it with a Lutheran model of church government. Through his Spiritual Regulation, drafted by Prokopovich, he created a body called the Holy Governing Synod to regulate the Russian Church. The Spiritual Regulation was based on the Swedish Lutheran *kirchenordnung* ("Church Constitution") of 1686, which had placed the Swedish Lutheran Church under a more full-blooded royal supremacy, transferring power from the bishops to the king. The Spiritual Regulation's Holy Governing Synod had 10 (later 12) members, all appointed by Peter, whom

Peter could also dismiss at will. The Synod's presiding officer was a lay Procurator: he could not vote, but he controlled agenda and membership. By the 19th century the Procurator had evolved into a very powerful official, ensuring that the Russian Orthodox Church was submissive to the tsarist state. Peter himself took the title "Supreme Judge of the Spiritual College".

The abolition of the patriarchate aroused protests, but Peter was powerful enough to ignore them contemptuously. A mere two years later, in 1723, the other Orthodox patriarchs of Constantinople, Antioch, Jerusalem, and Alexandria acquiesced in Peter's act, and recognized the Holy Synod as the Russian Church's new governing body. The Synod was to rule for 200 years; it would not be until 1917, and the fall of the tsarist state, that the Russian Church would restore the patriarchate.

It would probably be true to say that spiritually-minded Russian Orthodox submitted to the Holy Synod, rather than actually approving of it as a replacement for the patriarchate. In a Church already so wounded by the schism of the Old Believers, they may well have felt that any path other than submission would merely have inflicted even deeper injuries the Church could not afford to bear. In any event, the Holy Synod often worked quite efficiently; apart from the lay Procurator, the Synod's 12 members were all clergy or monks, who generally had an authentic concern for the Church's welfare. Certainly the "Synodical period" of Russian Orthodox history (1721–1917) was no less productive of brilliant theologians and heaven-breathing saints than any previous period.

Important people:

Konstantin Ostrozhskii (1526–1608)
Andrei Kurbskii (1528–83)
Theophilus Corydalleus (1563–1645)
Patriarch Cyril Lucaris (1572–1638)
Nicephorus Cantacuzinos (dates unknown)
Ivan Neronov (1591–1670)
Meletios Pantogalos (1596–1646)
Peter Moghila (1596–1646)
Patriarch Meletios Pegas (d.1601)

Patriarch Nikon (1605–81)
Avvakum Petrovich (c.1620–82)
Simeon Polotski (1629–80)
Dimitri Tuptalo (1651–1709)
Stefan Vonifatiev (d.1656)
Stefan Yavorsky (1658–1722)
Meletios Syrigos (d.1667)
Patriarch Dositheos II (1669–1707)
Joannikos Likoudes (d.1717)
Sophronios Likoudes (d.1730)
Feofan Prokopovich (1681–1736)

Royalty

Sultan Murad IV (1623–40)
Basil the Wolf of Moldavia (1634–53)
Tsar Alexei I (1645–76)
Regent Sophia Alekseyevna (1682–9)
Tsar Peter the Great (1682–1725)

Primary source material

Cyril Lucaris' Confession of Faith

In the name of the Father and of the Son and of the Holy Spirit. Cyril, Patriarch of Constantinople, publishes this short Confession to help those who wish to know about the faith and religion of the Greeks, that is, the Eastern Church, testifying before God and human beings with a clear conscience and without hypocrisy.

Chapter 1.

We believe in one true God, the Almighty, in three persons, the Father, the Son, and the Holy Spirit. The Father is unbegotten; the Son is begotten of the Father before all ages, of the same essence as the Father; the Holy Spirit proceeds from the Father by the Son, and has the same essence as the Father and the Son. These three persons in one essence we call the Holy Trinity, and the Trinity should be blessed, glorified, and worshipped by all creation.

Chapter 2.

We believe that Holy Scripture has been given by God, and that its sole author is the Holy Spirit. We should believe this without question, for it is written, "We have a more sure word of prophecy, to which you do well to pay attention, as a light shining in a dark place." We believe that the authority of the Holy Scripture is above the authority of the Church. It is very different to be taught by the Holy Spirit and to be taught by a human being; for a human being through ignorance can err, deceiving and being deceived, whereas the Word of God does not deceive nor is deceived, and cannot err. Indeed it is infallible, and has everlasting authority.

Chapter 3.

We believe that God most gracious has predestined His elect to glory before the creation of the world. This was not based on their works; there was no other impelling cause behind this election, apart from God's good-will and mercy. Likewise before the creation of the world, He rejected whom He would reject. Concerning this act of reprobation, if you look at the absolute decrees of God, His will is the cause; but if you look at the laws and principles by which good order exists in the world, which God's providence employs in governing the world, then His justice is the cause, for God is both merciful and just.

Chapter 4.

We believe that the one triune God, Father, Son, and Holy Spirit, is the Creator of all things visible and invisible. The invisible things are the angels; the visible things are the heavens above and everything beneath them. Because the Creator is good by nature, and cannot do any evil, He created all things good. If there is any evil, it flows either from the devil or from humanity. It should be a fixed principle with us that God is not the author of evil, and that sin cannot with any good reason be reckoned to Him.

Chapter 5.

We believe that everything is governed by God's providence. We should adore this providence rather than inquire into it. Because providence is beyond our grasp, we cannot truly understand its reason from the things themselves. Therefore we consider it better to practise silence in humility, rather than speak a multitude of words that do not edify.

Chapter 6.

We believe that God's first-created man fell in paradise. This was because he turned from God's command and surrendered to the deceitful word of the serpent. This is the wellspring of original sin in Adam's descendants, so that no human being is born according to the flesh without bearing this burden and experiencing its fruits in his life.

Chapter 7.

We believe that Jesus Christ our Lord made Himself of no account, that is, He took human nature into union with His own substance. He was conceived by the Holy Spirit in the womb of Mary Ever-Virgin, was born, suffered, died, was buried, and rose in glory, so that He might bring salvation and glory to all who believe. We look for Him to come again to judge both the living and the dead.

Chapter 8.

We believe that our Lord Jesus Christ sits at the right hand of His Father. There He intercedes for us, carrying out by Himself the function of a true and legitimate High Priest and Mediator. From there He looks after His people and governs His Church, beautifying and enriching her with many blessings.

Chapter 9.

We believe that no one can be saved without faith. Faith is what justifies in Christ Jesus. The life and death of our Lord Jesus Christ obtained this faith for us, the Gospel makes it known, and without it no one can please God.

Chapter 10.

We believe that the catholic Church is made up of all true believers in Christ, both those who have left this world and are in heaven, and those who dwell on earth and are still on the way to heaven. No mortal human can be the Head of this Church. The Head is Jesus Christ alone, and He holds in His own hand the rudder and government of the Church. However, since there are on earth particular visible Churches, each one of them has one leader. He is not strictly called the head of that particular Church, but he can loosely be called the head in the sense that he is the chief member of it.

Chapter 11.
We believe that the members of the catholic Church are holy, chosen for eternal life. Hypocrites are excluded from the number and the fellowship of this Church. In particular visible Churches, however, tares may be found in the midst of the wheat.

Chapter 12.
We believe that the Holy Spirit sanctifies and teaches the Church on earth, for the Spirit is the true Counsellor, whom Christ sends from the Father to teach the truth and to drive away darkness from the minds of the faithful. It is certainly true that the Church on earth is capable of erring; it may choose falsehood instead of truth. From this error, mortal man does not set us free, but only the light and teaching of the Holy Spirit sets us free, although this may take place through the means of the Church's faithful ministers and their labours.

Chapter 13.
We believe that humanity is justified by faith and not by works. However, when we say "by faith", we understand the corresponding object of faith, namely the righteousness of Christ. Faith grasps this like a hand, and applies it to us for our salvation. This is not detrimental to good works, because truth itself teaches us not to neglect works; they are necessary means to testify to the reality of our faith, and to confirm our calling. But human weakness shows that our works are not themselves sufficient to save us, nor can they enable us to stand before the judgment seat of Christ, nor can they bestow salvation by their merit. No, it is the righteousness of Christ applied to the repentant soul which alone justifies and saves faithful people.

Chapter 14.

We believe that free will in the unregenerate is dead, because they can do no good thing—whatever they do is sin. In the regenerate, however, by the grace of the Holy Spirit, the will is energized and truly works, although not without the help of grace. So in order that a person be born again and do good, prevenient grace is necessary. Without this, human nature is injured, having received as many injuries as he received who fell into the hands of thieves when travelling from Jerusalem down to Jericho. By himself, then, a person can do nothing.

Chapter 15.

We believe that the Church's Gospel-sacraments are those the Lord ordained in the Gospel. There are two. Only these have been delivered to us, and He who ordained them delivered to us no others. Further, we believe that the sacraments are made up of the Word and the Element, that they are seals of God's promises, and that they confer grace. But in order that the Sacrament be complete and whole, an earthly substance and an outward action must go along with the use of that element ordained by Christ our Lord. It must be joined with a true faith, because lack of faith harms the wholeness of the sacrament.

Chapter 16.

We believe that baptism is a sacrament ordained by the Lord. Unless a person has received it, he has no communion with Christ, from whose death, burial, and glorious resurrection the whole force and efficacy of baptism flows. Therefore we are certain that for those baptized in the form which our Lord commanded in the Gospel, both original and actual sins are remitted, so that everyone who has been washed in the name of Father, Son, and Holy Spirit is regenerate, cleansed, and justified. Concerning the repetition of baptism, we have no command to be rebaptized, and therefore we must refrain from this indecorous thing.

Chapter 17.

We believe that the other sacrament ordained by the Lord is what we call the eucharist. For on the night that the Lord offered up Himself, He took bread, blessed it, and said to the apostles, "Take, eat, this is My body." And when He had taken the cup, He gave thanks and said, "Drink of this, all of you. This is My blood which is shed for many; do this in remembrance of Me." And Paul adds, "For as often as you eat of this bread and drink of this cup, you show the Lord's death." This is the untainted and lawful institution of this wonderful sacrament. In its administration, we acknowledge the true and certain presence of our Lord Jesus Christ. That presence, however, is the presence which faith offers to us, not that which the invented doctrine of transubstantiation teaches. For we believe that the faithful eat the body of Christ in the Lord's Supper, not by breaking it with the teeth of the body, but by apprehending it with the sense and feeling of the soul. For the body of Christ is not the visible element in the sacrament. Rather His body is what faith spiritually apprehends and offers to us. From this it follows that, if we believe, we eat and partake, but if we do not believe, we are destitute of the entire fruit of it. We believe, therefore, that to drink the cup in the sacrament is to partake of the true blood of our Lord Jesus Christ, in the same way that we said about the body. As the Author of the sacrament commanded about His body, so He commanded about His blood. This command should not be dismembered nor mutilated, according to the fancy of human judgment. Indeed, the institution should be observed as it was delivered to us. So when we have partaken of the body and blood of Christ worthily and have concluded our communion, we confess ourselves to be reconciled with God, united to the Head of the body of which we are all members, with sure hope that we shall be co-heirs with Him in the future Kingdom.

Chapter 18.
We believe that the souls of the dead are either in blessedness or in condemnation, according to what each one has done. As soon as they leave the body, they go either to Christ or to hell. For as a person's condition is at his death, so he is judged. After this life, there is neither ability nor opportunity for repenting. In this life there prevails a season of grace, so that those who are justified

here will not be punished hereafter. But those who die without being justified, are consigned to eternal punishment. This makes it clear that the fable of Purgatory should not be given room. In truth it is appointed that each one should repent in this life, and obtain pardon of his sins by our Lord Jesus Christ, if he would be saved. Let this conclude our Confession.

We suspect that this short Confession of ours will be "a sign spoken against" by those who take pleasure in vilifying and persecuting us. However, our trust is in the Lord Jesus Christ, and we hope He will not abandon the cause of His faithful people, nor allow the rod of iniquity to rest heavy on the fortune of the righteous.

Avvakum's sufferings

An imperial edict arrived, decreeing that I be removed from Tobolsk, because I had spoken from the Scriptures and denounced Nikon for his heresy. I also got a letter from Moscow, which said that two of my brothers, who lodged in the Tsarina's quarters in the palace, had died of plague, along with their wives and their children, and indeed many others of my relatives and friends. God had outpoured the vials of His wrath on Russia, and yet the miserable troublemakers did not repent; they kept on making trouble in the Church. Neronov had frequently admonished the Tsar, saying, "Three judgments will fall in consequence of the split in the Church: plague, war, and division." This has now this very day occurred. But the Lord is gracious; after chastening us to bring us to repentance, He pardons us; after healing the maladies of our souls and bodies, He will grant us peace. My hope and trust are in Christ, I wait for His mercy, and I look for the resurrection of the dead!

Again I sailed off in my ship, in accordance with the vision I have already recounted. I went to the Lena River. When we came to Yeniseisk, another imperial edict ordered me to go to Dauria, which is some 20,000 versts[2] from Moscow; the edict

---

2. A verst is an archaic Russian unit of distance, approximating to 3,500 feet or 1.07 kilometres.

gave me over to Athanasy Pashkov and his troops. He was in charge of 600 men. Pashkov was a violent man (I was handed over to him for my sins), who burned, whipped, and tortured people endlessly. I had frequently tried to stop him, but I had at last fallen into his clutches. He had received from Moscow the command of Nikon to make my life miserable.

Once we departed from Yeniseisk, while we were coming to great Tunguska River, there was a storm that nearly destroyed my ship; full of water, it was adrift in the middle of the river, its sails ripped. Everything except the deck was inundated. My wife, looking indecent because she had no head-covering, dragged the children out of the water; raising my eyes heavenward, I cried out: "O Lord, help us and rescue us!" By God's will, a wind blew us toward the shoreline. The story is too long to tell. Two men from another ship were hurled overboard; they drowned. After we had got ourselves back into a settled state of mind on the shore, we continued our journey.

The Shaman rapids were now approaching, and we encountered a group of other people sailing on the river. In their company were two widows, one of them around 60 years old, the other even older; they were making their way to a convent to become nuns. Pashkov wanted them to force them to go home and get married. But I told him: "According to Church law, it is not right to make them marry." Rather than listen to what I said, he lost his temper and started torturing me. Once we arrived at the Long Rapids, he began forcing me out of the ship, saying: "It's your fault that the ship isn't making good speed, you heretic! Off with you into the mountains! You don't belong among Cossacks."

Alas for my fate! The mountains were steep, the woods were thick; those cliffs were like a great wall—you could snap your neck just looking up at them! Huge snakes inhabit these mountains; scarlet-plumed geese and ducks fly above your head, and dark ravens and drab-coloured jackdaws... Pashkov wanted to throw me out into these mountains, to dwell among the birds and the beasts. I penned a brief letter to him, beginning thus: "O man, have the fear of God in you! Fear Him who sits

above the cherubim, who watches over the deep! The powers of
heaven and all created things tremble in His presence, including
humankind. Only you scorn Him and upset the order of things!"
And so my letter went on. I put quite a lot into that letter, and
then I had it delivered to him. Some 50 men ran towards me,
seized my ship, and towed it to Paskov—he was some three
versts away. I made some porridge to feed the Cossacks, those
poor souls; they both ate and trembled together, and some of
them shed tears of pity for me.

Once my ship had been towed to the shoreline, executioners
grabbed hold of me and escorted me into Pashkov's presence.
There he stood, his sword in his hand, and quaking with anger.
He asked: "Are you a proper priest or a deposed one?" I replied:
"I am archpriest Avvakum. Speak! What do you want from me?"
He bellowed like a savage beast and hit me, first on one cheek,
then on the other. Then he struck me on the head, knocking me
down. As I lay there, he grabbed his battle-axe, and hit me on the
back three times. Then he ripped away my garment, and his men
gave me 72 lashes on the back. I cried out: "Lord Jesus Christ,
Son of God, come to my aid!" These words I kept on repeating,
and Pashkov was deeply provoked because I did not add: "Have
mercy." As each lash of the whip struck me, I said the prayer. And
then, in the course of the flogging, I cried out: "That's enough of
this whipping!" Pashkov ordered the men to stop flogging me.
Then I asked him: "Do you know why you whipped me? Do you
know why?" So he ordered his men to strike me in the ribs. Then
they released me. I shuddered and collapsed.

Pashkov had me put in the ship carrying the ammunition;
they chained my hands and feet, and tied me to a beam. It was
autumn, and all night the rain fell on me, as I hung exposed to
the deluge. During the flogging, I had not felt any pain, owing to
my prayer. Now, though, as I hung there, the thought came into
my mind: "Son of God, why did You allow me to undergo such a
hard thrashing? Did I not speak up for Your widows? Who shall
judge between You and me? While I was doing sinful things,
You did not bring such brutal afflictions on me. Now, I do not
know how I have sinned to deserve this." O what righteousness

I flaunted! I, another foul-smelling Pharisee, dared to challenge the justice of the Lord! Job was able to use such words because he was righteous and blameless. Also he did not know the Scriptures, because Job dwelt outside the realm of God's Law in heathen land; he only knew God through creation. But me, I am first of all a real sinner; secondly, I have the sustenance of the Law, being buttressed in all things by the Scriptures that say, "Through much tribulation we must enter the Kingdom of God." And yet I had done such a foolish thing as flaunt my righteousness! Alas for me! Why did the ship not sink and take me with it?

My bones now began to throb, my veins tightened, my heart failed me, and I came close to death. But the men blew water into my mouth, and I once again drew breath. I repented before the Lord. The Lord in His sweetness is gracious; He forgets our former sins when we repent. Once again, all my pain vanished.

From *The Life of Archpriest Avvakum by himself*

The Confession of Dositheos

Decree 3

We believe that the supremely good God has eternally predestined to glory those whom He has chosen, and has given over to condemnation those whom He has rejected; but not in such a way that He would justify the one, and give over and condemn the other, without reason. That would contradict the nature of God, who is the universal Father of all; He has no favourites, and desires all people to be saved and to come to the knowledge of the truth. However, since He foreknew that some would make a right use of their free will, and others a wrong use, He predestined the one, and condemned the other.

We understand the operation of free will as follows. God's illuminating grace, which we call prevenient grace, is by God's goodness bestowed as a light on those in darkness, that is, on all those who are willing to obey it (for it is of benefit only to the willing, not the unwilling) and cooperate with it in what it requires as needful for salvation. After this, there is granted particular grace, which cooperates with us, enables us, and makes us persevere in the love of God, that is to say, in performing the good works that God wishes us to do, and which His prevenient grace exhorts us to do, and justifies us, and puts us among the predestined. But those who will not obey and cooperate with grace, and therefore will not observe the things God wishes us to perform, and misuse in Satan's service the free will that God gave them that they might perform willingly what is good: these are given over to eternal condemnation.

To say, however, as the most wicked heretics do—and as we find contained in the Chapter corresponding to this[3]—that God, in predestining or condemning, had no sort of regard to the works of those predestined or condemned: this we know to be profane and ungodly. It would make Scripture contradict itself, since it promises the believer salvation through works, yet supposes God to be its only author, by His illuminating grace alone, which He bestows without preceding works...

But to affirm that God's will is solely and causelessly the author of their condemnation, what greater slander can be fastened on God? What greater insult and blasphemy can be offered to the Most High? For we know that God is not tempted by evil, and that He equally wills the salvation of all, since there is no favouritism with Him; and we confess that for those who, through their own wicked choice and their unrepentant heart, have become vessels of dishonour, there is justly decreed condemnation. But we never, never say that God is the author of eternal punishment, cruelty, ruthlessness, and inhumanity, for He tells us that there is joy in heaven over one sinner that repents. Far be it from us, while we have our senses, to believe or to think such things! We pronounce an eternal anathema on those who say and think such things, and we regard them as worse than unbelievers.

Decree 13
We believe that a person is not merely justified through faith alone, but through a faith that works through love, in other

---

3. Chapter 3 of Cyril's Confession.

words, through faith and works. But the idea that faith acting like a hand lays hold of the righteousness that is in Christ, and applies it to us for salvation: this we know to be far from all Orthodoxy. In that case, faith would be within everyone's grasp, so that no one could miss salvation, which is obviously false. On the contrary, we believe that it is not the corresponding object of faith, but the very faith that is in us, which justifies us through works before Christ. And we regard works not as witnesses that vindicate our calling, but as fruits in themselves, through which faith becomes effective; through the divine promises, our works in themselves merit that each of the faithful may indeed receive what is done in his own body, whether good or bad.[4]

The regime of Patriarch Nikon as seen by a visiting Greek

To judge by what we saw of the top men of Russia, they have little fear of the tsar, nor do they feel much awe of him. The one they more exceedingly fear is this patriarch [Nikon]. The patriarchs who went before him did not meddle at all in affairs of state; this man, however, by his astuteness, understanding, and knowledge, is adept in every art and craft concerning matters both of Church and state, in fact of all secular matters, owing to his having once been married, and his prior familiarity with the world at large. After completing his business with the visiting dignitaries, his custom is to turn once more to the icons, chanting "He is worthy" a second time. Then he blesses his visitors, sends them away, and sets off ahead of them to the church. For he never leaves off church service three times a day and night, in addition to assisting at the mysteries[5] and at vespers. On most days he celebrates the mysteries himself. On entering the church, and on leaving it, many people present him with *cholofilat*—accounts of their circumstances and business.

---

4. This assertion of merit is "as far from all Orthodoxy" as anything Cyril is alleged to have said!
5. The eucharist, routinely called "the mysteries" in the East.

They do this because no one can get an interview with him in his quarters, except the top people who see him in the mornings.

Beneath his array of chambers there are seven halls of justice, where seven judges hold court, accompanied by a battery of clerical officers. Each hall of justice is relevant to specific matters. One of the halls is given over to monks and convents, where all their cases are judged. Another hall is given over to the clergy; here, each man coming to be ordained priest, wherever in all Russia he is from, presents himself, along with testimonials from the inhabitants of his area. The ruler of this court, a monk who is also the patriarch's treasurer, piles up these testimonials until there are some 20 or 30 applicants. Then he takes the testimonials to the patriarch. The applicants stand before the patriarch, who walks around them carrying a service book. If any of them can read it easily, the patriarch signs a certificate for him, approving him. If anyone cannot read the book easily, the patriarch rejects him. In this matter the patriarch's authority is as great as the tsar's. Many of these applicants for the priesthood have travelled from as far away as a thousand versts, from Siberia and other regions. Neither the patriarch himself, nor any of the other top dignitaries in the Church, gets any financial contribution from his flock. They are paid directly from imperial funds. They also tax their priests, according to rank, on an annual basis.

Another court deals with inheritances. Here the patriarch claims ten per cent, on top of what the judge and his clerks take. Everyone being ordained as a parish priest also has to pay heavy fees...

Previously, no one could become an archimandrite[6] except by the tsar's decree, nor could an archimandrite be deposed save by the tsar. This man [Nikon] has overturned that rule; he now appoints or dismisses anyone he wishes, without asking anyone else about it. If God removes His protection, and unleashes His anger on anyone, it is surely the ecclesiastic who is guilty of any lapse or fault in the presence of the patriarch, or whom he knows has got drunk, or been lax in attending prayers. Such a man is

6. Head of a monastery.

instantly banished by the patriarch's command. The convents of Siberia use to be empty, but since coming to power, the patriarch has populated them with archimandrites, and top priests, and drunken miserable monks. If any priest has committed a fault, the patriarch instantly takes the black cap off his head, which is tantamount to disqualifying him from the priesthood. If the patriarch ever relents and pardons the offender, it has to come from his own personal will, because he does not permit anyone to intercede for offenders. In fact, other than the tsar himself, there is nobody with sufficient courage to intercede with him! He has been so infuriated with a good number of his clergy, that he has had them shaved bald, and banished them along with wives and children to Siberia, where they spend their days in a very miserable life. By such harshness, the patriarch makes everyone afraid of him, and his word is law.

Archdeacon Paul of Aleppo
The Travels of Macarius, Patriarch of Antioch,
written by his Archdeacon Paul of Aleppo

Glossary

AMYRALDIANISM
The theology associated with the 17th century French Reformed theologian Moise Amyraut (Latin "Amyraldus"). Amyraut strongly emphasised the universal dimensions of the atonement: Christ died to atone for the sins of all humanity, but the atonement's effect was conditional on faith. Hence, in terms of God's decrees, Amyraut placed the decree to provide atonement for all sinners prior to the decree of election which gave faith to some.

APOPHATIC
The method of Eastern Orthodox theology. We cannot know God's essence at all—it is absolutely incomprehensible. We can only know God's "energies" (His attributes in action) which flow from His essence but are not identical with it. Our knowledge of God's energies is more experiential than intellectual. *Apophatic* is from the Greek word for "denial".

ARMINIANISM
A movement within the Dutch Reformed Church to align Reformed theology more closely with Erasmian humanism. Named after the 17th century Dutch theologian Jacob Arminius. Arminius believed that the grace of Christ had supernaturally and universally restored a measure of freedom to the sin-bound human will, thus enabling each person to choose whether to respond to the Gospel. God's election was conditioned on this response, as divinely foreseen from eternity.

CAMBRIDGE PLATONISM
The outlook of a number of Anglican theologians who all trained at Cambridge University. They reacted against the perceived intolerance of Calvinism, and looked for inspiration to the early Greek fathers of the early church and to Platonist and Neoplatonist philosophy.

CONGREGATIONALISM
A form of church government where each congregation has final authority over its own affairs.

COVENANTERS
A movement for affirming and maintaining the Reformed theology and Presbyterian church government of the Scottish national church, and its independence from state control. Named from the National Covenant of 1637.

EPISCOPACY, EPISCOPALIANISM
Government of the church by diocesan bishops, with each bishop having authority over a regional group of congregations.

FEDERAL THEOLOGY
The typically Reformed way of giving a "shape" to the theology of the Bible, by organising its story and content under the concept of covenant (Latin *foedus*), beginning with God's covenant with pre-fall humanity, and culminating in the New Covenant in Christ.

GALLICANISM
The theory that the French Catholic Church and monarchy have certain rights of independence from the papacy.

INDEPENDENTS
Another term for Congregationalists.

INFRALAPSARIAN
A Reformed view of God's decrees which places the decree to permit the fall before the decree of election. Hence those chosen for life are chosen as sinners.

JANSENISM
A movement for the renewal of Augustinian theology within the Roman Catholic Church. Named after the 17th century Dutch Catholic theologian Cornelius Jansen.

LATITUDINARIANS
An influential group in the post-1660 Anglican Church who took a minimalist attitude to doctrine, instead emphasising moral life.

MOLINISM
A theological way of combining the freeness of God's grace with the reality of human free choice, involving the concept of *scientia media* ("middle knowledge"). Named after the 16th century Spanish Jesuit theologian Luis de Molina.

NONJURORS
Those Anglican clergy who refused to swear loyalty to the new English royal house of Orange after the 1689 Revolution, remaining loyal to the deposed house of Stuart.

OLD BELIEVERS
Those in Orthodox Russia who opposed the worship-reforms of patriarch Nikon in the 17th century, ultimately forming a separate body out of fellowship with the Moscow patriarchate.

PIETISM
A movement for the spiritual renewal of Lutheranism. Pietists emphasised practical Christian life and sanctification above doctrine, and were more open than traditional Lutherans to people from other Christians traditions, e.g. Roman Catholics and Reformed.

PRESBYTERIANISM
A form of church government where authority is vested in the whole body of pastors and elders from all congregations, meeting as a church court—ultimately a national assembly.

PURITANISM
A term almost impossible to define. I take it to refer to those Anglicans who aspired to further reformation of their Church in a more strongly Protestant, perhaps Presbyterian, direction.

QUAKERS
A nickname for the group associated with George Fox (1624-91). They located supreme spiritual authority in the "indwelling Christ" or "inner light" rather than the Bible, and had radically egalitarian social and religious attitudes.

QUIETISM
A type of Roman Catholic spirituality that emphasised the passivity of the human soul before God, and a "disinterested love" for God (loving God for His own sake, even though He might not save us).

RAMISM
A theological method named after the French Reformed thinker Peter Ramus (1515-72). He developed a system of logical analysis that relied on "dichotomy"—breaking concepts down into pairs, and then dividing each pair into another pair, until one finally arrived at basic axioms that could not be further divided.

RESTORATION
The re-establishment of the Stuart monarchy and the Anglican Church in 1660 after the upheavals of the civil wars.

SCIENTIA MEDIA
"Middle knowledge". A form of God's knowledge held to be somewhere between His knowledge of everything possible and everything actual. This middle knowledge is His knowledge of what actual persons would do in hypothetical circumstances. See MOLINISM.

SEPARATISM
Separatists were English Protestants who broke away entirely from the English national church, in the pre-Civil War era. Some were Congregationalists, some Baptists. Of the Baptists, some were Arminian, some Reformed.

SOLEMN LEAGUE AND COVENANT
The politico-religious treaty of 1643 between the English parliament and the Scottish Covenanters, which united them against King Charles I.

SUPRALAPSARIAN
A Reformed view of God's decrees which places the decree of election before the decree to permit the fall. Hence those chosen for life are not chosen as sinners, but simply as human beings whose creation has been decreed.

THOMISM
The theology of Thomas Aquinas (1225-74), greatest of the medieval scholastic theologians.

UNIATE CHURCHES
Churches originally from Eastern Orthodoxy that accepted the authority of the papacy. They are sometimes called "Greek Catholics". The papacy allowed them to keep most of their own traditions of worship and church life, e.g. a married priesthood.

Bibliography

This is a selection of materials used in the writing of this present work and recommended to readers for their own perusal. Other books formed the "deep background" to the work, shaping my outlook over a long period, but I have no note of actually consulting them specifically for this work, so I have not included them here. Chief among these are writings on 17th century English history in general and Puritanism in particular; and among such writings, pride of place must go to the writings of Christopher Hill, an erudite Marxist with a gift for words who found much to admire in the English Revolution, and wrote fine biographies of Oliver Cromwell and John Milton.

H. G. Alexander, *Religion in England 1558-1662* (London: Hodder and Stoughton, 1968).

Gerald H. Anderson (ed.), *Biographical Dictionary of Christian Missions* (New York: Erdmans, 1998).

Michael Angold (ed.), *The Cambridge History of Eastern Christianity* (Cambridge: Cambridge University Press, 2006).

Brian G. Armstrong, *Calvinism and the Amyraut Heresy* (Madison, Wisconsin: University of Wisconsin Press, 1969).

John W. Beardslee III, *Reformed Dogmatics: J. Wollebius, G. Voetius, F. Turretin* (New York: Oxford University Press, 1965).

Joel Beeke and Randall J. Pederson, *Meet the Puritans* (Grand Rapids: Reformation Heritage Books, 2007).

F. Bente, *Historical Introductions to the Lutheran Confessions* (St Louis: Concordia Publishing House, 2005).

Thomas Bokenkotter, *A Concise History of the Catholic Church* (New York: Doubleday, 1990).

Francis Bremer, *Congregational Communion* (Boston: Northeastern University Press, 1994).

J. H. S. Burleigh, *A Church History of Scotland* (London: Oxford University Press, 1960).

Douglas Bush, *English Literature in the Earlier Seventeenth Century 1600-1660* (London: Oxford University Press, 1973).

Nigel Cameron (ed.), *Dictionary of Scottish Church History and Theology* (Edinburgh: T & T Clark, 1993).

Martin Chemnitz, *Examination of the Council of Trent* (trans. with biographical introduction by Fred Kramer, 4 vols. Saint Louis: Concordia Publishing House, 1971-86).

G. R.Cragg, *From Puritanism to the Age of Reason* (Cambridge: Cambridge University Press, 1950).

— *The Church and the Age of Reason 1648-1789* (Harmondsworth: Penguin Books, 1966).

F. L. Cross and E .A. Livingstone, *The Oxford Dictionary of the Christian Church* (New York: Oxford University Press, 1997).

H. Daniel-Rops, *The Church in the Seventeenth Century* (London: J. M. Dent & Sons, 1963).

— *The Church in the Eighteenth Century* (London: J. M. Dent & Sons, 1964).

Gordon Donaldson, *The Faith of the Scots* (London: Batsford, 1990).

— *Scotland: James V – James VII* (Edinburgh: Mercat Press, 1994).

William Doyle, *Jansenism* (Basingstoke: Macmillan, 2000).

David L. Edwards, *Christian England* (Glasgow: Collins, 1989).

Peter Erb, *Pietists: Selected Writings* (New York: Paulist Press, 1983).

Georges Florovsky, *Ways of Russian Theology* (2 vols. Belmont, Massachusetts: Nordland Publishing Company, 1979-87).

Aza Goudriaan, *Reformed Orthodoxy and Philosophy, 1625-1750* (Leiden: Brill, 2006).

Tim Grass, *Modern Church History* (London: SCM Press, 2008).

Ole Peter Grell (ed.), *The Scandinavian Reformation: From Evangelical Movement to Institutionalisation of Reform* (Cambridge: Cambridge University Press, 1995).

Eric W. Gritsch, *A History of Lutheranism* (Minneapolis: Fortress Press, 2002).

George Hadjiantoniou, *Protestant Patriarch: The Life of Cyril Lucaris* (London: The Epworth Press, 1961).

Basil Hall, 'Puritanism: The Problem of Definition' in G. J. Cuming (ed.), *Studies in Church History, vol. 2* (Edinburgh: Thomas Nelson, 1965).

Robert T. Handy, *A History of the Churches in the United States and Canada* (Oxford: Clarendon Press, 1976).

Heinrich Heppe, *Reformed Dogmatics* (rev. and ed. Ernst Bizer, trans. G. T. Thomson. London: Wakeman Trust, n.d.).

Christopher Hill, *Milton and the English Revolution* (London: Faber and Faber, 1979).

Hajo Holborn, *A History of Modern Germany: The Reformation* [covers up to 1648] (Princeton, New Jersey: Princeton University Press, 1982).

—*A History of Modern Germany: 1648-1840* (London: Eyre & Spottiswoode, 1965).

Kenneth Hylson-Smith, *The Churches in England from Elizabeth I to Elizabeth II: Volume I. 1558-1688* (London: SCM, 1996).

Peter Y. de Jong (ed.), *Crisis in the Reformed Churches. Essays in Commemoration of the Great Synod of Dort, 1618-19* (Grand Rapids, Michigan: Reformed Fellowship Inc., 1968).

J. N. D. Kelly, *Oxford Dictionary of Popes* (Oxford: Oxford University Press, 1986).

Martin Kitchen, *The Cambridge Illustrated History of Germany* (Cambridge: Cambridge University Press, 1996).

Leszek Kolakowski, *God Owes Us Nothing: A Brief Remark on Pascal's Religion and the Spirit of Jansenism* (Chicago: University of Chicago Press, 1995).

Robert Kolb, *Confessing the Faith: Reformers Define the Church 1530-1580* (Saint Louis: Concordia Publishing House, 1991).

Robert Kolb and Timothy J. Wengert (eds.), *The Book of Concord* (Minneapolis: Fortress Press, 2000).

A. N. S. Lane, *Justification by Faith in Catholic-Protestant Dialogue* (Edinburgh: T & T Clark, 2002).

K. S. Latourette, *A History of the Expansion of Christianity. Three Centuries of Advance: 1500-1800* (Exeter: The Paternoster Press, 1971).

C. S. Lewis, *English Literature in the Sixteenth Century* (London: Oxford University Press, 1973).

Carter Lindberg (ed.), *The Pietist Theologians. An Introduction to Theology in the Seventeenth and Eighteenth Centuries* (Oxford: Blackwell, 2005).

William Lumpkin, *Baptist Confessions of Faith* (Valley Forge: Judson Press, 1969).

George A. Maloney, *A History of Orthodox Theology Since 1453* (Belmont, Massachusetts: Nordland Publishing Company, 1976).

H. Leon McBeth, *The Baptist Heritage* (Nashville, Tennessee: Broadman Press, 1987).

—*A Sourcebook for Baptist Heritage* (Nashville, Tennessee: Broadman Press, 1990).

Alister McGrath, *In the Beginning: The Story of the King James Bible* (London: Hodder and Stoughton, 2001).

John T. McNeill, *The History and Character of Calvinism* (New York: Oxford University Press, 1954).

—*Unitive Protestantism* (London: The Epworth Press, 1964).

Richard A. Muller, *Post-Reformation Reformed Dogmatics* (4 vols. Grand Rapids, Michigan: Baker Academic, 2003).

Stephen Neill, *A History of Christian Missions* (Harmondsworth: Penguin, 1964).

Mark Noll, *A History of Christianity in the United States and Canada* (London: SPCK, 1991).

Roger Olson, *Arminian Theology: Myths and Realities* (Downers Grove, Illinois: IVP Academic, 2006).

Geoffrey Parker (ed.), *The Thirty Years' War* (Abingdon: Routledge, 1997).

Prem Poddar, Rajeev S. Patke, and Lars Jensen, *A Historical Companion to Post-Colonial Literatures: Continental Europe and its Empires* (Edinburgh: Edinburgh University Press, 2008).

Richard H. Popkin and Arjo Vanderjagt (eds.), *Scepticism and Irreligion in the Seventeenth and Eighteenth Centuries* (Leiden: Brill, 1993).

Robert D. Preuss, *The Theology of Post-Reformation Lutheranism* (2 vols. Saint Louis: Concordia Publishing House, 1970-72).

Nicholas Riasanovsky, *A History of Russia* (New York: Oxford University Press, 1993).

Ruth Rouse, Stephen Neill, and Harold E. Fey (eds.),
  A History of the Ecumenical Movement 1517-1968 (London:
  SCM, 1993).

Steven Runciman, *The Great Church in Captivity: A Study of
  the Patriarchate of Constantinople from the Eve of the Turkish
  Conquest to the Greek War of Independence* (Cambridge:
  Cambridge University Press, 1985).

Philip Schaff, *Creeds of Christendom* (3 vols. Grand Rapids,
  Michigan: Baker, 1993).

G. Michael Thomas, *The Extent of the Atonement: A Dilemma
  for Reformed Theology from Calvin to the Consensus* (Carlisle:
  Paternoster, 1997).

Peter Toon, *God's Statesman: The Life and Work of John Owen*
  (Exeter: The Paternoster Press, 1971).

Carl Trueman and R. S. Clark (eds.), *Protestant Scholasticism*
  (Carlisle: Paternoster, 1999).

Leonard J. Trinterud, *Elizabethan Puritanism* (New York:
  Oxford University Press, 1971).

Francis Turretin, *Institutes of Elenctic Theology* (ed. James
  T. Dennison, Jr., trans. George Musgrave Giger, 3 vols.
  Phillipsburg, New Jersey: P&R, 1992-7).

Nicholas Tyacke, *Anti-Calvinists: The Rise of English
  Arminianism* (Oxford: Clarendon Press, 1990).

Gordon Wakefield, *John Bunyan the Christian* (London: Fount,
  1992).

Timothy Ware, *The Orthodox Church* (London: Penguin
  Books, 1997).

Nicolas Zernov, *Eastern Christendom* (London: Weidenfeld
  and Nicolson, 1963).

Index of Names

Le Gross, Nicolas, Gallican treatise 512

Grotius, Hugo 133-4, 139, 156, 229
  Church-State position 135-6

Grynaeus, Jacob, in Basel 107

Gurnall, William (Calvinist
  conformist) 302-3, 302n, 311, 341

Gustavus Adolphus, king of Sweden
  59, 82

Gustavus Vasa, king of Sweden 77

Guthrie, James 409-410, 411, 433

Guthrie, William 409n

Guyon, Madame (Madame Guyon)
  71, 73, 462, 545-51, 568
    Fénelon and 548-51
    Lacombe and 546-7
    poetry 572-3

Haag, Cornelius van, Cyril Lucaris
  and 584-5

Habsburgs, Holy Roman Empire
  and 54, 57, 58-60

Hackston, David (Covenanter) 419

Hadjiantoniou, George, *Protestant
  Patriarch: The Life of Cyril Lucaris*
  (1961) 585n, 586n

Hales, Sir Edward 330

Hall, Joseph 234, 272

Hamilton, James, marquis, Lord
  High Commissioner 392, 393

Hanna (or Hannay), James, Prayers
  Book Service in St Giles Kirk 387

Hardouin de Péréfixe, Abp of Paris,
  Port-Royal nuns dispersed 500

Harlay de Champvallon, François
  de, Abp of Paris
    and Mme Guyon 547
    régale crisis 539
    restrictions on Port-Royal 503-4

Harsnett, Samuel, Abp of York 231

Heermann, Johann (hymnist) 51, 82

Heidegger, Johann Heinrich 122-5,
  150, 156
    efficacious merit of Christ 166-7

and Protestant refugees 124

Helwys, Thomas 219-20, 272

Henderson, Alexander 246, 304,
  383-4, 388-9, 389, 391, 392, 394,
  403-4, 433

Henrietta Maria, queen consort of
  Charles I 232-3, 272, 461

Henry III, king of France 447-8

Henry IV, king of France 448, 522

Henry VIII, and English succession
  213

Herbert, Edward, Lord Herbert of
  Cherbury 237

Herbert, George 236-7, 272
  Love bade me welcome...(poem) 286

Hermanszoon, Jakob, *see also*
  Arminius

Heyling, Peter 78, 81

Hobbes, Thomas 312

Hodge, Charles, *Systematic Theology*
  122

Hoffman, William (Muhlheim
  Pietist) 72

Hoffmann, Daniel 35, 81

Hohenzollern, house of, in
  Brandenburg-Prussia 46, 51, 60, 66

Hooker, Richard 177, 178, 208-212,
  212n, 271, 277-8

Hooker, Thomas 239

Hope, Sir Thomas 388

Howe, John 151, 307, 331, 342

Humphrey, Laurence 184, 188, 271

Hurleston, Sir Ranulf 200n

Huss, John 55

Hyde, Edward, earl of Clarendon
  246, 299, 304, 342
    Clarendon Code restrictions
      303-310
    and the Scottish situation 412

Hyperius, Andreas 117, 156

Ingoli, Francesco, guidelines for
  Catholic mission 560, 568

Index of Subjects

333–4; under the Clarendon
Code 303–310, *see also*
Nonconformists
Dissenting academies 310, 338
divine right of kings 369, 385,
450–51
Dominican order, in China 566–7
Donauworth, religious riot 54
Dordrecht *see* Dort
Dort: canons of 31*n*, 106, 140–41,
149; Synod of (1618) 109–110,
138, 139–42, 480, 486
Dover, Treaty of (1670) 315
Dunbar, battle 400–401
Dunbar, battle (1650) 28
Dunkeld, battle (1689) 427
Dutch Reformed Church: Second
Dutch Reformation 114;
Statenbijbel (States Bible) (1637)
142; Three Forms of Unity 141
Dutch Republic: Arminian
controversy 127–42, 156; atheism
116; Church-state relations 131,
135–9; English Separatists 203,
205, 219–21, 239; Huguenot
settlers 556; Jansenism in
519–20; Jansen's *Augustinus*
praised 486; Old-Catholic church
520; Oldenbarnevelt's "Sharp
Resolution" 137–8; Reformed
faith/Calvinism 99, 109; religion
and politics 135–9; Remonstrant
congregations 135–9, 141, 142;
Third Anglo-Dutch War (1672-74)
315–16; Thirty Years' War and
55, 60; war of independence from
Spain 128, 136, 137, 142

Eastern Orthodoxy (Greek)
575–608; *Apophatic* theology 590,
639; Calixtus and 44–5; council
of Jassy (1642) 597–8, 603–4;
council of Jerusalem (1672) 598,

604; Macarius of Egypt 68–9;
modern views of Lucaris 585–6,
585*n*; preaching reinstated by
Cyril 593–4; pro-Rome parties
581–2, 593; Protestant influences
585–9; Roman Catholic
influences 597, 598, 601–8;
theological distinctives 587&*n*;
Westernising influences 601–2,
607–8, 620–22
Eastern Orthodoxy (Russian):
Greek style worship 611–13;
Holy Synod replaces Moscow
patriarchate 607, 622–3; Lutheran
ideas 621; Old Believers schism
609–618; theatre and 606;
Tuptalo 606; Zealots of Piety
(reform movement) 610
ecumenism: Amyraut and 148;
Calixtus and 43–5; Casaubon and
44; Pietist teaching 72; Reformed
(at Westminster) 250
Edgehill, battle (1642) 245
Edict of Nantes 449, 555; revoked
(1685) 67, 124, 329, 541, 556
education: Brandenburg-Prussia
69–70; conference method 195–7;
Dissenting academies 310, 338;
France 455–6, 502–3, 521; Jesuits
in Constantinople 592; Puritan
clergy 195
election *see* predestination and
election
Engagement treaty (1647), effect of
on England 398
Engand, Conventicle Act (1593)
205
England: allied to Louis XIII of
France 232; Amyraldians 151–2,
151*n*; Arminians 177, 182;
Bill of Rights (1689) 337–9;
Bloody Assizes (1685) 328–9,
329*n*; Calvinism questioned and

Grace Publications Trust

Grace Publication Trust is a not for profit organisation that exists to glorify God by making the truth of God's Word (as declared in the Baptist Confessions of 1689 and 1966) clear and understandable, so that:

- Christians will be helped to preach Christ
- Christians will know Christ better and delight in him more
- Christians will be equipped to live for Christ
- Seekers will come to know Christ

From its beginning in the late 1970s the Trust has published simplified and modernised versions of important Christian books written earlier, for example by some of the Reformers and Puritans. These books have helped introduce the riches of the past to a new generation and have proved particularly useful in parts of Asia and Africa where English is widely spoken as a second language. These books are now appearing in editions co-published with Christian Focus as *Grace Essentials*.

More details of the Trust's work can be found on the web site at:

www.gracepublications.co.uk.

Christian Focus Publications

Our mission statement –

STAYING FAITHFUL

In dependence upon God we seek to impact the world through literature faithful to His infallible Word, the Bible. Our aim is to ensure that the Lord Jesus Christ is presented as the only hope to obtain forgiveness of sin, live a useful life and look forward to heaven with Him.

Our books are published in four imprints:

CHRISTIAN FOCUS

Popular works including biographies, commentaries, basic doctrine and Christian living.

CHRISTIAN HERITAGE

Books representing some of the best material from the rich heritage of the church.

MENTOR

Books written at a level suitable for Bible College and seminary students, pastors, and other serious readers. The imprint includes commentaries, doctrinal studies, examination of current issues and church history.

CF4•K

Children's books for quality Bible teaching and for all age groups: Sunday school curriculum, puzzle and activity books; personal and family devotional titles, biographies and inspirational stories – because you are never too young to know Jesus!

Christian Focus Publications Ltd,
Geanies House, Fearn, Ross-shire,
IV20 1TW, Scotland, United Kingdom.
www.christianfocus.com